PELOUBET'S NOTES
1983-1984

*Based on the International Bible
Lessons for Christian Living
Uniform Series*

D1246249

by

Ralph Earle

110th ANNUAL VOLUME

Founded by Francis N. Peloubet

BAKER BOOK HOUSE ● GRAND RAPIDS, MICHIGAN 49506

ISBN: 0-8010-3389-6

Copyright 1983 by
Baker Book House Company

Lessons based on International Sunday School Lessons; the International Bible Lessons for Christian Teaching, copyright by the Committee on the Uniform Series.

New International Version, Copyright © New York International Bible Society, 1978. Used by permission.

Scripture quotations designated NASB are from the New American Standard Bible, © The Lockman Foundation 1960, 1962, 1963, 1968, 1971, 1972, and are used by permission.

Printed in the United States of America

CONTENTS

OUR BIBLICAL FAITH

Unit I: God Reveals Himself

7043984

Unit II: God Redeems His People

Unit III: God Relates to His People

STUDIES IN ISAIAH

Unit I: The Messianic Hope

Unit II: Themes from Isaiah 1-39

Unit III: Themes from Isaiah 40-66

THE GOSPEL OF MARK

Unit I: Jesus Ministers to Human Need

Unit II: Jesus Gives His Life for Sinners

THE LETTER OF JAMES

THE RISE AND FALL OF A NATION

Unit I: Establishment of the Monarchy

Unit II: The Two Kingdoms

Unit III: Judah Only

Quarter I
OUR BIBLICAL FAITH

Unit I: God Reveals Himself
Unit II: God Redeems His People
Unit III: God Relates to His People

GOD OF CREATION

DEVOTIONAL READING	Psalm 136:1-9
ADULTS AND YOUTH	**Adult Topic:** *God of Creation* **Youth Topic:** *Do You See What I See?* **Background Scripture:** Gen. 1:1; Ps. 19:1-6; 136:3-9; Acts 17:24-28; Rom. 1:20 **Scripture Lesson:** Gen. 1:1; Ps. 19:1-4a; Acts 17:24-28; Rom. 1:20 **Memory Verse:** *The heavens are telling the glory of God; and the firmament proclaims his handiwork.* Ps. 19:1
CHILDREN	**Topic:** *God Made the World* **Background Scripture:** Gen. 1:1; Ps. 19:1-6; 136:3-9; Acts 17:24-25 **Scripture Lesson:** Gen. 1:1; Ps. 19:1-4; Acts 17:24-28 **Memory Verse:** *In the beginning God created the heavens and the earth.* Gen. 1:1
DAILY BIBLE READINGS	**Aug. 29 M.:** The Great Deeds of the Creator. Ps. 136:1-9 **Aug. 30 T.:** The Glory of the Creator. Ps. 19:1-6 **Aug. 31 W.:** The Word of the Creator. Gen. 1:1-13 **Sept. 1 T.:** The Incomparability of the Creator. Isa. 40:18-26 **Sept. 2 F.:** The Wisdom of the Creator. Prov. 8:22-31 **Sept. 3 S.:** The Majesty of the Creator. Ps. 8:1-9 **Sept. 4 S.:** God of Creation and Resurrection. Acts 17:24-31
LESSON AIM	To emphasize that God has revealed Himself in creation.

LESSON OUTLINE	**God of Creation**
	I. **How It All Began:** Genesis 1:1
	II. **God Revealed in Creation:** Psalm 19:1-6
	   A. The Glory of God: v. 1
	   B. A Constant Revelation: v. 2
	   C. A Silent Witness: v. 3
	   D. A Worldwide Voice: v. 4a
	   E. The Sun in Its Glory: vv. 4b-6
	III. **The Greatness of God:** Acts 17:24-28
	   A. The Lord of Heaven and Earth: v. 24
	   B. The Source of All Life: v. 25
	   C. The Maker of Mankind: v. 26
	   D. The God Who Is to Be Sought: v. 27
	   E. The Source of All Being: v. 28
	IV. **The Revelation of God in Nature:** Romans 1:20

9

SUGGESTED
INTRODUCTION
FOR ADULTS

The general topic for this quarter of lessons is "Our Biblical Faith." Our Christian faith is not based on philosophical speculation or historical tradition but on divine revelation. This revelation is found primarily in the Bible, which is God's Word to us.

This quarter's study is divided into three units. Unit I (lessons 1-4) is called "God Reveals Himself." Unit II (lessons 5-8) is entitled "God Redeems His People." Unit III (lessons 9-13) is "God Relates to His People." So our focus this quarter is on who God is and what He does.

Today we study the "God of Creation." That is where the Bible begins, and so that is where we must begin. Next week we look at the "God of History," for God has wonderfully revealed Himself in history. The third lesson is on the "God of Inspired Prophets." These three lessons give us an overview of the Old Testament. In our fourth lesson of Unit I we move into the New Testament to study "God in Christ." That is the final revelation of God, as the Epistle to the Hebrews so eloquently tells us.

SUGGESTED
INTRODUCTION
FOR YOUTH

Our topic today is: "Do You See What I See?" All of us see what is around us—the sky above us, the green grass, the towering trees, and the many-colored flowers.

But do we merely see material objects, or do we see the great God of the universe revealed in His marvelous creation? Every true Christian can properly ask the question: "Do you see what I see?"

The sad fact is that most people do not see God in creation. Even those who revel in its beauty are too often guilty of enjoying only an aesthetic reaction, with no recognition of the Creator who made it all. When we see God reflected in a beautiful flower, it becomes a spiritual experience that has eternal value for our souls.

CONCEPTS FOR
CHILDREN

1. "God Made the World."
2. The truth that God made the world is stated in the first verse of the Bible.
3. God not only made the world, but He made us.
4. So we should give ourselves wholly to Him.

THE LESSON COMMENTARY

I. HOW IT ALL BEGAN:
Genesis 1:1

In the Septuagint (Greek translation of the Hebrew Old Testament, made about 250-150 B.C.) the first book of the Bible is labeled "Genesis," the Greek word for "beginning." Genesis tells us how the world began.

The first verse of the Bible appropriately reads, "In the beginning God created the heavens and the earth." The world began with God.

The opening phrase, "in the beginning," is one word in Hebrew, *Bereshith*. Thomas Whitelaw says that here it means "at the commencement of time" (*The Pulpit Commentary*, Genesis, p. 2). God has existed from all eternity. But here we have the beginning of time, as indicated by the six "days" of creation.

The Hebrew word for "God" is *Elohim*,

the most frequent designation of the Supreme Being in the Old Testament (about two thousand times). It is in the plural—*im* is the masculine plural ending for Hebrew nouns. This plural form probably expresses "the fulness of the Divine nature, and the multiplicity of the Divine powers," and also may be "intended to foreshadow the threefold personality of the Godhead"—or "both" (*PC*, p. 2). Yet verbs and adjectives with it are in the singular, suggesting the unity of the Godhead.

The verb "created" is *bara*, which is used exclusively of God. It is probably intended to suggest the idea of creation out of nothing (*PC*, p. 3), something that only God can accomplish.

"The heavens" (plural) takes in the region of air and clouds above us, as well as the stars in the far beyond. It may be thought of as including the rest of the universe, apart from the earth. God created it all at the beginning of time.

II. GOD REVEALED IN CREATION:
Psalm 19:1-6

A. The Glory of God: v. 1

The heavens declare the glory
of God;
the skies proclaim the work
of his hands.

There is a poetic majesty about the lines of Psalm 19. C. S. Lewis declared, "I take this to be the greatest poem in the Psalter and one of the greatest lyrics in the world" (*Reflections on the Psalms*, p. 63).

The first line literally says, "The heavens are declaring the glory of God." This is a continuous witness that goes on night and day, year in and year out. Part of "glory" is beauty. No intelligent, sensitive person can fail to be impressed with the beauty of blue sky and shining sun by day, or the moon and stars at night. Another part of glory is greatness. Here we need the help of astronomy to give us an

adequate picture. Scientists tell us that many of those tiny specks of light are really far larger than our sun. And God has made millions of them!

The modern telescope has enlarged our vision of the heavens. Today astronomers are discovering new galaxies of stars over three hundred million light years away. And a light year—the distance light travels in a year—is six trillion miles. When we multiply these two figures together we get a distance that is utterly beyond our comprehension. What a great God we have! True science does not rob us of our God, nor of our faith in Him. Rather, it shows us how great our God is. Certainly a God who could create such a vast universe is able to take care of us. And His love guarantees that He will!

"The skies" is literally "the firmament"—that is, the atmosphere around the earth. This proclaims the work of God's hands.

Putting these two lines together we see that there is no excuse for doubting the existence of the God of creation. No accident of evolution can account for the beginning of life, or of succession and motion. The universe as we find it demands an intelligent, eternal, all-powerful Creator—the uncaused First Cause.

Matthew Henry has a beautiful comment on this verse. He writes:

From the excellency of the work—that is, God's creation—"we may easily infer the infinite perfection of its great author. From the brightness of the heavens we may collect that the Creator is light; their vastness of extent bespeaks his immensity, their height his transcendency and sovereignty, their influence upon this earth his dominion, and providence, and universal beneficence: and all declare his almighty power, by which they were at first made, and continue to this day according to the ordinances that were then settled" (*Commentary on the Whole Bible*, 3:301).

B. A Constant Revelation: v. 2

Day after day they pour forth
   speech;
   night after night they display
   knowledge.

How sad that so few people listen to
the "speech" or profit by the "knowledge" of the heavens! It is there for all
to receive, but most simply ignore its
message. W. T. Purkiser comments
here:

> The universe is a mute but eloquent
> witness to its Source. There is the
> thought that this has always been,
> and will continue to be as long as the
> earth shall last. No one can outrun
> or outlive the voice of God in nature
> (*Beacon Bible Commentary*, 3:183).

This verse emphasizes not only the
continuousness of the natural revelation of God—"day after day . . . night
after night"—but also the profusion of
it: The heavens "pour forth speech"
and "display knowledge." It is constantly there in abundance for all to
hear and see.

C. A Silent Witness: v. 3

The translation and meaning of this
verse have been a matter of much
debate. The King James Version reads:
"There is no speech nor language, *where*
their voice is not heard." The use of
italics indicates words that are not in
the original Hebrew. So the New
American Standard Bible has:

> There is no speech, nor are there
>   words;
> Their voice is not heard.

This is also the wording of the Revised
Standard Version. George Rawlinson
helpfully interprets this as meaning:
"The speech which they utter is not
common speech—it is without sound,
without language; no articulate voice
is to be heard" (*PC*, The Book of Psalms,
p. 129). A. R. Fausset gives a similar
interpretation. He writes:

> This, in a negative form, expresses
> the powerfulness of the testimony

which the heavens give to the glory
of God. They need no speech; for
without it, in silent eloquence, they
proclaim His power and Godhead
(Jamieson, Fausset, and Brown, *A
Commentary . . . on the Old and New
Testaments*, 3:143).

The poet Addison expressed beautifully the apparent thought of this
verse in its context. He wrote:

> What though in solemn silence all
> Move round the dark terrestrial
>   ball?
> What though no real voice nor
>   sound
> Amid their radiant orbs be found?
> In reason's ear they all rejoice,
> And utter forth a glorious voice,
> For ever singing, as they shine,
> "The hand that made us is divine."
> (Quoted in *BBC*, 3:183.)

D. A Worldwide Voice: v. 4a

Their voice goes out into all the
   earth,
   their words to the ends of the
   world.

As indicated in a footnote in the
New International Version, instead of
"voice" (Septuagint, Jerome, and Syr-
iac) the Hebrew has "line" (KJV, NASB).
But Paul quotes this passage from the
Septuagint in Romans 10:18. Fausset
makes this interesting comment about
Paul: "In this he, by the Holy Spirit,
gives the virtual meaning of the
Hebrew" (*Commentary*, 3:143). So the
Revised Standard Version and New
International Version have "voice"
here.

In spite of the problems of exact
translation in verses 3 and 4a, the main
thrust of the passage seems clear. It is
this: Nature speaks in a common, universal language to people around the
globe.

E. The Sun in Its Glory: vv. 4b-6

In the heavens he has pitched
   a tent for the sun,
   which is like a bridegroom
      coming forth from his
      pavilion,

like a champion rejoicing
to run his course.

The focus is now narrowed to "the sun." Its "tent," or dwelling place, is "the heavens."

Each morning the sun is "like a bridegroom coming forth from his pavilion." Delitzsch puts it well:

> The morning light has in it a freshness and cheerfulness, a renewed youth. Therefore the morning sun is compared to a bridegroom, the desire of whose heart is satisfied, who stands as it were at the beginning of a new life, and in whose youthful countenance the joy of the wedding day still shines (quoted in John Peter Lange, ed., *Commentary on the Holy Scriptures*, Psalms, p. 152).

On the last line of verse 5 Delitzsch comments:

> As in its rise it is compared to a bridegroom, so in its rapid course... it is compared to a hero . . . , for it goes over its course anew, every time it steps forth, bestowing its light, and overcoming all things (*Commentary*, p. 152).

Each morning the sun comes out of its "pavilion," where it has spent the night. It bursts forth in the glory of a new day and eagerly runs its race across the sky. And so verse 6 declares:

It rises at one end of the heavens
and makes it circuit to the other;
nothing is hidden from its heat.

How conscious we are of this on a cold morning! To be bathed with the soothing rays of fresh sunlight is a delightful experience. Every new sunrise is a message from God that He loves us and wants His warmth and light to refresh us in body and soul.

III. THE GREATNESS OF GOD: Acts 17:24-28

A. The Lord of Heaven and Earth: v. 24

"The God who made the world and everything in it is the Lord of heaven and earth and does not live in temples built by hands."

This verse is a part of Paul's speech before the Areopagus (v. 22), the supreme court of Athens. He began by saying: "Men of Athens! I see that in every way you are very religious." He had observed that the city was "full of idols" (v. 16). But he had been particularly impressed with one altar that had the inscription: "TO AN UNKNOWN GOD" (v. 23).

Paul proceeded to tell them who this God was. First, He was the one "who made the world and everything in it"—the great Creator. Secondly, He was "the Lord of heaven and earth." Because of that, He "does not live in temples built by hands."

It is true that the Lord told Moses to build a tabernacle at Mount Sinai, with a sanctuary where His presence would be manifested. But the Maker of the universe is too great to be housed in a manmade building. And in the ancient tabernacle there was to be no image of God. For "God is spirit" (John 4:24) and cannot be represented by any material likeness.

The "temples" that God wants to live in are human hearts—made by Himself, not by human hands. One of the great miracles in which we should rejoice daily is that if we invite the Lord into our hearts He gladly comes in to dwell there (Rev. 3:20).

DISCUSSION QUESTIONS

1. a. Why is divine creation the most reasonable explanation of the beginning of things?
   b. How else could everything have started?
2. What are some things that creation reveals about the nature of God?
3. How is God's love revealed in nature?
4. a. How is the unity of the human race taught in the Bible?
   b. What implications does this have for us?

B. The Source of All Life: v. 25

"And he is not served by human hands, as if he needed anything because he himself gives all men life and breath and everything else."

We are still studying about the "God of Creation," our lesson title. He not only made the "world"—Greek *cosmos*, "orderly universe" (v. 24)—but He made man. As Creator He still "gives all men life and breath and everything else."

This is a tremendous statement. God is the source, the continuous supply, of all life. Without Him our breath would fail and we would die. We are only kept alive by His creative power. How grateful we ought to be to Him! The ingratitude of most people in utterly ignoring God is one of the great tragedies of history and also of our day.

C. The Maker of Mankind: v. 26

"From one man [that is, 'Adam,' the Hebrew word for 'man' in Genesis] he made every nation of men, that they should inhabit the whole earth, and he determined the times set for them and the exact places where they should live."

All nations made from one man! I have commented at this point:

Thus Paul asserted the unity of the human race and suggests God's displeasure with all racial prejudice, whether it be that of the Greeks and Jews of the first century or the white and colored peoples of the twentieth century (*BBC*, 7:462).

We are related to all other human beings.

D. The God Who Is to Be Sought: v. 27

"God did this so that men would seek him and perhaps reach out for him and find him, though he is not far from each one of us."

The previous verse says that God provided "the whole earth" for man to live in and planned where each nation should settle. He even "determined the times set for them," like a loving father with his children. Now we are told that He "did this so that men would seek him." That is His loving concern for all individuals. He wants them to "reach out for him and find him." Even those who are farthest from Him because of background and environment He wants to draw to Himself in redeeming love. God "is not far from each one of us." All we have to do is turn our hearts and minds toward Him, and He is right there to receive us. How tragic that people don't realize this and accept His salvation!

E. The Source of All Being: v. 28

This verse contains two quotations. The first, "For in him we live and move and have our being" is attributed to the Greek scholar Epimenides. The second, "We are his offspring" comes from the poet Aratus. The "his" refers to the god Zeus.

Paul quoted these two men because they had stated a great truth although they referred to a false god. Paul wisely hitched on to their statement to win his audience over to a knowledge of, and acceptance of, the true God. Incidentally, it also shows that Paul was familiar with Greek literature.

IV. THE REVELATION OF GOD IN NATURE: Romans 1:20

"For since the creation of the world God's invisible qualities—his eternal power and divine nature—have been clearly seen, being understood from what has been made, so that men are without excuse."

James Denney writes:

God's power, and the totality of the Divine attributes constituting the Divine nature, are inevitably impressed on the mind by nature (or, to use the scripture word, by creation). There is that within man which so catches the meaning of all that is without as to issue in an instinctive knowledge of God (*The Expositor's Greek Testament*, 2:592).

We have a responsibility to be recipients of this knowledge of God. William Greathouse observes:

> Ever since its origin creation has spoken to the reflective mind about God. Although God cannot be known directly through reason (1 Cor. 1:21), He is knowable. This knowledge, however, is not thrust upon a passive subject; to learn about God we must adopt a positive and receptive attitude. Creation exists as an invitation to dialogue with God. Certain things may be "clearly seen," but only if we are willing to see (*BBC*, 8:51).

Consequently, sinners and unbelievers are "without excuse." If they had followed the light they found in creation, it would have led them to God. In the judgment day they will have no valid excuse to offer for their failure to do so.

CONTEMPORARY APPLICATION

A famous painter stood before a beautiful painting of a gorgeous sunset. Rapturously he described what he saw. Finally a bystander interrupted him by flatly asserting: "I don't see all *that* in this painting!" The simple reply of the painter was: "Don't you wish you could?"

God is revealed in His creation. We are familiar with the poet's observation: "Only God can make a tree." Every flower that blooms shows us something of God's beauty. The sun, the moon, the stars—they all show us something of the greatness and grandeur of our God. But do we see *Him* in His creation? This is the pertinent question we should ask ourselves frequently.

So much of life seems drab and drear, gloomy and depressing. What we need is a daily glimpse of God's glory that will lift our souls and guide our footsteps. God is revealing Himself every day in His creation. Let's not miss that revelation.

GOD OF HISTORY

DEVOTIONAL READING	Deuteronomy 26:5-10
ADULTS AND YOUTH	**Adult Topic:** *God of History*
	Youth Topic: *Listen and Learn*
	Background Scripture: Deut. 26:5-10; Ps. 105; Acts 7:2-53
	Scripture Lesson: Ps. 105:4-11, 37-45
	Memory Verse: *Remember the wonderful works that he has done.* Ps. 105:5
CHILDREN	**Topic:** *The Bible Tells About God*
DAILY BIBLE READINGS	**Sept. 5 M.:** Mighty Acts Recited. Deut. 26:5-10
	Sept. 6 T.: Deliverance Praised. Exod. 15:1-10
	Sept. 7 W.: Deliverance Forgotten. Mic. 6:3-8
	Sept. 8 T.: Deliverance Hymned. Ps. 135:1-14
	Sept. 9 F.: Creation of Nation Remembered. Ps. 114:1-8
	Sept. 10 S.: Divine Purposes Resisted. Acts 7:51-60
	Sept. 11 S.: Faithfulness Required. Ps. 105:37-45
LESSON AIM	To help us see how our God is the God of history.
LESSON SETTING	**Time:** Psalm 105 covers a period of about seven centuries, from Abraham's time (about 2000 B.C.) to the conquest of Canaan (about 1300 B.C.).
	Place: Palestine, Egypt, and the desert of Sinai

God in History

  I. **Recognizing What God Has Done:** Psalm 105:1-3

  II. **Remembering God's Works:** Psalm 105: 4-6
- A. Seeking His Face: v. 4
- B. Remembering His Wonders: v. 5
- C. A Chosen People: v. 6

  III. **The Covenant-Keeping God:** Psalm 105:7-11
- A. Covenant Forever: vv. 7-8
- B. Covenant with Abraham and Isaac: v. 9
- C. Covenant with Jacob: vv. 10-11

  IV. **Deliverance from Egypt:** Psalm 105:37-38
- A. Abundant Provision: v. 37
- B. Egyptian Reaction: v. 38

  V. **Divine Care in the Desert:** Psalm 105:39-42
- A. The Guiding Cloud: v. 39
- B. Meat and Bread: v. 40
- C. Supply of Water: v. 41
- D. The Faithful God: v. 42

  VI. **The Promised Land:** Psalm 105:43-45

(LESSON OUTLINE)

16

SUGGESTED
INTRODUCTION
FOR ADULTS

Our background Scripture today includes Stephen's speech before the Sanhedrin, recorded in Acts 7:2-53. Stephen rehearsed God's dealings with three individuals: Abraham (vv. 2-8); Joseph (vv. 9-16); and Moses (vv. 17-43). The speech is a very striking presentation of the "God of History," the title of today's lesson.

Stephen was addressing the most august body of Jews in that day, the seventy members of the Sanhedrin, the supreme court of Israel. He reminded these opponents of Jesus that the "God of glory" had appeared to Abraham in Mesopotamia (v. 2) and called him to "go to the land I will show you" (v. 3). Abraham obeyed the call and finally arrived in Canaan (v. 4). God promised him that his descendants would possess that land (v. 5). He also warned him of the oppression the people would undergo in Egypt (v. 6).

Then Stephen told graphically the story of God's dealings with Joseph (vv. 9-10) and the coming of Jacob's family into Egypt (vv. 11-16). It was an important part of God's plan.

The central event of the Old Testament was the exodus from Egypt under Moses, a picture of our redemption through Christ. So Stephen devoted the major part of his speech to the life and ministry of Moses.

Our lesson today is centered entirely in Psalm 105. The importance of this psalm is highlighted by the fact that its first fifteen verses occur in exactly the same form in I Chronicles 16:8-22. There it is attributed to David.

SUGGESTED
INTRODUCTION
FOR YOUTH

"Listen and Learn"—that's what all of us need to do. Without listening there is no learning.

One important application of that truth is this: If we don't listen to the past, we will not live successfully in the present. Those who ignore history fail in life.

In our lesson today Israel was reminded to look back and consider God's dealings with the nation from the beginnings of its history. That assignment has worthwhile rewards for us today. We should also remember God's dealings with us in the past. That should stir up gratitude in our hearts and at the same time furnish warnings for the future. So let's listen and learn.

CONCEPTS FOR
CHILDREN

1. "The Bible Tells About God." That's why we need to read it.
2. Bible stories are not only fascinating but are also important for our lives today.
3. As God helped people in Bible days, He can also help us now.
4. We should express our thanks to God for His goodness.

THE LESSON COMMENTARY

I. RECOGNIZING WHAT GOD HAS DONE:
Psalm 105:1-3

The psalm begins by saying (v. 1):

Give thanks to the LORD, call on
     his name;
   make known among the nations
     what he has done.

One of the most tragic sins committed by people in almost all walks of life is the sin of ingratitude. We should give thanks to the Lord often each day. And we should call on His name in prayer.

The psalmist exhorts us (v. 2):

Sing to him, sing praise to him;
   tell of all his wonderful acts.

One of the best ways of giving thanks is by singing songs of praise. We beg for much from God. What we need to do more often is to praise Him for what He is and for what He has already done. Songs of praise will gladden our own hearts. We will also be blessed, as will others, if we "tell of all his wonderful acts."

The psalmist continues (v. 3):

Glory in his holy name;
   let the hearts of those who seek
     the LORD rejoice.

We can't glory in ourselves or in what we have done. But we can glory in God's holy name.

Do we want joy? Then let us "seek the LORD," and we will "rejoice." This is the secret of happy living.

II. REMEMBERING GOD'S WORKS:
Psalm 105:4-6

A. Seeking His Face: v. 4

Look to the LORD and his
     strength;
   seek his face always.

Most of the versions have "seek" at the beginning of both clauses. But

Fausset says of the first: "The Hebrew is different from 'seek' in the next clause of this verse. . . . Here it is 'enquire of,' or 'ask of' . . ." (Jamieson, Fausset, and Brown, *A Commentary . . . on the Old and New Testaments*, 3:328).

When we look to ourselves for strength to carry on, the result too often is failure. What we need to do is to look to the Lord and *His* strength, which is equal to every occasion. In times of heavy pressure, which seem more than I can bear, I turn to the Lord and claim His promise: "As thy days, so shall thy strength be" (Deut. 33:25, KJV)—or, as the New International Version has it: "And your strength will equal your days." God's strength is always sufficient. I have never found it to fail.

The psalmist also admonishes us to "seek his face always." The reason we sometimes fail to meet life adequately is that we neglect to seek God's face. We depend on our own strength and experience futility instead of fullness.

B. Remembering His Wonders: v. 5

Remember the wonders he has
     done,
   his miracles, and the judgments
     he pronounced.

All three terms—"wonders" and "miracles" and "judgments"—could well be applied to the plagues in Egypt, referred to in verses 28-36. The ten plagues are described in detail in Exodus 7:14—11:6. Here in Psalm 105 only eight are mentioned.

The psalmist here moves to the time when Joseph was taken to Egypt and "sold as a slave" there (v. 17) by his jealous brothers. Joseph was mistreated in Egypt:

They bruised his feet with
     shackles,
   his neck was put in irons (v. 18).

But finally the king released him and made him second in command in Egypt (vv. 20-22).

> Then Israel entered Egypt;
> Jacob lived as an alien in the
>   land of Ham.

It was because of a severe famine that Jacob and his family moved to Egypt. But the Egyptians hated the Israelites (v. 25) and oppressed them. Then God had mercy on His people (vv. 26-27):

> He sent Moses his servant,
>   and Aaron, whom he had
>   chosen.
> They performed his miraculous
>   signs among them,
> his wonders in the land of Ham.

This is what is referred to in verse 5. Now we look at how this is spelled out in verses 28-36.

The first plague mentioned here is darkness over the land of Egypt (v. 28). This was the ninth of the ten plagues. It is described in Exodus 10:21-23, where we read: "Yet all the Israelites had light in the places where they lived."

The next plague listed (v. 29) was number one (as given in Exodus):

> He turned their waters into blood,
>   causing their fish to die.

The account in Exodus (7:14-21) graphically tells us that the waters of Egypt were turned to blood—in "streams and canals," "ponds and all the reservoirs," and "even in the wooden buckets and stone jars." It ends by saying: "The fish in the Nile died, and the river smelled so bad that the Egyptians could not drink its water. Blood was everywhere in Egypt."

The second of the ten plagues comes next in Psalm 105, in verse 30:

> Their land teemed with frogs
>   which went up into the
>   bedrooms of their rulers.

The language here is an echo of Exodus 8:3, where Moses told Pharaoh: "The Nile will teem with frogs. They will come up into your palace and your bedroom and onto your bed, into the houses of your officials and your people."

Next in our psalm come the fourth and third plagues (v. 31):

> He spoke, and there came swarms
>   of flies,
> and gnats throughout their
>   country.

The plague of gnats is described in Exodus 8:16-19 and the plague of flies in 8:20-24. In the case of the latter a new feature appeared. The Lord said to Pharaoh through Moses: "But on that day I will deal differently with the land of Goshen, where my people live; no swarms of flies will be there, so that you will know that I, the LORD, am in this land" (8:22). The Israelites suffered with the Egyptians in the first three plagues, but not in the other seven. Thus God showed that the Israelites were His people.

Next in Psalm 105 comes the seventh plague (vv. 32-33):

> He turned their rain into hail,
>   with lightning throughout their
>   land;
> he struck down their vines and
>   fig trees
>   and shattered the trees of their
>   country.

And that is exactly what we read in Exodus 9:13-26. The account concludes (vv. 23b-26):

So the LORD rained hail on the land of Egypt; hail fell and lightning flashed back and forth. It was the worst storm in all the land of Egypt since it had become a nation. Throughout Egypt hail struck everything in the fields—both men and animals; it beat down everything growing in the fields and stripped every tree. The only place it did not hail was the land of Goshen, where the Israelites were.

The eighth plague, locusts, comes next in our psalm (vv. 34-35):

He spoke, and the locusts came,
    grasshoppers without number;
they ate up everything green in
        their land,
    ate up the produce of their soil.

Again we find a graphic description
in Exodus (10:1-20). "So Moses
stretched out his staff over Egypt, and
the LORD made an east wind blow
across the land all that day and all
that night. By morning the wind had
brought the locusts" (v. 13). We are
told, "Never before had there been such
a plague of locusts, nor will there ever
be again" (v. 14). The result was:
"Nothing green remained on tree or
plant in all the land of Egypt" (v. 15).

The last of the ten plagues was climactic; it was the death of all the
firstborn males throughout Egypt. We
read of it here in Psalm 105, verse 36:

Then he struck down all the
        firstborn in their land,
    the firstfruits of all their
        manhood.

This is predicted in Exodus 11 and
12:12, and described in 12:29-30:

At midnight the LORD struck down
all the firstborn in Egypt, from the
firstborn of Pharaoh ... to the firstborn of the prisoner.... Pharaoh and
all his officials and all the Egyptians
got up during the night, and there
was loud wailing in Egypt, for there
was not a house without someone
dead.

C. A Chosen People: v. 6

The psalmist addresses his listeners
as:

O descendants of Abraham his
        servant,
O sons of Jacob, his chosen ones.

The second line reads in the King
James Version: "ye children of Jacob
his chosen." The reader would naturally
suppose that "chosen" refers to Jacob.
But the Hebrew word is plural and so
clearly means "chosen ones" (NIV). It
refers to the "sons of Jacob," the

children of Israel. They were God's
chosen people, as we find frequently
indicated in the Bible.

III. THE COVENANT-KEEPING GOD: Psalm 105:7-11

A. Covenant Forever: vv. 7-8

The psalmist cries out in verse 7:

He is the LORD our God;
    his judgments are in all the
        earth.

"LORD" (Hebrew *Yahweh*) indicates
the personal, eternal God, "He who is."
So Matthew Henry writes:

He that is our God is self-existent
and self-sufficient, has an irresistible
power and incontestable sovereignty:
"His judgments are in all the earth";
he governs the whole world in
wisdom, and gives law to all nations,
even to those that know him not. The
earth is full of the proofs of his power
(*Commentary on the Whole Bible*,
3:634).

Then the psalmist goes on to show
what this eternal, self-existent God
does, in verse 8:

He remembers his covenant
        forever,
    the word he commanded, for a
        thousand generations.

Matthew Henry comments (3:634):

See here the power of the promise; it
is the word which he commanded
and which will take effect. See the
perpetuity of the promise; it is "the
word which he commanded to a
thousand generations," and the entail
of it shall not be cut off. In the parallel
place it is expressed as our duty
(I Chron. xvi.15), "Be you mindful
always of his covenant." God will not
forget it and therefore we must not.
The promise is here called a *covenant*,
because there was something required on man's part as the condition
of the promise.

B. Covenant with Abraham and Isaac: v. 9

the covenant he made with
Abraham,
the oath he swore to Isaac.

The covenant with Abraham is described in Genesis 15:18, where we read: "On that day the LORD made a covenant with Abram and said, 'To your descendants I give this land, from the river of Egypt to the great river, the Euphrates.'"

The casual reader might assume that "the river of Egypt" means the Nile. But most commentators agree that it probably refers to the *Wadi el Arish*, which marked the boundary between Palestine and Egypt. The Euphrates is sometimes referred to in the Bible simply as "the River" (e.g., Josh. 24:14, 15). Probably in this connection it means the headwaters of the Euphrates, near Hamath, not southern Mesopotamia. These were the ideal limits of the Promised Land, and they were practically reached in the reigns of David and Solomon. In I Kings 4:21 we read, "And Solomon ruled over all the kingdoms from the River to the land of the Philistines, as far as the border of Egypt" (cf. 2 Chron. 9:26).

The second line of verse 9 reads, "the oath he swore to Isaac."

The oath was originally sworn to Abraham. In Genesis 22:15-17 we read:

The angel of the LORD called to Abraham from heaven a second time and said, "I swear by myself, declares the LORD, that because you have done this and have not withheld your son, your only son, I will surely bless you and make your descendants as numerous as the stars in the sky and as the sand on the seashore."

Then the Lord appeared to Isaac and told him: "For to you and your descendants I will give all these lands and will confirm the oath I swore to your father Abraham" (Gen. 26:3b).

C. Covenant with Jacob: vv. 10-11

He confirmed it to Jacob as a
decree,
to Israel as an everlasting
covenant:
"To you I will give the land of
Canaan
as the portion you will inherit."

It was in connection with Jacob's dream at Bethel that this covenant was confirmed to him. In his dream he saw a ladder or "stairway" (NIV) stretching from earth to heaven. Above it stood the Lord, who said to Jacob: "I am the LORD, the God of your father Abraham and the God of Isaac. I will give you and your descendants the land on which you are lying" (Gen. 28:13). As the Lord had promised to Abraham (Gen. 22:18) and to Isaac (Gen. 26:4) so now He promised to Jacob: "All peoples on earth will be blessed through your offspring" (Gen. 28:14b). This promise, as Paul points out (Gal. 3:16), was fulfilled magnificently in Christ.

"Israel" in Psalm 105:10 probably refers again to Jacob (poetic parallelism), since the Lord changed his name from "Jacob" ("heel-grasper," or "deceiver") to "Israel" (Gen. 32:28), which perhaps in its fullest sense means "princely wrestler with God."

IV. DELIVERANCE FROM EGYPT: Psalm 105:37-38

A. Abundant Provision: v. 37

He brought out Israel, laden with
silver and gold,
and from among their tribes no
one faltered.

Now we move from God's covenant with the patriarchs (Abraham, Isaac, and Jacob) to the exodus of the Israelites from Egypt. We have already noted the plagues (vv. 28-36) that precipitated that deliverance from Egyptian bondage.

The Israelites came out of Egypt

"laden with silver and gold." Exodus 12:35 tells us where they got this wealth: "The Israelites did as Moses instructed and asked the Egyptians for articles of silver and gold and for clothing." Incidentally, the King James' rendering "borrow" (here and in Exodus 3:22), which has caused so much needless discussion, is really a mistranslation. George Rawlinson notes: "The Hebrew word means simply 'ask'" (*The Pulpit Commentary*, Exodus p. 58). That is the only meaning of the Greek verb *aiteo*, used here in the Septuagint.

Why did the Israelites need all this gold and silver in the desert? To construct the tabernacle for the Lord at Mount Sinai. They were collecting some of the unpaid wages that the Egyptians owed them!

B. Egyptian Reaction: v. 38

Egypt was glad when they left,
    because dread of Israel had
    fallen on them.

Our God is a God of justice. The Egyptians had oppressed the Israelites for hundreds of years. For this, and a stubborn refusal to listen to God's demands through Moses, they were severely punished by the ten plagues. By the time the Egyptian homes had all lost their firstborn males, the people were glad to see the Israelites leave. In Exodus 12:33 we read: "The Egyptians urged the people to hurry and leave the country. 'For otherwise,' they said, 'we will all die!'"

In all of this, God was trying to get a message across to the Egyptians that He was the true God of the universe, and they should repent and turn to Him. But they refused to listen and continued on in their idolatrous pagan worship. The result is that they suffered much in their subsequent history, as have all nations that reject God.

V. DIVINE CARE IN THE DESERT: Psalm 105:39-42

A. The Guiding Cloud: v. 39

He spread out a cloud as a
    covering,
and a fire to give light at night.

In Exodus 13:21 we read: "By day the LORD went ahead of them in a pillar of cloud to guide them on their way and by night in a pillar of fire to give them light, so that they could travel by day or night." This was a very gracious, loving provision. Also at the Red Sea the cloud acted as a "covering" for the Israelites, bringing darkness to the pursuing Egyptians (Exod. 14:19-20). The cloud may also have acted as "covering" for the Israelites, shading them from the hot sun in the burning desert.

Apparently the main purpose of the cloud was to guide the Israelites in their movements through the desert between Egypt and Palestine (Exod. 40:36-37). It was also, of course, a symbol of God's constant presence with them.

B. Meat and Bread: v. 40

They asked, and he brought them
    quail
and satisfied them with the
    bread of heaven.

In Exodus 16:2-3 we read:

DISCUSSION QUESTIONS

1. Why should we thank the Lord and praise Him?
2. How often should we seek God's face in prayer?
3. In what ways are we heirs of God's covenant with Abraham?
4. What "wonders" has God done in our day?
5. What are the most important "miracles" in our times?
6. What warning should we take from the Israelites grumbling in the desert?

In the desert the whole community grumbled against Moses and Aaron. The Israelites said to them, "If only we had died by the LORD's hand in Egypt! There we sat around pots of meat and ate all the food we wanted, but you have brought us out into this desert to starve this entire assembly to death."

In response the Lord said to Moses: "I have heard the grumbling of the Israelites. Tell them, 'At twilight you will eat meat, and in the morning you will be filled with bread'" (Exod. 16:12). And this is what took place (Exod. 16:13-14).

C. Supply of water: v. 41

He opened the rock, and waters
  gushed out;
  like a river it flowed in the
    desert.

This happened twice. The first time was at Rephidim, where Moses struck a rock and water came out (Exod. 17:1-6). The second time was at Kadesh. There the Lord told Moses to speak to the rock. But Moses was impatient and struck the rock twice. "Waters gushed out" and there was plenty of it (Num. 20:8, 11).

D. The Faithful God: v. 42

For he remembered his holy
  promise
  given to his servant Abraham.

In spite of the fact that the Israelites grumbled ten times in the desert, God dealt with them in mercy. He kept His promise to Abraham and brought the people into their appointed inheritance.

VI. THE PROMISED LAND: Psalm 105:43-45

Verse 43 says:

He brought out his people with
  rejoicing,
  his chosen ones with shouts of
    joy.

At first glance this would seem to refer to the Israelites' deliverance from Egypt. But the point at which it occurs here seems to favor linking it with the Israelites being brought out of the desert and into the land of Canaan, with great joy.

In verse 44 we read:

he gave them the lands of the
  nations,
  and they fell heir to what others
    had toiled for—

Moses told the people that the Lord was going to bring them

into the land he swore to your fathers, to Abraham, Isaac and Jacob, to give you—a land with large, flourishing cities you did not build, houses filled with all kinds of good things you did not provide, wells you did not dig, and vineyards and olive groves you did not plant (Deut. 6:10-11).

There was a twofold purpose in all of this, as we find in verse 45:

that they might keep his precepts
  and observe his laws.

This is God's purpose in all his faithfulness and kindness to us. We must not fail as Israel did.

The psalm ends with "Praise the LORD." The Hebrew is our word *Hallelujah*. This is a good note on which to conclude our lesson.

CONTEMPORARY APPLICATION

The history of Israel is full of valuable lessons for us. First, we see the faithfulness of God. Regardless of obstacles and difficulties, God kept His promises to Abraham, Isaac, and Jacob. He delivered a helpless people from the strong grasp of the great military power of that day. He cared for them forty years in a barren desert. He helped them conquer the powerful nations in the land He had promised to their forefathers. All He had said He would do, He did.

But there is another side to the picture. Over and over the Israelites missed God's best blessings because they disobeyed Him. It is a warning to all of us to be obedient.

GOD OF INSPIRED PROPHETS

DEVOTIONAL READING	Amos 7:1-9

Adult Topic: *God of Inspired Prophets*

Youth Topic: *Tune In to the Messengers*

Background Scripture: Deut. 18:15-22; Amos 7:10-15; 5:21-24; Mic. 6:8

ADULTS AND YOUTH

Scripture Lesson: Deut. 18:15-22; Amos 5:21-24; Mic. 6:8

Memory Verse: *I will raise up for them a prophet like you from among their brethren; and I will put my words in his mouth, and he shall speak to them all that I command him.* Deut. 18:18

CHILDREN

Topic: *God Speaks Through People*

Memory Verse: *Let me hear what God the Lord will speak.* Ps. 85:8

DAILY BIBLE READINGS

Sept. 12 M.: The Prophetic Role. Deut. 18:15-22
Sept. 13 T.: The Prophetic Call. Jer. 1:4-10
Sept. 14 W.: The Prophetic Commission. Ezek. 3:16-21
Sept. 15 T.: The Prophetic Responsibility. Amos 7:10-15
Sept. 16 F.: The Prophetic Cry for Justice. Amos 5:21-27
Sept. 17 S.: The Prophetic Cry of Woe. Amos 6:1-7
Sept. 18 S.: The Prophetic Cry of Hope. Hab. 3:16-19

LESSON AIM

To help us see the role of God's prophets.

LESSON SETTING

Time: The incident in Deuteronomy comes from about the fourteenth century B.C. Amos prophesied about 760 B.C., Micah about 740-700 B.C. (same as Isaiah).

Place: Deuteronomy, in Moab, east of the Jordan River. Amos in North Israel, especially Bethel, twelve miles north of Jerusalem. Micah, in the southern kingdom of Judah.

LESSON OUTLINE

God of Inspired Prophets

   I. **The Promise of a Prophet:** Deuteronomy 18:15-19
      A. Moses' Assurance: v. 15
      B. Human Request: v. 16
      C. Divine Provision: vv. 17-18
      D. Divine Warning: v. 19

   II. **False Prophets:** Deuteronomy 18:20-22
      A. Severe Penalty: v. 20
      B. Recognition of a False Prophet: vv. 21-22

   III. **Prophet and Priest:** Amos 7:10-15

IV. **Ritualism Versus Righteousness:** Amos 5:21-24
  A. Divine Abhorrence: v. 21
  B. Divine Rejection: vv. 22-23
  C. Call for Righteousness: v. 24

V. **The Divine Requirement:** Micah 6:8

Since people cannot hear the divine voice speaking audibly to them, God has raised up prophets to receive His messages and communicate them to people. Particularly in the Old Testament, these divinely appointed messengers played a very important role. In the historical books we read about such prophets as Samuel, Nathan, Elijah, and Elisha. And a considerable part of the Old Testament consists of the prophetic books: Isaiah, Jeremiah, Ezekiel, Daniel, and the twelve Minor Prophets. Prophecy had a very significant place in the history of Israel.

In the New Testament we read of prophets in the early church. Today we sometimes use the term *preacher* to refer to a prophet. As we shall see, anyone who truly proclaims God's message is rightly called a prophet. May we have more of them!

"Tune In to the Messengers" is our topic today. When the preacher in the pulpit proclaims God's message on Sunday morning or evening, are you tuned in to hear it?

We all know that if a radio is not tuned in to the right station, or the television to the right channel, we do not hear the program. Just so, if our hearts and minds are not tuned in properly to the message from the pulpit, we do not really hear it as we sit in the pew.

This means that in a church service we should not be whispering or looking around at others. We should be looking at the preacher with both eyes and listening with both ears, so as to receive the message that God has for us.

1. "God Speaks Through People."
2. We should listen carefully to the preacher as he speaks, and also to our Sunday school teacher.
3. God wants to speak to us through preachers and teachers.
4. We should always listen quietly.

THE LESSON COMMENTARY

I. THE PROMISE OF A
PROPHET:
Deuteronomy 18:15-19

A. Moses' Assurance: v. 15

"The LORD your God will raise up for you a prophet like me from among your own brothers. You must listen to him."

The first and obvious application of this prediction was to Joshua, who would take Moses' place as the prophet and leader of God's people. Moses had told the Israelites that he would not be leading them into the Promised Land (Deut. 3:23-28). Naturally they were concerned. He had led them out of Egypt and for forty years in the desert. They couldn't get along without him! So Moses assured them that God was going to raise up for them a prophet like himself, and they were to listen to him and follow his directions.

But when we turn to the New Testament we discover something else. Both Peter (on the Day of Pentecost) and Stephen (before the Sanhedrin) quote this prophecy (Deut. 18:15) and apply it to Christ (Acts 3:22; 7:37).

This underscores a very important principle for handling prophecies in the Old Testament. Many prophecies have a nearer partial fulfillment in the general period of the prophet who uttered them and also a distant complete fulfillment in Christ—either at His first coming or His second coming, or both. Failure to recognize both applications can lead to misunderstanding and distortion. Some people see only the fulfillment in Christ. Others see only the application to the Old Testament situation. We must see both.

B. Human Request: v. 16

"For this is what you asked of the LORD your God at Horeb on the day of the assembly when you said, 'Let us not hear the voice of the LORD our God nor see this great fire anymore, or we will die.'"

On the morning that the Israelites received the Ten Commandments (Exod. 20:2-17) Mount Sinai was covered with smoke, as the Lord descended on it in fire and with a loud trumpet blast (Exod. 19:18-19). "When the people saw the thunder and lightning and heard the trumpet and saw the mountain in smoke, they trembled with fear" (Exod. 20:18). They said to Moses: "Speak to us yourself and we will listen. But do not have God speak to us or we will die" (Exod. 20:19). They were afraid of God's holy presence, for they had frequently evidenced unbelief and disobedience.

C. Divine Provision: vv. 17-18

The Lord told Moses: "What they say is good. I will raise up for them a prophet like you from among their brothers; I will put my words in his mouth, and he will tell them everything I command him."

The language here indicates just what a true prophet is. He is one who stands (in a sense) in the place of God and speaks God's word to the people. W. L. Alexander says of "a prophet":

The Hebrew word so rendered (*nabhi*) signifies to tell, to announce; hence the primary concept of the word is that of announcer, or forthspeaker; and to this the word "prophet" (Greek *prophetes*, from *prophemi*, I speak before or in place of) closely corresponds; the prophet is one who speaks in the place of God, who conveys God's word to men, who is an interpreter of God to men (*The Pulpit Commentary*, Deuteronomy, p. 303).

Concerning the statement, "I will put my words in his mouth," Alexander comments: "will so reveal to him my mind, and so inspire him to utter it, that the words he speaks shall be really my words" (p. 304). This put a great responsibility on the prophets to be sure they got God's messages just right.

D. Divine Warning: v. 19

"If anyone does not listen to my words that the prophet speaks in my name, I myself will call him to account." This is a solemn warning to all of us. If we fail to listen to God's message through His appointed prophet, we will be held accountable by God Himself. We are responsible for what we do with the truth we hear preached.

We realize that it is a serious thing deliberately to reject God's word to us. But we must realize that the consequences are also tragic if we ignore or neglect it. The only safe path in life is the path of sincere, prayerful obedience to the whole will of God as it is revealed to us in His Word and through His messengers.

II. FALSE PROPHETS:
Deuteronomy 18:20-22

A. Severe Penalty: v. 20

"But a prophet who presumes to speak in my name anything I have not commanded him to say, or a prophet who speaks in the name of other gods, must be put to death."

One of the most serious sins a person can commit is to claim to speak for God when he is really speaking for himself. To claim to speak divine truth when one is actually promoting error is a form of blasphemy. The enormity of this crime, in God's sight, is shown by the death penalty prescribed for it. A false prophet was to be put to death.

B. Recognition of a False Prophet: vv. 21-22

Moses recognized that someone might ask: "How can we know when a message has not been spoken by the LORD?" (v. 21). The answer given here is this: "If what a prophet proclaims in the name of the LORD does not take place or come true, that is a message the LORD has not spoken. That prophet has spoken presumptuously. Do not be afraid of him" (v. 22). Some false prophets of our day have predicted dire events for a certain date, now past. According to this test, they have proved to be false prophets.

III. PROPHET AND PRIEST:
Amos 7:10-15

Amos prophesied in the middle of the eighth century before Christ (about 760 B.C.). His ministry was in the northern kingdom of Israel, especially at Bethel.

In this passage (a part of our background Scripture) we find "Amaziah the priest of Bethel" sending a message to "Jeroboam king of Israel" accusing Amos of "raising a conspiracy against you in the very heart of Israel" (v. 10). He quoted Amos as saying (v. 11):

"Jeroboam will die by the sword, and Israel will surely go into exile, away from their native land."

This was Jeroboam II, who reigned from 786 to 746 B.C. He was one of the most powerful kings of North Israel; but he did die and the people of the northern kingdom did go into exile to Assyria in 722 B.C., when the fall of Samaria took place.

Jeroboam I (922-901 B.C.) was the first king of the northern kingdom (Israel), which broke away from Solomon's son, Rehoboam (I Kings 12:1-24). To keep the people in the north from going down to Jerusalem to worship—and perhaps reverting to Rehoboam's rule—Jeroboam set up golden calves at Bethel, in the south, and Dan, in the north, saying to the people: "Here are your gods, O Israel, who brought you up out of Egypt" (I Kings 12:28). Bethel, which literally means "house of God" (Gen. 28:16-18), was only twelve miles north of Jerusalem. Jeroboam hoped this would catch any would-be pilgrims headed for Jerusalem. They would be urged to stop and worship at Bethel.

Amaziah, the priest of the false worship at Bethel, told Amos to go back to the land of Judah and prophesy there (v. 12). Bethel was "the king's sanctuary and the temple of the kingdom" (v. 13).

The answer of Amos is very interesting. He said: "I was neither a prophet nor a prophet's son, but I was a shepherd, and I also took care of sycamore-fig trees. But the LORD took me from tending the flock and said to me, 'Go, prophesy to my people Israel" (vv. 14-15). And the Lord is still calling people from secular occupations to go and preach His gospel.

Amos was from Tekoa, a village about ten miles south of Jerusalem and five miles south of Bethlehem. The quiet surroundings helped to breed a prophet of God.

IV. RITUALISM VERSUS RIGHTEOUSNESS: Amos 5:21-24

A. Divine Abhorrence: v. 21

"I hate, I despise your religious
    feasts;
I cannot stand your assemblies."

The eighth century B.C. was the high-water mark of Hebrew prophecy. The four great prophets of that period—Amos, Hosea, Isaiah, and Micah—all sounded the keynote that righteousness, not an empty ritualism, is what God desires.

The language here seems very strong: "I hate, I despise . . . I cannot stand." We find a similar thing in Isaiah 1:14, where we read:

"Your New Moon festivals and
    your appointed feasts
my soul hates.
They have become a burden to me;
    I am weary of bearing them."

Why did God abhor these religious festivals? The answer is given in the verses that follow in Isaiah (vv. 15b-17):

"Your hands are full of blood;
    wash and make yourselves
        clean.
Take your evil deeds
    out of my sight!
Stop doing wrong,
    learn to do right!"

God wants righteousness rather than ritual. A show of piety at religious gatherings is no substitute for right living.

B. Divine Rejection: vv. 22-23

"Even though you bring me burnt
    offerings and grain offerings,
I will not accept them.
Though you bring choice
    fellowship offerings,
I will have no regard for them.
Away with the noise of your songs!
I will not listen to the music of
    your harps."

Again we find a striking parallel in Isaiah. In 1:11, 13 the Lord says to the people:

"The multitude of your sacrifices—
    what are they to me?" says the
        LORD.
"I have more than enough of burnt
    offerings,
of rams and fat of fattened
    animals;
I have no pleasure
    in the blood of bulls and lambs
        and goats. . . .
Stop bringing meaningless
    offerings!
Your incense is detestable to
    me."

What is evident throughout this whole section is that God abhors insincere acts of worship. What He wants is sincere hearts and righteous lives. Only those whose hands (representing outward living) are clean should enter His presence.

C. Call for Righteousness: v. 24

"But let justice roll on like a river,
    righteousness like a never
        failing stream!"

Here we come to the heart of the message. It is a call for justice and righteousness.

Earlier in the chapter some of the unrighteous acts and attitudes of these people are enumerated. In verse 7 the Lord says:

You . . . turn justice into
    bitterness
And cast righteousness to the
    ground.

In verses 10-11 God declares:

You hate the one who reproves
    in court
and despise him who tells the
    truth.
You trample on the poor
    and force him to give you grain.

And in verse 12b God asserts:

You oppress the righteous and
take bribes
and you deprive the poor of
justice in the courts.

Oppression of the poor is one of the
main sins mentioned by these prophets
of the eighth century. Amos himself
had already quoted the Lord as saying
of the people (2:7a):

"They trample on the heads of the
poor
as upon the dust of the ground
and deny justice to the
oppressed."

And in 4:1 the Lord rebukes those
"who oppress the poor and crush the
needy."

Isaiah speaks out very strongly on
this point. In 3:14-15 he quotes the
Lord as saying to the elders and leaders
of the people:

"It is you who have ruined my
vineyard;
the plunder from the poor is in
your houses.
What do you mean by crushing
my people
and grinding the faces of the
poor?"

And in chapter 10, verses 1-2 Isaiah
writes:

Woe to those who make unjust
laws,
to those who issue oppressive
decrees,
to deprive the poor of their rights
and rob my oppressed people of
justice,
making widows their prey
and robbing the fatherless.

The mention of "widows" reminds
us of what Jesus said on the same
subject. Speaking of the teachers of
the law—the rabbis who taught in the
synagogues—Jesus declared: "They
devour widows' houses and for a show
make lengthy prayers. Such men will
be punished severely" (Mark 12:40;
Luke 20:47). These religious leaders
would take mortgages on poor widows'
homes and when the widows could not
make the payments they would fore-
close and take over the houses.

V. THE DIVINE
REQUIREMENT:
Micah 6:8

He has showed you O man, what
is good.
And what does the LORD
require of you?
To act justly and to love mercy
and to walk humbly with your
God.

This is universally recognized as
the central verse in the Book of Micah
and one of the most significant verses
in the Old Testament. It shows us what
kind of persons God wants us to be.

Verse 8 was in answer to the questions people had asked in verses 6-7:

With what shall I come before the
LORD
and bow down before the
exalted God?
Shall I come before him with
burnt offerings,
with calves a year old?
Will the LORD be pleased with
thousands of rams,
with ten thousand rivers of oil?
Shall I offer my firstborn for my
transgression,
the fruit of my body for the sin
of my soul?

DISCUSSION QUESTIONS

1. What is a true prophet of God
today?
2. How can we recognize a false
prophet?
3. a. In what ways can our wor-
    ship in church be displeasing to
    God?
    b. What can we do about it?
4. What is included in "righteousness"?
5. What does Micah 6:8 say to each
of us?

W. J. Deane comments:

> Micah exactly represents the people's feelings; they would do anything but what God required; they would make the costliest sacrifice, even, in their exaggerated devotion, holding themselves ready to make a forbidden offering; but they would not attend to the moral requirements of the law (*PC*, Micah, p. 88).

In answer to this question the prophet named three things that God requires of us. The first is "to act justly." Deane says that this means: "To act equitably, to hurt nobody by word or deed, which was the exact contrary of the conduct previously mentioned (ch. ii. 1, 2, 8; iii. 2, etc.)." The second requirement was "to love mercy." Deane defines this as: "To be guided in conduct to others by loving-kindness." He adds, "These two rules contain the whole duty to the neighbour" (p. 88).

The third requirement was "to walk humbly with your God." Deane comments:

> This precept comprises man's duty to God, humility and obedience. "To walk" is an expression implying "to live and act," as the patriarchs are said to have "walked with God," denoting that they lived as consciously under his eye and referred all their actions to him (p. 88).

In the Gospels we find that Jesus over and over emphasized humility as one of the main virtues of a godly life. Certainly no one can truly walk with God, the eternal, infinite One, unless he walks humbly.

CONTEMPORARY APPLICATION

The heart of this lesson is the truth that no amount of ritualism will take the place of righteous living. It is not our presence or performance in church on Sunday that satisfies God's requirements, but how we live during the week. We must be just and honest in all our dealings with others. Beyond that, we must be merciful and kind. And, most important of all, we must walk humbly with God, realizing that it is only His grace through Christ that really makes us Christians.

GOD IN CHRIST

DEVOTIONAL READING	John 1:14-18

Adult Topic: *God in Christ*

Youth Topic: *Meet God in Person*

ADULTS AND YOUTH

Background Scripture: John 1:14-18; 14:8-11; Heb. 1:1-4; I John 1:1-4

Scripture Lesson: John 14:8-11; Heb. 1:1-4; I John 1:1-4

Memory Verse: *In many and various ways God spoke of old to our fathers by the prophets; but in these last days he has spoken to us by a Son.* Heb. 1:1-2

CHILDREN

Topic: *Jesus Tells About His Father*

Memory Verse: *(Jesus said) "He who has seen me has seen the Father."* John 14:9

DAILY BIBLE READINGS

Sept. 19 M.: The Word Made Flesh in Christ. John 1:9-18
Sept. 20 T.: God Well-Pleased in Christ. Mark 1:1-11
Sept. 21 W.: The Hidden Mystery in Christ. Eph. 3:7-21
Sept. 22 T.: The Way in Christ. John 14:1-14
Sept. 23 F.: Servanthood Exalted in Christ. Phil. 2:5-10
Sept. 24 S.: God's Glory Reflected in Christ. Heb. 1:1-14
Sept. 25 S.: God Made Manifest in Christ. I John 1:1-10

LESSON AIM — To help us understand how God has spoken to us in Christ.

LESSON SETTING

Time: A.D. 30-95

Place: Jerusalem; Ephesus. The place of writing of Hebrews is unknown.

LESSON OUTLINE

God in Christ

  I. **God Seen in Christ:** John 14:8-11
    A. Philip's Request: v. 8
    B. Jesus' Answer: v. 9
    C. The Father Living in the Son: v. 10
    D. Evidence of the Miracles: v. 11

  II. **God Speaking in Christ:** Hebrews 1:1-4
    A. Variety of Previous Revelations: v. 1
    B. Final Revelation in Christ: v. 2
    C. The Being and Work of Christ: v. 3
    D. Superiority to Angels: v. 4

  III. **God Appearing in Christ:** I John 1:1-4
    A. The Word of Life: v. 1
    B. The Eternal Life: v. 2
    C. Seen and Heard: v. 3
    D. Purpose of Writing: v. 4

SUGGESTED
INTRODUCTION
FOR ADULTS

The background Scripture of our lesson today is John 1:14-18. Verse 14 is one of the greatest statements of the Incarnation to be found in the Bible.

In John 1:1 we read: "In the beginning was the Word, and the Word was with God, and the Word was God." Here we have the assertion that the Word (Greek, *Logos*) existed eternally with God and was God. The imperfect tense ("was") underscores this truth.

In verse 14 we shift to another verb and the aorist tense—"became." The eternal Son of God became Son of Man ("became flesh"), "and lived for a while [Greek, 'tented'] among us." The apostle declares, "We have seen his glory."

Some may wonder why the New International Version has "one and only" instead of "only begotten" (KJV). This is because the Greek word *monogenes* is clearly used in the former sense in the Septuagint (Greek translation of the Old Testament).

In verse 15 we have the testimony of John the Baptist to the superiority of Jesus, who though born after him was "before me." Then the apostle John resumes his testimony to Jesus in verses 16-18.

SUGGESTED INTRODUCTION FOR YOUTH

Our topic today is "Meet God in Person." That is what we all need to do if our religion is going to be worth anything. We need more than head religion; we need heart religion. And that involves persons.

How can we meet God in person? Only in Christ! Jesus Christ came to earth in human form to reveal God to us. What is God like? He is like the Jesus who lived among men to show them the true nature of God—that "God is love" (I John 4:8, 16).

We need to read the Gospels to see what Christ is like, and so what God is like. Someone has well said that Jesus is "God brought near." How thankful we ought to be that Jesus can come into our hearts and make God real to us!

CONCEPTS FOR CHILDREN

1. Christ makes God the Father real to us.
2. We should ask Jesus to come into our hearts.
3. Then we will have God's presence with us all the time.
4. God's presence can make life worthwhile.

THE LESSON COMMENTARY

I. GOD SEEN IN CHRIST: John 14:8-11

A. Philip's Request: v. 8

Chapters 14-16 of John's Gospel are generally referred to as the Last Discourse of Jesus, given to His disciples in the upper room the night before His crucifixion. It was followed by His high-priestly prayer, recorded in chapter 17.

Jesus began by saying: "Do not let your hearts be troubled. Trust in God; trust also in me" (14:1). The disciples were troubled because Jesus had told them He was going to leave them (13:33).

Then He told them why He was
leaving them: "I am going ... to prepare
a place for you. And if I go and prepare
a place for you, I will come back and
take you to be with me that you also
may be where I am" (14:3). Jesus added:
"You know the way to the place where
I am going" (v. 4).

Typically, Thomas said to Him:
"Lord, we don't know where you are
going, so how can we know the way?"
(v. 5). Jesus replied with the tremendous
statement: "I am the way and the truth
and the life" (v. 6). Then He added: "If
you really knew me, you would know
my Father as well. From now on, you
do know him and have seen him" (v. 7).
This was an amazing disclosure.

Our printed lesson begins at this
point. Philip said, "Lord, show us the
Father and that will be enough for us"
(v. 8). Philip was a very practical
person. This is shown in John 1:45-46
and 6:5-7. He wanted a concrete
demonstration!

B. Jesus' Answer: v. 9

Jesus replied, "Don't you know me,
Philip, even after I have been among
you such a long time?" We can almost
hear the pathos in Jesus' voice as He
asked this question. So many days,
weeks, months—about three years—
have passed and you still don't know
me!

Jesus went on to say, "Anyone who
has seen me has seen the Father." This
is one of the most startling statements
Jesus ever uttered. And we should face
up realistically to the implications of
this. If any of us made this statement
we would rightly be called the world's
worst fool and egotist. But Jesus made
the statement and got away with it.
Why? Because He was really what He
claimed to be—the eternal God appearing in human flesh. The centuries
have vindicated His claim.

In the past hundred years many
liberal theologians have said that Jesus
was a good man, a great teacher, but
not the eternal Son of God. They admire
His humanity but deny His deity. What

they fail to see is that if Jesus was not
God, He was not a good man; He was a
liar. Jesus declared, "Anyone who has
seen me has seen the Father"—that is,
has seen Deity. And in John 10:30 we
find this even more definite statement:
"I and the Father are one." No wonder
we read immediately: "Again the Jews
picked up stones to stone him" (v. 31)
for blasphemy. If Jesus is not truly
God, then He *was* guilty of blasphemy.
There is no middle ground here.

So the Master chided His disciples:
"How can you say, 'Show us the
Father'?" (14:9). They were seeing the
Father as revealed in the Son. This
shows the unreasonableness of unbelief.
For all those who are willing to stop
and look at Jesus—in the Bible, in
history—the evidence is clear: He *is*
the Son of God.

C. The Father Living in the Son:
  v. 10

"Don't you believe that I am in the
Father and that the Father is in me?
The words I say to you are not just my
own. Rather, it is the Father, living in
me, who is doing his work."

This verse highlights another truth.
Although Jesus is equal in divine
essence to the Father, He is subordinate
in office and work. He speaks what His
Father directs Him to say and does
what His Father commands Him to
do. That is why He is called "the Son of
God." As Son, He is subordinate to the
Father.

D. Evidence of the Miracles:
  v. 11

"Believe me when I say that I am in
the Father and the Father is in me; or
at least believe on the evidence of the
miracles themselves."

Unlike the authors of the synoptic
Gospels, John records only seven miracles of Jesus. And each one is called a
"sign." That is, each one signified
(sign-i-fied) some spiritual truth. For
instance, the feeding of the five thousand signified that Jesus was the Bread

of Life (see chapter 6). And in John 20:30-31 we read: "Jesus did many other miraculous signs in the presence of his disciples.... But these are written that you may believe that Jesus is the Christ, the Son of God...." The miracles were proofs of His deity.

II. GOD SPEAKING IN CHRIST: Hebrews 1:1-4

A. Variety of Previous Revelations: v. 1

"In the past God spoke to our forefathers through the prophets at many times and in various ways." This is a summary description of divine revelation in the Old Testament period.

"At many times" is one word in Greek, the adverb *polymeros*. *Poly*, which we have taken over as an English prefix, means "many." *Meros* means "part." So the adverb literally means "in many parts" or "in many portions" (NASB). It wasn't all given at once.

"In various ways" is the adverb *polytropos*. *Tropos* means "way." So the compound word means "in many ways," which suggests "in various ways."

Marcus Dods gives an excellent treatment of these two adverbs. He writes:

> *Polymeros* points to the fragmentary character of former revelations. They were given piece-meal, bit by bit, part by part, as the people needed and were able to receive them. The revelation of God was essentially progressive; all was not disclosed at once, because all could not at once be understood (*The Expositor's Greek Testament*, 4:247).

Dods goes on to say:

> His speaking was also *polytropos* ... not in one stereotyped manner but in modes varying with the message, the messenger, and those to whom the word is sent. Sometimes, therefore, God spoke by an institution [for instance, the Tabernacle and its offerings], sometimes by parable,

sometimes in a psalm, sometimes in an act of righteous indignation.... These features of previous revelations, so prominently set and expressed so grandiloquently, cannot have been meant to disparage them, rather to bring into view their affluence and pliability and many-sided application to the growing receptivity and varying needs of men (*EGT*, 2:248).

Even the written revelation from God that we find in the Old Testament was given over a period of about a thousand years—from Moses (about 1400 B.C.) to Malachi (about 400 B.C.). But before that revelations were given to Adam, Noah, Abraham, and the other patriarchs.

B. Final Revelation in Christ: v. 2

"But in these last days he has spoken to us by his Son, whom he appointed heir of all things, and through whom he made the universe."

We are apt to think of the expression "last days" as referring to the end of this church age. And it does seem to have that meaning in II Timothy 3:1, as well as in some other places in the New Testament. But on the Day of Pentecost Peter quoted Joel's prophecy of the "last days" and applied it to what had just taken place in the outpouring of the Spirit on Jesus' followers in the upper room (Acts 2:16-18). So in its largest connotation "the last days" means the days of the Messiah, or the messianic age. That is the meaning it clearly has here.

In the past God had spoken at many times and in various ways. But now He had spoken "by his Son." The Greek says *en whio*—literally, "in a son." This emphasizes the character of the new revelation in Christ; it was a *personal* revelation. The previous revelations had been in prophecies, types, and symbols. But an impersonal revelation of a person must always be an imperfect one. So at last God sent His Son. Only a personal revelation of a person can be a perfect revelation. Christ alone is the perfect revelation of God.

The author of Hebrews says further of Christ: "whom he appointed heir of all things." As the one and only Son of God, Jesus is heir to the whole estate. But Paul makes a startling declaration. He says that "we are God's children. Now if we are children, then we are heirs—heirs of God and co-heirs with Christ" (Rom. 8:16-17). What a fantastic privilege!

We also read of Christ: "through whom he made the universe." The Greek says *tous aionas*—literally, "the ages." B. F. Westcott observes:

The universe may be regarded either in its actual constitution as a whole (*ho cosmos*), or as an order which exists through time developed in successive stages. There are obvious reasons why the latter mode of representation should be adapted here (*The Epistle to the Hebrews*, p. 8).

This idea of Christ as Creator of all things is given strong emphasis by Paul in Colossians 1:16, as well as by John in his Gospel (1:3). It is one of the many glories attributed to Christ.

C. The Being and Work of Christ: v. 3

The being of Christ is expressed here in strong language: "The Son is the radiance of God's glory and the exact representation of his being." The Greek word for "radiance" (*apaugasmia*) is found only here in the New Testament. It means the "effulgence," or outshining, of God's presence. "Exact representation" is one word in Greek, *character* (only here in the New Testament), which we have taken over into English. It first meant "a tool for engraving," and then "a stamp or impress," as on a coin or seal. It is that by which a person or thing can be recognized. We recognize God in Christ.

What about the term "being" (KJV, "person") here? The Greek word is *hypostasis*, "underlying reality." Westcott says that Christ "is the expression

of the 'essence' of God. He brings the Divine before us at once perfectly and definitely according to the measure of our powers" (*Hebrews*, p. 13). Marcus Dods suggests: "To the English ear, perhaps, 'nature' or 'essence' better conveys the meaning" (*EGT*, 4:251). So we can use "nature" (NASB) or "being" (NIV).

Now how about Christ's "work"? First, we are told that He is "sustaining all things by his powerful word." Christ is not only the Creator of all life; He is the sustainer of all life. This truth is beautifully expressed by Paul. After saying that "all things were created by him [Christ]," he goes on to say, "and in him all things hold together" (Col. 1:16-17). Some years ago an eminent scientist declared, "If the creative force that holds our universe together were withdrawn for even a moment, the whole universe would collapse." Paul, under divine inspiration, tells us that this creative force is Christ. And He is not only the force that holds the universe together; He is the creative force that holds our individual lives together. Without Him, life falls apart.

Another work of Christ is indicated here in the verse we are studying. We read about Christ, "After he had provided purification for sins, he sat down at the right hand of the Majesty in heaven." He is not only the Creator and Sustainer of the universe; He is also its Redeemer. And His work of redemption is every bit as important as His work of creation.

D. Superiority to Angels: v. 4

The main theme of the first chapter of the Epistle to the Hebrews (see vv. 4-14) is the superiority of Christ to angels. This is introduced here by the statement: "So he became as much superior to the angels as the name he has inherited is superior to theirs."

What is that name of His? It is "son" (v. 5). The word "angel" comes directly from the Greek word *angelos*, which means "messenger." Christ is the Son of God, truly God, King of the universe (see v. 8). But angels are only servants in God's household. This is affirmed in the closing verse of the chapter: "Are not all angels ministering spirits sent to serve those who will inherit salvation?"

III. GOD APPEARING IN CHRIST: I John 1:1-4

A. The Word of Life: v. 1

"That which was from the beginning, which we have heard, which we have seen with our eyes, which we have looked at and our hands have touched—this we proclaim concerning the Word of life."

Alfred Plummer says of I John:

The first four verses are introductory. They are analogous to the first eighteen verses of the Gospel, and to the first three of Revelation. Like the Prologue to the Gospel, this Introduction tells us that the Apostle's subject is *the Word who is the Life* (*The Epistles of St. John*, p. 14).

Several good commentators insist that *logos* ("word") does not here mean the personal Son of God, as in the prologue of John's Gospel. Rather, it means the "word" (small "w") about Jesus (cf. RSV). But I prefer to take the terms as referring to Christ, as in the Gospel. Plummer says of the expression "of life": "More probably the genitive is one of apposition." He goes on to say: "'The Word which is the Life' is the meaning. Christ is at once the Word of God and the Life of man" (p. 16).

"That which"..."which"..."which" ..."which"—all four times in the Greek it is simply *ho*, which is a neuter pronoun. Plummer comments: "S. John employs the neuter as the most comprehensive expression to cover the attributes, words, and works of the Word and the Life manifested in the flesh" (p. 14).

John's Gospel begins by saying, "In the beginning was the Word" (*Logos*). Similarly we have here: "That which

was from the beginning." The Son of God did not come into being; He existed from all eternity.

John here makes four observations about the Word of Life. The first is: "which we have heard." With his own ears John had heard Jesus speak the tremendous truths that he recorded in his Gospel.

The second is: "which we have seen with our eyes." The Logos was no apparition. The disciples had seen Him with their own eyes, as He shared life with them day after day for a period of about three years.

In the third place John notes: "which we have looked at." The Greek verb used here indicates more than "see." George Abbott-Smith says that it means *"to behold, look upon, contemplate, view*... in NT apparently always in literal, physical sense of 'careful and deliberate visions which interprets... its object'" (*A Manual Greek Lexicon of the New Testament*, p. 203). It was not just a fleeting glimpse of Christ.

The fourth assertion made is: "our hands have touched." The disciples had been in close contact with Jesus over a considerable period of time.

Why did John pile up these clauses? The Epistle as a whole shows that he was combating Docetic Gnostic ideas that were permeating the atmosphere at Ephesus and threatening the faith of the Christians. The Docetists denied the humanity of Christ; He only *seemed* to have a physical body. John's answer

---

DISCUSSION QUESTIONS

1. How does Jesus reveal Himself to us today?
2. How can we learn to know Him better?
3. In what ways did God speak in Old Testament times?
4. In what ways is Christ superior to angels?
5. Why did Christ come in the flesh?
6. In what way is Christ eternal life?

was an emphatic "No! We have heard, seen, viewed, and touched Him. We know that He had a physical body." In his Gospel John emphasizes the deity of Jesus; in his Epistle he underscores Jesus' humanity.

Probably "we" is the editorial we. John was the last survivor of the twelve apostles. He speaks for them and from his own experience.

B. The Eternal Life: v. 2

"The life appeared; we have seen it and testify to it; and we proclaim to you the eternal life, which was with the Father and has appeared to us." This seems clearly to indicate a person, the Son of God, who "appeared" in His incarnation. Jesus declared in His Last Discourse: "I am . . . the life" (John 14:6).

C. Seen and Heard: v. 3

"We proclaim to you what we have seen and heard, so that you may have fellowship with us. And our fellowship is with the Father and with his Son, Jesus Christ." Here we have another favorite Johannine term: "fellowship" (Greek, *koinonia*), which occurs four times in this chapter (vv. 3, 6, 7). Paul also uses it four times in II Corinthians. The term basically means a "sharing"—in this case, of love.

D. Purpose of Writing: v. 4

"We write this to make our joy complete." This is what the earliest Greek manuscripts say. Plummer comments: "'*Our* joy' may mean either the *Apostolic* joy at the good results of Apostolic teaching; or the joy in which the recipients of the teaching share—'yours as well as ours'" (*St. John*, p. 21).

CONTEMPORARY APPLICATION

The question Jesus asked Philip (John 14:9)—"Don't you know me . . . , even after I have been among you such a long time?"—still confronts us today with a tremendous challenge. We have been a disciple of Jesus for years, yet we still don't know Him?

Fortunately, we have a significant advantage that Philip did not have. While he could see Jesus in physical form in daily action, which we cannot, we have the even greater advantage of the Holy Spirit in our hearts to reveal to us who and what Jesus really is (John 14:15-19, 26; 15:26; 16:12-15).

But our problem is this: Do we take time to listen to the Holy Spirit speaking in our hearts and trying to show us Jesus more clearly? He wants to do it, but we must let Him. And that takes time and attention.

THE PROBLEM: SIN

DEVOTIONAL READING	Romans 2:5-11

ADULTS AND YOUTH

Adult Topic: *The Problem: Sin*

Youth Topic: *You Have a Problem*

Background Scripture: Jer. 2:9-13; Rom. 1:18—2:29

Scripture Lesson: Jer. 2:9-13; Rom. 1:18, 28—2:1, 11

Memory Verse: *All have sinned and come short of the glory of God.* Rom. 3:23

CHILDREN

Topic: *Wrongdoing Makes Trouble*

Memory Verse: *Hate what is evil, hold fast to what is good.* Rom. 12:9

DAILY BIBLE READINGS

Sept. 26 M.: The Evils of God's People. Jer. 2:9-13
Sept. 27 T.: "My Sin Is Ever Before Me." Ps. 51:1-12
Sept. 28 W.: No Excuse. Rom. 1:18-23
Sept. 29 T.: "God Shows No Partiality." Rom. 2:1-11
Sept. 30 F.: "Doers of the Law." Rom. 2:12-16
Oct. 1 S.: "Will You Not Teach Yourselves?" Rom. 2:17-24
Oct. 2 S.: "A Matter of the Heart." Rom. 2:25-29

LESSON AIM

To help us see the seriousness of sin as the main problem of humanity.

LESSON SETTING

Time: Jeremiah prophesied 626-586 B.C. Romans was written about A.D. 56.

Place: Jeremiah prophesied in Jerusalem. Romans was written at Corinth.

LESSON OUTLINE

The Problem: Sin

I. **The Lord's Charge Against Judah:** Jeremiah 2:9-12
   A. Charges by the Lord: v. 9
   B. Worse Than the Pagans: vv. 10-11
   C. Horror at Judah's Sin: v. 12

II. **Two Sins of Judah:** Jeremiah 2:13
   A. Forsaking God: v. 13a
   B. Making Their Own Religion: v. 13b

III. **God's Wrath Against Sin:** Romans 1:18

IV. **The Sins of the Gentiles:** Romans 1:21-32
   A. Idolatry: vv. 21-23
   B. Immorality: vv. 24-27
   C. Inner Depravity: vv. 28-32

V. **God's Righteous Judgment:** Romans 2:1-11
   A. No Excuse: v. 1
   B. Fair Judgment: vv. 2-10
   C. No Favoritism: v. 11

SUGGESTED
INTRODUCTION
FOR ADULTS

We all have many problems that arise in our daily existence. That's a part of life in this world. But our lesson today, "The Problem: Sin," highlights an important truth: Sin is *the* problem of all humanity. Other problems—physical ailments, financial pressures, emotional upsets, social adjustments, job difficulties—are nothing compared to the problem of sin. We, with the help of other people, may be able to take care of those problems, but only God can take care of the problem of sin. Christ made provision for the solution of this problem at Calvary. We have to accept His finished work for us in order for the problem of sin to be solved in our own lives.

As our lesson tells us, God holds us accountable for our sins. We cannot blame them on heredity or environment. We have the responsibility to confess our sins and receive forgiveness for them—then quit sinning!

SUGGESTED
INTRODUCTION
FOR YOUTH

"You Have a Problem." I sometimes say to an audience, "I got problems; you got problems; all God's children got problems!" And that is true. But it is not only God's children who have problems. The worst problem is sin, and every individual who has reached the age of accountability faces that problem. Our key verse tells us, "All have sinned and fall short of the glory of God."

Not only does the Bible tells us that we have sinned, but our own conscience corroborates the fact. We all have that inner consciousness of having done wrong.

Thank God, there is a solution for this problem. John tells us: "If we confess our sins, he is faithful and just and will forgive our sins and purify us from all unrighteousness" (I John 1:9).

CONCEPTS FOR
CHILDREN

1. "Wrongdoing Makes Trouble"—always!
2. Even when we have done wrong, God loves us and wants to forgive us.
3. But we must ask God's forgiveness.
4. And we should ask God to help us not do wrong again.

THE LESSON COMMENTARY

I. THE LORD'S CHARGE AGAINST JUDAH:
Jeremiah 2:9-12

A. Charges by the Lord: v. 9

Jeremiah prophesied during the last forty years of the kingdom of Judah. This is indicated precisely in the first three verses of the book. "When the people of Jerusalem went into exile" (v. 3) was 586 B.C., when the Babylonian army destroyed Jerusalem (with its Temple) and took the people as captives.

This is called the Babylonian captivity. It was Jeremiah's assignment to warn the people of their coming captivity, and to see the event take place because they refused to repent and obey the Lord.

In 2:5 the Lord, through His prophet, asks a pathetic question:

"What fault did your fathers find
    in me,
    that they strayed so far from
    me?

They followed worthless idols
and became worthless
themselves."

This is always the price that people
pay when they forsake the true God to
follow false gods such as money,
pleasure, or self.

The condition of the nation was sad
indeed. Verse 8 shows that the priests,
the teachers of the law, the leaders,
and even the prophets had rebelled
against God and gone into idolatry. We
read:

"The priests did not ask,
'Where is the LORD?'
Those who deal with the law did
not know me,
the leaders rebelled against me.
The prophets prophesied by Baal,
following worthless idols."

Now we come to verse 9, the beginning of our printed lesson.

"Therefore I bring charges
against you again,"
declares the LORD.
"And I will bring charges
against your children's
children."

Criminals sometimes manage to
avoid having charges brought against
them by their fellowmen. But no one
who sins can evade God's charges of
guilt. For He sees all we do and hears
all we say, and even knows all we think.
There is no escaping His judgment for
our sins, except to confess them and
throw ourselves on His mercy. This
condemnation for sin extends to all
generations.

B. Worse Than the Pagans:
vv. 10-11

"Cross over to the coasts of
Kittim and look,
send to Kedar and observe
closely;
see if there has ever been
anything like this:
Has a nation ever changed its
gods?

(Yet they are not gods at all.)
But my people have exchanged
their Glory
for worthless idols."

The people of Judah were worse
than the pagan idolaters. The latter
were usually very loyal to their gods.
But the people of Judah had forsaken
the true God, "their Glory," to follow
worthless idols.

It is often true today that people of
other religions are much more zealous
in their worship than are professing
Christians. One thinks of the Moslems
praying five times a day. How many
Christians do that? When I was
teaching for two months in Beirut I
was awakened each morning at about
four o'clock by the loudspeaker from
the minaret of a nearby mosque. When
I visited the mosques at any time of
the day I usually found many people
there reading the Koran or praying to
Allah—the Moslem name for the
Supreme Being.

The nearest I have seen to this on
the part of Christians is in Korea. While
teaching there for about three months
I heard the chimes ringing from the
nearest church each morning at about
4:30. Looking out, I would see the
lights on at the church, where people
gathered at that hour seven mornings
a week to pray. I joined them one
morning, sitting on the floor, with no
heat on in the church and eight degrees
above zero outside! That is real dedication. No wonder Christianity is
flourishing in Korea more than in any
other non-Christian country!

There is another aspect of this that
should concern us. Are we less zealous
about our service for the Lord than
worldly people are about their secular
pursuits? The devotion that people
show to money, pleasure, and personal
interest puts most of us to shame. We
ought to serve the true God with more
zeal and dedication than people give
to their false gods, which are really
only "worthless idols."

C. Horror at Judah's Sin: v. 12

"Be appalled at this, O heavens,
    and shudder with great horror,"
            declares the LORD.

In John Peter Lange's *Commentary on the Holy Scriptures* we read this comment: "The greatness of the crime can be estimated by none so well as the over-arching heavens, which can behold and compare all that takes place" (Jeremiah, p. 32).

We find this appeal to the "heavens" at several places in prophetic poetry. Typical is the second verse of Isaiah:

Hear, O heavens! Listen, O earth!
    For the LORD has spoken:
"I reared children and brought
        them up,
    but they rebelled against me."

Matthew Henry comments:

Heaven itself is here called upon to stand amazed at the sin and folly of these apostates from God. . . . The earth is so universally corrupt that it will take no notice of it; but let the heavens and heavenly bodies be astonished at it. Let the sun blush to see such ingratitude and be afraid to shine upon such ungrateful wretches (*Commentary on the Whole Bible*, 4:408).

One of the greatest follies that mankind has ever committed is turning away from worshiping the Creator and bowing down to manmade idols. From every standpoint—intellectual, moral, spiritual—this is the abysmal depth of stupidity. When God's greatness and beauty abound before our eyes on every side, the least we can do is to turn to Him with gratitude and full devotion.

II. TWO SINS OF JUDAH: Jeremiah 2:13

A. Forsaking God: v. 13a

The Lord says: "My people have committed two sins: . . ." The first sin they committed was:

"They have forsaken me,
    the spring of living water."

When we think of all the Lord had done for His people, this seems incredible. He had delivered them from Egyptian slavery, led them safely across the desert, given them possession of the Promised Land, and helped them to build a strong, extensive kingdom under David and Solomon. And now they had forsaken Him and gone into idolatry.

The ten northern tribes had immediately turned to the worship of the images of the golden calves set up by Jeroboam I at Bethel and Dan. He set up the calves for political reasons, to keep the people from going back to Jerusalem for the annual religious festivals.

There was no excuse for the southern kingdom of Judah to go into idolatry. They had the Temple at Jerusalem and God's presence represented there in the Holy Place. They should have remained true.

B. Making Their Own Religion: v. 13b

God says here that His people have forsaken Him, "the spring of living water,"

"and have dug their own cisterns,
    broken cisterns that cannot
        hold water."

Jesus told the Samaritan woman at Jacob's well: "The water I give him will become in him a spring of water welling up to eternal life" (John 4:14). Since Jesus is eternal life, His presence in our hearts gives us eternal life.

But the people of Judah had forsaken God, the fountain of life, and had "dug their own cisterns, broken cisterns that cannot hold water." Archaeology has uncovered many cisterns in the Holy Land, where water is often scarce. When abundant rain does come at certain times of the year, the water is stored in these cisterns to prepare for the dry seasons.

The worthless idols the people had turned to were like broken cisterns; there was no "living water" in them. And this is true of all false religions. Why will people turn away from the true God and worship the gods they have made—their own selfish ambitions and pleasures? These only bring death.

III. GOD'S WRATH AGAINST SIN: Romans 1:18

"The wrath of God is being revealed from heaven against all the godlessness and wickedness of men who suppress the truth by their wickedness."

The King James Version says, "who hold the truth." The Greek verb *katecho* does sometimes mean "hold fast." But *katecho* is compounded of *echo*, "hold," and *kata*, "down." So its literal meaning is "hold down." William Sanday and Arthur C. Headlam observe: "It is the truth which is "held down," hindered, thwarted, checked in its free and expansive operation" (*A Critical and Exegetical Commentary on the Epistle to the Romans*, p. 42). They also comment: "They stifle and suppress the Truth within them, while they go on still in their wrong-doing" (p. 39). So the correct translation is "suppress" (RSV, NASB, NIV).

The expression "the wrath of God" causes some people to raise their eyebrows. How do we harmonize this with "God is love" (I John 4:8, 16)?

Frederick Godet writes: "In God, who is the living *Good*, wrath appears as the holy disapprobation of evil, and the firm resolve to destroy it" (*Commentary on St. Paul's Epistle to the Romans*, p. 99). I like A. M. Hunter's definition of God's wrath as "his holy love reacting against evil" (*Interpreting Paul's Gospel*, pp. 69-70).

IV. THE SINS OF THE GENTILES: Romans 1:21-32

A. Idolatry: vv. 21-23

These verses portray the tragic descent of man from the highest heights to the lowest depths. Man began with a knowledge of the true God; he "knew God" (v. 21) from the days of the Garden of Eden.

Then men took the first step downward: "they neither glorified him as God nor gave thanks to him." They did not give Him His proper place as the eternal, infinite God. And they were guilty of the horrible sin of ingratitude. When we fail to give God thanks, we are headed downward.

As a result of this, "their thinking became futile and their foolish hearts were darkened." When we turn away from God, who is Light (I John 1:5), we plunge ourselves into darkness.

Proudly claiming to be wise, "they became fools" (v. 22). Then they "exchanged the glory of the immortal God for images made to look like mortal man and birds and animals and reptiles" (v. 23). We have here not only the descent into idolatry, but also the descent *in* idolatry; worshiping images of "man," then of "birds," then of "animals," and finally of "reptiles."

B. Immorality: vv. 24-27

Idolatry naturally leads to immorality. We become like the object we worship. When people worship animals they live like animals. That is what happened in the pagan world.

Because the people forsook God and worshiped idols, "God gave them over in the sinful desires of their hearts to sexual impurity for the degrading of their bodies with one another" (v. 24). This describes much of society in our day.

Verses 26-27 present a sordid picture of homosexuality. This was the sin of ancient Sodom (Gen. 19:5, NIV). Secular writers of the time of Paul show that it was exceedingly common then. And how about our day? Every alert American knows the answer to that question. It may well be that there is more homosexuality practiced in the world today than at any time since the first century. It is one of the appalling sins of our day. It caused the fall of

Sodom and Rome, and it could cause the fall of western civilization in our time. It is not only prevalent in America, but also in western Europe.

C. Inner Depravity: vv. 28-32

"Furthermore, since they did not think it worthwhile to retain the knowledge of God, he gave them over to a depraved mind, to do what ought not to be done" (v. 28).

In verses 23-28 we find two significant expressions, each of which occurs three times. The first is "exchanged ... for" (vv. 23, 25, 26). What a bad bargain mankind struck when it made these exchanges!

The second expression describes what God did in judgment as a result. We read three times that God "gave them over" (vv. 24, 26, 28). The King James Version only twice says "gave them over." But the Greek is precisely the same in all three places, and "gave them over" is its true meaning.

What is the implication of this expression, which is one word in Greek (*paredoken*)? Sanday and Headlam state that the force of *paredoken* "is not merely *permissive* . . . , through God permitting men to have their way; or *privative* through His withdrawing His gracious aid; but *judicial;* the appropriate punishment of their defection" (*Romans*, p. 45). God is not only loving, but holy and just.

In verses 29-31 we find perhaps the longest list of vices to be found in the New Testament—no less than twenty-one of them. Godet divides these into four groups. He suggests that the four terms in the first group—"wickedness, evil, greed, and depravity"— "refer to injustices committed against the well-being and *property* of our neighbour." The five terms of the second group—"envy, murder, strife, deceit, and malice"—embrace "all the injustices whereby the person of our neighbour is injured." The six terms of the third group—"gossips, slanderers, God-haters, insolent, arrogant, and boastful"—"are those of which

pride is the centre." The six terms of the fourth group—"inventors of evil, disobedient to parents" (NASB), "senseless, faithless, heartless, ruthless"— refer to "the extinction of all the natural feelings of humanity, filial affection, loyalty, tenderness, and pity" (*Romans*, pp. 110-11).

Paul concludes by saying: "Although they know God's righteous decree that those who do such things deserve death, they not only continue to do these very things but also approve of those who practice them" (v. 32).

V. GOD'S RIGHTEOUS JUDGMENT: Romans 2:1-11

A. No Excuse: v. 1

"You, therefore, have no excuse, you who pass judgment on someone else, for at whatever point you judge the other, you are condemning yourself, because you who pass judgment do the same things."

In the last part of chapter 1 Paul gives a vivid portrayal of the sins of the Gentiles, against which "the wrath of God is being revealed from heaven" (v. 18). In chapter two he turns his attention to the sins of the Jews (see verses 17-29). Probably verse 1 here is addressed primarily to the self-righteous Jew, although it may include the moralistic Gentile.

Paul had said in 1:20 that men "are

DISCUSSION QUESTIONS

1. What parallels can be found between Jeremiah's day and ours?
2. What are some "idols" worshiped by Americans?
3. Have we in America been guilty of changing gods?
4. How does wickedness "suppress the truth"?
5. What does "a depraved mind" do to people?
6. How can we escape condemnation at the Judgment Day?

without excuse." As we have noted, the reference is primarily to Gentiles in chapter 1. But he declares likewise to the judgmental Jews: "You . . . have no excuse" for your sins, though they may be different from those of the Gentiles. Judging others harshly is in itself a sin. And Jesus' words to the Pharisees, recorded in the Gospels, show that He held them to be guilty of the very serious sins of inconsistency and bad attitudes.

B. Fair Judgment: vv. 2-10

"Now we know that God's judgment against those who do such things is based on truth" (v. 2). Judges and juries make unfair judgments because of not knowing the actual truth of a case, but God knows perfectly what the truth is. And His holy character guarantees that He will always be just in judging.

Because "a mere man" (v. 3) cannot judge rightly, we should leave all judgment to God. Jesus Himself warned: "Do not judge, or you too will be judged" (Matt. 7:1).

Verses 5-8 contain solemn warnings of divine judgment on those who do evil. There is no escaping God's "righteous judgment" (v. 5).

C. No Favoritism: v. 11

"For God does not show favoritism," or "partiality" (NASB). The Greek literally says: "For there is no receiving of face (*prosopolempsia*) with God." Earthly politicians often practice receiving someone's face for selfish advantage. But God deals fairly and justly with all individuals, great or small. Moses warned the Israelites: "For the LORD your God . . . shows no partiality and accepts no bribes" (Deut. 10:17).

CONTEMPORARY APPLICATION

Two things stand out in the lesson today. The first is the seriousness of sin. In both Jeremiah (Old Testament) and Romans (New Testament) we find severe condemnation pronounced on those who willfully sin against God. And a significant aspect of sin is conforming to the lifestyle of those around us. The Israelites were condemned for following the idolatrous patterns of their neighbors. And in Romans we are warned of the fatal consequences of living like the world.

A second point is the variousness of sin. As professing Christians we may feel that we are "righteous" before God, when actually we are guilty of wrong attitudes that will bring divine judgment on us. We need to keep close to God to be free from sin and guilt.

THE MOTIVE: GOD'S LOVE

DEVOTIONAL READING	John 3:16-18
ADULTS AND YOUTH	**Adult Topic:** *The Motive: God's Love* **Youth Topic:** *You Have a Friend* **Background Scripture:** Hos. 11:1-4, 8; 14:4-7; John 3:16-18; I John 4:8-12 **Scripture Lesson:** Hos. 11:1-4; 14:4-7; I John 4:8-9 **Memory Verse:** *He who does not love does not know God; for God is love.* I John 4:8
CHILDREN	**Topic:** *God Is Love*
DAILY BIBLE READINGS	Oct. 3 M.: "How Can I Give You Up?" Hos. 11:1-9 Oct. 4 T.: "I Will Heal Their Faithlessness." Hos. 14:1-9 Oct. 5 W.: "Thou Knowest Me Right Well." Ps. 139:7-18 Oct. 6 T.: "God So Loved the World." John 3:16-21 Oct. 7 F.: "The Free Gift of God." Rom. 6:15-23 Oct. 8 S.: "No Condemnation." Rom. 7:21—8:4 Oct. 9 S.: "Love Is of God." I John 4:7-12
LESSON AIM	To help us understand and appreciate the love of God.
LESSON SETTING	**Time:** Hosea prophesied about 750-736 B.C. I John was probably written about A.D. 95. **Place:** Hosea prophesied in the northern kingdom of Israel. I John was probably written in Ephesus.

LESSON OUTLINE	**The Motive: God's Love**
	
	I. **God's Love for Israel:** Hosea 11:1-4
	  A. Israel as a Child: v. 1
	  B. A Wayward Son: v. 2
	  C. Teaching Ephraim to Walk: v. 3
	  D. The Tenderness of God: v. 4
	
	II. **God's Compassion for Israel:** Hosea 11:8
	
	III. **God's Healing Love:** Hosea 14:4-7
	  A. Healing Their Backsliding: v. 4
	  B. Healthy Growth: vv. 5-7
	
	IV. **God Is Love:** I John 4:8-9
	  A. The Central Attribute of Deity: v. 8
	  B. Demonstration of Divine Love: v. 9

SUGGESTED INTRODUCTION FOR ADULTS	The Book of Hosea is the first of the so-called Minor Prophets. This does not mean that these books are less important. It simply recognizes that they are shorter than Isaiah, Jeremiah, and Ezekiel.

Hosea prophesied in the eighth century B.C., which marked the high-water level of Hebrew prophecy. His contemporaries were Isaiah, Amos, and Micah.

Hosea's book is the most dramatic of all the prophets. It is built around the story of his marriage to Gomer, her unfaithfulness to him, and his redemption of her from slavery. Their three children had names that symbolized God's message to Israel.

In *Meet the Minor Prophets* I have written this summary:

> The Book of Hosea divides itself very naturally into two sections. In the first three chapters we have the story of a broken heart and a broken home. In chapters four to fourteen, inclusive, we have God's message to Israel, based on this experience (p. 17).

SUGGESTED INTRODUCTION FOR YOUTH

"You Have a Friend." What wonderful news that is! Sometimes young people feel as if they don't have a friend in the world. Pastor, parents, school friends—no one understands them or really cares about them.

But you always have one friend who loves you all the time and wants to help you to have a happy, worthwhile life. That friend is Jesus. He showed His love for you by dying for you on the cross, paying the penalty for your sins. He shows His love for you now by coming to you and speaking to your heart. Respond to that love and you will experience life at its best.

CONCEPTS FOR CHILDREN

1. "God is love." This verse can be memorized in a few moments, but it has meaning all our lives.
2. We should accept God's love because we need it.
3. God's love is the love of a kind Father.
4. Because God loves us, He disciplines us.

THE LESSON COMMENTARY

I. GOD'S LOVE FOR ISRAEL: Hosea 11:1-4

A. Israel as a Child: v. 1

"When Israel was a child, I loved him,
and out of Egypt I called my son."

W. J. Deane comments: "The prophet goes back to that early period when the national life of Israel was in its infancy; it was then that a few patriarchs who had gone down to sojourn in Egypt were becoming a people" (*The Pulpit Commentary*, Hosea, p. 329).

He goes on to say: "The people of Israel is called God's son in consequence of God's choosing them and bringing them into close relationship to himself, such as that of a son to a father" (p. 330).

When God called Moses to return to Egypt and deliver His people, He instructed him to tell Pharaoh that the Lord says: "Israel is my firstborn son, and I told you, 'Let my son go, so he may worship me.' But you refused to let him go; so I will kill your firstborn son" (Exod. 4:22-23). Here we find the reason why the tenth, climactic plague in Egypt was the death of the firstborn.

God loved the Israelites as a father loves his young child. And that is why He, in mercy, delivered them out of Egyptian bondage.

B. A Wayward Son: v. 2

"But the more I called Israel,
    the further they went from me.
They sacrificed to the Baals
    and they burned incense to
        images."

The picture here is a familiar one. A father calls to his little boy, "Johnny, come here." Instead of obeying him, the child starts walking away. Again the father calls, *"Johnny, come here!"* But the boy starts running farther away as fast as he can.

That is the way young Israel had treated the Lord. Through His prophets ("they . . . them" [KJV, NASB] means the prophets of the Lord) God called His child to follow Him. But the more He called, the farther the nation went away from Him.

The Israelites went so far away from God that they even "sacrificed to the Baals" (Hebrew, *Baalim*). This was a general name for the male gods of the pagan nations of that time. The people who alone had the eternal God of heaven, the Creator of the universe, the Almighty One, forsook Him to burn incense to dumb idols. It is difficult for us today to understand how the people of Israel could do such a senseless thing. Their God had delivered them from the mighty empire, Egypt, given them the land of powerful nations in Canaan, cared for them lovingly across the years, and now they had forsaken Him to worship the dead idols of the nations that God had enabled them to defeat. What could be more utterly stupid? Yet that is what people do today when they turn their backs on a loving, redeeming God to follow the idols of this world.

C. Teaching Ephraim to Walk: v. 3

"It was I who taught Ephraim to
    walk,
    taking them by the arms;

but they did not realize
    it was I who healed them."

Again we have a vivid picture, that of a fond parent holding the arms of a toddling infant as he learns to take his first steps. It is a very tender scene: the great Creator of the universe, the One who inhabits eternity, lovingly teaching His child Israel to walk. What divine condescension!

The last two lines of this verse—"but they did not realize it was I who healed them"—sound a pathetic note.

God was doing everything to help Israel, but with blinded eyes and hardened hearts they ignored Him and actually turned away from Him.

Matthew Henry writes on this verse:

When they were in the wilderness God led them by the pillar of cloud and fire, showed them the way in which they should go, and bore them up, *taking them by the arms.* . . . He took them by the arms, to guide them, that they might not go astray, and to hold them up, that they might not stumble and fall. . . . When anything was amiss with them, or they were ever so little out of order, he was their physician: *"I healed them;* I not only took a tender care of them (a friend may do that), but wrought an effectual cure: it is a God only that can do that" (*Commentary on the Whole Bible,* 4:1181).

D. The Tenderness of God: v. 4

"I led them with cords of human
    kindness,
    with ties of love;
I lifted the yoke from their neck
    and bent down to feed them."

It was not with the heavy ropes of harsh slavery that God led the Israelites, but with ties of tender love. He treated them like helpless children who needed His gentle care.

The last two lines paint a picture that is unfamiliar to modern Americans. It is that of oxen lowering their heads to eat hay. The heavy wooden yokes on their necks slide down onto their heads, making it very difficult for them to eat. A kind owner lifts the yoke off the back of their heads. He might also go a step further: bend down and lift some hay to their mouths, to make eating easier for them. That is the way God was treating His people.

II. GOD'S COMPASSION FOR ISRAEL: Hosea 11:8

"How can I give you up, Ephraim?
How can I hand you over, Israel?
How can I treat you like Admah?
How can I make you like
Zeboiim?
My heart is changed within me;
all my compassion is aroused."

As noted in the Lesson Setting, Hosea was prophesying in the northern kingdom of Israel—called by that name in contradistinction from Judah in the south. The people in the north were also called Ephraim, since that was the main one of the ten tribes. So "Ephraim" and "Israel" here mean the same thing.

With tender compassion God cries out: "How can I give you up. . . . How can I hand you over?" Just as Hosea's heart was broken when his wife Gomer left him, so God was broken-hearted that His people would leave Him for other gods. This was shown later when Jesus "died of a broken heart" on the cross of Calvary. God doesn't want to give us up, to hand us over to our enemies. He wants to save us.

What is meant by the reference to Admah and Zeboiim? In Deuteronomy 29:23 we read a warning of what will happen to Israel if she breaks God's covenant with her: "The whole land will be a burning waste of salt and sulphur—nothing planted, nothing sprouting, no vegetation growing on it. It will be like the destruction of Sodom and Gomorrah, Admah and Zeboiim, which the LORD overthrew in fierce anger." But here God says, "How can I treat you like" these cities of the plain that perished with Sodom and Gomorrah? And so He cries out:

"My heart is turned over within
Me,
All my compassions are
kindled" (NASB).

In the Gospels we frequently read that when Jesus was confronted with human need He was "filled with compassion" or "moved with compassion." Jesus came to earth to show us what God was like, as we saw in a recent lesson. So we know that God's heart is gripped with compassion for us. And nowhere in the Old Testament is that portrayed more graphically than in Hosea.

III. GOD'S HEALING LOVE: Hosea 14:4-7

A. Healing Their Backsliding: v. 4

In the first two verses of this chapter the prophet is pleading with the people to repent. He exhorts them:

Return, O Israel, to the LORD
your God.
Your sins have been your
downfall!
Take words with you
and return to the LORD.
Say to him:
"Forgive all our sins
and receive us graciously."

Then in verse 4 we find the very gracious reply of Deity:

"I will heal their waywardness
and love them freely,
for my anger has turned away
from them."

What words could be more gracious and forgiving? Even though the people had forsaken the Lord, turned to other gods and terribly disobeyed the law God had given them, yet He agrees to answer their cry of repentance with tender compassion, His healing touch, His gracious love, His complete forgiveness. What a great God we have!

B. Healthy Growth: vv. 5-7

"I will be like the dew to Israel;
   he will blossom like a lily.
Like a cedar of Lebanon
   he will send down his roots;
   his young shoots will grow.
His splendor will be like an olive
      tree,
   his fragrance like a cedar of
      Lebanon.
Men will dwell again in his shade.
He will flourish like the grain.
He will blossom like a vine,
   and his fame will be like the
      wine from Lebanon."

This is a description of Israel when
God has healed its waywardness. Once
more the nation would flourish, when
it had repented and turned back to
God.

With regard to the "dew" (v. 5)
W. J. Deane writes:

In lands where there is little rain,
the dew, falling copiously, *fertilizes*
the earth, refreshes the languid
plants, revives the face of nature,
and makes all things grow. Thus the
dew becomes the source of fruitfulness. So God, by his Spirit's grace, is
the Source of Israel's spiritual fruitfulness (*PC*, Hosea, p. 433).

The Lord goes on to say, through
His prophet, that Israel "will blossom
like the lily." Deane comments:

This comparison suggests many
qualities, any one of which may
characterize, or all of which may
combine in, the spiritual growth thus
pictured. There is the purity of the
lily, the beauty of the lily, the fecun-
dity of the lily, the perfume of the
lily, the rapidity of its growth, the
stately slightness of its stem (p. 433).

Next God says that Israel will send
down its roots "like a cedar of Lebanon."
The emphasis here is on stability.
Deane quotes Jerome (fourth century)
as commenting:

As the trees of Lebanon, which strike
their roots as far down into the depths
as they lift their heads up into the

air, so that they can be shaken by no
storm, but by their stable massive-
ness maintain their position (p. 433).

The description may seem a bit exag-
gerated. But we should seek to send
our spiritual roots deep down into the
Word of God and prayer, so that our
Christian lives will be stable.

In verse 6 the splendor of revived
Israel is likened to that of an "olive
tree," and its fragrance to that of a
"cedar of Lebanon." Deane comments:

The olive has been called the crown
of the fruit trees of Palestine, but
besides, its fruitage so plentiful and
useful, the splendour of its green,
and the enduring freshness of its
foliage, make it a vivid picture of
that *beauty* of holiness or spiritual
graces which it is here employed to
represent (p. 433).

There is also to be a "fragrance"
about our Christian lives, the fragrance
of God's presence and also of our
devotion to our Lord (John 12:3, NIV).

Verse 7 declares, "Men will dwell
again in his shade." As Christians we
should be like shade trees to those who
are suffering in the scorching heat of
the pressures of life. Our presence
should be refreshing, not depressing.

It is also said that revived Israel
will "blossom like a vine." Anyone who
has seen a vineyard flourishing in the
springtime can appreciate this simile.

DISCUSSION QUESTIONS

1. Why did the Israelites turn
   away from the Lord?
2. a. What makes people from
      Christian homes go astray?
   b. What can we do to help
      prevent this?
   c. What part does love play in
      this?
3. What is the real meaning of
   compassion?
4. How can we grow spiritually?

IV. GOD IS LOVE:
I John 4:8–9

A. The Central Attribute
of Deity: v. 8

"Whoever does not love does not know God, because God is love." Here we find inescapable logic. If God is love, then those who know God in His saving grace show love in their lives. Church members who do not evidence this love for others belie their testimony that they are Christians. John says bluntly: "If anyone says, 'I love God,' yet hates his brother, he is a liar" (v. 20).

Very few things are equated absolutely with God in the Scriptures, but "love" is. And we find this repeated in verse 16, for emphasis. "God is love" is one of the first Scripture verses lisped on the lips of children in Sunday school. And yet it is one of the most profound statements in print, confounding the abilities of the greatest philosophers and theologians to fathom its depths. It will take us all our lives here and eternity to comprehend its full meaning.

John had already given us two great statements about the nature of God: "God is spirit" (John 4:24) and "God is light" (I John 1:5). Now he climaxes it with "God is love." Alfred Plummer writes: "Here, as in the other cases, the predicate has no article, and expresses not a quality which He *possesses*, but one which embraces all He *is*" (*The Epistles of St. John*, p. 100). He goes on to say:

And yet of the three great truths this is the chief. The other two are incomplete without it. The first, "God is spirit," is almost more negative than positive: God is not material.... The second might seem in making our idea of Him more definite to remove Him further away from us: God is perfect intelligence, perfect purity, perfect holiness. The third

not only makes His Nature far more clearly known, but brings Him very close to us. The spirit is shewn to be personal, the light to have warmth and life (p. 101).

It is no wonder that John has been called "the apostle of love." It would be well for us to pray that we, too, might become apostles of love in a loveless world.

It should be remembered, of course, that the Greek word for "love" here is not *eros*, physical love. This term came to describe behavior so lascivious in that day that it never occurs in the New Testament. From it we get our term "erotic." And there is altogether too much erotic love in our world today.

Neither is it the noun *philia*, which does occur once in the New Testament (James 4:4), where it is translated "friendship." *Philia* means affectionate love (the verb *phileo* is twice translated "kiss" [Matt. 26:48; Mark 14:44]) or friendship love.

The word here, as is commonly known, is *agape*. This is pure love, unselfish love, the love of full loyalty and true devotion, a love that always seeks the best good of its object. That is the kind of love that God is and that He shows to us.

If God is love, then we are not godly (Godlike) unless we have this divine love and show it in our lives. This is a daily challenge to all of us.

B. Demonstration of Divine
Love: v. 9

"This is how God showed his love among us: He sent his one and only Son into the world that we might live through him." There could be no greater demonstration of divine love than this. Flowing out of the heart of the infinite God, it encompasses the whole world. God give us more of this kind of love!

CONTEMPORARY APPLICATION

Jesus said to His disciples in John 20:21, "As the Father has sent me, I am sending you." This highlights the application of this lesson that we should make to our lives today. True love is outflowing, outgoing toward others. If we do not have this kind of love, we need to tarry before God until He implants it in our hearts.

God's love was the motive for creation and redemption. It must be our motive for Christian service today.

THE MEANS: GOD'S SON

DEVOTIONAL READING	Hebrews 3:1-6
ADULTS AND YOUTH	**Adult Topic:** *The Means: God's Son* **Youth Topic:** *God Made a Way* **Background Scripture:** Rom. 3:21-26; 5:6-11; Heb. 9:11-15; Col. 1:11-14 **Scripture Lesson:** Rom. 3:21-26; 5:6-11; Col. 1:13-14 **Memory Verse:** *While we were still weak, at the right time Christ died for the ungodly.* Rom. 5:6
CHILDREN	**Topic:** *Jesus, the Son of God* **Memory Verse:** *This is my beloved Son with whom I am well pleased.* Matt. 3:17
DAILY BIBLE READINGS	Oct. 10 M.: The Gift of Grace. Rom. 3:21-26 Oct. 11 T.: "Mediator of a New Covenant." Heb. 9:11-15 Oct. 12 W.: We Are Made Alive with Christ. Col. 2:8-15 Oct. 13 T.: Christ the Cornerstone. Eph. 2:11-22 Oct. 14 F.: The Faithfulness of Christ. Heb. 3:1-6 Oct. 15 S.: Reconciled Through Christ. Col. 1:13-23 Oct. 16 S.: "While We Were Yet Sinners." Rom. 5:6-11
LESSON AIM	To see the means God used to provide redemption for mankind.
LESSON SETTING	**Time:** Paul wrote Romans about A.D. 56, Colossians about A.D. 60. **Place:** Paul wrote Romans in Corinth, Colossians in prison at Rome.

LESSON OUTLINE	**The Means: God's Son**
	
	 I. Righteousness Through Faith: Romans 3:21-26
	   A. A Righteousness from God: v. 21
	   B. A Righteousness Through Faith: v. 22
	   C. All Have Sinned: v. 23
	   D. Justification by His Grace: v. 24
	   E. An Atoning Sacrifice: v. 25a
	   F. The Justice of God: vv. 25b-26
	
	 II. Christ's Death for Us: Romans 5:6-8
	   A. He Died for the Ungodly: v. 6
	   B. Demonstration of Divine Love: vv. 7-8
	
	 III. Results of Justification: Romans 5:9-11
	   A. Saved from God's Wrath: v. 9
	   B. Saved Through Christ's Life: v. 10
	   C. Rejoicing in God: v. 11

IV. **Redemption in Christ:** Colossians 1:13-14
   A. The Divine Rescue: v. 13
   B. The Forgiveness of Sins: v. 14

SUGGESTED
INTRODUCTION
FOR ADULTS

The Epistle to the Romans is the most theological book of the New Testament. Paul had been trained in rabbinical thinking, and he argues his points at considerable length, as the rabbis did. One must pay close attention to follow his train of thought.

The first eight chapters of the Epistle are doctrinal. The apostle treats three essential doctrines of Christianity in logical order: (1) sin (1:16—3:20); (2) justification (3:21—5:21); (3) sanctification (cc. 6-8). Today we are dealing with the matter of justification, in chapters 3 and 5.

Last week we studied the "motive" of our redemption, which was God's "love." Today we look at the "means" of our redemption, which is "God's Son"—specifically His atoning death for us on the cross. There was no other means by which our salvation could have been secured. We ought to feel eternally, and *daily*, thankful for God's love and Christ's sacrifice that made possible our salvation.

SUGGESTED
INTRODUCTION
FOR YOUTH

"God Made a Way." When there was no way, God made a way. And it was a costly way. It meant the death of His own Son on the cross of Calvary. Since God is love, as we noted last week, this makes His giving of His Son all the more magnanimous and magnificent. Think of what it cost our loving heavenly Father! No sacrifice that we make to follow Christ can repay the debt of love we owe. So let's give ourselves to Christ completely, and let Him have His way fully in our lives. That is the least, and the greatest way, we can show our gratitude.

CONCEPTS FOR
CHILDREN

1. God the Father said of Jesus: "This is my Son, whom I love; with him I am well pleased."
2. Jesus carried out His Father's will completely.
3. We can be well pleasing to God by doing His will for us.
4. God will help us to do His will.

THE LESSON COMMENTARY

I. RIGHTEOUSNESS THROUGH FAITH: Romans 3:21-26

A. A Righteousness from God: v. 21

The King James Version, Revised Standard Version, and New American Standard Bible all have "the righteousness of God" in verse 21, but the Greek does not have the definite article with *dikaiosyne*, "righteousness." So the New International Version, probably correctly, has "a righteousness from God" (genitive of source).

James Denney discusses three interpretations of the phrase, as it is found here and in 1:17 (where he discusses it at length). He begins by saying, "Plainly, *dikaiosyne theou* is something without which a sinful man cannot be saved; but what is it?" (*The Expositor's Greek Testament*, 2:589). He goes on to say:

> There can be no doubt that the fundamental religious problem for the Apostle—that which made a Gospel necessary . . . —was, How shall a sinful man be righteous before God? To Luther this suggested that *dikaiosyne theou* meant a righteousness valid before God, of which a man can become possessed through faith; for such a righteousness (as the condition of salvation) is the first and last need of the sinful soul (p. 590).

After expressing his approval of Luther's concept, Denney calls attention to the contrast in 10:3 between God's righteousness and man's own attempted righteousness. He then goes on to say:

> If this contrast were allowed to tell here, the righteousness of which Paul speaks would be one of which God is the source or author; we do not bring it to Him, He reveals it for our acceptance. . . . The broad sense of "a Divine righteousness" covers this second, which may be called the historical Protestant interpretation, as well as Luther's (p. 590).

Denney proceeds to mention a third interpretation. He says that Theodore Haering "argues that *dikaiosyne theou* means the judicial action of God in which He justifies His people and accomplishes their salvation" (p. 590).

Which of these interpretations is correct? Denney declares: "In substance all these three views are Biblical, Pauline and true to experience" (p. 591).

Denney's conclusion is this:

> The righteousness of God, conceived as a Divine attribute, may have appeared to Paul the great difficulty in the way of the justification of sinful man. God's righteousness in this sense is the sinner's condemnation, and no one will succeed in making him find in it the ground of his hope. What is wanted . . . is a righteousness which, as man cannot produce it, must be

> from God, and which, once received, shall be valid before God (p. 591).

Taking everything into consideration, I feel that "a righteousness from God" is the best translation here. I would agree, however, with William Greathouse when he notes the "much discussion" about whether the expression here means a divine attribute or a gift bestowed by God upon man ("a righteousness of which God is the author and man the recipient"), and concludes: "No doubt it is both of these" (*Beacon Bible Commentary*, 8:41).

We have labored this subject at considerable length. This is because, as Greathouse notes, we are dealing here with "the thematic topic of the Epistle" (*BBC*, 8:41).

There is another phrase in this verse that also needs careful interpretation. In the Greek it is *choris nomou*—literally, "apart from law" (RSV, NIV). Again we find "without the law" (KJV) and "apart from the Law" (NASB). But there is no definite article with *nomou*, "law." On the basis of this fact, Denney comments:

> It is plain that in this expression *nomos* does not signify O.T. revelation or religion as such, but that religion, or any other, conceived as embodied in statutes. It is statutory obedience which (as Paul has learned by experience) cannot justify (*EGT*, 2:609).

Paul declares that the righteousness God has provided to believers is witnessed by "the Law and the Prophets." This twofold expression was used by the Jews for their Holy Scripture, our Old Testament. In the fourth chapter of Romans Paul labors the point that Abraham was justified by faith, not works (law).

B. A Righteousness Through Faith: v. 22

"This righteousness from God comes through faith in Jesus Christ to all who believe. There is no difference, . . ." The earliest Greek manuscripts have simply "to all," not "unto all and upon all" (KJV).

This verse states the great central truth of the Epistle to the Romans. We receive God's righteousness through faith in Jesus Christ and what He did for us on the cross. Nothing we can do will merit it. Paul writes that "to the man who does not work but trusts God who justifies the wicked, his faith is credited as righteousness" (4:5). That truth is the heart of the gospel of salvation.

C. All Have Sinned: v. 23

Every human being needs this salvation, "for all have sinned and fall short of the glory of God." The first verb here is in the aorist tense, "for all have sinned"—a summary statement of the past. But the second verb is in the present tense of continuous action, "and fall short of the glory of God."

What is meant by "the glory of God"? Frederick Godet says it means "the divine splendor which shines forth from God Himself, and which He communicates to all that live in union with Him" (*Commentary on St. Paul's Epistle to the Romans*, pp. 148-49). He goes on to say:

> God can communicate this glory, because he possesses it Himself, and it belongs to His nature. He had communicated a ray of it to man when He created Him pure and happy; it was intended to shine more and more brightly in him as he rose from innocence to holiness. By sinning, man lost both what he had received of it and what he was yet to obtain (p. 149).

D. Justification by His Grace: v. 24

Paul then says that all who believe "are justified freely by his grace through the redemption that came by Christ Jesus."

There are two important words in this verse. The first is the verb "justify." The Greek verb is *dikaioo*. It is obviously related to the noun *dikaiosyne*, "righteousness," which we found in verse 21. The verb *dikaioo* means "declare righteous." But it also involves the idea of being made righteous. When God declares us righteous, because of our faith in Jesus Christ as our Savior, He also makes us righteous in heart. Otherwise He would be telling a lie. That is, God cannot say we are righteous unless we *are* righteous. So justification (in a legal sense) and regeneration (new spiritual life) take place simultaneously in the experience we call "conversion."

The second significant word here is "redemption." The Greek term is *apolytrosis*. It comes from *lytron*, which means a ransom price—used most frequently in that day for the ransom paid to free a slave. So "redemption" means the ransom price that was paid to free us from the slavery of sin.

William Sanday and Arthur C. Headlam note that some commentators wish to reduce the meaning of the Greek word here to merely that of deliverance, without any suggestion of "ransom." They counter this idea by observing:

> But in view of the clear resolution of the expression in Mark x.45 (Matt. xx.28) ... and in 1 Tim. ii.6 ..., and in view also of the many passages in which Christians are said to be "bought," or "bought with a price" ... we can hardly resist the conclusion that the idea of *lytron* retains its full force.... The emphasis is on the *cost* of man's redemption (*A Critical and Exegetical Commentary on the Epistle to the Romans*, p. 86).

They wisely conclude by sounding this salutary warning: "We need not press the metaphor yet a step further by asking (as the ancients did) to whom the ransom or price was paid" (p. 86).

E. An Atoning Sacrifice: v. 25a

Speaking of Christ Jesus, Paul wrote: "God presented him as a sacrifice of atonement, through faith in his blood." Here we are clearly told what the ransom price was that was paid for our salvation: It was "his [Christ's] blood."

"A sacrifice of atonement"—"a propitiation" (KJV, NASB)—is one word in the Greek, *hilasterion*. This is an adjective, but here, in the neuter, it is evidently used as a substantive. The only other place in the New Testament where this word occurs is Hebrews 9:5, where it is translated "mercy seat" (KJV, NASB) or "place of atonement" (NIV). The clear reference there is to the lid of the ark, on which the high priest sprinkled the blood of the sin offering on the annual Day of Atonement (Yom Kippur), to atone for the sins of all the people.

There has been a good deal of debate among commentators as to how *hilasterion* should be treated here. I have expressed my own conclusion this way:

It seems best to relate the term *hilasterion* to the mercy seat in the ancient Tabernacle, since all agree that it clearly has this meaning in the Septuagint and in the only other place where it occurs in the NT, Heb. 9:5. Just as the high priest once a year on the Day of Atonement, took the blood of the sin offering and sprinkled it on the mercy seat, so Christ as our great High Priest took the blood of His own sacrifice and offered it as the propitiation for our sins. The Epistle to the Hebrews seems clearly to indicate that Christ is himself the Priest, the Altar, and the Sacrifice. He is the Fulfillment of all the typology of the Tabernacle (*Word Meanings in the New Testament*, 3:83).

F. The Justice of God: vv. 25b-26

"He did this to demonstrate his justice, because in his forbearance he had left the sins committed beforehand unpunished—he did it to demonstrate his justice at the present time, so as to be just and the one who justifies the man who has faith in Jesus."

The point of division between verses 25 and 26 was very poorly chosen. The last part of verse 25 obviously belongs with 26. Sanday and Headlam say of

the beginning of verse 26: "to be closely connected with the preceding clause: the stop which separates this verse from the last should be wholly removed . . . we should represent it in English by a dash or semicolon" (*Romans*, p. 90). The New American Standard Bible uses the semicolon. The New International Version, with better English style, uses a dash.

Sanday and Headlam represent the various pauses in this passage in this way:

Whom God set forth as propitiatory—through faith—in His own blood—for a display of His righteousness; because of the passing-over of foregone sins in the forbearance of God with a view to the display of His righteousness at the present moment, so that He might be at once righteous (Himself) and declaring righteous him who has for his motive faith in Jesus (*Romans*, p. 90).

Some thoughtful people might well ask the question: "How could a holy God let sin go on so long, without direct punishment?" The answer is that in allowing His Son to be a sacrifice of atonement so that sincere believers could be saved, God showed His hatred of sin.

II. CHRIST'S DEATH FOR US: Romans 5:6-8

A. He Died for the Ungodly: v. 6

"You see, at just the right time, when we were still powerless, Christ died for the ungodly." When we were utterly powerless to save ourselves, Christ provided salvation for us by dying in our place on the cross.

B. Demonstration of Divine Love: vv. 7-8

"Very rarely will anyone die for a righteous man, though for a good man someone might possibly dare to die. But God demonstrates his own love for us in this: While we were still sinners, Christ died for us."

In verse 8 the King James Version has "his love." The Greek emphatically says "his own love." The greatest proof of God's unfathomable love for us is that He would plan for and permit His own precious Son to die on the cross for us sinners. There could be no greater demonstration of divine love. We show our gratitude for this, first by accepting Christ's atoning sacrifice for our sins, and then by sharing this good news with others.

III. RESULTS OF JUSTIFICATION: Romans 5:9-11

A. Saved from God's Wrath: v. 9

"Since we have now been justified by his blood, how much more shall we be saved from God's wrath through Him!"

Now that we are justified before God by the blood of Christ shed for us, we have the gracious assurance that on the day of final judgment we shall be saved from God's wrath. It is only as we are consciously in Christ through faith that we can feel no dread of divine judgment.

B. Saved Through Christ's Life: v. 10

"For if, when we were God's enemies, we were reconciled to him through the death of his Son, how much more, having been reconciled, shall we be saved through his life!"

One of the great marvels of salvation is that while we were actually "God's enemies" we were reconciled to Him through the death of His Son. The Greek word for "enemy," echthros, actually means "hateful" or "hostile." God loved us when we were hateful toward Him!

There is another aspect. I have put it this way: "This term shows the seriousness of sin. Reduced to final analysis, sin is rebellion against God. It is not only a failure, but a refusal, to do God's will. Only when understood

thus can the serious consequences of sin be properly appreciated" (Word Meanings, 3:102).

We are reconciled to God through Christ's death. But we are "saved through his life." The Greek may be translated "in (Greek, en) His life." It is only as Christ lives His life in us that we experience the beauty and fullness of salvation.

C. Rejoicing in God: v. 11

"Not only is this so, but we also rejoice in God through our Lord Jesus Christ, through whom we have received reconciliation."

The Greek word for "reconciliation" is katallage. James Denney comments: "Katallage is not a change in our disposition toward God, but a change in His attitude toward us. We do not give it . . . ; we receive it by believing in Christ Jesus" (EGT, 2:626). I prefer to say that it is both. We change our attitude in the act of reconciliation.

IV. REDEMPTION IN CHRIST: Colossians 1:13-14

A. The Divine Rescue: v. 13

"For he has rescued us from the dominion of darkness and brought us into the kingdom of the Son he loves.... . ."

As sinners we were in the "dominion" or "domain" (NASB) of darkness. John Nielson writes that the sinner "is delivered from the domination of Satan

---

DISCUSSION QUESTIONS

1. How do we get right with God?
2. What is "faith in Jesus Christ"?
3. How does Christ's sacrifice atone for our sins?
4. How did God demonstrate His justice?
5. What is the sinner "powerless" to do?
6. What does "reconciliation" involve?

into devotion to Christ, from bondage into freedom, from servitude into sonship, from darkness into light" (*Beacon Bible Commentary,* 9:375). What a glorious exchange!

B. The Forgiveness of Sins: v. 14

"... in whom we have redemption, the forgiveness of sins." We have already noted that "redemption" means the release of a captive or slave. Sinners are in captivity to sin. In Christ we find deliverance from slavery. We are now free to follow God's will in our lives and find the highest and best in life. But we must always remember that we have this freedom only *in Christ.*

CONTEMPORARY APPLICATION

The trouble with our world today is that most human beings are not right with God, and so not right with themselves or with each other. The result is hatred and strife that divides families, communities, and nations.

The only answer to this problem is Christ. He alone can make us righteous—right with God, right with ourselves, and right with others. We must let Him make us "righteous" and then seek to help others to get right.

THE RESULT: NEW PERSONS

DEVOTIONAL READING	Titus 3:3-8

ADULTS AND YOUTH

Adult Topic: *The Result: New Persons*

Youth Topic: *The New You*

Background Scripture: Eph. 4:17—5:2; II Cor. 5:14-21

Scripture Lesson: Eph. 4:17—5:2; II Cor. 5:17

Memory Verse: *If any one is in Christ, he is a new creation.* II Cor. 5:17

CHILDREN

Topic: *We Are Jesus' Helpers*

Memory Verse: *Be kind to one another, tenderhearted, forgiving one another as God in Christ forgave you.* Eph. 4:32

DAILY BIBLE READINGS

Oct. 17 M.: "A New Creation." II Cor. 5:14-21
Oct. 18 T.: "Heirs In Hope." Titus 3:3-8
Oct. 19 W.: "Alive to God in Christ Jesus." Rom. 6:1-11
Oct. 20 T.: "Walk By the Spirit." Gal. 5:13-26
Oct. 21 F.: "Put On the New Nature." Eph. 4:17-24
Oct. 22 S.: "Do Not Grieve the Holy Spirit." Eph. 4:25-32
Oct. 23 S.: "Be Imitative of God." Eph. 5:1-10

LESSON AIM

To help us see what it means to be a new person in Christ Jesus.

LESSON SETTING

Time: Paul wrote Ephesians about A.D. 60, II Corinthians about A.D. 55.

Place: Paul wrote Ephesians from prison in Rome, II Corinthians probably at Philippi.

LESSON OUTLINE

The Result: New Persons

I. **Life Without Christ:** Ephesians 4:17-19
   A. Futility of Mind: v. 17
   B. Separated from the Life of God: v. 18
   C. Moral Insensitivity: v. 19

II. **Life with Christ:** Ephesians 4:20-24
   A. Introduction: vv. 20-21
   B. Putting off the Old Self: v. 22
   C. Being Renewed in Mind: v. 23
   D. Putting on the New Self: v. 24

III. **A New Lifestyle:** Ephesians 4:25-32
   A. No Falsehood: v. 25
   B. No Sinful Anger: vv. 26-27
   C. No Stealing: v. 28
   D. No Unwholesome Talk: v. 29

E. No Grieving the Spirit: v. 30
F. No Malice: v. 31
G. Compassion: v. 32

IV. **A Life of Love:** Ephesians 5:1-2

V. **A New Creation:** II Corinthians 5:17

Today we finish Unit II of this quarter: "God Redeems His People." We first dealt with the problem of sin, which is the necessity for redemption. Then we looked at the motive of redemption: God's love. Next came the means of redemption: God's Son. Today we look at the result of redemption: new persons.

SUGGESTED
INTRODUCTION
FOR ADULTS

Those who claim to be in Christ but live the same old life belie their confession, for our key verse tells us: "If anyone is in Christ, he is a new creation." If we are not new persons, we are not really Christians.

Our lesson today surveys what it means for us to be new persons. We must lay aside the old life and live a new life in Christ. That means Christlike living. The old habits that are unchristlike must be put off and new Christian habits adopted.

The contrast between the old life and the new is spelled out in considerable detail. Let us search our hearts and check our lives carefully.

"The New You." Have you found that? If not, you can find it in Christ—and nowhere else, for it has to start inside, by Christ coming into your heart. He, and He alone, can bring new life.

SUGGESTED
INTRODUCTION
FOR YOUTH

The new life, however, is not only an inward change; it involves our outward living. It does begin with a new heart and the developing of new attitudes, but it definitely involves a new lifestyle. That is why we need to look carefully at our lesson today.

The passage in Ephesians gives us an important list of things we must put off and things we must put on. Let's ask the Lord to help us to comply with the instructions given here.

CONCEPTS FOR
CHILDREN

1. "We Are Jesus' Helpers." What a privilege!
2. We help Jesus by being kind to others.
3. We must also forgive others, as Christ forgave us.
4. Jesus can help us forgive others.

THE LESSON COMMENTARY

I. LIFE WITHOUT CHRIST: Ephesians 4:17-19

A. Futility of Mind: v. 17

"So I tell you this, and insist on it in the Lord, that you must no longer live as the Gentiles do, in the futility of their thinking."

Paul speaks with great urgency here: "I tell you . . . and insist on it in the Lord." This is no trifling matter; it is of the utmost importance how we live.

Paul is addressing Christians, but he firmly declares, "You must no longer live as the Gentiles do." The verb here is *peripatein* (imperatival infinitive), which literally means "walk." In the Gospels it is used about forty times of Jesus and others walking around, but here it clearly has the metaphorical meaning of "live." It includes all the activities of life.

In the two verses preceding our printed lesson the apostle has been talking about Christ, who is the Head of the church, His body. Charles W. Carter comments:

> From the sublime heights of his contemplation of the ideal, mystical union in the body of Christ Paul descends to the practical, workaday problems of sin and salvation—the old man and the new man of the present life. Throughout the remainder of chapter 4 the Apostle presents in bold and vivid contrast the old and new ways of life—the way of sin and the way of salvation in Jesus Christ. Verses 17-24 depict the old sinful life and its consequences without Christ, and Christ's call from this way to His new way of life. Verses 25-32 present the call to the principle and practices of the new way of life in Christ (*The Wesleyan Bible Commentary*, 5:412).

The "Gentiles" (non-Christians) live "in the futility of their thinking." The Greek word for "futility"—"vanity" (KJV)—is *mataiotes*, which occurs, in the Septuagint, nearly forty times in Ecclesiastes and many times in the Psalms. Its basic meaning is "emptiness." James Denney says of the Greek word: "The idea is that of looking for what one does not find—hence of futility, frustration, disappointment." Of the "vanity of vanities" in Ecclesiastes he says that it is "the complaint of the utter resultlessness of life" (*The Expositor's Greek Testament*, 2:649).

B. Separated from the Life of God: v. 18

"They are darkened in their understanding and separated from the life

of God because of the ignorance that is in them due to the hardening of their hearts."

The King James Version says "blindness" of their heart. But the Greek word *porosis* means "hardening . . . dullness, insensibility, obstinacy" (Arndt and Gingrich, *Greek-English Lexicon of the New Testament*, p. 732). E. K. Simpson comments:

> Unblushing obscenity and infamous orgies of lasciviousness were becoming a stupefying opiate, under whose narcotic fumes the sense of shame was vanishing from a bestialized community. An American traveler in Italy has noted how fully the demoralizing frescoes of Pompeii account for the downfall of Rome. It was not lava but lewdness that buried Herculaneum (*Commentary on the Epistles to the Ephesians and the Colossians*, p. 103).

This description fits in perfectly with the next verse, to which we now turn.

C. Moral Insensitivity: v. 19

"Having lost all sensitivity, they have given themselves over to sensuality so as to indulge in every kind of impurity, with a continual lust for more."

That this verse does not overstate the situation in the pagan society of Paul's day is abundantly corroborated by the evidence we have from the first century. It is not only on the walls of Pompeii and Herculaneum, which were buried many feet deep by a massive eruption of Mount Vesuvius in A.D. 79. The literature of that period reflects the kind of situation we find described here and in the closing part of the first chapter of Romans, as we noted in a recent lessson.

Willard Taylor gives a good commentary on this verse. He writes:

> Moral insensibility means shamelessness, haughtiness before God and man, and living without the restraint of conscience. The ultimate result is moral irresponsibility, in which sin runs rampant through the life. Paul

speaks of the Gentiles as having *given themselves over* or "abandoned themselves" (NEB) to sin. In Rom. 1:21-28, he declares that God gave them over to their own sinful ways, but here the apostle shows the other side. The tragedy is twofold—the man who abandons God in order to keep his sins, and the ultimate, reluctant act of God when He abandons the man whom He can no longer help (*Beacon Bible Commentary*, 9:215).

S. D. F. Salmond says of the Gentiles as described here that "they gave themselves willfully over to wanton sensuality, in order that they might practise every kind of uncleanness and do that with unbridled greedy desire" (*EGT*, 3:340).

II. LIFE WITH CHRIST:
Ephesians 4:20-24

A. Introduction: vv. 20-21

"You, however, did not come to know Christ that way. Surely you heard of him and were taught in him in accordance with the truth that is in Jesus."

Verse 20 literally says: "But you did not thus learn Christ." Simpson comments: "Usually we learn subjects, not persons; but the Christian's choicest lesson-book is his loveworthy Lord. Instruction about Him falls short of the mark; personal intimacy is requisite to rivet the bond of union with the Saviour" (*Ephesians and Colossians*, p. 104).

Paul had spent about three years in ministry at Ephesus (Acts 20:17, 31), so he knew that his readers had been taught about Christ "in accordance with the truth that is in Jesus" (v. 21). He wants them now to walk in the light of the truth they had received.

B. Putting off the Old Self: v. 22

"You were taught, with regard to your former way of life, to put off your old self, which is being corrupted by its deceitful desires."

Instead of "way of life" the King James Version has "conversation." This is one of the 830 words in the King James Version that has changed its meaning since that version came out in 1611. Actually, there are three different Greek words in the New Testament that are translated that way in the King James Version, and not one of them means what "conversation" means today!

The Greek word here is *anastrophe*. It literally means a "turning about." Interestingly that is what "conversation," from the Latin *converso*, meant in 1611. But today it simply means talking. Greek writers in the time of Christ and Paul used *anastrophe* for "manner of life," and that is what it means here.

Paul says that the Christian is to put off his "old self." The Greek literally says "old man." Salmond says that "the old man" is "the former unregenerate self in its entirety" (*EGT*, 3:342). John Eadie writes: "The words are . . . a bold and vivid personification of the old nature we inherit from Adam, the source and seat of original and actual transgression" (*Commentary on the Epistle to the Ephesians*, p. 339).

C. Being Renewed in Mind: v. 23

Paul likes long sentences! Verses 20-24 are all one sentence in the Greek. The man who made the verse divisions in the Bible cut this verse short: "to be made new in the attitude of your minds."

"To be made new" is the present infinitive in Greek, indicating continuous action. Taylor writes:

A continuous renewal of the inner life, that is, *the spirit of the mind*, is expected as one puts on the new nature (24). The dynamic character of the new life is denoted here. A parallel Pauline verse is Rom. 12:2: "And continue to be transformed by the renewing of your mind" (lit.). This renewal is not the result of human effort; it is the work of the Holy Spirit upon the human spirit. The transformation comes as the individual surrenders himself to the leadership of the Spirit (*BBC*, 9:222).

D. Putting on the New Self: v. 24

Paul went on to say: "and to put on the new self, created to be like God in true righteousness and holiness."

What is the difference between "righteousness" and "holiness"? Salmond suggests that "the former expresses the right conduct of the Christian man more distinctively in its bearings on his fellow-men, and the latter the same conduct distinctively in its relation to God" (*EGT*, 3:344).

Paul is not talking about a self-righteous attitude. Nor is he thinking of a legalistic, outward display of holiness, such as the Pharisees were guilty of in Jesus' day. True holiness is an inner attitude of humility, not pride. It is a sense of belonging wholly to God, not ourselves. As a result we are "created to be like God" in thought and purpose. That is, our spirits are so united to Christ that His presence and power make us truly godly.

III. A NEW LIFESTYLE: Ephesians 4:25-32

A. No Falsehood: v. 25

"Therefore each of you must put off falsehood and speak truthfully to his neighbor, for we are all members of one body."

"Put off" is in the aorist tense, suggesting an instantaneous act. "Speak" is in the present tense of continuous action. So the meaning is: "having put off falsehood, keep on speaking truth." Lying is one of the first sins a child commits and one of the most common sins of adults. A Christian must be done, once and for all, with lying. Then he must speak the truth the rest of his life.

The last clause of this verse seems to suggest that "neighbor" primarily means a fellow Christian. But there is also the sense in which all of humanity is "one body."

B. No Sinful Anger: vv. 26-27

"In your anger do not sin: Do not let the sun go down while you are still angry, and do not give the devil a foothold."

Verse 26 has caused a lot of raised eyebrows. Should a Christian be angry? The answer to that question, of course, is that Jesus was angry (Mark 3:5). So there is an anger that is holy and just.

H. C. G. Moule gives a good explanation of the difference between righteous and unrighteous anger. He writes:

Anger, as the mere expression of wounded personality, is sinful; for it means that self is in command. Anger, as the pure expression of repugnance to wrong is loyalty to God, is sinless where there is true occasion for it. The Apostle practically says, let anger, when you feel it, be *never* from the former motive, always from the latter (*Ephesian Studies: Lessons in Faith and Walk*, p. 122).

C. No Stealing: v. 28

"He who has been stealing must steal no longer, but must work, doing something useful with his own hands, that he may have something to share with those in need."

It is important to note that the main emphasis here is on the positive. It is not only "Don't steal," but do work and give some of your income to help the needy.

D. No Unwholesome Talk: v. 29

"Do not let any unwholesome talk come out of your mouths, but only what is helpful for building others up according to their needs, that it may benefit those who listen."

The Greek word for "unwholesome," *sapros*, does mean "decayed" or "rotten," and so might mean "filthy." But the rest of the verse suggests that it means anything that is bad or worthless. We should always seek to say what will be helpful and "edifying" (KJV)—literally, "building up."

E. No Grieving the Spirit: v. 30

"And do not grieve the Holy Spirit of God, with whom you were sealed for the day of redemption."

The connection with the preceding verse suggests that one way we may grieve the Spirit is by "unwholesome talk." We can also grieve the Spirit by disobedience. When He prompts us to do some good thing and we fail to obey, we grieve the loving Spirit. And because He is a personal guest in our hearts, we can grieve Him by simply ignoring Him.

F. No Malice: v. 31

"Get rid of all bitterness, rage and anger, brawling and slander, along with every form of malice."

We find here a list of six evil characteristics. The first five are separated from the sixth. Of these five B. F. Westcott says: "There is a natural progress: bitterness, passion, anger, loud complaint, railing accusation. All these must be utterly removed." Of the sixth he writes: "Ill-feeling is the spring of the faults which have been enumerated" (*Saint Paul's Epistle to the Ephesians*, pp. 74-75).

G. Compassion: v. 32

"Be kind and compassionate to one another, forgiving each other, just as in Christ God forgave you."

This is the positive side of the picture. It is not enough to avoid all the evil things mentioned in the previous verse. We must, as Christians, be kind, compassionate, and forgiving. When God has forgiven us all our debt of sin, certainly we can freely forgive others.

IV. A LIFE OF LOVE:
Ephesians 5:1-2

"Be imitators of God, therefore, as dearly loved children and live a life of love, just as Christ loved us and gave himself up for us as a fragrant offering and sacrifice to God."

The King James Version says, "Be ye therefore followers of God." But the Greek has a stronger term than that for "followers." It has *mimetai*, from which we get "mimic." It clearly means "imitators." We are not just to follow along behind God, as it were, but to imitate His character in our daily lives.

"Live a life of love." What a tremendous challenge that is to all of us! As we have noted before, we are not godly unless we are loving, for "God is love." So the Christian life must be a life of love.

It is not natural to love everybody; it is supernatural. But when we realize that "Christ loved us," even the worst of us, we know that it is our duty to love those that we may naturally not like. This can only be done as Christ's love fills our hearts.

V. A NEW CREATION:
II Corinthians 5:17

"Therefore, if anyone is in Christ, he is a new creation; the old has gone, the new has come!"

For the first half of this verse the Greek simply has: "So that if anyone in Christ, a new creation"—with no verb! J. H. Bernard translates it: "so that if any man be in Christ, there is a new creation" (*EGT*, 3:71). Clarence Zahniser writes:

To be *in Christ* means that a new being has been created, a new creation . . . has taken place. This is

---

DISCUSSION QUESTIONS

1. What causes spiritual hardening of the heart?
2. How can our consciences become insensitive?
3. Why is "holiness" important in the Christian life?
4. What is the only justifiable kind of anger?
5. What is "unwholesome" talk?
6. What does it mean to "live a life of love"?

due to the operation of the Holy Spirit changing man's inner nature. Peter speaks of a begetting (1 Pet. 1:3); John of the new birth (John 3:3-7); Paul of the new creation (*WBC*, 5:287).

"The old has gone, the new has come!" This is what happens in conversion.

The Greek language has two words for "new." One is *neos*, from which we get our word "new." It means new in time. But the word used twice in this verse is *kainos*, which means new in quality.

CONTEMPORARY APPLICATION

Too many professing Christians today have much the same lifestyle as the rest of society around them. But a true Christian is a Christed person; he or she must live a Christlike life.

This truth is emphasized graphically in our lesson today. It begins by telling us that we "must no longer live as the Gentiles do"—like the non-Christians around us. Then it describes conditions much like those that we see everywhere in our time.

These things of the old life we must lay aside. But we must also take on the Christlike characteristics indicated at the close of the lesson. Then we will be real Christians.

GOD'S GRACIOUS COVENANT

DEVOTIONAL READING	Jeremiah 31:31-34

Adult Topic: *God's Gracious Covenant*

Youth Topic: *One Promise You Can Count On*

ADULTS AND YOUTH

Background Scripture: Exod. 19:3-6; Jer. 31:31-34; Heb. 8:6-13

Scripture Lesson: Exod. 19:5-6a; Heb. 8:6-13

Memory Verse: *I will put my laws into their minds, and write them on their hearts, and I will be their God, and they shall be my people.* Heb. 8:10

CHILDREN

Topic: *Obeying God's Rules*

Memory Verse: *If you will obey my voice and keep my covenant you shall be my own possession.* Exod. 19:5

DAILY BIBLE READINGS

Oct. 24 M.: The Covenant with Israel. Exod. 19:1-6
Oct. 25 T.: The Conditions of the Covenant. Exod. 20:13-17
Oct. 26 W.: The Celebration of the Covenant. Exod. 24:1-8
Oct. 27 T.: Life in the Covenant. Deut. 30:15-20
Oct. 28 F.: The New Covenant Promised. Jer. 31:31-36
Oct. 29 S.: The New Covenant Celebrated. I Cor. 11:23-27
Oct. 30 S.: The New Covenant Proclaimed. Heb. 8:6-13

LESSON AIM

To see the nature and significance of the new covenant of grace.

LESSON SETTING

Time: Moses received the Law at Sinai probably about 1400 B.C. Hebrews was written about A.D. 63.

Place: Mount Sinai was in the southern part of the Sinai Peninsula. The place of writing of Hebrews is unknown.

LESSON OUTLINE

God's Gracious Covenant

I. **God's Covenant with Israel:** Exodus 19:3-6
 A. God Calling to Moses: v. 3
 B. God's Deliverance of Israel: v. 4
 C. God's Treasured Possession: v. 5
 D. God's Holy Nation: v. 6

II. **A Superior Covenant:** Hebrews 8:6-8a
 A. Jesus the Mediator: v. 6
 B. Need for a New Covenant: vv. 7-8a

III. **Announcement of the New Covenant:** Hebrews 8:8b-9
 A. A Covenant with Israel and Judah: v. 8b
 B. A Different Covenant: v. 9

67

IV. Nature of the New Covenant: Hebrews 8:10-12
  A. Written on the Heart: v. 10
  B. Knowledge of the Lord: v. 11
  C. Divine Forgiveness: v. 12

SUGGESTED
INTRODUCTION
FOR ADULTS

The Book of Genesis records covenants that God made with Adam, Noah, Abraham, Isaac, Jacob, and Joseph. The main covenant He made was with His people Israel at Mount Sinai, with Moses acting as mediator. That covenant dominates the remaining thirty-eight books of the Old Testament.

The old covenant was based on the Law, summarized in the Ten Commandments. If the Israelites obeyed God's law, and so kept His covenant with them, He would bless them.

Today we study "God's Gracious Covenant." The old covenant was a covenant of law, the new covenant a covenant of grace.

It is an amazing thing that God revealed the nature of this new covenant to the prophet Jeremiah six hundred years before Christ came to bring it in. Though the people had broken God's covenant and so were going into captivity, God was graciously providing a new covenant.

SUGGESTED
INTRODUCTION
FOR YOUTH

Our topic today is: "One Promise You Can Count On." All of us have had an experience of being promised something that didn't materialize. It was a real disappointment. But God's promises never fail.

God promised the people of Israel that if they would obey Him He would bless them. And across their history He fulfilled that promise many times.

In our lesson today we learn that God promised, through Jeremiah, a new covenant of grace. And that promise was fulfilled in the coming of Christ to earth and His death on the cross. To us God promises that if we confess our sins He will forgive us and make us His children. We can be very sure that He will keep this promise.

CONCEPTS FOR
CHILDREN

1. "Obeying God's Rules" is the only safe way to live.
2. If we fail to obey, we can ask forgiveness and start over again.
3. God has promised to help us if we turn to Him.
4. Obedience brings happiness.

THE LESSON COMMENTARY

**I. GOD'S COVENANT
   WITH ISRAEL:
   Exodus 19:3-6**

A. God Calling to Moses: v. 3

"Then Moses went up to God, and the LORD called to him from the mountain and said, 'This is what you are to say to the house of Jacob and what you are to tell the people of Israel: . . .'"

This chapter begins by saying: "In the third month after the Israelites left Egypt—on the very day—they came to the Desert of Sinai . . . and Israel camped there in the desert in front of the mountain" (vv. 1-2). Today Mount Sinai is generally identified with Jebel Musa (mountain of Moses) in the southern part of the Sinai Peninsula, between the Gulf of Suez and the Gulf of Aqaba. It is a rugged mountain peak, rising high above the plain.

"Moses went up to God." When the Lord called Moses at the burning bush, He told him: "When you have brought the people out of Egypt, you will worship God on this mountain" (3:12). So when the Israelites reached the place, Moses naturally ascended the mountain to meet God. Incidentally, it is called "Horeb" in 3:1; but "Sinai" and "Horeb" seem to be used interchangeably.

"And the LORD called to him from the mountain." Before Moses made the long, steep climb up the side of the mountain, the Lord kindly instructed him to go back down the hill and give a message to the people. Evidently God called to Moses from the top of the mountain.

The Lord's first words were: "This is what you are to say to the house of Jacob and what you are to tell the people of Israel: . . ." All the Israelites were descended from Jacob, whose name was changed to Israel (Gen. 35:10). "House" here of course means "family," including descendants. The term is still used this way in history books.

B. God's Deliverance of Israel: v. 4

The Lord's message to the Israelites began with these words: "You yourselves have seen what I did to Egypt, and how I carried you on eagles' wings and brought you to myself."

The Israelites at Sinai were very conscious of what God did to Egypt. The ten plagues, culminating in the death of the firstborn in each home, and the destruction of the Egyptian army at the Red Sea were fresh, vivid memories in the minds of the people. Yes, God had wrought a wonderful deliverance for them.

The Lord brought the Israelites to His special presence and ministry at Mount Sinai. They were very conscious that God was there, as we see in the latter part of this chapter (vv. 16-25).

The picture portrayed here—"carried you on eagles' wings"—is a beautiful one. When the eaglet becomes old enough to fly, the mother eagle pushes it out of the nest. The little eagle flutters in the air, trying desperately to fly. After it has fallen a bit in space, the mother swoops under it, takes it on her broad, powerful wings, and carries it safely back to the nest.

This lovely metaphor is developed further in Deuteronomy 32:10-11, where we read in the Song of Moses:

In a desert land he found him,
   in a barren and howling waste.
He shielded him and cared for
      him;
   he guarded him as the apple of
      his eye,
like an eagle that stirs up its nest
   and hovers over its young,
that spreads its wings to catch
      them
   and carries them on its pinions.

This passage shows the loving care that God had for His people. He still has the same loving care for us today, and we should appreciate it deeply. Incidentally, the verses we have just quoted highlight the marvelous combination of God's almighty strength and His tender love. We are safe in His care!

C. God's Treasured Possession: v. 5

"Now if you obey me fully and keep my covenant, then out of all nations you will be my treasured possession."

The word "peculiar" is used here in the King James Version in its original sense of indicating "private property, that which is one's own" (*Oxford English Dictionary*, 7:602). But today "peculiar" means "odd, eccentric, strange." So it does not communicate accurately to the modern reader what the original Hebrew (Old Testament) or Greek (New Testament) says.

If the Israelites were to be God's own "treasured possession," then they must "obey me fully and keep my covenant," and that is the requirement we face today. God's covenant with Israel was about to be given to the nation at Sinai, and God's new covenant with us is already available to us in what we call the "New Testament"—more properly, the "New Covenant."

In Psalm 135:4 we find the same beautiful truth expressed that we have in this verse:

For the LORD has chosen Jacob to
be his own,
Israel to be his treasured
possession.

What greater privilege and glory could any people have than this? And we, as the people of God today, have that same glorious privilege.

D. God's Holy Nation: v. 6

The Lord said to Israel: "You will be for me a kingdom of priests and a holy nation." This language is strikingly reflected in the New Testament: "But you are a chosen people, a royal priesthood, a holy nation, a people belonging to God" (I Peter 2:9). Also in Revelation 1:6 we are told that Jesus Christ "has made us to be a kingdom and priests to serve his God and Father."

God intended for Israel to be a holy nation, but she became a sinful nation. He also planned for the Israelites to be priests to the pagan nations, rightly representing Him and giving the Gentiles the knowledge of the true God. But in this they miserably failed. Instead of winning Gentiles to the worship of Yahweh, the Israelites were won over by the pagan religions and turned to idolatry. They lost a great opportunity, and lost their own souls as well.

II. A SUPERIOR COVENANT: Hebrews 8:6-8a

A. Jesus the Mediator: v. 6

The writer of Hebrews has been talking about the Aaronic priests who offered sacrifices and served in the sanctuary (vv. 4-5). Now he declares, "But the ministry Jesus has received is as superior to theirs as the covenant of which he is mediator is superior to the old one, and it is founded on better promises."

The key word of Hebrews is "better." The Greek term (*kreisson* or *kreitton*) occurs no less than twelve times in this Epistle and only six times in the rest of the New Testament.

So Hebrews is the book of better things. We find a "better hope" (7:19), a "better covenant" (7:22; 8:6), "better promises" (8:6), "better sacrifices" (9:23), "better possessions" (10:34), "a better country" (11:16), and "a better resurrection" (11:35). In reading the Epistle to the Hebrews we should feast our souls on better things and appreciate more our glorious heritage.

Jesus is declared to be "the mediator of a better covenant" (8:6, KJV, NASB), or "the mediator of a new covenant" (9:15; 12:24). The Greek for "mediator" is *mesites*, "one who stands in the middle." Aside from these passages, it occurs only three times in the New Testament—in Galatians 3:19, 20, and in the great theological statement: "For there is one God and one mediator between God and men, the man Christ Jesus" (I Tim. 2:5).

Charles W. Carter writes:

As Moses was the mediator of the old covenant in that he received the law from God on Sinai and then delivered and administered it to the people, so Christ was the Mediator and minister of the new covenant. This He did by providing salvation for all men in His atoning death on Calvary. He then ascended to the right hand of the Father where as man's Great High Priest He ministers the provisions of His own will or testament to believing men. It was His covenant of grace by promise to which the old covenant of the law was designed to direct the faith of man (*The Wesleyan Bible Commentary*, 6:106).

B. Need for a New Covenant: vv. 7–8a

"For if there had been nothing wrong with the first covenant, no place would have been sought for another" (v. 7). Carter makes this comparison of the two:

> In the first place, the old covenant was external and disciplinary (Gal. 3:24). The new is internal and gracious. The old was compulsion. The new is impulsion. The old promised. The new fulfilled the promise. The old directed. The new delivers. The old was a shadow of the new cast before. The new is the reality that cast that shadow. The old was temporary, dispensational. The new is eternal—timeless. The old was preparatory. The new is final (Gal. 4:4) (*WBC*, 3:106–7).

The first part of verse 8 reads literally: "For finding fault with them, He says" (NASB, cf. KJV). It is not stated that God found fault with the old covenant; it was "with them"—that is, with the people who failed to keep it that God found fault. To make this crystal clear for the reader, the New International Version has, "But God found fault with the people and said."

III. ANNOUNCEMENT OF THE NEW COVENANT: Hebrews 8:8b–9

A. A Covenant with Israel and Judah: v. 8b

Except for the last two lines of verse 9, verses 8b–12 are a nearly exact quotation of Jeremiah 31:31–34. This is one of the great passages of the Old Testament, portraying the new covenant of the Christian era. Here is what the Lord said through Jeremiah:

"The time is coming, declares the Lord,
 when I will make a new
  covenant
with the house of Israel
and with the house of Judah."

At that time the Israelites were divided into two areas, Israel in the north and Judah in the south. The kingdom of Israel had already been overthrown in 722 B.C. This was in the middle of Isaiah's ministry (740–700 B.C.) in Judah. It was also a hundred years before the beginning of Jeremiah's ministry (626 B.C.), ending with the overthrow of Jerusalem in 586 B.C. The Israelites—both north and south—had broken God's covenant; so they were being broken as nations. Now God had to make a new covenant.

B. F. Westcott points out well the significance of that moment in history. He writes:

> The context of the quotation gives it a special force. Jeremiah at the crisis of national calamity pictures the final result of the discipline of the exile into which Judah was now going. The united people 'Israel and Judah' are to return to their land (xxx.3). . . . The counsel of divine love finds certain accomplishment (xxxi.37). This issue is summed up in the establishment of a New Covenant, by which the fulfilment of the whole of God's purpose is assured, when trial had done its work. Under this Covenant, grace not law is the foundation of fellowship (*The Epistle to the Hebrews*, p. 220).

Westcott goes on to make this excellent observation:

> The whole situation is Messianic no less than the special words. The time of humiliation is the time of ardent hope. The fall of the Kingdom, which was of man's will, is the occasion of a greater promise (p. 220).

B. A Different Covenant: v. 9

"It will not be like the covenant
 I made with their forefathers

when I took them by the hand
  to lead them out of Egypt,
because they did not remain
    faithful to my covenant,
and I turned away from them,
      declares the LORD."

God had made a covenant with the Israelites' forefathers at Mount Sinai, when He delivered them from Egyptian bondage. But they had not been faithful to that covenant, and so He had abandoned them.

The word "covenant" occurs twice in this verse, as well as once in verse 8 and once in verse 10. So this might be a good place to examine its meaning.

The Greek word is *diatheke*, which occurs over three hundred times in the Septuagint and thirty-three times in the New Testament. In the King James Version it is translated "covenant" twenty times and "testament" thirteen times. But Westcott feels strongly that since the Septuagint always uses it in the sense of a covenant, that should be taken as its meaning in the New Testament. He writes: "There is not the least trace of the meaning 'testament' in the Greek Old Scriptures, and the idea of a 'testament' was indeed foreign to the Jews till the time of the Herods" (*Hebrews*, p. 299). Westcott would use "covenant" except in 9:15-17.

IV. NATURE OF THE NEW COVENANT: Hebrews 8:10-12

A. Written on the Heart: v. 10

"This is the covenant I will make
    with the house of Israel
  after that time, declares the
      LORD.
I will put my laws in their minds
  and write them on their hearts.
I will be their God,
  and they will be my people."

The old covenant was embodied in the Ten Commandments, which were written on stone tablets. But the laws of the new covenant in Christ would be inscribed on human hearts.

Westcott comments:

Under the Mosaic system the law was fixed and external: the new laws enter into the understanding as active principles to be realized and embodied by progressive thought. The old law was written on tables of stone: the new laws are written on the heart and become, so to speak, part of the personality of the believer (*Hebrews*, pp. 222-23).

Westcott also summarizes verses 10-12 in this way:

The positive character of the New Covenant, "the better promises" on which it rests, are to be found in (1) its spirituality (v. 10), (2) its universal efficacy (v. 11), (3) its assurance of free forgiveness (v. 12) (p. 222).

B. Knowledge of the Lord: v. 11

"No longer will a man teach his
    neighbor,
  or a man his brother, saying,
    'Know the Lord,'
because they will all know me,
  from the least of them to the
      greatest."

The old covenant was tied up closely with the Tabernacle, with its offerings and sacrifices. It was largely external. The scribes taught the Law to the people. With no printing—all writing was done by hand—individuals would

DISCUSSION QUESTIONS

1.   Why did God meet the delivered Israelites so soon at Sinai?
2.   Why do we need God's written Word?
3.   Why do people cling tenaciously to the outward forms of religion and fail to have true religion in their hearts?
4.   In what way is Jesus the Mediator of the new covenant?
5.   What does it mean to have God's laws written on our hearts?
6.   How do we come to know the Lord?

have to listen to the Law read and expounded.

But under the new covenant things would be different. Westcott puts it this way:

> The people are brought into true fellowship with God, and this involves an immediate knowledge of Him. No privileged class is interposed between the mass of men and God.... All have immediate access to the divine Presence (*Hebrews*, p. 224).

C. **Divine Forgiveness: v. 12**

"For I will forgive their
wickedness
and will remember their sins no
more."

One of the greatest blessings of the new covenant is the personal consciousness of sins forgiven through grace by faith in Jesus Christ. He sealed the covenant with His own blood, and now free forgiveness is available to all who will accept it.

CONTEMPORARY APPLICATION

There are still Christians today who live too much under a formal, legalistic concept of religion, such as belonged to the old covenant. They do not seem to realize that we cannot save ourselves by conformity to a legal code, by observance of certain forms of worship, or by any good works we do. We are saved only by accepting what Christ has done for us, by letting Him write His law of love on our hearts, and by living in close fellowship with Him on a spiritual plane. The new covenant is essentially a spiritual religion.

GOD'S STEADFAST LOVE

DEVOTIONAL READING	Psalm 107:1-9
ADULTS AND YOUTH	**Adult Topic:** *God's Steadfast Love*
	Youth Topic: *God Keeps on Loving Us*
	Background Scripture: Ps. 103; Eph. 1:3-10
	Scripture Lesson: Ps. 103:1-12; Eph. 1:5-10
	Memory Verse: *The Lord is merciful and gracious, slow to anger and abounding in steadfast love.* Ps. 103:8
CHILDREN	**Topic:** *God Loves Us*
	Memory Verse: *God is love.* I John 4:8
DAILY BIBLE READINGS	Oct. 31 M.: "O Give Thanks to the Lord." Ps. 107:1-9 Nov. 1 T.: "An Everlasting Love." Jer. 31:2-6 Nov. 2 W.: "They Who Wait for the Lord." Isa. 41:21-31 Nov. 3 T.: "Who Can Separate Us?" Rom. 8:31-39 Nov. 4 F.: "Every Spiritual Blessing." Eph. 1:3-10 Nov. 5 S.: "Bless the Lord, O My Soul." Ps. 103:1-14 Nov. 6 S.: "From Everlasting to Everlasting." Ps. 103:15-22
LESSON AIM	To help us appreciate the blessings that come to us from God's steadfast love.
LESSON SETTING	**Time:** Psalm 103: about 1000 B.C. Ephesians: about A.D. 60. **Place:** Psalm 103: Jerusalem. Paul wrote Ephesians from prison in Rome.

LESSON OUTLINE

God's Steadfast Love

I. **Praising the Lord:** Psalm 103:1-2
   A. With All One's Heart: v. 1
   B. For All God's Blessings: v. 2

II. **Personal Blessings:** Psalm 103:3-5
   A. Forgiveness and Healing: v. 3
   B. Salvation and Compassion: v. 4
   C. Satisfaction and Fresh Life: v. 5

III. **Blessings to All:** Psalm 103:6-12
   A. Deliverance of the Oppressed: vv. 6-7
   B. Compassion and Love: vv. 8-10
   C. Love and Forgiveness: vv. 11-12

IV. **Praise to God:** Ephesians 1:3-6
   A. For Every Spiritual Blessing: v. 3
   B. Chosen by God: vv. 4-5
   C. His Glorious Grace: v. 6

V. **God's Eternal Purpose:** Ephesians 1:7-10
   A. Redemption Through Christ: vv. 7-8
   B. Christ As Head of All: vv. 9-10

SUGGESTED
INTRODUCTION
FOR ADULTS

This is the second lesson of Unit III: God Relates to His People. Last week we found that God relates to His people by the covenant He makes with them. Today we note that He relates to His people in steadfast love.

Some love is superficial, undependable, short-lived. But God's love is steadfast, unchanging, always reaching out to us. And it is eternal. It is not only eternal but infinite. There is no way of measuring God's love. God's love reaches out to all people everywhere, seeking their salvation and their best interests.

If we are truly living godly lives, our love will be steadfast. Nothing else in our personalities or conduct will compensate for a lack of love. Intellectual brilliance, successful performance as the world sees it, wealth and fame—none of these will be acceptable to God in place of love. Love must always have the highest priority.

SUGGESTED
INTRODUCTION
FOR YOUTH

"God Keeps on Loving Us"—what a comforting thought! Others may give up on us, but God doesn't. His love is steadfast. And God's steadfast love is the greatest asset we have in life.

We ought to be deeply grateful for God's love. And we should express our gratitude by singing God's praises. That is what the psalmist did.

The Psalms were the hymns of the ancient Israelites, and they can still help us to express our praise. They make good devotional reading. "Let's just praise the Lord," we sing. And that is the way David talks in Psalm 103, which we will study today.

CONCEPTS FOR
CHILDREN

1. "God Loves Us"—all of us, all the time!
2. Even when we do wrong, God still loves us and wants to help us do right.
3. We can see God's love showing in the lives of good Christians.
4. We can show our love by doing good things for others.

THE LESSON COMMENTARY

I. PRAISING THE LORD: Psalm 103:1-2

A. With All One's Heart: v. 1

Praise the LORD, O my soul;
    all my inmost being, praise his
      holy name.

Using the traditional "bless," George Rawlinson comments:

To "bless" is more than to praise; it is to praise with affection and gratitude. The psalmist calls upon his own soul,

and so on each individual soul, to begin the song of praise, which is to terminate in a general chorus of blessing from all creation (vers. 20-22) (*The Pulpit Commentary*, Psalms, 2:382).

The psalmist added: "All my inmost being, praise his holy name." The Hebrew literally says: "all my inward parts." Some people join in singing hymns of praise with their lips, but their heart is not in it. David believed in a heartfelt religion.

David was concerned for God's "holy

name." In another Psalm (145:21b) he says:

> Let every creature praise his holy
> name
> for ever and ever.

And in the Book of Isaiah we find twenty-five times the expression, "the Holy One of Israel."

B. For All God's Blessings: v. 2

> Praise the LORD, O my soul,
> and forget not all his benefits.

The first line of verse 2 is the same as the first line of verse 1. And the psalm concludes with the same words. Following that, Psalm 104 begins with the same refrain and has it also in its last verse. We find it again in the first verse of Psalm 146. It was obviously a favorite line of poetry for those who wrote the Psalms.

The second line of our verse says: "and forget not all his benefits." Fausset says that this is "a hint to David's seed that they, too, should not (as the human heart is apt to do) forget all God's benefits" (Jamieson, Fausset, and Brown, *A Commentary . . . on the Old and New Testaments*, 3:321). Fausset goes on to say, "The very prosperity which is the gift of God is too often the occasion of the heart being lifted up so as to forget the Giver."

This truth is documented in Deuteronomy 32:15. Moses found it necessary to warn the Israelites: "When you have eaten and are satisfied, praise the LORD your God for the good land he has given you. Be careful that you do not forget the LORD your God" (Deut. 8:10-11).

II. PERSONAL BLESSINGS: Psalm 103:3-5

For verses 3-5 we quote the New American Standard Bible. The use of "my" for "your" (Heb.) in the New International Version is explained in a footnote. We hope to get this changed in a meeting of the Committee on Bible Translation in 1983.

A. Forgiveness and Healing: v. 3

> Who pardons all your iniquities;
> Who heals all your diseases.

Concerning the first line, Rawlinson comments: "This is the first and greatest of 'benefits,' and is therefore placed first, as that for which we ought, above all else, to bless God" (*PC*, p. 382). The Psalms often refer to God's forgiveness of sins (25:11, 18; 32:1; 51:9; 85:2; 86:5; etc.).

With regard to the second line Fausset writes:

> The maladies of the body, including all earthly sufferings . . . are associated with the soul's sicknesses, "iniquities." Christ came as the Healer of both. By removing sin, the cause, He will finally remove sickness and suffering, the effect (Isa. xxxiii.24). He gave an earnest of this in combining His forgiveness of the paralytic with His cure of his body (Mark ii.5, 10 . . .) (*Commentary*, p. 321).

B. Salvation and Compassion: v. 4

> Who redeems your life from the
> pit;
> Who crowns you with loving-
> kindness and compassion;

Again we have themes that are common to the Psalms. For the first line we might note Psalm 56:13:

> For you have delivered my soul
> from death
> and my feet from stumbling.

This is largely repeated in Psalm 116:8. God delivers us from danger and death more times than we are aware of. We ought to be very grateful for His loving care.

For the second line we also find a similar thought expressed in the familiar Psalm 23, verse 6:

> Surely goodness and love will
> follow me
> all the days of my life.

C. Satisfaction and Fresh Life: v. 5

Who satisfies your years with
  good things,
So that your youth is renewed
  like the eagle.

Instead of "years," the King James Version has "mouth." Most commentators agree that the Hebrew word does not mean "mouth" but "desire" (NASB margin; cf. NIV), as found in the Septuagint and other ancient versions.

For the second line Fausset quotes a Greek proverb: "The eagle's old age is as good as the lark's youth" (*Commentary*, p. 321). Isaiah said (40:31) of those who hope in the Lord: "They will soar on wings like eagles."

III. BLESSINGS TO ALL: Psalm 103:6-12

A. Deliverance of the Oppressed: vv. 6-7

The LORD works righteousness
  and justice for all the oppressed.
He made known his ways to
    Moses,
  his deeds to the people of Israel.

These two verses tie in together, for the outstanding example of God working justice for the oppressed was His deliverance of the Israelites from oppressive slavery in Egypt. In doing so, God "made known His ways to Moses" and "His deeds to the people of Israel." Of course, this also continued through the forty years in the desert.

The idea of God's care for the oppressed bulks large in Scripture. Not only do we find it in connection with the Israelites in Egypt (Exod. 2:23-25; 3:9), but in Judges 2:18 we read, "For the LORD had compassion on them as they groaned under those who oppressed and afflicted them." Psalm 9:9 says, "The LORD is a refuge for the oppressed." In 10:18 He is spoken of as "defending the fatherless and the oppressed." Psalm 146:7 declares, "He upholds the cause of the oppressed." God is concerned about oppression of people, even today.

B. Compassion and Love: vv. 8-10

The LORD is compassionate and
  gracious,
slow to anger, abounding in love.

What a beautiful description of God's character! As His children, we should be like that, too.

It was almost in these very words that God revealed Himself to Moses at Mount Sinai. There "the LORD came down in the cloud and stood there with him and proclaimed his name, the LORD" (Exod. 34:5). The Hebrew for "LORD" is *Yahweh*, the covenant-keeping God. In the next verse we read that the LORD passed in front of Moses, proclaiming, "The LORD, the LORD, the compassionate and gracious God, slow to anger, abounding in love and faithfulness." These words of God to Moses are also quoted by David in Psalm 86:15. They were evidently very precious to David and they should be to us.

The last clause of verse 8 reads in the King James Version: "plenteous in mercy." But scholars are agreed that the Hebrew word *chesed* does not mean "mercy" but "lovingkindness" (NASB) or "love" (NIV). The term occurs at least eighty times in the Psalms. In Psalm 136 it is found in the refrain of all twenty-six verses: "His love endures forever."

The psalmist goes on to say in verse 9:

He will not always accuse,
  nor will he harbor his anger
    forever.

Ezekiel 18:27 says, "But if a wicked man turns away from the wickedness he has committed and does what is just and right, he will save his life." And in II Peter 3:9 we read, "The Lord . . . is patient with you, not wanting anyone to perish, but everyone to come to repentance." His mercy always tempers His justice.

This thought is carried a step further in verse 10:

> He does not treat us as our sins
>   deserve
>   or repay us according to our
>   iniquities.

Rawlinson remarks: "God never punishes men so much as they deserve to be punished" (*PC*, p. 383). How true that is! If God punished us as we deserved, not one of us would ever get to heaven. He punishes us just enough to make us realize that we need to turn to Him and repent.

C. Love and Forgiveness:
   vv. 11-12

> For as high as the heavens are
>   above the earth,
>   so great is his love for those who
>   fear him;
> as far as the east is from the west,
>   so far has he removed our
>   transgressions from us.

In Psalm 36:5 we read:

> Your love, O LORD, reaches to the
>   heavens,
>   Your faithfulness to the skies.

Rawlinson rightly observes: "The metaphor is bold, yet inadequate; for God's mercy is infinite" (*PC*, p. 383). Again we would note that "mercy" (KJV) is not the correct translation. The Hebrew word *chesed* means "lovingkindness" (NASB) or "love" (NIV). It is God's love that is infinite, because God—the infinite One—is love.

"As far as the east is from the west" expresses infinite distance. We can measure the distance from north to south—from the north pole to the south pole—on this earth. But how far is it from east to west? No one can measure that. One can head west on this globe and keep going endlessly, but he will never reach east. So immeasurable is the distance God has removed our transgressions from us.

IV. PRAISE TO GOD:
   Ephesians 1:3-6

A. For Every Spiritual Blessing:
   v. 3

"Praise be to the God and Father of our Lord Jesus Christ, who has blessed us in the heavenly realms with every spiritual blessing in Christ." The Greek has the singular—"every spiritual blessing" (NASB, NIV)—not the plural—"all spiritual blessings" (KJV).

Three words in this one verse come from the same root: the adjective *eulogetos* ("blessed"), the verb *eulogeo* ("bless"), and the noun *eulogia* ("blessing"). The verb has two distinct meanings. One is "bestow blessings on," and that is what God does to us. The other is the literal meaning, "speak well of," "praise," and this is what we do to God. That is why the New International Version has "Praise be to God."

"In the heavenly realms"—"heavenly *places*" (KJV, NASB)—is the key phrase of Ephesians, occurring five times in this Epistle and nowhere else in the New Testament. It is literally "in the heavenlies." Ephesians describes life in the heavenlies in Christ.

We should note carefully the significance of the phrase "with every spiritual blessing." Scripture does not say "with every material blessing." God has not promised that every faithful follower of His will drive a Cadillac and live in an expensive home—contrary to what some have preached. But He does promise every *spiritual* blessing.

Where do we get these spiritual blessings? The answer is clear: "in the heavenlies in Christ"—that is, in heavenly fellowship with Christ. Without Christ we cannot have the blessings. And the greatest blessing any person can enjoy is the conscious presence of Christ in his or her heart.

We might say a further word about the expression "in Christ" (Greek, *en Christo*). It is the key phrase of Paul's Epistles, the heart of his theology.

Everything we get from God comes to us "in Christ."

B. Chosen by God: vv. 4-5

"For he chose us in him before the creation of the world to be holy and blameless in his sight." To what are we chosen? "To be holy and blameless in his sight." We cannot always escape blame in the eyes of men. But if our hearts are right, we can be blameless before God, because He sees our motives, not just our sometimes bungling actions.

The question as to whether the phrase "in love" should go with the preceding (KJV) or the following (RSV, NASB, NIV) is unsolvable. The Greek has no punctuation marks and no capital letters to indicate the beginning of sentences. So it is wholly a matter of editorial interpretation, and the decision could equally well go either way.

Including this phrase with verse 5 we read: "In love he predestined us to be adopted as his sons through Jesus Christ, in accordance with his pleasure and will." The first part of Ephesians has a strong emphasis on divine sovereignty. Whatever is God's will is going to be carried out, and it is His will, revealed in Scripture (e.g., John 3:16), that all who believe in Christ should have eternal life.

C. His Glorious Grace: v. 6

"To the praise of his glorious grace, which he has freely given us in the One he loves." The Greek word for "grace" is *charis*, while the verb "freely given" is *charitoo*, "bestow divine grace or favor." All we receive from God comes by His grace.

V. GOD'S ETERNAL PURPOSE: Ephesians 1:7-10

A. Redemption Through Christ: vv. 7-8

"In him we have redemption through his blood, the forgiveness of sins, in accordance with the riches of God's grace that he lavished on us with all wisdom and understanding."

We have already discussed rather carefully the meaning of "redemption" in lesson 7. It is interesting that this term occurs more frequently in Ephesians (1:7, 14; 4:30) than in any other book of the New Testament (twice in Romans and twice in Hebrews; once each in Luke, I Corinthians, and Colossians). We would simply note that the Greek word, *apolytrosis* comes from *lytron*, "ransom," and *apo*, "away from." So it meant *"buying back* a slave or captive, *making* him *free* by payment of a ransom" (Arndt and Gingrich, *Greek-English Lexicon of the New Testament*, p. 95). Buechsel writes: "It means 'setting free for a ransom,' and is used of prisoners of war, slaves, and criminals condemned to death" (*Theological Dictionary of the New Testament*, 4:352).

The ransom price of our redemption is "his blood"—Jesus' blood that was shed for us at Calvary. Because He was the Son of God, this is the highest price that could ever have been paid for our salvation. Nothing less would have procured our freedom.

The term "forgiveness" is a very important word in the New Testament. The Greek word, *aphesis*, is used in the inscriptions of that time for "remission from debt or punishment." R. C. Trench writes:

> He, then, that is partaker of the *aphesis*, has his sins forgiven, so that,

---

DISCUSSION QUESTIONS

1. What does it mean to praise the Lord?
2. What is the greatest blessing God gives us?
3. Why is love "the greatest thing in the world"?
4. Why did God choose us?
5. How do we find "forgiveness of sins"?
6. What are some spiritual blessings we have in Christ?

unless he bring them back upon himself by new and further disobedience (Matt. 18:32, 34; 2 Pet. 1:9; 2:20), they shall not be imputed to him, or mentioned against him any more (*Synonyms of the New Testament*, p. 119).

We have another beautiful truth expressed here. Paul says that the riches of God's grace He has "lavished" (NASB, NIV) on us. The Greek word is literally "made abundant." When we think of how God has *lavished* the *riches* of His grace on us, it surely ought to make us lavish with our praise to Him.

B. Christ As Head of All: vv. 9–10

And he made known to us the mystery of his will according to his good pleasure, which he purposed in Christ, to put into effect when the times will have reached their fulfillment—to bring all things in

heaven and on earth together under one head, even Christ.

The word "mystery" (v. 9) comes from the Greek *mysterion*. S. D. F. Salmond writes:

The word *mysterion*, which in classical Greek meant something *secret*, especially the secrets of religion communicated only to the initiated and by them to be kept untold, is used in the Apocryphal books of things hidden.... But its distinctive sense in the NT is that of something once hidden and now revealed, a secret now open (*The Expositor's Greek Testament*, 3:258).

The hidden secret, now revealed, is that God is going to bring all things "together under one head, even Christ" (v. 10). This does not teach universal salvation, but the final sovereignty of the Creator over all creation, when Christ's kingdom has been established.

CONTEMPORARY APPLICATION

Do we feel poor spiritually? If so, it is our fault. For God wants to bless us with "every spiritual blessing in Christ." If we are willing to give ourselves fully to Christ as our Savior and Lord and then take time for increasingly close fellowship with Him, we can enjoy these spiritual blessings in

abundant measure. Someone has said, "You can be as spiritual as you want to be."

Everything worthwhile in life is costly in some way. The finest things in life require mainly our time and devoted attention. Are we willing to pay that price?

GOD'S INDWELLING SPIRIT

DEVOTIONAL READING	Romans 8:1-8
ADULTS AND YOUTH	**Adult Topic:** *God's Indwelling Spirit* **Youth Topic:** *God Keeps on Helping Us* **Background Scripture:** John 4:24; 14:25-26; Rom. 8:9-17, 26-28 **Scripture Lesson:** John 14:25-26; Rom. 8:9-17, 26-28 **Memory Verse:** *You are not in the flesh, you are in the Spirit, if in fact the Spirit of God dwells in you.* Rom. 8:9
CHILDREN	**Topic:** *God Gives a Helper* **Memory Verse:** *God is spirit and they that worship him must worship him in spirit and in truth.* John 4:24
DAILY BIBLE READINGS	Nov. 7 M.: The Teaching of the Spirit. John 14:15-26 Nov. 8 T.: The Promise of the Spirit. Acts 1:1-11 Nov. 9 W.: The Power of the Spirit. John 20:19-23 Nov. 10 T.: The Pouring Out of the Spirit. Acts 2:14-21 Nov. 11 F.: The Life of the Spirit. Rom. 8:1-8 Nov. 12 S.: The Children of the Spirit. Rom. 8:9-17 Nov. 13 S.: The Intercession of the Spirit. Rom. 8:18-28
LESSON AIM	To help us appreciate more and understand better the ministry of the Holy Spirit.
LESSON SETTING	**Time:** John's Gospel was probably written about A.D. 95. Romans was written about A.D. 56. **Place:** John's Gospel was written at Ephesus, Romans at Corinth.

LESSON OUTLINE	**God's Indwelling Spirit**
	
	I. **God Is Spirit:** John 4:24
	
	II. **The Holy Spirit As Helper:** John 14:25-26
	
	III. **The Indwelling Spirit:** Romans 8:9-11
	   A. The Spirit in the Believer: v. 9
	   B. The Indwelling Christ: v. 10
	   C. The Life-Giving Spirit: v. 11
	
	IV. **The Spirit Versus the Flesh:** Romans 8:12-14
	
	V. **The Spirit of Sonship:** Romans 8:15-17
	   A. Assurance of Sonship: vv. 15-16
	   B. Heirs of God: v. 17
	
	VI. **The Spirit As Intercessor:** Romans 8:26-27
	
	VII. **God Working for Our Good:** Romans 8:28

SUGGESTED
INTRODUCTION
FOR ADULTS

Most Christians hear a great deal about Christ as Savior and Lord, but in too many places very little is said about the Holy Spirit. Yet the New Testament contains a considerable amount of teaching about the Spirit, and we should give attention to the subject.

It is significant that in Jesus' Last Discourse with His disciples, before going to the cross the next day, the main concern He had was to tell them about the Holy Spirit, who would come to take His place with them and teach them all things they needed to know. If Jesus were to visit us visibly today He probably would urge us to let the Holy Spirit make His presence more real and guide us more fully in our Christian lives.

SUGGESTED
INTRODUCTION
FOR YOUTH

"God Keeps on Helping Us." This is shown in our lesson today. Jesus had spent three years with His disciples, setting them an example of godly, dedicated living and teaching them how their heavenly Father wanted them to live. Now He was about to leave them, and their hearts were sad at His announcement of this fact.

But He told them, "Don't worry. The Holy Spirit will come to take my place, and He will keep on helping you—every day, all the way. With His help you can make it, no matter what comes." Paul, in the Book of Romans, tells us further how the Holy Spirit will help us.

CONCEPTS FOR
CHILDREN

1. "God Gives a Helper"—the Holy Spirit.
2. When we do wrong, the Holy Spirit convicts us and tells us to ask forgiveness.
3. The Holy Spirit will help us to do better next time.
4. We should ask the Holy Spirit to help us.

THE LESSON COMMENTARY

I. GOD IS SPIRIT:
John 4:24

"God is spirit, and his worshipers must worship in spirit and in truth."

This significant announcement came in an unusual setting. While Jesus was sitting one day beside Jacob's well, resting from a long walk, a Samaritan woman came to draw water. Jesus accosted her and asked for a drink. She rebuffed him a bit. Then He told her about the water of life that He could give her.

When she kept insisting on talking about physical water, when He was speaking of spiritual water, He startled her by saying, "Go, call your husband,

and come back" (v. 16). This was a forbidden subject, for she was living the life of a prostitute.

As people still sometimes do today, the woman tried to turn the conversation away from her sin. She raised a religious question: Where was she supposed to worship, on Mount Gerizim or at Jerusalem? She acted as if that was her greatest problem.

Jesus answered by emphasizing the fact that it is not primarily a matter of where we worship, but how we worship. "God is spirit, and his worshipers must worship in spirit and in truth." Wherever this woman went to worship, her worship would not be acceptable because she was living a sinful life.

The King James Version reads, "God is a Spirit"—as if He were one of many spirits. But the correct translation is: "God is spirit" (RSV, NASB, NIV). It is one of the great theological declarations of the Bible. God is pure spirit; He has no physical form. So the second of the Ten Commandments forbade the making of any image to represent God (Exod. 20:4).

The emphasis Jesus gave to worshiping "in spirit and in truth" should not be missed. Many people go to church on Sunday morning and participate in the ritual of the service without actually engaging in true worship, which is spiritual worship. Our hearts as well as minds must be involved. All of us need to be careful about this!

II. THE HOLY SPIRIT AS HELPER: John 14:25-26

"All this I have spoken while still with you. But the Counselor, the Holy Spirit, whom the Father will send in my name, will teach you all things and will remind you of everything I have said to you."

The Greek word translated "Counselor" is *paracletos*, which we have taken over into English as Paraclete. Theologians often refer to the Holy Spirit as "the Paraclete," a word which occurs five times in the New Testament. It is used only by John—four times in the Gospel (14:16, 26; 15:26; 16:7) and once in the First Epistle (2:1).

The noun comes from the verb *paracaleo*, which means "call alongside (to help)." That is why I personally felt happy when the New American Standard Bible came out with "Helper" in John's Gospel. The Holy Spirit helps us in many ways, in whatever way we need Him. In His Last Discourse (John 14-16), Jesus indicated a number of ways in which the Holy Spirit would help His disciples. "Comforter" (KJV) is only one aspect.

The New International Version translators felt, however, that since the main use of *paracletos* in the first century was for a "counselor," it would be best to translate it that way in John's Gospel. (In the Epistle it is Jesus who acts as *paracletos*, our legal advocate in the court of heaven.)

The term "counselor" is very meaningful today. Do we need guidance in some important matter? We seek counsel from someone who can give us the proper advice. What we need to realize is that the Holy Spirit is ready to help us with all our problems. All we need to do is to ask Him to guide us, strengthen us, and lead us in the way we ought to go.

Jesus said that the Holy Spirit "will teach you all things." We ought to turn to Him more frequently as our infallible Teacher.

III. THE INDWELLING SPIRIT: Romans 8:9-11

A. The Spirit in the Believer: v. 9

The Holy Spirit is mentioned only four times in the first seven chapters of Romans. By contrast He is referred to some twenty times in the eighth chapter, making this the greatest single chapter on the Holy Spirit in the New Testament. The greatest full passage on the Holy Spirit is Jesus' Last Discourse (John 14-16), from which our previous section of the lesson was taken.

In the second verse of this chapter we read: ". . . because through Christ Jesus the law of the Spirit of life set me free from the law of sin and death." Paul goes on to say that God sent His own Son to be a sin offering "in order that the righteous requirements of the law might be fully met in us, who do not live according to the sinful nature but according to the Spirit" (v. 4). Ultimately our lives will be dominated either by the selfish, self-centered sinful nature or by God's Holy Spirit.

This truth is highlighted in verse 5: "Those who live according to the sinful nature have their minds set on what that nature desires; but those who live in accordance with the Spirit have their minds set on what the Spirit desires." Paul concludes that paragraph by saying: "Those controlled by the sinful nature cannot please God" (v. 8). The New American Standard Bible reads, "and those who are in the flesh cannot please God" (cf. KJV). Yet Paul says elsewhere, "God was manifest in the flesh" (I Tim. 3:16), and he refers to himself as living "in the flesh" (Phil. 1:22)—obviously meaning "living in the body" (NIV).

It is clear that the Greek word *sarx* ("flesh") has two distinct senses in the New Testament: It is used literally for the physical body and metaphorically for the carnal self. But to the average person today in our society "flesh" means either the physical body, or more specifically "sex." To make it clear when the Scriptures are using it metaphorically, the New International Version calls it "sinful nature" in these passages.

This comes out clearly in verse 9: "You, however, are controlled not by the sinful nature but by the Spirit, if the Spirit of God lives in you." Paul goes on to say: "And if anyone does not have the Spirit of Christ, he does not belong to Christ." That is, every true believer has the Holy Spirit, for He is the One who comes in regenerating power when we accept Christ as our Savior.

Wilber Dayton says on this verse:

Again it is grace that triumphs. It is not human, self-righteous efforts but the indwelling Spirit of God (which every Christian has in a vital sense) that enthrones the spiritual. Of course the human must be obedient and cooperative. But, as always, it is God who enables (*The Wesleyan Bible Commentary*, 5:54).

B. The Indwelling Christ: v. 10

"But if Christ is in you, your body is dead because of sin, yet your spirit is alive because of righteousness."

This verse has caused much discussion, with considerable difference of interpretation. In the first place, what

is meant by the statement that the "body is dead"? Some think that Paul is anticipating verse 11 and saying that the physical body is "mortal." On the other hand, C. K. Barrett writes: "If Christ is in you, two consequences follow. On the one hand your body is dead. 'Your body' is 'you,' and you are dead; for this see vi.2-11; vii.1-6" (*Commentary on the Epistle to the Romans*, p. 159).

The second clause of this verse has caused even more debate: "but the Spirit is life because of righteousness" (KJV). Barrett comments: "On the other hand, the Spirit (of God) is life-giving.... The human self is dead—to sin; the Spirit is able to give life" (*Romans*, p. 159). But Wilber Dayton comments: "Now if, as we know *Christ* (himself) *is in* us, our human *spirit is life*—God-begotten, God-sustained life, beyond the reach of death" (*WBC*, 5:54). By using a small "s" both the New American Standard Bible and the New International Version follow the idea that the "spirit is alive." This is made even more definite in the New International Version by saying, "your spirit is alive."

C. The Life-Giving Spirit: v. 11

"And if the Spirit of him who raised Jesus from the dead is living in you, he who raised Christ from the dead will also give life to your mortal bodies through his Spirit, who lives in you."

William Greathouse gives a very helpful discussion of this verse. He writes:

Here both a future gift and a present grace merge with each other. The reference is undoubtedly to the resurrection of the body which will occur when Christ returns.... But as believers we now have "the first-fruits of the Spirit" (23). The resurrection of Christ was the beginning of every blessing that we have through Him. Through the risen Lord we have received even now the quickening power of the Holy Spirit. Thus Paul is thinking here of all those revivifying forces which broke into history with Christ's victory over death and which are mediated to us through the Spirit (*Beacon Bible Commentary*, 8:173).

I have more than once experienced that life-giving energy quickening my physical body. God gives us strength to accomplish what He calls us to do.

IV. THE SPIRIT VERSUS THE FLESH: Romans 8:12-14

Therefore, brothers, we have an obligation—but it is not to the sinful nature, to live according to it. For if you live according to the sinful nature, you will die; but if by the Spirit you put to death the misdeeds of the body, you will live, because those who are led by the Spirit of God are sons of God.

"You will die" . . . "you will live"— these two expressions obviously refer to spiritual, not physical, death and life. It is spiritual life that Paul is concerned with in this Epistle.

Greathouse advises us that verses 12-14 should be read together, as forming one thought. He goes on to say:

The alternative presented is a familiar one in Romans: life according to the flesh or life according to the Spirit. Equally known is the end to which each way leads: death or life (*BBC*, 8:174).

"Mortify the deeds of the body" does not mean "Practice asceticism." In Colossians Paul speaks out strongly against this false idea of religion. Rather, it is making the body subservient to the Spirit.

V. THE SPIRIT OF SONSHIP: Romans 8:15-17

A. Assurance of Sonship: vv. 15-16

"For you did not receive a spirit that makes you a slave again to fear, but you received the Spirit of sonship.

And by him we cry, 'Abba, Father'" (v. 15). We find a similar statement elsewhere by Paul: "Because you are sons, God sent the Spirit of his Son into our hearts, the Spirit who calls out, 'Abba, Father'" (Gal. 4:6).

Aside from these two passages the term *Abba* is found (in the New Testament) only in Mark 14:36, where Jesus used it in praying to His Father in Gethsemane. It is the Aramaic word for "Father." As far as we know, Aramaic was the common language of the home in Palestine in the first century. So *Abba* expresses familiar affection. When we have been adopted into the family of God, the Holy Spirit enables us to have a gracious sense of God's presence as our Father.

Verse 16 states: "The Spirit himself testifies with our spirit that we are God's children." It is unfortunate that the King James Version says "the Spirit itself." In English "itself" is neuter. But the Holy Spirit is not an "it"; He is a person.

How do we know that we are God's children? It is by a joint witness, as this verse declares. The Holy Spirit witnesses with our spirit. And that is all the assurance we need. But this "inner witness" is essential if we are to have complete certainty as to our relationship to God.

DISCUSSION QUESTIONS

1. How can we know the reality of spiritual things? (Heb. 11:1)
2. What are some of the ways in which the Holy Spirit can be our Helper?
3. Where did our sinful nature come from?
4. How can we be "led by the Spirit of God"?
5. How can we share Christ's sufferings?
6. What does sharing Christ's glory mean?

B. Heirs of God: v. 17

"Now if we are children, then we are heirs—heirs of God and co-heirs with Christ, if indeed we share in his sufferings in order that we may also share in his glory."

What a privilege our sonship brings! Imagine being an heir of the King of Kings and Lord of Lords! Yet that is our privilege in Christ. He is both the Creator of the universe and Heir to the universe. And we are co-heirs with Him.

But there is a price to pay, even as Christ paid a supreme price at Calvary. If we are going to share "in his glory" we must share "in his sufferings." This will involve a sacrificial burden for the salvation of the lost. But the wonderful thing is that He shares those sufferings with us.

VI. THE SPIRIT AS INTERCESSOR: Romans 8:26-27

In the same way, the Spirit helps us in our weakness. We do not know what we ought to pray, but the Spirit himself intercedes for us with groans that words cannot express. And he who searches our hearts knows the mind of the Spirit, because the Spirit intercedes for the saints in accordance with God's will.

As Christians we have two intercessors. At the right hand of the Father in heaven Christ is continually interceding for us, representing us as our attorney there (v. 34; I John 2:1). At the same time, the Holy Spirit is our Intercessor within.

With our limited knowledge, we do not know how to pray. But the Holy Spirit intercedes for us and through us with groans too deep for words. It is when we "pray in the Spirit" that our prayers are effective.

Always the Holy Spirit intercedes for us "in accordance with God's will." We need both His power and guidance in our praying.

VII. GOD WORKING FOR OUR GOOD: Romans 8:28

This is a favorite verse with Christians everywhere. The King James Version reads: "And we know that all things work together for good to them that love God, to them who are the called according to his purpose." But the earliest Greek manuscripts say: "And we know that in all things God works for the good of those who love him, who have been called according to his purpose." This is more meaningful and true. For it is God who is doing the working.

God works for the good of "those who love him." The word for "love" here indicates more than affection. It is the love of full loyalty and devotion. When we are completely committed to God and want only His will, He works effectively and continually on our behalf.

This means that even the hardship and disappointments of life can bring real blessing. What may seem to be material liabilities will turn out to be spiritual assets.

CONTEMPORARY APPLICATION

What does it mean to be "heirs of God and co-heirs with Christ"? Our inheritance is a spiritual one, not one of material wealth. But spiritual riches are eternal, whereas material wealth is only temporal. No intelligent person would choose something good that he can have for only a short time in preference to something far better that will last forever. It is only because "their understanding is darkened" that people choose earthly wealth instead of eternal riches. We have an immeasurable, incomparable inheritance. Let's hold on to it!

GOD'S CALLED-OUT PEOPLE

DEVOTIONAL READING	Colossians 3:1-12
ADULTS AND YOUTH	**Adult Topic:** *God's Called-Out People*
	Youth Topic: *God's Special People*
	Background Scripture: Col. 3:1-17; 4:5-6; I Peter 2:9-17
	Scripture Lesson: Col. 3:1-3; 4:5-6; I Peter 2:9-17
	Memory Verse: *You are a chosen race, a royal priesthood, a holy nation, God's own people, that you may declare the wonderful deeds of him who called you out of darkness into his marvelous light.* I Peter 2:9
CHILDREN	**Topic:** *God Helps Us Live Better*
	Memory Verse: *Do everything in the name of the Lord Jesus, giving thanks to God.* Col. 3:17
DAILY BIBLE READINGS	Nov. 14 M.: "Christ Is All." Col. 3:1-11
	Nov. 15 T.: "Put on Love." Col. 3:12-17
	Nov. 16 W.: "Continue Steadfastly in Prayer." Col. 4:2-6
	Nov. 17 T.: "A Living Sacrifice." Rom. 12:1-13
	Nov. 18 F.: "The Body of Christ." I Cor. 12:14-27
	Nov. 19 S.: "You Shall Be Holy." I Peter 1:13-25
	Nov. 20 S.: "God's Own People." I Peter 2:1-10
LESSON AIM	To help us understand better our privileges and responsibilities as God's people.
LESSON SETTING	**Time:** Colossians was written about A.D. 60, I Peter perhaps soon after that.
	Place: Both Epistles were written in Rome. Paul wrote Colossians while in prison.

God's Called-Out People

I. **Spiritual Elevation:** Colossians 3:1-4
   A. Earnest Desire: v. 1
   B. The Set of the Mind: v. 2
   C. A Safe Hiding Place: vv. 3-4

II. **Putting off the Old Life:** Colossians 3:5-11

LESSON OUTLINE

III. **Putting on the New Life:** Colossians 3:12-14

IV. **The Ideal Christian Life:** Colossians 3:15-17

V. **Relation to Outsiders:** Colossians 4:5-6

VI. **God's Special People:** I Peter 2:9-10

VII. **Different from the World:** I Peter 2:11-12

VIII. Submission to Authority: I Peter 2:13-17
  A. To Kings and Governors: vv. 13-14
  B. Good Example: v. 15
  C. Free, Yet Servants: v. 16
  D. Proper Respect: v. 17

SUGGESTED
INTRODUCTION
FOR ADULTS

As God's people we are called out of the world and out of sin and into a close walk with God. This lesson emphasizes that we should not be content with living spiritually on the lowest plane we think we can get by with. Rather, we should seek the highest levels of spiritual living.

Actually, this is the only safe way to live. To live life at the minimum is to risk losing it altogether. The safest way, and the happiest way, is to live as close to God as we can. That will help us to keep at a safe distance from the world, which poses a threat to us in these days of permissive morals.

SUGGESTED
INTRODUCTION
FOR YOUTH

As Christians we are "God's Special People." This fact suggests both privileges and responsibilities.

We learn in this lesson that we are "a chosen people, a royal priesthood." This puts us in a special class, far above worldly people around us. We are a very privileged people!

But it also puts on us a solemn responsibility to act the part! We are to glorify God by living holy lives and pointing people toward a higher way of life. This should not be a burden to us, but a joy to represent our Christ to others.

CONCEPTS FOR
CHILDREN

1. "God Helps Us Live Better"—if we will let Him.
2. We should try to please God in everything we do.
3. Doing "everything in the name of the Lord Jesus" means doing it as He would do it.
4. We should learn to be more and more thankful.

THE LESSON COMMENTARY

I. SPIRITUAL ELEVATION:
Colossians 3:1-4

A. Earnest Desire: v. 1

"Since, then, you have been raised with Christ, set your heart on things above, where Christ is seated at the right hand of God."

Having been raised with Christ from sin and selfish living, now "keep seeking the things above" (NASB). The Greek verb is *zeteo*, which means "seek." For this passage Arndt and Gingrich suggest it means "try to obtain, desire to possess" (*Greek-English Lexicon of the New Testament*, p. 339). The verb is in the present tense of continuous action (NASB). John Nielson observes: "*Seek those things which are above* becomes the lifelong pursuit of the man in Christ" (*Beacon Bible Commentary*, 9:410).

"Things above" means heavenly things. Since "Christ is seated at the right hand of God" and we are "in Christ" (as we saw in our previous lesson), we should seek to have fellowship with Him "in the heavenlies"—the main thrust of Ephesians. So we might say that "life in the heavenlies" is the emphasis here, as we found it was in Ephesians. These two Epistles (Colossians and Ephesians) were written by Paul at the same time and sent by the same messengers, and they have a great deal in common.

B. The Set of the Mind: v. 2

"Set your minds on things above, not on earthly things." The King James Version says, "Set your affection on things above." This comes from the Bishop's Bible. It should be remembered that the King James Version was a revision of the Bishop's Bible. The bishops of the Church of England had been brought up on the Latin Vulgate, and they loved their Latin. Many of the unfortunate translations in the King James Version reflect this Latin influence (e.g., "charity" in I Corinthians 13). The Greek word here means "mind," not "affection" (which we connect with the heart).

We are to set our mind on heavenly things, "not on earthly things." John Eadie wisely observes: "'Things on earth' are only subordinate and instrumental—'things above' are supreme and final" (*Commentary on the Epistle of Paul to the Colossians,* p. 215).

If we set our minds on earthly things, these will continually drag us down to lower levels. If we set our minds on heavenly things, they will draw us nearer to Christ.

C. A Safe Hiding Place: vv. 3-4

"For you died, and your life is now hidden with Christ in God."

What could be more wonderful than to be "hidden with Christ in God"? Here is safety, seclusion, divine fellowship, shelter from the enticements of the world—true heavenly living while on earth. We are constantly challenged to live this way.

How do we find such a life? The first answer is found here: "For you died." We have to die to self in order to become fully alive in fellowship with

Christ (Gal. 2:20). Dead to self and sin, we are alive in Christ.

Verse 4 carries us a step further: "When Christ, who is your life, appears, then you also will appear with him in glory." Every true Christian wants to go to heaven and enjoy eternal bliss and blessing with Christ there. The way that we can be sure that this will be our experience throughout eternity is to live a life "hidden with Christ in God." When Christ is our life, we have the firm assurance that we will share His "glory" when He returns.

II. PUTTING OFF THE OLD LIFE: Colossians 3:5-11

"Put to death, therefore, what belongs to your earthly nature" (v. 5)— literally, "the members that are upon the earth." T. K. Abbott says that this does not mean our hands, feet, etc., and of course this is obvious from the list that follows. Abbott says of *mele,* "members": "It is more natural to explain the word by the idea of the 'old man'.... The members spoken of are those which belong to the body as the instrument of the carnal mind" (*A Critical and Exegetical Commentary on the Epistles to the Ephesians and to the Colossians,* p. 280).

The words that follow explain what Paul means: "sexual immorality, impurity, lust, evil desires and greed, which is idolatry." In the King James Version the first item is "fornication." But the Greek word *porneia* is clearly used in the New Testament for adultery as well as fornication; it takes in all "sexual immorality." Also "evil concupiscence" (KJV) does not today communicate anything clearly. The Greek simply says "evil desire." All the things listed here are painfully apparent in modern society.

Paul goes on to say, "Because of these the wrath of God is coming" (v. 6). The added words, "on the children of disobedience" (KJV), are not found in our two oldest Greek manuscripts of Colossians (from the third and fourth centuries).

We are also to get rid of "anger, rage, malice, slander, and filthy language from your lips" (v. 8), as well as lying to each other (v. 9). This is because we have taken off the "old self with its practices and have put on the new self, which is being renewed in knowledge in the image of its Creator" (vv. 9-10). That is, as Christians we are to become continually more like Christ, reflecting His image in our lives.

It hardly needs to be said that the things Paul mentions in verses 8 and 9 are very common today. But they were also evident everywhere in his day, and that is why he enumerates them.

We are reminded here again that the life of the Christian is to be different from that of the world around him or her. We must show that we are God's called-out people.

III. PUTTING ON THE NEW LIFE:
Colossians 3:12-14

"Therefore, as God's chosen people, holy and dearly loved, clothe yourselves with compassion, kindness, humility, gentleness and patience" (v. 12). What a contrast to the list in verse 8!

The virtues listed here in verse 12 are not those of the natural man. They are found only in those who have been supernaturally changed by the grace of God. How different our world today would be if these characteristics were predominant in modern society. But we must show them more and more in our lives as Christians.

Paul goes on to say: "Bear with each other and forgive whatever grievances you may have against one another. Forgive as the Lord forgave you" (v. 13). The Lord forgave us freely and fully. Do we forgive people that way, even those who have hurt us deeply?

"And over all these virtues put on love, which binds them all together in perfect unity" (v. 14). Love is like the belt that holds things together. Without love, life falls apart. Love alone can produce "perfect unity."

IV. THE IDEAL CHRISTIAN LIFE:
Colossians 3:15-17

What is the ideal Christian life? Paul here gives us some important guidelines.

First he says: "Let the peace of Christ rule in your hearts, since as members of one body you were called to peace. And be thankful" (v. 15). We live in a world of constant strife, turmoil, and war. In such a world, we must "let the peace of Christ" rule in our hearts. And even in such a world we must "be thankful."

Paul goes on to say: "Let the word of Christ dwell in you richly as you teach and admonish one another with all wisdom, and as you sing psalms, hymns and spiritual songs with gratitude in your hearts to God" (v. 16). How far short we all come in living up to this beautiful standard set for us here! We need more heavenly things and less of the earthly.

Paul concludes his admonition here by saying: "And whatever you do, whether in word or deed, do it all in the name of the Lord Jesus" (v. 17). In the Scripture "name" means "nature." We are to show daily the nature of Christ.

V. RELATION TO OUTSIDERS:
Colossians 4:5-6

"Be wise in the way you act toward outsiders; make the most of every opportunity" (v. 5).

Too often we hear of people being turned against a church by the actions or words of some of its members. This is a very serious problem. It isn't primarily the reputation of the church that concerns us. Rather, it is two other things: the reputation of our Lord, and the salvation of souls. There is no question but that some people are lost eternally because of the unchristian attitudes or actions of professing Christians. This is tragic!

Paul goes on to say: "Let your conversation be always full of grace, seasoned with salt, so that you may know how to answer everyone" (v. 16).

Are we always gracious in our talk? We could all seek God's help at this point.

"Seasoned with salt." What does this mean? Abbott suggests, "pleasant but not insipid, nor yet coarse" (p. 298). Nielson says it "suggests that our words should be palatable and sensible" (*BBC*, 9:423). Too much conversation is "flat," insipid.

VI. GOD'S SPECIAL PEOPLE: I Peter 2:9-10

"But you are a chosen people, a royal priesthood, a holy nation, a people belonging to God, that you may declare the praises of him who called you out of darkness into his wonderful light" (v. 9).

In lesson 9 we looked at a similar passage in Exodus (19:5-6), as applied to Israel. Here it is applied to believers in Christ.

Peter first says that we are "a chosen people," or "race" (NASB). This is only because we are in Christ, God's Son.

Next he says that we are "a royal priesthood." This combination of kings and priests (Rev. 1:6) not only overwhelms us with the noble privileges it suggests but also challenges us with its tremendous responsibility. If we are kings, we should act in a kingly fashion—not looking, acting, or talking like worldly persons. If we are priests, we have a responsibility to minister to others, representing God to them and them to God—the twofold function of a priest. This involves a prayerful concern for their spiritual welfare. Being a priest is a costly business. It cost Christ His life's blood.

The third designation is "a holy nation." A holy God must have holy people to represent Him in an unholy world. Nothing less than a holy life will be pleasing to God and a proper witness to others.

The fourth description is "a people belonging to God." The Greek literally says "a people for (God's) own possession." The King James Version rendering, "a peculiar people," is most unfortunate. It does not at all communicate the correct meaning to the modern reader. "A precious people" would be far more accurate and helpful.

F. B. Meyer has this to say about "a people for God's own possession":

> Love yearns for proprietorship; nor can the heart of God be satisfied unless it can speak of some as its own. Oh, happy they who have obeyed his summons, and have made a complete surrender of themselves to Him! He has already taken them for his own possession. Enclosed as a garden; tilled as a field; inhabited as a home; guarded, kept, used, loved, with an emphasis none others know. Nor is there anything in God Himself which is not at the disposal of those who hold nothing back from Him (*Tried by Fire*, p. 74).

As such favored people, what is our responsibility? "That you may declare the praises of him who called you out of darkness into his wonderful light." Concerning "darkness" E. G. Selwyn writes:

> The metaphor expresses the deceit and concealment which accompany evil, and the bewilderment and misery which it causes. Light, on the other hand, was thought of, as from the Creation onwards the special characteristic of God, who dwells in it and imparts it to all who love truth and justice (*First Epistle of St. Peter*, p. 168).

Then Peter points out a further significant truth about Christians: "Once you were not a people, but now you are the people of God; once you had not received mercy, but now you have received mercy." F. B. Meyer writes:

> How can we repay Him for all He has done for us—when we compare what we are, with what we were? Once in darkness, now in marvellous light. Once not included among the people of God, now accounted as part

of them. Once without hope of mercy, now the happy recipients of untold mercy. What shall we say? Is it not our duty to praise Him, not only with our lips, but in our lives, casting our crowns at his feet, and bearing our part in the song of adoration? (*Tried by Fire*, p. 74).

VII. DIFFERENT FROM THE WORLD:
I Peter 2:11-12

Dear friends, I urge you, as aliens and strangers in the world, to abstain from sinful desires, which war against your soul. Live such good lives among the pagans that, though they accuse you of doing wrong, they may see your good deeds and glorify God on the day he visits us.

Peter emphasizes the fact that Christians are "aliens and strangers" (NASB, NIV) in the world. Since we are children of God we are aliens in an ungodly world. We should never allow ourselves to become entangled in its godless lifestyle. Charles Ball writes:

Christians are strangers in this world and cannot live by its standards; while residents upon the earth, they are on their way to a better country beyond. The warning to *abstain from fleshly lusts* has three reasons for Christians disciplining and directing their lives: (1) the fact of their heavenly citizenship, (2) the importance of their own well-being, and (3) their influence for God upon the unbelieving world around them" (*The Wesleyan Bible Commentary*, 6:259).

The word "conversation" (v. 12, KJV), as we have noted before, is a mistranslation today. The Greek word means "manner of life" or "behavior" (NASB).

VIII. SUBMISSION TO AUTHORITY:
I Peter 2:13-17

A. To Kings and Governors: vv. 13-14

"Submit yourselves for the Lord's sake to every authority instituted among men: whether to the king, as the supreme authority, or to governors, who are sent by him to punish those who do wrong and to commend those who do right."

Peter here is in close agreement with what Paul wrote in Romans 13:1-7. And Jesus enunciated this principle of submission to governmental authority when He said: "Give to Caesar what is Caesar's" (Matt. 22:21).

"The king" would refer primarily to the emperor at Rome. Peter was writing this Epistle to "God's elect, strangers in the world, scattered throughout Pontus, Galatia, Cappadocia, Asia and Bithynia" (1:1)—five Romans provinces in Asia Minor (modern Turkey). The "governors" would be those "sent by him" (the emperor) to govern the various provinces of the Roman Empire.

B. Good Example: v. 15

"For it is God's will that by doing good you should silence the ignorant talk of foolish men." To some degree this is an enlargement of "for the Lord's sake" in verse 13. Everything we do should be for *His* sake.

C. Free, Yet Servants: v. 16

"Live as free men, but do not use your freedom as a cover-up for evil; live as servants of God." The Greek word for "servants" is *douloi*,

---

DISCUSSION QUESTIONS
1.   What is the secret of becoming more spiritual?
2.   What should be our main goal in life?
3.   In what ways should we be different from the world?
4.   How do we put off the old self?
5.   What is the highest Christian virtue?
6.   What should be our relationship to our governmental authorities?

which means "bondslaves" (NASB). The only way we can be truly free in this world is to be the bondslaves of God, living in obedience to His will. (See further discussion in Contemporary Application.)

D. Proper Respect: v. 17

Peter enunciates an important principle here: "Show respect to everyone." Then he breaks it down into three applications: "Love the brotherhood of believers, fear God, honor the king."

On the general principle Roy S. Nicholson writes:

> This means that all men will be given the esteem they deserve as being created in God's image, redeemed by His Son, and designed for a place in His kingdom. There are different circumstances of life, but the Christian renders to each the regard and treatment to which he is entitled (*BBC*, 10:283).

There is to be a special "love" for our fellow Christians ("the brotherhood"). Above all, we are to "fear God." Peter has already told us how to "honor the king" in verse 13.

CONTEMPORARY APPLICATION

On the very important topic today of freedom (I Peter 2:16) Charles Ball has this to say:

> Too often liberty has been misinterpreted as license. False freedom means living according to the impulses of the flesh, or human nature apart from God. True freedom means living according to the will of God. Free people live by moral standards and can govern themselves. People without these inner controls have to be governed by an outside force and possibly by a police state. Liberty exists in proportion to the respect for moral law and the recognition of personal responsibility. Whether a man steals much or little depends upon the opportunity; whether he steals at all depends upon character (*WBC*, 6:261).

GOD'S WITNESSING PEOPLE

DEVOTIONAL READING	II Tim. 4:1-5
ADULTS AND YOUTH	**Adult Topic:** *God's Witnessing People*
	Youth Topic: *God's Sharing People*
	Background Scripture: Matt. 5:13-16; 28:18-20; II Cor. 5:18-21; II Tim. 4:1-5
	Scripture Lesson: Matt. 5:13-16; 28:18-20; II Cor. 5:18-21; II Tim. 4:1-2
	Memory Verse: *We are ambassadors for Christ, God making his appeal through us.* II Cor. 5:20
CHILDREN	**Topic:** *Sharing Jesus with Others*
	Memory Verse: *Go therefore and make disciples of all nations.* Matt. 28:19
DAILY BIBLE READINGS	Nov. 21 M.: The Call to Influence. Matt. 5:13-16
	Nov. 22 T.: The Call to Proclaim. II Tim. 4:1-5
	Nov. 23 W.: The Call to Make Defense. I Peter 3:8-17
	Nov. 24 T.: The Call to Love. I Cor. 13
	Nov. 25 F.: The Call to Persevere. Phil. 3:12-16
	Nov. 26 S.: The Call to Reconcile. II Cor. 5:16-21
	Nov. 27 S.: The Call to Witness. Matt. 28:16-20
LESSON AIM	To help us be good ambassadors for Christ.
LESSON SETTING	**Time:** Matthew 5 relates to about A.D. 28, chapter 28 to about A.D. 30. II Corinthians was written about A.D. 55, II Timothy about A.D. 61.
	Place: The Sermon on the Mount was given in Galilee. II Corinthians was written in Ephesus, II Timothy in Rome.
LESSON OUTLINE	**God's Witnessing People**

God's Witnessing People

   I. **Christians As Salt and Light:** Matthew 5:13-16
      A. Salt: v. 13
      B. Light: vv. 14-16

  II. **The Great Commission:** Matthew 28:18-20
      A. Divine Authority: v. 18
      B. Making Disciples: v. 19
      C. Teaching Converts: v. 20

 III. **The Ministry of Reconciliation:** II Corinthians 5:18-21
      A. Reconciled Through Christ: v. 18
      B. The Message of Reconciliation: v. 19
      C. Be Reconciled to God: v. 20
      D. Christ's Atoning Death: v. 21

IV. **The Charge to Preach:** II Timothy 4:1-5
   A. A Solemn Charge: v. 1
   B. Preach the Word: v. 2

SUGGESTED
INTRODUCTION
FOR ADULTS

As we come to the last lesson of the quarter, we might glance back to see what we have learned. Review is one of the phases of good pedagogy.

The general topic for the quarter was "Our Biblical Faith"—a broad field! This was treated in three units: (1) God Reveals Himself; (2) God Redeems His People; (3) God Relates to His People.

Logically, we started with "God of Creation," beginning our study at the very "beginning," Genesis 1:1. Then we moved to the "God of History," focusing especially on the history of the Israelites. The rest of the Old Testament was caught up in "God of Inspired Prophets." The climax, of course, was "God in Christ."

The second unit, on redemption, naturally started with the problem of sin and moved on to the motive for redemption in God's love; the means of redemption, God's Son; and the result, new persons.

The third unit, "God Relates to His People," logically started with God's gracious covenant and then moved on to God's steadfast love, His indwelling Spirit, His called-out people, and finally (today) "God's Witnessing People."

SUGGESTED
INTRODUCTION
FOR YOUTH

If we have something that we are enthusiastic about we like to share the good news with others. The truth is that we have the real Good News, the gospel, and we should be eager to share it. So our topic today is "God's Sharing People."

If we have found that Christ has lifted the load of sin from our hearts, let's tell other people. If we have found that Jesus is our best friend, who is always with us to strengthen and help us, let's share the good news.

CONCEPTS FOR
CHILDREN

1. Sharing Jesus with others helps us to enjoy Him more ourselves.
2. We can tell our friends and relatives what we have learned about Jesus in Sunday school.
3. We can encourage others to go to church with us.
4. We can also pray for others.

THE LESSON COMMENTARY

I. **CHRISTIANS AS SALT AND LIGHT:**
Matthew 5:13-16

A. Salt: v. 13

"You are the salt of the earth. But if the salt loses its saltiness, how can it be made salty again? It is no longer good for anything, except to be thrown out and trampled by men."

I have commented on this verse as follows:

Salt does two things: it *flavors* and *preserves*. Life without Christ is flat, insipid, tasteless. His followers are to add tone to life and zest to living, just as salt adds flavor to food. But Christianity must also be the preservative of human society. When Jesus spoke these words modern refrigeration was unknown. One of the most common ways to preserve food—such as fish shipped from the Lake of Galilee down to Jerusalem—was to salt it heavily. What would the world be today without the Church of Jesus Christ? (*The Wesleyan Bible Commentary*, 4:32).

We as Christians must not let our salt lose its saltiness, or we will become useless. We must guard the spiritual tone of our lives carefully and prayerfully.

B. Light: vv. 14-16

"You are the light of the world" (v. 14). We can see how Jesus, the Son of God, the Creator of light, could say: "I am the light of the world" (John 8:12; 9:5). But how could He say that *we* are the light of the world?

The Son of God is the Sun of righteousness (Mal. 4:2). There is a sense in which the church is the moon, shining in the darkness of the world's night.

Where does the moon get its light? It has no light of its own, but reflects the light of the sun. So we are to reflect the light of Christ shining on us. But perhaps we should also say that when Christ, the Light of the world, comes into our hearts He wants to shine out through our lives to darkened souls about us.

Jesus went on to say: "A city on a hill cannot be hidden." One sees many cities and towns sitting on hills in Palestine. They are in plain sight for everyone to see. Just so, Christians are on display and must be concerned about their influence on others.

Then Jesus said: "Neither do people light a lamp and put it under a bowl. Instead they put it on its stand, and it gives light to everyone in the house" (v. 15). The King James Version speaks of "candle" and "candlestick," but this is an anachronism. In Jesus' day the people used little clay lamps, small enough to fit into the palm of one's hand. These would be filled with olive oil and have a small lighted wick. The King James translators were used to having candles for light, so they changed "lamp" to "candle."

Also the King James Version speaks of hiding a lamp under a "bushel." Actually, the Greek word *modion* means a "peck measure" (NASB), or a "bowl" (NIV) holding that amount—perhaps a "meal-tub" (NEB) of that size, which held the flour ground fresh every day on the little handmill in each home.

Jesus concluded, "In the same way, let your light shine before men, that they may see your good deeds and praise your Father in heaven" (v. 16). So our good deeds are the light that people see in our lives—deeds of honesty, kindness, compassion, and love.

II. THE GREAT COMMISSION:
Matthew 28:18-20

A. Divine Authority: v. 18

After His resurrection Jesus met with His twelve apostles on a mountain in Galilee (vv. 16-17). There He said to them, "All authority in heaven and on earth has been given to me." The King James Version says "power," but the Greek word for that is *dynamis*, whereas the word here is *exousia*, "authority."

B. Making Disciples: v. 19

"Therefore go and make disciples of all nations, baptizing them in the name of the Father and of the Son and of the Holy Spirit...." The King James Version says "teach" all nations, but the Greek verb is *matheteuo*, from the noun *mathetes*, "disciple." So it means "make disciples."

C. Teaching Converts: v. 20

". . . and teaching them to obey everything I have commanded you."

Here the verb is *didasko*, which means "teach." New converts need to be taught many things. "Disciple" literally means "learner." As disciples of Jesus, we are to keep on learning.

The Gospel of Matthew closes with a beautiful promise: "And surely I will be with you always, to the very end of the age." The word for "always" is literally "all the days"; the bad days as well as the good days, He is with us.

III. THE MINISTRY OF RECONCILIATION: II Corinthians 5:18-21

A. Reconciled Through Christ: v. 18

"All this is from God, who reconciled us to himself through Christ and gave us the ministry of reconciliation: ..."

I have written elsewhere of verses 18-20:

> The two greatest passages on reconciliation in the NT are this one and Rom. 5:10-11.... The noun *katallage* occurs twice here (vv. 18, 19) and twice in Romans (5:11; 11:15), and nowhere else in the NT. The verb *katallasso* is found three times here (vv. 18, 19, 20) and once in Rom. 5:10. In the only other place where it occurs in the NT (1 Cor. 7:11) it is used of an estranged wife being reconciled to her husband (*Word Meanings in the New Testament*, 4:129).

Concerning Paul's "ministry of reconciliation" (*katallage*) Buechsel says: "It brings before men the action by which God takes them again into fellowship with Himself" (*Theological Dictionary of the New Testament*, 1:258).

Buechsel also discusses the verb. He writes:

> ... *katallassein* denotes a transformation or renewal of the state between God and man, and therewith of man's own state.... By reconciliation our sinful self-seeking is overcome and the fellowship with God is created in which it is replaced by living for Christ (*TDNT*, 1:255).

Without reconciliation there could be no salvation. If it were not for the reconciling work of Christ we would all be forever separated from God, lost in eternal darkness. And all this is because of man's sin. Frank Carver writes:

> Reconciliation involves the overcoming of personal alienation (Eph. 4:18) or hostility (Col. 1:21) caused by man's rebellion against his rightful Sovereign. The result is a new condition of peace (Rom. 5:1; Gal. 5:22; Eph. 2:12-17; Phil. 4:7) and the restoration of fellowship (*Beacon Bible Commentary*, 8:554-55).

From the many Scripture passages cited by Carver it will be seen that reconciliation is an important idea in the New Testament. Without it we are lost forever.

B. The Message of Reconciliation: v. 19

What is the message of reconciliation? "That God was reconciling the world to himself in Christ, not counting men's sins against them."

Paul here repeats his central emphasis that God is the one who initiates the reconciliation, bringing sinful man back into fellowship with Himself. And He effects this reconciliation "through" (v. 18) or "in" (v. 19) Christ. Commenting on this main thrust, especially as found in verse 18, Alfred Plummer writes:

> This is the usual language of the N.T., in which the change which brings about the reconciliation between God and men is regarded as taking place in them rather than in Him. Greeks thought of God as estranged from men, and it was He who needed to be won over. Jews thought rather that it was men who by their sins were estranged from God. ... St. Paul follows Jewish rather than Hellenic thought. It is man who is reconciled to God, rather than God to man (*The Second Epistle of Paul to the Corinthians*, p. 181).

Plummer also adds this comment on verse 19: "God did all that on His side is necessary for their being reconciled to Him; but not all men do what is necessary on their side" (p. 183).

The careful reader may have noted a change in word order from "God was in Christ reconciling" (KJV, NASB) to "God was reconciling . . . in Christ" (NIV). Several excellent commentators argue strongly for the latter, insisting that "was" goes grammatically with "reconciling." For instance, J. H. Bernard writes: "The A.V., 'God was in Christ, reconciling,' etc., is not accurate" (*The Expositor's Greek Testament*, 3:72). And Plummer says that this translation (KJV) "is to be rejected." He would translate the passage: "God in Christ was reconciling the world to Himself" (p. 183). In my estimation, the matter is not worth fighting over; the Greek could go either way.

C. Be Reconciled to God: v. 20

After noting "And he has committed to us the message of reconciliation" (v. 19), Paul enlarges on this in verse 20: "We are therefore Christ's ambassadors, as though God were making his appeal through us. We implore you on Christ's behalf: Be reconciled to God."

The office of ambassador is always considered a high honor. The thought of being an ambassador of the King of Kings and Lord of Lords is almost overwhelming! We should always remember that the high honor is matched by tremendous responsibility. As ambassadors of Christ we represent Him. How well do we represent Him?

D. Christ's Atoning Death: v. 21

"God made him who had no sin to be sin for us, so that in him we might become the righteousness of God."

The first significant point here is the sinlessness of Christ. We find a similar statement in I Peter 2:22: "He committed no sin." Jesus Christ was the only sinless person on earth.

The second significant point is the statement that God made Christ "to be

sin for us." On the basis of Old Testament usage, some suggest that this means "be a sin offering" (NIV footnote). But Bernard asserts that "*hamartia* cannot be translated 'sin-offering' . . . for it cannot have two different meanings in the same clause" (*EGT*, 3:73). Plummer agrees. He writes: "We must face the plain meaning of the Apostle's strong words. In some sense which we cannot fathom, God is said to have identified Christ with man's sin, in order that man might be identified with God's own righteousness" (*Corinthians*, p. 187). So perhaps we should not push the idea of "sin offering" here.

IV. THE CHARGE TO PREACH: II Timothy 4:1-5

A. A Solemn Charge: v. 1

"In the presence of God and of Christ Jesus, who will judge the living and the dead, and in view of his appearing and his kingdom, I give you this charge. . . ."

The New American Standard Bible says, "I solemnly charge you." It is unquestionably a very solemn setting that is presented here. Paul is standing his young protege Timothy in the presence of God and of Christ Jesus, who will judge all people on the basis of how well they obey Him. The charge is also given "in view of his appearing and his kingdom." This is no light

---

DISCUSSION QUESTIONS

1. What are some of the properties of salt that we can exhibit in our lives?
2. What will hinder us from letting our light shine?
3. How does the Great Commission affect us?
4. How can we be reconciling agents?
5. Why do people not seek reconciliation with God?
6. What is the message of reconciliation?

matter! N. J. D. White expresses it this way:

> I solemnly charge you, in view of the coming judgment, to be zealous in the exercise of your ministry while the opportunity lasts, while people are willing to listen to your admonitions (*EGT*, 4:175).

Verses 3-5 indicate that the time will come when people will not listen to the gospel.

D. D. Whedon notes that Paul's charge "has the nature of an oath, by which the imposer assumes to bind his disciple *before* God by the solemnities and penalties of the final judgment to do certain things which are specified in verse 2" (*Commentary on the New Testament*, 5:457). That is, the apostle is putting his young preacher under oath to perform his ministry well.

B. Preach the Word: v. 2

Paul charged Timothy: "Preach the Word; be prepared in season and out of season; correct, rebuke and encourage—with great patience and careful instruction."

The first and most important item in the charge was: "Preach the Word." The Greek verb here for "preach" is *kerysso*. It comes from the noun *keryx*, "herald." The noun is used in Xenophon's *Anabasis*, for instance, of one who would stand up in front of the army and make a proclamation for the commander, or make an important proclamation for the emperor. So the verb means "herald" or "proclaim." The preacher is not to air his own ideas but to make a proclamation for his Chief.

What is Timothy to preach? The answer here is: "the Word." J. Glenn Gould asserts: "No sermon is really a sermon unless it makes explicit some biblical truth" (*BBC*, 9:653). The preacher must soak himself in the Word of God until it permeates his mind and heart. Then he must preach it with conviction and in the power of the Spirit.

Paul goes on to say: "Be prepared in season and out of season." Walter Lock suggests that "in season and out of season" may be "semi-proverbial," meaning "at all times." He further defines this as: "*both* whether or not the moment seems fit to your hearers, 'welcome or not welcome' . . . *and* 'whether or not it is convenient to you' . . . 'on duty or off duty,' 'in the pulpit or out of it,' 'take or make your opportunity'" (*The Pastoral Epistles*, pp. 112-13).

Paul charged Timothy to have not only *persistence*, as we have just seen, but also *courage:* "correct, rebuke and encourage—with great patience and careful instruction." It takes real courage to correct and rebuke those who are not acting properly, who are hurting the work of the church by their actions or words. Sometimes the pastor, as the leader of the local church, has to fulfill this function—but always with love and patience.

CONTEMPORARY APPLICATION

As Christians we are supposed to be "God's Witnessing People." This command is not just for preachers and pastoral staffs; it is for all of us.

How can we witness? In the first place, we have to have personal experience of what we witness to. We must know Jesus as our personal Savior before we can witness about Him effectively to others.

There are numerous ways in which we can witness. Jesus said that by our "good deeds" we let our light shine before others. This is a silent witness that is sometimes the most effective witness for Christ. People are watching our lives to see if we practice what we profess. Let's not let them down!

Quarter II
STUDIES IN ISAIAH

A NEW DAY FOR GOD'S PEOPLE

DEVOTIONAL READING	Isaiah 65:17-25
ADULTS AND YOUTH	**Adult Topic:** *A New Day for God's People* **Youth Topic:** *Look to the Future* **Background Scripture:** Isa. 2:1-5; 62; 65:17-25 **Scripture Lesson:** Isa. 2:2-4; 62:1-3 **Memory Verse:** *They shall be called The holy people, The redeemed of the Lord.* Isa. 62:12
CHILDREN	**Topic:** *God's Promise of Peace* **Scripture Lesson:** Isa. 2:2-4 **Memory Verse:** *Seek peace, and pursue it.* Ps. 34:14
DAILY BIBLE READINGS	**Nov. 28 M.:** A World Transformed. Isa. 65:17-25 **Nov. 29 T.:** The Hope of Fulfillment. Rom. 8:18-25 **Nov. 30 W.:** "The Lord Will Comfort Zion." Isa. 51:1-12 **Dec. 1 T.:** "Your God Reigns." Isa. 52:7-12 **Dec. 2 F.:** The New Age of Peace. Mic. 4:1-5 **Dec. 3 S.:** The New Age of Peace. Isa. 2:1-5 **Dec. 4 S.:** The New Jerusalem. Isa. 62:1-12
LESSON AIM	To get a glimpse of God's plan for the future.
LESSON SETTING	**Time:** 740-700 B.C. **Place:** Jerusalem

LESSON OUTLINE	**A New Day for God's People**
	
	  I. **Prophecy of the Last Days:** Isaiah 2:2-4
	    A. The Temple Hill: v. 2
	    B. A Center of Worship: v. 3
	    C. No More War: v. 4
	
	 II. **The Glory of Zion:** Isaiah 62:1-5
	    A. Future Righteousness: v. 1
	    B. A New Name: v. 2
	    C. A Crown of Splendor: v. 3
	    D. A Change of Name: v. 4
	    E. Time of Rejoicing: v. 5
	
	III. **A New Jerusalem:** Isaiah 65:17-25
	    A. New Heavens and Earth: v. 17
	    B. Jerusalem a Delight: v. 18
	    C. No More Weeping: v. 19
	    D. Longevity of Life: v. 20
	    E. Fruitful Labor: vv. 21-23
	    F. A Listening God: v. 24
	    G. Universal Peace: v. 25

This quarter's lessons are devoted to a study of Isaiah. Since Isaiah is one of the longest books in the Bible, it will be impossible to cover the whole book. Thus our focus will be on some of Isaiah's major theological themes.

The first unit (four lessons) deals with "The Messianic Hope." Appropriately, this unit reaches its climax on Christmas Day.

SUGGESTED
INTRODUCTION
FOR ADULTS

Unit II (five lessons) is a study of "Themes from Isaiah 1-39." The emphases here are on God's judgment (especially for injustice and oppression), a prophet's vision and ministry, and loyalty to God as our ultimate security.

Unit III (four lessons) looks at "Themes from Isaiah 40-66." Here we shall study God's sovereign power as the Lord of history, the role of the servant of the Lord, and God's concern to change the condition of the oppressed and afflicted.

Young people should not have to be told to "Look to the Future," for most of their life lies ahead of them. But the expression here refers particularly to the future of God's people.

SUGGESTED
INTRODUCTION
FOR YOUTH

If we listen to the news on radio and television, the future looks dismal and gloomy. It seems as though almost everything is going wrong. Instead of peace and prosperity, we see war and recession.

In a time like this we need to look into God's Word and get the divine perspective. There we learn that God has a glorious future for those who obey Him. If we are His children, we know the future is bright.

CONCEPTS FOR
CHILDREN

1. We all wish for world peace.
2. Instead of peace we see war and strife.
3. War and strife are caused by sin and selfishness.
4. For those who follow the Lord, there is coming a time of universal peace.

THE LESSON COMMENTARY

I. PROPHECY OF THE LAST DAYS: Isaiah 2:2-4

A. The Temple Hill: v. 2

In the last days
the mountain of the LORD's
    temple will be established
    as chief among the mountains;
it will be raised above the hills,
    and all nations will stream to it.

Verses 2-4 are found almost verbatim in Micah 4:1-3. Isaiah and Micah wrote at about the same time and had much the same vision. The repetition of this passage alerts us to its importance.

In the preceding quarter we looked at the expression "in the last days" and found that in such passages as Acts 2:17 (quoting Joel 2:28) it clearly refers to the messianic age, which began with the first coming of Christ. So some commentators apply this whole passage to the church, into which people from all nations will "stream." I prefer to make a double application: to the church age and also to the millennial kingdom at the close of this age.

The necessity of including the latter

seems to be indicated by verse one of this chapter: "This is what Isaiah son of Amoz saw concerning Judah and Jerusalem." In view of the restoration of Jews to Palestine and the setting up of the nation of Israel in 1948, it would appear that the prophet is talking about a political and religious future for Judah and Jerusalem.

A. R. Fausset seems to be combining the two interpretations—literal and metaphorical—when he says of the expression "in the last days":

> i.e., Messiah's; especially the days yet to come, to which all prophecy hastens, when "the house of *Jacob*," viz., at Jerusalem, shall be the centre to which the converted nations shall flock together (Robert Jamieson, A. R. Fausset, and David Brown, *A Commentary . . . on the Old and New Testaments,* 3:570).

What is "the mountain of the LORD's temple"? Again Fausset suggests the double interpretation when he writes: "the temple on Mount Moriah: type of the Gospel, beginning at Jerusalem, and, like an object set on the highest hill, made so conspicuous that all nations are attracted to it" (*Commentary,* 3:570).

B. A Center of Worship: v. 3

Many peoples will come and say,
"Come, let us go up to the
        mountain of the LORD,
    to the house of the God of Jacob.
He will teach us his ways,
    so that we may walk in his
        paths."
The law will go out from Zion,
    the word of the LORD from
        Jerusalem.

On the first two poetical lines here Fausset comments, "If the curse foretold against Israel has been literally fulfilled, so shall the promised blessing be literal" (*Commentary,* 3:570). And concerning the next two lines he observes: "The Holy Ghost shall be poured out for a *general* conversion then, and the Jews shall be the

instruments whose ministry shall be blessed in effecting it" (3:570).

C. No More War: v. 4

He will judge between the nations
    and will settle disputes for
        many peoples.
They will beat their swords into
        plowshares
    and their spears into pruning
        hooks.
Nation will not take up sword
        against nation,
    nor will they train for war
        anymore.

The promises found in this verse have not yet been fulfilled. At this very hour nation is rising against nation, and people are training for war around the globe!

We shall never have peace on earth until the Prince of Peace comes to set up His kingdom on earth. It will be a kingdom of righteousness and peace. The reason we can't have peace among nations is that they do not practice righteousness.

II. THE GLORY OF ZION:
   Isaiah 62:1-5

A. Future Righteousness: v. 1

For Zion's sake I will not keep
        silent,
    for Jerusalem's sake I will not
        remain quiet,
till her righteousness shines out
        like the dawn,
    her salvation like a blazing
        torch.

There is some difference of opinion as to who the speaker ("I") is. Alexander Maclaren says that "the speaker is the personal Messiah" (*Expositions of Holy Scripture,* Isaiah, 2:200). George Rawlinson writes:

> In the past God has kept silence (ch. xlii.14; lvii.11). "The Servant" has not caused his voice to be heard. . . . But now there will be a change. God will lift up his voice, and the nations

will hear; and the "salvation" will be effected speedily (*The Pulpit Commentary,* Isaiah, 2:430).

A. R. Fausset treats the matter a bit differently. He comments:

> "I"—the prophet as representative of all the praying people of God who love and intercede for Zion . . . ; or else Messiah, the great Intercessor (cf. v. 6). So Messiah is represented as unfainting in His efforts for his people (*Commentary,* 3:753).

With regard to "her righteousness" Fausset says:

> not its own *righteousness* inherently, but imputed to it for its restoration to God's favour: hence *"salvation"* answers to it in the parallelism. "Judah" is to be *"saved"* through "the Lord *our* (Judah's and the Church's) *righteousness"* (*Commentary,* 3:753).

I would say "imparted" as well as "imputed."

Commentators are agreed that the Hebrew for "brightness" (KJV) suggests "the bright shining of the rising sun" (Fausset), and so "the dawn" (Rawlinson, NIV). Also "a lamp that burneth (KJV) should be "a blazing torch" (Fausset, NIV).

B. A New Name: v. 2

The nations will see your
　righteousness,
　and all kings your glory;
you will be called by a new name
　that the mouth of the LORD will
　bestow.

In both the Hebrew and the Greek the same word is used for "Gentiles" (KJV) and "nations" (RSV, NASB, NIV). This is because all the nations except Israel were referred to as "the Gentiles." We find the same thing in the New Testament, where in the King James Version the word *ethnos* (*ethnoi,* plural) is translated "Gentiles" ninety-three times and "nation" sixty-four times.

The parallel of "righteousness" and "glory" in the first two lines of this verse is significant. God's righteousness is our greatest glory.

The "new name" will reflect the new, restored condition of God's people. It must always be remembered that in the thinking of that time "name" indicated "nature." God would give His people a new name, as further indicated in verse 4.

C. A Crown of Splendor: v. 3

You will be a crown of splendor in
　the LORD's hand,
a royal diadem in the hand of
　your God.

This is a very striking statement. Israel will be "a crown of splendor" and "a royal diadem." There has been some discussion of why these are spoken of as in the Lord's "hand." Rawlinson helpfully comments:

> God will exhibit Israel to an admiring world, as a man might exhibit a "crown" or "diadem" which he held in his hand. They will look on with admiration and reverence—"for they shall perceive that it is his work" (Ps. lxiv.9) (*PC,* Isaiah, 2:430).

D. A Change of Name: v. 4

No longer will they call you
　Deserted,
　or name your land Desolate.
But you will be called Hephzibah,
　and your land Beulah;
for the LORD will take delight in
　you,
　and your land will be married.

The Hebrew for "Deserted" is *Azubah.* This was the name of the mother of Jehoshaphat, king of Judah (I Kings 22:42). As we have noted before, all Hebrew names have significant meanings. The Hebrew word for "Desolate" is *Shemamah.* In the Babylonian captivity, soon to take place, Judah would be "Forsaken" (KJV, NASB), because the nation had forsaken God and turned to idols. The land would be left "Desolate."

But then there would be a restoration, and the revived nation would be called "Hephzibah," the Hebrew for "My delight is in her," and the land would be called "Beulah," Hebrew for "Married." Incidentally, Hephzibah was the name of Hezekiah's wife, Manasseh's mother (II Kings 21:1). In John Peter Lange's *Commentary on the Holy Scriptures* we read:

> It is reasonable to suppose that the passage before us was written with allusion to the marriage of Hezekiah with Hephzibah, and that the imagery and form of expression here employed were suggested by that event. That marriage was evidently hailed with joy as full of promise (Isaiah, p. 665).

E. Time of Rejoicing: v. 5

As a young man marries a
    maiden,
  so will your sons marry you;
as a bridegroom rejoices over his
    bride,
  so will your God rejoice over
    you.

The idea of sons marrying their mother seems incongruous. Fausset makes this helpful suggestion: "But 'thy sons' mean simply, *thy citizens;* and 'shall marry thee' means, *shall dwell in thee*, Jerusalem" (*Commentary,* 3:754).

A wedding is traditionally a very happy event, so the restoration of Judah to the Promised Land after the time of captivity would be an event of great rejoicing.

III. A NEW JERUSALEM: Isaiah 65:17-25

A. New Heavens and Earth: v. 17

Behold, I will create
  new heavens and a new earth.
The former things will not be
    remembered,
  nor will they come to mind.

The language of this verse reminds us of Revelation 21:1, where we read, "Then I saw a new heaven and a new earth." This comes after the "thousand years" of Revelation 20 (vv. 2-7). As Fausset rightly observes on verse 17 here:

> This prophecy uses language which, whilst fulfilled on the millennial earth in a degree, shall receive its full accomplishment only in the regenerated earth, which shall succeed the post-millennial conflagration (*Commentary,* 3:762).

The last two lines of this verse are comforting. Rawlinson comments:

> The glory of the new heavens and earth would be such that the former ones would not only not be regretted, but would not even be had in remembrance. No one would so much as think of them (*PC,* Isaiah, 2:472).

B. Jerusalem a Delight: v. 18

But be glad and rejoice forever
  in what I will create,
for I will create Jerusalem to be a
    delight
  and its people a joy.

In Revelation 21:2 we read, "I saw the Holy City, the new Jerusalem, coming down out of heaven from God, prepared as a bride beautifully dressed for her husband." We find here in Isaiah God's promise that Jerusalem will be "a delight, and its people a joy." Rawlinson comments: "The 'new Jerusalem' was to be from the first all joy and rejoicing—a scene of perpetual gladness. Her people also were to be 'a joy' or 'a delight,' since God would delight in them" (*PC,* Isaiah, 2:475).

C. No More Weeping: v. 19

I will rejoice over Jerusalem
  and take delight in my people;
the sound of weeping and of
    crying
  will be heard in it no more.

We read in Lange's *Commentary:* "Where there is no more sin, there is no more trouble, and where there is no more trouble, there is no more pain" (Isaiah, p. 696). Sin is the ultimate cause of all our troubles.

D. Longevity of Life: v. 20

Never again will there be in it
an infant that lives but a few
   days,
or an old man who does not live
   out his years;
he who dies at a hundred
   will be thought a mere youth;
he who fails to reach a hundred
   will be considered accursed.

The literal Hebrew of this verse is a bit awkward to handle. "There shall be no more thence an infant of days" (KJV) hardly makes sense to the ordinary reader today. Both the New American Standard Bible and New International Version put it very clearly, and that is the responsibility of the modern translator.

As far as "sinner" (KJV) is concerned, the New American Standard Bible marginal note indicates that the Hebrew literally says "one who misses the mark"—that is, of becoming a hundred years old. But the expression may mean "sinner" (RSV)—"one who misses the mark."

This verse seems to speak of conditions in the millennial kingdom. At that time, under the direct reign of Christ, there will be longevity of life such as we find in the patriarchal period, described in the early chapters of Genesis. But still some will be considered "accursed." Fausset is probably right when he says:

This passage proves that the millennial age to come on earth, though much superior to the present, will not be a perfect state. Sin and death shall have place in it . . . , but much less frequently than now (*Commentary,* 3:763).

That is, the description here fits chapter 20 of Revelation, rather than chapters 21 and 22.

E. Fruitful Labor: vv. 21-23

What we have just said about verse 20 applies even more obviously to these three verses. Building houses and planting vineyards do not belong to our eternal life in heaven, but to life on earth. As noted above, the conditions described are much better than we know now, but fall short of the perfection we shall know in eternity.

Verse 23 speaks of bearing children. But Jesus told the Pharisees: "At the resurrection people will neither marry nor be given in marriage; they will be like the angels in heaven" (Matt. 22:30). So we are dealing here with the millennial kingdom, not eternity.

F. A Listening God: v. 24

Before they call I will answer;
while they are still speaking I will
   hear.

This is a wonderful twofold promise that I have seen fulfilled many times. Married in 1932, my wife and I knew what it was to live almost entirely without money. One day I was faced unexpectedly with the necessity of paying five dollars that day. I had no idea at all where I could get that

---

DISCUSSION QUESTIONS

1. Is there a future for the nation of Israel?
2. What does II Peter 3:8-9 tell us about God's delaying His judgment on the earth?
3. When was Israel deserted and her land left desolate?
4. What part did the Babylonian captivity play in Israel's history?
5. How does God express His love for Israel?
6. When will the new heavens and earth come?

amount. But in the mail there came a five dollar bill—from whom, I never knew. Days before I prayed desperately, God had already spoken to some friend to mail me the money I would need. He had already answered before I called, and while I was speaking the answer came.

G. Universal Peace: v. 25

The wolf and the lamb will feed
    together,
    and the lion will eat straw like
      the ox,
    but dust will be the serpent's
      food.
They will neither harm nor
    destroy
    in all my holy mountain.

When Adam sinned, he brought a curse not only on himself but on all creation (Gen. 3:17-18). In Romans 8:20-21 we read:

> For the creation was subjected to frustration, not by its own choice, but by the will of the one who subjected it, in hope that the creation itself will be liberated from its bondage to decay and brought into the glorious freedom of the children of God.

Under inspiration, Isaiah foretold the time when this would take place, when animals would live as God intended them to live. Instead of killing each other—as happens every day now—wild and domestic animals will at that time live together in perfect peace.

CONTEMPORARY APPLICATION

What does this lesson say to us? It tells us that for those who love the Lord a better time is coming. Every day we hear on radio and television news of hatred and strife, murder and violence. Is there no hope for the future?

Yes, for the child of God there is. God still sits on the throne. In His own appointed time He will bring an end to all war and strife. As His children we have His firm promise that some day all will be different. We can wait!

GOOD NEWS FOR THE AFFLICTED

DEVOTIONAL READING	Isaiah 61:8-9
ADULTS AND YOUTH	**Adult Topic:** *Good News for the Afflicted* **Youth Topic:** *When Life Gets Tough* **Background Scripture:** Isa. 61 **Scripture Lesson:** Isa. 61:1-7 **Memory Verse:** *The Lord has anointed me to bring good tidings to the afflicted.* Isa. 61:1
CHILDREN	**Topic:** *The Announcement of Jesus' Birth* **Background Scripture:** Isa. 61:1-11 **Scripture Lesson:** Isa. 61:1-7 **Memory Verse:** *I bring you good news of a great joy which will come to all the people.* Luke 2:10
DAILY BIBLE READINGS	**Dec. 5 M.:** A More Splendid Temple. Hag. 2:1-9 **Dec. 6 T.:** "Your Light Has Come." Isa. 60:1-7 **Dec. 7 W.:** "The City of the Lord." Isa. 60:8-14 **Dec. 8 T.:** A Land At Peace. Isa. 6:15-22 **Dec. 9 F.:** A People the Lord Blessed. Isa. 61:8-11 **Dec. 10 S.:** Impatient for the New Jerusalem. Isa. 62:1-12 **Dec. 11 S.:** "Good News to the Humble." Isa. 61:1-7
LESSON AIM	To help us see God's compassionate love for suffering humanity.
LESSON SETTING	**Time:** about 700 B.C. **Place:** Jerusalem

LESSON OUTLINE	**Good News for the Afflicted**
	
	I. **God's Care for the Afflicted:** Isaiah 61:1-3
	  A. Good News for the Poor: v. 1a
	  B. Freedom for Captives: v. 1b
	  C. The Year of the Lord's Favor: v. 2a
	  D. Comfort for Mourners: vv. 2b-3a
	  E. The Planting of the Lord: v. 3b
	
	II. **Restoration of the Land:** Isaiah 61:4-6
	  A. Rebuilding the Ruins: v. 4
	  B. Help of Foreigners: v. 5
	  C. Priests of the Lord: v. 6
	
	III. **A Double Inheritance:** Isaiah 61:7
	
	IV. **An Everlasting Covenant:** Isaiah 61:8-9
	  A. Divine Justice: v. 8
	  B. A Blessed people: v. 9

SUGGESTED
INTRODUCTION
FOR ADULTS

In Luke 4:18-19 we find quoted the substance of the
first two verses of our lesson today. Jesus was visiting
Nazareth, where He had been brought up, and on the
Sabbath (our Saturday) He went into the synagogue, "as
was his custom" (v. 16). Every Sabbath morning in the
synagogue two Scripture lessons were read—the first
from the Law and the second from the Prophets.

When the time came for the second Scripture, Jesus
"stood up to read" (v. 16). The synagogue attendant handed
Him the scroll of the prophet Isaiah (v. 17). He unrolled it
to the place where our lesson begins and read the equivalent
of the first two verses. (There were no verse divisions
then.)

After Jesus had read the Scripture, He "rolled up the
scroll, gave it back to the attendant and sat down" (v. 20).
The Jewish rabbis always stood to read the Scriptures
and then sat down to teach. Jesus began by saying to
them: "Today this scripture is fulfilled in your hearing"
(v. 21). By that declaration He clearly indicated that this
was a messianic passage, that the "me" (Isa. 61:1) referred
to Him as the promised Messiah. This gives us the setting
for our lesson today.

SUGGESTED
INTRODUCTION
FOR YOUTH

Our topic today is "When Life Gets Tough." Our godless,
permissive society has made it harder than ever for young
people to live as God wants them to live.

In such tough times we all need the Lord's help. Jesus,
in this beautiful passage, tells us that He will help us. As
we follow Him we find that He is always with us to
comfort, guide, and strengthen us, and to meet our every
need. So we need to claim His promises given here.

CONCEPTS FOR
CHILDREN

1. Isaiah predicted the coming of Jesus, the Messiah.
2. That would be a very happy event.
3. We should care about others, as Jesus does.
4. As Christians, we follow Christ's example.

THE LESSON COMMENTARY

I. GOD'S CARE FOR THE AFFLICTED: Isaiah 61:1-3

A. Good News for the Poor: v. 1a

The Spirit of the Sovereign LORD
    is on me,
because the LORD has anointed
    me to preach
good news to the poor.

As we noted in the Introduction for
Adults, Jesus applied this passage to
Himself as the promised Messiah who
had now come. He declared that "the

Spirit" was on Him. This had twice
already been predicted in Isaiah. In
11:2 we read:

The Spirit of the LORD will rest
    on him—
    the Spirit of wisdom and of
        understanding,
    the Spirit of counsel and of
        power,
    the Spirit of knowledge and of
        the fear of the LORD—

Then in 42:1 we find:

Here is my servant, whom I
    uphold,
my chosen one in whom I
    delight;
I will put my Spirit on him
and he will bring justice to the
    nations.

The fulfillment of these predictions is found in the Gospels. In all three of the Synoptics we read that at Jesus' baptism the Holy Spirit came upon Him like a dove (Matt. 3:16; Mark 1:10; Luke 4:22).

What is meant by "Lord GOD" (KJV, RSV, NASB), and why is it changed to "Sovereign LORD" (NIV)? The answer is that the Hebrew has *Adonai Yahweh.* In the Old Testament *Adonai* is usually represented in English by "Lord," *Yahweh* by "LORD." But "Lord LORD" is awkward English. So we find here "Sovereign LORD" (NIV). Elsewhere in the King James and other versions "LORD God" is *Yahweh Elohim* in the Hebrew. God the Father is meant.

The word "anointed" is especially appropriate here. Our term *Messiah* comes from the Hebrew *mashiah,* which means the "anointed one." The Greek translation is *christos,* from which we get "Christ." So it is appropriate for the Messiah to say here that "the LORD has anointed me." In the Bible (both Old Testament and New Testament) we read of people being anointed with oil (always olive oil). Oil is a type of the Holy Spirit.

The Messiah declares (prophetically here) that the Lord has anointed Him "to preach good news to the poor." The King James Version has "the meek." The Revised Standard Version and New American Standard Bible have "the afflicted," hence our lesson title: "Good News for the Afflicted." The New International Version rendering, "the poor," is based on the Septuagint, as quoted in Luke 4:18. Since the New Testament interprets it that way, this seems best for us. A. R. Fausset says that "the poor" means "those afflicted with calamity, poor in circumstances and in spirit (Matt. xi.5)" (Robert

Jamieson, A. R. Fausset, and David Brown, *A Commentary . . . on the Old and New Testaments,* 3:751-52).

B. Freedom for Captives: v. 1b

He has sent me to bind up the
    brokenhearted,
to proclaim freedom for the
    captives
and release for the prisoners.

George Rawlinson comments: "'Binding up' is an ordinary expression in Isaiah's writings for 'healing' (see ch. i.6; iii.7; xxx.26)" (*The Pulpit Commentary,* Isaiah, 2:415). On "proclaim freedom for captives" he says: "This was one of the special offices of 'the Servant' (see ch. xlii.7). The 'captivity' intended is doubtless that of sin" (2:415).

The "brokenhearted" need healing. They number in the millions today and merit our concern.

C. The Year of the Lord's Favor: v. 2a

to proclaim the year of the LORD's
    favor
and the day of vengeance of our
    God,

Fausset makes this comment:

The "acceptable time of grace" is a "year"; the time of "vengeance" but a "day." . . . Jesus (Luke iv.20, 21) "closed the book" before this clause; for the interval from His first to His second coming is "the acceptable year": "the day of vengeance" will not be till He comes again (2 Thess. i.7-9) (*Commentary,* 3:752).

These two lines of poetry highlight a significant combination of truths: the time of salvation and the time of judgment. Jesus came not only to preach good news to the poor, to heal the brokenhearted, to proclaim freedom for the captives of sin, and to proclaim the year of the Lord's favor, but also to proclaim the day of divine judgment on sinners. We would all like to proclaim the former glorious truths, but we are obligated to proclaim the other side also: sin brings judgment.

D. Comfort for Mourners: vv. 2b-3a

to comfort all who mourn,
    and provide for those who
        grieve in Zion—
to bestow on them a crown of
        beauty
    instead of ashes,
the oil of gladness
    instead of mourning,
and a garment of praise
    instead of a spirit of despair.

On the first two lines above Matthew Henry has this to say:

Christ not only provides comfort for them, and proclaims it, but he applies it to them. There is enough in him to *comfort all who mourn*, whatever their sore or sorrow is; but this comfort is sure to those who *mourn in Zion*, who sorrow *after a godly sort*, according to God, for his residence is in Zion,—who *mourn because of Zion's* calamities and desolations, and mingle their tears by a holy sympathy with those of all God's suffering people (*Commentary on the Whole Bible*, 4:358).

This thought is well brought out by the translation "grieve in Zion" (NIV). Sinners mourn, but saints "grieve" over the sins of others and pray for their salvation.

The next six lines of poetry (v. 3a) are particularly beautiful. Rather than "beauty" (KJV) or "a crown of beauty" (NIV), the Revised Standard Version and New American Standard Bible have "a garland." Picking this term up from the Revised Version, Alexander Maclaren writes of these six lines of poetry:

There we have two contrasted pictures suggested: one of a mourner with grey ashes strewed up his dishevelled locks, and his spirit clothed in gloom like a black robe;

and to him there comes One who, with gentle hand, smoothes the ashes out of his hair, trains a garland round his brow, anoints his head with oil, and, stripping off the trappings of woe, casts about him a bright robe fit for a guest at a festival. That is the miracle that Jesus Christ can do for every one, and is ready to do for us, if we will let Him (*Expositions of Holy Scripture*, Isaiah, 2:192).

In these six poetic lines that we are looking at we find "beauty," "gladness," and "praise." Here is indeed a joyous note. This leads Maclaren to declare: "Jesus Christ is the Joy-bringer to men because He is the Redeemer of men." He goes on to say that

it is Christ as the Emancipator, Christ as the Deliverer, Christ as He who brings us out of the prison of bondage of the tyranny of sin, who is the great Joy-giver. For there is no real, deep, fundamental and impregnable gladness possible to a man until his relations to God have been rectified, and until, with these rectified relations, with the consciousness of forgiveness and the divine love nestling warm at his heart, he has turned himself away from his dread and his sin, and has recognized in his Father God "the gladness of his joy" (*Expositions*, Isaiah, 2:193).

E. The Planting of the Lord: v. 3b

They will be called oaks of
    righteousness,
a planting of the LORD
    for the display of his splendor.

Instead of "trees of righteousness" (KJV), modern versions correctly have "oaks of righteousness" (RSV, NASB, NIV). The oak is one of the sturdiest of trees. It exhibits towering beauty and strength. God's people are to have lives like these oaks, "for the display of his splendor." Do we glorify God by our lives, or disgrace Him?

In verses 1-3 Matthew Henry finds five things that Christ, the Messiah, was to be: (1) a preacher; (2) a healer;

(3) a deliverer; (4) a comforter; (5) a planter. Christ wants to be all of those to us as individuals. Our responsibility is to let Him be all of those to each of us. If we fail to do so we not only suffer ourselves because of that, but we also deprive those around us of the blessings He wants to bring to them through us. Selfishness hurts both us and those we come into contact with.

II. RESTORATION
OF THE LAND: Isaiah 61:4-6

A. Rebuilding the Ruins: v. 4

They will rebuild the ancient
  ruins
  and restore the places long
  devastated;
they will renew the ruined cities
  that have been devastated for
  generations.

There seems to be a reference here first of all to the rebuilding of the ruined cities of Judah after the return from Babylonian captivity about 536 B.C. It was a long process, stretching over a century or so until Nehemiah went back to restore the walls of Jerusalem in 445 B.C.

But there is also a spiritual application to the rebuilding of ruined lives through the salvation that Christ provides. Too many people think of salvation only in terms of the forgiveness of sins or escape from eternal punishment. But it is much more than that: it is the rebuilding of our characters in the image of God. We are not only freed from guilt; we are to live a new life in Christ Jesus.

B. Help of Foreigners: v. 5

Aliens will shepherd your flocks;
  foreigners will work your fields
  and vineyards.

Rawlinson comments:

The Gentiles who join themselves with the Jews, and form with them one community, are constantly represented in the writings of Isaiah as occupying a subordinate position. In the New Testament Jew and Gentile are put upon a par (*PC*, Isaiah, 2:415).

It seems that perhaps we need the next verse to explain this one. So we turn to it now.

C. Priests of the Lord: v. 6

And you will be called priests of
  the LORD,
  You will be named ministers of
  our God.
You will feed on the wealth of
  nations,
  and in their riches you will
  boast.

Fausset comments here:

Ye shall have no need to attend to your flocks and lands: *strangers* will do that for you: *your* exclusive business will be the service of Jehovah as His "priests" (*Commentary*, 3:752).

While it may seem a bit difficult to interpret this in relation to Israel, the application to us is clear. Matthew Henry puts it this way:

Those whom God sets at liberty he sets to work; he *delivers them out of the hands of their enemies* that they may *serve him*, Luke i. 74, 75; Ps. cxvi.16. But his service is perfect freedom, nay, it is the greatest honour. When God brought Israel out of Egypt he took them to be to him a *kingdom of priests*, Exod. xix.16. And the gospel church is a royal priesthood (1 Pet. ii.9). All believers are made to our God kings and priests; and they ought to conduct themselves as such in their devotions and in their whole conversation, with *holiness to the Lord* written upon their foreheads, that men may *call them the priests of the Lord* (*Commentary*, 4:360).

III. A DOUBLE
INHERITANCE: Isaiah 61:7

Instead of their shame
  my people will receive a double
  portion,

and instead of disgrace
  they will rejoice in their
    inheritance;
and so they will inherit a double
    portion in their land
and everlasting joy will be theirs.

On this idea of a double inheritance
Rawlinson writes:

Instead of the shame and confusion
of face which were the portion of
Israel during the Captivity ... they
should after their restoration to
Palestine "have double" their former
glory and double their former territory. An increase of territory had
been already prophesied (ch.xlix.
18-21)—an increase which, however,
was not so much an extension of the
bounds of Palestine as a spread of
the Church over the whole earth
(comp. Zech. ix.12)(PC, Isaiah, 2:416).

There are many prophecies in the
Old Testament whose complete fulfill-
ment awaited the coming of Christ.
Some still await His second coming.

IV. AN EVERLASTING
    COVENANT: Isaiah 61:8-9

A. Divine Justice: v. 8

For I, the LORD, love justice;
  I hate robbery and iniquity.
In my faithfulness I will reward
    them
  and make an everlasting
    covenant with them.

Justice is one of the significant
attributes of Deity and it should always
mark God's people. God loves justice,
and so should we.
Rawlinson writes on this verse:

Jehovah will restore the Israelites to
their land because he "loves judgment" (equivalent to "justice") and
hates injustice. The Babylonian conquest, though a judgment sent by
him, is, so far as the Babylonians are
concerned, a wrong and a "robbery"
(PC, Isaiah, 2:416).

On "I hate robbery for burnt
offering" (KJV), Rawlinson comments:

"rather, *I hate robbery with wickedness.* ... The transplantation of nations
was a gross abuse of the rights of
conquest" (PC, 2:416). Of course, the
Babylonian conquest of Judah had not
yet taken place, but it did so not long
after this. And Isaiah looks beyond the
Babylonian captivity to the restoration
of the Jews to their own land.
  On "I will direct their work in truth"
(KJV), Rawlinson says: "rather, *I will
give them their recompense faithfully.*"
(Compare NASB and NIV.) Rawlinson
goes on to say:

As they have been wronged, they
shall be righted; they shall be faithfully and exactly compensated for
what they have suffered. Nay, more—
over and above this, God will give
them the blessing of an "everlasting
covenant" (PC, Isaiah, 2:416).

B. A Blessed People: v. 9

Their descendants will be
    known among the nations
    and their offspring among the
      peoples.
All who see them will
    acknowledge
  that they are a people the
    LORD has blessed.

There has without doubt been a
striking fulfillment of this prophecy
in relation to the Jewish nation. The
Jews have been outstanding in the
fields of science and in other areas.

DISCUSSION QUESTIONS

1. In what way can Isaiah 61:1
apply to us?
2. How far can we enter into
Christ's ministry?
3. What part does the Spirit play
in our ministering for Christ?
4. How can we bind up the broken-
hearted?
5. What could "ashes" represent
in our lives?
6. What is suggested by "garment
of praise"?

But the main fulfillment is in the case of Jesus Christ, who became the Savior of the world, and in the church, the spiritual Israel. Truly we are a blessed people.

Fausset does a good job of summing up the thrust of this great chapter of Isaiah. He writes:

> The grand theme of this prophecy is the Messiahship of the Saviour. He was described in various other aspects previously: here He is set before us as the Anointed One of the Lord Jehovah. In His first sermon in the synagogue at Nazareth He commenced by appropriating to Himself this prophecy. As three classes of typical personages—prophets, priests, and kings—used to be anointed with oil, to consecrate them to their function, so He, the great Antitype was anointed with antitypical oil, the fulness of the Spirit, to His function, which combines in one the prophetical, the priestly, and the kingly offices. As His prophetical function was prominent during His earthly ministry in the flesh, His priestly function at His death, and especially now in His session at the Father's right hand as our great High Priest in the heavens, so at His coming again His kingly office shall be visibly and prominently manifested (*Commentary*, 3:753).

CONTEMPORARY APPLICATION

As God's children in this age we have the right—and responsibility—to claim these promises made to ancient Israel, giving them a spiritual, rather than material, application. We can also enrich our understanding of who Jesus is and what His functions are.

We especially can rejoice in the comfort and joy that Jesus brings to us. No situation is too hard for Him to handle. He can rebuild the most ruined life when it is wholly turned over to Him.

PREPARING FOR GOD'S COMING

DEVOTIONAL READING	Isaiah 46:8-13
ADULTS AND YOUTH	**Adult Topic:** *Preparing for God's Coming*
	Youth Topic: *Prepare the Way*
	Background Scripture: Isa. 40-41
	Scripture Lesson: Isa. 40:3-11
	Memory Verse: *Prepare the way of the Lord, make straight in the desert a highway for our God.* Isa. 40:3
CHILDREN	**Topic:** *Birth of Jesus*
	Background Scripture: Isa. 9:1-7; 11:1-10; Luke 2:1-7
	Scripture Lesson: Luke 2:1-7; Isa. 9:6-7
	Memory Verse: *For to us a child is born, to us a son is given.* Isa. 9:6
DAILY BIBLE READINGS	Dec. 12 M.: In Might. Isa. 46:8-13 Dec. 13 T.: In Deliverance. Isa. 41:21-29 Dec. 14 W.: In Sovereignty. Isa. 41:21-29 Dec. 15 T.: In Affection. Isa. 54:1-10 Dec. 16 F.: In Victory. Isa. 54:11-17 Dec. 17 S.: In Greatness. Isa. 40:27-31 Dec. 18 S.: In Comfort. Isa. 40:1-11
LESSON AIM	To help us see how we may prepare the way for the Lord.
LESSON SETTING	**Time:** probably about 700 B.C.
	Place: Jerusalem

LESSON OUTLINE

Preparing for God's Coming

  I. **Comfort for God's People:** Isaiah 40:1-2
    A. Comfort: v. 1
    B. Assurance of Forgiveness: v. 2

  II. **Preparing the Way:** Isaiah 40:3-5
    A. A Way in the Desert: v. 3
    B. A Level Path: v. 4
    C. The Glory of the Lord: v. 5

  III. **The Cry of a Voice:** Isaiah 40:6-8
    A. Hesitation: v. 6a
    B. The Frailty of Humanity: vv. 6b-7
    C. The Enduring Word: v. 8

  IV. **The Good Proclamation:** Isaiah 40:9-11
    A. A Loud Voice: v. 9
    B. The Powerful Lord: v. 10
    C. The Gentle Shepherd: v. 11

SUGGESTED
INTRODUCTION
FOR ADULTS

The fortieth chapter of Isaiah is one of the most eloquent chapters of the Bible. Listening to it read by a competent person (both literarily and spiritually) can be a very moving experience. I have been thrilled more than once when it was presented by a mature, godly woman, who had taught speech many years. But recently I heard it given even more effectively, if possible, by a brilliant, spiritual college girl. Her presentation held the audience spellbound.

All of us would do well to read Isaiah 40 every once in awhile, to revel in its beauty and be inspired by its message. In a day when there is so much bad news on radio and television, here is good news. We have a great God!

SUGGESTED
INTRODUCTION
FOR YOUTH

"Prepare the Way." Today's lesson says two things to us. First, we need to prepare the way for the Lord to come into our own hearts and lives. As we shall see, this involves sincere repentance and earnest believing on our part.

Second, we should help prepare the way for the Lord to come to others. This means that we must live godly lives ourselves, setting the right example. It also requires that we should witness for Christ and try to lead people into a personal experience of salvation.

We should also try to prepare the way for the Lord to come to our church in a fresh, moving way. We do this by prayer and obedience.

CONCEPTS FOR
CHILDREN

1. Isaiah prophesied the coming of Christ.
2. The New Testament records the fulfillment of that promise.
3. God's Son was born as a baby and was laid in a manger.
4. This was to show God's love for us.

THE LESSON COMMENTARY

I. COMFORT FOR GOD'S PEOPLE: Isaiah 40:1-2

A. Comfort: v. 1

Comfort, comfort my people,
says your God.

The background for this chapter is found in the preceding chapter, where we find a prediction of the coming Babylonian captivity. Through His prophet Isaiah the Lord sent this message to King Hezekiah:

Hear the word of the LORD Almighty: The time will surely come when everything in your palace, and all that your fathers have stored up until this day, will be carried off to Babylon. Nothing will be left, says the LORD. And some of your descendants, your own flesh and blood who will be born to you, will be taken away, and they will become eunuchs in the palace of the king of Babylon (39:5-7).

We find the fulfillment of this prophecy described in Daniel 1:1-5.

Because of the change of tone here from judgment—very prominent in chapters 1-39—to comfort, many scholars have insisted that chapters 40-66 of Isaiah were written during the latter part of the Babylonian captivity by someone other than Isaiah. But I like

Matthew Henry's handling of the matter. He writes:

> We have here the commission and instructions given, not to this prophet only, but, with him, to all the Lord's prophets, and to all Christ's ministers, to proclaim comfort to God's people. 1. This did not only warrant, but enjoin this prophet himself to encourage the good people who lived in his own time, who could not but have very melancholy apprehensions of things when they saw Judah and Jerusalem by their daring impieties ripening apace for ruin, and God in his providence hastening ruin upon them. Let them be sure that, notwithstanding all this, God had mercy in store for them. 2. It was especially directed to the prophets that should live in the time of the captivity, when Jerusalem was in ruins; they must encourage the captives to hope for enlargement in due time. 3. Gospel ministers, being employed by the blessed Spirit as comforters, and as helpers of the joy of Christians, are here put in mind of their business (*Commentary on the Whole Bible*, 4:211).

Concerning the change of tone that we find at the beginning of chapter 40, A. R. Fausset writes:

> The latter part was written in the old age of Isaiah, as appears from the greater mellowness of style and tone which pervades it. It is less fiery and more tender and gentle than the former part (Robert Jamieson, A. R. Fausset, David Brown, *Commentary . . . on the Old and New Testaments*, 3:684).

On "Comfort, comfort" Fausset says: "twice repeated, to give double assurance" (3:685).

Alexander Maclaren makes this beautiful comment on verse 1: "What a world of yearning love there is . . . in the two little words 'my' and 'your'!" (*Expositions of Holy Scripture*, Isaiah, 1:245). God had not forsaken Israel.

B. Assurance of Forgiveness: v. 2

Speak tenderly to Jerusalem,
  and proclaim to her
that her hard service has been
    completed,
  that her sin has been paid for,
that she has received from the
    LORD's hand
  double for all her sins.

The King James Version translates the first line: "Speak ye comfortably to Jerusalem." The Hebrew literally says, "Speak to the heart of Jerusalem." This apparently means, "Speak tenderly to Jerusalem" (RSV, NIV). Maclaren comments: "The prophet's charge is laid upon all who would speak of Christ to men. Speak to the heart, not only to the head or to the conscience" (*Expositions*, Isaiah, 1:246).

The next line says, "and proclaim to her." John Peter Lange notes that the Hebrew phrase for "speak tenderly" means "to speak out over the heart, to charm the heart, to cover with words, to sooth, to quiet," whereas the Hebrew verb for "proclaim" ("call out," NASB) "involves rather the notion of loud, strong, and clear speaking" (*Commentary on the Holy Scriptures*, Isaiah, p. 421).

The next four lines have the perfect tense three times. This has caused some to insist that these words must have been written near the end of the Babylonian captivity. But George Rawlinson helpfully declares, "These perfects can only be viewed as 'perfects of prophetic certainty'" (*The Pulpit Commentary*, Isaiah, 2:66).

The first statement is that "her hard service has been completed." With regard to "warfare" (KJV, RSV, NASB), Fausset says that the Hebrew word *tzaba* means "her *term of service* and hardship—a military metaphor" (*Commentary*, 3:685).

The second statement is that "her sin has been paid for." This causes Maclaren to comment:

Of course, the captivity is in the foreground of the prophet's vision; but the wider sense of the prophecy embraces the worse captivity of sin under which we all groan, and the divine voice bids His prophets proclaim that Jehovah comes, to set us all free, to end the weary bondage, and to exact no more punishment for sins (*Expositions*, Isaiah, 1:246).

The third statement is:

that she has received from the
LORD's hand
double for all her sins

The word "double" has caused considerable comment. Interestingly, Fausset writes: "The 'double for her sins' must refer to the two-fold captivity—the Assyrian or Babylonian and the Roman" (*Commentary*, 3:685). The Assyrian captivity, of course, was that of northern Israel, while the Babylonian was that of southern Judah.

It seems more likely that there is an intended reference to Exodus 22:9, where we are told that in the case of illegal possession of someone else's property, "The one whom the judges declare guilty must pay back double to his neighbor." Rawlinson comments on our verse in Isaiah: "It is not here intended to assert that the law of Divine judgment is to exact double; but only to assure Israel that having been simply punished, she need fear no further vengeance" (*PC*, Isaiah, 2:66). That, of course, is the main point of these first two verses of the chapter. This is the "comfort" for God's people.

II. PREPARING THE WAY:
   Isaiah 40:3-5

A. A Way in the Desert: v. 3

A voice of one calling:
"In the desert prepare
the way for the LORD;
Make straight in the wilderness
a highway for our God."

Since the Hebrew Old Testament has no quotation marks, we cannot be positive as to whether "in the desert"

(or "wilderness") modifies "crieth" (KJV) or "prepare" (RSV, NASB, NIV). But the main principle of Hebrew poetry is parallelism, and this very strongly favors the latter interpretation—"in the desert" and "in the wilderness" being parallel to each other. Fausset notes that the "Hebrew accents" (in the Masoretic Text) favor the parallelism we have just noted (*Commentary*, 3:685).

Why, then, do we find in Matthew 3:3, "A voice of one calling in the desert"? The answer is that the Septuagint puts it this way, and Matthew follows the Septuagint here when he identifies the voice as that of John the Baptist (Matt. 3:1-3).

B. A Level Path: v. 4

"Every valley shall be raised up,
every mountain and hill made
low;
the rough ground shall become
level,
the rugged places a plain."

John the Baptist preached in a literal wilderness, or desert, but it was in a moral wilderness that the way of the Lord was to be prepared (v. 3). Now in verse 4 we find what kind of preparation was to be made. It is spelled out in four specifics: (1) filling in the valleys; (2) cutting down the hills; (3) leveling the rough ground; (4) smoothing out the bumps.

Fausset points out the background for these instructions: "Eastern monarchs send heralds before them in a journey, to clear away obstacles, make causeways over valleys, and level hills" (*Commentary*, 3:685). He goes on to say:

So John's duty was to bring back the people to obedience to the law, and remove all self-confidence, pride in national privileges, hypocrisy, and irreligion, so that they should be ready for His coming (Mal. iv.6; Luke 1:17) (*Commentary*, 3:685).

Rawlinson puts it this way:

The prophets are to see that the poor and lowly are raised up; the proud and self-righteous depressed; the crooked and dishonest induced to change their ways for those of simplicity and integrity; the rude, rough, and harsh rendered courteous and mild (*PC*, Isaiah, 2:66).

C. The Glory of the Lord: v. 5

"And the glory of the LORD will
　be revealed,
and all mankind together will see
　it.
For the mouth of the LORD has
　spoken."

In Luke 3:6 the middle line here is quoted, but instead of "it" we find "God's salvation." That is because Luke was using the Septuagint, which has that in place of "it." Of course, it was God's salvation that John the Baptist was preaching.

Matthew (3:3) and Mark (1:3) quote only verse 3 here. But Luke (3:4-6) quotes verses 3-5. All three synoptic Gospels apply this passage to the ministry of John the Baptist, whose main emphasis was on repentance, the main preparation for the coming of Christ to our hearts.

III. THE CRY OF A VOICE: Isaiah 40:6-8

A. Hesitation: v. 6a

A voice says, "Cry out."
And I said, "What shall I cry?"

There is considerable difference of opinion among commentators as to the identification of "a voice." Fausset simply says: "The same divine herald as in v. 3" (*Commentary*, 3:686). In contrast to this, Rawlinson writes, "It is a second voice, distinct from that of ver. 3, that now reaches the prophet's ear—a voice responded to by another" (*PC*, Isaiah, 2:66). He goes on to say, "The speakers seem to be angels, who contrast the perishable nature of man with the enduringness and unchangingness of God" (2:66-67).

When equally good and godly scholars disagree on their interpretation of precise points of minor importance, it should teach us a lesson. That is that we should not be dogmatic in insisting that our particular interpretation is the one and only correct one.

Should this verse read "he said" (KJV), "He answered" (NASB), or "I said" (RSV, NIV)? The New American Standard Bible offers the latter in the margin. We are not sure which it is.

B. The Frailty of Humanity: vv. 6b-7

"All men are like grass,
　and all their glory is like the
　　flowers of the field.
The grass withers and the flowers
　fall,
　because the breath of the LORD
　　blows on them.
　Surely the people are grass."

This is a familiar and obvious simile. It occurs several times in the Old Testament (Job 5:25; Ps. 90:5; 92:7). The transitory nature of human existence is a fact of which all thoughtful people are aware. Since we only have, at best, a short time on earth, and since life is so frail and fragile, we should all be concerned to live each day and hour at our best in God's will.

We have noted above several other passages in the Old Testament that speak of mankind as being like grass that withers. But we also find Ephraim compared to a "fading flower" (Isa. 28:1). Job 14:2 says of "man born of woman," "He springs up like a flower and withers away." Psalm 103:15 combines the two, as here:

As for man, his days are like
　grass,
　he flourishes like a flower of the
　　field;
　the wind blows over it and it is
　　gone.

C. The Enduring Word: v. 8

"The grass withers and the
   flowers fall,
but the word of our God stands
   forever."

What a contrast! Rawlinson asserts,
"Amid all human frailty, shifting-
ness, changefulness, there is one thing
that endures, and shall endure—God's
Word." He adds, "In the sureness of
God's promises is Israel's exceeding
comfort" (*PC*, Isaiah, 2:67).

Verse 8 repeats (in the first line)
what has already been said in verses 6
and 7. Maclaren makes this comment:

The repetition of the theme of man's
frailty is not unnatural, and gives
emphasis to the contrast of the
unchangeable stability of God's word.
An hour of the deadly hot wind will
scorch the pastures, and all the petals
of the flowers . . . will fall. So everything lovely, bright, and vigorous in
humanity wilts and dies. One thing
alone remains fresh from age to
age—the uttered will of Jehovah
(*Expositions*, Isaiah, 1:248-49).

IV. THE GOOD PROCLAMATION: Isaiah 40:9-11

A. A Loud Voice: v. 9

You who bring good tidings to
   Zion,
go up on a high mountain.
You who bring good tidings to
   Jerusalem,
lift up your voice with a shout,
lift it up, do not be afraid;
say to the towns of Judah,
"Here is your God!"

In lines one and three "Zion" and
"Jerusalem" are used interchangeably.
Strictly speaking, Zion was the mountain and Jerusalem the city. But more
and more the city, with its temple, came
to be referred to as "Zion."

The traditional translation (literal
Hebrew) makes Zion or Jerusalem the
bearer of good tidings (KJV, RSV, NASB).
But the oldest versions (Septuagint,

Vulgate, Arabic, etc.) have the good
tidings being brought to Zion (Jerusalem). This is the basis of the New
International Version rendering, which
is found in the margin of the King
James Version. Rawlinson favors this.
Since we cannot be sure, we may well
say that Jerusalem is both the recipient
and the hearer of the good tidings.

In any case, the herald of good news
is commanded to "go up on a high
mountain." In those days of no public
address systems, men often went to
the top of a hill in order to be seen and
heard by all the people (Judg. 9:7; Matt.
5:1).

The herald was also told to lift up
his voice with a shout, so that all could
hear the important message clearly.
He was not to be "afraid," regardless
of any opposition.

What was his message? "Here is
your God!" This proclamation was
primarily intended to bring comfort
to the towns of Judah, as the context
indicates, but it may also have carried
a note of admonition to act as God's
people.

B. The Powerful Lord: v. 10

See, the Sovereign LORD comes
   with power,
   and his arm rules for him.
See, his reward is with him,
   and his recompense accom-
   panies him.

DISCUSSION QUESTIONS

1. How do we become God's people?
2. Why is salvation the highest
comfort?
3. How was our sin paid for?
4. How can we prepare for God's
coming to our churches in a more
effective way?
5. How do we fill in valleys, cut
down hills, and smooth out rough
places?
6. What do valleys, hills, and rough
places represent in our lives?

The "arm" (line 2) is always a symbol of "power" (line 1) in the Old Testament. This powerful arm allows the Lord to rule effectively. As noted in our last lesson (on 61:1), "Sovereign LORD" represents accurately the Hebrew words *Adonai Yahweh.*

C. The Gentle Shepherd: v. 11

He tends his flock like a shepherd:
  He gathers the lambs in his
      arms
and carries them close to his
      heart;
  he gently leads those that have
      young.

The figure of the Lord as Shepherd is a favorite one in the Psalms (77:20; 78:52; 80:1) and occurs again in Isaiah (49:9-10). It combines beauty and sweetness, gentleness, and tenderness. One of Jesus' most comforting and meaningful declarations was, "I am the good shepherd" (John 10:11, 14).

We all can quote "God is love" (I John 4:8, 16). But Isaiah 40:11 spells out what this means to Christ's sheep, as He tenderly cares for them and supplies all their emotional as well as physical needs.

CONTEMPORARY APPLICATION

How do we prepare for God's coming? This question has several applications. The first is to His coming to our hearts as our Savior and Lord. The main preparation for this is repentance and humility on our part.

A second application is God's coming to others, through us. This requires our loving concern for others and a burden for their salvation.

A third application is to our preparation for the coming again of our Lord. This demands faithfulness in our personal devotion to Him and in service to others (Matt. 25).

A REIGN OF RIGHTEOUSNESS

DEVOTIONAL READING	Isaiah 12:1-6

Adult Topic: *A Reign of Righteousness*

Youth Topic: *A New Day Coming*

ADULTS AND YOUTH

Background Scripture: Isa. 9:1-7; 11:1-10

Scripture Lesson: Isa. 9:2-7; 11:1-3a

Memory Verse: *His name will be called "Wonderful Counselor, Mighty God, Everlasting Father, Prince of Peace."* Isa. 9:6

Topic: *The Wise Men Find Jesus*

Background Scripture: Matt. 2; Isa. 60:1-3

CHILDREN

Scripture Lesson: Matt. 2:1-2, 10-11

Memory Verse: *Where is he who has been born king of the Jews? For we have seen his star in the East, and have come to worship him.* Matt. 2:2

DAILY BIBLE READINGS

Dec. 19 M.: A Reign of Justice. Luke 1:46-55
Dec. 20 T.: A Reign of Deliverance. Luke 1:67-79
Dec. 21 W.: A Reign of Joy. Luke 2:1-7
Dec. 22 T.: A Reign of Righteousness. Isa. 32:1-8
Dec. 23 F.: A Reign of Hope. Isa. 12:1-6
Dec. 24 S.: A Reign of Light. Isa. 9:2-7
Dec. 25 S.: A Reign of Peace. Isa. 11:1-9

LESSON AIM

To show the nature of Christ's kingdom.

LESSON SETTING

Time: Eighth century B.C.

Place: Jerusalem

LESSON OUTLINE

A Reign of Righteousness

I. **A Hope for the Future:** Isaiah 9:2-5
    A. A Dawning Light: v. 2
    B. Increase of Joy: v. 3
    C. Deliverance from Oppression: v. 4
    D. Peace Instead of Strife: v. 5

II. **The Wonderful Christ:** Isaiah 9:6-7
    A. His Fourfold Name: v. 6
    B. His Righteous Reign: v. 7

III. **The Promised Messiah:** Isaiah 11:1-3a
    A. A Branch from Jesse: v. 1
    B. Endued with the Spirit: v. 2
    C. Delighting in the Fear of the Lord: 3a

121

SUGGESTED
INTRODUCTION
FOR ADULTS

Isaiah 9:6 is rightly considered to be one of the most beautiful verses in the entire Bible. Every Christmas time it comes alive for us in some rendition of Handel's great oratorio, "The Messiah." But it is a verse that should bless us every time we read it—even on a hot summer day! Meditating on the meaning of the four names for Christ can be a rewarding experience again and again.

I never cease to wonder at the fact that the prophet Isaiah could have such a receptive heart and perceptive mind that the Holy Spirit could reveal these marvelous truths to him, for divine revelation of the sacred Scriptures was not a matter of audible dictation. Rather, the Holy Spirit moved mightily on the hearts and minds of the writers, so that they thought the thoughts of God after Him. What majestic thoughts Isaiah had as he wrote these words for us to enjoy!

SUGGESTED
INTRODUCTION
FOR YOUTH

Our topic sparkles with hope: "A New Day Coming." Certainly we need a new day. Modern society has gone farther and farther away from God, flouting His laws and sneering at righteousness.

But some day Christ will come back to set up His kingdom of righteousness and peace—of peace because of righteousness. Then there will be no more flagrant miscarriage of justice in court or tolerance of wild evils such as we see today. If we have let Christ become Lord of all in our hearts and lives, that kingdom has already come for us inwardly. We can enjoy it now in our hearts.

CONCEPTS FOR
CHILDREN

1. The wise men brought gifts to Jesus.
2. The gift Jesus especially wants today is our heart.
3. Then we can add gifts of loving devotion and service.
4. Love is action as well as feeling.

THE LESSON COMMENTARY

I. A HOPE FOR THE FUTURE: Isaiah 9:2-5

A. A Dawning Light: v. 2

The people walking in darkness
   have seen a great light;
on those living in the land of the
   shadow of death
a light has dawned.

This verse is a good example of poetic parallelism, the main feature of Hebrew poetry. It is not a matter of sound but of sense—a parallelism of thought. So here we see that lines 1 and 3 say the same thing in somewhat different words, and so do lines 2 and

4. This is indicated helpfully in the New International Version by indenting lines 2 and 4.

Ross Price comments on verse 2 as follows:

Isaiah's expression *the people* now has reference to his nation whittled down to a mere remnant. But the darker the cloud, the brighter the rainbow. This *great light* first streamed forth in Galilee as Jesus began His ministry there. His person and message were like a great dawning upon forlorn and weary wanderers through *the land of the shadow of death* (II Cor. 4:6) (*Beacon Bible Commentary,* 4:61).

With his usual eloquence, Alexander Maclaren says this about verse 2:

First we have the picture of the nation groping in a darkness that might be felt, the emblem of ignorance, sin, and sorrow, and inhabiting a land over which, like a pall, death cast its shadow. On that dismal gloom shines all at once a "great light," the emblem of knowledge, purity, and joy. The daily mercy of the dawn has a gospel in it to a heart that believes in God; for it proclaims the divine will that all who sit in darkness shall be enlightened, and that every night but prepares the way for the freshness and stir of a new morning (*Expositions of Holy Scripture*, Isaiah, 1:49).

This verse is quoted in Matthew 4:16 as a prophecy of Isaiah that was fulfilled in the ministry of Jesus. He spent most of His time in Galilee (compare verse 1 here with Matt. 4:15).

B. Increase of Joy: v. 3

You have enlarged the nation
    and increased their joy;
they rejoice before you
    as people rejoice at the harvest,
as men rejoice
    when dividing the plunder.

The King James Version says, "Thou hast multiplied the nation, and not increased the joy." But a majority of the best commentators feel that "increased its joy" (RSV); or "increased their joy" is correct. The difference in the Hebrew for "not" and "its" is slight. The latter makes better sense.

The rejoicing of the people is compared to people rejoicing "at the harvest" or "when dividing the plunder" (after defeating the enemy in battle). Ross Price comments:

It is characteristic of the Judeo-Christian heritage that the "golden age" is never past, but always future. Isaiah's portrayal of that future declares it exuberant with rejoicing. *Joy in harvest* is proverbial for great delight. Men recently victorious in

battle are never happier than *when* they divide the spoil (*BBC*, 4:61-62).

C. Deliverance from Oppression: v. 4

For as in the day of Midian's defeat,
    you have shattered
the yoke that burdens them,
    the bar across their shoulders,
    the rod of their oppressor.

What was "the day of Midian's defeat"? George Rawlinson comments:

The "day of Midian" is probably the time of Israel's deliverance from the Midianite oppression by Gideon (Judg. vii.19-25). The special characteristic of the deliverance was, as Dr. Kay well observes, "that it was accomplished without military prowess by a small body of men selected out of Israel, selected expressly in order that Israel might not vaunt itself against the Lord, saying, My own hand hath saved me (Judg. vii.2)" (*The Pulpit Commentary*, Isaiah, 2:166).

Regarding the rest of this verse Rawlinson has this to say:

The coming of the Messiah sets the Israelites free, removes the yoke from off their neck, breaks the rod wherewith their shoulders were beaten, delivers them from bondage into the "glorious liberty of the children of God." Not, however, in an earthly sense, since the Messiah's kingdom was not of this world. The "yoke" is that of sin, the "oppressor" is that prince of darkness, who had well-night brought all mankind under his dominion when Christ came (*PC*, Isaiah, 2:166).

It is interesting to note that the Hebrew word for "oppressor" is the same as that which is used for the Egyptian taskmasters in Exodus 5:6. The Israelites of Isaiah's day would doubtless get the connection. Just as God had delivered them from Egyptian bondage, so He would deliver them from all foreign oppression.

We have to keep in mind constantly

a twofold application of the prophecies Isaiah is giving us here. Since they are messianic, as indicated by verses 6-7, we must refer them spiritually to Christ's first coming and perhaps more literally to His second coming.

D. Peace Instead of Strife: v. 5

Every warrior's boot used in
 battle
and every garment rolled in
 blood
will be destined for burning,
 will be fuel for the fire.

The first line here (NIV) is different from the King James Version. The New American Standard Bible has: "For every boot of the booted warrior in the *battle* tumult." Alexander Maclaren comments:

In any case, the whole accoutrements of the oppressor are heaped into a pile and set on fire; and as they blaze up, the freed slaves exult in their liberty. The bloody-drenched cloaks have been stripped from the corpses and tossed on the heap, and, saturated as they are, they burn. So complete is the victory that even the weapons of the conquered are destroyed. Our conquering King has been manifested, that He might annihilate the powers by which evil holds us bound. His victory is not by halves (*Expositions*, Isaiah, 1:51).

II. THE WONDERFUL CHRIST: Isaiah 9:6-7

A. His Fourfold Name: v. 6

For to us a child is born,
 to us a son is given,
 and the government will be on
  his shoulders.
And he will be called
 Wonderful Counselor, Mighty
  God,
 Everlasting Father, Prince of
  Peace.

"To us a child is born"—the Babe of Bethlehem. "To us a son is given"—the sinless Son of God given as the sacrifice

for our sins. "And the government will be on his shoulders"—the government of our lives, when we turn them over completely to Him to let Him be Lord of all in our lives; and also the government of the whole world. It is a glorious prospect, but what a small, tender beginning it had at Bethlehem. Who would have dreamed that the baby in the manger of a cave stable in a small village would become the Savior of the world, the King of Kings and Lord of Lords? No wonder Jesus' birth divides history into B.C. and A.D.!

The King James Version has five names for the coming Messiah. But most scholars are agreed that the Hebrew indicates four names: Wonderful Counselor, Mighty God, Everlasting Father, Prince of Peace. Each of these four names deserves careful attention.

First, Jesus is "Wonderful Counselor." He was wonderful in His supernatural birth; He was wonderful in His sinless life; He was wonderful in His sacrificial death; He was wonderful in His sudden resurrection; and He will be wonderful in His second coming. He is the wonderful Christ!

Specifically, Jesus is the Wonderful Counselor. Matthew Henry observes: "He is the *counsellor*, for he was intimately acquainted with the counsels of God from eternity" (*Commentary on the Whole Bible*, 4:60). Paul declares that "Christ Jesus . . . has become for us wisdom from God" (I Cor. 1:30). When we are in Christ we have the necessary wisdom for wise living in a foolish world.

In the second place, Jesus is "Mighty God." Part of the wonder of Christ is that He is both God and man—the only God-man who ever existed. In this He is utterly unique.

The term "Mighty God" occurs again in 10:21. There it seems to designate God the Father. This emphasizes Christ's oneness with the Father. Paul refers to Him as "our great God and Savior, Jesus Christ" (Titus 2:13). The deity of Jesus is the foundation doctrine of our Christian faith. Without a divine Savior we would still be lost in our sins.

As man, Jesus was "the son of David, the son of Abraham" (Matt. 1:1). But as God, He was truly "the Son of God" (Matt. 14:32). In Peter's confession near Caesarea Philippi, the Messiah ("Christ") is declared to be "the son of the living God" (Matt. 16:16). Again we say: Only Christ is both God and man. And He is the "Mighty God," able to take care of us and all our needs under all circumstances.

Third, Jesus is called "Everlasting Father." Though born a "child" at Bethlehem, in His deity He is Everlasting Father. Matthew Henry writes:

> He is *the everlasting Father,* or *the Father of eternity:* he is God, one with the Father, who is from everlasting to everlasting. His fatherly care of his people and tenderness towards them are everlasting. He is the author of everlasting life and happiness to them, and so is the Father of a blessed eternity to them (*Commentary,* 4:60).

To us the name "Everlasting Father" points in two directions. First, Jesus Christ has existed from all eternity and so is God (John 1:1). Only as God can He fully meet my needs. But the word "everlasting" also points toward the present and future: Christ is everlastingly with us. Combined with the beautiful term "Father," this suggests constant companionship. Whenever I need this Wonderful Counselor He is right there in my heart, ready to meet my every need. And He has a father's love for me, knowing what I need and lovingly wishing to meet my need. All I have to do is to turn to Him for help at any time, day or night.

The fourth name for the Messiah is "Prince of Peace." Peace—what a tantalizing term! Many of us have lived through two World Wars and on the verge of a third one ever since. But in the midst of hot wars and cold wars we can have perfect, personal peace if the Prince of Peace sits on the throne of our heart. His presence *is* peace. Or, to put it another way, peace is the consciousness of Christ's presence as the all-knowing, all-powerful, all-loving God in our hearts and lives. In Ephesians 2:14 we read of Christ, "For he himself is our peace." What a consolation!

"Peace" is an intriguing word, especially in its Hebrew background. Ross Price observes, *"Prince of Peace* is a name which indicates a successful rule in a blessed and true prosperity." He goes on to say, "The Hebrew term *shalom* indicates not only absence of war, but a condition of rich, harmonious, and positive well-being" (*BBC,* 4:63). Matthew Henry comments:

> As a King, he preserves the peace, commands peace, nay, he creates peace, in his kingdom. He is our peace, and it is his peace that both keeps the hearts of his people and rules in them. He is not only a peaceable prince, and his reign peaceable, but he is the author and giver of all good, all that peace which is the present and future bliss of his subjects (*Commentary,* 4:60).

B. His Righteous Reign: v. 7

Of the increase of his government
  and peace
  there will be no end.
He will reign on David's throne
  and over his kingdom,
establishing and upholding it
  with justice and righteousness
  from that time on and forever.
The zeal of the LORD Almighty
  will accomplish this.

The title of our lesson is "A Reign of Righteousness," and here we find it described. Five things are said in this verse about it.

First, it will be an increasing government, without end. As Matthew Henry says, "The bounds of his kingdom shall be more and more enlarged, and many shall be added to it daily" (*Commentary,* 4:60). This is what is happening in the spiritual reign of Christ today. In Acts 2:47 we read, "And the Lord added to their number daily those who were being saved."

Probably that has gone on every day since. In our own day thousands of people are being saved in the great missionary outreach around the world. Christ's reign is increasing!

Second, it will be a peaceable government, befitting the Prince of Peace. Matthew Henry says, "He shall rule by love, shall rule in men's hearts; so that wherever his government is there shall be peace" (*Commentary*, 4:60).

Third, it will be a rightful government. "He that is the Son of David shall reign upon the throne of David and over his kingdom, which he is entitled to" (*Commentary*, 4:60).

Fourth, it will be a righteous government: Christ will establish and uphold it "with justice and righteousness." Those characteristics are sadly lacking in manmade governments today. But in Christ's reign there will be no injustice, no unrighteousness. We need to pray more fervently and frequently, "Your kingdom come" (Matt. 6:10).

The fifth thing that is said here is that it will be an everlasting kingdom: "From that time on and forever." What a consolation to know that Christ's kingdom will never end!

How can all this happen?

The zeal of the LORD Almighty will accomplish this.

III. THE PROMISED MESSIAH: Isaiah 11:1-3a

A. A Branch from Jesse: v. 1

A shoot will come up from the stump of Jesse; from his roots a Branch will bear fruit.

Jesse was the father of King David. So the reference here is to the Messiah as a descendant of David. This fits in with the fact that "the son of David" was a main messianic title.

Of the word "stem" (KJV, NASB) A. R. Fausset writes: "lit., *the stump* of a tree cut close by the roots: happily

expressing the *depressed* state of the royal house of David . . . when Messiah should arise from it, to raise it to more than its pristine glory" (Robert Jamieson, A. R. Fausset, and David Brown, *A Commentary . . . on the Old and New Testaments*, 3:601). That is why the Revised Standard Version and New International Version have "stump" here.

The prophet goes on to say, "from his roots a Branch will bear fruit." Fausset points out that the Hebrew verb here translated "shall grow" (KJV, RSV) really means "will bear fruit" (NASB, NIV). Regarding "from his roots" he explains, "from the stump cut down to *the roots*" (*Commentary*, 3:601). It would seem that the royal line of David, cut off by the Babylonian captivity (in the near future) would never revive. But it did so magnificently in the coming of Christ, the Son of David.

B. Endued with the Spirit: v. 2

The Spirit of the LORD will rest on him—
the Spirit of wisdom and of understanding,
the Spirit of counsel and of power,
the Spirit of knowledge and of the fear of the LORD—

There are three pairs of characteristics that the Spirit of the Lord would bring to the Messiah—and in a

---

DISCUSSION QUESTIONS

1. Why do people walk in darkness?
2. In what way is Christ the light of the world?
3. How can we put the government of our lives on Christ's shoulders?
4. How can we experience Christ as our Wonderful Counselor?
5. What is Christ's kingdom?
6. How can Christ be to us the Prince of Peace?

measure to all those upon whom the Holy Spirit rests. Kenneth E. Jones suggests, "The first pair is *intellectual*, the second pair is *practical*, and the third pair is *spiritual*" (*The Wesleyan Bible Commentary*, 3:52). He goes on to say:

> The Messiah received the gifts of the Spirit in order to give them to us. He came in the power of the Spirit to do the work that was necessary for our redemption, then He offers to us the Spirit of God so that we can do the work of God. As these gifts of the

Spirit made Him capable of being King, so these gifts, in a measure, enable us to fill our places in the kingdom (3:52).

C. Delighting in the Fear of the Lord: v. 3a

and he will delight in the fear of the LORD.

In Psalm 40:8 David says: "I delight to do thy will, O my God" (KJV). This was always the attitude of Jesus, and it should always be our attitude as Christians.

CONTEMPORARY APPLICATION

In fifty-five years of preaching and fifty-four years of teaching, I have had many people come to me for counseling. I have listened to their tale of trouble, given the best counsel I could, and then had to confess, "I can't solve your problem or answer all your questions."

I am glad, however, that I haven't had to leave them defeated and frustrated, for I have been able to say: "But I have a Friend who can answer all your questions and solve all your problems. Let's talk to Him about it."

As I have told the Lord all about a person's difficulty, I have felt a sweet Presence stealing into the room. When I opened my eyes I saw tears still glistening on the cheeks of the counselee. But the face was now relaxed, and the person said quietly: "It's all right now. The Lord has shown me what to do." We have a Wonderful Counselor!

GOD'S CASE AGAINST HIS PEOPLE

DEVOTIONAL READING	Isaiah 3:1-7
ADULTS AND YOUTH	**Adult Topic:** *God's Case Against His People* **Youth Topic:** *Accountable to God* **Background Scripture:** Isa. 1; 2:6—3:15 **Scripture Lesson:** Isa. 1:2-6, 18-20 **Memory Verse:** *The Lord has taken his place to contend, he stands to judge his people.* Isa. 3:13
CHILDREN	**Topic:** *God Wants Us to Obey Him* **Scripture Lesson:** Isa. 1:2-3, 19-20 **Memory Verse:** *If you are willing and obedient, you shall eat the good of the land.* Isa. 1:19
DAILY BIBLE READINGS	**Dec. 26 M.:** Judgment on the Unrighteous. Isa. 1:21-28 **Dec. 27 T.:** Judgment on Reliance on Wealth. Isa. 2:6-11 **Dec. 28 W.:** Judgment on Idolatry. Isa. 2:12-22 **Dec. 29 T.:** Judgment on Leaders of Society. Isa. 3:1-9 **Dec. 30 F.:** Judgment on Exploiters of People. Isa. 3:10-15 **Dec. 31 S.:** Lament Over the Nation. Isa. 1:1-9 **Jan. 1 S.:** Futility of Worship Without Righteousness. Isa. 1:10-17
LESSON AIM	To see why the people of Judah had earned God's judgments on them.
LESSON SETTING	**Time:** 740-700 B.C. **Place:** Jerusalem

LESSON OUTLINE	**God's Case Against His People**
	
	  I. **Israel's Apostasy:** Isaiah 1:2-3
	    A. Rebellious Children: v. 2
	    B. Senseless People: v. 3
	
	  II. **A Sinful Nation:** Isaiah 1:4
	
	  III. **A Sick People:** Isaiah 1:5-6
	    A. The Result of Rebellion: v. 5a
	    B. Completely Sick: vv. 5b-6
	
	  IV. **A Desolate Country:** Isaiah 1:7-9
	
	  V. **God's Plea and Promises:** Isaiah 1:18-20
	    A. The Plea: v. 18a
	    B. The Promise of Cleansing: v. 18b
	    C. The Promise of Prosperity: v. 19
	    D. A Careful Warning: v. 20

SUGGESTED
INTRODUCTION
FOR ADULTS

Today we begin our study of Unit II: "Themes from Isaiah 1-39." The lesson planners tell us, "Themes treated include God's judgment on injustice and oppression, a prophet's vision and mission, and loyalty to God as our ultimate security." Unit II consists of five lessons. The first lesson is taken from the first chapter of Isaiah.

In most of the prophetic books of the Old Testament the first one or two verses give the title of the book. Here we find that Isaiah 1:1 reads, "The vision concerning Judah and Jerusalem that Isaiah son of Amoz saw during the reigns of Uzziah, Jotham, Ahaz and Hezekiah, kings of Judah." This was about 740-700 B.C., the latter part of the eighth century before Christ. This traditional dating has been challenged by scholars in recent years, but no firm consensus has been achieved. With such uncertainty one may still use approximately 740-700 B.C.

SUGGESTED
INTRODUCTION
FOR YOUTH

Our topic today is "Accountable to God." This is one of the most important subjects we can consider. We realize that we are all accountable to our government—national, state, county, and community. If we refuse to acknowledge that, we can get into real trouble.

But our ultimate accountability is to God. This is far more serious, for God not only hears what we say and sees what we do but He knows fully our inner thoughts, attitudes, and motives. That means that every day, all the time, we must be careful what we think and purpose to do. Romans 14:12 warns us: "So then, each of us will give an account of himself to God." We should live every hour in the light of that fact.

CONCEPTS FOR
CHILDREN

1. "God Wants Us to Obey Him" for our best good.
2. Obedience brings happiness.
3. Disobedience to parents and to God makes us unhappy.
4. Those who disobey suffer for it.

THE LESSON COMMENTARY

I. ISRAEL'S APOSTASY: Isaiah 1:2-3

A. Rebellious Children: v. 2

Hear, O heavens! Listen, O earth!
  For the LORD has spoken:
"I reared children and brought
    them up,
  But they rebelled against me."

This invoking of heaven and earth is found a number of times in Deuteronomy. After warning the Israelites against disobeying God and going into idolatry, Moses said, "I call heaven and earth as witnesses against you this day that you will quickly perish from the land that you are crossing the Jordan to possess" (4:26). He speaks similarly in Deuteronomy 30:19 and 31:28. The Song of Moses begins in much the same way as we find here in Isaiah. In 32:1 we read:

Listen, O heavens, and I will
    speak;
  hear, O earth, the words of my
    mouth.

This invocation adds solemnity to what the Lord is now going to say through His prophet. F. Delitzsch observes:

> The time had now arrived for heaven and earth, which are always existing, and always the same, and which had accompanied Israel's history thus far in all places and at all times, to fulfil their duty as witnesses, according to the word of the lawgiver. And this was just the special, true, and ultimate sense in which they were called upon by the prophet, as they had previously been by Moses, to "hear" (C. F. Keil and F. Delitzsch, *Biblical Commentary on the Old Testament*, Isaiah, 1:75).

The Lord begins by saying:

"I reared children and brought
        them up,
    but they have rebelled against
        me."

The Israelitess had their childhood stage in Egypt, where God had cared for them and finally rescued them from slavery. One might speak of their time in the desert as their adolescent stage. In the land of Canaan they had reached maturity and had become a great nation on earth. "Brought them up" literally means "made them great." That is what God had done for the Israelites, but they had rebelled against Him and gone into idolatry.

Speaking of Isaiah, Alexander Maclaren writes:

> And how lovingly, as well as sternly, God speaks through him! That divine lament which heralds the searching indictment is not unworthy to be the very words of the Almighty Lover of all men, sorrowing over His prodigal and fugitive sons. Nor is its deep truth less than its tenderness. For is not man's sin blackest when seen against the bright background of God's fatherly love? (*Expositions of Holy Scripture*, Isaiah, 1:2)

B. Senseless People: v. 3

"The ox knows his master,
    the donkey his owner's manger,
but Israel does not know,
    my people do not understand."

As indicated by quotation marks in the Revised Standard Version, New American Standard Bible, and New International Version, it is the Lord who is speaking directly in the last half of verse 2 and all of verse 3. It is a very plaintive note that He sounds here.

The ox and donkey are often thought of as being among the least intelligent of domesticated animals, yet they know their master and the place where he feeds them. How tragic that human beings should fall short of this! Maclaren comments:

> Man's neglect of God's benefits puts him below the animals that "know" the hand that feeds and governs them. Some men think it is a token of superior "culture" and advanced views to throw off allegiance to God. It is a token that they have less intelligence than their dog (*Expositions*, Isaiah, 1:2).

Animals know enough to stay with those who care for them. But "Israel"—"my people"—had wandered away from God in deep rebellion. It was indeed the most stupid thing they could do.

But how about people today who ignore their Creator and Redeemer, the only one who can save them from sin and its eternal punishment? How can people be so utterly unwise?

II. A SINFUL NATION:
   Isaiah 1:4

Ah, sinful nation,
    a people loaded with guilt,
a brood of evildoers,
    children given to corruption.
They have forsaken the LORD;
    they have spurned the Holy One
        of Israel
and turned their backs on him.

As noted above, the words of the Lord end with verse 3. Now we have Isaiah's denunciation of the people for their sins. They had mistreated his Lord, and he protested strongly.

Israel was supposed to be a "holy nation." At Mount Sinai God had instructed Moses to tell the people: "Now if you obey me fully and keep my covenant, then out of all nations you will be my treasured possession.... You will be for me a kingdom of priests and a holy nation" (Exod. 19:5-6). Instead they were a "sinful nation." What a pity that they had missed their high and noble calling and had sunk down into sin!

Isaiah also calls the Israelites "a people loaded with guilt."

Next Isaiah says that they are "a brood of evildoers." The Israelites were to be the holy seed of Abraham, God's friend. Instead they had become "an evildoing seed."

Fourth, Isaiah labels them as "children given to corruption." We read in verse 21:

> See how the faithful city has
> become a harlot!
> She once was full of justice;
> righteousness used to dwell in
> her—
> but now murderers!

The prophet was deeply stirred as he uttered these first four lines of verse 4. Delitzsch comments that "his words pour out with violent rapidity, like flash after flash, in climactic clauses having no outward connection, and each consisting of only two or three words" (*Commentary*, 1:79).

After these four brief, sharp, interjectional clauses, we find three declaratory clauses in the rest of the verse. They describe a tragic apostasy on the part of the people.

The first charge is, "They have forsaken the LORD." Though they were still carrying on their offering of sacrifices in the temple (vv. 11-15), in their hearts they had forsaken God. Outward forms of worship will never take the place of the right inner attitudes toward the Lord.

Second, "they have spurned the Holy One of Israel." The verb may also be translated "despised" (NASB) or "scorned." They had shown this attitude by disobeying God's law.

"The Holy One of Israel" is a name

that "constitutes the keynote of all Isaiah's prophecy." Delitzsch goes on to say:

> It was sin to mock at anything holy; it was a double sin to mock at God, the Holy One; but it was a threefold sin for Israel to mock at God, the Holy One, who had set Himself to be the sanctifier of Israel, and required that as He was Israel's sanctification, He should also be sanctified by Israel according to His holiness (*Commentary*, Isaiah, 1:81).

The title "the Holy One of Israel" is a favorite one with Isaiah, in whose book it occurs twenty-five times (only seven times in all the rest of the Old Testament). George Rawlinson rightly observes, "According to Isaiah's conception of God, holiness is the most essential element of his nature" (*The Pulpit Commentary*, Isaiah, 1:3). In fact, the holiness of God is emphasized throughout much of the Old Testament. The New Testament declares that "God is love" (I John 4:8, 16). Holy love (*agape*) is meant here.

The final insult to God is found in the last line of verse 4, where we are told that the Israelites "turned their backs on him." Everywhere in the world it is considered discourteous to turn one's back toward another person, but in the Eastern culture it is high insult.

III. A SICK PEOPLE: Isaiah 1:5-6

A. The Result of Rebellion: v. 5a

> Why should you be beaten
> anymore?
> Why do you persist in rebellion?

George Rawlinson comments, "The Authorized Version does not express the sense, which is that suffering *must* follow sin—that if they still revolt, they must still be smitten for it—why, then, will they do it?" (*PC*, Isaiah, 1:3). Ezekiel has a similar question: "Why will you die, O house of Israel?" (18:31). And that is a solemn query that every human individual ought to face realistically. The Bible tells us that "the wages of sin is death" (Rom. 6:23). Why go on sinning, then, and collect these wages throughout eternity?

B. Completely Sick: vv. 5b-6

Your whole head is injured,
   your whole heart afflicted.
From the sole of your foot to the
      top of your head
   there is no soundness—
only wounds and welts
   and open sores,
not cleansed or bandaged
   or soothed with oil.

Commenting on verse 5b, Rawlinson says, "The head and the heart represent respectively the intellectual and moral natures" (*PC*, Isaiah, 1:3). Both are sick because of wilful sin.

The first two lines of verse 6 emphasize the totality of the sickness: it stretches from the sole of the foot to the top of the head. Israel was completely diseased. A. R. Fausset suggests another way of interpreting this: "From the lowest to the highest of the people" (Robert Jamieson, A. R. Fausset, and David Brown, *A Commentary . . . on the Old and New Testaments*, 3:567).

On the last four lines of verse 5 Rawlinson makes this comment:

The general sentiment of the entire passage is that there has been no medical treatment of the wounds of any kind; they have been left to themselves, to spread corruption over the whole body—no attempt has been made to cure them" (*PC*, Isaiah, 1:3).

IV. A DESOLATE COUNTRY: Isaiah 1:7-9

Verse 7 reads:

Your country is desolate,
   your cities burned with fire;
Your fields are being stripped by
      foreigners right before you
   laid waste as when overthrown
      by strangers.

Rawlinson comments here:

Metaphor is now dropped, and the prophet describes in strong but simple language the judgments of God, which have already followed the sins of the nation. First of all, their land is "a desolation." It has been recently ravaged by an enemy; the towns have been burnt, the crops devoured (*PC*, Isaiah, 1:3).

The loneliness of the city of Jerusalem and its inhabitants is described graphically in verse 8:

The Daughter of Zion is left
   like a shelter in a vineyard,
like a hut in a field of melons,
   like a city under siege.

Instead of "shelter" and "hut" the King James Version has "cottage" and "lodge." But the reference is to a small booth in a vineyard and a tiny hut in a melon patch. One can still see these in the Holy Land.

Then the prophet goes on to say in verse 9:

Unless the LORD Almighty
      had left us some survivors,
   we would have become like
         Sodom,
   we would have been like
         Gomorrah.

Sodom and Gomorrah were two very wicked cities that were destroyed in the days of Abraham (Gen. 19:24-25). Even today "sodomy" is a term used for homosexuality, the besetting sin of Sodom.

Fausset comments on this verse as follows:

we should have been (treated judicially) *as Sodom*. We, as a State, are become like Sodom in morals (as v. 10 expressly declares). It is well for us that God has not dealt with us judicially, as He did with Sodom, according to our condition morally (*Commentary*, 1:567).

This comparison of Jerusalem with Sodom is made again in 3:9. It is also developed at considerable length in Ezekiel 16:44-56. It is indeed a sad commentary on the morals of Judah in Isaiah's day.

V. GOD'S PLEA AND PROMISES: Isaiah 1:18-20

A. The Plea: v. 18a

"Come now, let us reason
    together,"
says the LORD.

This whole verse is one of the great evangelistic texts of the Old Testament. But, for the moment, we want to look at these first two lines.

God is pleading with His people, Israel, to pause and come into a conference so that they can "reason together." If people today would stop their mad rush in the things of the world and be willing to sit down, as it were, and let God reason with them, their lives could be radically changed.

God's offer of salvation to those who will believe and obey Him is the most reasonable proposition that has ever been presented to any individual. God is always reasonable. He never asks from us the impossible. All He wants us to do is to listen to Him and accept His free, gracious offer of salvation. What could be more reasonable, or more worthwhile?

B. The Promise of Cleansing: v. 18b

"Though your sins are like scarlet,
    they shall be as white as snow;
though they are red as crimson,
    they shall be like wool."

Rawlinson suggests that "scarlet" and "crimson" means "open, evident, glaring." He adds, "Or there may be an allusion to their bloodguiltiness (see vers. 15, 19)" (PC, Isaiah, 1:6). In any case, the awfulness and visibility of sin is emphasized. It stains us red.

These scarlet, crimson sins will become "as white as snow" and "like wool." One is reminded of a dirty, obnoxious sight in the evening that becomes a beautiful, dazzling white overnight from a fresh fall of snow.

We find a striking parallel to this passage in Psalm 51:7, where we read:

Cleanse me with hyssop, and I
    will be clean;
wash me, and I will be whiter
    than snow.

Why stay filthy in our sins when we can be cleansed? This is the question that every sinner should face. Thank God that He has provided a cleansing from sin!

C. The Promise of Prosperity: v. 19

"If you are willing and obedient,
    you will eat the best from the
        land;"

The first line of this verse could be paraphrased thus: "If you consent in your wills, and are also obedient in your actions" (quoted by Rawlinson). The second line suggests protection from any invasion of the Israelites' land. Instead of their crops being destroyed, or the people being taken into captivity, they would enjoy the best crops of their land. It is a strong contrast to verse 7.

DISCUSSION QUESTIONS

1. In what ways did God rear our nation?
2. What are the sins in our society that most dangerously threaten our future?
3. What can be done about the sins in our society that threaten our future?
4. How can we sound God's warning to the people?
5. In what ways is sin like a disease?
6. What are the conditions for cleansing from sin?

D. A Careful Warning: v. 20

"but if you resist and rebel,
   you will be devoured by the
      sword."

This was a kind, but solemn, warning, that further disobedience and rebellion would lead to defeat in war.

And this is exactly what happened some time later in the Babylonian captivity.

Why will people refuse to learn from history? Rebellion against God has brought suffering again and again. Let's obey Him!

CONTEMPORARY APPLICATION

In a real sense what happened to the people of Judah in the fall of Jerusalem in 586 B.C. and the Babylonian captivity that followed, happened again to Jerusalem in A.D. 70 when the Romans destroyed that city and took many captives to Rome. It seems that people never learn from the past!

But what about us in America today? We have the example of Sodom and Gomorrah, mentioned in our lesson today. And yet the sin of sodomy is becoming increasingly prevalent, and is widely accepted in society. What can we expect God to do to our country if this continues?

SONG OF THE VINEYARD

DEVOTIONAL READING	Isaiah 24:1-13
ADULTS AND YOUTH	**Adult Topic:** *Song of the Vineyard* **Youth Topic:** *What God Expects* **Background Scripture:** Isa. 5 **Scripture Lesson:** Isa. 5:1-7 **Memory Verse:** *I planted you a choice vine, wholly of pure seed. How then have you turned degenerate and become a wild vine?* Jer. 2:21
CHILDREN	**Topic:** *God Wants Us to Be Thankful* **Background Scripture:** Isa. 5; Matt. 21:33-41 **Scripture Lesson:** Matt. 21:33-41 **Memory Verse:** *I am the true vine, and my Father is the vinedresser.* John 15:1
DAILY BIBLE READINGS	**Jan. 2 M.:** Parable Against a Nation. Matt. 21:33-46 **Jan. 3 T.:** Lament Over Evil Doers. Isa. 5:8-17 **Jan. 4 W.:** Lament Over Evil Doers. Isa. 5:18-23 **Jan. 5 T.:** "His Hand Is Stretched Out Still." Isa. 5:24-30 **Jan. 6 F.:** Parable Against Abimelech. Judg. 9:7-16 **Jan. 7 S.:** Parable Against David. II Sam. 12:1-7 **Jan. 8 S.:** Parable Against a Nation. Isa. 5:1-7
LESSON AIM	To see how God felt toward wayward Israel.
LESSON SETTING	**Time:** Eighth century B.C. **Place:** Jerusalem

LESSON OUTLINE	**Song of the Vineyard**
	
	  I. **Preparation of the Vineyard:** Isaiah 5:1-2
	  A. On a Fertile Hillside: v. 1
	  B. Cleared and Planted: v. 2a
	  C. Watchtower and Winepress: v. 2b
	  D. Bad Fruit: v. 2c
	
	 II. **A Great Disappointment:** Isaiah 5:3-4
	  A. Call for Judgment: v. 3
	  B. Divine Protest: v. 4
	
	III. **Destruction of the Vineyard:** Isaiah 5:5-6
	  A. Divine Pronouncement: v. 5a
	  B. Wholesale Destruction: v. 5b
	  C. A Wasteland: v. 6a
	  D. No Rain: v. 6b

IV. **Identification of the Vineyard:** Isaiah 5:7
   A. The House of Israel: v. 7a
   B. The Men of Judah: v. 7b
   C. Wickedness of the People: v. 7c

In our first lesson of this quarter we studied Isaiah 2:1-5 under the title, "A New Day for God's People." There we saw a rosy picture of Israel's future.

Then in last week's lesson, the first of Unit II, we looked at chapter one and 2:6—3:15. There we discovered "God's Case Against His People." Today our lesson is taken from the fifth chapter of Isaiah.

By way of introduction we want to glance at the intervening material. In 3:16 we find a divine description of the women of Jerusalem. The Lord says:

> "The women of Zion are haughty,
>   walking along with outstretched necks,
>   flirting with their eyes.
>   tripping along with mincing steps,
>   with ornaments jingling on their ankles."

SUGGESTED
INTRODUCTION
FOR ADULTS

They sound like the "flappers" of the 1930's!

What will be the result of the women's behavior? The Lord continues in verse 17:

> "Therefore the LORD will bring sores on the
>   heads of the women of Zion;
>   the LORD will make their scalps bald."

The women will lose all their seductive attraction and will become repulsive to look at.

In 3:18-26 we find a detailed picture of the spoiling of all the spectacular finery of these women. There is nothing like it elsewhere in the Bible. This carries over to 4:1, where we find these women in abject destitution. But in the rest of chapter 4 (vv. 2-6) we find that the remnant "will be called holy" (v. 3), as the nation returns to God.

SUGGESTED
INTRODUCTION
FOR YOUTH

Our topic for today is a challenging one: "What God Expects." From our lesson we learn that God expects us to produce good fruit in our lives. If we bear bad fruit, our lives will be ruined and destroyed. The challenge is ours to meet.

God has made ample provision for us to live fruitful lives and be a blessing, not a curse, in this world. It is up to us to cooperate with Him for His glory and our good.

CONCEPTS FOR
CHILDREN

1. "God Wants Us to Be Thankful."
2. We should express our gratitude to God for all the good things He gives us.
3. Ingratitude is a serious sin.
4. Being grateful makes us feel happy.

THE LESSON COMMENTARY

I. PREPARATION OF THE VINEYARD: Isaiah 5:1-2

A. On a Fertile Hillside: v. 1

I will sing for the one I love
a song about his vineyard.

In all three synoptic Gospels we find a parable of a vineyard (Matt. 21:33-41; Mark 12:1-9; Luke 20:9-16). The resemblance with the Song of the Vineyard here in Isaiah is that in both cases Israel is condemned and judged severely for failing to obey God.

The New American Standard Bible introduces this "song" with the words: "Let me sing now for my well-beloved a song of my beloved concerning his vineyard." Commentators seem agreed that "for" is better than "to" (KJV). A. R. Fausset says it should be "concerning" or "for." He notes that the latter could mean:

in the person of my beloved, as His representative (Vitringa). Or *for*— i.e., in honour of God, my Beloved (*Grotius*), on whose account I am jealous lest the Israelites should transfer their affection to another (*Calvin*) (Robert Jamieson, A. R. Fausset, and David Brown, *A Commentary . . . on the Old and New Testaments*, 3:577).

The first two lines (NIV), quoted above, could be put in prose (as in the NASB). They are introductory to the song itself, which begins at the middle of verse one. George Rawlinson comments:

The song consists of eight lines, beginning with "My Well-beloved," and ending with "wild grapes." It is in a lively, dancing measure, very unlike the general style of Isaiah's poetry. The name "Well-beloved" seems to be taken by the prophet from the Song of Songs, where it occurs above twenty times. It well expresses the feeling of a loving soul towards its Creator and Redeemer (*The Pulpit Commentary*, Isaiah, 1:77).

The Song of Songs (called The Song of Solomon in the KJV) immediately precedes Isaiah in our Bibles. It is the last of the so-called poetical books of the Old Testament.

Matthew Henry describes the poetry we find here in the Song of the Vineyard:

This parable was put into a song that it might be the more moving and affecting, might be the more easily learned and exactly remembered, and the better transmitted to posterity; and it is an exposition of the song of Moses (Deut. xxxii), showing that what he then foretold was now fulfilled (*Commentary on the Whole Bible*, 4:29).

The first two lines of the Song of the Vineyard are found in the second half of verse one:

My loved one had a vineyard
on a fertile hillside.

To anyone who has traveled in the Holy Land this is a familiar picture. The important town of Bethlehem is set on a knoll, surrounded by vineyards on the terraced hillsides. As one drives the roads of Judea, Samaria, or Galilee, he frequently sees the hillsides covered with vineyards. This is one of the most common sights in Israel today.

In the Hebrew "a fertile hillside" is literally "a horn of the son of oil." Fausset says that this is used "poetically for *very fruitful.* Suggestive of *isolation, security,* and a *sunny aspect*" (*Commentary*, 3:577). Similarly Rawlinson comments:

So the passage is generally understood, since *keren*, horn, is used for a height by the Arabs (as also by the Germans, e.g. Matterhorn . . .), and "son of oil" is a not unlikely Orientalism for "rich" or "fruitful" (*PC*, Isaiah, 1:78).

In keeping with this, Delitzsch translates these two lines: "My beloved had a vineyard on a fatly nourished mountain-horn" (C. F. Keil and F. Delitzsch, *Biblical Commentary on the Old Testament,* Isaiah, 1:160).

B. Cleared and Planted: v. 2a

He dug it up and cleared it of
    stones
  and planted it with the choicest
    vines.

In the King James Version the first clause reads: "And he fenced it." That is what the Septuagint has. Unfortunately the Hebrew verb here is not found anywhere else, and so the meaning is uncertain. "Dug it up" (NIV) is the translation offered by Delitzsch. He comments, "The plough could not be used, from the steepness of the mountain slope: he therefore dug it up, that is to say, he turned up the soil which was to be made into a vineyard with a hoe" (*Commentary,* Isaiah, 1:161).

Having dug up the soil, he planted it with the "choicest vines." The Hebrew word is *sorek,* which Delitzsch says was "the finest kind of eastern vine, bearing small grapes" (*Commentary,* Isaiah, 1:161). Fausset comments: "It perhaps takes its name from Sorek, mentioned in Judg. xvi. 4, not far from Eshcol, which was famed for its grapes. The name of the Sorek grape appears still in Morocco, *serki.* The grapes had scarcely perceptible stones" (*Commentary,* 3:577). God planted the very best vines in the persons of the patriarchs Abraham, Isaac, and Jacob.

Those who live in some parts of the United States may not be familiar with the phrase "cleared it of stones" (before planting). I was brought up on a farm in Massachusetts, where this was very meaningful. Every year we would go through a freshly plowed field with a two-horse wagon, picking up stones by the hundreds. Otherwise, the crops would have been greatly hindered from growing.

The same condition exists in the Holy Land. I have seen fields there where it seemed that a goat would

hardly be able to get his nose between the stones to get a sprig of grass! Clearing away the stones is a very important exercise in the rocky soil of Israel. And it was metaphorically true in the beginning stages of planting the Israelites in the Promised Land.

C. Watchtower and Winepress: v. 2b

He built a watchtower in it
  and cut out a winepress as well.

In a vineyard near the top of the hill Samaria one can see today a typical watchtower. A fairly large platform rests on poles stuck in the ground. When the fruit was ripe a watchman would sit there at night to guard it. Rawlinson observes, "Towers had to be built in gardens, orchards, and vineyards, that watch might be kept from them against thieves and marauders" (*PC*, Isaiah, 1:78). The rabbis specified that these must be fifteen feet high and six feet square at the top. Watchtowers are mentioned numerous times in the Bible.

In preparing the vineyard the subject of this song also "cut out a winepress." Ross Price describes what this was like:

> A wine vat was made of stone on two levels. The upper and larger vat was shallower and in it the grapes were thrown and trodden (cf. Isa. 63:3). The lower one was smaller and deeper. Into it the grape juice would flow by a channel from the upper vat. From thence it was dipped up and poured into the goatskin bottles (such as are still used for water today in some parts of Palestine) for carrying and preservation (*Beacon Bible Commentary,* 4:44, n. 10).

In the Garden of the Empty Tomb one can still see a winepress used in Jesus' day. This is a short distance from the north wall of Jerusalem, between the Damascus Gate and Herod's Gate.

D. Bad Fruit: v. 2c

Then he looked for a crop of good
  grapes,
  but it yielded only bad fruit.

Matthew Henry gives a good discussion of these closing words of the Song of the Vineyard. He writes:

God expects vineyard-fruit from those that enjoy vineyard-privileges, not leaves only, as Mark xi.13. A bare profession, though ever so green, will not serve: there must be more than buds and blossoms. Good purposes and good beginnings are good things, but not enough; there must be fruit; a good heart and a good life, vineyard fruit, thoughts and affections, words and actions, agreeable to the Spirit, which is the fatness of the vine (Gal. v.22, 23). . . . Such fruit as this God expects from us . . . and his expectations are neither high nor hard, but righteous and very reasonable (*Commentary on the Whole Bible*, 4:30).

II. A GREAT DISAPPOINTMENT: Isaiah 5:3-4

A. Call for Judgment: v. 3

"Now you dwellers in Jerusalem
  and men of Judah,
  judge between me and my
  vineyard."

Jesus made somewhat the same kind of a "pitch" at the end of His parable of the tenants. After describing what the wicked tenants had done, He asked His hearers: "Therefore, when the owner of the vineyard comes, what will he do to those tenants?" The people replied: "He will bring the wretches to a wretched end" (Matt. 21:40, 41).

There are striking parallels between the Song of the Vineyard in Isaiah 5 and the Song of Moses in Deuteronomy 32. There we read in verse 6:

Is this the way you repay the
  LORD,
O foolish and unwise people?
Is he not your Father, your
  Creator,
  who made you and formed you?

B. Divine Protest: v. 4

"What more could have been done
  for my vineyard
  than I have done for it?
When I looked for good grapes,
  why did it yield only bad?"

Combining this with verse 3, Delitzsch makes these comments:

To any one with spiritual intuition . . . the parabolical meaning and object of the song would be at once apparent; and even the inhabitants of Jerusalem and the men of Judah . . . were not so stupefied by sin, that they could not perceive to what the prophet was leading. It was for them to decide where the guilt of this unnatural issue lay—that is to say, of this thorough contradiction between the "doing" of the vineyard and the "doing" of the Lord; that instead of the grapes he hoped for, it brought forth wild grapes (*Commentary*, Isaiah, 1:162).

Fausset puts it well: "God has done all that could be done for the salvation of sinners, consistently with His justice and goodness" (*Commentary*, 3:578). No man will have any excuse to give at the judgment.

III. DESTRUCTION OF THE VINEYARD: Isaiah 5:5-6

A. Divine Pronouncement: v. 5a

"Now I will tell you
  what I am going to do to my
  vineyard."

Delitzsch suggests: "The Lord of the vineyard breaks the silence of the umpires, which indicates their consciousness of guilt. They shall hear from Him what He will do at once to His vineyard" (*Commentary*, Isaiah,

1:163). There were no reasonable answers that could be given to the questions that the Lord asked in verse 4, so He took over the stage and said, "Now I will tell you." The time had come for judgment to begin at the house of God, and a declaration must be made.

B. Wholesale Destruction: v. 5b

"I will take away its hedge,
      and it will be destroyed;
I will break down its wall,
      and it will be trampled."

Rawlinson comments:

Vineyards were usually protected either by a hedge of thorns, commonly of the prickly pear, or else by a wall; but the rabbis say that in some cases, for additional security, they were surrounded by both. God had given his vineyard all the protection possible (*PC*, Isaiah, 1:78).

Ross Price says about the vineyard:

To take away the hedge (5) would be to place it at the mercy of straying goats which delight to crop off the tender branches. To destroy *the wall* would be to allow any cloven-footed devil to romp across it at pleasure (*BBC*, 4:44).

This is the metaphorical picture of the vineyard. What actually happened was that God's protection of the nation was finally taken away, and the result was the Babylonian captivity. Matthew Henry puts it well:

They shall no longer be protected as God's people, but left exposed. God will not only suffer the wall to go to decay, but he will break it down, will remove all their defenses from them, and then they will become an easy prey to their enemies, who have long waited for an opportunity to do them a mischief, and will now tread them down and trample upon them (*Commentary*, 4:31).

C. A Wasteland: v. 6a

"I will make it a wasteland,
      neither pruned nor cultivated,
      and briers and thorns will grow
         there."

As Delitzsch says, "Further pruning and hoeing would do it no good, but only lead to further disappointment: it was the will of the Lord, therefore, that the deceitful vineyard should shoot up in thorns and thistles" (*Commentary*, Isaiah, 1:164).

D. No Rain: v. 6b

"I will command the clouds
      not to rain on it."

Palestine has always been a very dry country, dependent on its meager fall and spring rains. When these fail, the result is catastrophe. Delitzsch comments:

In order that it might remain a wilderness, the clouds would also receive commandment from the Lord not to rain upon it. There can be no longer any doubt who the Lord of the vineyard is. He is Lord of the clouds, and therefore the Lord of heaven and earth. It is He who is the prophet's beloved and dearest one (*Commentary*, Isaiah, 1:164).

DISCUSSION QUESTIONS

1.   What "stones" does God want to clear out of our lives?
2.   What are the "choicest vines" in our case?
3.   How do we care for our own vineyard?
4.   What might "briers and thorns" represent?
5.   What does "the garden of his delight" suggest to you?

IV. IDENTIFICATION
OF THE VINEYARD:
Isaiah 5:7

A. The House of Israel: v. 7a

The vineyard of the LORD
Almighty
is the house of Israel.

Finally we are told beyond equivocation what the vineyard is: It is "the house of Israel." Here the term is rather clearly not limited to the northern kingdom of Israel, which had broken away under Jeroboam. It takes in all the descendants of Jacob, whose name was changed to Israel. These were God's people, His vineyard that He cared for.

B. The Men of Judah: v. 7b

and the men of Judah
are the garden of his delight.

Since Isaiah was prophesying in the southern kingdom of Judah, at Jerusalem, it was natural that he should single out the men of Judah for special mention. They were especially the garden of God's delight, staying closer to Him in their temple worship and keeping true to Him longer than their idolatrous brothers in the north.

C. Wickedness of the People:
v. 7c

And he looked for justice, but saw
bloodshed;
for righteousness, but heard
cries of distress.

Isaiah is fond of a play on words, and we have a good example here. The Hebrew says, "God looked for *mishpat*, but behold *mispah;* for *sedakah*, but behold *se'akah!'"*

God had good reason to expect justice and righteousness in His people. But instead he found bloodshed and cries of distress. In spite of the laws given at Sinai, the Israelites had rejected the right way. Matthew Henry writes:

It is sad with a people when wickedness has usurped the place of judgment. . . . It is very sad with a soul when instead of the grapes of humility, meekness, patience, love, and contempt of the world, which God looks for, there are the wild grapes of pride, passion, discontent, malice, and contempt of God—instead of the grapes of praying and praising, the wild grapes of cursing and swearing (*Commentary,* 4:31).

CONTEMPORARY APPLICATION

Just as Israel had a great heritage and the wonderful love and protection of the Lord, so we Christians have both. To depart from God and disobey His laws is to earn His well-deserved judgment. The Christian church has a great heritage from the past. We must be true to that heritage.

But there is a positive thrust here that we must not miss. God expects us to bear "the fruit of the Spirit" (Gal. 5:22-23). If we fail to do that, we are failing Him. And where the fruit of the Spirit is conspicuously absent, "the acts of the sinful nature" ("works of the flesh") will soon be increasingly manifest in our lives. Ultimately we will display one set or the other.

VISION AND MISSION

DEVOTIONAL READING	Isaiah 30:15-18

Adult Topic: *Vision and Mission*

Youth Topic: *God's Mission for Me*

ADULTS AND YOUTH

Background Scripture: Isa. 6

Scripture Lesson: Isa. 6:1-8

Memory Verse: *I heard the voice of the Lord saying, "Whom shall I send, and who will go for us?" Then I said, "Here am I! Send me."* Isa. 6:8

CHILDREN

Topic: *God Calls—Who Will Go?*

Scripture Lesson: Isa. 6:8

Memory Verse: *Here am I! Send me.* Isa. 6:8

DAILY BIBLE READINGS

Jan. 9 M.: The King of the Universe. Ps. 47:1-9
Jan. 10 T.: The King of the World. Ps. 93:1-5
Jan. 11 W.: The Head of the Heavenly Council. Jer. 23:18-22
Jan. 12 T.: The Sinfulness of the Nation. Isa. 1:4-9
Jan. 13 F.: A Prayer for Forgiveness. Amos 7:1-6
Jan. 14 S.: The Insensitivity of the People. Matt. 13:10-15
Jan. 15 S.: The Call of a Messenger. Isa. 6:1-13

LESSON AIM

To help us understand that a worthwhile mission in life requires a vision of God's will.

LESSON SETTING

Time: Eighth century B.C.

Place: Jerusalem

LESSON OUTLINE

Vision and Mission

I. **The Vision of God:** Isaiah 6:1-4
  A. The Exalted Lord: v. 1
  B. The Reverent Seraphs: v. 2
  C. The Seraphs' Cry: v. 3
  D. The Divine Impact: v. 4

II. **The Vision of Himself:** Isaiah 6:5

III. **The Vision of the Remedy:** Isaiah 6:6-7
  A. The Live Coal: v. 6
  B. The Divine Forgiveness: v. 7

IV. **The Mission:** Isaiah 6:8
  A. The Divine Call: v. 8a
  B. The Human Response: v. 8b

SUGGESTED
INTRODUCTION
FOR ADULTS

We may look at ourselves and feel satisfied. Apparently this is the way with most people, for they do little to improve themselves. We may look at others and be complacent about the comparison. This is too often true, for people tend to commend themselves and condemn others.

But we can never look at God and feel complacent. For when we see Him in His utter holiness and perfection, we keenly sense how imperfect we are. Augustine, the great church father of the fourth century, put it well when he said, "The surest evidence of perfection is the consciousness of our imperfections." And that is certainly logical, for the closer we draw to God the more we realize how far we fall short of perfect Christlikeness. Then we ask Him for help and receive it, as Isaiah did.

SUGGESTED
INTRODUCTION
FOR YOUTH

"God's Mission for Me"—that is the most important thing that should engage our attention. Our first concern as Christians should be: What does God want me to do with my life?

The world offers many attractions: career, fame, money, success. But all of these can turn out to be a hollow mockery and end in frustration and futility if we miss God's will. One of the greatest consolations in life is the consciousness that we are where God wants us to be and doing what He wants us to do. That really makes life worthwhile. It gives us a sense of fulfillment rather than frustration. Let's ask God what *He* wants us to do and then follow His directions.

CONCEPTS FOR
CHILDREN

1. "God Calls—Who Will Go?"
2. The important question is: Will *you* go?
3. We should ask the Lord what we can do to help others.
4. Young children can receive a divine call to Christian service.

THE LESSON COMMENTARY

I. THE VISION OF GOD:
Isaiah 6:1-4

A. The Exalted Lord: v. 1

"In the year that King Uzziah died, I saw the Lord seated on a throne, high and exalted, and the train of his robe filled the temple."

The words, "in the year that King Uzziah died," are very significant. That great godly king had raised the kingdom of Judah to its highest heights of peace and prosperity since the days of David and Solomon. The young patriot, Isaiah, was doubtless filled with great hope for the future. It seemed that the golden age of his people lay just ahead. The glorious promises of God were about to be fulfilled.

But then something went wrong. In a moment of self-will King Uzziah took a censer, filled it with incense, and entered the Holy Place of the temple, where only the priests had a right to go. Eighty of the priests followed him in and told him: "It is not right for you, Uzziah, to burn incense to the LORD. That is for the priests, the descendants of Aaron, who have been consecrated to burn incense to the LORD" (II Chron. 26:16-18).

Instead of appreciating and heeding their admonition, Uzziah "became angry." Then we read, "While he was raging at the priests in their presence before the incense altar in the LORD's temple, leprosy broke out on his forehead" (v. 19), and he was hurried out of the temple (v. 20) to live a lonely life in a leprosarium the rest of his days.

This was the most traumatic hour in Isaiah's life. It seemed that all those aircastles he had built so high in the heavens came crashing down on his head and lay in ruins around his feet. All he could see ahead of him was a black, blank wall. He probably knew that Uzziah's son, Jotham, was a weak man, and he may have sensed that the grandson, Ahaz, would be a wicked ruler. The prospects for Judah were sad indeed.

In that tragic hour Isaiah did what all of us must do in times like that: he went to the place of prayer. Kneeling in the temple, he wept out the sorrow of his soul. Lifting tear-dimmed eyes, he saw the empty throne of Judah sinking slowly out of sight, and his heart sank with it.

But then he saw another throne, and it wasn't empty. He records: "I saw the Lord seated on a throne, high and exalted." In that hour Isaiah realized that though earthly kingdoms may crumble and fall, and everything seems to go wrong, yet God still sits supreme on the throne, serene in the calm consciousness of His eternal power and absolute deity. That is the assurance we need to have when everything goes to pieces on the earthly scene or in our own circumstances.

We read of the Lord that "the train of his robe filled the temple." Eastern kings of that day wore long, flowing robes when they sat on the throne. Isaiah saw God throned in majesty, splendor, and authority.

According to tradition, in Manasseh's reign Isaiah was "sawed in two"

(Heb. 11:37) because he testified that he had seen the Lord. High spiritual experiences can sometimes be costly!

B. The Reverent Seraphs: v. 2

Above the Lord "were seraphs, each with six wings: With two wings they covered their faces, with two they covered their feet, and with two they were flying."

We might say a word about the term "seraphims" in the King James Version. The singular word is *seraph*, which means "fiery one." The masculine plural ending of Hebrew nouns is "-*im*." So *seraphim* is already plural. To use "seraphims" is like saying "I have three childrens"; it simply is not correct.

These holy creatures, made to dwell in the presence of Deity, draped their faces and their feet in awe and reverence before God. How much more should we come into God's presence in the sanctuary on Sunday morning with holy awe and reverence for Him. That is not the place and time for gabbing, but for quiet meditation and sincere worship. We are in the presence of the King of Kings and Lord of Lords!

Alexander Maclaren has some helpful comments about these seraphs. He writes:

> The significance of their attitude has been well given by Jewish commentators, who say, "with two he covered his face that he might not see, and with two he covered his body that he might not be seen," and we may add, "with two he stood ready for service, by flight withersoever the King would send." Such awe-stricken reverence, such humble hiding of self, such alacrity for swift obedience, such flaming ardours of love and devotion, should be ours (*Expositions of Holy Scripture,* Isaiah, 1:19-20).

The position of the seraphs in relation to the King is described this way by Kenneth E. Jones: "The statement that the seraphim stood *above* the Lord is a Hebrew idiom which simply expresses the fact that they were standing near Him ready to be of service, while He was *sitting*" (*The Wesleyan Bible Commentary*, 3:33).

C. The Seraphs' Cry: v. 3

The seraphs were calling to one another:

"Holy, holy, holy is the LORD Almighty;
 the whole earth is full of his glory."

In Revelation 4:6-8 we find a striking parallel to this. There we read of four living creatures, each having six wings (like the seraphs). We are told that day and night they never stop saying:

"Holy, holy, holy
is the Lord God Almighty."

The so-called Trisagion (thrice-holy) has often been taken as suggesting the Trinity, a doctrine that is not clearly stated in the Old Testament. It may have been intended especially for emphasis, as in Jeremiah 7:4; 22:29. At any rate, it accords with the doctrine of the Trinity. It also suggests that God is completely holy.

It is impossible for our finite minds to grasp the full significance of the "Holy, holy, holy." But Delitzsch suggests something of its thrust. He writes:

God is in Himself the *Holy One* (*kadosh*), *i.e.* the separate One, beyond or above the world, true light, spotless purity, the perfect One. His *glory* (*cabod*) is His manifested holiness, . . . just as, on the other hand, His holiness is His veiled or hidden glory. The design of all the work of God is that His holiness should become universally manifest, or, what is the same thing, that His glory should become the fulness of the whole earth (C. F. Keil and F. Delitzsch, *Biblical Commentary on the Old Testament*, Isaiah, 1:192).

Delitzsch goes on to say:

The whole book of Isaiah contains traces of the impression made by this ecstatic vision. The favourite name of God in the mouth of the prophet, viz., "the Holy One of Israel" (*kedosh Yisrael*), is the echo of this seraphic *sanctus;* and the fact that this name already occurs with such marked preference on the part of the prophet in the addresses contained in ch. i.2–iv.5, supports the view that Isaiah is here describing his own first call (1:192–94).

The seraphs linked the holiness and glory of God, as we see in the second line of their cry: "the whole earth is full of his glory." But few have eyes to see it, or ears to hear it, or hearts to feel it. God's glory is manifested in every flower that blooms, in every towering tree, in every bird that sings, in every sunrise and sunset, in the starry sky above at night, and in the beautiful blue sky of the daytime. It is all around us; it fills the whole earth— but how pitifully little of it ever gets inside of us!

People pay all kinds of money to experience the glamorous baubles that man creates. But it doesn't cost one single penny to view the glory of God. All it takes is a little time and attention—to stop and look at a flower or stand enrapt before a gorgeous sunset. What we all need is to take more time to expose ourselves to the glory of God and absorb it into our souls, until it will shine out through our personalities. There is nothing more beautiful on earth than the glow of God's glory on a human countenance. We see it too seldom!

D. The Divine Impact: v. 4

"At the sound of their voices the doorposts and thresholds shook and the temple was filled with smoke."

Delitzsch comments:

Every time the choir of seraphim . . . began their song, the support of the threshold of the porch in which Isaiah was standing trembled. The building was seized with reverential awe throughout its whole extent, and in its deepest foundations (*Commentary*, Isaiah, 1:194).

We also read that "the temple was filled with smoke." There is considerable difference of opinion among commentators as to the meaning of this. For instance, Maclaren writes: "'The house was filled with smoke,' which, since it was an effect of the seraph's praise, is best explained as referring to the fragrant smoke of incense which, as we know, symbolized 'the prayers of saints'" (*Expositions, Isaiah,* 1:20–21). Fausset says it was "the shekinah cloud, the symbol of 'the glory of the Lord'" (Robert Jamieson, A. R. Fausset, and David Brown, *A Commentary . . . on the Old and New Testaments,* 3:582). I like this better than Rawlinson's suggestion that it was an indication of God's presence in anger.

Not only did Isaiah feel the threshold shaking beneath his feet, but he felt earthquake disturbances down deep in his soul. His self-satisfaction was shattered to pieces and his self-complacency was dealt a death blow. He was all "shook up" inside. This is shown by the next verse, to which we now turn.

II. THE VISION OF HIMSELF: Isaiah 6:5

"Woe to me!" I cried. "I am ruined! For I am a man of unclean lips, and I live among a people of unclean lips, and my eyes have seen the King, the LORD Almighty."

We never really see ourselves as we actually are until we see God. In the light of His holiness we see the darkness of our own sin. As with Isaiah, the vision of God must precede the vision of ourselves.

The King James Version reports Isaiah as saying, "I am undone." But the Hebrew literally says, "I am cut off." Isaiah saw a gap between his soul and God he couldn't close, a canyon he couldn't cross, a chasm he couldn't bridge. And so he cried out in despair, "I am cut off!"

Isaiah went on to say, "I am a man of unclean lips, and I live among a people of unclean lips." Jones comments:

As Isaiah heard the voices of the heavenly creatures praising God with their heaven-pure lips, he felt with his whole being that his own lips were sinfully unfit to speak the words of God, for with the lips one speaks what is in the heart. He knew that his own heart needed to be cleansed, and that the hearts of the people of his nation needed the same cleansing (*WBC,* 3:34).

One more thing Isaiah added as a reason for his being "ruined": "My eyes have seen the King, the LORD Almighty." Matthew Henry comments:

He saw God's sovereignty to be incontestable—he is the King; and his power irresistible—he is the Lord of hosts. These are comfortable truths to God's people, and yet they ought to strike an awe upon us. . . . A believing sight of God's glorious majesty should affect us all with reverence and godly fear (*Commentary on the Whole Bible,* 4:40).

Kenneth Jones writes on the effects of seeing God's holiness:

A vision of God always brings to man a sense of awe and reverence, which imparts true humility, the only proper attitude of man toward God. Any true experience of worship should involve the kind of experience of the presence of God that brings a deepened sense of true Christian humility. This is the kind of thing that should happen every Sunday, and in every occasion of private worship (*WBC,* 3:34).

DISCUSSION QUESTIONS

1. How can we see God today?
2. How can people be so complacent in their sins?
3. How can some professing Christians be so self-satisfied?
4. What kind of cleansing do we all need?
5. What is the relation between heart and mouth?
6. How should we respond to God's call to us?

III. THE VISION
OF THE REMEDY:
Isaiah 6:6-7

A. The Live Coal: v. 6

"Then one of the seraphs flew to me with a live coal in his hand, which he had taken with tongs from the altar."

When we sincerely confess our sinfulness and call on God for help, He is always ready to answer. Isaiah had received a vision of God, which brought a vision of himself, and now he had a vision of the remedy for his condition. When he cried out for help, he saw a seraph winging his way across the vast spaces. With tongs, for protection, the seraph lifted a live coal from the altar.

What altar was this? Fausset says that it was the altar "of burnt offering, in the court of the priests before the temple"—that is, the sanctuary itself. He adds, "The fire on it was at first kindled by God (Lev. ix.24), and was kept continually burning" (*Commentary*, 3:582). This typified the fact that all our cleansing from sin comes from Christ's altar of sacrifice for us.

B. The Divine Forgiveness: v. 7

"With it he touched my mouth and said, 'See, this has touched your lips; your guilt is taken away and your sin atoned for.'"

Isaiah had confessed, "I am a man of unclean lips" (v. 5). So it was appropriate for the seraph to apply the burning coal to his lips to cleanse them.

But the cleansing went deeper than that. The seraph announced that Isaiah's guilt was taken away and his sin atoned for.

In the King James Version the last verb is "purged." Ross Price comments:

The Hebrew word, *Kaphar*, is in the Hebrew *Pual* (passive) verb form

here, which Gesenius notes is perhaps best translated "obliterated" or "deleted" since it is both passive and intensive in form. Hence the KJV translation is valid (*BBC*, 4:51, n. 19).

It is interesting to note that Alexander Maclaren writes: "The next stage in Isaiah's experience is that sin recognized and confessed is burned away. Cleansing rather than forgiveness is here emphasized" (*Expositions*, Isaiah, 1:21).

IV. THE MISSION:
Isaiah 6:8

A. The Divine Call: v. 8a

"Then I heard the voice of the LORD saying, 'Whom shall I send? And who will go for us?'"

It has often been remarked that "us" in the second question implies the Trinity. This seems to be a fair enough deduction, even though some discount it.

As we have already noted, this whole passage seems to describe Isaiah's initial call to be God's prophet to His people. The preceding chapters were perhaps placed first for emphasis on the spiritual condition of Judah at that time.

B. The Human Response: v. 8b

"And I said, 'Here am I. Send me!'"

With all that had transpired, Isaiah was now ready to accept God's call. His lips had been cleansed by the burning coal (type of the Holy Spirit), so that He could speak the messages a holy God would give him. Without this vision and cleansing he could never have done it.

We, too, must first be cleansed before we can convey God's truth. Let's submit to both the cleansing and the call to service.

CONTEMPORARY APPLICATION

Christ has closed the *gap* between Deity and humanity. He has crossed the *canyon* that yawned so deep and wide between heaven and earth. He has bridged the *chasm* that separated man from God. With one foot planted in eternity, He planted another in time. He who was the eternal Son of God became the Son of Man. And across this bridge, Christ Jesus, we can come into the presence of the eternal, holy God.

TURN TO THE LORD

DEVOTIONAL READING	Psalm 107:1-9

ADULTS AND YOUTH

Adult Topic: *Turn to the Lord*

Youth Topic: *Learning to Trust*

Background Scripture: Isa. 30-31

Scripture Lesson: Isa. 31:1-7

Memory Verse: *In returning and rest you shall be saved; in quietness and in trust shall be your strength.* Isa. 30:15

CHILDREN

Topic: *God Wants Us to Depend on Him*

Scripture Lesson: Isa. 31:1, 6-7

Memory Verse: *Blessed is the man who makes the Lord his trust, who does not turn to the proud, to those who go astray after false gods!* Ps. 40:4

DAILY BIBLE READINGS

Jan. 16 M.: The Holy Purpose of God. Isa. 10:5-15
Jan. 17 T.: "A Covenant with Death." Isa. 28:14-22
Jan. 18 W.: Learn from the Farmer. Isa. 28:23-29
Jan. 19 T.: A Rebellious People. Isa. 30:1-7
Jan. 20 F.: The Suicide of Rejecting Faith. Isa. 30:12-17
Jan. 21 S.: The Compassionate God. Isa. 30:18-26
Jan. 22 S.: No Substitute for Faith in God. Isa. 31:1-7

LESSON AIM	To see the importance of trusting fully in the Lord.

LESSON SETTING

Time: Eighth century B.C.

Place: Jerusalem

LESSON OUTLINE

Turn to the Lord

I. **Relying on Egypt for Help:** Isaiah 31:1-3
   A. Woe to Those Who Do: v. 1
   B. Divine Wisdom: v. 2
   C. The Folly of Looking to Egypt: v. 3

II. **The Lord's Care for Judah:** Isaiah 31:4-5
   A. Protecting Mount Zion: v. 4
   B. Shielding Jerusalem: v. 5

III. **A Call for Repentance:** Isaiah 31:6-7
   A. Returning to the Lord: v. 6
   B. Rejecting Idolatry: v. 7

IV. **Downfall of Assyria:** Isaiah 31:8-9
   A. Divine Judgment: v. 8
   B. Divine Terror: v. 9

Our background Scripture takes in chapter 30 along with chapter 31, so we want to look at part of chapter 30 by way of introduction. We shall deal particularly with verses 8-14.

The Lord told the prophet to write the divine message on a tablet and inscribe it on a scroll (v. 8). What was the message?

We find the essence of it in verse 9:

> These are rebellious people, deceitful children,
>   children unwilling to listen to the LORD's
>   instruction.

God is speaking of the people of Judah. As descendants of Abraham, they were God's people, but they were a rebellious people. They were also God's children, but they were deceitful children.

Then the accusation becomes more definite in verses 10 and 11:

SUGGESTED
INTRODUCTION
FOR ADULTS

> They say to the seers,
>   "See no more visions!"
> and to the prophets,
>   "Give us no more visions of what is right!
> Tell us pleasant things,
>   prophesy illusions.
> Leave this way,
>   get off this path,
> and stop confronting us
>   with the Holy One of Israel!"

We have a counterpart of this today in that people prefer to believe that they are all children of God and will be saved. They don't want preachers to tell them they are lost sinners and need Christ as Savior.

God warns the people that because they have rejected His message they will suddenly experience total disaster (vv. 12-14). This is the message that sinners need to hear and heed today.

SUGGESTED
INTRODUCTION
FOR YOUTH

"Learning to Trust" is the most important lesson we can learn. Young people, for many reasons, tend to feel insecure. In a world like ours, this is very understandable.

What we need to learn is that we can put our total, ultimate trust only in God, not in human beings. The worst of people let us down all the time, and even best friends disappoint us sometimes. But God never will!

CONCEPTS FOR
CHILDREN

1. "God Wants Us to Depend on Him."
2. God has promised to protect His own.
3. We can always trust God to guide us, if we ask Him to.
4. If we love God, we know we can trust Him.

THE LESSON COMMENTARY

I. RELYING ON EGYPT
FOR HELP:
Isaiah 31:1-3

A. Woe to Those Who Do: v. 1

Woe to those who go down to
    Egypt for help,
  who rely on horses,
who trust in the multitude of their
    chariots
and in the great strength of
    their horsemen,
but do not look to the Holy One of
    Israel,
  or seek help from the LORD.

The word "woe"—Hebrew *oy* or
hoy—occurs no less than twenty-one
times in Isaiah. Actually, we have in
this section of Isaiah (cc. 28-33) a series
of six woes. They are pronounced on
drunken politicians (c. 28), formalists
in religion (29:1-14), those who hide
their plans from God (29:15-24), the
pro-Egyptian party (c. 30), those who
trust in horses and chariots (cc. 31-32),
and the Assyrians (c. 33).

Here the woe is pronounced on
"those who go down to Egypt for help."
The historical background for this is
that the Assyrian Empire was ex-
panding westward. At this point it
was threatening Israel and Judah from
the north. In fact, in the middle of
Isaiah's ministry (722 B.C.), the Assyrians captured Samaria and took the
northern kingdom of Israel into
captivity.

Living in constant fear of the Assyrians, many of the politicians in Judah
turned southward to Egypt for help.
We call them the pro-Egyptian party.

The Assyrians had horses and a
multitude of chariots. This is because
they lived in the level Tigris-Euphrates
Valley. But Palestine is a hilly, rocky
country where chariots cannot maneuver well. Lacking these means of
warfare, the people of Judah were
turning to Egypt, which was famous
for its horses and chariots. Diodorus
says that one Pharaoh had twenty-

seven thousand chariots. This is doubtless an exaggeration. But we do read
that the pharaoh of the Exodus had
six hundred (Exod. 14:7), and that
Shishak had twelve hundred (II Chron.
12:3). Egypt exported chariots to the
neighboring countries (I Kings 10:29).
George Rawlinson says that Egypt
"was at this time the only power which
seemed capable of furnishing such a
chariot-force as could hope to contend
on tolerably even terms with the force
of Assyria" (*The Pulpit Commentary,*
Isaiah, 1:510).

The Lord had already warned
Judah, through His prophet, not to seek
a military alliance with Egypt against
Assyria. We read in the first two verses
of chapter 30:

"Woe to the obstinate children,"
    declares the LORD,
"to those who carry out plans that
    are not mine,
    forming an alliance, but not by
        my Spirit,
    heaping sin upon sin;
who go down to Egypt
    without consulting me;
who look for help to Pharaoh's
    protection,
    to Egypt's shade for refuge."

The ridiculousness of the people of
Judah in doing this is readily apparent from what happened back at the
time of the Exodus. The Lord delivered
the Israelites—helpless slaves—out of
Egypt, destroying the horses and
chariots of Pharaoh at the Red Sea.
Why should the nation—now relatively
strong militarily—turn to its ancient
enemy and oppressor, Egypt, for help?
The Lord could and would deliver the
people again, if they would turn to
Him for help, rather than to Egypt.
The trouble was that God's people had
turned away from Him to worship
false gods, and that is why they were
threatened.

In verses 3-5 of chapter 30 the Lord
goes on to say:

"But Pharaoh's protection will be
  to your shame,
Egypt's shade will bring you
  disgrace.
Though they have officials in Zoan,
  and their envoys have arrived
    in Hanes,
everyone will be put to shame
  because of a people useless to
    them,
who bring neither help nor
  advantage,
but only shame and disgrace."

Zoan (v. 4) was evidently Tanis,
in the fertile delta of Egypt. Hanes
was perhaps between Memphis and
Thebes, although the location is somewhat uncertain. The "officials" or
"envoys" went to both places. It is
thought that Egypt was in something
of a turmoil at this time, with rival
princes in both these places. This
makes the Israelites' plea for help from
Egypt all the more unreasonable.

The Lord told His people that
everyone would be put to shame
"because of a people useless to them"
(v. 5). Rawlinson comments:

> The reference is not to the ambassa-
> dors, who felt no shame in their
> embassy . . . but to the subsequent
> feelings of the Jewish nation, when
> it was discovered by sad experience
> that no reliance was to be placed on
> "the strength of Egypt" (*PC*, Isaiah,
> 1:489).

In verses 6–8 of chapter 30 we find
"An oracle concerning the animals of
the Negev" (v. 6). The word *Negev*
means "south" and is applied today to
the southern part of Israel. But here it
seems clear that the term applies to
the desert between Palestine and
Egypt. The prophet writes in verses
6–7:

Through a land of hardship and
  distress,
of lions and lionesses,
of adders and darting snakes,
the envoys carry their riches on
  donkeys' backs,
their treasures on the humps of
  camels,

to that unprofitable nation,
  to Egypt, whose help is utterly
    useless.
Therefore I call her
  Rahab the Do-Nothing.

The picture is that of a caravan of
camels and donkeys loaded with rich
treasures to buy Egypt's support for
the expected war against Assyria.
The caravan, led by envoys from
Jerusalem, passes through the dangerous, snake-ridden desert between
Judea and Egypt. The Lord warns the
people through His prophet that the
difficult trip will be in vain. They are
carrying these hard-won riches to "that
unprofitable nation," Egypt, "whose
help is utterly useless." Time, effort,
and money are all being completely
wasted. The Lord's name for Egypt is
"Rahab the Do-Nothing." Kenneth
Jones comments:

> Since *Rahab* (strength?) was the
> name of a mythological dragon, and
> had been applied in a figurative way
> to Egypt, Isaiah mockingly calls
> that nation Rahab that sitteth still
> (. . . Smith-Goodspeed: "Rahab Sit
> Still"; Moffat: "Dragon Do-Nothing")
> (*Wesleyan Bible Commentary*, 3:88).

Ross Price carries the meaning of
"Rahab" a step further. He writes:

> "Dragon do-nothing" is the name
> Isaiah gives to Egypt. The "Rahab"
> symbol for Egypt seems to specify
> the Nile "river-horse" (*hippopotamus
> amphibius*). This huge, sluggish
> beast constitutes a fitting symbol in
> Isaiah's mind for the Empire on the
> Nile which brags and boasts, but does
> not stir from its place to help another
> (*Beacon Bible Commentary*, 4:129).

We return now to the first verse of
our printed lesson (31:1). Here the woe
is pronounced on "those who go down
to Egypt for help, who rely on horses,"
and "trust in . . . chariots, and in the
great strength of their horsemen." The
sad thing is that they "do not look to
the Holy One of Israel, or seek help
from the LORD." Jones comments:

It was easy for the people of Judah to be jealous of the horses, horsemen, and chariots of Egypt, because that country had so many and they had so few. Of course, such aids to warfare were far more suitable to the flat land of lower Egypt than to the hills of Judah; and this, together with the expense involved, led to their having so few horses and chariots. But when they were threatened by Assyria, they felt that they would be secure if they could only have the horses and chariots of Egypt on their side. Isaiah warned them that they would not find security that way (WBC, 3:92).

B. Divine Wisdom: v. 2

Yet he too is wise and can bring
       disaster;
   he does not take back his words.
He will rise up against the house
       of the wicked,
   against those who help
       evildoers.

The "he" of this verse is obviously the Lord. Rawlinson calls the first clause of this verse "Intense irony." He goes on to say: "Wisdom is not wholly confined to the human counsellors whose advice Judah follows (ch. xxix. 14). He (Jehovah) is 'wise' too, and could give prudent counsel if his advice were asked" (PC, Isaiah, 1:510).

God does not take back his words; He never has to retract what He says. Almost all human beings have to do this at times, but God never! He is infinite in both knowledge and power. He knows what to say, and He has the ability to carry out His commands and declarations.

The prophet asserts that the Lord "will rise up against the house of the wicked" (Judah) and "against those" (the Egyptians) who help evildoers. Both Judah and Egypt will suffer.

C. The Folly of Looking to Egypt: v. 3

But the Egyptians are men and
       not God;
   their horses are flesh and not
       spirit.

When the LORD stretches out his
       hand,
   he who helps will stumble,
   he who is helped will fall;
   both will perish together.

One can hardly imagine greater folly than that of the people of Judah in turning away from their omniscient "God" and seeking help from the Egyptians, who were only men. Yet how many people do that very thing today! Rawlinson comments: "Judah relied on Pharaoh, as on a sort of God, which indeed he was considered in his own country. . . . Isaiah asserts the contrary in the strongest way: the Egyptians, are men—mere men" (PC, Isaiah, 1:510).

The last part of this verse echoes and enforces what was said in the second half of the previous verse. "He who helps" (Egypt) "will stumble" and "he who is helped" (Judah) "will fall." The prophet adds, "both will perish together."

This final prediction was fulfilled in large measure by the Babylonian conquest of Judah that eventually came. And Egypt was invaded and its famous city of Thebes sacked by the Assyrians (664 B.C.).

II. THE LORD'S CARE FOR JUDAH: Isaiah 31:4-5

A. Protecting Mount Zion: v. 4

The Lord said to Isaiah:

"As a lion growls,
   a great lion over his prey—
and though a whole band of
       shepherds
   is called together against him,
he is not frightened by their
       shouts
   or disturbed by their clamor—
so the LORD Almighty will come
       down
   to do battle on Mount Zion and
       on its heights."

The first six lines of this verse describe a familiar scene for the people of that day. Rawlinson puts it this way:

> The lion has seized his prey, and is crouching over it; the shepherds gather themselves together against him, and seek to scare him away; but he remains firm, undaunted by their threats and cries, never for a moment relinquishing the body of which he has made himself the master. The image is best explained as representing Jehovah, standing over and keeping guard on Jerusalem, which he will allow no one to rend from him (*PC*, Isaiah, 1:511).

That the lion represents the Lord is indicated by the last two lines of the verse:

"so the LORD Almighty will come down
   to do battle on Mount Zion and
      on its heights."

"Mount Zion" represents Jerusalem. Regardless of what is done by anybody else, God will defend Jerusalem. This is confirmed by the next verse.

B. Shielding Jerusalem: v. 5

"Like birds hovering overhead,
   the LORD Almighty will shield
      Jerusalem;
he will shield it and deliver it,
   he will 'pass over' it and will
      rescue it."

Just as the figure of verse 4 emphasizes God's almighty power, so the one in this verse stresses His solicitous care. Price observes:

> As birds flying is meant to suggest the parent eagle hovering over the nest when its little ones are in peril, and swooping down with fury upon any who would molest them. Not only protection but deliverance is indicated. *Passing over* is the root of *pesah*, from which the word "passover" is derived (*BBC*, 4:133).

It is difficult to understand how the people of Judah could ignore God's loving words through Isaiah. Yet people do the same today.

III. A CALL FOR REPENTANCE: Isaiah 31:6-7

A. Returning to the Lord: v. 6

"Return to him you have so greatly revolted against, O Israelites."

Our key verse for today (30:15) is the best commentary on this verse in chapter 31. It reads:

"In repentance and rest is your
   salvation,
   in quietness and trust is your
      strength."

How sad that the last line of that verse has to add, "but you would have none of it."

The consequences of that spirit of refusal to repent are given in 30:16-17. But then the passage ends on a beautiful note of divine compassion and love (v. 18):

Yet the LORD longs to be gracious
   to you;
   he rises to show you compassion.
For the LORD is a God of justice.
   Blessed are all who wait for
      him!

B. Rejecting Idolatry: v. 7

"For in that day every one of you will reject the idols of silver and gold your sinful hands have made."

This promise was not fulfilled until

DISCUSSION QUESTIONS

1. Of what is Egypt always a type in the Bible?
2. To what wrong sources may we be tempted to turn for help today?
3. What applications from our lesson might be made to our nation, to our church, and to us as individuals?
4. How can we learn to rest in the Lord?
5. What is meant by "repentance"?
6. What does it mean to "trust" the Lord?

the "day" of the Babylonian captivity. In that traumatic experience the Jews were finally cured of idolatry, and they have never returned to it since.

IV. DOWNFALL OF ASSYRIA: Isaiah 31:8-9

A. Divine Judgment: v. 8

"Assyria will fall by a sword that
     is not of man;
   a sword, not of mortals, will
     devour them.
They will flee before the sword
   and their young men will be put
     to forced labor."

The fulfillment of this prediction in the destruction of the Assyrian forces is graphically told in II Kings 19:35-36. The Assyrian army camped before Jerusalem and announced its intention to take the city. But then we read:

> That night the angel of the LORD went out and put to death a hundred and eighty-five thousand men in the Assyrian camp. When the people got up the next morning—there were all the dead bodies! So Sennacherib king of Assyria broke camp and withdrew. He returned to Nineveh and stayed there.

But we read in verse 37 that Sennacherib's two sons "cut him down with the sword." So the Assyrian threat against Judah was ended. Sad to say, because of the continued disobedience of the people of Judah they were later taken into captivity by the Babylonians.

B. Divine Terror: v. 9

"Their stronghold will fall
     because of terror;
   at sight of the battle standard
     their commanders will
     panic,"
declares the LORD,
   whose fire is in Zion,
   whose furnace is in Jerusalem.

The first line of this verse suggests the fall of Nineveh, the capital and "stronghold" of the Assyrian Empire. This city did fall in 612 B.C.

The names "Zion" and "Jerusalem" are used interchangeably here, as elsewhere in the Old Testament. Regarding the "fire" and "furnace" Rawlinson has this to say:

> Jehovah was at once a Light to his people, and "a consuming fire" (Heb. xii.29) to his enemies. His presence, indicated by the Shechinah in the holy of holies, was at once for blessing and for burning (PC, Isaiah, 1:511).

We, as the people of Isaiah's day, choose which of these two God's presence will be for us. It may warm our hearts, or it may destroy us forever.

CONTEMPORARY APPLICATION

Our key verse (Isa. 30:15) expresses the main thrust of this lesson:

In repentance and rest is your
     salvation,
   in quietness and trust is your
     strength.

Spiritual salvation comes through our repenting of our sins and then resting in Jesus as our Savior. For the people of Judah in Isaiah's day it primarily meant repentance for their idolatry and disobedience, and then trusting in God's protection rather than Egypt's help. But we can apply it to our salvation from sin and also to our deliverance from any fears that may afflict us in life. If God is on our side, who can be against us?

A DAY OF JOY AND GLADNESS

DEVOTIONAL READING	Isa. 26:7-11

ADULTS AND YOUTH

Adult Topic: *A Day of Joy and Gladness*

Youth Topic: *Joy Unlimited*

Background Scripture: Isa. 35

Scripture Lesson: Isa. 35:1-6a, 8-10

Memory Verse: *The ransomed of the Lord shall return, and come to Zion with singing.* Isa. 35:10

CHILDREN

Topic: *God Promises Us Happiness*

Scripture Lesson: Isa. 35:5-6, 10

Memory Verse: *Everlasting joy shall be upon their heads; they shall obtain joy and gladness.* Isa. 35:10

DAILY BIBLE READINGS

Jan. 23 M.: Praise for Final Victory. Isa. 26:1-6
Jan. 24 T.: Prayer for a Sorrowing People. Isa. 26:7-19
Jan. 25 W.: "No Kingdom There." Isa. 34:1-12
Jan. 26 T.: "For Violence Done to Your Brother." Obad. 10-18
Jan. 27 F.: "To You Also the Cup Shall Pass." Lam. 4:18-22
Jan. 28 S.: "Remember, O Lord, . . . the Edomites." Ps. 137
Jan. 29 S.: A Glad Restoration. Isa. 34:1-10

LESSON AIM

To show that there will be a glorious future for God's people.

LESSON SETTING

Time: Eighth century B.C.

Place: Jerusalem

LESSON OUTLINE

A Day of Joy and Gladness

  I. **From Desert to Splendor:** Isaiah 35:1-2
    A. A Blossoming Wilderness: vv. 1-2a
    B. A Place of Beauty: v. 2b

  II. **Divine Salvation:** Isaiah 35:3-4
    A. Strengthening the Feeble: v. 3
    B. Saving the Fearful: v. 4

  III. **Healing for the Handicapped:** Isaiah 35:5-6a
    A. The Blind and the Deaf: v. 5
    B. The Lame and the Dumb: v. 6a

  IV. **Abundance of Water:** Isaiah 35:6b-7
    A. Streams in the Desert: v. 6b
    B. Bubbling Springs: v. 7a
    C. New Vegetation: v. 7b

V. The Way of Holiness: Isaiah 35:8-10
  A. A New Highway: v. 8a
  B. A Restricted Way: v. 8b
  C. No Dangerous Beasts: v. 9
  D. Gladness and Joy: v. 10

SUGGESTED
INTRODUCTION
FOR ADULTS

The major part of the first thirty-nine chapters of the Book of Isaiah consists of messages of judgment on the people of Judah, and particularly Jerusalem, because of their sins. But every once in awhile we find a beautiful passage of hope and promise for a splendid future. Such is the thirty-fifth chapter that we study today.

We have already seen a few of these glimpses of future glory. The first is found in 2:1-5, and it paints a very bright picture of what will happen "in the last days."

Chapter 4 presents the messianic "Branch of the LORD." Chapter 9 tells of a child to be born, who will be called (v. 6):

Wonderful Counselor, Mighty God,
Everlasting Father, Prince of Peace.

Another beautiful messianic passage is found in chapter 11, followed by songs of praise in chapter 12. Then come prophecies against foreign nations (cc. 13-21, 23, 34), with a few touches of hope, as in 30:15-18.

Today we study the "Joy of the Redeemed" (NIV heading). It is a thrilling picture of what God will do for those who repent and put their trust in Him.

SUGGESTED
INTRODUCTION
FOR YOUTH

"Joy Unlimited." That's impossible! No, not for those who are willing to pay the price of living in God's presence.

But this "Joy Unlimited" is the "Joy of the Redeemed." We must accept Christ's redemption for us, which He purchased on the cross. Then we must give Him our hearts and lives, to follow and obey Him. As we do so, we will find this joy in increasing measure. It will be limited only by our failure to live close to the Lord, in the center of His will. It costs something to experience it, but it is well worth the price.

CONCEPTS FOR
CHILDREN

1. "God Promises Us Happiness."
2. It is a joy for anyone to be restored from illness to full physical health.
3. Just so, it is a great joy to receive spiritual health when we give our hearts to Christ.
4. God wants His children to have the joy of His presence.

THE LESSON COMMENTARY

I. FROM DESERT TO SPLENDOR: Isaiah 35:1-2

A. A Blossoming Wilderness: vv. 1-2a

The desert and the parched land
    will be glad;
the wilderness will rejoice and
    blossom.
Like the crocus, it will burst into
    bloom;
it will rejoice greatly and shout
    for joy.

The previous chapter of Isaiah is filled with "Judgment Against the Nations." On the contrast between chapters 34 and 35 Kenneth Jones has this to say:

Here is another of the sudden changes with which Isaiah moves from woe to wealth, or from threat to mercy. This is one of the most dramatic. After the terrible and graphic descriptions of destruction in chapter 34, the prophet turns suddenly to the wonders awaiting the righteous. Both chapters are in the same poetic structure and have many similarities in form, which show that they were written to complement each other like two sides of a coin. Yet the beauty of the poem is most unusual. It is a masterpiece (*The Wesleyan Bible Commentary*, 3:99-100).

Judgment on sin must precede divine blessing. But the latter comes to those who repent.

The description given here doubtless had some literal fulfillment in the return of the Jews from Babylonian captivity and God's blessing on their land, which had been cursed because of their sin. But it has its largest fulfillment in the spiritual blessings that come to God's redeemed people.

Bible readers are familiar with the expression: "blossom as the rose" (v. 1, KJV). But a glance at modern versions will show that the accepted translation of the Hebrew is: "Like the crocus, it will burst into bloom" (NIV)—or, "blossom abundantly" (RSV), or "blossom profusely" (NASB). A. R. Fausset affirms: "The rose is not mentioned in the Hebrew Bible" (Robert Jamieson, A. R. Fausset, and David Brown, *A Commentary . . . on the Old and New Testaments*, 3:670). So we shall have to drop the familiar phrase as incorrect. Archaeological research has given us a far more accurate understanding of the fauna and flora of the Bible than translators had nearly four centuries ago.

The desert, parched land, and wilderness are pictured as rejoicing. It is even said that they will "rejoice greatly and shout for joy." Anyone who has seen green grass flourish again, and beautiful flowers appear, when refreshing rains come after a long, hot drought, can appreciate the language here. All nature seems to come alive with spontaneous joy.

B. A Place of Beauty: v. 2b

The glory of Lebanon will be
    given to it,
the splendor of Carmel and
    Sharon;
they will see the glory of the
    LORD,
the splendor of our God.

The name "Lebanon" has been much in the news in recent years. We know it as a country just north of Israel, sandwiched in between Syria and the Mediterranean Sea. Its capital is Beirut, once a beautiful seaport city, but now badly damaged.

In Bible times this country was called Phoenicia, with Tyre and Sidon (south of Beirut) as its main cities. The Phoenicians were the great sea-travelers of ancient times, pushing their way the full length of the Mediterranean Sea and even out into the Atlantic Ocean, forming colonies on the west coast of Africa.

But "Lebanon" here, and throughout the Bible, refers to the Lebanon Mountains, as they are now called. They were especially famous for the cedars of Lebanon, a grove of which one can still see up in the mountains. These cedar trees were especially noted for their "firmness" (the meaning of the Hebrew word used). It will be remembered that Solomon built the temple in Jerusalem of cedar wood from Lebanon (I Kings 5-10).

The cedars of Lebanon were also noted for their massive size. They can grow to a height of 120 feet, and may be thirty to forty feet in circumference.

They were especially admired for their beauty and fragrance. It is claimed that insect pests do not attack them, and so their wood has remarkable lasting qualities. The cedar of Lebanon has been called "the monarch of the evergreens." In Psalm 92:12 we read:

The righteous will flourish like a
    palm tree,
  they will grow like a cedar of
    Lebanon.

And Hosea 14:5-6 says of Israel:

Like a cedar of Lebanon
  he will send down his roots; . . .
His splendor will be like an olive
    tree,
  his fragrance like a cedar of
    Lebanon.

Our verse in Isaiah also speaks of "the splendor of Carmel and Sharon." The name "Carmel" is given to a mountain range, which almost juts out into the Mediterranean, rising above the modern seaport city of Haifa, and then stretches southeast for about thirty miles to the plain of Dothan. It varies in height from less than five hundred feet near Haifa to 1,742 feet at its highest elevation. It was famous in antiquity as the "garden with fruit trees." It was regarded as a symbol of beauty (Song of Sol. 7:5), fruitfulness (here), and majesty (Jer. 46:18).

"Sharon" was the name given to the plain that stretched along the Mediterranean from Joppa (now Jaffa-Tel Aviv) northward to Caesarea. It was about fifty miles long and ten miles wide and was known commonly as the most fertile part of Palestine. Today it is largely filled with citrus groves, so that Jaffa oranges are sold throughout Europe.

So these three terms signify beauty, fragrance, and fruitfulness. They were in a sense, symbols of "the glory of the LORD" and "the splendor of our God," which the redeemed would see at last.

II. DIVINE SALVATION: Isaiah 35:3-4

A. Strengthening the Feeble: v. 3

Strengthen the feeble hands,
  steady the knees that give way;

The people of Judah were getting weak and feeble in their hands, as shown by the fact that they were turning to Egypt for help. Their knees were tottering so they could hardly walk as a nation. The Lord told His prophet to strengthen these weak hands and steady these tottering knees.

B. Saving the Fearful: v. 4

say to those with fearful hearts,
  "Be strong, do not fear;
your God will come,
  he will come with vengeance;
with divine retribution
  he will come to save you."

At the beginning of the next chapter we are told that "Sennacherib king of Assyria attacked all the fortified cities of Judah and captured them." Then he "sent his field commander with a large army from Lachish to King Hezekiah at Jerusalem" (36:1-2). These were fearful days, and the people needed the prophet's assurance.

III. HEALING FOR THE HANDICAPPED: Isaiah 35:5-6a

A. The Blind and the Deaf: v. 5

Then will the eyes of the blind be
    opened
  and the ears of the deaf
    unstopped.

We have numerous cases of Jesus healing physically blind eyes while He was here on earth (Matt. 9:27; 12:22; 20:29-34; 21:14; and especially John 9:1-7). He also healed those who were deaf (Matt. 11:5; Mark 7:32).

B. The Lame and the Dumb: v. 6a

Then will the lame leap like a
    deer,
and the tongue of the dumb
    shout for joy.

We find Jesus healing the lame (Matt. 15:30; John 5:8), and also Peter doing it after Pentecost (Acts 3:2). As for the tongue of the dumb being healed, we see Jesus doing this too (Matt. 9:32).

Jesus told the disciples of John the Baptist: "Go back and report to John what you hear and see: The blind receive sight, the lame walk, those who have leprosy are cured, the deaf hear, the dead are raised..." (Matt. 11:4-5). These healing miracles were proofs that Jesus was the long-awaited Messiah (Matt. 11:2-3).

But these miracles also had spiritual significance. George Rawlinson comments:

Our Lord's miracles of bodily healing, performed during the three years of his earthly ministry, were types and foreshadowings of those far more precious miracles of spiritual healing, which the great Physician is ever performing on the sick and infirm of his Church, by opening the eyes of their understandings, and unstopping the deaf ears of their hearts, and loosening the strings of their tongues to hymn his praise, and stirring their paralyzed spiritual natures to active exertions in his service (*The Pulpit Commentary*, Isaiah, 1:569).

Alexander Maclaren gives an even wider spread of interpretation. He goes back to the first word of verse 5 and writes:

What is the period of that emphatic "then" at the beginning of our text?

The return of the Jews from exile? Yes, certainly; but some greater event shines through the words. Some future restoration of that undying race to their own land? Yes, possibly, again we answer, but that does not exhaust the prophecy. The great coming of God to save in the gift of His Son? Yes, that in an eminent degree. The second coming of Christ? Yes, that too. All the events in which God has come for men's deliverance are shadowed here; for in them all, the same principles are at work, and in all, similar effects have followed. But mainly the mission and work of Jesus Christ is pointed at here— whether in its first stage of Incarnation and Passion, or in its second stage of coming in glory, "the second time without sin, unto salvation" (*Expositions of Holy Scripture*, Isaiah, 1:216).

In other words, we here find symbolized Christ's great work of redeeming man from his lost condition and making him whole. Jesus is the Great Physician of both body and soul.

IV. ABUNDANCE OF WATER: Isaiah 35:6b-7

A. Streams in the Desert: v. 6b

Water will gush forth in the
    wilderness
and streams in the desert.

This promise was fulfilled particularly in the coming of Christ. He told the Samaritan woman at Jacob's Well that He could give her a spring of living water "welling up to eternal life" (John 4:14). A little later He declared, "Whoever believes in me, as the Scripture has said, streams of living water will flow from within him" (John 7:38).

B. Bubbling Springs: v. 7a

The burning sand will become a
    pool,
    the thirsty ground bubbling
    springs.

This promise was fulfilled in a beautiful way in the case of the Samaritan woman. Her life was certainly made up of "burning sand." But

Jesus put in her heart a bubbling spring of the water of life.

C. New Vegetation: v. 7b

In the haunts where jackals once
    lay,
    grass and reeds and papyrus
       will grow.

"Papyrus" is the name of a plant that still grows in the Nile River and in northern Galilee. The pith of this plant was cut into strips to form the writing material of that day, and we get our word *paper* from it.

V. THE WAY OF HOLINESS: Isaiah 35:8-10

A. A New Highway: v. 8a

And a highway will be there;
    it will be called the Way of
      Holiness.

The King James Version has: "And an highway shall be there, and a way." But commentators and translators are agreed that only one way is being spoken of. The second "and" could very well be translated "even." There is only one way to heaven: Christ said, "I am the way" (John 14:6).

On the first line of this verse Ross Price comments as follows:

This verse is the sparkling point of the entire chapter. *And an highway shall be there.* Translated freely from the Greek of the Septuagint it reads: "There shall be a clean way and it shall be called a holy way, and there shall by no means pass over there anything unclean, neither shall there be an unclean way. But the dispersed ones shall proceed upon it, and they shall in no wise be deceived [i.e., caused to err]." Paraphrasing from the Hebrew we may read it:

A stainless highroad shall
    appear,
  Its name "the Holy Way";
No unclean soul shall travel
    here.
Nor godless foot e'er stray
(*Beacon Bible Commentary,* 4:147).

Kenneth Jones makes this observation: "It is called *The way of holiness* because only the holy can walk on it. It leads not merely to Jerusalem, but eventually to the 'new Jerusalem'—the glorified Church in heaven (Rev. 21:2)" (*WBC,* 3:101).

B. A Restricted Way: v. 8b

The unclean will not journey on it;
    it will be for those who walk in
      that Way;
    wicked fools will not go about
      on it.

Since this is the Way of Holiness, it naturally follows that the unclean cannot journey on it, and so defile it. This Holy Way is only for those who are willing to walk as holy pilgrims.

The last line of this verse is translated in the King James Version: "the wayfaring men, though fools, shall not err *therein.*" Ross Price warns us that this "hardly means, 'Even simpletons cannot miss it.' The Hebrew seems to indicate that no impious heathen will travel this road" (*BBC,* 4:147).

Ross Price makes this further comment:

This is God's highway. Hence it is for the redeemed and cleansed one, not for the profane, the polluted, or the hypocrite. Nor is it intended for those who live for the world and love selfish pleasures more than this heavenly,

---

DISCUSSION QUESTIONS

1. What signs of new life can be seen in the spiritual wilderness of western countries?
2. What can the glory of Lebanon, Carmel, and Sharon mean to us?
3. How can we strengthen the feeble and fainthearted?
4. Why do we need our souls to be watered?
5. What does "the Way of Holiness" mean to us?
6. What part do joy and gladness play in our lives?

homeward way. Isaiah sets forth here the true moral quality of God's people (*BBC*, 4:148).

C. No Dangerous Beasts: v. 9

No lion will be there,
nor will any ferocious beast get up on it:
they will not be found there.
But only the redeemed will walk there,

There is safety and security for those who sincerely walk the Way of Holiness. God is with them, and no ferocious beast can attack them. We are perfectly safe in His care.

D. Gladness and Joy: v. 10

and the ransomed of the LORD will return.
They will enter Zion with singing; everlasting joy will crown their heads.

Alexander Maclaren has caught the atmosphere of this last verse. He writes:

The pilgrims do not plod wearily in silence, but, like the tribes going up to the feasts, burst out often, as they journey, into song.... The Christian life should be a joyful life, ever echoing with the "high praises of God." However difficult the march, there is good reason for song, and it helps to overcome the difficulties. "A merry heart goes all the day, a sad heart tires in a mile." Why should the ransomed pilgrims sing? For present blessings, for deliverance from the burden of self and sin, for communion with God, for light shed on the meaning of life, and for the sure anticipation of future bliss (*Expositions*, Isaiah, 1:233).

Ross Price waxes eloquent in his closing paragraph on this great chapter. He summarizes:

This is the "song of the open road" and of the holy people on their homecoming day. Let the desert rejoice! Let the fainthearted take courage! Let the ailing ones be healed! They may travel through beauty and blessing, pitch their tents by nature's luscious growth, travel the holiness highway assured of sanctity, safety, security, and singing. They are the pilgrims whom the Lord has set free indeed, all homeward bound from earth's threescore years and ten of captive sojourn! "Lord, I want to be in that number, when those saints come marching home" (*BBC*, 4:149).

CONTEMPORARY APPLICATION

Streams in the Desert. That line of this beautiful poem, Isaiah 35, has been made famous by Mrs. Charles Cowman's book with that title. She and her husband were for many years missionaries in mainland China and co-founders, with the Kilbournes, of the Oriental Missionary Society. It was my privilege to know her.

For nearly a generation China has been a "desert" and "parched land" spiritually, but now things are beginning to blossom again. House churches are springing up everywhere. Bubbling springs are appearing in the burning sand. Recently a new printing of *Streams in the Desert* was being circulated widely in China and read avidly by faithful Christians there.

I AM THE LORD

DEVOTIONAL READING	Exodus 19:1-6

ADULTS AND YOUTH

Adult Topic: *I Am the Lord*

Youth Topic: *No Other God*

Background Scripture: Isa. 43; 45

Scripture Lesson: Isa. 43:1-7

Memory Verse: *Turn to me and be saved, all the ends of the earth! For I am God, and there is no other.* Isa. 45:22

CHILDREN

Topic: *God Cares for Us*

Scripture Lesson: Isa. 43:1-3

Memory Verse: *Trust in the LORD with all your heart, and do not rely on your own insight.* Prov. 3:5

DAILY BIBLE READINGS

Jan. 30 M.: Thanksgiving for God's Care. Ps. 65:1-12
Jan. 31 T.: Fear Not; Trust God. Isa. 41:8-16
Feb. 1 W.: The New Exodus. Isa. 43:14-28
Feb. 2 T.: God's Amazing Choice. Isa. 45:1-8
Feb. 3 F.: Who Dares Deny God's Choice? Isa. 45:9-13
Feb. 4 S.: God's Invitation to All People. Isa. 45:14-25
Feb. 5 S.: God, Your Deliverer. Isa. 43:1-7

LESSON AIM

To enforce the truth that there is only one God, the Lord.

LESSON SETTING

Time: Eighth century B.C.

Place: Jerusalem

LESSON OUTLINE

I Am the Lord

   I. **The God of Israel:** Isaiah 43:1-4
     A. The Creator: v. 1a
     B. The Redeemer: v. 1b
     C. The Protector: v. 2
     D. The Savior: v. 3
     E. The Restorer: v. 4

   II. **Gathering the Scattered Children:** Isaiah 43:5-7
     A. From East and West: v. 5
     B. From North and South: v. 6a
     C. God's Own Children: vv. 6b-7

SUGGESTED INTRODUCTION FOR ADULTS

Today we begin our study of the third and last unit of this quarter. It is entitled "Themes from Isaiah 40-66."

The title of our previous unit was "Themes from Isaiah 1-39." This suggests that the Book of Isaiah has a major break between chapters 39 and 40, dividing the book into two differing parts.

Much has been made of this by liberal scholars. They claim that while Isaiah, the prophet of the eighth century B.C., may have written the first thirty-nine chapters, the rest of the book was written by someone else, a Second Isaiah. (Some even postulate a Third Isaiah.)

The main emphasis of the first thirty-nine chapters is on judgment, whereas the constantly recurring note of chapters 40-66 is comfort and promise. So these scholars claim that the second part of the book was written toward the end of the Babylonian captivity, in the sixth century B.C.

In answer to these contentions I would call attention to the fact that the divine name, "the Holy One of Israel"—found twenty-five times in Isaiah and only seven times elsewhere in the Old Testament—occurs equally in the two parts: twelve times in chapters 1-39 and thirteen times in chapters 40-66. I believe in the unity of Isaiah.

SUGGESTED INTRODUCTION FOR YOUTH

Our topic today is "No Other God." That is the main emphasis of chapters 40-46, which stress the folly of idolatry. The so-called "gods" of the pagans are only dumb, lifeless idols, that cannot see, hear, speak, or act. To worship them is the greatest folly the human mind can commit.

Instead we have as our God the Creator of the universe, the Savior from sin, the Almighty One who can care for all needs of spirit, soul, and body. We should let Him become Lord of all in our lives.

CONCEPTS FOR CHILDREN

1. "God Cares for Us."
2. We should trust God fully.
3. We should submit to God as our Lord.
4. Trust and obedience go together.

THE LESSON COMMENTARY

I. THE GOD OF ISRAEL: Isaiah 43:1-4

A. The Creator: v. 1a

But now, this is what the LORD says—
he who created you, O Jacob,
he who formed you, O Israel:

The opening words, "But now," mark a strong contrast between the closing part of chapter 42 (vv. 18-25) and the opening part of chapter 43 (vv. 1-7). In the former passage we find this description of Judah (v. 22):

But this is a people plundered and
looted,
all of them trapped in pits
or hidden away in prisons.
They have become plunder,
with no one to rescue them;
they have been made loot,
with no one to say, "Send them
back."

This sounds like a prophetic description of the Babylonian captivity. Judah is looted of its people, and no one says, "Send them back." But finally Cyrus did.

Then the prophet asks (v. 24):

Who handed Jacob over to become
      loot,
   and Israel to the plunderers?

And the answer comes:

Was it not the LORD,
   against whom we have sinned?

Chapter 42 ends on a very sad note
of judgment for the people of Judah
(v. 25):

So he poured out on them his
      burning anger,
   the violence of war.
It enveloped them in flames, yet
      they did not understand;
   it consumed them, but they did
      not take it to heart.

God's wrath against wilful sin, which
we find stressed in both the Old and
New Testaments, brought divine judgment on His people who had turned
away from Him.

"But now," in chapter 43, we find
the other side of the coin. Here we
read, "this is what the LORD says"—the
One who created Jacob and formed
Israel. Of course, God created all men,
but He especially created the children
of Israel to be His own people, enjoying
the covenants He made with Abraham,
Isaac, and Jacob.

Concerning the contrast here with
what precedes, F. Delitzsch writes:

The tone of the address is now
suddenly changed. The sudden leap
from reproach to consolation was
very significant. It gave them to
understand that no meritorious work
of their own would come in between
what Israel was and what it was to
be, but that it was God's free grace
which came to meet it (C. F. Keil and
F. Delitzsch, *Biblical Commentary
on the Old Testament*, Isaiah, 2:189).

B. The Redeemer: v. 1b

"Fear not, for I have redeemed
      you;
   I have called you by name; you
      are mine."

It has often been pointed out that
redemption is the main theme of both
the Old and New Testaments. God had
redeemed Israel from Egypt. The
Hebrew word for "redeem," *gaal*,
means "to ransom by a price paid for
delivering a captive." Its final fulfillment, of course, is in Christ.

We find here a very beautiful touch:
"I have called you by name; you are
mine." We need always to remember
that God is a person, a very loving
person! He calls us each by name and
makes us His own treasured possession.
What a privilege is ours!

Alexander Maclaren raises the
question: "What does God's calling a
man by his name imply?" He gives
this threefold answer: (1) "intimate
knowledge"; (2) "loving friendship";
(3) "designation and adaptation to
work" (*Expositions of Holy Scripture*,
Isaiah, 1:297).

George Rawlinson says this about
the four main verbs in verse 1:

An ascending series of benefits. First,
creation, like that of formless matter
out of nought; then, formation, or
putting of the formless matter into
shape; thirdly, redemption, or making them all his own; lastly, calling
them by their name, and so con-
ferring on them a proud and enviable
distinction. On this fourfold ground
God claims Israel as his own (*The
Pulpit Commentary*, Isaiah, 2:136).

The most comforting statement in
this verse is: "You are mine." Nothing
could be more precious than that!

C. The Protector: v. 2

"When you pass through the
      waters,
   I will be with you;
and when you pass through the
      rivers,
      they will not sweep over you."

We have two examples of what is
said here in the history of the Israelites:
(1) their passing through the waters of
the Red Sea with the Egyptians in hot
pursuit; (2) their crossing the Jordan

River into Canaan. In the first instance, God was with them in a remarkable way, protecting them from Pharaoh's chariots and causing the Egyptians to be drowned as the sudden inflow of water overcame them. In the second instance, the flood waters of the Jordan did "not sweep over" the Israelites. We read in Joshua 3:15-16:

> Now the Jordan is at flood stage all during harvest. Yet as soon as the priests who carried the ark reached the Jordan and their feet touched the water's edge, the water from upstream stopped flowing. It piled up in a heap a great distance away . . . , while the water flowing down to the Sea of the Arabah (the Salt Sea) was completely cut off.

It was a marvelous miracle!

The last part of verse 2 says:

> "When you walk through the fire, you will not be burned;
> the flames will not set you ablaze."

The most obvious example of this, of course, is the case of the three Hebrew youths who were thrown into the fiery furnace at the command of furious King Nebuchadnezzar. God was visibly present with them in the person of His Son (Dan. 3:25). We read: "So Shadrack, Meshach and Abednego came out of the fire. . . . the fire had not harmed their bodies, nor was a hair of their heads singed; their robes were not scorched, and there was no smell of fire on them" (Dan. 3:26-27). God will do the same for His faithful people today when they find themselves in the furnace of oppression or affliction.

The psalmist put it well when he wrote (Ps. 66:12):

> we went through fire and water, but you brought us to a place of abundance.

Trials successfully endured always leave us much richer in our spiritual experience.

D. The Savior: v. 3

> "For I am the LORD, your God,
> the Holy One of Israel, your Savior;
> I give Egypt for your ransom,
> Cush and Seba in your stead."

Again God emphasizes the fact that He is the "LORD" (Hebrew, *Yahweh*), "your God" (Hebrew, *Elohim*). And once more we find Isaiah's favorite designation, "the Holy One of Israel" (see Introduction). He also asserts that He is Israel's "Savior." This last term is emphasized in the later chapters of Isaiah, being found no less than eight times (cf. v. 11; 45:15, 21; 47:15; 49:26; 60:16; 63:8). It is no wonder that this book is sometimes called "The Gospel of Isaiah."

The Lord had certainly demonstrated that He was Israel's Savior. He had saved them from Pharaoh (Exod. 14:23-31), from Jabin (Judg. 4), from Midian (Judg. 7), from the Philistines (II Sam. 8:1), and from Sennacherib, king of Assyria (Isa. 37:36). God had abundantly and repeatedly shown Himself to be the Savior of His people. And He wants to be our Savior.

The Lord went on to say:

> "I give Egypt for your ransom,
> Cush and Seba in your stead."

"I give" is literally "I have given," or "I gave" (KJV, NASB). The reason the New International Version has "I give" is that this is the prophetic perfect of something that God has purposed and so will surely carry out, though it has not yet taken place.

The Lord said that He was giving "Egypt for your ransom." The Persian Empire finally conquered Egypt as the fulfillment of this prophecy. Also Cush and Seba were to be taken instead of Judah. As the footnote in the New International Version indicates, "Cush" means "the upper Nile region" (sometimes identified as the Sudan). The Septuagint indicates "Ethiopia" (cf. KJV, NASB margin). The identification of "Seba" is debated. Some equate it with "Sheba" and so place it in southern Arabia (see *New Bible Dictionary*, ed. J. D. Douglas, p. 1157).

Rawlinson interprets these two lines as meaning: "In my counsels I have already assigned to the Persians, as compensation for letting thee go free, the broad countries of Egypt, Ethiopia, and Seba" (*PC*, Isaiah, 2:136). It was Cyrus, king of Persia, who made the decree that the Jewish captives were free to return to their own land (Ezra 1:1-4).

E. The Restorer: v. 4

"Since you are precious and
honored in my sight,
and because I love you,
I will give men in exchange for
you,
and people in exchange for your
life."

This is a further elaboration of the previous verse. "Ransom" (v. 3) and "exchange" (v. 4) refer to the same thing—these other nations being taken over by Persia in exchange for Persia's letting Judah go free again.

Notice why the Lord said he would do this: "you are precious and honored in my sight," and "I love you." Through His covenant with Abraham, Isaac, Jacob, and David, the Lord had a special love-relationship to His chosen people.

This verse refers ultimately to God's giving of His Son in redeeming, ransoming love for all mankind, His creation. What an ungrateful world we live in! God gave His only Son and that Son shed His precious blood that all might be saved. But few accept the free offer of salvation!

II. GATHERING THE SCATTERED CHILDREN: Isaiah 43:5-7

A. From East and West: v. 5

"Do not be afraid, for I am with
you;
I will bring your children from
the east
and gather you from the west."

The first line of this verse expresses the most comforting thought that can come to any of us. We are not to be afraid because we have the divine promise: "I am with you." In a very real sense, God's presence can and will supply our every need, if we welcome and recognize that presence. He is able to care for all our needs—physical, financial, social, psychological, spiritual—as we fully obey and trust Him. We sometimes sing, "Jesus is all I need." That is true. It takes both obedience and trust to guarantee freedom from all fear, but this is the way God intended we should live. He has not promised us luxury or riches, as some have mistakenly suggested, but He has promised to supply all our needs (Phil. 4:19).

God's special promise to Judah at this time was that He would gather its scattered children from the places where they had gone, whether east or west. And He was able to keep His promise.

B. From North and South: v. 6a

"I will say to the north, 'Give
them up!'
and to the south, 'Do not hold
them back.'"

God had once commanded Pharaoh of Egypt: "Let my people go" (Exod. 5:1). For some time Pharaoh resisted that command, but finally he was compelled to let the Israelites leave his land. So it would be with the people

---

DISCUSSION QUESTIONS

1. What does it mean to be redeemed?
2. In what way are we called by Christ's name?
3. What kind of "waters" and "fire" do we have to pass through?
4. What ransom did God give for us?
5. Why does God love us?
6. Why were we created?

of Judah at the end of the Babylonian captivity and at later times.

Rawlinson writes at this point:

> The actual extent of the Jewish *diaspora* in Isaiah's day has been greatly exaggerated by some modern critics. . . . Israel had been carried captive into Mesopotamia and into Media . . . , perhaps also into other regions belonging at that time to Assyria, as Babylonia, Assyria Proper, Syria. Two hundred thousand Jews had been taken to Nineveh by Sennacherib . . . and planted probably by him in outlying portions of his dominions. But such transplantation would not carry the dispersion further than Cilicia and Cyprus towards the west, Armenia towards the north, Media towards the east, and the shores of the Persian Gulf towards the south (*PC*, Isaiah, 2:137).

On the other side of the ledger, Ross Price, writing more recently, makes this observation: "By Isaiah's time a fairly wide dispersion of the Hebrews had taken place, as archaeologists now recognize" (*BBC*, 4:180).

C. God's Own Children: vv. 6b-7

"Bring my sons from afar
and my daughters from the
ends of the earth—
everyone who is called by my
name,
whom I created for my glory,
whom I formed and made."

On the first two lines A. R. Fausset comments: "The feminine joined to the masculine expresses the complete *totality* of anything (Zech. ix.17)" (*Commentary*, 3:698). The Bible gives proper attention to women, as many passages show.

The word "Bring" here is significant. Rawlinson says:

> The nations are called upon, not merely to "let Israel go," but to conduct and escort them from the places of their abode to their own country. (On the need of such an escort, see Ezra viii.22, 31. On the actual furnishing of an escort in one case by a Persian king, see Neh. ii.7, 8.) (*PC*, Isaiah, 2:137).

It should be recognized that "the ends of the earth" did not mean in that day what it does to us—in our day of round-the-world jet travel, and live satellite television that makes Japan nearer than the house next door. The "earth" was confined pretty much to what we now call the Middle East.

Who was to be brought back home? "Everyone who is called by my name." Rawlinson observes, "The very name of 'Israel' meant 'prince of God,' or 'soldier of God,' and thus every Israelite was 'called by God's name'" (*PC*, Isaiah, 2:137).

The Lord adds:

"whom I created for my glory,
whom I formed and made."

Rawlinson comments:

> The third verb, perhaps, would be best translated, "I have perfected," or "I have completed (him)." All three acts—creation, formation, and completion—are done by God for his own glory (comp. Prov. xvi.4) (p. 137).

CONTEMPORARY APPLICATION

I can think of two contemporary applications of this lesson, especially of the last part. One would be to the return of the Jews to the Holy Land and their organization of the State of Israel—after nearly two thousand years of being scattered from their Promised Land.

The other application is to the bringing of God's children from the ends of the earth into the kingdom in the great outreach of world missions today. They are truly coming from every continent and country.

We live in exciting days. We ought to rejoice at the privilege of being alive and serving Christ.

THE SERVANT OF THE LORD

DEVOTIONAL READING	Isaiah 50:4-11
ADULTS AND YOUTH	**Adult Topic:** *The Servant of the Lord*
	Youth Topic: *Your Stand-In*
	Background Scripture: Isa. 42:1-4; 49:1-6; 50:4-11; 52:13—53:12
	Scripture Lesson: Isa. 42:1-4; 49:5-6; 53:4-6
	Memory Verse: *Behold my servant, whom I uphold, my chosen, in whom my soul delights.* Isa. 42:1
CHILDREN	**Topic:** *God Gives Us His Son*
	Scripture Lesson: Isa. 42:1, 4a
	Memory Verse: *God so loved the world that he gave his only Son.* John 3:16
DAILY BIBLE READINGS	Feb. 6 M.: In the Synagogue at Nazareth. Luke 4:16-30
	Feb. 7 T.: "The Good News of Jesus." Acts 8:26-29
	Feb. 8 W.: "Justice to the Nations." Isa. 42:1-9
	Feb. 9 T.: "Light to the Nations." Isa. 49:1-13
	Feb. 10 F.: "Set Like a Flint." Isa. 50:4-11
	Feb. 11 S.: "A Man of Sorrows." Isa. 53:1-6
	Feb. 12 S.: "An Offering for Sin." Isa. 53:7-12
LESSON AIM	To give a better understanding of the expression, "The Servant of the Lord."
LESSON SETTING	**Time:** Eighth century B.C.
	Place: Jerusalem

The Servant of the Lord

LESSON OUTLINE

   I. **The Lord's Servant:** Isaiah 42:1-4
      A. His Chosen One: v. 1a
      B. Spirit-Anointed: v. 1b
      C. A Gentle Servant: v. 2
      D. A Considerate Servant: v. 3a
      E. Establisher of Justice: vv. 3b-4

  II. **The Servant's Call:** Isaiah 42:5-6
      A. The God Who Calls: v. 5
      B. A Covenant for the People: v. 6

 III. **The Servant's Mission:** Isaiah 49:5-6
      A. Restorer of Israel: v. 5
      B. A Light for the Gentiles: v. 6

 IV. **The Humble Servant:** Isaiah 53:1-3
      A. An Unbelieving World: v. 1

B. A Root out of Dry Ground: v. 2
C. Despised and Rejected by Men: v. 3

V. **The Suffering Servant:** Isaiah 53:4-6
A. Taking Our Infirmities: v. 4
B. Punished for Our Sins: v. 5
C. Bearer of Our Iniquity: v. 6

SUGGESTED
INTRODUCTION
FOR ADULTS

Isaiah's greatest theological contribution consists of his presentation and description of "The Servant of the Lord." In chapters 42-53 we find four "Servant Songs." The first is 42:1-9, a part of which we shall be looking at in the beginning of our lesson today. The second is 49:1-13, which we shall also be glimpsing. The third is in 50:4-11, which is included in our background Scripture. The fourth song, the longest and best known, covers 52:13-53:12. We will look at this in the final part of our lesson.

Isaiah 53 is often spoken of by Christians as giving us the nearest to the New Testament revelation of the gospel that can be found anywhere in the Old Testament. It leads us unmistakably to the cross at Calvary, where Christ died for our sins. We shall note in our study how these passages in Isaiah are picked up in the New Testament and quoted at considerable length. No message from Isaiah could be more important than what we study today.

SUGGESTED
INTRODUCTION
FOR YOUTH

Our topic today is "Your Stand-In"—that is, someone who takes your place in a crucial situation. Jesus took our place on the cross. All of us have sinned (Rom. 3:23), and our consciences confirm it. "The wages of sin is death" (Rom. 6:23), so someone had to die for our sins. As the guilty ones, we were naturally appointed to that spiritual, eternal death. But Christ "stood in" for us. He took our place as the object of God's righteous judgment. He died in our stead. Our sins were placed on Him, as we see in today's lesson. Because He is infinite, His death atoned for the sins of all the human race. By believing in Him and accepting Him as our Savior, we can have all our sins forgiven. What a Savior!

CONCEPTS FOR
CHILDREN

1. "God Gives Us His Son."
2. Jesus' life was the greatest gift ever given.
3. Jesus' death expressed God's infinite love for us.
4. We should accept the gift of salvation.

THE LESSON COMMENTARY

I. THE LORD'S SERVANT: Isaiah 42:1-4

A. His Chosen One: v. 1a

"Here is my servant, whom I uphold,
my chosen one in whom I delight;"

In 41:8 the epithet "my servant" is applied by the Lord to Israel, but not so here. F. Delitzsch has an excellent discussion of this point. He writes:

But the servant of Jehovah who is presented to us here is distinct from Israel, and has so strong an individuality and such marked personal features, that the expression cannot possibly by merely a personified collective. Nor can the prophet himself be intended; for what is here affirmed of this servant of Jehovah goes infinitely beyond anything to which a prophet was ever called, or of which a man was ever capable. It must therefore be the future Christ; and this is the view taken in the Targum (C. F. Keil and F. Delitzsch, *Biblical Commentary on the Old Testament*, Isaiah, 2:174).

Jews today commonly apply all the passages in Isaiah 42–53 to Israel as the Lord's servant. But Delitzsch cites the Targum (Aramaic paraphrase) as identifying the servant with the Messiah. This was the original Jewish interpretation.

That Isaiah 42:1-4 does apply to Christ is proved conclusively by Matthew 12:15-21. Jesus had just healed a man in the synagogue on the Sabbath (Saturday). Angry at Him for doing this, "the Pharisees went out and plotted how they might kill Jesus" (v. 14). The Master withdrew but kept on healing people (vv. 15-16). Then we find the statement of the writer of this Gospel: "This was to fulfill what was spoken through the prophet Isaiah." Verses 18-21 consist of a quotation (almost verbatim) of Isaiah 42:1-4. So the Holy Spirit, through Matthew, identifies Jesus as "my servant." He alone could fulfill all that is said here in Isaiah about the servant of the Lord.

Why is it here "my servant" instead of "my Son"? A. R. Fausset observes: "'Servant' was the position assumed by the Son of God throughout His humiliation" (Robert Jamieson, A. R. Fausset, and David Brown, *A Commentary . . . on the Old and New Testaments*, 3:693).

George Rawlinson says that "my servant" means

my true and perfect servant, utterly obedient (John iv.34; Heb. iii.2); not, like Israel, my rebellious and faithless servant; not even, like my prophets, yielding an imperfect obedience (*The Pulpit Commentary*, Isaiah, 2:116-17).

Regarding "uphold" in the first line, Delitzsch says that the Hebrew verb means "to lay firm hold of and keep upright" (p. 175)—that is, "sustain." As God's Servant on earth, Jesus was continually sustained by the Father.

The Messiah is further described as "My chosen one in whom I delight." This reminds us of the words that came to Jesus from heaven at the time of His baptism: "You are my Son, whom I love; with you I am well pleased" (Mark 1:11). Christ was the Father's chosen servant to carry out the work of redemption.

B. Spirit-Anointed: v. 1b

"I will put my Spirit on him
  and he will bring justice to the
    nations."

Again we are reminded of the baptismal scene. All three synoptic Gospels say that the Holy Spirit came down on Jesus like a dove (cf. Mark 1:10). Luke records that after His temptation by the devil, "Jesus returned to Galilee in the power of the Spirit" (Luke 4:14). If Jesus needed to be anointed with the Holy Spirit for His ministry, how much more do we for ours!

Finally verse one declares, "and he will bring justice to the nations." The term "justice" has first of all a legal connotation; people go to court to secure justice. It also has a wider, moral application. Most significantly, it has a spiritual meaning, being equivalent to "righteousness." That is what Christ now brings to all who will accept it.

C. A Gentle Servant: v. 2

"He will not shout or cry out,
  or raise his voice in the streets."

Rawlinson comments:

His methods shall be quiet and gentle. He shall not seek to recommend his teaching by clamour or noisy demonstrations. There shall be a marked unobtrusiveness in all his doings (*PC*, Isaiah, 2:117).

Anyone who reads the Gospels will see how Christ fulfilled this description. One could cite, for instance, Matthew 8:4; 9:30; 12:15; 14:13; John 5:13; 6:15; 7:3, 4; 8:59; 10:40. He is the gentle Jesus.

D. A Considerate Servant: v. 3a

"A bruised reed he will not break, and a smoldering wick he will not snuff out."

Considering the figure in the first line—"a bruised reed"—Rawlinson says that "here the image represents the weak and depressed in spirit, the lowly and dejected. Christ would deal tenderly with such, not violently." With regard to the second figure—"a smoldering wick"—he writes:

Where the flame of devotion burns at all, however feebly and dimly, Messiah will take care not to quench it. Rather he will tend it, and trim it, and give it fresh oil, and cause it to burn more brightly (PC, Isaiah, 2:117).

Ross Price also puts it well: He says:

Tender pastoral care will be His course of action toward a bruised and battered humanity, burdened to the point of discouragement and death amidst life's injustices. All such He will seek to save and not destroy (Beacon Bible Commentary, 4:176).

Writing on these two lines, as quoted by Matthew, Henry Alford says that these metaphors represent "a proverbial expression for 'He will not crush the contrite heart, nor extinguish the slightest spark of repentant feeling in the sinner'" (The Greek Testament, 1:127).

E. Establisher of Justice: vv. 3b-4

"In faithfulness he will bring forth justice;
he will not falter or be discouraged
till he establishes justice on earth.
In his law the islands will put their hope."

On the first line here Rawlinson has this to say:

But with all this tenderness, . . . this allowance for the shortcomings and weaknesses of individuals, he will be uncompromising in his assertion of absolute justice and absolute truth. He will sanction nothing short of the very highest standard of moral purity and excellence (PC, Isaiah, 2:117).

The first line of verse 4 reads: "he will not falter or be discouraged." In the Hebrew this literally says, "he will not burn dimly nor be bruised." This ties it in with the first two lines of verse 3. Rawlinson comments:

He will himself show no signs of that weakness which he will compassionate in others. As a "Light" (Luke ii.32; John 1:4-9), he will burn brightly and strongly; as a Reed, or Rod, he will be firm and unbroken (PC, Isaiah, 2:117).

The second line of verse 4 carries us back to the last line of verse one. As we noted before, "justice" has its fullest meaning in "righteousness." So it could mean, as several commentators suggest, that Christ will finally establish true religion throughout the earth.

The last line of this paragraph reads, "In his law the islands will put their hope." Actually, the word "islands" occurs twelve times in chapters 40-66. It seems to equal "lands"—perhaps, especially, lands around the Mediterranean. Matthew quotes this line as, "In his name the nations will put their hope."

II. THE SERVANT'S CALL: Isaiah 42:5-6

A. The God Who Calls: v. 5

This is what God the LORD says—
he who created the heavens and stretched them out,
who spread out the earth and all that comes out of it,
who gives breath to its people,
and life to those who walk on it:

The first line here stands by itself, as indicated by the dash. Rawlinson makes this suggestion as to the reason for this:

> The entire utterance, vers. 1-4, is the utterance of God; but, as that fact is gathered by inference, not asserted, the prophet suddenly stops, and makes a new beginning. It must be made perfectly clear that the announcement of the "Servant of the Lord" and his mission are from the Almighty; and so we have the solemn announcement of the present verse (*PC*, Isaiah, 2:117).

The fact that in verses 1-4 the Lord is speaking directly is helpfully indicated by quotation marks in the New American Standard Bible and New International Version. Now the speaker is identified as "God the LORD"—the only true God and the one Lord of all the earth—and further described as He who created the heavens and spread out the earth. He is also the source of all life and breath to all His creatures.

This is a tremendous truth. As we noted in a previous lesson, Christ the Creator is also the sustaining force in the universe. Particularly, He gives breath to all animal life (including human beings), without which physical life would come to an end. We have a great God!

B. A Covenant for the People: v. 6

Now the Lord speaks again directly to His Servant:

> "I, the LORD, have called you in righteousness;
> I will take hold of your hand.
> I will keep you and will make you to be a covenant for the people and a light for the Gentiles,"

On the idea of the Lord's Servant being a covenant Rawlinson has this to say:

> The covenant between God and his people being in Christ, it is quite consistent with Hebrew usage to

transfer the term to Christ himself, in whom the covenant was, as it were, embodied. So Christ is called "our Salvation" and "our Peace," and again, "our Redemption" and "our Life." This is the ordinary tone of Hebrew poetry which rejoices in personification and embodiment (*PC*, Isaiah, 2:117).

III. THE SERVANT'S MISSION: Isaiah 49:5-6

A. Restorer of Israel: v. 5

And now the LORD says—
> he who formed me in the womb to be his servant
> to bring Jacob back to him and gather Israel to himself,
> for I am honored in the eyes of the LORD
> and my God has been my strength—

These verses are a part of the second Servant Song (see Introduction). The second line has reference to Jesus' virgin birth. He had to be "born of a woman" in order to become a human being, so that He could die for us on the cross.

The first mission of the Servant of the Lord was:

> to bring Jacob back to him and gather Israel to himself.

Both "Israel" and "Jacob" are used to represent the Israelites.

"Though Israel be not gathered" (KJV) is almost universally recognized as incorrect. As one scholar says, "It entirely spoils the symmetry of the verse." The problem was probably due to the fact that scribes often wrote from dictation, and some heard the same word one way and other another way. The correct meaning is represented in the Revised Standard Version, New American Standard Bible, and New International Version.

Jesus brought many Jews back to God during His earthly ministry, so that He was seen after His resurrection by more than five hundred believers at one time (I Cor. 15:6). So He was "honored in the eyes of the LORD."

B. A Light for the Gentiles: v. 6

God said to His servant:

"It is too small a thing for you to
be my servant
to restore the tribes of Jacob
and bring back those of Israel I
have kept.
I will also make you a light for the
Gentiles,
that you may bring my
salvation to the ends of the
earth."

The fulfillment of this verse comes in the Book of Acts and in the world missionary outreach of modern times. Jesus—who declared, "I am the light of the world" (John 8:12)—has become "a light for the Gentiles," bringing salvation "to the ends of the earth." His first task was to restore Jews to God, but that was "too small a thing" for His ultimate ministry. And so He was divinely ordained as a light to the Gentiles.

The last two lines of this verse were quoted by Paul and Barnabas at Pisidian Antioch on their first missionary journey (Acts 13:47). This marked the beginning of world missions on a large scale.

IV. THE HUMBLE SERVANT: Isaiah 53:1-3

A. An Unbelieving World: v. 1

"Who has believed our message
and to whom has the arm of the
LORD been revealed?"

This is a part of the fourth and last Servant Song (52:13-53:12). The prophet laments the rejection of the message of redeeming love by a world that refuses to listen to it. One reason the message was spurned by the Jews was that Jesus had died a disgraceful, criminal's death on the cross. Surely He was not the Son of God! He was an impostor, who made false, even blasphemous, claims. The reasons for rejecting Him are spelled out further in the next two verses.

B. A Root out of Dry Ground: v. 2

"He grew up before him like a
tender shoot,
and like a root out of dry
ground.
He had no beauty or majesty to
attract us to him,
nothing in his appearance that
we should desire him."

The King James Version says: "For he shall grow up before him as a tender plant." But all the verbs here are in the past tense. They are "perfects of prophetic certitude."

Rawlinson has a very good treatment of this verse. He says of the first line: "The Messiah will be a fresh sprout from the stump of a tree that has been felled; i.e. from the destroyed Davidic monarchy" (*PC*, Isaiah, 2:294). Concerning "out of dry ground" he comments, "Either out of the 'dry ground' of a corrupt age and nation, or out of the arid soil of humanity" (p. 294). On the third line he observes:

> It is scarcely the prophet's intention to describe the personal appearance of our Lord. What he means is that "the Servant" would have no splendid surroundings, no regal pomp nor splendour—nothing about him to attract men's eyes, or make them think him anything extraordinary (*PC*, Isaiah, 2:295).

On "no beauty" he says specifically: "The spiritual beauties of holy and sweet expression and majestic calm could only have been spiritually discerned" (*PC*, Isaiah, 2:295).

C. Despised and Rejected by Men: v. 3

"He was despised and rejected by
men,
a man of sorrows, and familiar
with suffering.
Like one from whom men hide
their faces
he was despised, and we
esteemed him not."

The word "despised" is none too strong. Anyone who reads the four Gospel accounts of Jesus' treatment in the hours of that fateful Friday would heartily agree. The attitudes and actions of Herod and his soldiers (Luke 23:11), of Pilate's soldiers (Matt. 27:27-31), and of the chief priests and others at the crucifixion (Matt. 27:39-44) all reveal something of the unbelievable depths of the depravity of unregenerated human hearts. He who was divine love incarnate was hated, despised, and beaten unmercifully.

On "man of sorrows" Rawlinson says:

> The word translated "sorrows" means also pains of any kind. But the beautiful rendering of our version may well stand, since there are many places where the word used certainly means "sorrow" and nothing else.... The "sorrows" of Jesus appear on every page of the Gospels (*PC*, Isaiah, 2:295).

And they were deeper sorrows than we will ever know!

V. THE SUFFERING SERVANT: Isaiah 53:4-6

A. Taking Our Infirmities: v. 4

"Surely he took up our infirmities
    and carried our sorrows,
yet we considered him stricken by
        God,
    smitten by him, and afflicted."

Commentators emphasize the great importance of the pronouns in the first two lines. *He* (the Servant of the Lord) took up *our* infirmities and carried *our* sorrows. Rawlinson says of Isaiah:

> Twelve times over within the space of nine verses he asserts, with the most emphatic reiteration, that all the Servant's sufferings were vicarious, borne for man, to save him from the consequences of his sins, to enable him to escape punishment (*PC*, Isaiah, 2:295).

This truth, of course, is central to the New Testament. In Matthew 20:28 we read, "the Son of Man did not come to be served, but to serve, and to give his life a ransom for many." Galatians 3:13 asserts, "Christ redeemed us from the curse of the law by becoming a curse for us." And I Peter 2:24 reads, "He himself bore our sins in his body on the tree, so that we might die to sins and live for righteousness; by his wounds you have been healed."

B. Punished for Our Sins: v. 5

"But he was pierced for our
        transgressions,
    he was crushed for our
        iniquities;
the punishment that brought us
        peace was upon him,
    and by his wounds we are
        healed."

The term "pierced" is much stronger than "wounded" (KJV). Ross Price notes:

> The Hebrew term *meholal* means pierced, transfixed, or bored through, hence nailed. Nailed for our *pesha'*, *transgressions*, which were really rebellions. Hence, "He was pierced on account of our rebellions." The pain was *His*, in consequence of the sin that was *ours*. Rebellion is the primary element in all human sin. *Bruised for our iniquities* indicates that the Redeemer was shattered for our "inborn crookedness." The

---

DISCUSSION QUESTIONS

1. How did the Holy Spirit function in Jesus' life?
2. How should He function in our lives?
3. Why did Jesus not "raise his voice"?
4. How can we be "a light to the nations"?
5. Why do people not believe the gospel message?
6. What do we mean by the vicarious atonement?

Hebrew, *medhukkah*, means utterly crushed or shattered, and *awonoth* means not only "iniquities" but "twisted and perverted crookedness." The sin principle is basically an incorrigible perversity (*BBC*, 4:224).

All Christ did was for us. How undeserving we are, and how grateful we should be!

C. Bearer of Our Iniquity: v. 6

"We all, like sheep, have gone
       astray,
   each of us has turned to his own
       way;
and the LORD has laid on him
   the iniquity of us all."

Alexander Maclaren catches the spirit of this verse. He writes:

The sad picture of humanity painted in that simile of a scattered flock lays stress on the universality of transgression, on its divisive effect, on the solitude of sin, and on its essential characteristic as being self-willed rejection of control. But the isolation caused by transgression is blessedly counteracted by the concentration of the sin of all on the Servant. Men fighting for their own hand, and living at their own pleasure, are working to the disruption of all the sweet bonds of fellowship. But God, in knitting together all the black burdens into one, and loading the Servant with that tremendous weight, is preparing for the establishment of a more blessed unity, in experience of the healing brought about by His Sufferings (*Expositions of Holy Scripture*, Isaiah, 2:101).

CONTEMPORARY APPLICATION

The picture of Jesus not breaking a bruised reed or snuffing out a smoldering wick carries a lesson for us as Christians. We tend to become impatient with those who show little evidence of vital spiritual life and growth. We are tempted to cast them aside as hopeless.

But Jesus' example bids us strengthen the bruised reed and encourage the flickering lamp. "Where there's life, there's hope." It's sad to think of souls suffering because of our inattention or pessimism. Let's try to do better!

COME TO THE FEAST

DEVOTIONAL READING	Isaiah 56:1-8

ADULTS AND YOUTH

Adult Topic: *Come to the Feast*

Youth Topic: *A New Kind of Satisfaction*

Background Scripture: Isa. 55

Scripture Lesson: Isa. 55:1-3, 6-11

Memory Verse: *Seek the Lord while he may be found, call upon him while he is near.* Isa. 55:6

CHILDREN | **Topic:** *God Offers Love*

DAILY BIBLE READINGS

Feb. 13 M.: God's Unfailing Love. Isa. 54:1-10
Feb. 14 T.: "The Lord Reigns." Ps. 93:1-5
Feb. 15 W.: Praise to the King and Judge. Ps. 98:1-9
Feb. 16 T.: The Heavenly Banquet. John 6:32-41
Feb. 17 F.: "Hold Fast to My Covenant." Isa. 56:1-8
Feb. 18 S.: Invitation to the Covenant. Isa. 55:1-5
Feb. 19 S.: Invitation to Repentance. Isa. 55:6-13

LESSON AIM | To increase our appreciation for the offer of free salvation as God's gift to man.

LESSON SETTING

Time: Eighth century B.C.

Place: Jerusalem

LESSON OUTLINE

Come to the Feast

I. **Invitation to the Feast:** Isaiah 55:1-3
   A. No Cost: v. 1
   B. The Best Food: v. 2
   C. An Everlasting Covenant: v. 3

II. **A New Leader:** Isaiah 55:4-5
   A. A Commander of the Peoples: v. 4
   B. Endowed with Splendor: v. 5

III. **A Call to Repentance:** Isaiah 55:6-7
   A. Seek the Lord: v. 6
   B. Forsake Evil: v. 7

IV. **The Higher Way:** Isaiah 55:8-9
   A. The Divine Versus the Human: v. 8
   B. Infinitely Higher: v. 9

V. **God's Unfailing Word:** Isaiah 55:10-11
   A. Like Rain and Snow: v. 10
   B. Accomplishing Its Purpose: v. 11

Chapter 55 of Isaiah is in striking contrast to chapter 53, which we studied last week. There we looked at the horrible sufferings that the Servant of the Lord must go through in order to purchase our salvation. Here we find the gracious offer of that salvation, free of charge. No money can buy it. But Christ has paid the price for it, and so we are invited to come and receive it freely from His hand.

In between lies chapter 54. Here we find depicted the future glory of God's people. They are urged to enlarge their habitation, "for you will spread out to the right and to the left" (v. 3). God will take away their former shame and disgrace (v. 4). Now, "your Maker is your husband" and "the Holy One of Israel is your Redeemer" (v. 5). The Lord promises never to remove His covenant of peace from them (vv. 9-10).

"O afflicted city" (v. 11) is Jerusalem. It is to enjoy future splendor (vv. 11-15). The complete fulfillment will come in the new Jerusalem that we read about in Revelation (c. 21).

Today we study about "A New Kind of Satisfaction." Every person wants satisfaction, but how can he get it?

Unfortunately, most young people seek satisfaction in pleasure, in the things of the world. But anyone who takes that route finds out ultimately that it leads to nowhere. As we are admonished in this lesson, why spend money and labor "on what does not satisfy"?

Man is spirit, as well as body. And the human spirit can be satisfied only with spiritual blessings. These we find in Christ, who offers them freely to us. The smart thing to do is to give ourselves to Him, and so let Him give Himself to us. It is true: only Jesus satisfies.

1. "God Offers Love" to all of us.
2. The best things in life cannot be bought with money.
3. We should accept God's love, and then show it toward others.
4. God loves and cares for children.

THE LESSON COMMENTARY

I. INVITATION TO THE FEAST: Isaiah 55:1-3

A. No Cost: v. 1

"Come, all you who are thirsty,
   come to the waters;
and you who have no money,
   come, buy and eat!
Come, buy wine and milk
   without money and without
      cost."

In chapter 53, which we studied last week, we saw the provisions for our salvation in the sufferings and death of our Lord Jesus, the Servant of the Lord. Today we have the invitation to come and accept that salvation as a free gift from God.

The words of the first line here remind us of the fourth Beatitude:

Blessed are those who hunger and
   thirst for righteousness,
for they will be filled (Matt. 5:6).

They are thirsty, hungry souls who are ready to receive God's blessings.

Alexander Maclaren writes:

> Who are invited? There are but two conditions expressed in verse 1, and these are fulfilled in every soul. All are summoned who are thirsty and penniless. If we have in our souls desires that all the broken cisterns of earth can never slake—and we all have these—and if we have nothing by which we can procure what will still the gnawing hunger and burning thirst of our souls—and none of us has—then we are included in the call (*Expositions of Holy Scripture,* Isaiah, 2:135).

The term "waters" perhaps suggests abundance of supply. And water is the most basic physical need we have. One can go without food for some time, but not long without water. So "waters" represents our fundamental spiritual need.

The call to the thirsty here reminds us of what Jesus did on the last day of the Feast of Tabernacles. He said "in a loud voice," so all could hear, "If a man is thirsty, let him come to me and drink" (John 7:38). Jesus probably had these words of Isaiah in mind when He gave that gracious invitation.

The call is universal. We read, "Come, all you who are thirsty." Ross Price comments: "It is that grand word 'Whosoever,' sounded centuries later by the Saviour of the world (John 3:16)" (*Beacon Bible Commentary,* 4:232).

Not only is water offered here, but wine and milk. Price observes: "*Water* in Isaiah's prophecy is always a symbol of God's presence in the world. *Water* is for thirst (Ps. 42:2). *Milk* is for strengthening and growth (1 Pet. 2:2). *Wine* is for rejoicing and happiness (Zech. 10:7; Matt. 26:29)" (*BBC,* 4:232). F. Delitzsch puts it a bit differently. He says that water, wine, and milk are "figurative representations of spiritual revival, recreation, and nourishment (cf. 1 Pet. ii.2, 'the sincere milk of the word')" (C. F. Keil and F. Delitzsch, *Biblical Commentary on the Old Testament,* Isaiah, 2:353).

The thirsty ones are invited to buy wine and milk "without money and without cost." Price comments:

> God's provision is *free.* . . . The humble seeker comes in self renunciation, saying: 'Nothing in my hand I bring; simply to Thy cross I cling.' In simple self-surrender he accepts the blessing. The best gifts of life cannot be earned by labor nor purchased with money. The simple requirement is a hungering and a thirsting after righteousness (*BBC,* 4:232).

God's spiritual gifts to us have to be free, for no amount of money could possibly buy them. Job declared that "the price of wisdom is beyond rubies" (Job 28:18).

Maclaren asserts: "All that any man needs or desires is to be found in Christ" (*Expositions,* Isaiah, 2:135). Then he raises the question, "How does He become ours?" To that question he gives this answer:

> The paradox of buying with what is not money is meant, by its very appearance of contradiction, to put in strongest fashion that the possession of Him depends on nothing in us but the sense of need and the willingness to accept. We buy Christ when we part with self, which is all that we have, in order to win Him. We must be full of conscious emptiness and desire, if we are to be filled with His fulness. Jesus interpreted the meaning of "come to the waters" when He said, "He that cometh to Me shall never hunger, and he that believeth on Me shall never thirst." Faith is coming, faith is drinking, faith is buying (2:136).

Christ not only gave Himself *for* us, on the cross, but He wants to give Himself *to* us. To accept Him is the greatest decision any person can make.

B. The Best Food: v. 2

"Why spend money on what is not bread,
  and your labor on what does not satisfy?

Listen, listen to me, and eat what
is good,
and your soul will delight in the
richest of fare."

George Rawlinson says that the
expression "for that which is not
bread" (KJV) means "for that which
has no real value—which cannot sustain you, which will do you no good"
(*The Pulpit Commentary*, Isaiah, 2:329).
On "hearken diligently unto me" he
comments: "rather, *hearken, oh, heark-
en unto me*. The phrase is one of earnest
exhortation. It implies the strong dis-
inclination of Israel to listen, and seeks
to overcome it" (2:329). That is why
the New International Version has:
"Listen, listen to me."

Why should we spend labor on what
does not satisfy? James D. Smart
declares:

> Men are always willing to spend some
> time and money on religion if they
> think that through it they can secure
> the things they want. But the water
> of life and the bread of life cannot be
> purchased or earned by any human
> effort. They have to be accepted as
> gifts that put one evermore in debt
> to God, gifts that one can never
> deserve, because in giving them God
> gives himself, and in receiving them
> man receives God himself, the sov-
> ereign God, to be the center of his
> life (*History and Theology in Second
> Isaiah*, p. 221).

To those who "eat what is good," the
food that Christ gives us, the promise
is: "and your soul will delight in the
richest of fare." Rawlinson comments:

> The spiritual blessings of the Messi-
> anic kingdom are richer dainties
> than any that this world has to offer.
> The soul that obtains them "delights"
> in them, and is satisfied with them
> (*PC*, Isaiah, 2:329).

The psalmist wrote (Ps. 34:8), "Taste
and see that the LORD is good."
Everyone who has heeded this exhortation has found that its promise is
true. There is nothing sweeter in this
world than the sense of God's presence.
It satisfies the deepest desires of our
hearts and fills us with a "deli-
cious," delightful sense of complete
satisfaction.

C. An Everlasting Covenant: v. 3

"Give ear and come to me;
hear me, that your soul may
live.
I will make an everlasting
covenant with you,
my unfailing kindnesses
promised to David."

Again, for the fourth time, we hear
the gracious voice of God saying,
"Come." We are reminded of Jesus'
beautiful invitation: "Come to me, all
you who are weary and burdened, and
I will give you rest" (Matt. 11:28). Those
who accept the invitation find rest and
satisfaction. Those who refuse it only
hurt themselves by doing so. Only those
who "hear" can have their souls really
"live."

Then God promises, "I will make
an everlasting covenant with you." Last
quarter, on October 30, we studied
"God's Gracious Covenant." As there,
so here, the reference is to the "new
covenant" that God makes with us in
Christ.

Regarding the last line of this verse
Rawlinson writes:

> The "sure mercies of David" are the
> loving and merciful promises which
> God made to him. These included
> the promise that the Messiah should
> come of his seed, and sit on his throne,
> and establish an everlasting king-
> dom (Ps. lxxxix.2-5, 19-37), and
> triumph over death and hell (Ps.
> xvi.9, 10), and give peace and happi-
> ness to Israel (Ps. cxxxii.15-18). The
> promises to David, rightly under-
> stood, involve all the essential points
> of the Christian covenant (*PC*, Isaiah,
> 2:329).

II. A NEW LEADER:
Isaiah 55:4-5

A. A Commander of the Peoples:
v. 4

"See I have made him a witness to
the peoples,
a leader and commander of the
peoples."

The pronoun "him" would seem naturally to refer to David. But we would agree with Rawlinson when he affirms that "the Messiah is intended." He goes on to say:

> It is certainly difficult to see how the historical David could be, at this time and in the future, a "leader and commander to the peoples" who were about to flock into the Messianic kingdom (*PC*, Isaiah, 2:330).

But Christ was "witness" and "leader" and "commander" in the fullest sense.

B. Endowed with Splendor: v. 5

"Surely you will summon nations
  you know not,
and nations that do not know
  you will hasten to you,
because of the LORD your God,
  the Holy One of Israel,
  for he has endowed you with
    splendor."

Rawlinson comments:

> The great cause of the attraction will be the "glory" which God the Father has bestowed upon his Son, by raising him from the dead, and exalting him to a seat at his right hand in heaven (Acts ii.32-35; iii.13-15)(*PC*, Isaiah, 2:330).

III. A CALL TO REPENTANCE: Isaiah 55:6-7

A. Seek the Lord: v. 6

Seek the LORD while he may be
  found;
  call on him while he is near.

Isaiah is fond of double imperatives, which have occurred dozens of times in the passages we have been studying. So now we have here: "Seek . . . call." We are to seek while the Lord may be found and call on Him while He is near. Ross Price comments:

> God is not always providentially available, not because He is unwilling and unconcerned, but simply because the hinges on the door of salvation

are providential circumstances. We may as well recognize the fact that at some times it is easier to find the Lord than it is at others. *While he may be found* is spoken to remind us that divine grace is no excuse for human complacency (Ps. 95:7-9; Rom. 6:1; Heb. 3:7-19). *While he is near* is the time when the human soul is psychologically sensing His presence, and hearing the summons to salvation (BBC, 4:234).

The time to seek the Lord is when the Holy Spirit is pleading with us. Only He can lead us to God.

B. Forsake Evil: v. 7

Let the wicked forsake his way
  and the evil man his thoughts.
Let him turn to the LORD, and he
  will have mercy on him
and to our God, for he will
  freely pardon.

It seems obvious that "his way" refers more to the outward life and "his thoughts" more to the inner life. Many people think they are getting by because they are careful how they conduct themselves in public. But if they entertain evil thoughts, these are recorded in God's books, and they are sinners in His sight. If we are going to get by with God we must avoid evil thoughts as surely as wicked ways. Psalm 94:11 says:

The LORD knows the thoughts of
  man;
  he knows that they are futile.

The Lord will have mercy on those who turn to Him, and God will "freely pardon"—literally, "multiply to pardon"—those who turn to Him. Here we have true repentance rewarded by a full and free pardon. Psalm 130:7 declares:

for with the LORD is unfailing
  love
and with him is full redemption.

IV. THE HIGHER WAY:
Isaiah 55:8-9

A. The Divine Versus the Human: v. 8

"For my thoughts are not your
thoughts,
neither are your ways my ways,"
        declares the LORD.

Rawlinson comments:

Though man is made in God's image
(Gen. 1:27), yet the nature of God in
every way infinitely transcends that
of man. Both the thoughts and the
acts of God surpass man's understanding. Men find it hard to pardon
those who have offended them; God
can pardon, and "pardon abundantly"
(*PC*, Isaiah, 2:330).

Maclaren has some good observations on this subject. He writes:

Notice the profound truth here in
regard to the essential and deepest
evil of all our evil. "*Your* thoughts";
"*your* ways"—self dependence, and
self-confidence are the master evils
of humanity. And every sin is at
bottom the result of saying—"I will
not conform myself to God, but I am
going to please myself, and take my
own way." My own way is never God's
way; my own way is always the
devil's way. And the root of all sin
lies in these two strong, simple words,
"*Your* thoughts are not Mine; *your*
ways not Mine" (*Expositions*, Isaiah,
2:156).

B. Infinitely Higher: v. 9

"As the heavens are higher than
the earth,
so are my ways higher than
your ways
and my thoughts than your
thoughts."

In view of the mention of repentance
and pardon in the immediately preceding verses (6, 7), Maclaren suggests:
"*The* special 'thought' and 'way' which
is meant here is God's thought and way
about sin" (*Expositions*, Isaiah, 2:158).
He then goes on to say, "There are three

points here on which I would touch for
a moment." The first is: "God's way of
dealing with sin is lifted above all
human example" (2:158). Maclaren
declares that "all the forgiveness of
the most placable and long-suffering
and gladly pardoning of men is but as
earth to heaven compared with the
greatness of His" (2:158).

The second point Maclaren makes
is: "God's way of dealing with sin sur-
passes all our thought" (*Expositions*,
Isaiah, 2:159). The mystery of divine
forgiveness is solved in Jesus Christ
and in Him alone.

The third point is: "God's way of
dealing with sin is the very highest
point of His self-revelation" (*Expositions*, Isaiah, 2:160). He not only
pardons but purifies. He completely
takes care of the sin problem for those
who will let Him.

V. GOD'S UNFAILING WORD:
Isaiah 55:10-11

A. Like Rain and Snow: v. 10

"As the rain and the snow
come down from heaven,
and do not return to it
without watering the earth
and making it bud and flourish,
so that it yields seed for the
sower and bread for the
eater,"

Ross Price comments: "Nothing
grows on earth without *rain* from
above. This verse includes almost every

DISCUSSION QUESTIONS

1. In what way are people
"thirsty"?
2. What are people receiving for
their money these days?
3. Why can only God satisfy the
human heart?
4. What is God's "everlasting
covenant"?
5. What is true repentance?
6. In what ways are God's thoughts
higher than our thoughts?

element in Jesus' parables of agriculture (especially that of the soils)" (*BBC*, 4:236). In line with this E. H. Plumptre writes:

> The "rain" and the "dew" are the gracious influences that prepare the heart; the seed is the Divine Word, the sower is the Servant of the Lord, i.e., the Son of Man (Matt. 13:37); the "bread" the fruits of holiness that in their turn sustain the life of others (*Ellicott's Commentary on the Whole Bible*, The Book of the Prophet Isaiah, *ad.loc.*).

"Snow" has been called the poor man's fertilizer. There was not much snow in Palestine, but what did come was important for the crops.

B. Accomplishing Its Purpose: v. 11

"so is my word that goes out from
    my mouth:
It will not return to me empty,
but will accomplish what I desire
    and achieve the purpose for
      which I sent it."

Rawlinson observes: "God's word is creative. With the utterance the result is achieved" (*PC*, Isaiah, 2:330). The great example of this is: "And God said, 'Let there be light,' and there was light" (Gen. 1:3). This is echoed by the psalmist (Ps. 33:6):

By the word of the LORD were the
    heavens made,
  their starry host by the breath
    of his mouth.

Also in Psalm 148:5 we read:

Let them praise the name of the
    Lord,
  for he commanded and they
    were created.

The Lord declares that His word "will not return to me empty." Instead it accomplishes what He desires and achieves the purpose for which He sent it.

This should encourage us as we give out God's Word in various ways. No Word of His is without power. The Holy Spirit can take the Word home to hearts with convicting force that will accomplish the divine purpose.

CONTEMPORARY APPLICATION

Our key verse for today (Isa. 55:6) is very important:

Seek the LORD while he may be
    found;
  call on him while he is near.

We are apt to quote this as a warning to sinners not to put off their repentance and their acceptance of Jesus Christ as Savior. And this is unquestionably the main application of this verse.

But this verse also has a message for us as Christians. We should seek to create in our church services and in our personal contacts a setting in which the Lord "may be found" by those who need him. Especially we should pray and plan that the Lord's presence will be so graciously felt in our church services that the unsaved will feel He is "near" and they will be drawn to Him.

THE SERVICE GOD SEEKS

DEVOTIONAL READING	Isaiah 59:9-15
ADULTS AND YOUTH	**Adult Topic:** *The Service God Seeks*
	Youth Topic: *Lend a Hand*
	Background Scripture: Isa. 58-59
	Scripture Lesson: Isa. 58:5-11
	Memory Verse: *He has showed you, O man, what is good; and what does the Lord require of you but to do justice, and to love kindness, and to walk humbly with your God?* Mic. 6:8
CHILDREN	**Topic:** *God Wants Us to Love Others*
	Scripture Lesson: Isa. 58:5-7, 10-11

DAILY BIBLE READINGS

Feb. 20 M.: Who Can Be God's Guest? Ps. 15:1-5
Feb. 21 T.: God, the King of Glory. Ps. 24:1-10
Feb. 22 W.: Condemnation of Corrupt Leaders. Isa. 57:9—58:2
Feb. 23 T.: Crimes of Corrupt Leaders. Isa. 57:3-13
Feb. 24 F.: God's Promise to the Contrite. Isa. 57:14-21
Feb. 25 S.: "Is Such the Fast . . . I Choose?" Isa. 58:1-5
Feb. 26 S.: "If You Take Away . . . the Yoke." Isa. 58:6-14

LESSON AIM   To show us the nature of true religion.

LESSON SETTING

Time: Eighth century B.C.

Place: Jerusalem

LESSON OUTLINE

The Service God Seeks

I. **A Rebellious People:** Isaiah 58:1-3a
   A. Divine Declaration: v. 1
   B. False Profession: v. 2
   C. People's Complaint: v. 3a

II. **Wrong Kind of Fasting:** Isaiah 58:3b-5
   A. Exploitation of Workers: v. 3b
   B. Quarreling and Strife: v. 4
   C. False Humility: v. 5

III. **Right Kind of Fasting:** Isaiah 58:6-7
   A. Justice and Mercy: v. 6
   B. Kindness to the Needy: v. 7

IV. **Divine Blessing:** Isaiah 58:8-11
   A. Healing: v. 8
   B. God's Presence: v. 9a
   C. Light Instead of Darkness: vv. 9b-10
   D. Divine Guidance: v. 11

SUGGESTED
INTRODUCTION
FOR ADULTS

Today we complete thirteen weeks of studies in Isaiah. We spent four weeks on "The Messianic Hope"—which, incidentally, crops up all through the Book of Isaiah. Then we had five lessons on "Themes from Isaiah 1-39." Now we are finishing four lessons on "Themes from Isaiah 40-66." We have seen that Yahweh, Israel's Lord, is the only true God; that the Messiah would come as "The Servant of the Lord," to provide redemption for the human race; that, as a result of His sacrificial death for us, we are all invited to the wonderful feast of salvation.

In today's lesson we look at "The Service God Seeks." A clear distinction is made between false religion—formal, ceremonial, outer, insincere—and true religion: spiritual, moral, inner, sincere. The service that God seeks comes from the heart. It is a service of love, not of empty profession. It is concern for others, not just for oneself. The emphases we see here are needed today just as much as in the time of Isaiah.

SUGGESTED
INTRODUCTION
FOR YOUTH

"Lend a Hand." That's what God did for us when we were helpless and hopeless in our sins. He reached down from heaven with a loving hand of redeeming love, in the person of His Son, and lifted us "out of the miry pit."

Now He says to us: "That's what I want you to do for others who need *your* help." All around us are people who are hurting, struggling, crying for help. If we have God's love in our hearts, we will reach out a hand of love to lift those in need.

Jesus said to His disciples: "Freely you have received, freely give" (Matt. 10:8). That is a challenge to us for a life of loving, sometimes sacrificial, service to others. And this kind of service has rich rewards, both here and hereafter.

CONCEPTS FOR
CHILDREN

1. "God Wants Us to Love Others."
2. We should always be kind and helpful.
3. Even as children, we must choose between right and wrong.
4. Choosing the right way makes us happy.

THE LESSON COMMENTARY

I. A REBELLIOUS PEOPLE: Isaiah 58:1-3a

A. Divine Declaration: v. 1

"Shout it aloud, do not hold back.
  Raise your voice like a trumpet.
Declare to my people their
    rebellion
  and to the house of Jacob their
    sins."

"Shout it aloud" is literally "cry from the throat." The Lord wanted His prophet to shout to get the attention of the people, for He had a crucial message to give to His people, a warning that they were rebellious, and needed to repent.

To make it doubly emphatic, the Lord added, "Raise your voice like a trumpet." The trumpet was used to sound an alarm, like our modern sirens. Similarly the Lord said to Hosea: "Put the trumpet to your lips!" (Hos. 8:1). And to Joel He gave the command (2:1):

> Blow the trumpet in Zion;
>   sound the alarm on my holy hill.

The Lord also told His prophet (line 1): "Do not hold back." Ross Price comments: "Unceasingly and without restraint must come this loud call that penetrates marrow and bone as it were. Intrenched perversity calls for dynamic and radical exposure if men are to be convicted and repent" (*Beacon Bible Commentary,* 4:245).

The Lord went on to say, "Declare to my people their rebellion." The Hebrew word for "rebellion" is *pasha,* which Price says "has reference to trespasses and acts of rebellion, covenant breaking, and the like" (*BBC,* 4:245). Delitzsch translates it as "apostasy" (C. F. Keil and F. Delitzsch, *Biblical Commentary on the Old Testament,* Isaiah, 2:384). The Hebrew word for "sins" (next line) is *chatta,* which means "missing the mark"—the same as the most common Greek word for "sin" in the New Testament, *hamartia.* This is a comprehensive term, which in a sense covers all sins—missing the mark of God's will for us.

Concerning "my people" (line 3), A. R. Fausset says that it means "the Jews in Isaiah's time and again in the time of our Lord, more zealous for externals than for inward holiness" (Robert Jamieson, A. R. Fausset, and David Brown, *A Commentary . . . on the Old and New Testaments,* 3:743). This has always been the bane of formal religion.

B. False Profession: v. 2

> "For day after day they seek me out;
>   they seem eager to know my ways,
> as if they were a nation that does what is right
>   and has not forsaken the commands of its God."

Ross Price observes, "Religiosity may become a substitute for spirituality" (*BBC,* 4:245). This was true in Isaiah's time, and it is sadly true today.

C. People's Complaint: v. 3a

> "'Why have we fasted,' they say,
>   and you have not seen it?
> Why have we humbled ourselves,
>   and you have not noticed?'"

The only fast prescribed in the law was the Day of Atonement (Lev. 16:29-31), known today by its Hebrew name, Yom Kippur. This is the main Jewish religious day in the fall each year. But in Zechariah 8:19 we read of "The fasts of the fourth, fifth, seventh and tenth months," commemorating calamities such as the beginning of the siege of Jerusalem, its capture, its destruction, and the murder of Gedaliah (see Keil and Delitzsch, p. 385). In addition to this, we find that the Pharisees of Jesus' day went much further, fasting twice every week (Luke 18:12). Fasting had become a very important part of religion.

II. WRONG KIND OF FASTING: Isaiah 58:3b-5

A. Exploitation of Workers: v. 3b

The Lord began His answer to the people's complaint by saying:

> "Yet on the day of your fasting,
>   you do as you please
>   and exploit all your workers."

"You do as you please" seems to catch the correct meaning better than "ye find pleasure" (KJV). Fausset suggests that the Hebrew *cheephetz* "must be taken as we sometimes use 'your pleasure'—i.e., *your own will* or *desire*" (*Commentary,* 3:743). Delitzsch translates the clause: "Ye carry on your business" (*Commentary,* Isaiah, 2:385). On the Day of Atonement no work was to be done (Lev. 16:29). "The true reason for fasting is prayer, meditation, and penitence" (Price, *BBC,* 4:246). But these hypocrites were using their fast days as work days, for selfish gain. The New American Standard Bible translates the last line: "And drive hard all your workers." George Rawlinson paraphrases it: "require of your servants and subordinates all the services they have to render on other days."

B. Quarreling and Strife: v. 4

"Your fasting ends in quarreling
    and strife,
    and in striking each other with
        wicked fists."

Delitzsch says that "when fasting they are doubly irritable and ill-tempered; this leads to quarrelling and strife, and even to striking with angry fists" (*Commentary*, Isaiah, 2:386). He goes on to say:

> Whilst the people on the fast-day are carrying on their worldly, selfish, everyday business, the fasting is perverted from a means of divine worship and absorption in the spiritual character of the day to the most thoroughly selfish purposes: it is supposed to be of some worth and to merit some reward (2:386).

Delitzsch describes their attitude as "This work-holy delusion, behind which self-righteousness and unrighteousness were concealed" (2:387).

C. False Humility: v. 5

"Is this the kind of fast I have
    chosen,
    only a day for a man to humble
        himself?
Is it only for bowing one's head
    like a reed
    and for lying on sackcloth and
        ashes?
Is that what you call a fast,
    a day acceptable to the LORD?"

Jesus dealt with this question in His Sermon on the Mount. He told His disciples:

> "When you fast, do not look somber as the hypocrites do, for they disfigure

their faces to show men they are fasting. I tell you the truth, they have received their reward in full. But when you fast, put oil on your head and wash your face, so that it will not be obvious to men that you are fasting, but only to your Father, who is unseen; and your Father, who sees what is done in secret, will reward you" (Matt. 6:16-18).

Fausset comments on this verse in Isaiah: "The *pain* felt by abstinence is not the *end* to be sought, as if it were meritorious; it is of value only so far as it leads us to amend our ways (vv. 6, 7)" (*Commentary*, 3:744).

Fasting is intended only as an aid to earnest, uninterrupted prayer. This is illustrated in Acts 13:2-3, which marked the beginning of the great world mission enterprise. Because these church leaders at Antioch were waiting on the Lord in prayer and fasting, the Holy Spirit was able to speak to them clearly and call the first missionaries.

Fasting for effect, to impress others with our piety, is sheer hypocrisy. Fasting as an aid to soul-searching prayer may be fruitful.

III. RIGHT KIND OF FASTING: Isaiah 58:6-7

A. Justice and Mercy: v. 6

"Is not this the kind of fasting I
    have chosen:
to loose the chains of injustice
    and untie the cords of the yoke,
to set the oppressed free
    and break every yoke?"

When the Babylonian army was on the verge of taking Jerusalem, Zedekiah king of Judah made a covenant with all the people in Jerusalem to free their Hebrew slaves; "no one was to hold a fellow Jew in bondage" (Jer. 34:9). "They agreed, and set them free. But afterward they changed their minds and took back the slaves they had freed and enslaved them again" (vv. 10-11).

Through His prophet the Lord

reminded the people that at Sinai He made a covenant with the Israelites that included this stipulation: "Every seventh year each of you must free any fellow Hebrew who has sold himself to you. After he has served you six years, you must let him go free" (v. 14). The Israelites had disobeyed this command, and clearly this sin was being committed in the time of Isaiah. The people were ostentatiously having their fast days, but disobeying God's command. Now He tells them to "untie the cords of the yoke."

B. Kindness to the Needy: v. 7

"Is it not to share your food with
    the hungry
  and to provide the poor
      wanderer with shelter—
when you see the naked, to clothe
    him,
  and not to turn away from your
    own flesh and blood?"

Rawlinson makes this observation: "Days of religious observance, even under the Law, were always intended to be days of kindly forbearance toward the poor, of the remission of burdens, or even of actual giving of relief" (PC, Isaiah, 2:373). But the people of Judah in Isaiah's time were failing miserably at this point. Selfishness was the order of the day. God's love showing itself toward the needy was missing.

What Jesus said about the sheep and the goats is very appropriate here. To the sheep on His right hand the King will say, "Come." Why? "For I was hungry and you gave me something to eat, I was thirsty and you gave me something to drink, I was a stranger and you invited me in, I needed clothes and you clothed me" (Matt. 25:34-36). To the goats on His left He said, "Depart." Why? Just because they had failed to do those very things (vv. 41-43). The lesson is very clear.

III. DIVINE BLESSING:
Isaiah 58:8-11

A. Healing: v. 8

"Then your light will break forth
    like the dawn,
  and your healing will quickly
    appear;
then your righteousness will go
    before you,
  and the glory of the LORD will
    be your rear guard."

In this verse we find four beautiful promises. If we meet the conditions laid down in verses 6 and 7, God promises light, health, righteousness, and protection.

On the first of these four Delitzsch observes:

The love of God is called "light" in contrast with His wrath; and a quiet cheerful life in God's love is so called, in contrast with a wild troubled life spent in God's wrath. This life in God's love has its dawn and its noon-day. When it is night both within and around a man, and he suffers himself to be awakened by the love of God to a reciprocity of love; then does the love of God, like the rising sun, open for itself a way through man's dark night and overcome the darkness of wrath (Commentary, Isaiah, 2:389).

In the second line the King James Version has "health." But the Hebrew suggests "healing" (NIV), or "recovery" (NASB), from the sickness of sin.

The third promise is: "your righteousness will go before you." It will be our vanguard. Fausset comments, "Thy conformity to the divine covenant acts as a leader, conducting thee to peace and prosperity" (Commentary, 3:744). Our righteousness, which is Christ's righteousness in us, points the way ahead for us.

The fourth promise is: "and the glory of the LORD will be your rear guard." Just as the pillar of cloud and fire protected the Israelites from the pursuing Egyptians, so God's glory will protect us from any attacks from the rear as we move on in God's will.

B. God's Presence: v. 9a

"Then you will call, and the LORD
  will answer;
  you will cry for help, and he
  will say: Here am I."

This is really a fifth promise, as indicated by the repeated "Then." Ross Price says of this beautiful promise:

Here mankind's two great needs are met: the need for a response and recognition, and the need for the sense of a Presence. Silence and aloneness are thus removed. God himself is the real answer to prayer and the true evidence of sanctification (Luke 11:13). God's best gift is himself (*BBC*, 4:247).

C. Light Instead of Darkness: vv. 9b-10

"If you do away with the yoke of
  oppression,
  with the pointing finger and
  malicious talk,
and if you spend yourselves on
  behalf of the hungry
  and satisfy the needs of the
  oppressed,
then your light will rise in the
  darkness,
  and your night will become like
  the noonday."

In verses 8 and 9 we have seen God's gracious promises that He makes to His people. But they are conditional. We are warned of this by the threefold "then" in those verses. But now it is made more definite by the twofold "if" in verses 9b and 10. The people of Judah must "do away with the yoke of oppression" (see comments on v. 6), and "the pointing finger" of scorn or contempt, and "malicious talk"—the Hebrew is worse than "speaking vanity" (KJV), as commentators agree. On the positive side they must spend themselves in behalf of the hungry and satisfy the needs of the oppressed. Kindness, even sacrificial love, is required of those who obey God's will.
    Again we have "then." For those who fulfill these conditions just enumerated, the promise is given:

then your light will rise in the
  darkness,
  and your night will become like
  the noonday.

When we walk in the light, we find plenty of light on our pathway. Disobedience brings darkness; obedience brings light. We make the choice!
    As has often been said, we can choose our course in life, but we cannot choose the consequences. The consequences are fixed by the course we choose. One of my favorite verses in the Bible is Proverbs 4:18. It reads:

The path of the righteous is like
  the first gleam of dawn,
  shining ever brighter till the
  full light of day.

The next verse in Proverbs says:

But the way of the wicked is like
  deep darkness;
  they do not know what makes
  them stumble.

Why should anyone choose to walk in the dark when offered the choice of walking in the light? Yet most people choose the former.

DISCUSSION QUESTIONS

1. What part does fasting have in the Christian life?
2. What is the main purpose and function of fasting?
3. How can we avoid a self-righteous attitude in our fasting?
4. What are some results of legalism?
5. How can we minister to the needy?
6. How can we be sure of divine guidance?

D. Divine Guidance: v. 11

"The LORD will guide you always;
   he will satisfy your needs in a
      sun-scorched land
and will strengthen your frame.
You will be like a well-watered
      garden,
   like a spring whose waters
      never fail."

The first line of this verse is another favorite promise. One of the greatest needs we all have in life is for proper guidance. Losing one's way often has very serious consequences. Taking the wrong path can lead to disaster.

But how can we get sure guidance? The answer is given here: "The LORD will guide you always." What more comforting words could we hear? He—the all-knowing, all-loving, all-powerful One—has promised to be our unfailing guide, "always"! What more could we ask?

The price of continuous divine guidance is full and constant obedience. If we follow the Lord closely, He will guide us all the way.

CONTEMPORARY APPLICATION

Much of our lesson today deals with the matter of fasting. The negative side—the wrong kind of fasting—was illustrated in one Christian businessman I heard about some time ago.

He fasted regularly one day a week. But the secretaries and others working in his office soon became very much aware of the fact that on his fast days he was irritable and hard to get along with. So they would often warn each other: "Today's his fast day. We'll have to be extra careful that we don't upset him."

Needless to say, that didn't help the man's Christian testimony with his employees. His fasting probably did more harm than good!

JESUS BEGINS HIS MINISTRY

DEVOTIONAL READING	Luke 3:7-17

Adult Topic: *Jesus Begins His Ministry*

Youth Topic: *Ready to Follow*

ADULTS AND YOUTH

Background Scripture: Mark 1

Scripture Lesson: Mark 1:14-28

Memory Verse: *The time is fulfilled, and the kingdom of God is at hand; repent and believe in the gospel.* Mark 1:15

CHILDREN — **Topic:** *Jesus Begins His Work*

DAILY BIBLE READINGS

Feb. 27 M.: Get Ready for the Lord. Mark 1:1-8
Feb. 28 T.: John's Forecast. Luke 3:7-14
Feb. 29 W.: Jesus' Baptism and Temptation. Mark 1:9-13
Mar. 1 T.: The Right Time Has Come. Mark 1:14-20
Mar. 2 F.: A Man with an Evil Spirit. Mark 1:21-28
Mar. 3 S.: Jesus Heals Many People. Mark 1:29-34
Mar. 4 S.: Ministering in New Places. Mark 1:35-39

LESSON AIM — To see the central emphasis in Jesus' ministry.

LESSON SETTING

Time: about A.D. 27

Place: Galilee

LESSON OUTLINE

Jesus Begins His Ministry

  I. **Mark's Introduction:** Mark 1:1-13

 II. **The Beginning of Jesus' Ministry:** Mark 1:14-15
     A. The End of John's Ministry: v. 14
     B. The Message of Jesus: v. 15

III. **The Calling of the First Disciples:** Mark 1:16-20
     A. Simon and Andrew: v. 16
     B. Jesus' Call: v. 17
     C. Their Obedience: v. 18
     D. James and John: v. 19
     E. Called and Obedient: v. 20

 IV. **Driving Out an Evil Spirit:** Mark 1:21-26
     A. Teaching in the Synagogue: v. 21
     B. Amazement at His Teaching: v. 22
     C. A Demon-possessed Man: v. 23
     D. The Demon's Challenge: v. 24
     E. Jesus' Command: v. 25
     F. Divine Deliverance: v. 26

  V. **Reaction of the People:** Mark 1:27-28
     A. Amazement: v. 27
     B. Publicity: v. 28

SUGGESTED
INTRODUCTION
FOR ADULTS

This quarter we have eight lessons from the Gospel of Mark and five from the Epistle of James. These two books have in common an emphasis on the importance of good works, of ministering to the needs of people.

The Gospel of Mark is the "Gospel of Action." It does not have the long discourses of Jesus, as found in Matthew and Luke. There are more of Jesus' doings and less of His teachings in Mark than in any of the other Gospels. For instance, Mark has eighteen of the miracles of Jesus but only four of His parables, compared with fifteen parables in Matthew and nineteen in Luke.

Two things may help to account for this type of record. The early church held that Mark gives us the preaching Peter, who was always a man of action. In the second place, Mark wrote for the Romans, who, unlike the Greeks, majored on action rather than words.

In the first half of the Gospel of Mark we see Jesus as the Miracle Worker, helping afflicted and needy people, mainly in Galilee. In the second half we see Him as the Suffering Servant (of Isaiah), giving His life for the salvation of mankind.

For Mark's Gospel we have two units of four lessons each: Unit I: Jesus Ministers to Human Need (chapters 1-9); Unit II: Jesus Gives His Life for Sinners (chapters 10-16).

SUGGESTED
INTRODUCTION
FOR YOUTH

Our topic today is "Ready to Follow." The four fishermen, whom Jesus called as His first disciples, were ready to follow. We read that "at once" they left their boats and nets and followed Jesus as He went around Galilee preaching, healing, and performing various other miracles. It cost something for them to do this, but they obeyed Christ's call without any hesitation. That is what we must do.

Jesus' call was not just to follow Him for the three years of His public ministry on earth; it was a lifelong assignment. After Jesus' death, resurrection, and ascension, the disciples waited to be filled with the Holy Spirit on the Day of Pentecost and then went out to spend the rest of their lives preaching Christ and His salvation. This is what we find reflected in the Book of Acts.

As Christ calls us, let's be ready to follow Him—all the way. That is the only life worth living.

CONCEPTS FOR
CHILDREN

1. We study today how Jesus began His ministry.
2. Jesus wants us all to follow Him.
3. We follow Jesus by obeying what He tells us to do.
4. Jesus wants to use us to help others.

THE LESSON COMMENTARY

I. MARK'S INTRODUCTION: Mark 1:1-13

The first verse of Mark gives us the heading for this Gospel: "The beginning of the gospel about Jesus Christ, the Son of God." Some take this as simply the heading for the preaching of John the Baptist (vv. 2-8), but it seems best to take it as suggested above; that is the beginning of the gospel—the Good News—comprised the life, death, and resurrection of Jesus.

In these first thirteen verses we have (besides the heading) the ministry of John the Baptist (vv. 2-8), the baptism of Jesus (vv. 9-11), and the temptation of Jesus (vv. 12-13). These were the three main preparations for Jesus' public ministry, which begins in verse 14.

Matthew has 76 verses of introduction before he begins the public ministry in 4:12. Luke has 183 verses before he comes to that point in 4:14. But Mark has only 13 verses. He omits all the so-called infancy narratives of the other two synoptic Gospels because he is eager to get right into the exciting action of Jesus' ministry of meeting human needs.

II. THE BEGINNING OF JESUS' MINISTRY: Mark 1:14-15

A. The End of John's Ministry: v. 14

"After John was put in prison, Jesus went into Galilee, proclaiming the good news of God."

Jesus had no desire to operate in competition with John the Baptist, or to interfere with John's ministry as the forerunner and introducer of the Messiah. But after His forty days of temptation by Satan in the desert of Judea (vv. 12-13), Jesus heard that John had been imprisoned by Herod Antipas, the ruler of Galilee, so Jesus went north to Galilee to begin His public ministry (cf. Matt. 4:12).

In Galilee Jesus was "proclaiming the good news of God." Incidentally, "of the kingdom" (KJV) is omitted in the Revised Standard Version, New American Standard Bible, and New International Version because it is not in our two fourth-century manuscripts, as well as in the best minuscule manuscripts of a later date.

In the Greek New Testament there are two words for "preach." One is *euangelizo*, which means "announce good news." It comes from the noun *euangelion*, "good news," translated here as "gospel" (KJV). But the Greek verb in this verse is *kerysso*. It comes from the noun *keryx*, which meant "a herald"—one who made a proclamation for the emperor or military commander. So the distinctive emphasis of the participle here is "proclaiming" (NIV).

B. The Message of Jesus: v. 15

"The time has come," he said. "The kingdom of God is near. Repent and believe the good news!"

The word used for "time" here is not *chronos*, passing of time, but *kairos*, "the appointed time, right season, opportune moment." I have written:

> God's clock was striking the hour. It was the time for the ushering in of the kingdom of God, the rule or reign of God. The great moment of opportunity for the Jewish nation had arrived. But, as has happened multiplied times with both individuals and groups, there was no recognition and seizing of the opportunity, and it finally passed. The Jewish nation lapsed into deeper darkness, and instead of a religious revival there took place the awful judgment of A.D. 70 when Jerusalem was destroyed by the Romans (*The Gospel According to Mark*, p. 33).

In Matthew 3:2 and 4:17 we find exactly the same message preached by both John the Baptist and Jesus: "Repent, for the kingdom of heaven is near." Repentance was the main emphasis of John's preaching, as we see from Mark 1:4. Jesus now added, "Believe the good news!" The good news at that point in time was that the Messiah had now come to be the Savior of mankind.

What is repentance? The Greek verb used here, *metanoeo*, literally means "change one's mind." True repentance means a change of attitude toward God, ourselves, and sin. It does not mean simply "being sorry," as often defined, but being sorry enough to quit! It is turning our backs on sin and turning to God.

III. THE CALLING OF THE FIRST DISCIPLES: Mark 1:16-20

A. Simon and Andrew: v. 16

"As Jesus walked beside the Sea of Galilee, he saw Simon and his brother Andrew casting a net into the lake, for they were fishermen." The New International Version has retained "Sea of Galilee," because that is the familiar name, but when the word "sea" stands alone, it has changed it to "lake." The so-called Sea of Galilee was only about twelve miles long and six miles wide. Today we would call that a "lake," not a "sea." J. A. Alexander comments: "This use of the word *sea*, though lost in modern English, is retained in German (*See*) with specific reference to inland lakes" (*The Gospel According to Mark*, p. 15).

Walking beside the lake, Jesus saw "Simon." This is a Hellenized form of the Hebrew *Simeon*. There are seven Simons mentioned in the Gospels. Josephus, the Jewish historian of that period, mentions twenty-five in his writings. It is claimed that Simon was the most common name for male Jews in the first century. This Simon is better known as "Peter" (Greek *petros*, "rock"), a name that Jesus gave to him (Matt. 16:18). "Andrew" is an old Greek name (*Andreas*), which shows the influence of the Greek language in Palestine at this time. Peter is mentioned first as the older of the two. He may well have been the oldest of all the twelve apostles that Jesus called, and so he naturally became the leader and spokesman for the group.

These two brothers were "casting a net into the lake." The Greek verb is not the simple *ballo*, "cast," but the compound *amphiballo*, "cast about," or from side to side. This was not a large dragnet, pulled behind the boat, but a hand net, probably thrown into the water first on one side of the boat and then on the other.

Simon and Andrew were "fishermen," as were also the two sons of Zebedee—all four of the first men called as disciples. These rugged fishermen were accustomed to hard work and to exposure to danger in the severe storms on the Lake of Galilee. They also had been forced to learn the art of watchful waiting, of patient perseverance. All these qualities were to stand them in good stead as followers of Jesus and fishers of men.

B. Jesus' Call: v. 17

Jesus said to these two brothers, "Come, follow me, and I will make you fishers of men." The Greek literally says, "Come after me." This would be understood by the Jews of that day as meaning, "Be my disciples." The rabbis called on young men to follow them as their disciples.

Instead of catching fish, these men were to become "fishers of men." Fishing lost men out of the devil's deep waters of despair is the greatest occupation that anyone can have.

C. Their Obedience: v. 18

"At once they left their nets and followed him." The Greek for "at once" is *euthys*. It occurs eighty times in the New Testament, and half of these are in the Gospel of Mark. In the King James Version the two most common translations are "immediately" (thirty-five times) and "straightway" (thirty-two times). Twice (Luke 17:7; 21:9) the King James Version has "by and by," which to the modern reader says exactly the opposite of the Greek.

This word underscores the main characteristic of Mark's Gospel, which is rapidity of action. But here we note that it indicates prompt obedience. These two fishermen did not stop to argue or debate. Of course it would cost them their source of income, but "at once" they left their nets and followed Jesus. And we may be sure that they never regretted this immediate response.

D. James and John: v. 19

"When he had gone a little farther, he saw James son of Zebedee and his brother John in a boat, preparing their nets."

The Greek, like the Hebrew Old Testament, has "Jacob." But the earliest English Bible, that of Wyclif (1382) has "James" for the New Testament. His brother's name was "John," a very common name among the Jews of that day.

These two brothers were in a "boat." The King James Version says "ship," which, of course, is incorrect. Wyclif correctly had "boat." But Tyndale, in the first *printed* English New Testament (1525), used "ship." Unfortunately the translators of the King James Version followed Tyndale rather closely, and so this mistranslation got into our traditional version. These craft on the Lake of Galilee were small fishing boats, propelled by sails or oars. By no stretch of the imagination would they be called "ships."

The two fishermen were "preparing their nets." The Greek verb was used at that time for setting a broken bone. It is thought they were also washing the nets in preparation for using them the next day.

E. Called and Obedient: v. 20

"Without delay" (*euthys*) "he called them and they left their father Zebedee in the boat with the hired men and followed him."

Both "left" and "followed" are in the aorist tense in Greek, suggesting prompt action. The same is true in verse 18. All four fishermen promptly obeyed. They found the highest and best in their lives by obeying the divine call. When we fail or refuse Christ's call, we are the sufferers.

"With the hired men" is found only in Mark. It is important to note that their father, Zebedee, was not left to carry on the work alone; he had helpers.

Before leaving this incident, there is one point that we should notice, and that is that this was not the first contact these men had had with Jesus. In John 1:35-42 we read of an earlier meeting.

There we are told that John the Baptist was with two of his disciples when he saw Jesus passing by. He cried, "Look, the Lamb of God!" (v. 36).

Then we read that one of these two was "Andrew, Simon Peter's brother" (v. 40). The next two verses say: "He found first his own brother Simon.... He brought him to Jesus" (NASB).

The other of the two disciples is not named. This has led many scholars to suggest that it was John, the son of Zebedee, the writer of that Gospel, who never mentions himself by name in his Gospel. Several scholars also hold that the meaning of verse 41 is that as Andrew "first" found his brother Simon and brought him to Jesus, so John, in the second place, found his brother James and brought him to Jesus. It was only some time later that Jesus called these four men to leave all and follow Him in full-time service.

IV. DRIVING OUT AN EVIL SPIRIT: Mark 1:21-26

A. Teaching in the Synagogue: v. 21

"They went to Capernaum, and when the Sabbath came, Jesus went into the synagogue and began to teach."

In Matthew 4:12-13 we read: "When Jesus heard that John had been put in prison, he returned to Galilee. Leaving Nazareth, he went and lived in Capernaum." The little obscure village of Nazareth was up in the hills. Jesus wanted to be with people in order to minister to them. So He left His hometown and made His headquarters in Capernaum, a busy commercial city, located on the north shore of the Lake of Galilee, near the west side. One can now see the ruins of ancient Capernaum spread out for more than a mile along the north shore of the lake. The four fishermen disciples may all have lived here.

"... When the Sabbath came, Jesus went into the synagogue and began to teach" (v. 21). It must always be remembered that "the Sabbath," as for Jews today, was Saturday, not Sunday. Actually it lasted from sunset on Friday to sunset Saturday. The *synagogue* (Greek word for "a gathering together") first meant the congregation. But, as with our word *church*, it soon came to be applied to the building in which the congregation met for worship.

It may seem surprising to read that Jesus went into the synagogue "and began to teach." But it was the custom not only for the rabbis to teach but also to let qualified others function in this capacity, as we see from Acts 13:14-15.

B. Amazement at His Teaching: v. 22

"The people were amazed at his teaching, because he taught them as one who had authority, not as the teachers of the law."

The scribes, or teachers of the law, were in the habit of quoting the various opinions of earlier rabbis, but Jesus spoke with direct divine authority, to the amazement of his hearers.

One may wonder why the New International Version has changed the traditional "scribes" of most versions to "teachers of the law," thus a word of explanation is in order. The word

"scribe" today, from the Latin verb *scribo*, "I write," is generally taken as indicating a secretary, but the so-called "scribes" of the Gospels were far above this. They were the official "teachers of the law" in the synagogue and need to be so designated.

C. A Demon-possessed Man: v. 23

"Just then a man in their synagogue who was possessed by an evil spirit cried out...." The Greek literally says "in an unclean spirit"—that is, under its power. Henry Barclay Swete says of the construction "in a spirit" in the New Testament: "Most of the examples refer to the Holy Spirit, but there is nothing in the formula to forbid its application to evil spirits in their relation to men under their control" (*The Gospel According to St. Mark*, p. 18).

D. The Demon's Challenge: v. 24

"What do you want with us, Jesus of Nazareth? Have you come to destroy us? I know who you are—the Holy One of God!"

"What do you want with us" is very brief in the Greek: literally, "what to us and to you" (sing.). R. C. H. Lenski says that here it has the sense: "Do thou leave us alone!" (*Interpretation of the New Testament*, Mark, p. 788). A simple meaning would be: "What is there between us, or common to us?"

DISCUSSION QUESTIONS

1. Why did Jesus spend most of His time in Galilee?
2. What is meant by "the kingdom of God"?
3. How can we show true repentance?
4. Why did Jesus go to the big city?
5. Is demon possession real in our day?
6. How should demon possession be dealt with?

Goodspeed translates it: "What do you want of us?" Vincent Taylor prefers "Why dost thou meddle with us?" (*The Gospel According to St. Mark*, p. 174). Interestingly, the King James Version gives a double translation: "Let *us* alone; what have we to do with thee?"

The demon addressed Jesus as: "Jesus Nazarene" (literal Greek). He feared that Jesus had come to destroy him and his fellow demons. Then he made the startling assertion: "I know who you are—the Holy One of God!" This was a very appropriate expression for the *unclean* spirit to use. On other occasions the demons addressed Jesus as "Son of God" (Matt. 8:29), and as "Son of the Most High God" (Mark 5:7). It is obvious that demons (fallen angels) believe in the deity of Jesus, even though many intellectuals don't! One is reminded of what James says in his Epistle about demons believing there is one God (2:19).

E. Jesus' Command: v. 25

"'Be quiet!' said Jesus sternly. 'Come out of him!'" The command, "Be quiet!" is literally, "Be muzzled!" In other words, "Shut your mouth and keep it shut!" It was strong language, fitting a drastic situation.

Why did Jesus silence the demon? I have suggested:

> Probably He objected to testimony coming from this source. It is also likely that He was not yet ready to have His Messiahship proclaimed publicly. He was not anxious to have His teaching ministry interrupted by the precipitation of a political revolution (*Mark*, p. 36).

F. Divine Deliverance: v. 26

"The evil spirit shook the man violently and came out of him with a shriek."

"Evil spirit" is literally "unclean spirit." Mark uses this expression ten times, compared with twice in Matthew and six times in Luke. The demon convulsed this victim, let out a loud scream, and came out of the man. We see something here of the hateful cruelty of demons, of their malicious meanness. How different is the Holy Spirit in His influence!

V. REACTION OF THE PEOPLE: Mark 1:27-28

A. Amazement: v. 27

"The people were all so amazed that they asked each other, 'What is this? A new teaching—and with authority! He even gives orders to evil spirits and they obey him.'"

It must be remembered that in the original Greek there are no punctuation marks whatever, so different translations punctuate the verse different ways. But the basic meaning is clear.

We might mention that "doctrine" (KJV) is simply "teaching" in the Greek and should be so translated. It does not mean a theological "doctrine."

The thing that astonished the crowd was that Jesus cast out demons by a simple, authoritative command. The Jews of that day practiced exorcism of demons by repeating magical formulae.

B. Publicity: v. 28

"News about him spread quickly over the whole region of Galilee."

The casting out of the demon in the synagogue at Capernaum is the first miracle of Jesus recorded in Mark and Luke. (Matthew omits it.) It caused great excitement throughout Galilee.

CONTEMPORARY APPLICATION

Jesus calls busy people—like the four fishermen—to do His work. Lazy people just don't qualify.

John Trapp, a Puritan divine, puts it this way:

God calls men when they are busy; Satan, when they are idle. For idleness is the hour of temptation, and an idle person the devil's tennis-ball, which he tosses at pleasure and sets to work as he likes and lists (*The Biblical Illustrator*, Mark, p. 31).

Much of our safety in the Christian life lies in our being occupied every hour of every day with things that are good and profitable.

JESUS ENCOUNTERS HOSTILITY

DEVOTIONAL READING	Mark 2:1-12
ADULTS AND YOUTH	**Adult Topic:** *Jesus Encounters Hostility*
	Youth Topic: *Putting People First*
	Background Scripture: Mark 2:1—3:6
	Scripture Lesson: Mark 2:15-17, 23—3:6
	Memory Verse: *I came not to call the righteous, but sinners.* Mark 2:17
CHILDREN	**Topic:** *Jesus and His Enemies*
	Memory Verse: *Those who are well have no need of a physician, but those who are sick.* Mark 2:17
DAILY BIBLE READINGS	**Mar. 5 M.:** Jesus Claims His Authority. Mark 2:1-12
	Mar. 6 T.: Finding New Meaning in Traditions. Mark 2:18-22
	Mar. 7 W.: Lord of the Sabbath. Mark 2:23-28
	Mar. 8 T.: Healing on the Sabbath. Mark 3:1-6
	Mar. 9 F.: Many Heard About Jesus. Mark 3:7-12
	Mar. 10 S.: Jesus Gathers His Twelve. Mark 3:13-19
	Mar. 11 S.: Jesus Reveals His Purpose. Matt. 9:9-13
LESSON AIM	To see how Jesus met hostility.
LESSON SETTING	**Time:** about A.D. 28
	Place: Galilee

LESSON OUTLINE

Jesus Encounters Hostility

   I. **The Call of Levi:** Mark 2:13-14

  II. **The Dinner at Levi's House:** Mark 2:15-17
     A. The Guests: v. 15
     B. Complaint of the Pharisees: v. 16
     C. Jesus' Answer: v. 17

 III. **Sabbath Controversy:** Mark 2:23-28
     A. Picking Grain: v. 23
     B. Pharisees' Objection: v. 24
     C. Example of David: vv. 25-26
     D. Reason for the Sabbath: v. 27
     E. Lord of the Sabbath: v. 28

 IV. **Healing on the Sabbath:** Mark 3:1-6
     A. Man with the Shriveled Hand: v. 1
     B. Critical Legalists: v. 2
     C. Coming out in the Open: v. 3
     D. Question of Jesus: v. 4
     E. Healing a Man: v. 5
     F. Plot to Kill Jesus: v. 6

SUGGESTED INTRODUCTION FOR ADULTS

Last week we studied the beginning of Jesus' ministry, as described in the first chapter of Mark's Gospel. Today we find, already in chapter two, hostility against Jesus. In loving mercy Jesus was healing the sick. Meanwhile the Pharisees were standing on the sidelines criticizing Him.

In the first part of chapter two we have a typical example of this. A paralytic was brought to Jesus, carried by four men (v. 3). When they found the way blocked, in desperation they took him up the outside stairs to the flat roof, dug a hole, and lowered him down before the Master (v. 4). Jesus said to the paralytic, "Son, your sins are forgiven" (v. 5). Teachers of the law who were sitting there thought to themselves: "Why does this fellow talk like that? He's blaspheming! Who can forgive sins but God alone?" (v. 7).

Knowing what they were thinking, Jesus asked them this question: "Which is easier to say to the paralytic, 'Your sins are forgiven,' or to say, 'Get up, take your mat and walk'?" It would be easier to say the former, since there would be no outward evidence of failure as to whether it happened or not.

To prove that He had authority to forgive the man's sins, Jesus told the paralytic to get up and walk. When the man did so, that demonstrated Jesus' power to heal both soul and body.

SUGGESTED INTRODUCTION FOR YOUTH

"Putting People First" is our topic today. The Pharisees put their rules and regulations first, regardless of how these affected people in need. Jesus put people first.

The legalistic Pharisees didn't want Jesus to heal a poor paralytic on the Sabbath because that was contrary to their tradition of the elders, which they elevated above God's Word (Matt. 15:1-6). But Jesus had compassion on the needy, and so must we have.

CONCEPTS FOR CHILDREN

1. Jesus healed those who were sick in body or soul.
2. Jesus had compassion for all who were in need.
3. The legalistic Pharisees criticized Jesus' way of helping others.
4. We must love people and try to help them.

THE LESSON COMMENTARY

I. THE CALL OF LEVI:
Mark 2:13-14

Once more Jesus went outside the city of Capernaum and was teaching a large crowd of people beside the Lake of Galilee. "As he walked along, he saw Levi son of Alphaeus sitting at the tax collector's booth." The Hebrew name "Levi"—held by one of the twelve sons

of Jacob—is used for this disciple only here and in Luke 5:27, 29. In the parallel account in the First Gospel (Matt. 9:9) he is called Matthew. This may have been the name that Jesus gave him, as He gave Simon the name Peter.

Levi was sitting at the *telonion*—"the receipt of custom" (KJV). It could have been a tollhouse on the great caravan road from Damascus to the Mediterranean coast, where customs duties were paid, or it may have been a place where duty was paid on fish caught in the lake. It is often translated "tax office" (RSV, NASB). But since it was not what we would think of as a modern tax office, the New International Version has "tax collector's booth."

Jesus said to Levi, "Follow me." Obediently, "Levi got up and followed him." The four fishermen could conceivably have returned to their nets, but Levi gave up his profitable job once and for all.

II. THE DINNER AT LEVI'S HOUSE: Mark 2:15-17

A. The Guests: v. 15

"While Jesus was having dinner at Levi's house, many tax collectors and 'sinners' were eating with him and his disciples, for there were many who followed him."

The King James Version says that Jesus "sat at meat" in Levi's house. But the Greek says that He was "reclining" at the table. The Greeks and Romans had the custom of reclining on couches while eating, and this custom had been adopted by the upper classes in Palestine. Vincent Taylor says that it was "universal in the time of Jesus" (*The Gospel According to St. Mark*, p. 204).

Many "tax collectors" were eating with Jesus. The King James Version calls them "publicans," getting this term from the Latin Vulgate. But the *publicani* were wealthy men, to whom Rome farmed out the taxes of large areas. The actual collection of taxes was done by local "tax collectors," or "tax gatherers" (NASB), and these are always the men who are mentioned in the Gospels.

Elsewhere I have written:

Taxes in Palestine were oppressive in Jesus' day. Water, meat and salt were taxed. There were road taxes, city taxes, house taxes, besides the poll tax. It is not surprising that tax collectors were classed as robbers and ruffians, whose money was not acceptable for alms, and whose testimony was not valid in court (*The Gospel According to Mark*, p. 45).

The tax collectors were also hated because they represented the domination of a foreign power—the Roman Empire. They were despised as traitors. Added to this, the pious Jews held them in contempt because they were defiled by frequent contact with Gentiles. Also, because they were careless about observing all the ceremonial cleansings of the law of Moses, they were "unclean."

Someone might raise the question as to why "sinners" is put in quotation marks here in the New International Version. The answer is that these people were not necessarily immoral, as we think of sinners today, but they were classed as "sinners" by the Pharisees because they did not live sufficiently "separated" lives.

B. Complaint of the Pharisees: v. 16

"When the teachers of the law who were Pharisees saw him eating with the 'sinners' and tax collectors, they asked his disciples: 'Why does he eat with tax collectors and "sinners"?'"

The best Greek text has "the scribes of the Pharisees" (RSV, NASB), rather than "the scribes and Pharisees" (KJV). The New International Version expresses this helpfully as "the teachers of the law who were Pharisees."

The name "Pharisee" means "separatist." The Pharisees prided themselves on being separated from the common people, who were careless about keeping all the numerous rules and regulations of the law of Moses and "the tradition of the elders." They felt that they were in a special sense God's "holy people." But this was a very legalistic, unloving type of holiness.

C. Jesus' Answer: v. 17

Jesus replied, "It is not the healthy who need a doctor, but the sick."

Apparently this was an old proverb, which fit the situation perfectly. I have written:

> It is the duty of a doctor to visit those afflicted with disease, even at the risk of contagion. How much more should He visit those diseased with sin, in order to save them. He should no more shrink from the ceremonial contamination than the physician shrinks from physical contagion. Such was Jesus' reasoning with these critics. Though religious leaders, they were not concerned for the salvation of these poor sinners. The common people found it very difficult to observe all the minute and multitudinous regulations of "the tradition of the elders." Hence they were contemptuously referred to by the Pharisees as *Amhaarez*, i.e., "people of the land." The typical attitude of the strict Jews is reflected in this rabbinical saying: "A disciple of the wise must not sit at table with the *Amhaarez*" (*Mark*, p. 46).

Then Jesus applied the proverb to himself: "I have not come to call the righteous, but sinners." The added "to repentance" is not found here in the oldest and best manuscripts. It was later added here from Luke 5:32, where it is genuine.

III SABBATH CONTROVERSY: Mark 2:23-28

A. Picking Grain: v. 23

"One Sabbath Jesus was going through the grainfields, and as his disciples walked along, they began to pick some heads of grain."

The King James Version paints a picture here that is quite misleading to the modern American reader. It says that Jesus was going through "the corn fields" and that His disciples began to pluck "the ears of corn." All grain is called "corn" in the British Isles. For instance, the famous "Corn Laws" had to do with the importation of wheat. Indian maize, which is called "corn" in the United States, was unknown in the Old World, although we have seen large fields of it in several European countries in very recent years. But for American readers "corn" must be changed to "grain." And the "heads of grain" were certainly not what we know in this country as "ears of corn." This is just one of many instances that underscores the need for using a contemporary American version of the Bible.

B. Pharisee' Objection: v. 24

The Pharisees said to Jesus, "Look, why are they doing what is unlawful on the Sabbath?"

I have written:

> The eager, ever-present Pharisees were on hand as usual to criticize. They challenged the conduct of the disciples as unlawful. It was not that Christ's followers were stealing, for what they were doing was expressly allowed in the Mosaic law (Deut. 23:25). The entire objection was to manual labor on the Sabbath day. In the eyes of the pedantic Pharisees plucking the grain was reaping, and rubbing of the husks or shells was threshing. Perhaps, also, blowing the loose chaff out of their hands was winnowing! Such was the narrow legalism of rabbinic interpretation (*Mark*, p. 49).

The rabbis specified thirty-nine different kinds of work that were not allowed on the Sabbath. Later they listed six subheads under each of the thirty-nine!

C. Example of David: vv. 25-26

Jesus answered the Pharisees' question with a counter-question, appealing to Scripture. This was a favorite method in rabbinical arguments, and Jesus beat them at their own game. He asked them: "Have you never read what David did when he and his companions were hungry and in need? In the time of Abiathar the high priest, he entered the house of God and ate the consecrated bread, which is lawful only for priests to eat. And he also gave some to his companions."

David was the greatest single hero in the history of Israel—at least after Moses. He had founded a dynasty that lasted down to the Babylonian captivity. The expected Messiah was called "the Son of David." Yet this great hero, looked up to by all the Jews, had actually eaten the "shewbread." (The Hebrew expression means "bread of the Presence"; that is, symbolizing the divine Presence.) In doing this he assumed the prerogative of a priest. But human need is a higher law than religious ritualism.

Actually, Jesus was meeting the Pharisees on their own ground, for the rabbis had dealt with this strange action of David and had come to the conclusion that a man was justified in eating the sacred bread rather than starving. They declared that God's laws were given that men might live, not die. But they were not practicing this sensible deduction very well!

I have commented further on this verse:

> The reference in verse 26 to "Abiathar the high priest" has caused a great deal of comment, for in 1 Samuel 21 it is stated definitely that Ahimelech, Abiathar's father, was priest of the tabernacle at Nob, near Jerusalem, when David asked for and received the sacred loaves. Morison, in his excellent commentary, lists no less than ten proposed solutions for the problem. The interpretation which he prefers—and which seems best to us—would make the passage mean "in the lifetime of the high priest," rather than during his term of office. Since Abiathar became the prominent high priest in the reign of David, his name is used rather than his father's (*Mark*, p. 49).

D. Reason for the Sabbath: v. 27

Jesus then said to His critics: "The Sabbath was made for man, not man for the Sabbath."

The Jewish rabbis themselves had said: "The Sabbath is delivered unto you, and ye are not delivered to the Sabbath." But again they had failed to follow their own teachings. Jesus echoed the rabbinical saying but made it more definite. Jesus knew that a human being needs one day a week for rest for his body and mind, and spiritual refreshment for his soul. I have suggested, "to ignore this law is only to prove its necessity." Adam Clarke well said, "Had we no Sabbath, we should soon have no religion" (*Commentary on the Whole Bible*, abridged by Ralph Earle, p. 838). And J. C. Ryle wrote, "National prosperity and personal growth in grace are intimately bound up in the maintenance of a holy Sabbath" (*Expository Thoughts on the Gospels*, Mark, p. 42).

E. Lord of the Sabbath: v. 28

"So the Son of Man is Lord even of the Sabbath." Some eighty times, as recorded in the Gospels, Jesus referred to Himself as "the Son of Man." It was His favorite designation for Himself. As the Messiah, and as the Head of the race, He was Lord of the Sabbath. Someone has well said that Jesus is Lord of the Sabbath "to own it, to interpret it, to preside over it and to ennoble it, by merging it in 'the Lord's day.'"

IV. HEALING ON THE SABBATH: Mark 3:1-6

A. Man with the Shriveled Hand: v. 1

"Another time he went into the synagogue, and a man with a shriveled hand was there."

This incident is the last of a series of five conflicts between Jesus and the Pharisees, as recorded in Mark 2:1—3:6. The first was triggered by Jesus' healing of the paralytic (2:1-12), the second by Jesus eating with tax collectors and "sinners" (2:13-17), the third by the question of fasting (2:18-22), the fourth by picking heads of grain on the Sabbath (2:23-28), and the fifth by healing on the Sabbath (3:1-6).

Whereas in Jerusalem Jesus found Himself in conflict with the chief priests who were in charge of the Temple, in Galilee it was with the Pharisees, who controlled the synagogues in all the cities and towns.

Again (cf. 1:21) Jesus went into the synagogue "as was his custom" (Luke 4:16). Today we would say that Jesus was in the habit of going to church. If we are His true followers, we will have the same habit.

In the synagogue that Saturday morning was a man "with a shriveled hand"—literally, "having his hand dried up." This would suggest that he was not born that way.

B. Critical Legalists: v. 2

"Some of them were looking for a reason to accuse Jesus, so they watched him closely to see if he would heal him on the Sabbath."

Wyclif, who put out the first English version of the Bible, caught the correct idea when he translated it: *"Thei aspieden Hym."* The Pharisees were acting as spies to trap Jesus. It is not at all unlikely that they "planted" the man there that morning to see what Jesus would do.

I have written:

The Jews allowed healing on the Sabbath day, but only in cases of life or death. Obviously this chronic ailment did not come under that category. If Jesus healed the man, He would be guilty of disregarding "the tradition of the elders," the rabbinic interpretation of the Mosaic law. His enemies were on the lookout for a chance to accuse Him. Morison aptly describes them as "ecclesiastical bloodhounds" (*Mark*, p. 50).

C. Coming out in the Open: v. 3

"Jesus said to the man with the shriveled hand, 'Stand up in front of everyone.'"

Jesus was not intimidated by the hostile Pharisees. He could have waited until after the synagogue service was over, taken the man to a quiet place, and healed him. Instead He said to him: "Rise into the midst" (literal Greek). The full force of the expression would be: "Rise and come into the midst," where everybody could see him. Christ deliberately made the affair as public as possible. If His critics wanted to see what He would do, He would give them ample opportunity.

D. Question of Jesus: v. 4

"Then Jesus asked them, 'Which is lawful on the Sabbath: to do good or to do evil, to save life or to kill?' But they remained silent."

This question went right to the heart of the issue between Jesus and the Pharisees. One way of interpreting it is that if a person does not do good when he (or, she) can, that person thereby does evil. Morison puts it this way: "To refuse to do good is to choose to do evil" (*A Practical Commentary on the Gospel According to St. Mark*, p. 67).

I have commented elsewhere:

The second part of the question suggests the other interpretation. The Greek word for "save" is used in the Gospels, Acts, and James for physical healing and throughout the New Testament for spiritual salvation. While Jesus on the Sabbath was planning to heal the afflicted man the pious Pharisees were plotting to kill the Healer. Who was desecrating the Sabbath, He or they? Here is the

---

DISCUSSION QUESTIONS

1. Does it pay to leave a lucrative vocation to follow Jesus?
2. Should we avoid eating with "sinners"?
3. Why did Jesus eat with sinners?
4. What "work" is wrong on Sunday?
5. What "work" is justified on Sunday?
6. When is it proper for a Christian to be angry?

real question that Jesus was asking: "Is it right on the sabbath to bless or to injure?" The query is a very penetrating one, with sweeping implications for modern observance of the Lord's Day. . . . "They kept silent." As in other instances, when Jesus' enemies found themselves cornered by His clear reasoning they maintained a stubborn, sullen silence. They could not deny His arguments, and they refused to admit their validity (*Mark*, p. 51).

We often hear the statement: "Silence is golden." That is not always true. By remaining silent, one can deliberately act a lie. We have to know when to keep still and when to speak.

E. Healing a Man: v. 5

"He looked around at them in anger and, deeply distressed at their stubborn hearts, said to the man, 'Stretch out your hand.' He stretched it out, and his hand was completely restored."

Jesus angry? Yes, Scripture says so. But we should note that "looked around" is the aorist participle of instantaneous action—"having quickly looked around"—while "deeply distressed" is the present participle of continuous action: "being grieved." The flash of anger was accompanied by a continuing feeling of distress. The Christian attitude is that of anger against sin, combined with grief for the sinner.

Then Jesus gave an impossible command: "Stretch out your hand." How could the man do it? But he obeyed, and his hand was "completely restored." Our responsibility is to obey our Lord; it is His responsibility to enable us to do what He tells us to do.

F. Plot to Kill Jesus: v. 6

"Then the Pharisees went out and began to plot with the Herodians how they might kill Jesus."

The Herodians are mentioned three times in the New Testament (here; 12:13; Matt. 22:16). They were the supporters of Herod Antipas, the ruler of Galilee, who represented the Roman regime. Ordinarily the Pharisees, who hated the Roman government, would have nothing to do with the Herodians. But these two mutual enemies got together in their common hostility toward Jesus.

CONTEMPORARY APPLICATION

As we have already noted, two of the occasions of conflict between Jesus and the Pharisees had to do with Sabbath observance. Jesus' answer was that "the Son of Man is Lord even of the Sabbath."

This divine assertion has important implications for us as Christians. What should we do on the Sabbath? It is "the Lord's Day," and we should always do what we believe is pleasing to our Lord.

JESUS USES HIS POWER

DEVOTIONAL READING	Mark 4:10-20
ADULTS AND YOUTH	**Adult Topic:** *Jesus Uses His Power* **Youth Topic:** *Help When You Need It* **Background Scripture:** Mark 4:35—5:43 **Scripture Lesson:** Mark 4:37-41; 5:35-43 **Memory Verse:** *Do not fear, only believe.* Mark 5:36
CHILDREN	**Topic:** *Jesus Has Power* **Background Scripture:** Mark 4:37-41; 5:35-43 **Scripture Lesson:** Mark 4:35-40 **Memory Verse:** *And he awoke . . . and said to the sea, "Peace! Be Still!"* Mark 4:39
DAILY BIBLE READINGS	**Mar. 12 M.:** Jesus Teaches with Parables. Mark 4:10-20 **Mar. 13 T.:** Jesus Calms the Storm. Mark 4:35-41 **Mar. 14 W.:** Power Against Evil Spirits. Mark 5:1-13 **Mar. 15 T.:** Witnessing the Miracle. Mark 5:14-20 **Mar. 16 F.:** Jesus Walks on the Water. Mark 6:45-52 **Mar. 17 S.:** Woman Who Touched Jesus' Cloak. Mark 5:25-34 **Mar. 18 S.:** Jarius' Daughter. Mark 5:35-43
LESSON AIM	To see how Jesus displayed divine power.
LESSON SETTING	**Time:** about A.D. 29 **Place:** the Lake of Galilee and its western shore

LESSON OUTLINE	**Jesus Uses His Power**
	
	 I. **Stilling the Storm:** Mark 4:35-41
	   A. Need for a Vacation: v. 35
	   B. Crossing the Lake: v. 36
	   C. A Furious Squall: v. 37
	   D. Terrified Disciples: v. 38
	   E. Divine Command: v. 39
	   F. Reproof of Disciples: v. 40
	   G. The Disciples' Reaction: v. 41
	
	 II. **Raising Jairus' Daughter:** Mark 5:21-43
	   A. Jairus' Plea: vv. 21-24
	   B. Healing a Sick Woman: vv. 25-34
	   C. Distressing News: v. 35
	   D. Jesus' Reaction: v. 36
	   E. The Three Disciples: v. 37
	   F. Loud Commotion: v. 38
	   G. Jesus' Intervention: vv. 39-40a

H. Divine Command: vv. 40b-41
I. Immediate Healing: v. 42
J. Human Care: v. 43

SUGGESTED
INTRODUCTION
FOR ADULTS

In the passages between last week's lesson and today's lesson we get glimpses of Jesus' popularity. We are told that large crowds followed Him—not only from Galilee, but also "from Judea, Jerusalem, Idumea, and the regions across the Jordan and around Tyre and Sidon" (3:8). To keep from being crowded (perhaps even pushed into the lake!) Jesus got into a small boat and sat in it a short distance from shore (3:9). It was His healing ministry that especially drew the crowds (3:10).

Next Jesus chose twelve of His disciples to be His appointed apostles (3:13-19). This was very important for the continuation of His ministry after He went back to heaven.

In chapter 4 we find three parables of Jesus: the Sower (vv. 1-20), the Growing Seed (vv. 26-29), and the Mustard Seed (vv. 30-34). As already noted, Mark gives only four of Jesus' great parables, and he records three of them right here together. Most of Mark's Gospel is taken up with Jesus' miracle-working ministry, rather than His teaching ministry.

Because He is the Son of God as well as the Son of man, Jesus has power. When He walked the earth He demonstrated divine power in healing the sick, stilling the storm, casting out demons, and in other ways.

SUGGESTED
INTRODUCTION
FOR YOUTH

Our topic today is "Help When You Need It." Jesus used His power not to make an impression or to gain fame, but to help those in need.

We have striking examples of that in today's lesson. When the disciples were terrified in the storm, Jesus stilled the storm and calmed their fears. When Jairus was feeling desperate at the prospect of his darling daughter's death, Jesus intervened and—though the daughter had died—raised her from the dead. Jesus is equal to any emergency in our lives today.

CONCEPTS FOR
CHILDREN

1. "Jesus Has Power."
2. Jesus uses that power to help others.
3. Jesus wants to help us when we need Him.
4. When we feel upset by what happens to us in life, Jesus can calm our fears.

THE LESSON COMMENTARY

I. STILLING THE STORM:
Mark 4:35-41

A. Need for a Vacation: v. 35

In his very helpful book, *The Synoptic Gospels and Acts*, D. A. Hayes refers to Mark as "The Gospel of the Strenuous Life." He says, "Mark alone has recorded the fact that twice in his ministry neither Jesus nor those who were working with Him had even time to eat" (p. 129). These statements are found in 3:20 and 6:31.

But this fact is matched by a strange supplementary one—that this Gospel calls special attention to the retirements of Jesus from public life. Philip Schaff writes:

Mark lays emphasis on the periods of pause and rest which rhythmically intervene between the several great victories achieved by Christ. He came out from his obscure abode in Nazareth; each fresh advance in his public life is preceded by a retirement, and each retirement is followed by a new and greater victory (*History of the Christian Church*, 1:635).

These retirements are mentioned in 1:12; 3:7; 4:35; 6:31; 7:24; 9:2; 14:32. I have suggested, "If Jesus needed to retire often for fresh power for service, His followers cannot hope to get along without such periods" (*The Story of the New Testament*, p. 28).

Jesus had had a busy day of teaching in parables (vv. 1-34), so when evening came He said to His disciples, "Let us go over to the other side." He spent most of His time teaching on the west side of the Lake of Galilee, where there was a large population. Now He was seeking a quiet retreat on the east side, which has always been relatively unpopulated, because of high hills on or near the shore.

B. Crossing the Lake: v. 36

"Leaving the crowd behind, they took him along, just as he was, in the boat."

This is probably the same boat in which Jesus had been sitting while He taught the large crowd on the shore (v. 1). It was very probably Peter's fishing boat.

The disciples took Jesus "as he was," weary and worn from the constant crowds. He badly needed rest and quiet.

This incident of the stilling of the storm is recorded also in Matthew (8:23-27) and Luke (8:22-25). Mark alone mentions "other boats with him." James Morison makes this suggestion:

It would appear that while our Lord was engaged in teaching the people, who stood crowding far and wide on the shore, there had been individuals who availed themselves of the opportunity of the adjoining boats for getting nearer His person, and into a more favourable position for listening to His discourse. Hence a little fleet had gathered round the boat in which our Saviour sat (*A Practical Commentary on the Gospel According to St. Mark*, pp. 111-12).

Mark adds many such little details in his Gospel. They doubtless came from Peter, who was a very observant person. As we previously noted, the early church tradition is that Mark's Gospel gives us the preaching of Peter.

C. A Furious Squall: v. 37

"A furious squall came up, and the waves broke over the boat, so that it was nearly swamped."

I have written:

Suddenly a storm broke over the lake. The word used by Mark and Luke (*lailaps*) indicates a storm "marked by frequent great gusts of winds" (ICC, p. 85); in other words, a cyclone. Plummer suggests "the swishing slap with which the wind struck" (p. 135). Such storms are rather common on the Lake of Galilee, lying, as it does, with its surface nearly 700 feet below sea level and surrounded by mountain gorges that act like gigantic funnels to draw down the cold winds from the mountains. The shallow waters of the lake are churned into fury by them (*The Gospel According to Mark*, p. 68).

I well remember an incident that took place on one of my many trips to the Holy Land. With a party of about forty my wife and I had just eaten a fish dinner at a fishing village on the east shore of the Lake of Galilee. While we were eating, a storm blew up. By the time our boat pulled out from the pier, the waves were furious. It seemed that when we went over a crest and down into the trough between, we were going to the bottom of the lake!

The King James Version says that the boat "was now full." But if the boat had been full of water it would have been at the bottom of the lake, not still floating on the surface! By the use of the present infinitive of action as *taking place*, not completed, the Greek very clearly says that the boat was "already filling." The disciples could not bail out the water fast enough to keep the boat from gradually filling up, and they were naturally very scared. So the correct translation here is "was already filling up" (NASB) or "was nearly swamped" (NIV).

D. Terrified Disciples: v. 38

"Jesus was in the stern, sleeping on a cushion." This shows how very weary He was. He had stretched out on a cushion, probably on the steersman's seat at the rear of the boat. By the time they got well on the way, He was sound asleep.

How soundly Jesus slept is highlighted by the fact that the furious storm and the activity of the twelve disciples bailing out water did not waken Him. We read, "The disciples woke him and said to him: 'Teacher, don't you care if we drown?'" The Greek literally says: "Teacher, is it not a care to you that we are perishing?" They apparently expected to drown at any moment. No wonder they were terrified!

E. Divine Command: v. 39

"He got up, rebuked the wind and said to the waves, 'Quiet! Be still!' Then the wind died down and it was completely calm."

The first word Jesus spoke literally means, "Be silent." The second literally says, "Be muzzled." Alfred Plummer comments, "The rare perfect imperative indicates that what is commanded is to continue in its effects: *be still* and remain so" (*The Gospel According to St. Mark*, p. 136).

Christ, the Creator, spoke with divine authority. As soon as He gave the command, "the wind died down and it was completely calm."

This was a double miracle. The first miracle was that the wind obeyed its Creator and ceased to blow. But the second miracle was even more remarkable. Normally when a heavy wind stops blowing on the water, the waves continue to roll heavily for a long time afterward. But this time the water "was completely calm." Contrary to nature, both the "wind" and the "waves" obeyed the Master's voice and became still. Jesus can still the storms in our lives and give us a great calm inside.

F. Reproof of Disciples: v. 40

Jesus then said to His disciples: "Why are you so afraid? Do you still have no faith?" The word "afraid" refers to cowardly terror. Although these disciples were seasoned sailors, they became terror-stricken in the face of this tempest. Jesus suggested that the cure for fear is faith.

G. The Disciples' Reaction: v. 41

"They were terrified and asked each other, 'Who is this? Even the winds and the waves obey him!'"

I have commented:

It was a different fear that now marked their attitude toward Jesus. They were filled with awe at His majestic presence and power. . . . It is to be noted that Jesus did not rebuke the disciples for their new fear of Him (*Mark*, p. 69).

II. RAISING JAIRUS' DAUGHTER: MARK 5:21-43

A. Jairus' Plea: vv. 21-24

The first twenty verses of this chapter tell about Jesus going across to the east side of the Lake of Galilee, "to the region of the Gerasenes" (v. 1).

There He cast a legion of demons out of a man.

Now we read in verse 21: "When Jesus had again crossed over by boat to the other side"—that is, the west side—"a large crowd gathered around him." As we have previously noted, the west side of the lake was heavily populated.

A synagogue ruler named Jairus had been eagerly awaiting Jesus' return, for his daughter was desperately ill. When he saw Jesus, "he fell at his feet and pleaded earnestly with him, 'My little daughter is dying. Please come and put your hands on her so that she will be healed and live.' So Jesus went with him" (vv. 22-24).

B. Healing the Sick Woman: vv. 25-34

In the large crowd that "followed and pressed around him" (v. 24) was a woman "who had been subject to bleeding for twelve years" (v. 25). She slipped up behind Jesus, touched His cloak, and "immediately her bleeding stopped" (v. 29)

C. Distressing News: v. 35

Jesus paused to carry on a conversation with the woman (vv. 30-34). We can easily imagine how Jairus was feeling: "Why is He wasting all this precious time while my daughter is dying? Doesn't He care at all?"

Just at that moment some men came hurrying up to Jairus and said: "Your daughter is dead. Why bother the teacher any more?" Poor Jairus must have been almost overcome with frustration. "If Jesus hadn't stopped to talk with that woman, He might have reached my house in time to save my daughter." It was just too much!

D. Jesus' Reaction: v. 36

The King James Version says, "As soon as Jesus heard the word that was spoken." But the Greek verb for "heard" is not the common *akouo*, which means

"hear," but *parakouo*. This compound literally means "hear beside" (*para*). So it first was used in the sense of "overhear" (cf. NASB). But later it came to mean "hear without heeding, take no heed" (Abbott-Smith, *A Manual Greek Lexicon of the New Testament*, p. 341). In the only other place in the New Testament where it occurs (Matt. 18:17, twice), it clearly means "neglect to hear" (KJV), or "refuses to listen" (NASB, NIV). So it would seem that the wisest translation here is "ignoring" (NIV). H. B. Swete notes, "In the Septuagint *parakouein* is uniformly to neglect or refuse to hear, or to act as if one did not hear. . . . The Lord heard the words said . . . but spoke as if He had not heard" (*The Gospel According to St. Mark*, p. 101). Moulton and Milligan confirm this meaning from the papyri of that period. And Vincent Taylor argues in favor of it (*The Gospel According to St. Mark*, p. 294).

And so we read, "Ignoring what they said, Jesus told the synagogue ruler, 'Don't be afraid; just believe.'" The Greek literally says: "Do not go on being afraid; only keep on believing." Jairus' heart had sunk at the shattering news of his daughter's death. Jesus urged him not to lose faith.

E. The Three Disciples: v. 37

"He did not let anyone follow him except Peter, James and John, the brother of James."

This is one of three instances where Jesus took only these three disciples with Him. The other two places were the Mount of Transfiguration and the Garden of Gethsemane. I have commented:

Added privilege brought added responsibility. One pays a greater price for being in the inner circle; but there is also greater glory. Peter was the preacher at Pentecost. James was the first of the apostles to die a martyr's death. John lived the longest of the apostles and according to tradition suffered much for Christ. But he left an invaluable legacy in his writings. This was a great trio (*Mark*, p. 76).

F. Loud Commotion: v. 38

"When they came to the home of the synagogue ruler, Jesus saw a commotion, with people crying and wailing loudly."

Swete draws this picture of the scene:

> The Lord has dismissed one crowd only to find the house occupied by another. . . . For the moment He stands gazing at the strange spectacle. . . . the uproarious crowd within consisted of mourners. . . . The mourners were probably professional; among them were musicians . . . and wailing women. . . . "even the poorest of Israel will afford his dead wife not less than two minstrels and one woman to make lamentations" (J. Lightfoot), and this was the house of an *archisynagogos* (*St. Mark*, p. 102).

Today we like quiet during a time of mourning, but the Jews of that day actually paid professional mourners to weep and wail—the louder the better! The relatives would also be wailing loudly. The din must have been terrific.

G. Jesus' Intervention: vv. 39-40a

"He went in and said to them, 'Why all this commotion and wailing? The child is not dead but asleep.' But they laughed at him."

As the conqueror of death and master of life Jesus walked into the home. The first thing He did was to reprove the noisy crowd for its loud commotion. Then He indicated why it was not appropriate: "The child is not dead but asleep."

Both terms, "dead" and "asleep," are to be taken in a figurative sense. The girl really had died, but her death was only temporary, so it was more like a sleep.

We find this use of the term in other places in the New Testament. The first of these is also on the lips of Jesus. In John 11:11 we read that Jesus said to His disciples: "Our friend Lazarus has fallen asleep; but I am going . . . to wake him up." Actually, Lazarus had died two days before, and his dead body was right then lying in a tomb. When the disciples misunderstood their Master, we read this explanation: "Jesus had been speaking of his death, but his disciples thought he meant natural sleep" (v. 13).

Second, in I Thessalonians 4:13-16 we read about "those who fall asleep" (v. 13), "those who have fallen asleep in him" (v. 14) and again, "those who have fallen asleep" (v. 15). But in verse 16 these are referred to as "the dead in Christ." They are asleep in Jesus.

A third use of the term "asleep" is particularly striking. In Acts 7:58 we read that the religious leaders stoned Stephen. He fell on his knees and asked the Lord to forgive his persecutors. Then we read that when he had done that, "he fell asleep." The Greek verb there gives us our English word "cemetery," a place where "the dead in Christ" actually "sleep."

H. Divine Command: vv. 40b-41

Putting all His mockers (v. 40a) out of the house, Jesus took the child's father and mother and His three disciples "and went in where the child was." The scene was too sacred for noisy

---

DISCUSSION QUESTIONS

1. Why did Jesus need times of retirement?
2. What do the Gospels indicate as to the relationship of Jesus' divine and human natures?
3. What was Jesus' attitude toward desperate need?
4. Why did Jesus keep Jairus waiting?
5. Why did Jesus take the three disciples with Him?
6. Why did Jesus avoid publicity?

wailing. Furthermore, miracles require an atmosphere of faith, not of cynical laughter.

Then we read: "He took her by the hand and said to her, *'Talitha koumi!'* (which means, 'Little girl, I say to you, get up!')." The common language of the home at that time in Palestine was Aramaic, which the Jews had learned in their Babylonian captivity. The two Aramaic words which Jesus used, *talitha koumi,* are explained here in Greek for Mark's Roman readers, who would not know Aramaic.

I. Immediate Healing: v. 42

"Immediately the girl stood up and walked around (she was twelve years old)." The statement in parentheses is perhaps added to show that this "little girl" was old enough to walk, not an infant.

J. Human Care: v. 43

"He gave strict orders not to let anyone know about this, and told them to give her something to eat."

Swete says that in this last command "We have fresh evidence of the sympathetic tenderness of the Lord, and His attention to small details in which the safety or comfort of others was involved." He goes on to say, "But life restored by miracle must be supported by ordinary means; the miracle has no place where human care or labour will suffice" (*St. Mark*, p. 104). That is a sensible lesson which some people have failed to learn.

CONTEMPORARY APPLICATION

We have heard the remark: "I don't believe in vacations. The devil never takes a vacation!" But are we supposed to be following the devil's example or Jesus' example? Our Lord *did* take vacations while here on earth, though they sometimes turned out to be interrupted (or invaded) times of hoped-for rest.

As noted in the lesson commentary, on several occasions Jesus withdrew from the crowds, but He sometimes found a crowd awaiting Him at the proposed vacation spot, as in the incident of the feeding of the five thousand (c. 6). If Jesus felt the need for times of physical and spiritual renewal, surely we need them.

JESUS CALLS PERSONS TO MINISTER

DEVOTIONAL READING	Mark 9:33-41

ADULTS AND YOUTH

Adult Topic: *Jesus Calls Persons to Minister*

Youth Topic: *Choosing the Best Way*

Background Scripture: Mark 8:27—9:50

Scripture Lesson: Mark 8:27-38

Memory Verse: *If any man would come after me, let him deny himself and take up his cross and follow me.* Mark 8:34

CHILDREN

Topic: *Jesus Wants Children to Know Him*

Background Scripture: Mark 8:27-38

Scripture Lesson: Mark 8:27-30

Memory Verse: *Peter answered him, "You are the Christ."* Mark 8:29

DAILY BIBLE READINGS

Mar. 19 M.: Peter's Declaration About Jesus. Mark 8:27-31
Mar. 20 T.: Jesus' Transfiguration. Mark 9:2-8
Mar. 21 W.: Prophecies About Elijah. Mark 9:9-13
Mar. 22 T.: Jesus Shows His Disciples How to Minister. Mark 9:17-27
Mar. 23 F.: Passion Foretold and True Greatness. Mark 9:30-41
Mar. 24 S.: Consistent Christian Lifestyle. Mark 9:42-50
Mar. 25 S.: Jesus Calls for Disciples. Mark 8:34—9:1

LESSON AIM

To see what it means to follow Jesus.

LESSON SETTING

Time: A.D. 29 or 30

Place: northern Galilee

LESSON OUTLINE

Jesus Calls Persons to Minister

I. **Peter's Confession:** Mark 8:27-30
  A. Jesus' Question: v. 27
  B. The Disciples' Answer: v. 28
  C. Personal Question: v. 29a
  D. Peter's Answer: v. 29b
  E. Strange Warning: v. 30

II. **Prediction of the Passion:** Mark 8:31-33
  A. Death and Resurrection: v. 31
  B. Peter's Rebuke: v. 32
  C. Jesus' Rebuke of Peter: v. 33

III. **The Cost of Discipleship:** Mark 8:34-38
   A. Three Requirements: v. 34
   B. Losing to Save: v. 35
   C. Value of the Human Soul: vv. 36-37
   D. Divine Retribution: v. 38

SUGGESTED INTRODUCTION FOR ADULTS

We have already noted that Mark is the "Gospel of Action." We find many fast-moving events between last week's lesson and today's study. The first event is Jesus' rejection by His own townspeople at Nazareth (6:1-6). Then we find Him sending out His twelve apostles on a mission of healing and preaching (6:7-13). The gruesome story of John the Baptist being beheaded by Herod Antipas follows (6:14-29). Then comes the only miracle of Jesus recorded in all four Gospels, the feeding of the five thousand (6:30-44). Following that we find Jesus walking on the Lake of Galilee (6:45-56). And so we have five important events, all in one chapter.

In chapter 7 we have only three incidents. The first is Jesus' conflict with the Pharisees over the subject of cleanness and uncleanness (vv. 1-23). Then follows the interesting account of the amazing faith of a Syro-Phoenician woman (vv. 24-30). The final incident is Jesus' healing of a deaf and dumb man in the Decapolis (vv. 31-37).

Chapter 8 records the feeding of the four thousand (vv. 1-10), another controversy with the Pharisees (vv. 11-13), Jesus' talk about the yeast of the Pharisees and Herod (vv. 14-21), and the healing of a blind man at Bethsaida. That brings us to our lesson for today.

SUGGESTED INTRODUCTION FOR YOUTH

We have a very important topic today: "Choosing the Best Way." Too many young people—even professing Christians—choose something less than the best in life. This is tragic. Life is too short and eternity is too long for us to waste our opportunities here and pay the penalty forever.

You say, "How can I know what is best?" Read your Bible daily. Pray each day, and ask God to show you what is His best for you in life. He has promised to guide us if we ask Him to. We are told in Proverbs 3:5-6:

> Trust in the LORD with all your heart
>   and lean not on your own understanding;
> in all your ways acknowledge him,
>   and he will direct your paths (margin).

That is the best way to live!

CONCEPTS FOR CHILDREN

1. "Jesus Wants Children to Know Him."
2. Jesus can make Himself real to children.
3. Children can be happy Christians.
4. Children should listen to their Christian parents.

THE LESSON COMMENTARY

I. PETER'S CONFESSION: Mark 8:27-30

A. Jesus' Question: v. 27

"Jesus and his disciples went on to the villages around Caesarea Philippi. On the way he asked them, 'Who do people say I am?'"

Caesarea Philippi has an interesting history. It was near one of the main sources of the Jordan River, north of the Lake of Galilee. Here the river seems to *leap* out of a subterranean cavern and dance over the rocks in sheer excitement. For this reason it is thought to have been a chief center for the ancient worship of Baal. When the Greeks took it over, following Alexander the Great, they made it into a shrine for their god Pan, and named it Paneion. The surrounding district was called Paneas, and this survives in the present name of the city, Banias. It is about twenty-five miles north of Bethsaida Julias, which is on the north shore of the Lake of Galilee, and it is at the foot of Mount Hermon (elevation 9,166 feet). Herod the Great's son Philip named the city after the emperor Tiberius Caesar. He added Philippi to distinguish it from the Caesarea his father had built on the shores of the Mediterranean.

The Greek word *pan* means "all." It was in this center of the worship of the All-god that Jesus called for the confession of His Messiahship and deity.

We note that Jesus and His disciples went to "the villages around Caesarea Philippi." It may very well be that they avoided going into the city because Jews considered it an unclean place on account of its strong pagan associations.

On the way to Caesarea Philippi Jesus asked His disciples, "Who do people say I am?"—literally, "say me to be?" Of course, Jesus was not asking for information. Some extreme liberals have gone so far as to say that Jesus had begun to wonder who He might be after all. Perhaps somewhat plaintively, after brooding over the question during their long walk northward, He finally asked His disciples, "Who do people say I am?" Still groping for light He said, "Who do you say I am?" To His great relief Peter confirmed Jesus' own budding suspicions!

Of course this whole reconstruction is completely contrary to the biblical account. Before Jesus began His public ministry, the voice of the Father from heaven had declared, "You are my Son" (1:11). From the very beginning of His ministry Jesus was conscious of His messianic mission.

B. The Disciples' Answer: v. 28

In answer to Jesus' question, "Who do people say I am?" the disciples replied. "Some say John the Baptist; others say Elijah; and still others, one of the prophets."

Jesus had preached the same basic message of repentance that John the Baptist had proclaimed (Matt. 3:2; 4:7). So it is not surprising that some had made this identification. We read earlier in Mark that some were saying about Jesus, "John the Baptist has been raised from the dead, and that is why miraculous powers are at work in him" (6:14). Then Herod Antipas himself declared, "John, the man I beheaded, has been raised from the dead!" (6:16). Herod's conscience had doubtless bothered him ever since he had John the Baptist put to death, and it is not surprising that he reacted this way.

Others were saying that Jesus was "Elijah." Since that great prophet had not died, but had been taken up to heaven (II Kings 2:11), it was expected that he would return to earth and finally die. People found support for this in Malachi 4:5, where we read, "See, I will send you the prophet Elijah before that great and dreadful day of the LORD comes."

Still others were saying, "one of the prophets." In Mark 6:15 we read that some claimed, "He is a prophet, like one of the prophets of long ago." They found many things in their Scriptures (our Old Testament) that seemed paralleled in the ministries of the ancient prophets, such as Moses, Samuel, and Elisha.

The surprising thing is that apparently no one suggested that Jesus was the Messiah. In Mark 1:24 the demons in a demon-possessed man right in the synagogue on the Sabbath, with many people present, cried out: "What do you want with us, Jesus of Nazareth? . . . I know who you are—the Holy One of God." Again we read that whenever demons saw Jesus they fell down before him and cried out, "You are the Son of God" (3:11; cf. 5:7). Evidently the people did not care to accept this testimony.

C. Personal Question: v. 29a

It was interesting to hear what others thought about Jesus. But now He confronted the disciples with a very personal question: "But what about you? Who do you say I am?" The New International Version brings out the force of the original Greek: "But *you*"—emphatic in the Greek—"who do you say me to be?" What others thought about Jesus was, of course, important, but what the disciples thought about His identity was *all*-important.

D. Peter's Answer: v. 29b

Peter, as the usual spokesman for the twelve apostles, gave a very definite reply: "You are the Christ." The Greek word *christos* means "anointed." It is equivalent to the Hebrew *maschiah*, from which we get the familiar term "Messiah." Peter declared, "You are the Messiah." And the "you" here is also very emphatic in the Greek: *"You* are the Christ."

Matthew reports Jesus as replying to Peter: "Blessed are you, Simon son of Jonah, for this was not revealed to you by man, but by my Father in heaven" (16:17). Only a divine revelation could have enabled Peter to answer so positively. It was not "I think," but "you are!"

E. Strange Warning: v. 30

"Jesus warned them not to tell anyone about him."

The verb here translated "warned" (NASB, NIV), or "charged" (KJV, RSV), occurs twenty-nine times in the New Testament. All but five of these times it is translated "rebuke" (KJV). Except for two cases (II Tim. 4:2; Jude 9) it occurs only in the synoptic Gospels. It is used of Jesus rebuking demons, the wind, and here the disciples. It is found again in verses 32 and 33, where Peter rebukes Jesus, and in turn Jesus rebukes him.

Why is such a strong term used here? I have suggested:

> Probably the main reason is to be found in the erroneous ideas of Messiahship held by the disciples. Jesus did not want them beginning to talk about His setting up an earthly kingdom and delivering the Jews from Roman oppression. Before the disciples could preach Jesus as the Messiah their hearts must be purified at Pentecost and their minds must be enlightened by the Holy Spirit to understand. Then, too, an open declaration of His Messiahship at this time would probably have precipitated a revolution against Rome or caused the premature death of Jesus (*The Gospel According to Mark*, p. 105).

Up to this point in the Gospel of Mark, Jesus had been dealing mainly with the multitudes, healing and teaching. From now on we find Him majoring on instructing His disciples, in preparation for the climactic events and His leaving them.

Harvie Branscomb has put it well. He writes:

> At this point in the Gospel a definite change takes place both in content and in tone. To this point we have

had accounts of Jesus as a public figure, teaching the multitudes, healing the sick, sending His disciples out to proclaim His message. In the section now beginning the primary interest is in the relationship of Jesus to His more intimate disciples, their recognition of Him as the Messiah, and His teaching of them as to the necessity of His sufferings and death (*The Gospel of St. Mark*, p. 143).

The last item here includes what is said in verse 31. So we turn immediately to that.

II. PREDICTION OF THE PASSION: Mark 8:31-33

A. Death and Resurrection: v. 31

"He then began to teach them that the Son of Man must suffer many things and be rejected by the elders, chief priests and teachers of the law, and that he must be killed and after three days rise again."

Of verses 31-33 I have written:

This paragraph marks a new departure in the teaching of Jesus. This is suggested by the word "began." Plummer (CGT, p. 203) remarks: "It was indeed a new beginning." All else that Jesus had taught was but leading up to the great truth of His death and resurrection. The passion was the central purpose of His presence on earth. Now for the first time Jesus told the disciples of His imminent suffering. The cross must be the prelude to the kingdom (*Mark*, p. 105).

Verse 31 contains the first of three announcements that Jesus made concerning His coming death and resurrection. The other two are found in 9:31 and 10:32-34. It is significant that all of these come after Peter's confession of Jesus' Messiahship. Because the disciples shared the popular ideas about the Messiah—as evidenced by Acts 1:6—it was necessary for Jesus to correct their erroneous concept by telling them what was really predicted about the Messiah, the Servant of the

Lord. We have been prepared for this by our study of that topic in Isaiah.

Verse 31 is closely paralleled in the other two synoptic Gospels (Matt. 16:21; Luke 9:22). All three accounts use the Greek word *dei*, "must, it is necessary."

Why "must" He suffer? Ezra Gould answers that question this way:

The necessity arises, first, from the hostility of men; secondly, from the spiritual nature of his work, which made it impossible for him to oppose force to force; and thirdly, from the providential purpose of God, who made the death of Jesus the central thing in redemption (*A Critical and Exegetical Commentary on the Gospel According to St. Mark*, p. 153).

It was, of course, this third point that made Jesus' death inevitable, as the expression of divine love for lost humanity. There was no other way that we could be saved from sin.

Since this verse is of paramount importance, I should like to quote from my commentary on Mark:

Jesus declared that He would be rejected by the elders and the chief priests and the scribes. The repetition of the definite article in the Greek underscores the responsibility of each of these classes for His death. The chief priest would include the high priest, ex-high priests and perhaps those in charge of the various courses of priests. The elders would perhaps originally be older men, but had probably by now become a rather distinct class. The name was evidently applied in general to rulers of the nation. The scribes were the teachers of the law. These three groups comprised the Great Sanhedrin at Jerusalem, which condemned Jesus to death (*Mark*, p. 106).

"Rejected" is the Greek verb *apo-dokimazo*, which literally means to disapprove after examination. "The Sanhedrin held an investigation of Jesus' claims to be the Messiah, rejected these claims, and condemned Him to death as a false Messiah, an imposter" (*Mark*, p. 106).

Jesus predicted not only His death, but also His resurrection. "After three days" is equivalent to Matthew's and Luke's "on the third day." The Jewish method of reckoning would include the day of His death and that of His resurrection, as well as the one full day between. Parts of days were treated as whole days.

B. Peter's Rebuke: v. 32

"He spoke plainly about this, and Peter took him aside and began to rebuke him." He was deeply disturbed about the line Jesus was taking. I have observed, "Peter is not the only follower of Jesus who thought he knew more than the Master about some things" (*Mark*, p. 106).

C. Jesus' Rebuke of Peter: v. 33

"But when Jesus turned and looked at his disciples, he rebuked Peter. 'Out of my sight, Satan!' he said. 'You do not have in mind the things of God, but the things of men.'"

These words of Jesus are certainly startling. It is the same expression that He used when the devil tempted Him (Matt. 4:10). How can we explain this?

I have suggested:

It is evident that Jesus saw in the solicitude of Peter the same temptation to avoid suffering and choose the easy way which Satan had presented to Him at the beginning of His ministry. As the time of His passion drew near the temptation would gain in point and poignancy. Already the shadow of the cross was beginning to fall across His path; why not turn aside? Jesus could not trifle a moment with this idea (*Mark*, pp. 106-7).

The closing statement of Christ— "You do not have in mind the things of God"—is similar to what Paul wrote in Romans 8:5 and Colossians 3:2. Peter's mind was filled with earthly affairs rather than heavenly truths.

He was materially minded rather than spiritually minded.

H. B. Swete comments:

It is not merely the officiousness of Peter which is rebuked, but the grave error which led him to interfere. His resistance to the thought of the Passion revealed a deep cleavage between his mind and the Mind of God (*The Gospel According to St. Mark*, 107-8).

The thing that distinguished Jesus from all other men was His perfect conformity to the divine will. That should be our goal as Christians.

III. THE COST OF DISCIPLESHIP: Mark 8:34-38

A. Three Requirements: v. 34

Calling the crowd to Him, along with His disciples, Jesus declared: "If anyone would come after me, he must deny himself and take up his cross and follow me."

This is one of Jesus' most important sayings. I have commented:

In this saying, as in many others, Jesus cut squarely across the world's philosophy of life. Over the portals of the path supposedly leading to worldly success are the words: "Assert yourself!" At the entrance of the pathway of eternal life one finds the words: "Deny yourself!" The first, the philosophy of Friedrich

---

DISCUSSION QUESTIONS

1. What are some opinions of Jesus today?
2. How can we *know* that Jesus is the Son of God?
3. Why did the religious leaders condemn Jesus?
4. Why did Jesus have to suffer so much?
5. What does "take up his cross" mean to you?
6. How can one "forfeit his soul"?

Nietzsche, has plunged this generation into bloodshed and destruction. The second, the philosophy of Jesus Christ, the Healer of nations, leads to life eternal. The first marks the path of self-love; the second shows the way of divine love. Each person must choose which path he will take (*Mark*, p. 107).

To take up one's cross is to accept the will of God as his or her will, no matter what the cost. It is having the old self crucified with Christ (Rom. 6:6). It is saying an everlasting no to self and an everlasting yes to God.

It is worth noting that "deny" and "take up" are in the aorist tense of instantaneous action, whereas "follow" is in the present tense of continuous action. Self-denial and self-crucifixion are crucial experiences of surrender to the will of God. One must go on following Christ as long as he or she lives.

B. Losing to Save: v. 35

"For whoever wants to save his life will lose it, but whoever loses his life for me and for the gospel will save it."

What Jesus here declares is that to save one's life in the highest way one must lose himself in service to God. Every consecrated Christian has found that the best life comes through losing one's self in unselfish living for God and others. "One of the greatest compensations that a Christian worker has is in the multiplication of his own life in the lives of those he helps. In this way lies the path of true happiness and deep joy" (Earle, *Mark*, p. 108).

C. Value of the Human Soul: vv. 36–37

"What good is it for a man to gain the whole world, yet forfeit his soul? Or what can a man give in exchange for his soul?"

The Greek word for "soul" in verses 36 and 37 is the same as for "life" in verse 35. It is *psyche*, which has both meanings. The distinction in translation here (found in most versions) seems logical.

If a man forfeits his soul through rejecting God's offer of salvation, what "exchange" or ransom price can he give for it? To ask the question is to answer it.

D. Divine Retribution: v. 38

This verse contains a stern truth. If we are ashamed of Christ and His words in this sinful world, He will be ashamed of us when He comes in His kingdom. The word "adulterous" should be taken in its Old Testament prophetic sense of "apostate, unfaithful to God." If we turn away from Christ, we are responsible for the consequences.

CONTEMPORARY APPLICATION

The heart of our lesson is expressed in our key verse for today: "If any man would come after me, he must deny himself and take up his cross and follow me."

The oldest Christian church in the world is the Church of the Nativity in Bethlehem. Built in the fourth century, it was rebuilt in the sixth century and still stands—an impressive building over the manger below.

One would expect a large entrance to a great church like this. Instead one has to bow low, or, for a tall person, almost crawl to get in. One can see the outlines of the original massive door. But in the Middle Ages the Turks used to ride in on horseback on Sunday and kill the worshipers. So the doorway was largely blocked in. The tiny entrance is now called "The Door of Humiliation." It is a parable of the entrance to the Christian life: "Let him deny himself."

THE WAY OF THE SERVANT

DEVOTIONAL READING	Mark 10:23-31

Adult Topic: *Not to Be Served but to Serve*

Youth Topic: *The Way to Greatness*

ADULTS AND YOUTH

Background Scripture: Mark 10

Scripture Lesson: Mark 10:32-45

Memory Verse: *The Son of man also came not to be served but to serve, and to give his life as a ransom for many.* Mark 10:45

Topic: *Jesus Has a Difficult Time*

Background Scripture: Mark 10:1-52

CHILDREN

Scripture Lesson: Mark 10:35-45

Memory Verse: *For the Son of man also came not to be served, but to serve, and to give his life.* Mark 10:45

DAILY BIBLE READINGS

Mar. 26 M.: The Sacredness of Marriage. Mark 10:1-12
Mar. 27 T.: Blessing the Children. Mark 10:13-16
Mar. 28 W.: The Rich and the Kingdom. Mark 10:17-31
Mar. 29 T.: Passion Told the Third Time. Mark 10:32-34
Mar. 30 F.: Making Blind Bartimaeus See. Mark 10:46-52
Mar. 31 S.: A Mother's Request. Matt. 20:20-24
Apr. 1 S.: Greatness Comes in Serving. Mark 10:35-45

LESSON AIM

To see how Jesus fulfilled the role of a servant, and how we should do the same.

LESSON SETTING

Time: about A.D. 30

Place: Perea, east of the Jordan River

LESSON OUTLINE

The Way of the Servant

  I. **Third Prediction of the Passion:** Mark 10:32-34
     A. The Courage of the Master: v. 32
     B. The Prediction of His Death: vv. 33-34

  II. **The Request of James and John:** Mark 10:35-40
     A. Their Approach: v. 35
     B. Jesus' Reply: v. 36
     C. Their Request: v. 37
     D. Jesus' Challenge: v. 38
     E. Their Superficial Answer: v. 39a
     F. Jesus' Final Answer: vv. 39b-40

  III. **The True Role of a Christian:** Mark 10:41-45
     A. Indignation of the Ten: v. 41
     B. Worldly Rulers: v. 42
     C. True Greatness: vv. 43-44
     D. The Example of Jesus: v. 45

SUGGESTED
INTRODUCTION
FOR ADULTS

Today we begin our study of Unit II: "Jesus Gives His Life for Sinners." This was not only the climax but the most important part of Jesus' ministry on earth. He did not come primarily to teach or to work miracles but in the words of our memory verse for today—"to give his life as a ransom for many."

In last week's lesson we found Jesus in the far north of Galilee, near Caesarea Philippi (Mark 8:27). There the Transfiguration took place (9:2-13). Next we see Him in Capernaum (9:33), the headquarters of His great Galilean ministry. But in 10:1 we read: "Jesus then left that place and went into the region of Judea and across the Jordan." The Greek word for "across" is *peran.* So this region east of the Jordan River was called "Perea" in Jesus' day. In modern times it has been known as Transjordan. Today it is the Hashemite Kingdom of the Jordan, usually referred to as simply "Jordan."

**SUGGESTED
INTRODUCTION
FOR YOUTH**

Our topic today is "The Way to Greatness." It is not wrong to want to be great, but there are two problems connected with this desire.

The first is: Why do we want to be great? Is it because we want to make a big name for ourselves? (Incidentally, not all famous people are really great people!) Or is it because we want to be big enough to do a great work for God and humanity?

The second problem is the nature of true greatness. Jesus clearly told His disciples that the main mark of true greatness is humility—not pride, self-assertion, or exercise of authority. As Christians we are not to accept the world's standards, but Jesus' standards. He is our example and our Lord.

**CONCEPTS FOR
CHILDREN**

1. Jesus did not come to be served, but to serve.
2. Too often children are selfish and want others to wait on them.
3. If we are true followers of Jesus we will wish to serve others.
4. Jesus can help us to do this in our daily lives.

THE LESSON COMMENTARY

I. THIRD PREDICTION OF THE PASSION:
Mark 10:32-34

A. The Courage of the Master: v. 32

"They were on their way up to Jerusalem, with Jesus leading the way, and the disciples were astonished, while those who followed were afraid."

We have already noted (in the Introduction) that in verse one we found Jesus in Perea, east of the Jordan. Verse 46 says, "Then they came to Jericho," which was on the west bank of the Jordan River. So Jesus and His disciples were still in Perea at this time.

This was Jesus' last, fateful journey to Jerusalem. John's Gospel indicates that Jesus went up to Jerusalem each year for the Passover festival. But this time He was to be slain as the Passover Lamb, sacrificed for the sins of all humanity. It was a crucial time.

Jesus was "leading the way," walking ahead of His disciples, who were "astonished." Meanwhile, "those who followed were afraid." Some scholars have suggested that only one group is mentioned—the disciples. But the New International Version (and somewhat the NASB) reflects the opinion of the majority of commentators that there were two groups. H. B. Swete writes:

> The Lord walked in advance of the Twelve with a solemnity and determination which foreboded danger. . . . His manner struck awe into the minds of the Twelve, who were beginning at length to anticipate an impending disaster . . . whilst the rest of the company, . . . the crowd who usually hung upon the Lord's footsteps, . . . or His fellow-travellers on their way to the Passover, were conscious of a vague fear. . . . There was risk of a real panic, and the Lord therefore checks His course, till the Twelve have come up to Him (*The Gospel According to St. Mark*, p. 219).

The look of firm determination on the face of Jesus must have impressed the disciples greatly, since He had told them He was going up to Jerusalem to die (9:31). They were astonished at His marching forward so fearlessly toward certain death. And the crowd of Passover pilgrims following behind was also moved by the sight. James Morison comments:

> The evangelist distinguishes between the apostles who would be nearest to our Lord, though at a distance, and the miscellaneous crowd who had been looking on wistfully, and listening as they had opportunity, and "following." To them the Saviour was an impenetrable Mystery; He was entirely unique and unearthly; and as He strode along sublimely, in advance of His chosen disciples, their reverence rose up into a weird feeling of awe, under which they began to tremble and be afraid (*A Practical Commentary on the Gospel According to St. Mark*, p. 292).

"Again he took the Twelve aside and told them what was going to happen to him." As we shall now see, this was the third prediction of the Passion.

B. The Prediction of His Death: vv. 33–34

Here is what Jesus told His disciples: "We are going up to Jerusalem, and the Son of Man will be betrayed to the chief priests and teachers of the law. They will condemn him to death and will hand him over to the Gentiles, who will mock him and spit on him, flog him and kill him. Three days later he will rise."

In last week's lesson we studied the first prediction of the Passion (8:31). There we noted that it came right after Peter's confession at Caesarea Philippi that Jesus was the Messiah (8:27–30). The second prediction, in 9:31, is somewhat briefer: "The Son of Man is going to be betrayed into the hands of men. They will kill him, and after three days he will rise."

The third prediction, quoted above, is much more full and specific. Swete writes:

> Six successive steps are clearly enumerated, and in their actual order—(1) the betrayal . . . , (2) the sentence of the Sanhedrin . . . , (3) the handing over of the Prisoner to the Roman power . . . , (4) the mockery and its details . . . , (5) the Crucifixion . . . , (6) the Resurrection (*St. Mark*, p. 220).

Why did the Sanhedrin have to "hand him over to the Gentiles?" Two answers to this question may be given. The first is that the Roman government had taken away from the Jewish supreme court the right to administer capital punishment. To get Jesus executed, the Sanhedrin had to turn Him over to the governor, Pilate.

The second answer is that the Scriptures had to be fulfilled. One of the outstanding messianic psalms is

Psalm 22. It pictures a scene of crucifixion. The Jewish method of capital punishment was by stoning, as often noted in the Old Testament (e.g., Deut. 13:10; 17:5; 22:21, 24). But it was God's will that Jesus should suffer the most ignominious death, crucifixion, which was used for slaves and criminals.

How does Psalm 22 picture death by crucifixion? Verse 14 says: "All my bones are out of joint." That would be true of a person hanging on a cross for hours. "They have pierced my hands and my feet" (v. 16) was literally fulfilled in Jesus' crucifixion. And especially appropriate to a crucifixion scene are the words of verse 17: I can count all my bones; people stare and gloat over me.

II. THE REQUEST OF JAMES AND JOHN: Mark 10:35-40

A. Their Approach: v. 35

"Then James and John, the sons of Zebedee, came to him. 'Teacher,' they said, 'we want you to do for us whatever we ask.'" This was a most unreasonable request for anyone to make. Asking a person to agree to do whatever we might ask before we state our petition is nothing short of insulting.

B. Jesus' Reply: v. 36

Very properly the Master answered His two disciples by saying, "What do you want me to do for you?" He was not going to make a blanket promise before hearing their request. More than one person has run into trouble by failing to observe this common-sense procedure.

C. Their Request: v. 37

James and John stated their request plainly: "Let one of us sit at your right and the other at your left in your glory." Matthew (20:20-21) has "the mother of Zebedee's sons" coming to Jesus with her sons, kneeling down before Him, and making this request. She may have originated the idea, out of maternal ambition or pride. Or the sons may have solicited her help. It should be noted that in Matthew (20:22) as well as Mark (10:38) Jesus addressed Himself directly to the sons. They probably had their mother ask first, thinking that Jesus would be more lenient toward her, and then joined her in making the petition.

The timing of this petition is almost unbelievable. Jesus had just made the third and most detailed prediction of His passion, and now two of His leading disciples furnish a most shocking spectacle of self-ambition. I have written elsewhere:

> How it must have hurt the Master to see how far short His disciples had fallen in understanding what He had just said about His coming sufferings. While He was thinking of a cross, they were thinking of crowns. His burden was matched by their blindness, His sacrifice by their selfishness. He wanted only to give, they to get. His motive was service; theirs was self-satisfaction. What a revelation of the carnal mind! And the thing that makes it all the sadder is that James and John had recently been with Him on the Mount of Transfiguration. But that experience only fired their zeal for first place in His glory (*The Gospel According to Mark*, p. 130.

It perhaps goes without saying that the seat on the right was the place of highest honor, while that on the left was the place of second highest honor. Josephus clearly indicates that this was the custom in the first century (*Antiquities* vi.11.9).

It has been suggested that James and John were trying to steal a march on Peter, the other member of the inner circle (Mark 9:2). Furthermore, Jesus had singled him out for special commendation (Matt. 16:17-18). Jealousy among the closest disciples of Jesus is indeed a sad spectacle!

D. Jesus' Challenge: v. 38

The Master said to His two self-ambitious disciples: "You don't know what you are asking." I have suggested, "Perhaps that is the answer Christians today would hear to some of their praying, if only their spiritual ears were keen enough to catch it" (*Mark*, p. 130). Selfishness almost always makes us ask for the wrong things.

Then Jesus challenged James and John with this momentous question: "Can you drink the cup I drink or be baptized with the baptism I am baptized with?" The figure of drinking the cup would be familiar to the Jews (Ps. 75:8). The meaning of baptism would also be understood as suggesting overwhelming floods of sorrows (Isa. 43:2). We speak today of a person undergoing a "baptism of fire," meaning deep suffering. Henry Alford says that the cup "here seems to signify more the *inner* and spiritual bitterness, resembling the agony of the Lord Himself—and the *baptism* . . . more the *outer* accession of persecution and trial" (*The Greek Testament*, 1:204).

E. Their Superficial Answer: v. 39a

Blithely the two disciples replied, "We are able" (KJV). Little did they realize how inappropriate this assertion was. Where were they when Jesus was drinking His cup of sorrow and undergoing His baptism of fire? These two men, along with Peter, were sleeping while He was agonizing in prayer in Gethsemane (14:32-41). When Jesus was arrested in the garden, they, along with all the rest of the apostles, "deserted him and fled" (14:50). No, they certainly proved that they were not able to share His sufferings at that time.

F. Jesus' Final Answer: vv. 39b-40

Jesus said to these two disciples: "You will drink the cup I drink and be baptized with the baptism I am baptized with, but to sit at my right or left is not for me to grant. These places belong to those for whom they have been prepared."

The first part of this (v. 39b) seems to contradict what we have just said. It is true that James—in A.D. 44, fourteen years later—did become the first apostolic martyr, being put to death by Herod Agrippa I (Acts 12:2). And John was banished to the Island of Patmos, doubtless suffering much persecution for the faith. But all of this took place after they were filled with the Holy Spirit at Pentecost. Before that event we find the disciples fearful, hiding behind locked doors (John 20:19, 26). There is no evidence before Pentecost of these two disciples being willing to risk suffering for the sake of Jesus. It is very clear from the scriptural account that it was the Holy Spirit who empowered them to be really "able" to endure the cup and baptism of suffering that Jesus referred to here.

In verse 40 Jesus declared that it was not His prerogative to assign the seats of honor—"These places belong to those for whom they have been prepared." I have observed, "History demonstrates that important places of service, and often honor, go to those who prepare themselves for such places rather than seek them selfishly" (*Mark*, p. 131). James Morison comments (on v. 38), "The degree of exaltation in ultimate glory is not to be a matter of capricious or arbitrary determination. It must be regulated by the degree of the spirit of self-sacrifice during probation" (*St. Mark*, p. 294).

III. THE TRUE ROLE OF A CHRISTIAN: Mark 10:41-45

A. Indignation of the Ten: v. 41

"When the ten heard about this, they became indignant with James and John."

Only here in the New Testament do we find the expression "the ten." Obviously Peter was a part—probably the leader—of this anger and resentment. One could wish that these disciples were showing righteous indignation, but it was evidently an outburst of envy and jealousy. Some of them may even have wished that they had thought to ask first! The disciples still had carnal, selfish hearts.

B. Worldly Rulers: v. 42

Jesus called the disciples together and said to them: "You know that those who are regarded as rulers of the Gentiles lord it over them, and their high officials exercise authority over them."

The Master took advantage of the opportunity to teach a lesson on true greatness. James and John wanted to be great in the kingdom of God. Jesus would show them what was involved in really being great, by drawing a sharp contrast between the pattern of the kingdom of heaven and that of earthly rulers. Gentile rulers "lord it over" their subjects, as the Greek literally says. This was the common attitude of most of the rulers of Jesus' day, as we know from history.

C. True Greatness: vv. 43-44

"Not so with you. Instead, whoever wants to become great among you must be your servant, and whoever wants to be first must be slave of all."

I have commented:

In the kingdom of God greatness is measured by service, not by self-assertiveness. Eternity will furnish a startling revelation of God's appraisal of who are the greatest. It is striking to realize that many shining stars in public life may be low in the heavenly scale, while some obscure, unheard of saints who have lived sacrificial lives will become the "five star generals" (*Mark*, p. 131).

The translation "minister" (KJV) at the end of verse 43 is misleading for the modern reader. In popular usage today "minister" means "pastor," and that is not at all the meaning here. The Greek word *diaconos* simply means "servant." It was first used for one who waited table, a servant in the home, and that was a humble position.

Also the translation "servant" (KJV) in verse 44 is inadequate. The Greek word *doulos* means a "bound" person, and so a "slave" (NASB, NIV). If one wants to be "great" in the kingdom, he must fill the role of a servant. And if one wants "first" place, he must take the lowest place. Paul expresses beautifully his attitude of being a servant, to serve all God's people (I Cor. 9:19; II Cor. 4:5; Gal. 5:13).

D. The Example of Jesus: v. 45

"For even the Son of Man did not come to be served, but to serve, and to give his life as a ransom for many."

The Greek verb for "serve" is *diakoneo*, which simply means to serve—not "minister" (KJV). I have commented:

Jesus not only preached this principle of true greatness; He practiced it. He did not come to be served, but to serve. It seems that not all of His professed followers are really following His example at this point. All attitudes of superiority, of condescension toward those lower than we are in position or attainment, are absolutely contrary to the spirit of Christ (*Mark*, p. 131).

DISCUSSION QUESTIONS

1. Why did Jesus face suffering so courageously?
2. How do you explain the action of James and John?
3. Why is self-seeking unwise as well as wrong?
4. What place does suffering have in our lives?
5. What should be the attitude of church officials?
6. How can we follow Jesus' example?

The word "ransom" here is very significant. The Greek noun *lytron* comes from the verb *lyo*, "loose." It was used for the price paid to release a slave. So Jesus paid the ransom price, His own blood, to free us from the slavery of sin. He took our place on the cross, suffering the penalty we deserved. How grateful we ought to be!

CONTEMPORARY APPLICATION

Self-seeking is a serious sin in God's sight. Instead of seeking a high position in the church, we should seek to serve to the best of our ability. And we should keep improving that ability, so as to be able to serve better.

Are we always wanting others to wait on us? If so, we are not true followers of Christ. He came to earth to serve all humanity, not to sit down and be served.

Jesus put this principle in brief, graphic language when He declared: "It is more blessed to give than to receive." This is a basic philosophy of life for all those who are truly Christians. Jesus gave His life; can we refuse to give ourselves in service?

CONFRONTATION IN JERUSALEM

DEVOTIONAL READING	Mark 12:28-34
ADULTS AND YOUTH	**Adult Topic:** *Confronting Entrenched Evil*
	Youth Topic: *Stand Up and Be Counted*
	Background Scripture: Mark 11:1—12:44
	Scripture Lesson: Mark 11:8-10, 15-19, 27-33
	Memory Verse: *The very stone which the builders rejected has become the head of the corner.* Mark 12:10
CHILDREN	**Topic:** *Jesus Visits Jerusalem*
	Scripture Lesson: Mark 11:15-19
	Memory Verse: *And he taught . . . my house shall be called a house of prayer for all the nations.* Mark 11:17
DAILY BIBLE READINGS	**Apr. 2 M.:** Entry into Jerusalem. Mark 11:1-11
	Apr. 3 T.: Cleansing the Temple. Mark 11:15-19
	Apr. 4 W.: Questioning Jesus' Authority. Mark 11:27-33
	Apr. 5 T.: Parable of the Vineyard. Mark 12:1-12
	Apr. 6 F.: Paying Taxes. Mark 12:13-17
	Apr. 7 S.: Questions About the Resurrection. Mark 12:18-27
	Apr. 8 S.: The Great Commandment. Mark 12:28-34
LESSON AIM	To see how Jesus was treated in His own "Holy City."
LESSON SETTING	**Time:** A.D. 30
	Place: Jerusalem
LESSON OUTLINE	**Confrontation in Jerusalem**

I. **Entering Jerusalem:** Mark 11:8-11
   A. A Royal Carpet: v. 8
   B. A Royal Welcome: vv. 9-10
   C. A Visit to the Temple: v. 11

II. **Cleansing the Temple:** Mark 11:15-19
   A. Abolishing the Market: v. 15
   B. Forbidding Merchandise: v. 16
   C. A Desecrated Temple: v. 17
   D. Reaction of Religious Leaders: v. 18
   E. Leaving the City: v. 19

III. **Confronted by the Sanhedrin:** Mark 11:27-33
   A. Composition of the Sanhedrin: v. 27
   B. Challenging Jesus: v. 28
   C. Jesus' Reply: vv. 29-30
   D. Perplexity of the Leaders: vv. 31-32
   E. Conclusion of the Discussion: v. 33

It was the last Sunday of Jesus' public ministry. He had finished His evangelization of Galilee and Perea. Now He and His disciples were coming up the Jericho Road to Jerusalem.

Chapter 11 begins by saying: "As they approached Jerusalem and came to Bethphage and Bethany at the Mount of Olives, Jesus sent two of his disciples." Bethany probably means "house of dates." Bethphage (pronounced beth-fa-jee) means "house of unripe figs." (*Beth* is the Hebrew word for "house.") Both dates and figs grow on the slopes of the Mount of Olives, just east of Jerusalem.

The location of Bethany is fairly certain. It is identified with modern El-Azariyeh, "Village of Lazarus," which is about two miles from Jerusalem on the southeast slope of the Mount of Olives. Since the Jewish Talmud speaks of Bethphage as being very near Jerusalem, it is thought that this village may have been on the west slope of the Mount of Olives, facing the Holy City. It was here that Jesus sent two of His disciples to get the colt on which He would ride into Jerusalem (cf. Matt. 21:1).

"Stand Up and Be Counted" is a good motto for all of us. It is especially important for young people in our modern permissive society. When moral issues arise, as they often do in school, we need to let our peers know where we stand. Though they may not have high standards of conduct, we must insist on maintaining ours as Christians. Otherwise we are failing Christ and hurting ourselves.

People knew where Jesus stood. Though they opposed Him, and even threatened Him, He "stood by His guns." And so must we. It is better to displease people than to please them and displease God, and so lose our souls.

1. God's house should always be kept sacred.
2. Jesus found His Father's house, the temple in Jerusalem, "a den of robbers."
3. So Jesus cleansed the Temple.
4. We should have our lives clean in God's sight.

THE LESSON COMMENTARY

I. ENTERING JERUSALEM: Mark 11:8-11

A. A Royal Carpet: v. 8

"Many people spread their cloaks on the road, while others spread branches they had cut in the fields."

All three synoptic Gospels (cf. Matt. 21:8; Luke 19:36) say that people spread their cloaks on the road as Jesus rode over the Mount of Olives toward Jerusalem. This was just about the highest honor they could give Him, one customarily reserved for kings. Other people, "cut branches from the trees and spread them on the road" (Matt. 21:8). They were paying Jesus the highest homage.

John's Gospel (12:13) says that the crowd "took palm branches and went out to meet him," acclaiming Him as "the King of Israel." That is why today the Sunday before Easter is called "Palm Sunday." In Jesus' day palms were a symbol of victory. Putting that together with the exultant cry of the crowd, this incident is referred to as "The Triumphal Entry."

Why was Jesus riding on the colt of a donkey? Matthew (21:4-5), writing to Jews, tells us that it was to fulfill what was spoken through the prophet Zechariah (9:9):

"Say to the Daughter of Zion,
'See, your king comes to you,
gentle and riding on a donkey,
on a colt, the foal of a donkey.'"

This shows that Jesus was intentionally presenting Himself to the nation of Israel as its promised Messiah. A. M. Hunter writes:

This prophesy Jesus now deliberately acted out. By his action he proclaimed that he was the Messiah, but a Messiah contrary to all their dreaming, a Messiah without arms or an army, who was riding in lowly pomp that road of the spirit marked out for the Servant of the Lord, a road upon which ever darker fell the shadow of a cross (*The Gospel According to St. Mark*, p. 109).

B. A Royal Welcome: vv. 9-10

The crowd of Passover pilgrims, probably mostly from Galilee where Jesus had performed many miracles, was overwhelmed with excitement. This was the day they had been waiting for. We read in John 6:15 that after Jesus had fed the five thousand the people "intended to come and make him king by force." But Jesus withdrew from the crowd, because His appointed hour had not yet come. Now it seemed to the people that the actual time had arrived for the setting up of the reign of the Messiah. So those who went ahead and those who followed shouted:

"Hosanna!"
"Blessed is he who comes in the name of the Lord!"
"Blessed is the coming kingdom of our father David!"
"Hosanna in the highest!"

"Hosanna" is a Greek transliteration of the Hebrew expression meaning "Save now" (so interpreted in the Septuagint). It probably carries the connotation "Save, we pray." But here it seems to be an exclamation of praise rather than prayer, like "God save the King!" (or "Queen"). The cry in verse 9 is quoted from Psalm 118:25, 26, where "Hosanna" may be translated "O LORD, save us" (NIV).

Verse 10 seems to indicate that the cry of the Passover pilgrims had messianic significance. They were looking for the messianic kingdom to be set up by "the Son of David"—a popular title for the Messiah (Mark 10:48). We might also note that the last line—"Hosanna in the highest!"—suggests that we have here an exclamation of praise.

We have already seen that this incident (vv. 8-10) is commonly referred to as "The Triumphal Entry" of Jesus into Jerusalem. But it hardly turned out to be that. Luke tells us that when Jesus "approached Jerusalem and saw the city, he wept over it" (Luke 19:41). Then He said, in weeping tones: "If you, even you, had only known on this day what would bring you peace—but now it is hidden from your eyes" (v. 42). He then went on to predict the coming siege of Jerusalem (v. 43), and added: "They will dash you to the ground, you and your children within your walls. They will not leave one stone on another, because you did not recognize the time of God's coming to you" (v. 44). So the "Triumphal Entry" ended in a tragedy of tears. And what Jesus predicted was literally and horribly fulfilled in the destruction of Jerusalem by the Romans in A.D. 70.

C. A Visit to the Temple: v. 11

"Jesus entered Jerusalem and went into the temple. He looked around at everything, but since it was already late, he went out to Bethany with the Twelve."

The next item we study in our lesson today is the cleansing of the Temple. A person reading Matthew's account (21:1-17) would probably get the impression that this incident took place on Sunday, following the so-called Triumphal Entry. But Mark indicates clearly that it was "the next day" (v. 12) that Jesus cleansed the Temple—that is on Monday. We know from many passages that Matthew has the habit of telescoping two or three incidents together closely, without indicating the breaks in time between them.

II. CLEANSING THE TEMPLE: Mark 11:15-19

A. Abolishing the Market: v. 15

"On reaching Jerusalem, Jesus entered the temple area and began driving out those who were buying and selling there. He overturned the tables of the money-changers and the benches of those selling doves. . . ."

The first messianic act of Jesus in the final week before the Crucifixion was His entrance into Jerusalem on a donkey, in fulfillment of Zechariah 9:9. The second messianic act was the cleansing of the Temple. This was in line with the prophecy of Malachi 3:1-4.

The Greek New Testament has two words for "temple." The first, *naos*, means "sanctuary." It refers to the Holy Place and Holy of Holies. But only the priests were allowed to enter that sacred building.

The other word, which is used here, is *hieron*. It refers to the whole area enclosed within the walls of the "temple." So the New International Version wisely uses "temple area" (eight times) or "temple courts" (twenty-two times) to indicate this. Altogether the courts of the Temple covered about twenty-five acres, as a visitor to Jerusalem can see today. The outer Court of the Gentiles was by far the largest. Here was located the busy market where sheep, oxen, and doves were sold for sacrifices (cf. 2:14). The law specified that these must be "without defect" (Exod. 12:15), so it was safer to buy these in the Temple market, which was run by relatives of the high priest. Everything bought there would be automatically approved. Another factor is that it would be inconvenient for the worshipers from Galilee to bring an animal on that journey of a hundred miles or more on foot. The poor people were allowed to offer "doves." Many of these would be sold every day. Those selling were making a handsome profit.

Not only did Jesus drive these busy merchants out of the Temple area, but He also "overturned the tables of the money-changers." The Greek word for "table" in the New Testament is *trapeza*. Today this is the regular Greek word for "bank." One can see it on the front of all the many banks in Athens. This is due to the fact that the earliest banks were money-changers' tables.

What were these doing in the Temple area? The annual Temple tax, which every adult male Jew had to pay, was required to be paid with a Phoenician silver half shekel. But the Jews of that time were using the Greek drachma and Roman denarius. So they had to get their money exchanged. It is said that the priests were allowed to collect one-fourth to one-third of a denarius for the exchange of half a shekel (that is, about five cents on thirty-three cents, or about 15 percent). This, of course, was exorbitant.

One can imagine the noisy, smelly atmosphere of this cattle market. But the greedy exchange of money was even more "smelly." No wonder Jesus drove the whole stinking mess out of the sacred Temple area.

B. Forbidding Merchandise: v. 16

Jesus also "would not allow anyone to carry merchandise through the temple courts." The sacred area was being turned into a secular thoroughfare.

C. A Desecrated Temple: v. 17

Jesus reminded the culprits that it was "written" (in Isa. 56:7): "My house will be called a house of prayer for all nations." Then He declared: "But you have made it 'a den of robbers.'" The King James Version says "thieves." But the Greek New Testament uses two distinct words. "Thief" is *kleptes*, from which we get "kleptomaniac." But the word here is *lestes*, which means "robber"—that is, one who takes by force. Incidentally, Jesus was not crucified between two "thieves" (as the KJV wrongly says) but between two "robbers" (15:27).

It was indeed a sad situation. I have written elsewhere:

> Christ's condemnation of the operators of the Temple market as "robbers" finds ample support in the rabbinical writings. They speak of the "Bazaars of the sons of Annas"— the former high priest who was succeeded by five of his sons, and whose son-in-law Caiaphas was high priest at this time (*Beacon Bible Commentary*, 6:192).

Alfred Edersheim, a converted Jew, calls attention to this statement:

> The Sanhedrin, forty years before the destruction of Jerusalem [i.e., A.D. 30, the year of the Crucifixion], transferred its meeting-place from "the Hall of Hewn Stones" (on the south side of the Court of the Priests . . .) to "the Bazaars," and then afterwards to the City (*The Life and Times of Jesus the Messiah*, p. 371).

Edersheim goes on to say that "popular indignation, three years before the destruction of Jerusalem, swept away the Bazaars of the family of Annas" (p. 372). He then makes this shocking statement:

> The Talmud also records the curse which a distinguished Rabbi of Jerusalem (Abba Shaul) pronounced upon the High-Priestly families (including that of Annas), who were "themselves High-Priests, their sons treasurers, and their sons-in-law assistant-treasurers, while their servants beat the people with sticks (p. 372).

D. Reaction of Religious Leaders: v. 18

"The chief priests and the teachers of the law heard this and began looking for a way to kill him, for they feared him, because the whole crowd was amazed at his teaching." Jesus was gaining in popularity, and the religious leaders couldn't take it!

A. M. Hills expresses the situation well when he writes: "The Temple Cleansing was both a challenge and a threat. Jesus threw down the gage to the authorities: he threatened both their prestige and their pockets" (*The Gospel According to St. Mark*, p. 111).

This is the first time in the synoptic Gospels that we find the chief priests in opposition to Jesus. Up to this point it had been the Pharisees, and particularly the teachers of the law. But now the rulers of the Temple sought His death.

E. Leaving the City: v. 19

"When evening came, they went out of the city." Jesus had done a tremendous day's work, and now it was time to retire for the night. And it was not safe for Him to stay in Jerusalem.

DISCUSSION QUESTIONS

1. Is religious enthusiasm ever justifiable?
2. What word has taken the place of "Hosanna" today?
3. Why was Jesus so concerned about the Temple?
4. What activities are improper in a church building?
5. How should we meet opposition from critics?

III. CONFRONTED BY THE SANHEDRIN: Mark 11:27-33

A. Composition of the Sanhedrin: v. 27

"They arrived again in Jerusalem, and while Jesus was walking in the temple courts, the chief priests, the teachers of the law and the elders came to him."

These were the three groups that comprised the great Sanhedrin at Jerusalem, the supreme court of Israel (seventy members). The "chief priests" included the high priest, the several ex-high priests and perhaps those in charge of the twenty-four courses of priests. They had charge of the Temple in Jerusalem. The "teachers of the law" were the ones who taught the Scriptures in the synagogues. The "elders" may have been the older men or at least the members who were not chief priests or teachers of the law.

B. Challenging Jesus: v. 28

These members of the Sanhedrin asked Jesus: "By what authority are you doing these things? And who gave you authority to do this?" The obvious reference is to the cleansing of the Temple. Did He act by *human* or *divine* authority?

C. Jesus' Reply: vv. 29-30

"I will ask you one question. Answer me, and I will tell you by what authority I am doing these things. John's baptism—was it from heaven, or from men? Tell me!"

"From heaven" obviously means "from God." Jesus' question, was a very clever one. The correct answer to *His*

question would be the correct answer to *their* question! Both Jesus and John acted by divine authority. But the Jewish leaders would not admit it in either case, even though Jesus sternly commanded, "Tell me!"

D. Perplexity of the Leaders: vv. 31-32

"They discussed it among themselves and said, 'If we say, "From heaven," he will ask, "Then why didn't you believe him?" But if we say, "From men. . . ."' (They feared the people, for everyone held that John really was a prophet.)"

I have written on this point:

Their utter lack of moral honesty shows up clearly in these verses. They were not at all concerned for truth, but only for expediency. When they said, "We do not know," they lied with stubborn willfulness. Morison rather quaintly remarks: "It was an unconscientious answer" (*The Gospel According to Mark*, p. 141).

E. Conclusion of the Discussion: v. 33

"So they answered Jesus, 'We don't know.'

"Jesus said, 'Neither will I tell you by what authority I am doing these things.'"

This was a fair enough reply. Since the Jewish leaders would not answer Jesus' question, He would not answer their question. If they had been honest and sincere, Jesus would have reasoned with them. But it was of no use. They did not care what was true. All they were concerned with was: "What will this do to us?" Under the circumstances Jesus was fully justified in refusing to answer their question.

CONTEMPORARY APPLICATION

The adult topic today is: "Confronting Entrenched Evil." That is what Jesus confronted, and we sometimes

may find ourselves in the same position. What do we do?

What did Jesus do? He moved firmly

against what He found wrong in God's house. And we might have to take this stand, though we hope not! In any case we should act in love, and only after much prayer.

Jesus got into trouble with the chief priests because He threatened their dishonest gains. When Martin Luther attacked the unholy sale of indulgences, which sent wagon loads of gold over the Alp Mountains to Rome, the papal wrath fell on him, but out of this came the great Protestant Reformation!

IN THE SHADOW OF THE CROSS

DEVOTIONAL READING	Mark 14:3-9
ADULTS AND YOUTH	**Adult Topic:** *In the Shadow of the Cross*
	Youth Topic: *First Things First*
	Background Scripture: Mark 14
	Scripture Lesson: Mark 14:22-36
	Memory Verse: *Remove this cup from me; yet not what I will, but what thou wilt.* Mark 14:36
CHILDREN	**Topic:** *Jesus Is Betrayed*
	Scripture Lesson: Mark 14:10-12, 17-21
	Memory Verse: *Truly, I say to you, one of you will betray me.* Mark 14:18
DAILY BIBLE READINGS	**Apr. 9 M.:** The Plot Against Jesus. Mark 14:1-2, 10-11
	Apr. 10 T.: Anointing for Burial. Mark 14:3-9
	Apr. 11 W.: The Last Supper. Mark 14:17-31
	Apr. 12 T.: Praying at Gethsemane. Mark 14:32-42
	Apr. 13 F.: The Arrest of Jesus. Mark 14:43-52
	Apr. 14 S.: On Trial. Mark 14:53-65
	Apr. 15 S.: Peter Denies Jesus. Mark 14:66-72
LESSON AIM	To seek to understand Jesus' feelings as He faced His crucifixion.
LESSON SETTING	**Time:** A.D. 30
	Place: Jerusalem

In the Shadow of the Cross

LESSON OUTLINE

   I. **Institution of the Lord's Supper:** Mark 14:22-26
      A. The Bread: v. 22
      B. The Cup: v. 23
      C. Significance of the Cup: v. 24
      D. A New Institution: v. 25
      E. Closing Hymn: v. 26

  II. **Prediction of Betrayal:** Mark 14:27-31
      A. Fulfillment of Scripture: v. 27
      B. Future Meeting: v. 28
      C. Peter's Declaration of Loyalty: v. 29
      D. Prediction of Denial: v. 30
      E. Peter's Protest: v. 31

 III. **Prayer in Gethsemane:** Mark 14:32-36
      A. Instructions to the Eight: v. 32
      B. Deep Distress of Jesus: v. 33
      C. Instructions to the Three: v. 34
      D. Overwhelming Agony: v. 35
      E. Jesus' Prayer: v. 36

It was the "first day of the Feast of Unleavened Bread, when it was customary to sacrifice the Passover lamb" (Mark 14:12). Jesus' disciples asked Him, "Where do you want us to go and make preparations for you to eat the Passover?"

In response, Jesus sent two of His disciples into the city of Jerusalem—they were out at Bethany, two miles away (v. 3)—with instructions as to how to find the right house (vv. 13-14). There they would discover "a large upper room, furnished and ready," where they would prepare for the meal (v. 15).

That evening "Jesus arrived with the Twelve" (v. 17). "While they were reclining at the table eating," Jesus made a startling announcement: "I tell you the truth, one of you will betray me—one who is eating with me" (v. 18). We are already told (vv. 10-11) that Judas Iscariot had made arrangements with the chief priests to betray Jesus to them.

The tragedy was deepened by the Master's next words: "It is one of the Twelve, one who dips bread into the bowl with me" (v. 20). It was necessary that Jesus should die, but "woe to that man who betrays the Son of Man" (v. 21).

Our topic today is "First Things First." This is a very important motto for all young people to follow. One of the most significant things in life is our choice of priorities.

With Jesus there was only one thing that mattered ultimately. He expressed it this way: "I always do what pleases him"—that is, His Father (John 8:29). When we have one real purpose each day and that is to please God in all we do, then we are putting first things first.

In His humanity Jesus naturally shrank from the Cross and all the terrible physical, mental, and spiritual suffering it involved. That is why He agonized in the Garden of Gethsemane. But He refused to turn aside from carrying out God's will, no matter what the cost. And that must be our attitude.

1. Jesus was betrayed by one of His chosen associates.
2. This betrayal caused Jesus deep pain and suffering.
3. We must be completely loyal to Jesus.
4. Jesus is always faithful to us.

THE LESSON COMMENTARY

I. INSTITUTION OF THE LORD'S SUPPER: Mark 14:22-26

The institution of the Lord's Supper is recorded in all three synoptic Gospels and in I Corinthians 11:24-26. Five items occur in all four accounts:

taking bread, thanksgiving or blessing, breaking bread, "This is my body," the mention of the cup.

A. The Bread: v. 22

"While they were eating, Jesus took bread, gave thanks and broke it, and gave it to his disciples, saying, 'Take it, this is my body.'"

The bread of the Passover meal was unleavened, as required by the law (Exod. 34:18; Lev. 23:6). That is why bread without yeast is used today in many, if not most, Communion services. James Morison makes this interesting observation:

> The bread of course would be such as was lying on the table, *unleavened bread*. But it would be finical to insist, at the present day, on using the same kind of bread. It is not now so much *the bread of affliction* that we need to eat as *the bread of true nourishment, the bread of life. The best bread is in itself the best bread for us to use* (*A Practical Commentary on the Gospel According to St. Mark*, p. 391).

Jesus then "gave thanks." The Greek verb is *eulogeo*, which literally means "speak well of." For this and the parallel passage in Matthew (26:26) Arndt and Gingrich suggest "give thanks," though "perhaps" we could say "bless" (*Greek-English Lexicon of the New Testament*, p. 322). Luke uses the verb *eucharisteo*, "give thanks" (22:19), from which we get the name "Eucharist" for the Communion service. I prefer to bring out the distinction of the different Greek verbs by using "blessed" in Matthew and Mark and "gave thanks" in Luke.

Jesus then "broke" the bread. We must not think of our modern large loaves. The "loaf" of that day, as now in Arab countries, was about the size of a small pancake or a very flat biscuit.

As He gave the small pieces of bread to His disciples, He said, "Take it." The King James Version adds "eat," but this is not found in any of the early Greek manuscripts. The very late manuscripts that have it evidently borrowed it from Matthew 26:26.

"This is my body" is a significant statement that we need to look at carefully. J. A. Alexander notes that it has been "the occasion and the subject of the most protracted and exciting controversy that has rent the church within the last thousand years" (*The Gospel According to Mark*, p. 381). He refers, of course, to the Roman Catholic doctrine of transubstantiation—that the bread and wine of the Eucharist are actually changed into the body and blood of our Lord by the blessing of the priest—and to Martin Luther's insistence on consubstantiation—that the elements of Communion *are* actually the body and blood of Christ. Both doctrines have the fault of taking the "is" very literally. We understand that "is" must be taken metaphorically, in the sense of "represents." Moffatt translates, "means my body."

Alexander goes on to say:

> Until the strong unguarded figures of the early fathers had been petrified into a dogma . . . these words suggested no idea but the one which they still convey to every plain un-biassed reader, that our Saviour calls the bread his body in the same sense that he calls himself a door (John 10:9), a vine (John 15:1), a root (Rev. 22:16), a star, and is described by many other metaphors in scripture. . . . The bread was an emblem of his flesh, as wounded for the sins of men, and as administered for their spiritual nourishment and growth in grace (*Mark*, p. 381).

B. The Cup: v. 23

"Then he took the cup, gave thanks and offered it to them, and they all drank from it."

"Gave thanks" here is the verb *eucharisteo*, which regularly has this meaning. Then Jesus offered His disciples the cup, "and they all drank from it." In line with the customs of that day, a single cup was passed around the circle and each person took a sip from it. Due to our modern sensitivity to sanitation, most groups now use individual small glasses for Communion.

C. Significance of the Cup: v. 24

"This is my blood of the covenant, which is poured out for many," Jesus said. Once more we note that "This is" has to mean "this represents," for the blood of Jesus was right then in His physical body.

Instead of "testament" (KJV) almost all modern versions have "covenant." The Greek word is *diatheke*, which has both meanings. In the New Testament of the King James Version this word is translated "testament" only thirteen times but "covenant" twenty times. Our word "testament," meaning a "will," comes from the Latin *testamentum*. But whereas the Greeks and Romans made wills or testaments, the Jews made covenants. B. F. Westcott declares, "There is not the least trace of the meaning 'testament' in the Greek Old Scriptures, and the idea of a 'testament' was indeed foreign to the Jews till the time of the Herods" (*The Epistle to the Hebrews*, p. 299).

It was common among the people of Old Testament times to seal a very solemn covenant with their own blood. So God's covenant with us is sealed with the blood of His own Son, shed at Calvary.

The word "new" (KJV) is not in the oldest Greek manucripts. It was probably imported here by some later scribe from Luke 22:20 or I Corinthians 11:25, where it is genuine. Of course it *was* a new covenant, but Mark does not say so here.

D. A New Institution: v. 25

"I tell you the truth, I will not drink again of the fruit of the vine until that day when I drink it anew in the kingdom of God."

J. A. Alexander comments: "The simplest explanation of these words is that which makes them a solemn though figurative declaration, that the Jewish Passover was now to be forever superseded by the Lord's Supper as a Christian ordinance" (p. 382).

Vincent Taylor writes of this verse:

The saying shows that at the Supper Jesus looked forward, beyond death, to the perfect fellowship of the consummated Kingdom. The drinking

of the cup is a present participation in that fellowship so far as it can exist here and now (*The Gospel According to St. Mark*, p. 547).

So the Supper ended on a note of hope and triumph. The best was yet to come.

E. Closing Hymn: v. 26

"When they had sung a hymn, they went out to the Mount of Olives."

The closing hymn of the Passover meal was the latter part of the Great Hallel ("praise"), which consisted of Psalms 115-118. It is still appropriate for us to end our services with a hymn of praise.

II. PREDICTION OF BETRAYAL: Mark 14:27-31

A. Fulfillment of Scripture: v. 27

"You will all fall away," Jesus told them, "for it is written:

"'I will strike the shepherd,
and the sheep will be scattered.'"

In the King James Version the first part of Jesus' statement reads: "All ye shall be offended because of me this night." Two things need to be said about this. The first problem is that "because of me this night" is not found in any of the earliest and best manuscripts. It obviously was imported from Matthew 26:31. The second thing is that "offended" is not at all a correct translation for the modern reader. Today we say that a person is "offended" at something that is said or done. But the Greek verb here is *scandalizo*. It comes from the noun *scandalon*, which first meant the bait-stick in a snare or the trigger on a trap. Then it came to be used for the trap or snare itself. So the literal meaning is "ensnare" or "trap." Arndt and Gingrich say it means "cause to sin" (*Lexicon*, p. 752). So "fall away" (NASB, NIV) is the correct meaning.

The quotation in this verse is taken from Zechariah 13:7. Jesus was the "shepherd" (John 10:11); the "sheep" were His own followers (John 10: 14-16). The reference here is to Christ's divinely ordained death, which would result in His sheep, the disciples, being scattered temporarily in fear and confusion. But Pentecost brought them together in the unity and power of the Spirit.

B. Future Meeting: v. 28

"But after I have risen, I will go ahead of you into Galilee." We find a repetition of this in 16:7, in Jesus' words to the women.

Vincent Taylor comments here:

Is the meaning that, while the little flock will be scattered in consequence of the smiting of the shepherd, after His Resurrection Jesus, the Shepherd, will reconstitute His community and lead them to Galilee? (*St. Mark*, p. 549).

That such took place is recorded in Matthew 28:16, where we read: "Then the disciples went to Galilee, to the mountain where Jesus had told them to go." Also in John 21 we find Jesus meeting with His disciples on the shore of the Lake of Galilee.

C. Peter's Declaration of Loyalty: v. 29

"Peter declared, 'Even if all fall away, I will not.'"

This follows Jesus' disturbing announcement in verse 27. As usual, Peter spoke out impulsively, asserting that regardless of what others did he would not deny his Lord. Poor Peter; he did not recognize his own weakness! He meant well, but that was not enough.

D. Prediction of Denial: v. 30

Jesus answered Peter: "I tell you the truth, today—yes, tonight—before the rooster crows twice, you yourself will disown me three times."

The Greek is very emphatic: "*Amen* I say to you that *you* today, in this night...." Peter had boldly proclaimed his loyalty. In response, Jesus emphatically predicted his failure.

"Today" and "tonight" go together. It was now late in the evening, after the Last Supper in the Upper Room. But the Jewish day began at sunset. Even though Peter's denials probably took place after midnight, it was still "today" in the Jewish reckoning— Friday, which had already begun as they met for the Passover meal.

Someone may raise the question as to why the traditional rendering "deny" has been changed to "disown" (NIV). The answer is that with us the usual meaning of "deny" is now "declare untrue" or "contradict." We *deny* a statement but *disown* a person.

Mark is the only one who mentions the rooster crowing "twice." Some critics have claimed an inconsistency here. But Alexander observes:

The difference is the same as that between saying *before the bell rings* and *before the second bell rings* (for church or dinner), the reference in both expressions being to the last and most important signal, to which the first is only a preliminary (*Mark*, p. 384).

Ezra Gould puts it well when he says, "These two fatal cock-crowings had stuck in Peter's memory, and so find their way into the Gospel which gets its inspiration from him" (*A Critical and Exegetical Commentary on the Gospel According to St. Mark*, p. 267).

E. Peter's Protest: v. 31

"But Peter insisted emphatically, 'Even if I have to die with you, I will never disown you.' And all the others said the same."

Instead of praying, "Lord, help me!"—as he should have—Peter kept on asserting vehemently that even if it meant death, he would "never" (double negative in the Greek) disown his Master. E. Bickersteth well says: "The true remedy against temptation is the consciousness of our own weakness, and supplication for Divine strength" (*The Pulpit Commentary*, St. Mark, 2:233).

It is interesting to note the added statement that all the other disciples chimed in and asserted the same thing. They were all sadly unaware of their inner weakness.

III. PRAYER IN GETHSEMANE: Mark 14:32-36

A. Instructions to the Eight: v. 32

"They went to a place called Gethsemane, and Jesus said to his disciples, 'Sit here while I pray.'"

The name "Gethsemane" means "oil press"—that is, a place where the oil was pressed out of olives. It was evidently situated on the west slope of the Mount of Olives facing Jerusalem. Today one is shown the Roman Catholic site, near the foot of the mount, and also the Russian site, farther up the hill. The former is much more impressive, with its many old olive trees. A beautifully frescoed Church of All Nations adjoins the "garden." In John 18:1 it is called "an olive grove."

Since the next verse mentions Peter, James, and John as going farther with Jesus, it was eight apostles to whom He said, "Sit here while I pray." Judas Iscariot had already left (John 13:30).

B. Deep Distress of Jesus: v. 33

"He took Peter, James and John along with him, and he began to be deeply distressed and troubled."

These three men comprised the inner circle—the only disciples that had been with Jesus when He raised Jairus' daughter (5:37) and when He was on the Mount of Transfiguration (9:2). In contrast to those times of triumph and glory, they were now to witness His agony in Gethsemane. Great privileges involve great responsibilities, and often heavy burdens.

As Jesus walked into Gethsemane "he began to be deeply distressed and

troubled." The first infinitive is a strong compound, *ekthambeomai*, found only in Mark (here; 9:15; 16:5, 6). It means "to be amazed or terrified." The second is *ademoneo*, which means "be distressed." Concerning the first verb H. B. Swete says: "The Lord was overwhelmed with sorrow..., but His first feeling was one of terrified surprise. Long as He had foreseen the Passion, when it came clearly into view its terrors exceeded His anticipations" (*The Gospel According to St. Mark*, p. 322). He goes on to say that the second verb represents "the distress which follows a great shock" (p. 322).

C. Instructions to the Three: v. 34

To Peter, James and John, Jesus said: "My soul is overwhelmed with sorrow to the point of death. Stay here and keep watch." So burdened was Jesus that He said, in effect: "My sorrow is killing me!"

He told the three disciples to "watch." Alexander suggests that the word is used "either in the primary and strict sense of the verb both in Greek and English, i.e. keep awake, or in the secondary but more useful sense, be upon your guard" (*Mark*, p. 386).

DISCUSSION QUESTIONS

1. What should we be praying as we partake of the Communion bread? of the cup?
2. How can we avoid Peter's self-confidence?
3. What did Paul mean by "the fellowship of his sufferings" (Phil. 3:10)?
4. How can we avoid disowning Jesus?
5. What "crosses" fall across our lives?
6. How can we take care of our "crosses" successfully?

D. Overwhelming Agony: v. 35

"Going a little farther, he fell to the ground and prayed that if possible the hour might pass from him."

I have written:

> So burdened was He that He "was falling on the ground." The imperfect seems to suggest the picture of Jesus staggering and stumbling until He fell on the ground, crying aloud in agony of soul. This is one of the most sacred scenes ever witnessed, across which must be drawn the veil of reverence (*The Gospel According to Mark*, p. 170).

E. Jesus' Prayer: v. 36

"*Abba*, Father, . . . everything is possible for you. Take this cup from me. Yet not what I will, but what you will."

Abba is the Aramaic word for "father." It is followed immediately by the Greek *pater*. Aramaic was the familiar language spoken by the people of Palestine at that time.

What was the "cup" from which He asked to be delivered? I have written:

> Some scoffers have called Jesus a coward. They have remarked that while martyrs have gone singing to the stake, He cringed at the thought of the cross and shrank from impending death. But such have not entered at all into the mysteries of Calvary. His was no martyr's death. It was not physical suffering that He dreaded, but separation from His Father's face when He took man's place as a condemned sinner. It was the premonition of that moment when He would cry out, "My God, My God, why hast thou forsaken me?" that caused Him now to pray, "Take away this cup from me" (*Mark*, p. 170).

But His prayer did not end there. He went on to say: "Yet not what I will, but what you will." The highest prayer any Christian can pray is "Your will, Lord, be done."

CONTEMPORARY APPLICATION

We shall never be called upon to face what Jesus confronted in Gethsemane. But He has left us an example of what we should do when the most overwhelming sorrows strike us, or the most unbearable crises face us. We have a right to ask God to deliver us from such: Jesus did! But, like Him, we must always finally say: "Yet not what I will, but what you will."

CRUCIFIED AND RAISED FROM DEATH

DEVOTIONAL READING	Mark 15:6-15
ADULTS AND YOUTH	**Adult Topic:** *He Has Risen!* **Youth Topic:** *Death Defeated!* **Background Scripture:** Mark 15:1—16:20 **Scripture Lesson:** Mark 15:31-39; 16:1-7 **Memory Verse:** *You seek Jesus of Nazareth, who was crucified. He has risen.* Mark 16:6
CHILDREN	**Topic:** *Jesus Lives!* **Memory Verse:** *He has risen.* Mark 16:6
DAILY BIBLE READINGS	**Apr. 16 M.:** Jesus Before Pilate. Mark 15:1-5 **Apr. 17 T.:** Sentenced to Death. Mark 15:6-15 **Apr. 18 W.:** Jesus Made Fun Of. Mark 15:16-20 **Apr. 19 T.:** Jesus Is Crucified. Mark 15:21-32 **Apr. 20 F.:** The Death of Jesus. Mark 15:33-41 **Apr. 21 S.:** The Burial of Jesus. Mark 15:42-47 **Apr. 22 S.:** The First Easter. Mark 16:1-15
LESSON AIM	To understand the meaning of Jesus' crucifixion and resurrection.
LESSON SETTING	**Time:** A.D. 30 **Place:** Jerusalem

LESSON OUTLINE	**Crucified and Raised from the Dead**
	
	 I. **The Place of Crucifixion:** Mark 15:22-24
	  A. Golgotha: v. 22
	  B. Refusal of Sedative: v. 23
	  C. Dividing His Clothes: v. 24
	
	 II. **The Setting:** Mark 15:25-32
	  A. The Time of the Crucifixion: v. 25
	  B. The Written Charge: v. 26
	  C. The Two Robbers: v. 27
	  D. Insults from Passersby: vv. 29-30
	  E. Mockery from Religious Leaders: vv. 31-32
	
	 III. **The Climax:** Mark 15:33-39
	  A. Darkness over the Land: v. 33
	  B. The Cry of Abandonment: v. 34
	  C. Misunderstanding of Onlookers: v. 35
	  D. A Man's Offer: v. 36
	  E. Death of Jesus: v. 37
	  F. The Torn Curtain: v. 38
	  G. The Centurion's Confession: v. 39

IV. The Resurrection: Mark 16:1-7

    A. Dedicated Women: v. 1

    B. Concerned Women: vv. 2-3

    C. The Problem Solved: v. 4

    D. The Angel: v. 5

    E. Message of the Angel: vv. 6-7

SUGGESTED INTRODUCTION FOR ADULTS

Last week we studied about Jesus' last evening with His disciples in the Upper Room, as He inaugurated the Lord's Supper. Then we followed Him to the Garden of Gethsemane, where He prayed in agony as His disciples slept.

It was there that Jesus was arrested, betrayed by His own disciple, Judas Iscariot (14:43-50). All eleven apostles, who had asserted their loyalty (14:31), "deserted Him and fled" (14:50).

Jesus was taken before the Sanhedrin, where He underwent His Jewish trial (14:53-65). There He was condemned as worthy of death for blasphemy (v. 64) and beaten by the guards (v. 65).

Then we have the sad story of Peter's three denials that he was a follower of Christ (14:66-72). It ends with the statement that Peter "broke down and wept."

Next was the Roman trial of Jesus before the governor Pilate (15:1-15). The chief priests stirred up the crowd to demand His crucifixion (vv. 11-14). So Pilate "had Jesus flogged, and handed him over to be crucified" (v. 15). After the soldiers had mocked Jesus, "they led him out to crucify him" (v. 20).

SUGGESTED INTRODUCTION FOR YOUTH

Our topic today is "Death Defeated!" Young people may not think much about death because it seems so remote. But we must all face the certainty of death, if Jesus tarries.

It is not only the inevitability of physical death that we need to face but also the peril of spiritual, eternal death, for physical death does not end existence.

By His own death on the cross Christ has conquered death, so that we no longer need to fear it if we are in Him as our Savior. Paul notes, "The sting of death is sin" (I Cor. 15:56). Then he joyfully writes: "But thanks be to God! He gives us the victory through our Lord Jesus Christ" (v. 57). True Christians will finally discover: "Death has been swallowed up in victory" (v. 54).

CONCEPTS FOR CHILDREN

1. "Jesus Lives!"
2. Because Jesus lives, we can also live—spiritually and eternally in Him.
3. The happy Easter announcement is: "He has risen!" (our memory verse for today).
4. We can enjoy Easter in our hearts every day.

THE LESSON COMMENTARY

I. THE PLACE OF CRUCIFIXION: Mark 15:22-24

A. Golgotha: v. 22

"They brought Jesus to the place called Golgotha (which means, The Place of the Skull)."

Golgotha is a modified transliteration of the Aramaic word for "skull." In our English versions "skull" is the translation of the Greek word *cranion*, which we have taken over into English in its Latin form, "cranium."

The location of Golgotha, or Calvary—*calvarium* is the Latin for "skull"—is disputed. The traditional site is the Church of the Holy Sepulcher, which is inside the present walls of the Old City of Jerusalem. Many Protestants prefer "Gordon's Calvary"—a skull-shaped hill just north of the city, between Herod's Gate and the Damascus Gate—as the site of Jesus' crucifixion.

B. Refusal of Sedative: v. 23

"Then they offered him wine mixed with myrrh, but he did not take it."

The rabbinical writings inform us that this wine drugged with myrrh was provided by the women of Jerusalem for condemned criminals, to deaden the sense of pain. Jesus refused it because He wanted to keep His mind clear and also because He chose to endure all the agonies that He knew awaited Him. H. B. Swete puts it this way: "He had need of the full use of His human faculties, and the pain which was before Him belonged to the cup which the Father's will had appointed" (*The Gospel According to St. Mark*, p. 358).

We, too, may sometimes, for the sake of helping others, have to bypass the opportunity of escaping pain. In all cases the question is: What is best for the person in need? Sometimes it is a fellowship of suffering.

C. Dividing His Clothes: v. 24

"And they crucified him. Dividing up his clothes, they cast lots to see what each would get."

We are not sure of the exact procedure of execution. Probably the cross was laid on the ground and Jesus' body stretched out on it. Then nails were driven through His hands and feet. Next, the soldiers lifted the cross into an upright position and dropped it with a thud into the hole made for it. We can only imagine the agony of pain!

John, who was an eyewitness at the cross (John 19:26), gives a fuller description of how the soldiers divided Jesus' clothes (John 19:23-24), but there is no confusion between the two accounts.

II. THE SETTING; Mark 15:25-32

A. The Time of the Crucifixion: v. 25

"It was the third hour when they crucified him."

Some have claimed that we have here a contradiction of John 19:14, where we find Jesus before Pilate at "about the sixth hour." It was later, of course, when He was crucified. How could it be "the third hour"?

The simple explanation is that Mark, in common with the other synoptic Gospels, uses Jewish time, which was reckoned from sunset and sunrise. So "the third hour" was nine o'clock in the morning. John, writing his Gospel in the city of Ephesus near the end of the first century (ca. A.D. 95), naturally used Roman time, which began at midnight. So there is no contradiction here. (For more extended discussion, see Gleason Archer's excellent new book, *Encyclopedia of Bible Difficulties*, pp. 363-64).

B. The Written Charge: v. 26

"The written notice of the charge against him read: THE KING OF THE JEWS."

The exact wording of this inscription is different in all four Gospels. Mark's form is the shortest, and it is incorporated in each of the other three (Matt. 27:37; Luke 23:38; John 19:19). John tells us that the inscription was written in three languages: "Aramaic, Latin and Greek" (19:20). There may have been some variation in these (see Archer, *Encyclopedia*, pp. 345-46). In any case, the central emphasis is the same in all four: "The King of the Jews."

C. The Two Robbers: v. 27

"They crucified two robbers with him, one on his right and one on his left."

On the basis of the King James Version we hear constantly that Jesus was crucified between two "thieves." But this is incorrect. The Greek has two very different words for "thief" and "robber." And the Greek term used here not only meant "robber," but it was used by Josephus at that time for murderous insurrectionists against the Roman government. Mark tells us that Barabbas was one of these (15:7). The evidence seems clear that Barabbas was to have died on the middle cross between his two henchmen. Instead, Jesus was hung there and died for the sins of all humanity—including the sins of Barabbas!

D. Insults from Passersby: vv. 29-30

"Those who passed by hurled insults at him. . . ." What a contrast between the loving Savior and sinful, hateful humanity!

E. Mockery from Religious Leaders: vv. 31-32

"In the same way the chief priests and the teachers of the law mocked him among themselves. 'He saved others,' they said, 'but he can't save himself!'" (v. 31).

In this taunt these leaders spoke better than they realized. Jesus could not save Himself from death on the cross and at the same time save lost sinners. Had He chosen to "save himself" in that hour, we would be without any hope of salvation.

"The chief priests" (Sadducees) and "the teachers of the law" (Pharisees) went on to say sarcastically: "Let this Christ, this King of Israel, come down now from the cross, that we may see and believe" (v. 32). But if they wouldn't believe Him on the basis of His loving, healing, miracle-working ministry, we may be sure they would not have believed Him now.

Then we have the added statement of the Evangelist: "Those crucified with him also heaped insults on him." Luke (23:39-41) has one malefactor railing at Jesus and the other defending Him. Evidently both insulted Him at first, and then one changed his attitude as he saw the true nature of Jesus displayed.

III. THE CLIMAX: Mark 15:33-39

A. Darkness over the Land: v. 33

"At the sixth hour darkness came over the whole land until the ninth hour." This would be from noon until three o'clock in the afternoon.

All three synoptic Gospels record this period of three hours of darkness (cf. Matt. 27:45; Luke 23:44). The Greek word for "land" is *ge* (pronounced "gay"), which means "earth, land, or ground." The King James Version shows a strange inconsistency in having "the whole land" here in Mark but "the whole earth" in Luke 23:44, when the Greek is exactly the same in both cases. Some, indeed, have thought that the darkness did cover the whole earth, but it was probably just the land of Judah, or, at most, all Palestine. It should be noted that an ordinary eclipse of the sun could not have taken place at the Passover, when the moon was full. It would seem that black storm clouds, suggesting God's judgment, would suit the occasion. This was the utterly unique time of God's judgment on human sin placed on His Son.

B. The Cry of Abandonment: v. 34

"And at the ninth hour Jesus cried out in a loud voice, '*Eloi, Eloi, lama sabachthani?*'—which means, 'My God, my God, why have you forsaken me?'"

At three o'clock in the afternoon, just when the evening sacrifice was being offered in the Temple, Jesus uttered this cry. It is commonly referred to as "the cry of dereliction"— that is, of abandonment.

The actual Aramaic words that Jesus used are recorded here, and then translated into Greek, closely in line with the Septuagint. They are basically a quotation of Psalm 22:1. This is unquestionably the most significant of the "seven sayings" from the cross.

Jesus first cried, "My God, my God." James Morison observes:

> The repetition denotes intensity and urgency of feeling. Wave, as it were, surges upon wave. The *My* indicates clinging and trust. The use of the word *God*, instead of *Father*, shows that it was in the human element of our Lord's complex personality that the darkness and agony had been experienced (*A Practical Commentary on the Gospel According to St. Mark*, p. 435).

We shall never be able to plumb the depths of the agonizing question Jesus asked, "Why have you forsaken me?" It was, of course, because He had taken our sins on Himself. John Wesley speaks of Jesus "lamenting His Father's withdrawing the tokens of His love, and treating Him as an enemy, while He

bore our sins" (*Explanatory Notes Upon the New Testament*, p. 192).

This does not mean that Jesus' divine nature left Him at this time, for then His sacrifice could not have atoned for sin. He had to be man in order to die on the cross. But He had to be God for His sacrificial death to have infinite worth. Morison comments:

> He had been *forsaken* or *left* by the Father; not, of course, physically or metaphysically, but politically or governmentally. In the sphere of the Divine moral government He was, as the world's Representative and Substitute "left" alone with the world's sin, "bearing" it (*St. Mark*, p. 435).

C. Misunderstanding of Onlookers: v. 35

"When some of those standing by heard this, they said, 'Listen, he's calling Elijah.'"

Probably this remark was just a cruel joke, a piece of heartless mockery. It does not seem that the bystanders actually understood Jesus to be calling for Elijah. J. A. Alexander observes: "Most interpreters are now agreed that this was not an actual error, but a bitter irony or sarcasm, which affected to mistake the meaning" (*The Gospel According to Mark*, p. 426). What the onlookers perhaps meant was: "This poor deluded 'Messiah' thinks Elijah will come to his rescue."

D. A Man's Offer: v. 36

"One man ran, filled a sponge with wine vinegar, put it on a stick, and offered it to Jesus to drink. 'Leave him alone now. Let's see if Elijah comes to take him down,' he said."

It is generally held that this man was a Roman soldier, one of the guards at the cross. But would a Roman know about Elijah or even repeat the name?

It is admittedly difficult to harmonize this verse with Matthew 27:49. But it may be that the bystander's words came first (Matthew) and then the man spoke similarly. Ezra Gould suggests this explanatory paraphrase for the last part of the verse here in Mark: "Let me give him this, and so prolong his life, and then we shall get an opportunity to see whether Elijah comes to help him or not" (*A Critical and Exegetical Commentary on the Gospel According to St. Mark*, p. 295).

E. Death of Jesus: v. 37

"With a loud cry, Jesus breathed his last."

"Breathed his last"—"gave up the ghost" (KJV)—is one word in the Greek. It literally means "breathed out." The modern equivalent is perhaps "expired." John (19:30) says that he "gave up his spirit." Mark's statement could mean much the same.

F. The Torn Curtain: v. 38

"The curtain of the temple was torn in two from top to bottom."

The Greek word for "temple" here is *naos*, "sanctuary," not *hieron*, "temple area." The "curtain" was the inner veil in front of the Holy of Holies, not the outer veil in front of the Holy Place. The significance of this startling event is that the way was now opened for every believer in Christ to enter the very presence of God (see Heb. 9:1-14; 10:19-22). What a glorious privilege is ours!

G. The Centurion's Confession: v. 39

"And when the centurion, who stood there in front of Jesus, heard his cry and saw how he died, he said, 'Surely this man was the Son of God!'"

Mark, writing to the Romans, uses the Latin word (in Greek transliteration, *centyrion*). Matthew and Luke use the regular Greek equivalent. The term meant an officer over a hundred soldiers (cf. our term "century").

In the Greek there is no article before "Son" (see NASB margin). Luke,

writing to Greeks, reports this Gentile centurion as saying, "Surely this was a righteous man" (Luke 23:47). This would be equivalent to "a son of God"—that is a godly man.

IV. THE RESURRECTION: Mark 16:1-7

A. Dedicated Women: v. 1

"When the Sabbath was over, Mary Magdalene, Mary the mother of James, and Salome bought spices so that they might go to anoint Jesus' body."

These same three women are mentioned in 15:40 as watching the death of Jesus. We are told, "In Galilee these women had followed him and cared for his needs" (v. 41). Luke (23:56) tells us that the women "went home and prepared spices and perfumes. But they rested on the Sabbath in obedience to the commandment." The Jewish Sabbath began at sunset on Friday, and so they did not have time to get back to the tomb that day. No work was to be done on the Sabbath.

Now we are told in Mark: "When the Sabbath was over"—at sunset Saturday evening—the women hurried to buy spices for anointing the body of Jesus. But darkness overtook them, and they had to wait until Sunday morning.

DISCUSSION QUESTIONS

1. How can one explain the way the religious leaders, who had our Old Testament, treated Jesus?
2. What did the darkness over the land symbolize?
3. Why did God the Father have to forsake His Son?
4. Why was the angel at the empty tomb?
5. Who first discovered Jesus' resurrection?
6. Why weren't Christ's disciples at the tomb?

B. Concerned Women: vv. 2-3

"Very early on the first day of the week, just after sunrise, they were on their way to the tomb and they asked each other, 'Who will roll the stone away from the entrance of the tomb?'"

They knew that Joseph of Arimathea had "rolled a stone against the entrance of the tomb" (15:46). How were they going to be able to get to the body of Jesus to anoint it with spices? But their extreme dedication—in contrast to the disciples' lack of it!—is shown by their going anyway.

C. The Problem Solved: v. 4

"But when they looked up, they saw that the stone, which was very large, had been rolled away."

I have written on this:

"Having looked up"—apparently their heads had been bowed with grief—they saw that the stone was already rolled away from the door. It was "very great"—perhaps some four or five feet in diameter and round like a millstone. The literal "has been rolled back" reproduces the excited exclamation of the women. The mind can almost picture them pointing suddenly and crying out: "Look! The stone has been rolled back!" Their worries on this point were over (*The Gospel According to Mark*, p. 190).

D. The Angel: v. 5

"As they entered the tomb, they saw a young man dressed in a white robe sitting on the right side, and they were alarmed."

Matthew identifies this "young man" as the angel who rolled away the stone (28:2). Luke mentions "two men" who appeared to the women. But there is surely no disharmony here—just different details reported by the different writers.

E. Message of the Angel: vv. 6-7

The angel said to the women: "Don't be alarmed. You are looking for Jesus the Nazarene, who was crucified. He has risen! He is not here. See the place where they laid him. But go, tell his disciples and Peter, 'He is going ahead of you into Galilee. There you will see him, just as he told you.'"

"He has risen!" That is the glorious message of Easter. And the empty tomb is its happy symbol. We do not worship a dead Christ, but a living Lord.

The "and Peter" gives a beautiful, tender touch. Jesus knew how terrible Peter was feeling for having thrice disowned Him. So, through the angel, He sent a special message to him.

CONTEMPORARY APPLICATION

In 1968 I spent Easter time in Jerusalem. On Good Friday I walked in a procession of the cross from Pilate's Praetorium to the Church of the Holy Sepulchre. It was a solemn occasion, but a moving one for my spirit. Then I enjoyed the Garden Tomb on Sunday morning, where I spoke at an Easter sunrise service.

The next Friday I was in Athens and found that the Greek Orthodox Church was celebrating Good Friday a week later than the Roman Catholics and Protestants. There I saw another procession of the cross. But the glorious sight was on Sunday morning—their Easter. From my hotel window overlooking Constitution Square I saw that place filled with banners saying in Greek, "He has risen." What a glorious message! Thank God for our risen Redeemer!

BE A DOER OF THE WORD

DEVOTIONAL READING	James 1:12-18

Adult Topic: *Be a Doer of the Word*

Youth Topic: *Believing Means Doing*

ADULTS AND YOUTH

Background Scripture: James 1

Scripture Lesson: James 1:1-6, 19-27

Memory Verse: *Be doers of the word, and not hearers only.* James 1:22

CHILDREN

Topic: *Learning to Be a Wise Helper*

Scripture Lesson: James 1:1-26

DAILY BIBLE READINGS

Apr. 23 M.: James, the Brother of Jesus. Matt. 13:53-58
Apr. 24 T.: James' Leadership. Acts 15:12-21
Apr. 25 W.: Faith and Trials. James 1:1-8
Apr. 26 T.: Being Poor Is Rich. James 1:2-11
Apr. 27 F.: Words of Hope. Isa. 40:3-8
Apr. 28 S.: Being Tested. James 1:12-18
Apr. 29 S.: Hearing and Doing. James 1:19-27

LESSON AIM — To help us see the importance of obedience.

LESSON SETTING

Time: possibly about A.D. 45; more likely in the A.D. 60s

Place: probably Jerusalem

LESSON OUTLINE

Be a Doer of the Word

I. **Salutation:** James 1:1
   A. Addressor: v. 1a
   B. Addressees: v. 1b
   C. Greetings: v. 1c

II. **Perseverance Under Trial:** James 1:2-6
   A. Rejoicing in Trials: vv. 2-3
   B. Perseverance and Perfection: v. 4
   C. Asking for Wisdom: v. 5
   D. Asking in Faith: v. 6

III. **Moral Emphasis:** James 1:19-21
   A. Avoiding Anger: vv. 19-20
   B. Avoiding Immorality: v. 21

IV. **Listening and Doing:** James 1:22-25
   A. Doers, Not Just Listeners: v. 22
   B. Simple Illustration: vv. 23-24
   C. The Right Way: v. 25

V. **True Religion:** James 1:26-27
   A. Worthless Religion: v. 26
   B. True Religion: v. 27

After eight sessions on the Gospel of Mark, we now spend five sessions in the study of the Epistle of James—one session on each chapter.

James is the first of the General Epistles—so called because they are written to the whole church, not just to a local church like most of Paul's Epistles. The latter are named after the place to which each was written: Romans, Corinthians, and so on. But the General Epistles are named after the writers: James, Peter, John, and Jude. They contain a great deal of practical instruction on how to live the Christian life.

SUGGESTED INTRODUCTION FOR ADULTS

The main emphasis in the Epistle of James is righteousness. It has many affinities with the Wisdom Literature of the Old Testament (especially Proverbs) and the Minor Prophets Hosea, Amos, and Micah, as also the Sermon on the Mount in the New Testament. Paul's Epistles are filled with a great deal of doctrine; he was a great theologian. But James is concerned primarily with practical Christian living.

SUGGESTED INTRODUCTION FOR YOUTH

"Believing Means Doing." That statement is correct if we recognize what real "believing" is. If we think of it merely as mental comprehension and acceptance, it would not be true. But in the biblical sense, believing is not only mental comprehension but moral commitment. To believe in Jesus means to put our trust in Him as our Savior and Lord, and this involves doing His will. In other words, true faith requires obedience.

A person may say emphatically and dogmatically, "I believe the Bible!" But if he is not obeying its precepts, he is telling a lie. He doesn't really believe God's Word unless he obeys it.

And so our memory verse warns us: "Do not merely listen to the word. . . . Do what it says" (NIV). That is what Christian living is.

CONCEPTS FOR CHILDREN

1. You should be "Learning to Be a Wise Helper."
2. Children have to undergo temptations.
3. We should listen to what God's Word tells us.
4. We should also listen to our Christian teachers.

THE LESSON COMMENTARY

I. SALUTATION:
James 1:1

A. Addressor: v. 1a

All of Paul's Epistles begin with the name of the writer (addressor), an indication of those to whom he is writing (addressees), and then the greeting. Here we find all three of these wrapped up briefly in verse 1. We have hundreds of papyrus letters from the first century (when the New Testament was written), and all of them follow this general pattern.

Who was the "James" who wrote this Epistle: We would naturally think first of James the apostle, the son of Zebedee—one of the inner circle of three disciples of Jesus, as we found recently in our study of Mark. But Paul, in nine of his thirteen Epistles, identifies himself as "an apostle," and so does Peter in both of his Epistles. This James does not.

There is general agreement among New Testament scholars that the author of this Epistle was James the brother of Jesus. He was evidently the head pastor of the Jewish Christian community in Jerusalem (Acts 12:7) and also acted as moderator of the Council of Jerusalem (Acts 15:13, 19). James the apostle, the son of Zebedee, had been martyred several years before this (Acts 12:2).

James identifies himself as "a servant of God and of the Lord Jesus Christ." The Greek word for "servant" is *doulos*. It comes from the verb *deo*, "bind," and so means a bond-servant—that is, a slave. James was a love slave of the Lord, committed to obey Him implicitly and always. Incidentally, this Epistle and that of Jude are the only ones in the New Testament where the writer calls himself simply a "servant." Jude also was not an apostle.

B. Addressees: v. 1b

"To the twelve tribes scattered among the nations."

There has been a great deal of discussion as to what these words mean. In his monumental commentary on the Greek text of the Epistle of James, Joseph B. Mayor holds that the reference is to the twelve tribes of the Diaspora: the dispersion that took place after the destruction of Samaria in 722 B.C. and Jerusalem in 586 B.C. James was concerned about those of his own race (*The Epistle of James*, pp. 29-31). But James addresses his readers as "believers in our glorious Lord Jesus Christ" (2:1). So they clearly were Christians.

At the opposite extreme is James H. Ropes, who also wrote a thorough commentary on the Greek text of this Epistle. He interprets this second line of the Epistle as meaning: "'To the dispersed People of God,' i.e. the

Christian church at large" (*A Critical and Exegetical Commentary on the Epistle of St. James*, p. 123). He further enlarges on this in these words: "To that body of Twelve Tribes, the new Israel, which has its centre in Heaven, and whose members, in whatever place on earth they may be, are all equally away from home and in the dispersion!" (pp. 125-26).

I prefer an interpretation between these two extremes. It seems to me that James is writing primarily to Christian Jews scattered abroad.

C. Greetings: v. 1c

"Greetings" is just one word in the Greek, *chairein*, the present infinitive of the verb *chairo*, "rejoice" or "be glad." This is the regular word for "greetings" that we find after the addressor and addressee in the papyrus letters of that period. In the New Testament it is found only here, in Acts 23:26 (the letter of Lysias to the governor Felix), and in Acts 15:23 (the letter from the Jerusalem Council, probably drawn up by James). This fits in well with James being the author of this Epistle.

II. PERSEVERANCE IN TRIAL: James 1:2-8

A. Rejoicing in Trials: vv. 2-3

"Consider it pure joy, my brothers, whenever you face trials of many kinds, because you know that the testing of your faith develops perseverance."

"My brothers" is a favorite expression with James. We find it again in 2:1, 14; 3:1, 10, 12; 5:12, 19. And he says "my dear brothers" in 1:16, 19; 2:5. He also has "brother" alone in 4:11; 5:7, 9, 10. This shows a warm, loving spirit on the part of James.

To his "brothers" he says, "Consider it pure joy"—literally, "all joy"—"whenever you face trials of many kinds." Mayor wisely observes that James does not say "that trial *is* all joy; he bids us *count* it joy, that is, look at it from the bright side, as capable of being turned to our highest good"

(*James*, p. 33). A. T. Robertson says of trials: "The way to face them all is with joy in the heart and a smile on the face" (*Studies in the Epistle of James*, p. 55).

The King James Version speaks of "divers temptations." (Instead of "divers" we now say "diverse.") But it is generally agreed that "temptations" is not the best translation here. Ropes comments, "In the passage before us *peirasmois* evidently means 'trials,' i.e. adversities, which befall us from without and against our will. According to James (vv. 13ff.) 'temptations' spring mainly from within and could not be a subject for rejoicing" (*St. James*, p. 133).

C. Leslie Mitton pursues the matter a bit further. He writes:

> In the Greek the word translated "trials" has a wider meaning than this single English word. It may refer either to inward impulses (temptations) prompting a man to evil (as it does in 1:13-14) or to outward trouble of different kinds. It may be used, for instance, of those disappointments, sorrows, hardships, which befall us all; or it may indicate special suffering inflicted upon the Christians by hostile pagan neighbours or government officials. All these may be called "trials," and the very use of this word interprets the way in which they were to be regarded. They were felt to be experiences which "tried," "tested," or "proved" the faith of the Christian (*The Epistle of James*, p. 19).

How can we count it all joy when we experience these various trials? Verse 3 gives us the answer: "because you know that the testing of your faith develops perseverance." The King James Version says "patience." But Ropes declares that the Greek word *hypomone*—literally, "a remaining under"—means "steadfastness," "staying power," not "patience" (*St. James*, p. 135). He goes on to say, "In the N.T. *hypomone* is chiefly used in this sense of unswerving constancy to faith and piety in spite of adversity and suffering" (p. 136). So the better translation

is "steadfastness" (RSV), "endurance" (NASB), or "perseverance" (NIV). And this goes for all the many occurrences of this word in the New Testament (e.g., Heb. 12:1).

B. Perseverance and Perfection: v. 4

"Perseverance must finish its work so that you may be mature and complete, not lacking anything."

In the Greek the two adjectives in the middle clause of this verse are *teleios* and *holokleros*. Ropes observes, "As *teleios* means 'complete' in the sense of 'perfect,' 'finished,' so *holokleros* means 'complete in all its parts,' no part being wanting or inadequate" (*St. James*, p. 138). The best translation here is "perfect and complete" (NASB). Mitton writes: "'Perfect' means 'having reached full development.' 'Complete' means 'with no unfinished part'" (*James*, p. 24). We might note that the adjective *teleios* comes from the noun *telos*, which means "end," while the first part of *holokleros* gives us our word "whole."

C. Asking for Wisdom: v. 5

"If any of you lacks wisdom, he should ask God, who gives generously to all without finding fault, and it will be given to him."

"Wisdom" is an important word in this Epistle (see 3:13, 15, 17). Mayor goes so far as to say, "To St. James . . . wisdom is 'the principal thing,' to which he gives the same prominence as St. Paul to faith, St. John to love, St. Peter to hope" (*James* p. 38).

What is this "wisdom"? The Greek word is *sophia*. Ropes correctly observes that this word is "not to be taken in the popular Stoic sense of 'Science.'" He goes on to say, "It is rather 'Wisdom,' the supreme and divine quality of the soul whereby man knows and practices righteousness" (*St. James*, p. 139). A. T. Robertson puts it this way: "With James wisdom is the right use of one's opportunities in holy living" (*James*, p. 63).

If we ask God for this kind of wisdom "it will be given" to us, for He "gives generously to all without finding fault." Ropes says that this last phrase "describes God's giving as full and free, in contrast to the meanness which after a benefaction calls it unpleasantly to the mind of the one benefacted" (*St. James*, p. 140).

D. Asking in Faith: v. 6

"But when he asks, he must believe and not doubt, because he who doubts is like a wave of the sea, blown and tossed by the wind."

We must always pray in faith, not doubting. Jesus told His disciples: "If you believe, you will receive whatever you ask for in prayer" (Matt. 21:22). Incidentally, real faith includes obedience. We cannot really believe unless we obey. Mark records this saying of Jesus in even fuller form: "Therefore I tell you, whatever you ask for in prayer, believe that you have received it, and it will be yours" (11:24). We cannot actually "believe" for anything that is contrary to the will of God. We should seek to ascertain His will and then ask.

James went on to say that the one who doubts "is like a wave of the sea, blown and tossed by the wind." Mayor says of this, "Like a cork floating on the wave, now carried towards the shore, now away from it; opposite to those who have 'hope as an anchor of the soul, sure and steadfast' . . . Heb. 6:19" (*James*, p. 41).

III. MORAL EMPHASIS: James 1:19-21

A. Avoiding Anger: vv. 19-20

"My dear brothers, take note of this: Everyone should be quick to listen, slow to speak and slow to become angry, for man's anger does not bring about the righteous life that God desires."

"Quick to listen, slow to speak"—

what a combination! Any reasonable, thoughtful person realizes the importance of this admonition. And in it all we should avoid anger. A. T. Robertson writes:

> Anger inflames one to hasty and unguarded talk. In turn the words act as fuel to the flames. The talk inflames the anger and the anger inflames the talk. The more one talks the angrier he becomes, like a spitfire. If one stops talking, his anger will cool down for lack of fuel (*James*, p. 91).

Who of us has not seen this kind of a performance? But we all realize the truth of what James asserts here: that "man's anger does not bring about the righteous life that God desires." If we are going to display God's righteousness in our lives, we must heed this admonition.

B. Avoiding Immorality: v. 21

"Therefore, get rid of all moral filth and the evil that is so prevalent, and humbly accept the word planted in you, which can save you."

"Get rid" is literally "putting aside" (NASB). It was used of putting off clothing, but also of removing dirt from the body. "Moral filth" represents a rare Greek word (only here in the New Testament) which means "filthiness" (KJV, NASB). Ropes says, "Evil habits and propensities in general seem to be meant" (*St. James*, p. 170).

"Therefore" seems to tie this verse to the preceding one, about anger. In view of this, Mitton writes, "Anger makes a man dirty and offensive to God" (*James*, p. 63).

Instead of "the evil that is so prevalent," the King James Version has "superfluity of naughtiness." Mitton observes:

> "Superfluity" or "excess" cannot, however, represent its real meaning here, since that would seem to imply that wickedness which is not excessive may be tolerated. Calvin suggested as the translation the

"immense chaos of wickedness"—that is, *all* evil in the overwhelming abundance with which it confronts us (*James*, p. 63).

"Naughtiness" today is a flippant term. It does not represent the true text here.

We are to "humbly accept the word." This is "the word of truth" (v. 18), the message of the gospel.

IV. LISTENING AND DOING: James 1:22-25

A. Doers, Not Just Listeners: v. 22

"Do not merely listen to the word, and so deceive yourselves. Do what it says."

I like the "punch" in that last sentence. It almost seems to deserve an exclamation point.

The Greek word for "doers" (KJV, NASB) is found only six times in the New Testament, and four of those times are in James. This fits well with the central emphasis of James on obedience as the evidence of faith.

Also the word for "hearers" (KJV, NASB) is found three times in James (1:22, 23, 25) and only once elsewhere in the New Testament (Rom. 2:13). Ropes comments that it "naturally suggests hearing the public reading of the Scriptures in Jewish or Christian worship" (*St. James*, p. 175). We must remember that in those days all copies of the Scriptures were written laboriously by hand, and so were very expensive. Most people had access to them only when they heard them read in the synagogue or church service. The Word of the Lord was truly "precious" in those days. Before the age of printing it is said that a man gave a load of hay for a few pages of the first English Bible (Wyclif's), which was copied by hand. How fortunate we are! We must read and obey God's Word.

B. Simple Illustration: vv. 23-24

"Anyone who listens to the word but does not do what it says is like a man who looks at his face in a mirror and, after looking at himself, goes away and immediately forgets what he looks like."

The King James Version says "in a glass." But they did not have glass mirrors in those days. The mirrors were made of copper or a similar metal, so "glass" is incorrect. The correct translation is "mirror."

The picture presented here is of a man looking at his face in a mirror, seeing something that needs to be changed (a spot washed away or his hair combed more neatly), going away and forgetting to do anything about it. God's Word is a mirror. When we hear it or read it, it shows us what we really are. But we have to take the initiative of doing something about it, of making necessary changes in our lives.

How many of us have been pricked by something in the sermon on Sunday morning, as the Spirit made the application? We resolved to do something about it. Then we went home and forgot what we resolved!

C. The Right Way: v. 25

"But the man who looks intently into the perfect law that gives freedom, and continues to do this, not forgetting what he has heard, but doing it—he will be blessed in what he does."

This verse fits in perfectly with our situation today. We have our Bibles,

---

DISCUSSION QUESTIONS

1. How can we face trials with joy?
2. Why is "perseverance" important in the Christian life?
3. How important is faith?
4. What are the dangers of anger?
5. Why do we need to listen as well as talk?
6. How can we practice true religion?

and we should search them "intently" to know God's will for us, and then proceed to carry out that will. If we do so, we will be blessed in what we do.

The verb translated "looks intently" (NASB, NIV) literally means "stoops down," in order to have a close look (John 20:5, 11). Mitton observes, "It is a word that suggests that very close attention is being given to what is being examined" (*James*, p. 70). On the expression "the law of liberty" (KJV, NASB), he writes:

Law often appears to be something that curbs freedom. But this is only when the Law represents a requirement which we do not want to fulfil. If the Law prescribed exactly what we *wanted* to do . . . , then freedom to do what we liked, and obedience to the Law, would become identical. This is what has happened to the real Christian (p. 72).

V. TRUE RELIGION:
James 1:26-27

A. Worthless Religion: v. 26

"If anyone considers himself religious and yet does not keep a tight rein on his tongue, he deceives himself and his religion is worthless."

The Greek word for "religious" (*threskos*, only here in the New Testament) is defined by Abbott-Smith as *"religious*, careful of the outward forms of divine service" (*A Manual Greek-English Lexicon of the New Testament*, p. 208). Similarly, Mitton says that it means "given to religious observances" (*James*, p. 181).

Outward religion is "worthless" if it does not come from a changed heart. James gives a rather surprising test here. He says that if a man does not bridle his tongue, his religious profession is worthless, no matter how carefully he observes the outward forms of worship.

Mitton suggest three tests we should apply to what we say about another person: (1) "Is it true?"; (2) "Is it kind?"; (3) "Am I doing any good by repeating it?" (*James*, p. 76). A lot of trouble would be saved if we submitted carefully to these three tests.

B. True Religion: v. 27

"Religion that God our Father accepts as pure and faultless is this: to look after orphans and widows in their distress and to keep oneself from being polluted by the world."

Two characterizations of true religion are given here. As every well-informed Christian knows, the so-called Liberals have accented the first, while Evangelicals have emphasized the second.

The correct concept, as this verse clearly shows, includes both. We are not to read the first and ignore the second, nor do we have any biblical basis for skipping over the first and giving all our attention to the second.

Jesus pointed the way for us in His words recorded in Matthew 25. First, He told the parable of the Ten Virgins, emphasizing inward spiritual experience in readiness for the Second Coming. Then He gave the parable of the Talents—we must be busy in the Master's business. But He also presented His disciples with the story of The Sheep and the Goats, which emphasized social concern for the needs of those about us. This also is a part of true religion.

CONTEMPORARY APPLICATION

Our memory verse today says, "Be doers of the word, and not hearers only." We need to read the Bible diligently, every day, and seek to learn what it has for us. Then we must "Do what it says" (NIV).

How can we accomplish this? The best pattern for successful obedience is to start each day with our private devotions, getting immediately related to God and His Word. I have found that it helps my time of prayer if I begin by reading carefully a passage of Scripture, asking God to show me His will as I read the Word. The Holy Spirit, who inspired the Word, can then show me how the Scripture can be applied to daily living.

SHOWING YOUR FAITH THROUGH WORKS

DEVOTIONAL READING	Leviticus 19:15-18
ADULTS AND YOUTH	**Adult Topic:** *Be Faithful Through Works* **Youth Topic:** *Let Your Action Do the Talking* **Background Scripture:** James 2 **Scripture Lesson:** James 2:1-7, 14-24 **Memory Verse:** *Faith by itself, if it has no works, is dead.* James 2:17
CHILDREN	**Topic:** *Learning to Accept All People* **Background Scripture:** James 2; Acts 10:30-44 **Scripture Lesson:** Acts 10:30-34 **Memory Verse:** *Truly I perceive that God shows no partiality.* Acts 10:34
DAILY BIBLE READINGS	**Apr. 30 M.:** Don't Be Prejudiced. James 2:1-7 **May 1 T.:** Love Your Neighbor. James 2:8-13 **May 2 W.:** Laws of Justice. Lev. 19:13-18 **May 3 T.:** Faith and Actions. James 2:14-18 **May 4 F.:** Abraham and Rahab's Actions. James 2:19-26 **May 5 S.:** Abraham Obeys God. Gen. 22:1-14 **May 6 S.:** Rahab's Good Deed. Josh. 2:1-14
LESSON AIM	To help us see the importance of faith being demonstrated in works.
LESSON SETTING	**Time:** probably in the A.D. 60s **Place:** Jerusalem

LESSON OUTLINE	**Showing Your Faith Through Works**
	
	I. **Warning Against Favoritism:** James 2:1-4
	   A. Favoritism Forbidden: v. 1
	   B. False Discrimination: vv. 2-4
	
	II. **The Rich and the Poor:** James 2:5-7
	   A. Divine Blessing on the Poor: v. 5
	   B. Faults of the Rich: vv. 6-7
	
	III. **Faith Without Works Is Dead:** James 2:14-17
	   A. Inadequate Faith: v. 14
	   B. False Faith: vv. 15-16
	   C. Dead Faith: v. 17
	
	IV. **A False Dichotomy:** James 2:18-19
	   A. Faith or Deeds: v. 18
	   B. Faith of Demons: v. 19

V. **The Example of Abraham:** James 2:20-24
  A. Scriptural Evidence: vv. 20-23
  B. Justification by Faith with Works: v. 24

We speak of the Bible as *The Book*. But actually it is a library of sixty-six books. Why don't we have just *one* book, written by *one* person?

The answer is partly that the Bible is God's revealed truth for a variety of people, so it was proper to have it written by people of varying personalities, who could understand different aspects and emphases of divine truth. Moses and Isaiah, for instance, were different types of men with different roles, but both give us very important segments of divine revelation.

We find the same thing in the New Testament. Right away we discover that there are four Gospels, not one. And so we get four important presentations of Christ. When we come to the Epistles, we find that Paul and James differ significantly in their main emphases. Paul, in reaction to the damaging work of the Judaizers, says that we are justified by faith (Galatians and Romans). James, plagued by inroads of antinomianism into the church, declares that faith without works is dead. They are not contradicting each other, but supplementing one another.

Our topic today is: "Let Your Action Do the Talking." We have often heard the quip: "Actions speak more loudly than words." Put another way, it goes: "Your actions speak so loudly that I can't hear what you say." One of the great demands of life is that our actions and words must be consistent.

This is what James emphasizes strongly in his Epistle, and especially in our lesson today. He says that if you claim to believe in God but don't live a godly life, you are deceiving yourself. Faith must show itself in good works. If it doesn't, it isn't real faith.

This is a very important truth for all of us to face. It is not enough to say that we believe in Jesus as our Savior. We must live Christlike lives to demonstrate the validity of that faith.

1. God does not show favoritism.
2. We should be kind to all people.
3. God loves all kinds of children.
4. We should be careful about our attitudes toward others.

THE LESSON COMMENTARY

I. WARNING AGAINST
FAVORITISM:
James 2:1-4

A. Favoritism Forbidden: v. 1

"My brothers, as believers in our glorious Lord Jesus Christ, don't show favoritism."

The Greek compound for "favoritism"—"respect of persons" (KJV)—literally means "receiving of face." Paul uses it three times (Rom. 2:11; Eph. 6:9; Col. 3:25), declaring that God does not show favoritism.

J. B. Mayor cites a number of passages in both the Old and New Testaments where this ban on favoritism is emphasized. He then observes, "In all these passages there is signified a bias of judgment owing to the position, rank, circumstances, popularity, and externals generally of the person judged." He goes on to say, "In its strict sense the Greek would mean to accept the outside surface for the inner reality, the mask for the person" (*The Epistle of James*, p. 78). It is interesting to note that the Greek word for "face," *prosopon*, sometimes means "mask." To accept the mask for the real person is certainly the height of folly and injustice.

B. False Discrimination: vv. 2–4

Suppose a man comes into your meeting wearing a gold ring and fine clothes, and a poor man in shabby clothes also comes in. If you show special attention to the man wearing fine clothes and say, "Here's a good seat for you," but say to the poor man, "You stand there," or, "Sit on the floor by my feet," have you not discriminated among yourselves and become judges with evil thoughts?

The Greek word for "meeting" ("assembly," KJV, NASB) is *synagoge*, which we have taken over as "synagogue." It is very significant that James is the only New Testament writer who uses this Jewish term for a Christian assembly. It fits in with his strong Jewish background and the fact that he is writing to Christian Jews. Incidentally, it is generally agreed that "synagogue" here means a gathering of Christians for worship. The Greek word literally means "a gathering together." It is not primarily a building that is meant. Such early church writers as Hermas use *synagoge* for an assembly of Christians.

James pictures two men coming into a Sunday morning worship service. One is wearing a gold ring and "fine clothes." The latter expression literally means "bright" or "brilliant" clothing—that is, elegant clothes. The other man has on "shabby clothes." The "vile raiment" of the King James Version is due to the fact that the Greek root for the adjective translated "shabby" (NIV) is the same as for the noun rendered "filthiness" (KJV, NASB) in 1:21. So "dirty clothes" (NASB) is possible here. At any rate, the wearer is "a poor man."

"Show special attention" (v. 3) is literally "look upon"—that is, with favor, and so "have regard." Who is the "you" that does this? J. H. Ropes suggests: "Doubtless the speaker is one of the dignitaries of the congregation" (*A Critical and Exegetical Commentary on the Epistle of St. James*, p. 190).

This one says to the luxuriously clothed stranger, "Here's a good seat for you." But to the poor man he says either, "You stand there," or "Sit on the floor by my feet."

C. L. Mitton points out the significance of the use of "my" here—"my feet." He writes:

The unhappy implication of the "my" is that not only is the poor man treated worse than the rich man, but worse even than the Christian who receives him. This Christian official has a seat, but he does not offer it to the poor newcomer, who is not important enough for that. If the church member had given up his own seat to the rich man, and himself had been content to sit on the floor with the poor man, the situation would not have been so deplorable as it is; but he too has a seat as well as the rich man (*The Epistle of James*, p. 84).

Mitton also gives a beautiful illustration of the right attitude. He records this incident:

Behind the fighting lines in the first world war a Christian group of men opened rest houses for Christian fellowship, in which all soldiers, irrespective of rank, were welcome. . . . Over the entrance was a parody of a famous quotation: "Abandon all rank, ye who enter here." Whatever differences of rank had to be observed in the military world outside, within the Christian fellowship all were equal. So it should be within the church (*James*, p. 82).

A. T. Robertson points out the logical effect of the action pictured in verses 2 and 3:

> The soul of the poor man is all the more embittered since he came in perhaps in a sort of desperation from the hardness of the world outside, a world that has economic and social laws that make the battle a difficult one. And now in the temple of God the worshipers of Jesus show the same pride of wealth and station as at a social function (*Studies in the Epistle of James*, p. 113).

The tragic result is that the poor man's soul is apt to be lost eternally because of the reception he was accorded "at church."

II. THE RICH AND THE POOR: James 2:5-7

A. Divine Blessing on the Poor: v. 5

"Listen, my dear brothers: Has not God chosen those who are poor in the eyes of the world to be rich in faith and to inherit the kingdom promised those who love him?"

It is an incontestable fact that throughout history the poor have been more apt to be pious than the rich. This is probably because the wealthy tend to feel a greater sense of security and self-sufficiency. So they do not turn to God for help. Mayor remarks, "In the Psalms 'the poor' is almost equivalent to 'the godly'" (*James*, p. 87).

Those whom the world looks down on as "poor," God has chosen for special blessings. Mitton comments, "When God chooses a 'poor man' it is to make him rich, but not as the world counts riches. He is to become RICH IN FAITH" (*James*, p. 86). Jesus spoke about "true riches" (Luke 16:11) and "treasures in heaven" (Matt. 6:20).

The "poor" people, "rich in faith" are to "inherit the kingdom promised to those who love him." What a glorious

inheritance—better than any rich man can provide!

B. Faults of the Rich: vv. 6-7

"But you have insulted the poor. Is it not the rich who are exploiting you? Are they not the ones who are dragging you into court? Are they not the ones who are slandering the noble name of him to whom you belong?"

Here we find a very similar emphasis to what is prominent in the Minor Prophets, especially Hosea, Amos, and Micah. All three of them spend considerable time condemning the rich for oppressing the poor.

This gross sin of oppression has always been predominant in human society and probably always will be until Jesus returns. It simply underscores the fact that the crowning sin of the unregenerate human heart is selfishness. Only God can deliver us from this vile, vicious sin, as we turn our wills over to His will and ask Him to give us the mind of Christ. Apart from grace, man lives for self. In Christ we are enabled to live for others. Being "poor" financially does not guarantee piety. Piety comes only to the poor who are "rich in faith."

III. FAITH WITHOUT WORKS IS DEAD: James 2:14-17

A. Inadequate Faith: v. 14

"What good is it, my brothers, if a man claims to have faith but has no deeds? Can such faith save him?"

The Greek word for "deeds" is *erga*, which literally means "works." But Ropes observes, "*Erga* seems here a recognized term for good deeds" (*St. James*, p. 204).

James brings up the case of a man who claims to have faith but is not showing any good deeds in his life. Then he asks, "Can faith save him?" (KJV). But the Greek word for faith (*pistis*) has the definite article with it—"*the* faith." And in Greek the definite article—the Greek language has no indefinite article—often has the force of a demonstrative pronoun: "that" or "this." So the proper meaning here is "that faith" (NASB). To make this clear the New International Version has "such faith"—that is, a faith that has no good deeds accompanying it. James is not saying that true faith will not save a person. What he clearly declares is that a faith without works will not.

B. False Faith: vv. 15–16

"Suppose a brother or sister is without clothes and daily food. If one of you says to him, 'Go, I wish you well; keep warm and well fed,' but does nothing about his physical needs, what good is it?"

James gives the illustration of a person who is cold and hungry. The use of "brother or sister" suggests that this is a fellow Christian. In Galatians 6:10 Paul says, "Therefore, as we have opportunity, let us do good to all people, especially to those who belong to the family of believers." Our first responsibility is to our brothers and sisters in the Lord. And then our kindness should reach out to others.

But James describes those who profess to have faith but do not show it in good deeds. They say to the poor person in need, "Go in peace" (NASB), but do nothing to help. Mayor writes:

> The sight of distress is unpleasant to these dainty Christians. They bustle out the wretched-looking brother or sister with seeming kindness and what sounds like an order to others to provide for their immediate relief, but without taking any step to carry out the order (*James*, pp. 97–98).

C. Dead Faith: v. 17

"In the same way, faith by itself, if it is not accompanied by action, is dead."

Again we note that James is not here talking about true faith but about a false profession of faith. Mayor observes, "The absence of works, the

natural fruit of faith, proves that the faith is in itself lifeless, just as compassion which expands itself in words is only counterfeit" (*James*, p. 99). And Ropes wisely remarks, "The two things which are opposed are not faith and works (as with Paul) but a living faith and a dead faith" (*St. James*, p. 207).

Mitton comments here:

> Love which consists only of nice words and feelings, but does not go on to actions is a poor ineffective thing. So too, says James, is faith. If it is a matter only of nice feelings and easy words, and does not lead on to costly action for the service of others, it is not really faith at all; at best it is a lifeless, ineffective thing. It is as it were only the corpse of faith (*James*, p. 102).

These are strong words, and they ought to jolt us. We need to check ourselves carefully.

IV. A FALSE DICHOTOMY: James 2:18–19

A. Faith or Deeds: v. 18

"But someone will say, 'You have faith; I have deeds.' Show me your faith without deeds, and I will show you my faith by what I do."

We have headed this section (vv. 18-19) "A False Dichotomy"—that is, between faith and works. John insists that they go together.

Ropes pictures a "supposed bringer of excuses" as saying, "One has preeminently faith, another has preeminently works." In answer to this, James asserts, "A live faith and works do not exist separately" (*St. James*, p. 208). On the last part of the verse Ropes expresses the meaning as being: "From the very existence of righteous conduct the fact of faith can be demonstrated, for without faith I could not do the works" (p. 210).

A. T. Robertson comments:

> Here James pits over against each other the two sorts of faith—the true faith which James claims to possess and which is proved by works, and

the false faith which is a mere profession and entirely apart from works (*James*, p. 134).

B. Faith of Demons: v. 19

"You believe that there is one God. Good! Even the demons believe that—and shudder."

The belief in one true God is an oft-repeated emphasis in the Old Testament. Every devout Jew was supposed to repeat every morning and evening the so-called *Shema* (Deut. 6:4): "Hear, O Israel: the LORD our God, the LORD is one." In contrast to all the nations around them, the Israelites had a monotheistic religion. This was the center of their faith.

So, in response to the assertion of monotheism, James says, "Good!" But then he adds a shocking statement: "Even the demons believe that."

The King James Version incorrectly has "devils" here, as also throughout the Gospels. The Greek word for "devil" is *diabolos;* there is only one devil. The word here is the plural of *daimonion,* from which we get our word "demon." It is misleading to speak of "devils"; we should always say "demons"—of which there are many.

V. THE EXAMPLE OF ABRAHAM: James 2:20-24

A. Scriptural Evidence: vv. 20-23

"You foolish man, do you want evidence that faith without deeds is useless?" (v. 20).

The last word here is somewhat in dispute, because the earliest Greek manuscripts of James (fourth and fifth centuries) are divided. Some have the Greek word meaning "dead" (KJV) while some have a word that means "useless" (NASB, NIV). We cannot be certain which was original, but both mean about the same thing.

James then proceeds to give the "evidence." He says in verse 21: "Was

not our ancestor Abraham considered righteous for what he did when he offered his son Isaac on the altar?"

This touching scene is recorded in Genesis 22. God told Abraham to offer his son Isaac as a burnt offering (v. 2). Without any argument the patriarch cut wood for the fire and started out (v. 3). He bound his son Isaac and laid him on top of the wood he had placed on the altar (v. 9). Finally he took a knife in his hand to slay his son as a sacrifice (v. 10). Only then did God intervene and provide a ram to be used in place of Isaac (v. 13). Abraham had dramatically proved the genuineness of his faith by his act of obedience. That is the point that James is making here.

James then goes on to make the application in verses 22 and 23: "You see that his faith and his actions were working together, and his faith was made complete by what he did. And the Scripture was fulfilled that says, 'Abraham believed God, and it was credited to him as righteousness,' and he was called God's friend." Paul gives this same quotation from Genesis 15:6 in Galatians 3:6 and Romans 4:3. He puts more stress on the aspect of faith: Abraham was saved by faith, not works (Rom. 4:2). But James beautifully combines the two: Abraham's "faith and his actions were working together, and his faith was made complete by what he did."

DISCUSSION QUESTIONS

1. What are the causes of favoritism?
2. What are the consequences of favoritism?
3. Why is it illogical, as well as wrong, to pay special attention to the rich?
4. How may poverty contribute to piety?
5. What is the proper relationship between faith and works?
6. What kind of works are the evidence of true faith?

So it is with all of us, James would say. When our faith and our deeds work together, we demonstrate that we have true, saving faith.

B. Justification by Faith and Works: v. 24

Now James scores his final point in this argument: "You see that a person is justified by what he does and not by faith alone." Unless one shows his faith by his good works he actually does not have the faith that justifies us before God.

Ropes sounds a good warning here. He says:

It is not to be inferred that James held to a justification by works without faith. Such a misunderstanding is so abhorrent to his doctrine of the inseparability of faith and works that it does not occur to him to guard himself against it. And the idea itself would have been foreign to Jewish as well as to Christian thought (*St. James*, pp. 223-24).

When Paul emphasizes in Galatians and Romans that a person cannot be saved by works, he is thinking of the works of the Old Testament law (e.g., Rom. 3:28). James, on the other hand, is thinking of the good works of love and mercy that follow out of faith. Properly understood, there is no contradiction between James and Paul.

CONTEMPORARY APPLICATION

Mitton gives a wonderful example of the kind of works that demonstrate true faith and bring glory to God. He writes:

Rev. Dr. W. E. Sangster, for sixteen years minister at Westminster Central Hall, London, was supreme as an evangelical preacher. When, however, the bombing made normal life in London impossible from 1940-45 he made the deep cellars of the Hall into shelters for frightened and homeless people, and himself slept in them for five years, supervising the welfare of thousands and bringing them love and cheer. His son in the biography of his father writes: "'Service before services' was his motto" (*James*, p. 79).

BE CAREFUL WHAT YOU SAY

DEVOTIONAL READING	Ezekiel 33:1-9

Adult Topic: *Be Careful What You Say*

Youth Topic: *Watch Your Words*

ADULTS AND YOUTH

Background Scripture: James 3

Scripture Lesson: James 3:1-10, 13-18

Memory Verse: *Death and life are in the power of the tongue, and those who love it will eat its fruits.* Prov. 18:21

Topic: *Learning to Be Responsible*

Background Scripture: James 3:1-10, 13-18; Acts 6:1-7

CHILDREN

Scripture Lesson: Acts 6:1-7; James 3:1-5

Memory Verse: *And the word of God increased; and the number of the disciples multiplied.* Acts 6:7

DAILY BIBLE READINGS

May 7 M.: Mistakenly Speaking. James 3:1-5
May 8 T.: Speaking Can Hurt. James 3:6-12
May 9 W.: Ezekiel Is a Watchman. Ezek. 33:1-9
May 10 T.: Accepting Consequences of Words. Prov. 18:17-21
May 11 F.: Warning Against Arrogance. James 3:13-18
May 12 S.: Example of a Loving Heart. I Thess. 3:6-13
May 13 S.: Boasting for the Lord. I Cor. 1:26-31

LESSON AIM

To help us see the importance of watching our words.

LESSON SETTING

Time: probably in the A.D. 60s

Place: Jerusalem

Be Careful What You Say

LESSON OUTLINE

I. **Responsibility of Teachers:** James 3:1-2
   A. Judged More Strictly: v. 1
   B. Human Frailty: v. 2

II. **Metaphors of the Tongue:** James 3:3-6
   A. Bits in Horses' Mouths: v. 3
   B. Rudders on Ships: v. 4
   C. A Small Spark: vv. 5-6

III. **The Untamable Tongue:** James 3:7-8

IV. **A Sad Dilemma:** James 3:9-10
   A. Praising God and Cursing Men: v. 9
   B. A Bad Combination: v. 10

V. **Two Kinds of Wisdom:** James 3:13-18
   A. Demonstration in Life: v. 13
   B. Earthly Wisdom: vv. 14-16
   C. Heavenly Wisdom: vv. 17-18

SUGGESTED INTRODUCTION FOR ADULTS

Our memory verse today suggests an important truth: "Death and life are in the power of the tongue." The words that we say can bring death or life to people. Whole nations have been involved in destructive wars, with great loss of life, as a result of a few words uttered by a key individual. Only God could possibly compute the total damage done by the tongue! It would run into countless billions of dollars and millions of lost lives.

We cannot be too careful about what we say. It is easier to put on the brakes, as it were, and avoid uttering some hasty words, than to have to face the consequences or try to repair the damage. The results of a few careless words can go on for many years, defiling many individuals and even destroying the work of God.

We need to give careful attention to what James says here about the tongue and to heed the warning: "Be Careful What You Say."

SUGGESTED INTRODUCTION FOR YOUTH

"Watch Your Words" is very wholesome advice. And it is one of the most significant warnings for us to hear and heed.

Probably more friendships have been ruined by the speaking of a few careless words than by any other single cause. Harsh words are a major contributing cause to divorce. They can also spoil the happy fellowship of Christian young people. I have seen a joyous party turned into a time of tension by a single sentence from a careless youth.

We have all heard the slogan: "Think before you speak." Too many people speak first and then think afterwards. This can be catastrophic. You may decide not to voice what you had planned to say if you think first. And that might be the smartest decision you make all day!

CONCEPTS FOR CHILDREN

1. "Learning to Be Responsible" is a vital part of childhood experience.
2. We must give attention to being dependable.
3. Being dependable involves carrying out what we promise to do.
4. God will help us fulfill our promises if we ask Him.

THE LESSON COMMENTARY

I. RESPONSIBILITY OF TEACHERS: James 3:1-2

A. Judged More Strictly: v. 1

"Not many of you should presume to be teachers, my brothers, because you know that we who teach will be judged more strictly."

The King James Version reads: "My brethren, be not many masters." One of the earliest meanings of "master" was "teacher." Shakespeare used "master" that way in 1599, just before the King James Version came out, but it does not carry that meaning today. The Greek word here is *didascaloi*, which means "teachers."

One of the problems that Paul had with the church at Corinth was that there were too many would-be teachers in the congregation, wanting to tell everybody else what to do. James here warns his readers against that tendency.

Why should not many act as teachers? "Because you know that we who teach will be judged more strictly." If we humbly seek to do our best, instead of telling everybody else what to do, we can get by a lot more easily. The more we teach others, the more strictly we will be judged.

B. Human Frailty: v. 2

"We all stumble in many ways. If anyone is never at fault in what he says, he is a perfect man, able to keep his whole body in check."

The first sentence of this verse is rendered in the King James Version "For in many ways we offend all." But this is not what the Greek says. The Greek word for "all" (*pantes*) is not in the accusative case (direct object) but in the nominative case (subject). It is not true that we offend all people. But what the inspired Greek text does say is true: "We all stumble in many ways" (NASB, NIV). The verb *ptaio* does not mean "offend," but "stumble," and is correctly translated that way in Romans 11:11 in the King James Version.

On this first sentence James H. Ropes makes this helpful observation: "All men stumble, and of all faults those of the tongue are the hardest to avoid. Hence the profession of teacher is the most difficult mode of life conceivable" (*A Critical and Exegetical Commentary on the Epistle of St. James*, p. 228). This introduces the problem of the tongue that takes in all of chapter three.

James goes on to say: "If anyone is never at fault in what he says, he is a perfect man, able to keep his whole body in check." The Greek verb for "keep . . . in check" is found (in the New Testament) only here and in James

1:26 ("keep a tight rein," NIV). It literally means "lead with a bridle," and so, metaphorically, "to bridle, restrain" (G. Abbott-Smith, *A Manual Greek Lexicon of the New Testament*, p. 478).

This last clause has to be interpreted in the light of the next verse. As J. B. Mayor notes, "by the bridle in the mouth we turn the horse as we will, so by controlling our words we can regulate our whole activity" (*The Epistle of James*, p. 108).

The rest of the chapter emphasizes the fact that the tongue is the most unruly part of the body (cf. vv. 7-8). So if we can control it, we can control the rest.

II. METAPHORS OF THE TONGUE: James 3:3-6

A. Bits in Horses' Mouths: v. 3

"When we put bits into the mouths of horses to make them obey us, we can turn the whole animal."

The Greek word for "bits" literally means "bridles," and is so translated in the only other place in the New Testament where it occurs (Rev. 14:20). It fits very well there. But you can't put a bridle into a horse's mouth! You slip the metal "bit" into his mouth first, and then the rest of the "bridle," made of leather, over his head. The ends of the metal bit, on either side of the horse's mouth, have leather reins attached to them. By pulling on either rein, the rider on horseback (or in a buggy or wagon behind) can turn the horse to the right ("Gee") or to the left ("Haw"), as he wishes.

The "bit" is just a small metal mouthpiece. That is the point that James is trying to make here, as he spells out more clearly in verse 4 and applies in verse 5. But even here in verse 3 it is the small "bit" that enables one to "turn the whole animal." As C. L. Mitton says, "The bit in the horse's mouth is tiny compared with the bulk of the horse itself, yet by it the horse can be controlled and directed" (*The Epistle of James*, p. 123).

B. Rudders on Ships: v. 4

"Or take ships as an example. Although they are so large and are driven by strong winds, they are steered by a very small rudder wherever the pilot wants to go."

Whenever I read this verse I am reminded of the two trips my wife and I took in 1958 and 1968 on the Queen Elizabeth I—at that time the largest passenger ship afloat. After traversing the length of the ship (nearly one thousand feet) on both sides, we stood at the stern. There we looked down at the small rudder. How could such a relatively small piece of equipment turn that giant hull? Yet we saw that little rudder safely maneuver the massive ship into a narrow harbor. The contrast between "so large" a ship and "a very small rudder" was impressive even in James' day.

C. A Small Spark: vv. 5-6

"Likewise the tongue is a small part of the body, but it makes great boasts. Consider what a great forest is set on fire by a small spark" (v. 5).

My father was forest fire warden of the area where we lived in Massachusetts (which is heavily wooded). Once I traced the origin of a fire by walking against the wind to the small point where it all began. There I picked up a handful of ashes, held them to my nose, and got a strong smell of tobacco. A discarded cigarette butt had been responsible for burning acres of land.

After presenting these three very striking metaphors, James now makes the application. He writes: "The tongue also is a fire, a world of evil among the parts of the body. It corrupts the whole person, sets the whole course of his life on fire, and is itself set on fire by hell" (v. 6).

This is about as strong language as one could use on the subject of the tongue. James declares that it "is a

fire." And what fiery tongues some people do have. They can enter a peaceful situation and with a few words start a great conflagration!

James goes on to say that the tongue is "a world of evil among the parts of the body," causing more damage than any other part. "It corrupts the whole person, sets the whole course of life on fire"—that is, "all that is contained in our life" (Mayor, *James*, p. 118).

James concludes this almost unbelievable description of the tongue by saying that it "is itself set on fire by hell." The Greek word is *Gehenna*, the place of fiery punishment, as held by the Jews.

III. THE UNTAMABLE TONGUE: James 3:7-8

"All kinds of animals, birds, reptiles and creatures of the sea are being tamed and have been tamed by man, but no man can tame the tongue. It is a restless evil, full of deadly poison."

In verse 7 there is probably a reference to the account of creation. God said: "Let us make man in our image, in our likeness, and let them rule over the fish of the sea and the birds of the air, over the livestock, over all the earth, and over all the creatures that move along the ground" (Gen. 1:26). Many animals have been tamed for domestic use. Others, more wild and dangerous, have been tamed for performance in circus shows. Even snakes have been charmed.

But, asserts James, "no man can tame the tongue." A. T. Robertson writes:

> The eye of man can subdue the lion, the tiger, the serpent as Jesus subdued the untamable demoniac (Mark 5:4). . . . In many cases animals have become so domesticated that they feel no longer at home elsewhere. Man is proud of his lordship over beast and bird. . . . But he cannot control his own tongue (*Studies in the Epistle of James*, p. 162).

James goes on to say of the tongue: "It is a restless evil, full of deadly poison." Alexander Maclaren says of James:

> He adds a characterization of the tongue, which fits in with his "image of an untamable brute: 'It is a restless evil,' like some caged but unsubdued wild animal, ever pacing uneasily up and down its den; 'full of deadly poison,' like some captured rattlesnake. The venom spurted out by a calumnious tongue is more deadly than snake poison. Blasphemous words, or obscene words, shot into the blood by one swift dart of the fangs, may corrupt its whole current ..." (*Expositions of Holy Scripture*, Hebrews and James, p. 435).

Mitton may come a little closer to where we live when he writes:

> Poison makes an apt name for hurtful gossip. It spreads an evil atmosphere through the whole of the community, lowering morale, and destroying the character of innocent people who have no means of stopping or answering the whispered slanders (*James*, p. 130).

IV. A SAD DILEMMA:
James 3:9-10

A. Praising God and Cursing Men: v. 9

"With the tongue we praise our Lord and Father, and with it we curse men, who have been made in God's likeness."

Probably no one would deny that every Sunday there are people who sit in church and join others in singing hymns of praise to God, and yet who during the week use curse words in addressing their fellowmen.

Again Mitton comes close to home. He says:

> "Cursing" may mean speaking words of abuse either to a person or about him; it may also mean uttering words which are believed to have potency to inflict injury on him. Here it probably refers primarily to angry words of abuse spoken to those whom

we regard as subordinate to us, as well as bitter denunciation (in their absence) of others whom we do not care to criticize to their face (*James*, p. 131).

B. A Bad Combination: v. 10

"Out of the same mouth come praise and cursing. My brothers, this should not be." Any true Christian would say a hearty "Amen!" to this verdict.

V. TWO KINDS OF WISDOM: James 3:13-18

A. Demonstration in Life: v. 13

"Who is wise and understanding among you? Let him show it by his good life, by deeds done in the humility that comes from wisdom."

Mitton comments:

> James proceeds to insist that true wisdom and understanding are not to be identified with a merely intellectual cleverness. Their genuineness is proved by the quality of conduct which they produce. Just as "faith" (or what claims to be "faith") is proved not to be real faith, unless it issues in "good works" of mercy and love, so wisdom is shown to be sham and unreal unless it leads to a good life expressed in good works (*James*, p. 134).

In a similar vein Robertson writes:

> The test is the acid test of deeds, not words. We may quibble over words and talk like a wise man, but time will prove our words by our deeds.... People have learned to discount mere talk when it stands alone (*James*, p. 174).

We should not fail to note that the main evidence of wisdom cited here is humility. No proud person can be a truly wise person. The wise person is aware of how little he knows!

B. Earthly Wisdom: vv. 14-16

Now we have a picture of false "wisdom," the kind that James is warning us against. He first says, "But if you harbor bitter envy and selfish ambition in your hearts, do not boast about it or deny the truth" (v. 14).

What a contrast to humility, the mark of true wisdom! Both "bitter envy" and "selfish ambition" are tragic evidences of carnal pride. These two attitudes are to be carefully avoided by Christians. Mitton comments:

> There is, perhaps no greater sign of the effective power of the grace of God in any community than when members of it live happily together, enjoying each other's company, appreciating each other's good qualities, and entirely free from "bitter jealousy" (*James*, p. 136).

"Selfish ambition" is one word in Greek. Ropes says, "The word denotes the inclination to use unworthy and divisive means for promoting one's own views or interest" (*St. James*, p. 246).

There were "teachers" in the churches (v. 1) who were not showing the right attitudes. Instead of having humility and piety, they were proud and selfish.

James goes on to say, "Such 'wisdom' does not come down from heaven but is earthly, unspiritual, of the devil" (v. 15).

Ropes comments:

> These three words, "earthly, sensual, devilish," describe the so-called wisdom, which is not of divine origin, in an advancing series—as pertaining to the earth, not to the world above; to mere nature, not to the Spirit; and to the hostile spirits of evil, instead of to God (*St. James*, p. 248).

Then James puts it right on the line: "For where you have envy and selfish ambition, there you find disorder and every evil practice" (v. 16). This is inevitable. Envy and selfish ambition always cause trouble between people. Mitton puts it this way: "True wisdom, as God gives it, has the effect of drawing people together and building them up into a stable and enduring society. But earthly wisdom separates them in rivalry and antagonism, and

produces 'disorder' or 'disharmony'" (*James*, p. 139). There was too much of this in the early church, as I Corinthians shows.

C. Heavenly Wisdom: vv. 17-18

"But the wisdom that comes from heaven is first of all pure; then peace-loving, considerate, submissive, full of mercy and good fruit, impartial and sincere" (v. 17).

It is important to note the priority here: heavenly wisdom is "first of all pure." Nothing takes the place of this. In these days of loose morals this needs to be emphasized afresh.

"Then" introduces the list of subordinate characteristics. The first is "peaceable" (KJV, NASB). From the Greek adjective here we get our word "irenic." A Christian who is not "peace-loving" is not wise!

The next adjective, "gentle" or "considerate," translates a distinctive Greek word. Ropes says it means "reasonable," "considerate," "moderate," "gentle" (*St. James*, p. 249).

Ropes defines the next adjective as "'obedient,' 'ready to obey'; here perhaps 'willing to yield,' the opposite of 'obstinate'" (*St. James*, p. 249). So "reasonable" (NASB) and "submissive" (NIV) both fit.

The remaining adjectives are treated much the same way in the different versions. They are all characteristics

---

DISCUSSION QUESTIONS

1. Why should we seek to serve, rather than have a position?
2. How can we learn to control our tongues?
3. What place does humility have in the Christian life?
4. What is the biblical concept of wisdom?
5. What causes envy and selfish ambition?
6. Why is purity placed first in describing heavenly wisdom?

of true wisdom, which comes from heaven.

The chapter closes with this observation: "Peacemakers who sow in peace raise a harvest of righteousness" (v. 18). If we want our lives filled with righteousness we must daily "sow in peace"—for we reap what we sow!

CONTEMPORARY APPLICATION

We would all do well to live in this chapter throughout this coming week. Perhaps it would help most if we read it each day for our private devotions, asking God to show us how to possess and display more of the wisdom that comes from above. Prayerful reading of this chapter for a week could have a marked influence for good on our lives.

Especially important would be going through verse 17, word by word, asking the Lord to help us to have each of these characteristics in increasing measure. There is plenty of room for growth in grace in all of us!

BE RESPONSIBLE TO GOD

DEVOTIONAL READING	I Peter 4:7-19
ADULTS AND YOUTH	**Adult Topic:** *Draw Near to God*
	Youth Topic: *Getting Close to God*
	Background Scripture: James 4
	Scripture Lesson: James 4:1-10, 13-17
	Memory Verse: *Draw near to God and he will draw near to you.* James 4:8
CHILDREN	**Topic:** *Learning to Depend on God*
	Memory Verse: *You ask and do not receive, because you ask wrongly.* James 4:3
DAILY BIBLE READINGS	**May 14 M.:** Source of Quarrels and Fights. James 4:1-6
	May 15 T.: Selfish Human Desires. Rom. 7:5-12
	May 16 W.: Managing God's Gifts. I Peter 4:7-19
	May 17 T.: Come Near to God. James 4:7-12
	May 18 F.: Humility Is Greatness. Matt. 23:1-12
	May 19 S.: Be Examples to the Flock. I Peter 5:1-7
	May 20 S.: Trusting in God. James 4:13-17
LESSON AIM	To help us see that the only way to be what we ought to be is to draw near to God for His help.
LESSON SETTING	**Time:** probably in the A.D. 60s
	Place: Jerusalem
LESSON OUTLINE	**Be Responsible to God**

Be Responsible to God

  I. **Cause of Quarrels:** James 4:1-3
    A. The Cause: vv. 1-2a
    B. The Remedy: vv. 2b-3

 II. **Adulterous People:** James 4:4-6
    A. Friends of the World: v. 4
    B. Proud, Not Humble: vv. 5-6

III. **Need for Repentance:** James 4:7-10
    A. Submit to God: v. 7
    B. Come Near to God: v. 8
    C. Mourning over Sins: v. 9
    D. Humble Yourselves: v. 10

IV. **Boasting About Tomorrow:** James 4:13-17
    A. False Confidence: v. 13
    B. Nature of Life: v. 14
    C. The Lord Willing: v. 15
    D. Evil Boasting: v. 16
    E. Sins of Omission: v. 17

In our last lesson we found that James has a lot to say about the human tongue. It can cause all kinds of trouble in society and in the church. He pictures the tongue as an untamable wild animal, causing all kinds of trouble.

In today's lesson we go behind the tongue to the human heart, to discover the cause of the tongue's misbehavior. We find that it lies in wrong attitudes, wrong desires, and wrong motives. The real problem is inward, rather than outward.

SUGGESTED INTRODUCTION FOR ADULTS

How is this awful condition going to be taken care of? James answers, "Wash your hands, you sinners, and purify your hearts, you double-minded" (v. 8).

How can this be brought about? Again James gives the necessary answer: "Come near to God and he will come near to you" (v. 8). That is why our adult topic today is: "Draw Near to God."

It is an admonition that we all need. The only way to succeed in life is to draw near to God and let Him guide us in all we do.

SUGGESTED INTRODUCTION FOR YOUTH

"Getting Close to God" is the most important thing for all of us to do. And the best time to do it is when we are young. I am very thankful that I turned my life completely over to the Lord when I was fifteen years old, a junior in high school. The result is that the sixty years since then have been wonderfully blessed, with a glorious sense of fulfilment, rather than frustration.

And so I would say to all young people: Draw near to God *now*, and let Him have His way in your life. We need to get close to God so that we can hear Him as He softly whispers in our hearts what He wants us to do.

Many Christian young people want God to be close to them. The responsibility is ours: "Come near to God and he *will* come near to you."

CONCEPTS FOR CHILDREN

1. We need to learn to depend on God.
2. We cannot depend wholly on others, because they may fail us.
3. God will never fail us—"Jesus Never Fails."
4. God is our Father; we can depend fully on Him.

THE LESSON COMMENTARY

I. CAUSE OF QUARRELS:
James 4:1-3

A. The Cause: vv. 1-2a

"What causes fights and quarrels among you? Don't they come from your desires that battle within you? You want something but don't get it. You kill and covet, but you cannot have what you want. You quarrel and fight."

It is worth noting that James does not address his readers (until v. 11) as "brothers." The description given here obviously does not apply to genuine Christians, although they probably were church members.

On the two words, "fights" and

"quarrels," James Ropes says that the first means "feuds" or "quarrels" and the second "conflicts" or "contentions." He adds, "The two words cover the chronic and the acute hostilities in the community" (*A Critical and Exegetical Commentary on the Epistle of St. James*, p. 253). In somewhat the same vein, J. B. Mayor writes, "These need not be limited to their narrow sense: the former denotes any lasting resentment, the latter any outburst of passion" (*The Epistle of James*, p. 133).

A. T. Robertson indicates what the "narrow sense" of these two words is and offers a helpful comment. He observes:

> We need not press the distinction between "wars" (*polemoi*) and "fightings" (*machai*), though the first means a state of war and the lasting resentment connected with it, while the second refers to battles or outbursts of passions which occur during a state of war. James does not, of course, here refer to wars between nations, but to the factional bickerings in the churches, the personal wrangles that embitter church life. "Among you" (*en hymin*), he adds, to drive the question home (*Studies in the Epistle of James*, pp. 192-93).

So instead of "wars and fightings" (KJV) it is better to say "quarrels and conflicts" (NASB) or "fights and quarrels" (NIV). These are personal, not national.

James answers his first question by asking a second question: "Don't they come from your desires that battle within you?" The Greek word translated "desires"—"lusts" (KJV)—is *hedonon*, which is usually translated "pleasures" (cf. our "hedonism"). In fact, the same word (in the dative plural) is rendered "pleasures" at the end of verse 3. The New American Standard Bible has "pleasures" in both places. The reason for "desires" (v. 1) in the New International Version is that in that verse it seems to be more desire for pleasure than pleasure itself.

Speaking particularly of verse one, Robertson says, "The word for pleasure does not necessarily mean sensual pleasures..., but what is sweet (*hedys, hedone*) and leads to sinful strife (like ambition, love of money or power)" (*James*, p. 194).

James goes on to say, "You want something but don't get it." So what do they do? "You kill and covet, but you cannot have what you want. You quarrel and fight."

The expression "kill and covet" has caused a great deal of discussion by commentators. There are two problems. The first is the order of the words: "covet" seems like an anticlimax after "kill." This can be averted by placing a period after "kill." The next part then makes a logical unit: "You covet, but you cannot have what you want." The second problem is the use of "kill" in relation to church members. Although many object to diluting this strong word, it seems to me that we could possibly apply John's statement: "Anyone who hates his brother is a murderer" (I John 3:15).

The Bible declares that "the love of money is a root of all kinds of evil" (I Tim. 6:10). Covetousness leads to all kinds of crime. It certainly leads to quarreling and fighting, as this verse plainly indicates. And it may lead to actual murder. It is too dangerous to permit in our hearts and minds.

B. The Remedy: vv. 2b-3

"You do not have, because you do not ask God. When you ask, you do not receive, because you ask with wrong motives, that you may spend what you get on your pleasures."

James tells his readers: "You do not have, because you do not ask God." They might reply: "We *do* pray." He then informs them: "You ask with wrong motives." C. L. Mitton says, "True satisfaction is to be found only when we want the right things, and these God readily grants to those who ask for them in prayer" (*The Epistle of James*, p. 151). Mitton goes on to say:

> The trouble with the people rebuked in verses 1 and 2 is that what they are seeking is not God's will for them. . . . True prayer begins with a willingness to learn God's will, and a readiness to submit our hearts to God to have them made to want His will. "If we ask anything according to His will, He hears us" (I John 5:14). The essence of prayer is not to get what we want out of God, but to have ourselves so changed by God that we come to want what He wants for us, to "love what God commands and to desire what He promises" (*James*, p. 15).

Ropes suggests that James' principle is: "Make the service of God your supreme end, and then your desires will be such as God can fulfil in answer to your prayer (cf. Mt. 6:31-33)" (*St. James*, p. 258).

III. ADULTEROUS PEOPLE: James 4:4-6

A. Friends of the World: v. 4

"You adulterous people, don't you know that friendship with the world is hatred toward God? Anyone who chooses to be a friend of the world becomes an enemy of God."

The King James Version says, "Ye adulterers and adulteresses." But the first part—"adulterers and"—is not found in any Greek manuscript earlier than the ninth century; it clearly is not genuine. Christians compose the bride of Christ. If any Christian is unfaithful to Jesus, being involved with the world, that person thereby becomes an "adulteress." A bride cannot be an "adulterer."

The Greek word for "friendship," *philia*, is found only here in the New Testament. It suggests an affection for the world. James uses strong language here when he declares that "friendship with the world is hatred toward God." He further declares, "Anyone who chooses to be a friend (*philos*) of the world becomes an enemy of God." Robertson wisely points out:

> World (*cosmos*) here is not the earth with all its beauty and charm (God's world made by him. Cf. Psa. 19), nor mankind, for whom Christ died (John 3:16), but that world of selfish pleasure and sin out of which Christ called his disciples and which in turn hated them as it hated Christ (John 15:18ff) (*James*, p. 200).

B. Proud, Not Humble: vv. 5-6

"Or do you think the Scripture says without reason that the spirit he caused to live in us tends toward envy, but he gives us more grace? That is why the Scripture says:

'God opposes the proud,
    but gives grace to the humble.'"

The first part of verse 5 presents two problems. The first is that we do not find any such quotation of "Scripture" in the Old Testament. But Mayor notes that "we have other instances of quotations in the N.T. which remind us rather of the general sense of several passages than of the actual words of any one particular passage in the O.T." (*James*, p. 140). John Wesley voiced much the same opinion two hundred years ago. This problem is really minor.

The second one, however, is more difficult. In the New American Standard Bible verse 5 reads, "Or do you think that the Scripture speaks to no purpose:'He jealously desires the spirit which He has made to dwell in us!'?" That is, God has placed in us a human spirit which he jealously, out of His infinite love, desires to bless and control. On the other hand, the New International Version (see above) makes "the spirit" the subject of the verb. Both of these two recent evangelical versions of the Bible give in their margin basically what is found in the other. Which is right?

No honest scholar today would presume to give a categorical answer to that question. The Greek word for "spirit," *pneuma*, is neuter, and in Greek the same form is used in the neuter for both the nominative and accusative cases. So we have no way of knowing whether "spirit" is the subject or the object of the verb. The fact that *pneuma* follows the verb does not determine which it is, for in Greek, as in Latin, the subject often comes after the verb instead of before it. So the only thing we can do is to allow both translations and interpretations. Ropes prefers the New American Standard Bible rendering, taking "desires" as "yearns over"—"of the longing affection of the lover." This appeals to me, too. "God is a jealous lover" (Ropes, *St. James*, p. 264).

A possible third interpretation is reflected in the King James Version translation: "The spirit that dwelleth in us lusteth to envy" (cf. NIV margin). But this seems to me the least likely one.

Verse 6 ends with a quotation from Proverbs 3:34:

"God opposes the proud,
    but gives grace to the humble."

This should be a constant warning to us. Are we really proud or humble?

III. NEED FOR REPENTANCE: James 4:7-10

A. Submit to God: v. 7

"Submit yourselves, then, to God. Resist the devil, and he will flee from you."

The Greek verb for "submit" is used widely in the New Testament. Peter uses it seven times in his two Epistles, and Paul twenty-four times in his thirteen Epistles. Altogether it is found forty times in the New Testament. Our greatest responsibility is to submit our wills wholly to God's will. Only thus can we find the highest and best in life.

But there is another side of the coin: "Resist the devil." This command is accompanied by the promise: "and he will flee from you." It is our responsibility to obey the command and God's responsibility to keep His promise.

B. Come Near to God: v. 8

"Come near to God and he will come near to you." This is one of the most important passages in the Bible for both the sinner and the saint. Admittedly the main emphasis in this passage is on the sinner drawing near to God in humble repentance. But we can daily discover that as we draw near to God (as in our morning devotions) He *does* draw near to us.

That this invitation is directed especially to sinners is shown by the rest of verse 8: "Wash your hands, you sinners, and purify your hearts, you double-minded." The last expression, it is true, may very well describe the one who has both the mind of the Spirit and the mind of the flesh. This double-mindedness can be ended by complete submission of our will to God's will.

C. Mourning over Sins: v. 9

"Grieve, mourn and wail. Change your laughter to mourning and your joy to gloom."

Ropes comments on this verse:

This is primarily a call to repentance; but, more than that, it is a vehemently expressed recommendation of sober earnestness as the proper mood of a Christian, in contrast to a light and frivolous spirit (*St. James*, p. 270).

Undoubtedly the first emphasis here is on repentance, on a "godly sorrow" for sin (II Cor. 7:10). But Mitton makes a further application:

The word "MOURN" may also mean distress for someone else's sorrows rather than our own. Since James has already administered sharp rebukes to those who show a callous disregard for the crying needs of others (e.g. at 2:15-16), it may be that here too he is summoning his readers to a more sympathetic attitude to others' distresses, even to the point of feeling those distresses as if they were their own (*James*, pp. 161-62).

D. Humble Yourselves: v. 10

"Humble yourselves before the Lord, and he will lift you up."

Mitton comments: "This verse takes up the thought of verse 6, which ends with the promise that God 'gives grace to the humble'" (*James*, p. 163). He goes on to say:

> To be humble before God means to be sharply aware of His unapproachable majesty, and of our unworthiness, even at our best, to be received by Him. It means to acknowledge His right to command and order our lives, and our readiness to submit our wills to His perfect will. To be humble before God also implies a willingness to be humble in our treatment of others, to follow ways of unnoticed service (Luke 22:26), without seeking prominence over or deference from others (*James*, p. 163).

A careful reading of Jesus' teachings in the Gospels will show that He emphasized humility as one of the primary Christian virtues. It is something we should all seek to exemplify.

IV. BOASTING ABOUT TOMORROW: James 4:13-17

A. False Confidence: v. 13

"Now listen, you who say, 'Today or tomorrow we will go to this or that city, spend a year there, carry on business and make money.'"

The Jews of that day were scattered around the Mediterranean world. They were often the leading merchants in the largest cities. Often they moved from city to city, as suggested here.

In the New Testament we have the interesting example of Aquila and Priscilla, who were Jewish tentmakers. Aquila was born in Pontus, in Asia Minor. But he and his wife were in business in Rome until Emperor Claudius ordered all Jews to leave that city. They then carried on their trade in Corinth, where Paul lived and worked with them (Acts 18:1-3). Then they moved to Ephesus (vv. 18-19). Corinth and Ephesus were the main centers of commerce in the eastern Mediterranean. From Romans 16:3 it appears that they were later back in Rome under a different emperor. Second Timothy 4:19 seems to indicate that about ten years later they were back in Ephesus (cf. I Tim. 1:3). So Jewish Christian merchants moved from city to city, as James suggests here.

We may be sure that Priscilla and Aquila did not display the false confidence James is warning against. But apparently some Jewish Christian merchants did.

Mitton comments on this verse:

> James's rebuke is not a condemnation of wise planning in advance.... What is condemned is the attitude of mind which enters into such planning without a humble recognition that it is God, not we ourselves, with whom lies the authority to determine whether we are alive this time next year or even tomorrow (*James*, p. 169).

DISCUSSION QUESTIONS

1. Why do professing Christians quarrel?
2. What is the right motive for asking God for things?
3. What is meant by "friendship with the world"?
4. How can we "resist the devil"?
5. What does it mean to be "double-minded"?
6. What are some sins of omission?

B. Nature of Life: v. 14

James declares, "Why, you do not even know what will happen tomorrow." Then he asks a very pertinent question: "What is your life?" Finally, he provides an answer: "You are a mist that appears for a little while and then vanishes." No thoughtful person would deny this statement about our life on earth.

The word translated "mist" could also be rendered "steam" or "vapor" (NASB) or "a puff of smoke"—something fleeting and passing, here for a few moments, and then gone. That is what life on earth is, compared with eternity.

The Bible gives several significant figures for life: "the evening shadow" (Ps. 102:11); "a breath" (Job 7:7); "a cloud" (Job 7:9); "grass" (Ps. 103:15). The last simile is especially fitting for Palestine, where the green grass of spring is quickly scorched and withered by the hot winds of summer.

C. The Lord Willing: v. 15

"Instead, you ought to say, 'If it is the Lord's will, we will live and do this or that.'"

Even the Jewish rabbi Ben Sira said: "Let no man say he will do anything without prefixing to it 'If the Lord will'" (quoted by Mayor, *James*, p. 152). We often hear Christians say something like this: "I'll be there on that day, the Lord willing." And in letters we find after a promise: "D.V." This represents the Latin *deo volente*. As Paul left Ephesus he promised, "I will come back if it is God's will" (Acts 18:21). He wrote to the Corinthians: "I

will come to you very soon, if the Lord is willing" (I Cor. 4:19). This is the proper habit for us as Christians to follow today.

D. Evil Boasting: v. 16

"As it is, you boast and brag. All such boasting is evil."

A. T. Robertson writes: "It is bad enough to ignore God as so many men, alas, do.... However, a positive refusal to do God's known will is worse. . . . These men were exalting themselves at the expense of God" (*James*, p. 222).

Concerning "boast" Mitton says:

It refers not so much to spoken words (as our English word "boast" suggests) as to an attitude of mind. It represents human self-confidence and self-congratulation. This may find expression in defiance of God, in disregard for God, and also in the service of God (*James*, p. 171).

E. Sins of Omission: v. 17

"Anyone, then, who knows the good he ought to do and doesn't do it, sins."

Most people think of sin as doing something evil. But James says that the failure to do good is also sin.

Here we find again that James reflects Jesus' teaching in a meaningful way. Jesus scored the Pharisees heavily for their sins of omission. They tithed carefully, but Jesus condemned them for neglecting the "more important matters" of "justice, mercy, and faithfulness" (Matt. 23:23). He also pictures "the King" at the judgment day pronouncing eternal doom on those who failed to do acts of kindness and compassion (Matt. 25:41-43).

CONTEMPORARY APPLICATION

Our memory verse for today says: "Draw near to God and he will draw near to you." If God seems rather far off, His presence not real to us, it is because we have failed to obey this

command, and so to enjoy this beautiful promise.

A very important application of this verse is to our devotional life. It should begin with our first waking moments each morning—in fact, with any waking moments we may have during the night. Instead of counting sheep when we can't sleep, we ought to draw near to God in prayer, praise, and repeating familiar Scripture verses to ourselves. If we do this, those sleepless times could become the most precious experiences of our lives.

Then we should begin each day with Bible reading and prayer. As we do so, God will draw near to us, and His presence will give us strength and courage for the day.

BE PATIENT BEFORE GOD

DEVOTIONAL READING	I Timothy 6:3-10
ADULTS AND YOUTH	**Adult Topic:** *Be Patient and Steadfast*
	Youth Topic: *You Are Responsible*
	Background Scripture: James 5
	Scripture Lesson: James 5:7-18
	Memory Verse: *The prayer of a righteous man has great power in its effects.* James 5:16
CHILDREN	**Topic:** *Learning to Be Patient*
	Background Scripture: James 5; Acts 1:4-9, 12-15, 21
	Scripture Lesson: Acts 1:4-9; James 5:8-11
	Memory Verse: *Be patient, therefore, brethren.* James 5:7
DAILY BIBLE READINGS	**May 21 M.:** The Folly of Riches. James 5:1-6
	May 22 T.: Be Fair to the Poor. Deut. 24:10-15
	May 23 W.: Rich in Faith. I Tim. 6:3-10
	May 24 T.: Endure Patiently. James 5:7-11
	May 25 F.: Job's Patience. Job 1:13-22
	May 26 S.: Power of Prayer. James 5:12-20
	May 27 S.: Speak Honestly. Matt. 5:33-37
LESSON AIM	To learn better how to be patient.
LESSON SETTING	**Time:** probably the A.D. 60s
	Place: Jerusalem
LESSON OUTLINE	**Be Patient Before God**

  I. **Patient Waiting:** James 5:7-9
   A. Example of the Farmer: v. 7
   B. Nearness of Christ's Coming: v. 8
   C. The Judge at the Door: v. 9

 II. **Patience in Suffering:** James 5:10-12
   A. Example of the Prophets: v. 10
   B. Job's Perseverance: v. 11
   C. Avoiding Swearing: v. 12

III. **Prayer for the Sick:** James 5:13-16
   A. Praying and Praising: v. 13
   B. Prayer and Anointing: v. 14
   C. The Prayer of Faith: v. 15
   D. Prayer of a Righteous Person: v. 16

 IV. **Elijah, a Man of Prayer:** James 5:17-18
   A. Praying for Drought: v. 17
   B. Praying for Rain: v. 18

SUGGESTED
INTRODUCTION
FOR ADULTS

In the mad rush of modern life, patience is a rare virtue. We are used to flipping a switch and instantly having light. In the past we cranked our cars to get them started. Now we turn a switch and expect immediate results. We can't spend an hour driving a horse seven miles to church, as in former days. Instead we jump into our car and get there in ten minutes. We grab a phone and call someone a mile or two away, instead of walking to see him. The truth is that we are rather "spoiled." We get impatient very quickly if things don't move fast.

All this tends to affect our spiritual life. It is hard for us to "wait on the Lord" until we receive the assurance of the answer to our prayers. We get restless and frustrated when results come slowly in our church work.

Patience comes by gearing into eternity, by broadening our perspectives. Maybe our lesson today will help us a bit.

SUGGESTED
INTRODUCTION
FOR YOUTH

Our topic today is "You Are Responsible." Some young people like to shift responsibility to others—parents, pastor, Sunday-school teacher, or even a schoolteacher. But we all need to face reality and recognize that ultimately each one of us is responsible for what he does with his life. We are responsible to God, to ourselves, and to our fellow human beings. We must develop a wholesome sense of responsibility and live by it.

We must not get into the habit of blaming others every time we fail. We need to ask, "Did I do my best? Not only in my own strength and wisdom, but did I ask the Lord to help me, and then cooperate with Him in succeeding?" These are questions we need to face honestly.

God is ready to help all of us who will let Him. He is available, but we must turn to Him in prayer and faith. Prayer is the key to success.

CONCEPTS FOR
CHILDREN

1. "Learning to Be Patient" is one of the most important lessons in life.
2. Children are often impatient; they want things right *now.*
3. When parents say, "Not now," we should say, "All right" and not get angry.
4. As we turn to God for help, we learn patience.

THE LESSON COMMENTARY

I. PATIENT WAITING:
James 5:7-9

A. Example of the Farmer: v. 7

"Be patient, then, brothers, until the Lord's coming. See how the farmer waits for the land to yield its valuable crop and how patient he is for the fall and spring rains."

James H. Ropes introduces this section of James that we study today by saying: "With v. 7 begin the Counsels for the Christian Conduct of Life, which occupy the rest of the chapter and are contrasted with the censure of Worldliness in 4:1–5:6" (*A Critical and Exegetical Commentary on the Epistle of St. James*, p. 293). It is noticeable that "brothers" occurs only once in chapter 4 (v. 11), whereas in chapter 5 we have "brothers" twice (vv. 7, 10) and "my brothers" twice (vv. 12, 19). In this chapter James is definitely addressing Christians.

James first bids his "brothers" in Christ to "be patient." The verb literally means be "long suffering"—that is, putting up with hardships and disappointments without complaining to people or finding fault with God.

The particular admonition here is to be patient "until the Lord's coming." The Greek word for "coming" is *parousia*, which literally means "being beside," and so "presence." But it was used in those days for an official visit of a king to some part of his kingdom. In the New Testament it is the term most frequently used for what we now call the Second Coming of Christ (Matt. 24:3, 27, 37, 39; I Cor. 15:23; I Thess. 2:19; 3:13; 4:15; 5:23; II Thess. 2:1, 8; James 5:7, 8; II Peter 1:16; 3:4, 12; I John 2:28). It is the technical term we now use for the Second Coming—the Parousia.

We are to wait for Christ's coming as patiently as the farmer waits for his crops to grow. Specifically, he has to be patient as he waits for "the early and latter rain" (KJV). Ropes observes:

> The "early rain" normally begins in Palestine in late October or early November, and is anxiously awaited because, being necessary for the germination of the seed, it is the signal for sowing. In the spring the maturing of the grain depends on the "late rain," light showers falling in April and May. Without these, even heavy winter rains will not prevent failure of the crops (*St. James*, p. 295).

B. Nearness of Christ's Coming: v. 8

"You too, be patient and stand firm, because the Lord's coming is near."

In verse 8 "be patient" translates exactly the same Greek form as in verse 7. But here James adds a new note: "stand firm," or "strengthen your hearts" (NASB). Ropes paraphrases this, "make your courage and purpose firm" (*St. James*, p. 297).

Why do this? "Because the Lord's coming is near." First and Second Thessalonians show us that this matter of expecting Christ's return at once had caused some troubles in the church. The New Testament clearly teaches us that we should be ready for the Second Coming to occur at any time. In His great Olivet Discourse Jesus admonished His disciples: "So you also must be ready, because the Son of Man will come at an hour when you do not expect him" (Matt. 24:44). At the end of His parable of the Ten Virgins He warned: "Therefore keep watch, because you do not know the day or the hour" (Matt. 25:13). The main emphasis in Jesus' teaching on His return was that we must watch and be ready all the time. That is where we should put the emphasis today, without setting dates.

Even when Peter wrote his Second Epistle it seemed that a long time had passed by without Christ's return. So he writes: "First of all, you must understand that in the last days scoffers will come, scoffing and following their own evil desires. They will say, 'Where is this "coming" he promised?'" (II Peter 3:3–4). But Peter has an answer to this objection: "With the Lord a day is like a thousand years, and a thousand years are like a day" (v. 8). So, even in our day, on God's calendar only two days have gone by since Jesus promised to return.

C. The Judge at the Door: v. 9

"Don't grumble against each other, brothers, or you will be judged. The Judge is standing at the door!"

The Greek word for "grumble" literally means "groan"; but we would say "grumble." It seems to express the idea of criticizing and finding fault.

If we grumble against our fellow

Christians, we will be judged. Jesus said, "Do not judge, or you too will be judged" (Matt. 7:1). And He, the Judge, "is standing at the door," listening to all we say.

II. PATIENCE IN SUFFERING: James 5:10-12

A. Example of the Prophets: v. 10

"Brothers, as an example of patience in the face of suffering, take the prophets who spoke in the name of the Lord."

In the Sermon on the Mount Jesus said: "Blessed are you when people insult you, persecute you and falsely say all kinds of evil against you because of me. Rejoice and be glad, because great is your reward in heaven, for in the same way they persecuted the prophets who were before you" (Matt. 5:11-12).

Jeremiah is perhaps the outstanding example of a suffering prophet. We read, "Jeremiah was put into a vaulted cell in a dungeon, where he remained a long time" (Jer. 37:16). Later we find it worse: "They lowered Jeremiah by ropes into the cistern; it had no water in it, only mud, and Jeremiah sank down into the mud" (Jer. 38:6). This was the way Jeremiah was treated for preaching God's message to the people. Surely his patient endurance of all this should serve as a worthy example to us in our lesser trials!

B. Job's Perseverance: v. 11

"As you know, we consider blessed those who have persevered. You have heard of Job's perseverance and have seen what the Lord finally brought about. The Lord is full of compassion and mercy."

Bible readers are familiar with the expression "the patience of Job" (KJV), and it is often quoted from this verse. But the truth is that Job was not very patient with his three would-be "comforters." He castigated them rather severely and even addressed them sarcastically (Job 12:1):

"Doubtless you are the people,
and wisdom will die with you!"

Unfortunately the King James translators failed to note the change of words in the Greek from verses 7, 8, and 10 to verse 11. In verses 7 and 8 we find the verb *macrothymeo* and in verse 10 the noun *macrothymia*. These mean "long-suffering" and are rightly translated "patient" ("patience"). But here in the first part of verse 11 we find the verb *hypomoneo*, which literally means "remain under" and is correctly translated "endure" in the King James Version. However the noun with Job is incorrectly translated "patience" in the King James Version. The Greek has *hypomone*, which means "endurance" (NASB) or "perseverance" (NIV). Job's patience ran out, but his perseverance held steady all the way through. He remained true and steadfast to the end, and God gave him a double reward.

"Have seen the end of the Lord" (KJV) has obvious problems for the reader today. The correct meaning is: "have seen the outcome of the Lord's dealings" (NASB) or "have seen what the Lord finally brought about" (NIV). That is, we can see "the end" of the Lord's dealings with Job, and so we can rest assured that if we "persevere" in being true to the Lord we shall not miss *our* reward.

James then makes the beautiful affirmation: "The Lord is full of compassion and mercy." Again we find the King James Version offering a "pitiful" translation for our day: "the Lord is very pitiful." When we say that a person is "pitiful," it is a deprecating statement, not a compliment. The Greek compound, *polysplangchnos* (only here in the New Testament) literally means "much compassionate." God is "full of compassion" (NASB, NIV). He is also *oiktirmon*, "merciful" (only here and in Luke 6:36).

C. Avoiding Swearing: v. 12

"Above all, my brothers, do not swear—not by heaven or by earth or by anything else. Let your 'Yes' be yes, and your 'No,' no, or you will be condemned."

Again we see the close dependence of James on Jesus' Sermon on the Mount. What we have here is a brief summary of Matthew 5: 34-37 (which should be read at this point). The wording is much the same.

James has had much to say about the tongue (c. 3). Mitton comments:

Here the fault in the tongue which James is most concerned to rebuke is the dishonesty of speech which has become so widespread that some special safeguard is needed to secure truthfulness. That safeguard was the oath. So low had ordinary standards of truthfulness sunk that a statement or a promise was felt to be valueless unless it was supported by a solemn oath. Moreover such an oath could itself be manipulated by tricks of phrasing so that though it sounded impressive and convincing, it was not regarded by the speaker as binding (Matt. 23:16-23) (*James*, p. 191).

III. PRAYER FOR THE SICK: James 5:13-16

A. Praying and Praising: v. 13

"Is any one of you in trouble? He should pray. Is anyone happy? Let him sing songs of praise."

The Greek for "is . . . in trouble" is the verb *kakopatheo*, which literally means "suffer evil." This could be evil of various kinds. A. T. Robertson comments:

It includes any kind of ill of body or mind. It means literally having had experiences and refers to the natural depression as a result of such misfortunes. The remedy is not in despondency or in suicide. The remedy lies in prayer. . . . Prayer is a blessing to the heart and to the mental life. It is good to talk with God. The worry disappears in God's presence and often the very ill itself disappears. But if it does not go, he gives us grace sufficient to bear the burden. So then prayer is the proper outlet for the depressed Christian (*James*, p. 252).

The Greek word for "pray" is in the present tense of continuous action. Prayer must be a habit.

What about the happy person? James says, "Let him sing songs of praise." This is all one word in Greek. It means "Let him sing a hymn." We owe God praise for all the things that make us happy.

B. Prayer and Anointing: v. 14

"Is any one of you sick? He should call the elders of the church to pray over him and anoint him with oil in the name of the Lord."

This prescription is followed widely today. The "elders of the church" could be thought of as ordained ministers or pastors (Acts 20:17, 28; Titus 1:5, 7; I Peter 5:1-4).

"Oil" in the Bible always means olive oil—never petroleum products! It is well known that oil was a common medicine in Bible times (Isa. 1:6; Luke 10:34). Greek physicians of New Testament times, as well as other writers of that period, refer to the medicinal use of oil. On the basis of this, Donald Burdick asserts that "James is prescribing prayer and medicine" (*The Expositor's Bible Commentary*, 12:204).

Since oil is a type of the Holy Spirit, it may be that anointing with oil symbolizes the Spirit's presence there to heal the person. Romans 8:11 says that God "will also give life to your mortal bodies through his Spirit." This is one of the functions of the Holy Spirit in our lives.

C. The Prayer of Faith: v. 15

"And the prayer offered in faith will make the sick person well; the Lord will raise him up. If he has sinned, he will be forgiven."

It is the prayer of faith that brings

healing. On the basis of my own experience I would suggest that when it is God's will to heal a certain individual He will enable one to pray the prayer of faith; when it is not His will, He does not give the assurance to the one praying for that healing. In that case we say, "Thy will be done," and submit, as Paul did (II Cor. 12:7-9).

The last part of the verse declares, "If he has sinned, he will be forgiven." This suggests that sickness may sometimes—though certainly not always—be the result of sin. Sickness may be sent "as a disciplinary agent (cf. I Cor. 11:30)," as Donald Burdick suggests (*The Expositor's Bible Commentary*, 12:204). He also notes that the "if" here indicates that not all sickness is the result of sin.

After Jesus had healed the impotent man at the Pool of Bethesda, He said to him: "Stop sinning or something worse may happen to you" (John 4:14). This is significant.

D. Prayer of a Righteous Person: v. 16

"Therefore confess your sins to each other and pray for each other so that you may be healed. The prayer of a righteous man is powerful and effective."

The King James Version says, "Confess your faults one to another." But the Greek has the most common word for "sin" in the New Testament, *hamartia*. So the correct translation is: "Confess your sins" (NASB, NIV). The word *hamartia* means "a missing the mark." So the broadest definition of "sin" would take in any missing the mark of God's perfect will for us.

The clear teaching hear is that confessing of sin should accompany our praying for healing. But how often is the biblical injunction carried out? My observation is that it is seldom done, even when this passage is read aloud at the time—as often, if not usually, happens.

James goes on to say that "the prayer of a righteous man is powerful and effective." In the context it might be suggested that this is one who has no unconfessed sin.

IV. ELIJAH, A MAN OF PRAYER: James 5:17-18

A. Praying for Drought: v. 17

"Elijah was a man just like us. He prayed earnestly that it would not rain, and it did not rain on the land for three and a half years."

In I Kings 17:1 we are told that Elijah the prophet said to wicked King Ahab: "As the LORD, the God of Israel, lives, whom I serve, there will be neither dew nor rain in the next few years except at my word." And so it happened.

Elijah was a man "with a nature like ours" (NASB). The King James Version says, "subject to like passions as we are." But that is too strong a translation, as Mitton notes. The Greek word is *homoiopathes*. Of this term Mitton says:

> The same word is used of Paul and Barnabas in Acts 14:15. The word suggests that Elijah, no less than ourselves, was sometimes unduly influenced by his feelings. It recalls the mood of depression which overwhelmed him, soon after his spectacular triumph over the priests of Baal (1 Kings 19:4), from which he had to be aroused by God's sharp

---

DISCUSSION QUESTIONS

1. Why is a farmer a good example of patience?
2. What should be our attitude toward the Second Coming of Christ?
3. Why did the Old Testament prophets suffer so much?
4. How did Job show his "perseverance"?
5. How can we pray "the prayer of faith"?
6. Does God always heal sick people?

rebuke (1 Kings 19:9, 15). In this we realize that he is one with us. Since his frailties link him with us, his achievements should serve us as an example that we may emulate (*James*, p. 207).

B. Praying for Rain: v. 18

"Again he prayed, and the heavens gave rain, and the earth produced its crops."

After Elijah's great victory on Mount Carmel (I Kings 18:16-40) he told Ahab, "Go, eat and drink, for there is the sound of a heavy rain" (v. 41).

While the king was eating and drinking, "Elijah climbed to the top of Carmel, bent to the ground, and put his face between his knees" (v. 42). Seven times he told his servant to go and look toward the Mediterranean Sea (v. 43). The seventh time the servant reported seeing "a cloud as small as a man's hand" (v. 44). Then the rain came (v. 45). This is a lesson to us that sometimes we have to keep on praying for something.

CONTEMPORARY APPLICATION

There are some who would equate patience with perseverance. But the former can be a bit more negative in our thinking, the latter more positive. If a fellow doesn't explode under provocation or "blow his top" when everything seems to be going against him, we say that he is patient. But he may sit still and do nothing.

On the other hand, if a person remains steadfast and firm under severe trial, keeps going forward instead of quitting, that person shows perseverance. And perseverance is exactly what it takes to live victoriously in a world such as ours. We should constantly persevere in our full devotion to God and His will, no matter what the circumstances of life.

Quarter IV
THE RISE AND FALL OF A NATION

Unit I: Establishment of the Monarchy
Unit II: The Two Kingdoms
Unit III: Judah Only

THE PEOPLE'S DEMAND FOR MONARCHY

DEVOTIONAL READING	I Samuel 8:4-9

Adult Topic: *The People's Choice*

Youth Topic: *The People's Choice*

ADULTS AND YOUTH

Background Scripture: I Samuel 8; 12

Scripture Lesson: I Samuel 12:14-25

Memory Verse: *Fear the Lord, and serve him faithfully with all your heart; for consider what great things he has done for you.* I Sam. 12:24

Topic: *The People Ask for a King*

Background Scripture: I Sam. 12

CHILDREN

Scripture Lesson: I Sam. 12:12-15, 24-25

Memory Verse: *Fear not; you have done all this evil, yet do not turn aside from following the Lord, but serve the Lord with all your heart.* I Sam. 12:20

DAILY BIBLE READINGS

May 28 M.: The People's Request for a King. I Sam. 8:4-9
May 29 T.: The Secret Choice of Saul. I Sam. 9:24b—10:1b
May 30 W.: Saul's Initiatory Religious Experience. I Sam. 10:1c-13
May 31 T.: The Choice of Saul by Lot. I Sam. 10:17-27
June 1 F.: Saul's Maintenance of National Security. I Sam. 11:1-11
June 2 S.: Public Choice of Saul. I Sam. 11:12-15
June 3 S.: Samuel's Farewell Address. I Sam. 12:14-25

LESSON AIM

To warn us against making our own choices without seeking divine guidance.

LESSON SETTING

Time: about 1020 B.C.

Place: Gilgal

LESSON OUTLINE

The People's Demand for Monarchy

  I. **Samuel's Challenge:** I Samuel 12:1-5

  II. **Previous Leaders:** I Samuel 12:6-11

  III. **People's Request for a King:** I Samuel 12:12-13

  IV. **Warning to Obey God:** I Samuel 12:14-15
    A. Challenge to Obedience: v. 14
    B. Warning Against Disobedience: v. 15

  V. **Divine Displeasure:** I Samuel 12:16-19
    A. Announcement: v. 16

B. Evil request: v. 17
C. Thunder and Rain: v. 18
D. People's Reaction: v. 19

VI. **Samuel's Farewell Words:** I Samuel 12:20-25
A. A Word of Comfort: v. 20
B. Warning Against Idolatry: v. 21
C. Divine Concern: v. 22
D. Samuel's Continued Concern: v. 23
E. Reminder of God's Goodness: v. 24
F. Final Warning: v. 25

SUGGESTED
INTRODUCTION
FOR ADULTS

In the fall quarter of 1982 we studied "Origins of God's Chosen People." That study took us through the period of the judges, as described in the Book of Judges.

This quarter we pick up Israel's history with the beginning of the period of monarchy, at about 1020 B.C., and follow it down to the Babylonian captivity of Judah in 586 B.C. Our biblical material will be taken from Samuel and Kings. Each of these was one book in the original Hebrew text. The Hebrew alphabet has no vowels. When the Hebrew text was translated into Greek (the Septuagint, about 250-150 B.C.), the inclusion of the Greek vowels lengthened the books so much that each book had to be put on two rolls or scrolls. (They had no bound books in those days.) The result is that in our Bibles we have I and II Samuel and I and II Kings. Our lesson materials for this quarter will be taken from all four books.

The quarter's lessons are divided into three units. The first is entitled "Establishment of the Monarchy." It includes the reigns of the first three kings—Saul, David, and Solomon. The second unit, "The Two Kingdoms," deals with the period from the division of the kingdom under Rehoboam and Jeroboam to the fall of Israel in 722 B.C. The third unit, "Judah Only," studies the reforms under Hezekiah and Josiah and ends with the destruction of Jerusalem in 586 B.C.

SUGGESTED
INTRODUCTION
FOR YOUTH

Our topic today is "The People's Choice." As happens too often, the people made a wrong choice. The people of Israel wanted to be like the other nations around them, with a king ruling over them.

We make a mistake when we choose to live like the worldly people around us. We, as Christians, are God's people and should live as His Word tells us to. That is the only way we can live happy, useful lives.

CONCEPTS FOR
CHILDREN

1. Children often want what other children have.
2. We should choose what God wants us to have.
3. What we want may not be good for us.
4. We should pray for our leaders.

THE LESSON COMMENTARY

I. SAMUEL'S CHALLENGE: I Samuel 12:1-5

To get the background for chapter 12 we have to look at chapter 8. Samuel was the last of a long line of "judges," or leaders, over Israel. God had used him in a wonderful way. When he grew old he appointed his sons to succeed him (8:1). Unfortunately, "his sons did not walk in his ways. They turned aside after dishonest gain and accepted bribes and perverted justice" (v. 3). It is a sad thing when a godly man does not discipline his sons and they turn out to be rascals.

One result of this was that the elders of Israel came to Samuel and said to him: "You are old, and your sons do not walk in your ways; now appoint a king to lead us, such as all the other nations have" (v. 5). Samuel was displeased and prayed about the matter (v. 6). The Lord told him to listen to the people, for "it is not you they have rejected as their king, but me" (v. 7). Samuel was to warn the people, however, that their choice was unwise (v. 9).

The man of God proceeded to do this. He told them that their new king would draft their sons into military service (vv. 11-12) and make their daughters work for him (v. 13). He would take the best of their land (v. 14) and a tenth of their crops (v. 15) and flocks (v. 17). The people would become the slaves of their king.

The people refused to heed Samuel's warning. Instead they said: "We want a king over us. Then we will be like all the other nations, with a king to lead us and go out before us and fight our battles" (vv. 19-20). They ignored the fact that God had chosen them to be His own special people, different from the nations around them. This desire to be "like the world" has been the besetting sin of professed followers of the Lord in all periods of time.

Properly, Samuel reported to the Lord what the people had said. God's answer was, "Listen to them and give them a king" (v. 22). The choice was theirs.

Obediently Samuel anointed a man named Saul as the first king of Israel (10:1). Then he summoned the people of Israel to meet before the Lord at Mizpah (v. 17). Then he warned them that they had rejected God as their leader (v. 19). But he proceeded to the designation of Saul (vv. 20-21). The people shouted, "Long live the king!" (v. 24). Samuel carefully wrote down "the regulations of the kingship" on a scroll and "deposited it before the LORD" (v. 25).

Confronted immediately by a military crisis, Saul won a great victory over the enemy forces (11:1-11). The result was that Samuel said to the people, "Come, let us go to Gilgal and there reaffirm the kingship" (v. 14). This they proceeded to do, holding "a great celebration" (v. 15).

Now we turn our attention to chapter 12. "Samuel said to all Israel, 'I have listened to everything you said to me and have set a king over you'" (v. 1). As we have just seen, God told him to do this (8:22).

Samuel went on to say, "I have been your leader from my youth until this day" (v. 2). Then he challenged the people to bring any accusation against him of having confiscated any of their property, cheated or oppressed anyone, or accepted a bribe to pervert justice (v. 3). His sons had been guilty (8:3), but not he.

The people were quick to respond: "You have not cheated or oppressed us. You have not taken anything from anyone's hand" (v. 4). Samuel knew that his record was clean, and the people confirmed this. He had been an exemplary, godly leader of the nation throughout most of his life.

In reply to the people's affirmation, Samuel said, "The LORD is witness against you, and also his anointed [Saul] is witness this day, that you have not found anything in my hand." The people responded, "He is witness" (v. 5).

As we see many times in the Old Testament, the rulers of that day were notorious for cheating the people; but Samuel's record was clear.

II. PREVIOUS LEADERS:
I Samuel 12:6-11

Samuel reminded the people, "It is the LORD who appointed Moses and Aaron and brought your forefathers up out of Egypt. Now then, stand here, because I am going to confront you with evidence before the LORD as to all the righteous acts performed by the LORD for you and your fathers" (vv. 6-7). Moses and Aaron were the first two leaders of the nation of Israel. They had led the people out of Egypt and to the borders of Canaan.

Samuel went on to tell how the Israelites had disobeyed God and so had suffered at the hands of surrounding nations. But they had repented and confessed: "We have sinned; we have forsaken the LORD and served the Baals and the Ashtoreths" (v. 10). "Baals" was a general name for the male gods of the pagan nations. "Ashtoreths," or "Ashtaroth" (NASB), were the female gods.

Now Samuel mentioned four more leaders whom God had raised up to deliver Israel (v. 11). Jerub-Baal is another name for Gideon. Barak is "Bedan" in the Hebrew (cf. NASB). Jephthah was one of the great judges. Samuel was the last judge.

III. PEOPLE'S REQUEST
FOR A KING:
I Samuel 12:12-13

We are now told what precipitated the people's demand for monarchy. Samuel said: "But when you saw that Nahash king of the Ammonites was moving against you, you said to me, 'No, we want a king to rule over us'— even though the LORD your God was your king." This threat is not mentioned in chapter 8, but that should not create

any problem, as we are told of previous Ammonite invasions of Israelite territory.

Samuel was certainly being fair and considerate. He went on to say, "Now here is the king you have chosen, the one you asked for; see, the LORD has set a king over you" (v. 13). R. Payne Smith writes:

We have here the two sides of the transaction. The people had desired a king, chosen and appointed by themselves, to represent the nation in temporal matters; Jehovah gave them a king to represent himself, with authority coming from God, and limited by God (*The Pulpit Commentary*, I Samuel, p. 210).

IV. WARNING TO OBEY GOD:
I Samuel 12:14-15

A. Challenge to Obedience: v. 14

"If you fear the LORD and serve and obey him and do not rebel against his commands, and if both you and the king who reigns over you follow the LORD your God—good!"

The New American Standard Bible follows the King James Version in treating only the first part of the verse as the protasis and making the second half an apodosis, inserting "then." But in John Peter Lange's *Commentary* we find this statement: "The 'if' introduces a *protasis* which includes all of ver. 14, and has no *apodosis*." He goes on to say that "the absence of the apodosis is easily explained by the length of the protasis, and its content apparent from the context = 'well,' or 'it will be well with you'" (*Commentary on the Holy Scriptures*, Samuel, p. 176).

R. Payne Smith agrees completely with this, rejecting the King James Version translation. On the last part of the verse he comments, "'To follow Jehovah' implies willing and active service as his attendants, going with him where he will, and being ever ready to obey his voice" (*PC*, I Samuel, p. 210).

B. Warning Against Disobedience: v. 15

"But if you do not obey the LORD, and if you rebel against his commands, his hand will be against you, as it was against your fathers."

This verse balances the previous one. Obedience brings God's blessing, but disobedience brings God's curse. We make the choice as to which we experience. It is a solemn responsibility!

Our topic today is "The People's Choice." The strong emphasis of the lesson is on the freedom of choice that we all possess. We can choose to believe and obey God, and so experience the best and highest in this life and throughout eternity. Or we can choose to disobey God, and then we reap the consequences of that choice both now and forever.

We can choose what we sow, but we cannot choose what we reap. If we sow wheat, we reap wheat; if oats, then oats. And if we sow wild oats, we will reap wild oats, and that is mighty bitter eating!

V. DIVINE DISPLEASURE: I Samuel 12:16-19

A. Announcement: v. 16

"Now then, stand still and see this great thing the LORD is about to do before your very eyes!" The beginning of this verse is the same as in verse 7. Samuel is alerting the people to what is to follow.

B. Evil Request: v. 17

"Is it not wheat harvest now? I will call upon the LORD to send thunder and rain. And you will realize what an evil thing you did in the eyes of the LORD when you asked for a king."

The wheat harvest was usually in May or June. Jerome, in his commentary on Amos 4:7, says that he had never seen rain in Palestine during June and July. So, to have

thunder and rain at this time would be very unusual.

This sign of divine displeasure would dramatically show the Israelites that their request for a human king was "an evil thing." It was a refusal to accept and acknowledge God as their king and sovereign ruler.

C. Thunder and Rain: v. 18

"Then Samuel called upon the LORD, and that same day the LORD sent thunder and rain. So all the people stood in awe of the LORD and of Samuel."

As we have just noted, this was not the rainy season, so the sudden thunderstorm startled the people. They stood in awe of the Lord because they knew that He was the one who "sent" the storm. They stood in awe of Samuel because he had such prevailing power with God.

D. People's Reaction: v. 19

"The people all said to Samuel, 'Pray to the LORD your God for your servants so that we will not die, for we have added to all our other sins the evil of asking for a king.'" It is too bad that people have to be *scared* into repentance by a display of divine judgment!

Samuel was God's prophet. One of his main functions was that of intercessory prayer for the people. We find him saying to them, "I will intercede with the LORD for you" (7:5). In time of danger they begged him, "Do not stop crying out to the LORD our God for us" (7:8).

In relation to verses 18 and 19 of our lesson Alexander Maclaren makes these observations:

> So the result of the thunder-burst was twofold—they "feared Jehovah and Samuel," and they confessed their sin in desiring a king. They were rude and sense-bound men, like children in many respects; their religion was little more than outward worship and a vague awe; they needed "signs" as children need

picture-books. The very slightness and superficiality of their religion made their confession easy and swift, and neither the one nor the other went deep enough to be lasting. The faith that is built on "signs and wonders" is easily battered down; the repentance that is due to a thunderstorm is over as soon as the sun comes out again. The shallowness of the contrition in this case is shown by two things,—the request to Samuel to pray for them, and the boon which they begged him to ask, "that we die not." They had better have prayed for themselves, and they had better have asked for strength to cleave to Jehovah (*Expositions of Holy Scripture*, Deuteronomy-I Samuel, p. 321).

The people here were like Simon Magus. He asked Paul to pray for protection from judgment (Acts 8:24).

VI. SAMUEL'S FAREWELL WORDS:
I Samuel 12:20-25

A. A Word of Comfort: v. 20

Samuel said to the people: "Do not be afraid. You have done all this evil; yet do not turn away from the LORD, but serve the LORD with all your heart."

After the consoling words, "Do not be afraid," Samuel wisely reminds the people of their sin—"all this evil." They must keep a repentant state of mind if they are going to enjoy God's favor.

Then, as frequently in his exhortations, Samuel combines the negative and the positive. The negative is: "Do not turn away from the LORD." The positive is: "Serve the LORD with all your heart." This means that "the undivided, complete devotion of the heart, the innermost life to the Lord is inseparably connected with not turning aside from Him" (Lange, *Commentary*, Samuel, p. 177).

On this verse Maclaren comments:

Samuel's closing words are tender, wise, and full of great truths. He begins with encouragement blended with reiteration of the people's sin. It is not safe for a forgiven man to forget his sin quickly. The more sure he is that God has forgotten, the more careful he should be to remember it, for gratitude, humility, and watchfulness. But it should never loom so large before him as to shut out the sunshine of God's love, for no fruits of goodness will ripen in character without that light. It is a great piece of practical wisdom always to keep one's forgiven sin in mind, and yet not let it paralyse hopefulness and effort. "Ye have indeed done all this evil, . . . yet do not turn aside from following Jehovah." That is truly evangelical exhortation. The memory of past failures is never to set the tune for future service (*Expositions*, Deuteronomy-I Samuel, p. 322).

B. Warning Against Idolatry: v. 21

"Do not turn away after useless idols. They can do you no good, nor can they rescue you, because they are useless."

The Hebrew literally says, "Do not turn away after *tohu* . . . because they are *tohu*." This Hebrew word is translated "formless" in Genesis 1:2. R. Payne Smith comments, "It means anything *empty, void,* and so is often used, as here, for 'an idol,' because, as St. Paul says, 'an idol is nothing in the world' (1 Cor. viii.4)" (*PC*, I Samuel, p. 210).

DISCUSSION QUESTIONS

1. Was God's choice of government for His people democracy, monarchy, or theocracy?
2. What does the New Testament say about the relation of Christians to government?
3. What weak point did Samuel have? Why?
4. What responsibility do we have in praying for others?
5. What "great things" has God done for us?
6. How can we avoid a shallow religion?

The words "then ye should go" in the King James Version (also NASB) are in italics, indicating that they are not in the original. Both the *The Pulpit Commentary* and Lange's *Commentary* prefer the New International Version handling of the textual problem here.

C. Divine Concern: v. 22

"For the sake of his great name the LORD will not reject his people, because the LORD was pleased to make you his own."

This verse is an important part of Samuel's farewell speech. R. Payne Smith writes:

> Though Samuel in ver. 14 had described their well-being as dependent on their own conduct, yet in a higher light it depended on God's will. He had chosen Israel not for its own sake (Deut. vii.7, 8), but for a special purpose, to minister to the Divine plan for the redemption of all mankind, and so, though individuals might sin to their own ruin, and the nation bring upon itself severe chastisements, yet it must continue according to the tenor of God's promises . . . and through weal and woe discharge the duty imposed upon it (*PC*, I Samuel, p. 210).

God would unfailingly glorify "his great name." His plan of salvation *would* be carried out.

D. Samuel's Continued Concern: v. 23

"As for me, far be it from me that I should sin against the LORD by failing to pray for you. And I will teach you the way that is good and right."

With the accession of Saul as king, the office of "judge" or "leader" (v. 2) ended. But Samuel continued his more important role as prophet. This office focused on two functions: praying and teaching. Both were of supreme importance.

E. Reminder of God's Goodness: v. 24

"But be sure to fear the LORD and serve him faithfully with all your heart; consider what great things he has done for you."

The repetition of the phrase "with all your heart" (cf. v. 20) is significant. God wants our wholehearted service and worship. On the last clause of the verse Smith comments, "Literally it is, 'For consider how grandly he hath wrought with you'" (*PC*, I Samuel, p. 210).

F. Final Warning: v. 25

"Yet if you persist in doing evil, both you and your king will be swept away."

Samuel knew only too well how fickle the Israelites were, so he closed with a warning. Unfortunately, the Israelites failed to heed it, and they were "swept away" into captivity.

CONTEMPORARY APPLICATION

As we have just seen, Samuel closed his farewell address to the nation of Israel with a solemn warning of the results of persistence in evil. The warning went unheeded, and Israel and Judah went into captivity.

Christianity was born in the period of the Roman Empire. Yet the people of that day became increasingly wicked, and the Empire perished.

Today we see an alarmingly similar thing happening in supposedly Christian America and western Europe. Homosexuality and pornography flourish on every side. We cannot help wondering how long our civilization can survive under such flouting of God's laws.

WHEN JEALOUSY DOMINATES

DEVOTIONAL READING	Genesis 37:12-24

Adult Topic: *When Jealousy Dominates*

Youth Topic: *Controlled by Jealousy*

ADULTS AND YOUTH

Background Scripture: I Sam. 18:1-29

Scripture Lesson: I Sam. 18:5-16

Memory Verse: *Saul has slain his thousands, and David his ten thousands.* I Sam. 18:7

CHILDREN

Topic: *When Jealousy Controls*

Memory Verse: *For jealousy makes a man furious, and he will not spare when he takes revenge.* Prov. 6:34

DAILY BIBLE READINGS

June 4 M.: War with the Philistines. I Sam. 13:1-7
June 5 T.: The Breach Between Saul and Samuel. I Sam. 13:8-15a
June 6 W.: The Rejection of Saul. I Sam. 15:7-22
June 7 T.: The Anointing of David. I Sam. 16:1-13
June 8 F.: David's Position at Saul's Court. I Sam. 16:14-23
June 9 S.: David's Slaying of Goliath. I Sam. 17:41-51
June 10 S.: Saul's Jealousy of David. I Sam. 18:5-16

LESSON AIM	To show the sad effects of jealousy.

LESSON SETTING

Time: about 1000 B.C.

Place: southern Palestine

LESSON OUTLINE

When Jealousy Dominates

  I. **David and Jonathan:** I Samuel 18:1-4

 II. **David's Success:** I Samuel 18:5-7
   A. High Rank in the Army: v. 5
   B. Honored by the Women: vv. 6-7

 III. **Saul's Jealousy:** I Samuel 18:8-9
   A. Saul's Anger: v. 8
   B. A Jealous Eye: v. 9

 IV. **Attempted Murder:** I Samuel 18:10-11
   A. An Evil Spirit on Saul: v. 10
   B. Attempt to Kill David: v. 11

  V. **Saul's Fear of David:** I Samuel 18:12-16
   A. Cause of Fear: v. 12
   B. Sending David Away: v. 13
   C. Great Success of David: v. 14
   D. Saul's Increasing Fear: v. 15
   E. David Loved by the People: v. 16

 VI. **Saul's Intrigues Against David:** I Samuel 18:17-29

SUGGESTED
INTRODUCTION
FOR ADULTS

Aside from a brief genealogical reference at the end of Ruth (4:17, 22), David is first mentioned in the sixteenth chapter of I Samuel, where his name occurs six times. At the Lord's bidding, Samuel anointed David to be Saul's successor as king (16:13).

Plagued by an evil spirit, Saul sent for David to come and play the harp to quiet his upset feelings (v. 19). So his father Jesse sent him to Saul (v. 20). Then we read, "David came to Saul and entered his service. Saul liked him very much, and David became one of his armor-bearers" (v. 21). So Saul asked Jesse to allow David to remain at the royal court (v. 22). David proved to be a real help: "Whenever the spirit from God came upon Saul, David would take his harp and play. Then relief would come to Saul; he would feel better, and the evil spirit would leave him" (v. 23).

In chapter 17 we have the well-known account of David killing Goliath. This forms the background for our lesson today.

SUGGESTED
INTRODUCTION
FOR YOUTH

King Saul became controlled by jealousy because he allowed himself to become more and more jealous, instead of repudiating a wrong attitude at once.

There *is* a good jealousy. In the Ten Commandments we find the Lord saying, "For I, the LORD your God, am a jealous God" (Exod. 20:5). The point there is that He will not tolerate the worship of other gods. So it is with the true husband or wife who does not want any other "lover" to enter the picture and form a triangle that will destroy marriage.

The main point of this lesson is that we must avoid wrong, selfish jealousy when others surpass us. This jealousy is highly destructive, as we see in today's lesson.

CONCEPTS FOR
CHILDREN

1. Some people get jealous when we do well.
2. We should never be jealous of others when they are more popular or praised than we are.
3. Jealousy damages our character.
4. We should be happy when others do well.

THE LESSON COMMENTARY

I. DAVID AND JONATHAN:
I Samuel 18:1-4

The exciting story of David killing the giant Goliath is told at length in I Samuel 17. Saul's son Jonathan became greatly attached to David. We read that "Jonathan became one in spirit with David, and he loved him as himself" (v. 1). It was evidently a mutual attraction of spirits.

In chapter 17 we read that "David went back and forth from Saul to tend his father's sheep at Bethlehem" (v. 15). But now we find: "From that day Saul kept David with him and did not let him return to his father's house" (18:2). This allowed the friendship between David and Jonathan to become closer. Verse 3 says, "And Jonathan made a covenant with David because he loved him as himself." He took off the robe and tunic he was wearing and gave them to David, "and even his sword, his bow and his belt" (v. 4). He could do no more!

II. DAVID'S SUCCESS:
I Samuel 18:5-7

A. High Rank in the Army: v. 5

"Whatever Saul sent him to do, David did it so successfully that Saul gave him a high rank in the army. This pleased all the people, and Saul's officers as well."

The King James Version says that David "behaved himself wisely." This alternative idea is given in the margin of the New American Standard Bible and New International Version. R. Payne Smith writes, "This is the primary meaning of the verb; but as success is the result of wise conduct, it constantly signifies *to prosper*" (*The Pulpit Commentary*, I Samuel, p. 339). In John Peter Lange's *Commentary on the Holy Scriptures* we read: "The verb ... means 'to act prudently, wisely' and then 'to be successful,' as in Josh. i.7" (Samuel, p. 241)—where the King James Version has "prosper."

Regarding the last part of the verse, Lange's *Commentary* observes, "David's *winning loveliness of character* is here brought out more strongly by the statement that he did not excite the envy and jealousy of his fellow-officials at court" (Samuel, p. 241).

B. Honored by the Women: vv. 6-7

When the men were returning home after David had killed the Philistine, the women came out from all the towns of Israel to meet King Saul with singing and dancing, with joyful songs and with tambourines and lutes. As they danced, they sang:

"Saul has slain his thousands,
    and David his tens of thousands."

The noisy reception that the women gave the returning warriors is typical of that time. It is usually held that two

groups of women sang antiphonally, one saying, "Saul has slain his thousands" and the other group responding, "and David his tens of thousands."

This mention of "thousands," coupled with verse 5, has led some commentators to take "the Philistine" David killed as not being Goliath but the nation as such. But the death of Goliath precipitated a great slaughter of Philistines (17:51-53). So there is no problem here in referring the singular to Goliath.

III. SAUL'S JEALOUSY:
I Samuel 18:8-9

A. Saul's Anger: v. 8

"Saul was very angry; this refrain galled him. 'They have credited David with tens of thousands,' he thought, 'but me with only thousands. What more can he get but the kingdom?'"

The concluding question is significant. Samuel had already told Saul, "You have rejected the word of the LORD, and the LORD has rejected you as king over Israel" (15:26). He added even more specifically, "The LORD has torn the kingdom of Israel from you today and has given it to one of your neighbors—to one better than you" (15:28). Naturally, Saul would be looking around suspiciously, and perhaps eagerly, to see who his chosen successor might be. The women's song seemed to point toward the possibility that David might be the one. It was bad enough to have to listen to the women's song without this context, but the combination of circumstances was enough to make Saul "very angry."

B. A Jealous Eye: v. 9

"And from that time on Saul kept a jealous eye on David."

Saul's jealousy was a natural reaction to his situation. How many men in high position can stand to hear one of their subordinates lauded more highly than they? It was indeed a bitter cup for Saul to drink.

Alexander Maclaren adds this observation:

> It will be more to the purpose that we take care lest we do the very same thing in our little lives and humble spheres; for envy and jealousy of those who threaten to out-shine, or in any way to out-do, us is not confined to people in high places or with great reputations. The roots of them are in all of us, and the only way to keep them from growing up rank is to think less of our reputation and more of our duty, to count it a very small matter what men think of us, and the all-important matter what God thinks (*Expositions of Holy Scripture*, Deuteronomy–I Samuel, p. 350).

IV. ATTEMPTED MURDER: I Samuel 18:10-11

A. An Evil Spirit on Saul: v. 10

"The next day an evil spirit from God came forcefully upon Saul. He was prophesying in his house, while David was playing the harp, as he usually did."

As we noted in the Introduction, the sixteenth chapter tells of the evil spirit tormenting Saul (v. 14). Some of Saul's attendants suggested that he find a good harpist who could offset the influence of the evil spirit (vv. 15-16). One of Saul's servants volunteered: "I have seen a son of Jesse of Bethlehem who knows how to play the harp. He is a brave man and a warrior. He speaks well and is a fine-looking man. And the LORD is with him" (v. 18). All this sounded very good, and Saul sent for David (v. 19). Now we learn that David was still serving in this capacity.

B. Attempt to Kill David: v. 11

"Saul had a spear in his hand and he hurled it, saying to himself, 'I'll pin David to the wall.' But David eluded him twice."

Jealousy quickly turns into murder. That is one reason why we cannot trifle with it. It must be shunned like a rattlesnake.

On the actions described in verses 10 and 11 Maclaren has this to say:

> What a striking picture is given of Saul, worn with passion and swept away by ungovernable impulses, "prophesying" or "raving" with wild gestures and uttering wilder sounds; and of David, young, calm, giving forth melodies on his harp and songs from his lips, that sought to soothe the paroxysms of fury.... It has been suggested that Saul did not "cast" his spear, but only brandished it in his fierce threat to pin David to the wall. But the youthful harper would scarcely have "avoided out of his presence" for a mere threat and the flourish of a lance; and a man, raging mad and madly hostile, would not be likely to waste breath in mere threats (*Expositions*, Deuteronomy–I Samuel, p. 352).

Maclaren goes on to observe: "Envy, allowed to have its way, becomes murderous. Let us suppress its beginning. A tiger pup can be held in and its claws cut, but a full-grown tiger cannot (p. 352).

V. SAUL'S FEAR OF DAVID: I Samuel 18:12-16

A. Cause of Fear: v. 12

"Saul was afraid of David, because the LORD was with David but had left Saul."

As a result of David's obedience to God and Saul's disobedience, the contrast between the two becomes ever sharper. Maclaren says of Saul here:

> It is a pathetic picture of the gradual creeping over a strong man of a nameless terror. Ever-thickening folds of cold dread, like a wet mist, wrap a soul once bright and energetic. And the reason is twofold: first, that God had left that tempestuous, rebellious soul because it had left Him; and second, that, in its desolate solitude, in which there was no trace of softening or penitence, that lightning-riven soul knew that the sunshine, which it had repelled, was now pouring on David. Saul's suspicions were hardened into

certainties. He was sure now that what his jealousy had whispered, when the women chanted their chorus, was grim fact. And he could but helplessly watch his supplanter's steady advance in favor with men and God (*Expositions*, Deuteronomy-I Samuel, pp. 352-53).

B. Sending David Away: v. 13

Verse 12 told us that Saul was afraid of David. Now we read, "So he sent David away from him and gave him command over a thousand men, and David led the troops in their campaigns."

Saul evidently was no longer comfortable with David around. As we read in Lange's *Commentary*, "Enmity against David (born of envy and jealousy) and fear of him (as one specially blessed by God) led Saul to *remove him from his presence*" (Samuel, p. 243).

In view of what we find later in this chapter (vv. 17-29), we may also probably assume that Saul wished to expose David to the danger of death by making him the commander of a thousand men. In those days military officers led their troops in battle, moving out in front of them. It was an easy way to get killed.

It is indeed pathetic and unbelievable that David should himself later have employed this same tactic to get rid of Uriah, who had done him no harm (II Sam. 11:14-16). Sin is a terrible thing!

C. Great Success of David: v. 14

It is said of David: "In everything he did he had great success, because the LORD was with him."

In his sermon at Pisidian Antioch, Paul the apostle quoted God as saying: "I have found David son of Jesse a man after my own heart; he will do everything I want him to do" (Acts 13:22). David had a humble, obedient spirit. Throughout most of his illustrious career he earnestly sought to know and do God's will. The one outstanding

exception was what we have just noticed—the tragic combination of adultery and murder in the case of Uriah.

The secret of David's success was that "the LORD was with him." But this was because he stayed close to the Lord. The Bible over and over emphasizes the principle that the Lord is with those who will let Him be near them. Disobedience drives God away. Obedience assures His constant presence with us and His blessing on all we do.

D. Saul's Increasing Fear: v. 15

"When Saul saw how successful he was, he was afraid of him." Instead of emulating David's beautiful spirit of humility and obedience, Saul went on in his own self-will and stubborn disobedience.

The difference between David and Saul is highlighted by Maclaren in this way:

The two processes of growing darkness and growing light go on side by side in the two men, and each makes the other more striking by contrast. Twice it is repeated that Saul was in awe of David. Twice it is repeated that Jehovah was with David, and that he "behaved himself wisely," which last statement includes in the Hebrew word both the idea of prudence and that of success. So, on the one hand, there is a steady growth in all good, godly, and happy qualities and experiences; and on the other, a

---

DISCUSSION QUESTIONS

1. What did Saul have in his favor at the beginning?
2. How can we account for Saul's losing out?
3. What were Saul's main traits that ruined him?
4. How can we avoid wrong jealousy?
5. What does bad jealousy do to people who have it?
6. What is the primary secret of success in life?

tragical increase of darkness and gloom, godlessness and despair. And yet Saul had begun so well! And Saul might have been what David was,—companioned by God, prosperous, and the idol of his people. Two souls stand side by side for a moment on the same platform, with the same divine goodness and love encircling them, and the one steadily rises, while the other steadily sinks. How awful are the endless possibilities of progress in either direction that lies open for every soul of man! (*Expositions*, Deuteronomy-I Samuel, p. 353).

E. David Loved by the People: v. 16

"But all Israel and Judah loved David, because he led them in their campaigns."

Israel and Judah had not yet become two kingdoms—Israel in the north and Judah in the south. This happened after the death of Solomon. But the two areas were already distinct. At the death of Saul, Judah accepted David as king (II Sam. 2:4), but the northern tribes made Saul's son their king (vv. 8-9). So the mention here of Israel and Judah does not prove a late date for the writing of I Samuel.

David was lovable, and so was loved by all the people. He was now their main protector in battle.

VI. SAUL'S INTRIGUES AGAINST DAVID: I Samuel 18:17-29

"Saul said to David, 'Here is my older daughter Merab. I will give her to you in marriage; only serve me bravely and fight the battles of the LORD.' For Saul said to himself, 'I will not raise a hand against him. Let the Philistines do that!'" (v. 17).

When Saul observed that all the people of Israel and Judah loved David, he dared not assassinate him directly. So he contrived a way to get him killed by the Philistines—the main enemy of the Israelites during this period. The Philistines lived on the coast of the Mediterranean and were a constant threat to the safety of God's people. Saul hoped that by urging David to press the fight against the Philistines, he would soon see David killed in battle.

David protested that he was not worthy of the honor of marrying the king's daughter (v. 18), and she was given to another man (v. 19). But when Saul heard that his younger daughter Michal had fallen in love with David, he was pleased (v. 20). He thought to himself, "I will give her to him, so that she may be a snare to him and so that the hand of the Philistines may be against him" (v. 21). Even though David protested again (v. 23), Saul pursued his objective. This time he set a far higher price: "a hundred Philistine foreskins." The account adds: "Saul's plan was to have David fall by the hands of the Philistines" (v. 25).

Now David "was pleased to become the king's son-in-law" (v. 26), perhaps partly because he loved Michal (not Merab). So he and his men went out and killed two hundred Philistine men. They brought their foreskins as a double price for the purchase of Michal. As a result, David and Michal were married (v. 27). Saul's hope that David would get killed was disappointed.

The old process continued. "When Saul realized that the LORD was with David and that his daughter Michal loved David, Saul became still more afraid of him, and remained his enemy the rest of his days" (vv. 28-29). The king now had a divided family and was very unhappy about it. Instead of accepting God's will, he opposed God's man.

CONTEMPORARY APPLICATION

The story of Saul and David, as portrayed in our lesson today, carries an important truth: we control our own destiny. We can obey God fully and find the highest and best in life, or we can disobey God and suffer the tragic consequences. No one else can choose for us—no other human being, not even God Himself. We determine our own destiny.

Another lesson we can learn from our study is the sad deterioration of character, as well as tragic circumstances, that comes through continued refusal to let God have His way. The spectacle of Saul's downward path—spiritually, psychologically, socially—is dismal. On the other hand, David climbed steadily. And so can we.

AN ANOINTED SHEPHERD

DEVOTIONAL READING	Psalm 23
ADULTS AND YOUTH	**Adult Topic:** *God's Choice of a Leader* **Youth Topic:** *The Number One Choice* **Background Scripture:** II Sam. 5-7 **Scripture Lesson:** II Sam. 5:1-3; 7:8-16 **Memory Verse:** *I took you from the pasture, from following the sheep, that you should be prince over my people Israel.* II Sam. 7:8
CHILDREN	**Topic:** *David Becomes King* **Memory Verse:** *You shall be shepherd of my people Israel, and you shall be prince over Israel.* II Sam. 5:2
DAILY BIBLE READINGS	**June 11 M.:** David's Elegy Over Saul and Jonathan. II Sam. 1:17-27 **June 12 T.:** David's Punishment of Ish-bosheth's Murderers. II Sam. 4:1-12 **June 13 W.:** David King Over All Israel. II Sam. 5:1-5 **June 14 T.:** Establishment of Jerusalem as Capital. II Sam. 5:6-16 **June 15 F.:** War with Philistines. II Sam. 5:17-25 **June 16 S.:** Bringing of Ark to Jerusalem. II Sam. 6:1-15 **June 17 S.:** Establishment of David's House. II Sam. 7:8-16
LESSON AIM	To see how God blessed His obedient servant David.
LESSON SETTING	**Time:** about 1000 B.C. **Place:** Jerusalem
LESSON OUTLINE	**An Anointed Shepherd** I. **Choice of David as King of Israel:** II Samuel 5:1-5 A. Chosen by All the Tribes: vv. 1-2 B. Anointed as King: v. 3 C. Length of David's Reign: vv. 4-5 II. **David's Conquest of Jerusalem:** II Samuel 5:6-12 III. **David's Desire to Build a Temple:** II Samuel 7:1-3 A. Proposal to Nathan: vv. 1-2 B. Nathan's Reply: v. 3 IV. **Message from the Lord:** II Samuel 7:5-16 A. Introduction: vv. 5-7 B. Reminder of Humble Beginning: v. 8 C. Promise of Greatness: v. 9

D. Promise of Protection: vv. 10-11a
E. Establishment of Dynasty: vv. 11b-12
F. Successor to Build the Temple: v. 13
G. God as Father: v. 14
H. Assurance of Continued Love: v. 15
I. An Everlasting Kingdom: v. 16

V. David's Prayer: II Samuel 7:18-29

SUGGESTED
INTRODUCTION
FOR ADULTS

Last week we studied I Samuel 18. Today we study the fifth and seventh chapters of II Samuel. Many events happened in between, but we can mention only a few here.

The main thing we discover in the intervening chapters is Saul's continued efforts to kill David. In 19:1 we read, "Saul told his son Jonathan and all the attendants to kill David." Jonathan, of course, protected his friend whom he loved dearly, as portrayed at great length in chapters 19 and 20.

The remaining chapters of I Samuel describe David's repeated efforts to escape Saul's murderous hounding. He had to run from place to place and even from country to country. First Samuel ends with Saul's suicidal death (c. 31).

The first chapter of II Samuel gives David's lengthy lament over Saul and Jonathan. Then David was anointed king of Judah at Hebron (2:1-4). The remainder of chapter 2 is taken up with the war between the houses of David and Saul. We are told, "The war between the house of Saul and the house of David lasted a long time. David grew stronger and stronger, while the house of Saul grew weaker and weaker" (3:1). Finally Abner shifted over from leading the army of Saul's son to siding with David (3:6-21). But Joab, David's military commander, assassinated Abner (3:27).

SUGGESTED
INTRODUCTION
FOR YOUTH

David was Israel's "Number One Choice" as king. That was because God was David's number one choice as Lord of his life. And that's the way it should be with us. If we make the Lord the number one choice in our lives, God will make good choices for our best good.

God chose David as king of Israel because He saw that David would seek His will at all times. Does He see that spirit of devotion in us? If so, we can enjoy His best for us.

CONCEPTS FOR
CHILDREN

1. We have to be good followers before we can be good leaders.
2. We must let the Lord lead us if we are going to help others.
3. If we let God have His way in our hearts, He will make our lives happy.
4. Doing God's will is the secret of a good life.

THE LESSON COMMENTARY

I. CHOICE OF DAVID AS KING OF ISRAEL: II Samuel 5:1-5

A. Chosen by All the Tribes: vv. 1-2

All the tribes of Israel came to David at Hebron and said, "We are your own flesh and blood. In the past, while Saul was king over us, you were the one who led Israel on their military campaigns. And the LORD said to you, 'You will shepherd my people Israel, and you will become their ruler.'"

David had been anointed at Hebron as king over Judah (2:4). But the ten tribes in the north had chosen Saul's son Ish-Bosheth as king of Israel (2:8, 9). However, when Ish-Bosheth insulted Abner, his military leader (3:70), the latter forsook Saul's dynasty and pledged himself to "transfer the kingdom from the house of Saul and establish David's throne over Israel and Judah from Dan to Beersheba" (3:10). (Dan was the northernmost city in Israel and Beersheba the southernmost in Judah.) Joab's murder of Abner (3:28) prevented the latter from carrying out his promise.

The next significant event was the murder of Ish-Bosheth, king of Israel (4:5-6). Interestingly, David had the two murderers put to death for their crime (4:9-12). The way was now prepared for all the tribes of Israel to come to David at Hebron (south of Bethlehem) and ask him to be their king.

They began by saying, "We are your own flesh and blood." All of them, including David, were descended from Jacob, whose name was changed to Israel (Gen. 32:28). So they should all be one nation, with David as king. He had "led Israel on their military campaigns," so he was best fitted to be the leader of the nation. Furthermore, God had chosen him for the place: "You will shepherd my people Israel, and you will become their ruler."

If this meeting at Hebron is the same one described in I Chronicles 12:23-40, a great host of armed men came "fully determined to make David king over all Israel. All the rest of the Israelites were also of one mind to make David king" (v. 38). It was a popular demonstration of loyalty to God's chosen leader.

B. Anointed as King: v. 3

"When all the elders of Israel had come to King David at Hebron, the king made a compact with them at Hebron before the LORD, and they anointed David king over Israel."

It was the proper duty of the elders to make the compact and anoint the king. We note that David was always careful to put God first in every event. It was "before the LORD" that the compact, or "covenant" (NASB), was made.

Alexander Maclaren writes on this verse:

So David has reached the throne at last. Schooled by suffering, and in the full maturity of his powers, enriched by the singularly varied experiences of his changeful life, tempered by the swift alternations of heat and cold, polished by friction, consolidated by heavy blows, he has been welded into a fitting instrument for God's purposes. Thus does He ever prepare for larger service. Thus does He ever reward patient trust. Through trials to a throne is the law for all noble lives in regard to their earthly progress, as well as in regard to the relation between earth and heaven (Expositions of Holy Scripture, II Samuel-II Kings 7, p. 10).

C. Length of David's Reign: vv. 4-5

"David was thirty years old when he became king, and he reigned forty years. In Hebron he reigned over Judah seven years and six months, and in

Jerusalem he reigned over all Israel and Judah thirty-three years."

In 2:10 we are told that Ish-Bosheth "reigned two years" over Israel. It is also stated (2:11), as here, that David reigned seven and a half years in Hebron. There is disagreement among commentators as to where the difference of about five years fits—before or after the death of Ish-Bosheth. Some think that it took that length of time for Ish-Bosheth to get control of the throne in Israel. Others feel strongly that it was five years after the death of Ish-Bosheth before the tribes in the north were willing to ask David to be their king. The matter is still an open question.

II. DAVID'S CONQUEST OF JERUSALEM: II Samuel 5:6-12

Hebron, about twenty miles below Jerusalem, was too far south to serve as a good capital for all Israel, so David decided to capture Jerusalem and make it his capital. The Jebusites taunted him when he appeared with his army (v. 6). But David captured "the fortress of Zion, the City of David" (v. 7). This was by the south wall of the city. He evidently took the whole city, with Joab as leader of the attack (I Chron. 11:4-9).

We are further told:

> David then took up residence in the fortress and called it the City of David. He built up the area around it, from the supporting terraces inward. And he became more and more powerful, because the LORD God Almighty was with him (vv. 9-10).

The fact that David was held in high esteem is shown by the statement that "Hiram king of Tyre sent messengers to David, along with cedar logs and carpenters and stonemasons, and they built a palace for David" (v. 11). Then "David knew that the LORD had established him as king over Israel and had exalted his kingdom for the sake of his people Israel" (v. 12).

III. DAVID'S DESIRE TO BUILD A TEMPLE: II Samuel 7:1-3

A. Proposal to Nathan: vv. 1-2

> After the king was settled in his palace and the LORD had given him rest from all his enemies around him, he said to Nathan the prophet, "Here I am, living in a palace of cedar, while the ark of God remains in a tent."

Chapter 6 is taken up with the story of how David brought the ark, in two stages, to Jerusalem. There it was "set in its place inside the tent that David had pitched for it, and David sacrificed burnt offerings and fellowship offerings before the LORD" (v. 17). Then "he blessed the people in the name of the LORD Almighty" (v. 18), and they had a great time of celebration (v. 19).

Understandably, David did not feel happy living in a palace while the ark of God was housed in a tent. It was proper and gracious of him to try to do something to remedy the situation.

B. Nathan's Reply: v. 3

"Whatever you have in mind, go ahead and do it, for the LORD is with you." It was natural that Nathan should feel this way about housing the ark, and he spontaneously expressed his own feelings.

IV. MESSAGE FROM THE LORD: II Samuel 7:5-16

A. Introduction: vv. 5-7

As we have just noted, Nathan gave his own approval to David's words. In doing so he was speaking as a private individual, not as a prophet. But God had other plans. And so "that night the word of the LORD came to Nathan" (v. 4).

The message is a rather long one (vv. 5-16). Verses 5-7 are introductory. Nathan was to tell David, "This is what the LORD says: Are you the one to build me a house to dwell in?" (v. 5). This was the important question.

The Lord went on to remind David that He had not dwelt in a house—the ark represented His presence—since the day He brought the Israelites up out of Egypt. In those early days of moving about His presence dwelt in a tent (v. 6).

Then the Lord raised an interesting question: "Wherever I have moved with all the Israelites, did I ever say to any of their rulers whom I commanded to shepherd my people Israel, 'Why have you not built me a house of cedar?'" (v. 7). In other words, God had not initiated such an idea.

B. Reminder of Humble Beginning: v. 8

"Now then, tell my servant David, 'This is what the LORD Almighty says: I took you from the pasture and from following the flock to be ruler over my people Israel.'" Shepherding was considered a very humble, lowly occupation. David had not come from a royal family, or even a wealthy home.

R. Payne Smith takes the term "servant" here to be significant. He calls it "word of high dignity, applied to but few persons in the Old Testament." He continues: "It signifies the prime minister, or vicegerent of Jehovah, as the theocratic king, and is the special title of Moses. ... But it is in the last twenty-seven chapters of Isaiah that the title reaches its full grandeur." There, "the servant is the Messiah, as being the personal representative of God upon earth." Smith concludes:

The title is now given to David as the type of Christ's kingly office, and also as the sweet singer, who added a new service to the worship of God, and made it more spiritual, and more like the service of angels round God's throne (The Pulpit Commentary, II Samuel, p. 183).

C. Promise of Greatness: v. 9

"'I have been with you wherever you have gone, and I have cut off all your enemies from before you. Now I will make your name great, like the names of the greatest men of the earth.'"

As before, the Lord reminded David of how He had been always with him and had cut off his enemies. But then He went on to give a tremendous promise for the future. David's name would be made great, beyond any human expectation. His reign typified that of the coming Messiah. As Smith notes, "if Messiah was to be 'David's Son,' it was necessary that the king should hold a special place in the hearts of all Israelites" (PC, II Samuel, p. 183).

D. Promise of Protection: vv. 10-11a

"And I will provide a place for my people Israel and will plant them so that they can have a home of their own and no longer be disturbed. Wicked people will not oppress them anymore, as they did at the beginning and have done ever since the time I appointed leaders over my people Israel."

This prophecy had a partial fulfillment in the reign of David. It will have its complete fulfillment in the millennial kingdom.

E. Establishment of Dynasty: vv. 11b-12

"The LORD declares to you that the LORD himself will establish a house for you: When your days are over and you rest with your fathers, I will raise up your offspring to succeed you, who will come from your own body, and I will establish his kingdom."

Saul's son reigned for only two years, and that only over the northern tribes. But the Lord promises David that his son will have a lasting kingdom. And, of course, this is exactly what happened. Solomon was a very prosperous ruler over a firmly established kingdom.

F. Successor to Build
the Temple: v. 13

"'He is the one who will build a house for my Name, and I will establish the throne of his kingdom forever.'"

Now we come to the main subject that had precipitated this revelation from the Lord. David was not to build the Lord's house; his son and successor would do this.

We have to turn to I Chronicles 28:2-3 to discover the reason why God would not allow David to build the Temple. There we read that the aged king said to his officials:

> Listen to me, my brothers and my people. I had it in my heart to build a house as a place of rest for the ark of the covenant of the LORD, for the footstool of our God, and I made plans to build it. But God said to me, "You are not to build a house for my Name, because you are a warrior and have shed blood...."

This does not mean that David had done wrong in fighting those many battles. But it was fitting that the Temple should be built by a man of peace, which Solomon was. Furthermore, it was helpful to build in a time of peace. Added to this, Solomon had adequate resources for building a suitable house for the God of glory.

The "forever" in the last part of verse 13 points forward to the messianic kingdom for its fulfillment. In Christ, the Son of David, the dynasty will be everlasting, literally "forever."

G. God as Father: v. 14

Speaking of Solomon, God said: "I will be his father, and he will be my son. When he does wrong, I will punish him with the rod of men, with floggings inflicted by men."

God's fatherly care of His children is beautifully expressed here. Like every good father, He knows that His children need discipline for their own good. If Solomon did wrong, as he surely did, God would have to punish him. And this happened in the latter part of Solomon's life. The story of his pagan wives who led him astray is a familiar one. In I Kings 11:4 we read, "As Solomon grew old, his wives turned his heart after other gods, and his heart was not fully devoted to the LORD his God, as the heart of David his father had been." We next read: "Then the LORD raised up against Solomon an adversary.... And God raised up against Solomon another adversary" (vv. 14, 23). Solomon had ample warning, but he paid no attention.

H. Assurance of Continued
Love: v. 15

The Lord went on to say to David concerning his son Solomon, "But my love will never be taken away from him, as I took it away from Saul, whom I removed from before you."

As Smith notes, "Saul's was a royalty for one generation; David's throne was to be established forever" (*PC*, II Samuel, p. 185). God would not fail to keep His promise.

One wonders if this verse might be taken as suggesting that Solomon repented of his sins before he died. The matter is not certain.

In I Chronicles 28:9 we have David's charge to Solomon:

> "And you, my son Solomon, acknowledge the God of your father, and serve him with wholehearted devotion and with a willing mind, for the LORD

DISCUSSION QUESTIONS

1. What were some of David's strong points?
2. What were some of David's weak points?
3. What would you say about David's desire to build the Temple for God?
4. Why does God call people from humble circumstances?
5. Why did Solomon fail?
6. In what ways is David a type of Christ?

searches every heart and understands every motive behind the
thoughts. If you seek him, he will be
found by you; but if you forsake him,
he will reject you forever."

Those are words that we all do well to
heed!

I. An Everlasting Kingdom:
v. 16

The Lord's final promise to David
was: "Your house and your kingdom

will endure forever before me; your
throne will be established forever."

V. DAVID'S PRAYER:
II Samuel 7:18-29

If time permits, read this prayer of
David aloud in class. It is one of the
most beautiful prayers in all the
Bible.

CONTEMPORARY APPLICATION

The life of David is a constant challenge to all of us to give ourselves
unreservedly to God and seek to follow
Him obediently every step of the way.
God has better things for us than any
of us could choose for ourselves. Why
not find out what "great things" He
can do in our lives?

David never dreamed what great
plans God had for him and for his
family. I have discovered that the
working out of God's plan for my life
has far exceeded my fondest expectations. It pays to serve Jesus!

FAMILY REBELLION

DEVOTIONAL READING	II Samuel 14:25-33
ADULTS AND YOUTH	**Adult Topic:** *Family Rebellion* **Youth Topic:** *Trouble in the Making* **Background Scripture:** II Sam. 13:20—18:16; I Kings 1 **Scripture Lesson:** II Sam. 15:2-12 **Memory Verse:** *Absalom stole the hearts of the men of Israel.* II Sam. 15:6
CHILDREN	**Topic:** *An Unhappy Family* **Background Scripture:** II Sam. 13:1-19; 15; I Kings 1 **Scripture Lesson:** II Sam. 15:2-12 **Memory Verse:** *And a messenger came to David, saying, "The hearts of the men of Israel have gone after Absalom."* II Sam. 15:13
DAILY BIBLE READINGS	**June 18 M.:** David's Prayer of Gratitude. II Sam. 7:18-29 **June 19 T.:** David's Wars and Victories. II Sam. 8:1-14 **June 20 W.:** David's Kindness to Mephibosheth. II Sam. 9:1-13 **June 21 T.:** A Rebuke by the Prophet Nathan. II Sam. 12:1-7a **June 22 F.:** Festivities of Sheepshearing Time. II Sam. 13:22-29 **June 23 S.:** Absalom's Estrangement from David. II Sam. 14:28-33 **June 24 S.:** The Revolt of Absalom. II Sam. 15:1-14
LESSON AIM	To show the tragic results of bad family relationships.
LESSON SETTING	**Time:** tenth century B.C. **Place:** Jerusalem

LESSON OUTLINE	**Family Rebellion**
	
	I. **Absalom's Ambition:** II Samuel 15:1-6
	    A. Military Escort: v. 1
	    B. Meeting the People: v. 2
	    C. Flattering the People: v. 3
	    D. Wooing the People: v. 4
	    E. Winning the People: vv. 5-6
	
	II. **Absalom's Conspiracy:** II Samuel 15:7-12
	    A. Deceitful Request: v. 7
	    B. Dishonest Reason: v. 8
	    C. David's Generosity: v. 9

D. Absalom's Treason: v. 10
E. Innocent Accomplices: v. 11
F. Growth of Conspiracy: v. 12

One of David's sons, Amnon, had raped Tamar, the sister of Absalom, who was another son of David. This sordid story is told in II Samuel 13:1-19.

When King David heard about it, "he was furious" (v. 21), but apparently he did nothing about it.

On the other hand, Absalom "hated Amnon because he had disgraced his sister Tamar" (v. 22). As a result, he saw to it that Amnon was killed (vv. 23-29). To flee his father's wrath, Absalom escaped to Talmai, the king of Geshur (v. 37), his maternal grandfather (3:3; I Chron. 3:1-4). There he stayed for three years (v. 38). David "longed to go to Absalom" (v. 39) but he did nothing about it. This was his first mistake in the case.

Joab, David's chief general, "knew that the king's heart longed for Absalom" (14:1). Working in rather subtle fashion through "a wise woman," he finally got the king to tell him to go and get Absalom (vv. 2-21). But when Joab brought Absalom back to Jerusalem, David said, "He must go to his own house; he must not see my face" (v. 24). That was the second serious mistake that David made, and he paid a tragic price for it. He should have welcomed Absalom with a kiss of forgiveness. It was only after two years of exclusion from the king's presence that Absalom finally forced a meeting and received his father's kiss (vv. 28-33). But by then it was too late.

"Trouble in the Making" is what we find in the sad story of David and his son Absalom. The unforgiving spirit of his father finally drove Absalom to become a rebel and seize the throne, making his father flee for his life.

In this unhappy situation both father and son were at fault. This teaches us that there must be cooperation and kindness in all family relationships or serious trouble will be brewing. Real love is the secret.

1. Children, as well as parents, can help to make the home happy.
2. We must first be honest with each other.
3. Then we must show love and kindness.
4. Concern for each other is important.

THE LESSON COMMENTARY

I. ABSALOM'S AMBITION:
II Samuel 15:1-6

A. Military Escort: v. 1

"In the course of time, Absalom provided himself with a chariot and horses and with fifty men to run ahead of him."

Absalom was filled with selfish ambition. To make a great impression on the public he put on this display. It must have been quite a sight to see him riding down the road in a magnificent chariot, with fifty men running ahead of the horses. Absalom was eager to catch the eyes of the people. As Alexander Maclaren says, "Absalom begins operations by dazzling people with ostentatious splendour" (*Expositions of Holy Scripture*, II Samuel-II Kings 7, p. 85).

B. Meeting the People: v. 2

He would get up early and stand by the side of the road leading to the city gate. Whenever anyone came with a complaint to be placed before the king for a decision, Absalom would call to him, "What town are you from?" He would answer, "Your servant is from one of the tribes of Israel."

Absalom's ambition led him to "get up early" and be on hand to greet those who were coming to see the king. He would intercept them before they entered the city gate.

Each newcomer received a warm greeting: "What town are you from?" Absalom showed a personal interest in each one who came along. He was a very adept politician! People want their leaders to be interested in them individually, not simply in the mass.

On this verse Robert Jamieson writes:

Public business in the East is always transacted early in the morning—the kings sitting an hour or more to hear causes or receive petitions in a court held anciently, and in many places still, in the open air at the city gateway; so that as those whose circumstances led them to wait on King David required to be in attendance on his morning levees, Absalom had to rise up early and stand beside the way of the gate (Robert Jamieson, A. R. Fausset, and David Brown, *A Commentary, Critical, Experimental, and Practical on the Old and New Testaments*, 2:251).

C. Flattering the People: v. 3

"Then Absalom would say to him, 'Look, your claims are valid and proper, but there is no representative of the king to hear you.'"

Absalom flattered the people by telling them that their claims were "valid and proper." In other words, *he* would give a favorable decision to each one. Naturally this won their hearts.

Then he went a step further by saying, "but there is no representative of the king to hear you." Jamieson makes this comment:

Through the growing infirmities of age, or the attack of a malignant sickness (Ps. xxxviii, xxxix, xli), and the occupation of the government with foreign wars, many private causes had long lain undecided, and a deep feeling of discontent prevailed amongst the people. This dissatisfaction was artfully fomented by Absalom, who addressed himself to the various suitors, and after briefly hearing their tale, gratified every one with a favourable opinion of his case (*Commentary*, 2:251).

I agree with Maclaren that there may have been a deeper, more serious cause for the situation. He writes:

Ever since his great sin, the king seems to have been stunned into inaction. The heavy sense of demerit had taken the buoyancy out of him, and, though forgiven, he could never regain the elastic energy of purer days.... If we suppose that he was much in the seclusion of his palace, a heavily-burdened and spirit-broken man, we can understand how his condition tempted his heartless, dashing son to grasp at the reins which seemed to be dropping from his slack hands, and how his passivity gave opportunity for Absalom's carrying on his schemes undisturbed...(*Expositions*, II Samuel-II Kings 7, p. 86).

We have already noted that it was a serious sin that David committed—a combination of adultery and murder. His two older sons were also guilty— Amnon of rape and Absalom of murder. David certainly had much reason to feel depressed in his old age. Sin takes its toll. Even when we are spiritually forgiven, there are natural consequences that sometimes plague us the rest of our lives.

D. Wooing the People: v. 4

"And Absalom would add, 'If only I were appointed judge in the land! Then everyone who has a complaint could come to me and I would see that he gets justice.'"

Jamieson comments:

> Studiously concealing his ambitious designs, he expressed a wish to be invested with official power, only that he might accelerate the course of justice, and advance the public interests. His professions had an air of extraordinary generosity and disinterestedness; and, together with his fawning arts in lavishing civilities on all, made him a popular favourite. Thus, by forcing a contrast between his own display of public spirit and the dilatory proceedings of the court, he created a growing disgust with his father's government, as weak, careless, or corrupt, and seduced the affections of the multitude, who neither penetrated the motives nor foresaw the tendency of his conduct (*Commentary,* 2:252).

E. Winning the People: vv. 5-6

"Also, whenever anyone approached him to bow down before him, Absalom would reach out his hand, take hold of him and kiss him" (v. 5).

Since Absalom was the king's son, it was altogether natural that people would bow before him. Then he would practice his "fawning arts," reaching out, taking hold, and kissing. Personal contact and warm attention are what people want, and Absalom was giving them what they were not receiving from the king.

"Absalom behaved in this way toward all the Israelites who came to the king asking for justice, and so he stole the hearts of the men of Israel" (v. 6).

Evidently this process went on for a long time and so affected a lot of people. Everyone appreciated Absalom's friendly concern. R. Payne Smith writes:

> By professing anxiety to devote himself to the hearing and deciding of the people's causes, by flattering each one with the assurance that his case was so good that it needed only a hearing to be decided in his favour, and by his affability, made the more charming by his personal beauty, he won the love of the people almost without their knowing how devoted they had become to him (*The Pulpit Commentary,* II Samuel, p. 367).

II. ABSALOM'S CONSPIRACY: II Samuel 15:7-12

A. Deceitful Request: v. 7

"At the end of four years, Absalom said to the king, 'Let me go to Hebron and fulfill a vow I made to the LORD.'"

We are confronted here with a textual problem. The Hebrew manuscripts have "forty" (KJV). But King James Version reference Bibles have this note in the margin: "Forty years from David's anointing as recorded in I Sam. 16:1. Or, four years from Absalom's return." The New American Standard Bible retains "forty." The New International Version has "four," with the footnote: "Some Septuagint manuscripts, Syriac and Josephus; Hebrew *forty.*" R. Payne Smith says that "the reading 'forty' is evidently incorrect" (*PC,* II Samuel, p. 367). Jamieson, who is basically conservative, agrees (*Commentary,* 2:252). The German commentator on Second Samuel in Lange's *Commentary on the Holy Scriptures* says, "We must read '*four years*'" (Samuel, p. 503). But his American translators append this observation: "Though the number *four* is more probable than *forty*, it is after all only a conjecture, though a well-supported one; the chronology must here be regarded as uncertain" (Samuel, p. 503). This seems to be the best conclusion. Fortunately, the matter is of no serious consequence, since both readings make sense.

Absalom was deceitful when he asked permission to go to Hebron to "fulfill a vow." He had other plans—to launch a revolution, as we shall soon see.

B. Dishonest Reason: v. 8

"While your servant was living at Geshur in Aram, I made this vow: 'If the LORD takes me back to Jerusalem, I will worship the LORD in Hebron.'"

This seems to have been a lie. At any rate, the succeeding verses show that he was not going to Hebron to worship the Lord. He was going there to drive the Lord's anointed servant from the throne. His purposes were evil.

Alexander Maclaren observes:

> The pretext of the sacrifice at Hebron, in pursuance of a vow made by Absalom in his exile, was meant to touch David's heart in two ways,— by appealing to his devotional feelings, and by presenting a pathetic picture of his suffering and devout son vowing in the land where his father's wrath had driven him (*Expositions of Holy Scripture*, II Samuel-II Kings 7, p. 87).

"Aram" is the Hebrew name for "Syria" (KJV, NASB). Since ancient *Aram* did not have the same boundaries as modern Syria, the Committee on Bible Translation chose to use the more precise biblical name.

C. David's Generosity: v. 9

"The king said to him, 'Go in peace.' So he went to Hebron."

How David could have failed to know what his rebellious son was doing near the city gate is a mystery. As it was, he generously told Absalom to go in peace.

And so Absalom "went to Hebron." As we have noted before, this place was about twenty miles south of Jerusalem. R. Payne Smith makes this comment:

> Absalom chose this town, both as being his birthplace, and also because

it was on the road to Geshur (1 Sam. xxvii.8), whither flight might be necessary should the enterprise fail. He hoped also to win to his cause some of the powerful tribe of Judah, though it generally was the mainstay of David's throne. Local sacrifices were still customary . . . and the visit of the king's son for such a purpose would be celebrated by a general holiday and much feasting at Hebron. As Ewald remarks, David's confidence and want of suspicion were the results of a noble-minded generosity (*PC*, II Samuel, p. 367).

D. Absalom's Treason: v. 10

"Then Absalom sent secret messengers throughout the tribes of Israel to say, 'As soon as you hear the sound of the trumpets, then say, "Absalom is king in Hebron."'"

Jamieson makes the following helpful comment on this verse:

> These emissaries were to sound the inclinations of the people, to further the interests of Absalom, and to exhort all the adherents of his party to be in readiness to join his standard as soon as they should hear that he had been proclaimed king. As the summons was to be made by the sound of trumpets, it is probable that care had been taken to have trumpeters stationed on the heights, and at convenient stations—a mode of announcement that would soon spread the news over all the country, of his inauguration to the throne (*Commentary*, 2:252).

It is sad to see Absalom getting revenge on his father for the unforgiving spirit that David had shown toward him. When David heard about Amnon's rape of Tamar, we read that "he was furious" (13:21). But what did he do about it? As king and father he should have punished his son for this unspeakable crime. Instead he apparently did nothing.

That caused Absalom to take the matter into his own hands and have Amnon killed, as we have seen. Then David turned against Absalom and the latter had to flee. Instead of calling him back and forgiving him, David rejected his son. Now the son was rejecting him. It is a sad story all the way through.

E. Innocent Accomplices: v. 11

"Two hundred men from Jerusalem had accompanied Absalom. They had been invited as guests and went quite innocently, knowing nothing about the matter."

Absalom had planned everything carefully and had maintained a surprising amount of secrecy about his plans. R. Payne Smith writes about the two hundred men:

> These, doubtless, were courtiers and men of rank, who were so accustomed to Absalom's love of display, that, when . . . invited, they would go without suspicion. To Absalom their attendance was most important, not only because, being compromised, many would join him, and even all of them for a time be forced to yield obedience, but because they would make the people of Hebron suppose that Absalom had a powerful body of supporters at Jerusalem (PC, II Samuel, p. 368).

Absalom showed a lack of honesty and moral responsibility in executing this revolt against his father. All he was thinking about was himself.

F. Growth of Conspiracy: v. 12

"While Absalom was offering sacrifices, he also sent for Ahithophel the Gilonite, David's counselor, to come from Giloh, his home town. And so the conspiracy gained strength, and Absalom's following kept on increasing."

The religious display that Absalom made reveals the depth of his depravity. Outwardly he was worshiping God with expensive sacrifices and a great display of piety. Inwardly he was spurning God's will and defying God's plans for Israel. It is a great tragedy when people make an outward display of religion to cover up their criminal purposes.

Absalom had the gall to send for Ahithophel, David's counselor, who lived in Giloh, a few miles south of Hebron. R. Payne Smith writes:

> The desertion of David by Ahithophel is in every way remarkable, even if he were Bathsheba's grandfather [as Jewish writers claim]. For he was far too subtle a man to have joined the conspiracy unless he had felt reasonably sure that it would be successful. Successful it would have been had his advice been followed [see c. 17]; but so correctly did he estimate the result if David were allowed time to gather his friends, that, when his counsel was rejected, he withdrew immediately to Giloh, and committed suicide (PC, II Samuel, p. 368).

David probably was referring to Ahithophel when he wrote (in Ps. 41:9):

> Even my close friend, whom I
>   trusted,
>   he who shared my bread,
>   has lifted up his heel against
>   me.

And this verse was quoted by Jesus at the Last Supper concerning Judas Iscariot, who was about to betray Him to His enemies (John 13:18).

The fact that Ahithophel was now living in his home town, Giloh, has caused considerable comment. If he was "David's counselor," why was he not at the royal palace in Jerusalem?

DISCUSSION QUESTIONS

1. Why do Christian parents sometimes show an unforgiving spirit?
2. What can we learn from the mistakes of David?
3. Why is monogamy required in Christianity?
4. What are some of the consequences of sins that have been forgiven?
5. Did David stay on the throne too long?
6. What are some consequences of incompetency?

Several commentators suggest that he had already turned against David because of the latter's sin against Bathsheba and had perhaps linked himself with Absalom before he left Jerusalem.

The latter part of verse 12 reads: "And so the conspiracy gained strength, and Absalom's following kept on increasing." Jamieson comments:

> The rapid accession of one place after another, in all parts of the kingdom, to the party of the insurgents, shows that deep and general dissatisfaction existed at this time against the person and government of David. The remnant of Saul's partizans, the unhappy affair of Bathsheba, the overbearing insolence and crimes of Joab, negligence and obstruction in the administration of justice, were some of the principal causes that contributed to the success of this wide-spread insurrection (*Commentary*, 2:252).

We cannot help but feel that one of David's worst mistakes was in marrying so many women. In II Samuel 3:2-5 (also I Chron. 3:1-3) we find a list of six sons born to David in those early years at Hebron. Each one had a different mother. With so many wives and their children, David was bound to have "An Unhappy Family" (children's topic)!

CONTEMPORARY APPLICATION

In our lesson today we see wrong attitudes taken not only by a wayward, self-ambitious son, but also by a godly father. It is not only our children who are to blame for trouble in the home, but sometimes it is good Christian parents who are unwise in the attitudes they take toward their children.

From the beginning there must be full love and acceptance in the home. A son rejected by his father—no matter what he has done—will pretty surely be a son who rejects his father, sometimes in a dangerous way. Love and forgiveness are what keep a home together.

SOWING SEEDS OF DESTRUCTION

DEVOTIONAL READING

II Peter 2:17-21

ADULTS AND YOUTH

Adult Topic: *Sowing Seeds of Destruction*

Youth Topic: *Wrong Choice!*

Background Scripture: I Kings 9:1—11:13

Scripture Lesson: I Kings 9:1-7; 11:9-12

Memory Verse: *If you turn aside from following me, you or your children, . . . then I will cut off Israel from the land which I have given them.* I Kings 9:6-7

CHILDREN

Topic: *Following a Good Example*

Background Scripture: I Kings 9:1-11; 13

Scripture Lesson: I Kings 9:1-7; 11:9-12

Memory Verse: *Walk before me, as David your father walked.* I Kings 9:4

DAILY BIBLE READINGS

June 25 M.: Solomon's Prayer for Wisdom. I Kings 3:3-15
June 26 T.: Solomon's Vision. I Kings 9:1-9
June 27 W.: The Forced Levy. I Kings 9:15-22
June 28 T.: Visit of the Queen of Sheba. I Kings 10:1-13
June 29 F.: Solomon's Wealth. I Kings 10:14-25
June 30 S.: Solomon's Business Enterprises. I Kings 10:26-29
July 1 S.: Judgment on Solomon. I Kings 11:1-13

LESSON AIM

To remind us that we reap what we sow.

LESSON SETTING

Time: about 960 B.C.

Place: Jerusalem

LESSON OUTLINE

Sowing Seeds of Destruction

I. **Second Appearance to Solomon:** I Kings 9:1-9
   A. Completion of Temple: vv. 1-2
   B. Response to Prayer: v. 3
   C. Challenge to Obedience: v. 4
   D. Reward of Obedience: v. 5
   E. Warning Against Disobedience: v. 6
   F. Results of Disobedience: v. 7
   G. Disgrace and Dishonor: vv. 8-9

II. **Divine Judgment:** I Kings 11:9-13
   A. God's Anger: v. 9
   B. Solomon's Disobedience: v. 10
   C. Loss of Kingdom: v. 11
   D. Delayed Execution: v. 12
   E. Retention of One Tribe: v. 13

SUGGESTED
INTRODUCTION
FOR ADULTS

Last week we studied Absalom's aborted rebellion against his father David. It ended with the death of the rebel aspirant to the throne (II Sam. 18:1-16).

Another of David's sons, Adonijah, decided to take the throne (I Kings 1:5), but David hastened to install Solomon as his successor (vv. 28-40). That brought an end to Adonijah's plans, and he was put to death (2:25). Joab, who had supported Adonijah, was also executed (2:34). Then we read, "The kingdom was now firmly established in Solomon's hands" (2:46).

Unfortunately, Solomon made some bad moves early in his reign. "Solomon made an alliance with Pharaoh king of Egypt and married his daughter" (3:1). David had strengthened his kingdom by military might. His son was a politician; he made political alliances with former enemies. But his marriages to pagan women, in order to strengthen foreign alliances, finally caused his downfall.

SUGGESTED
INTRODUCTION
FOR YOUTH

Solomon was the richest and wisest king of his day, but he became enamored of his wealth and great display of pomp and glory, and this proved to be his downfall.

His "Wrong Choice!" was to marry "seven hundred wives of royal birth." These were all women who had been brought up in pagan religions. They wanted to continue worshiping their heathen gods, and Solomon humored them (11:7-8). The result was that his own heart was turned away to idolatry (11:4), and he brought divine judgment on Israel.

We cannot be too careful about making our life choices. One of the most important choices we make is that of a life companion. It is absolutely essential that we marry a godly person, who worships the Lord.

CONCEPTS FOR
CHILDREN

1. "Following a Good Example" is very important.
2. That example can be godly parents or our Sunday school teacher.
3. Solomon started out following his father's example.
4. Unfortunately, he failed to keep this up.

THE LESSON COMMENTARY

I. SECOND APPEARANCE TO SOLOMON: I Kings 9:1-9

A. Completion of Temple: vv. 1-2

"When Solomon had finished building the temple of the LORD and the royal palace, and had achieved all he had desired to do...."

In I Kings 6:1 we read: "In the four hundred and eightieth year after the Israelites had come out of Egypt, in the fourth year of Solomon's reign over Israel... he began to build the temple of the LORD." This is generally identified as 966 B.C. In 6:38 we are told that he "had spent seven years building it." So it was completed in 959 B.C. It was a magnificent building, one of the greatest of ancient times. We are told in I Chronicles 22:14 that David had provided for the Temple of the Lord "a hundred thousand talents of gold" and "a million talents of silver." Since a talent weighed seventy-five pounds, this means about 3,750 tons of gold and about 37,500 tons of silver (see footnotes in NIV). When one considers how much an ounce of gold or silver is worth today, it is easy to see how utterly astronomical was the cost of the Temple in terms of money today!

The verse that we are now studying (I Kings 9:1) also says that Solomon had finished building "the royal palace." This took him "thirteen years" (7:1). At first sight it might seem unreasonable that he would spend almost twice as long building his palace as he did in building the Lord's house, but he doubtless had a much larger work force for the construction of the Temple than for his own palace, as it was the project of the whole nation, and David had prepared a massive amount of materials for it.

The second verse of our lesson says of Solomon that "the LORD appeared to him a second time, as he had appeared to him at Gibeon." Turning back to 3:5 we read: "At Gibeon the LORD appeared to Solomon during the night in a dream, and God said, 'Ask for whatever you want me to give you.'"

Solomon's response was beautiful. After noting God's kindness to David (v. 6), he went on to say:

"Now, O LORD my God, you have made your servant king in place of my father David. But I am only a little child and do not know how to carry out my duties.... So give your servant a discerning heart to govern your people and to distinguish between right and wrong" (vv. 7-9).

What a humble prayer!

We are not surprised to read, "The LORD was pleased that Solomon had asked for this" (v. 10). He had not asked selfishly, for his own glory (v. 11). So the Lord promised, "I will do what you have asked. I will give you a wise and discerning heart, so that there will never have been anyone like you, nor will there ever be" (v. 12). God added, "Moreover, I will give you what you

have not asked for—both riches and honor—so that in your lifetime you will have no equal among kings" (v. 13). We are not surprised to read later: "Solomon's wisdom was greater than the wisdom of all the men of the East, and greater than all the wisdom of Egypt" (4:30).

B. Response to Prayer: v. 3

The Lord said to Solomon: "I have heard the prayer and plea you have made before me; I have consecrated this temple, which you have built, by putting my Name there forever. My eyes and my heart will always be there."

The "prayer" referred to is Solomon's prayer of dedication of the Temple, recorded at length in 8:23-53. It is a prayer of adoration (v. 23) and appreciation (v. 24), and a plea for the fulfillment of God's promise to David (vv. 25-26).

Then Solomon appropriately exclaims: "But will God really dwell on earth? The heavens, even the highest heaven, cannot contain you. How much less this temple I have built!" (v. 27). Yet he prays: "May your eyes be open toward this temple night and day" (v. 29). The rest of the prayer is taken up with the plea that when the Israelites sin and then come to the Temple asking God's forgiveness He will forgive them (vv. 31-51).

Now the Lord assures Solomon that He has heard his prayer and will answer it in full. Specifically He promises, "My eyes and my heart will always be there."

C. Challenge to Obedience: v. 4

"As for you, if you walk before me in integrity of heart and uprightness, as David your father did, and do all I command and observe my decrees and laws...."

Alexander Maclaren comments:

The first requisite is to walk before God; that is, to nourish a continual consciousness of His presence, and to regulate all actions and thoughts under the thrilling and purifying sense of being "ever in the great Taskmaster's eye." Only we are not to think of Him only as a Taskmaster, but as a loving Friend and Helper. A child is happy in its little work or play when it knows that its father is looking on with sympathy. The sense of God's eye being on us should "make sunshine in a shady place," should lighten labour and sweeten care. It is at the root of practical obedience, as its place in this sequence shows; for there follow it, in verse 4, "integrity of heart and uprightness," on which again follow obedience to all God's commandments (*Expositions of Holy Scripture*, II Samuel-II Kings 7, p. 191).

D. Reward of Obedience: v. 5

"... I will establish your royal throne over Israel forever, as I promised David your father when I said, 'You shall never fail to have a man on the throne of Israel.'"

In a previous lesson we have already studied this promise to David: "Your house and your kingdom will endure forever before me: your throne will be established forever" (II Sam. 7:16). We noted then that "forever" must necessarily include the messianic kingdom. In I Kings 2:4 David reminds Solomon of the Lord's promise to him in extended form: "If your descendants watch how they live, and if they walk faithfully before me with all their heart and soul, you will never fail to have a man on the throne of Israel."

E. Warning Against Disobedience: v. 6

"But if you or your sons turn away from me and do not observe the commands and decrees I have given you and go off to serve other gods and worship them. . . ."

In this verse the singular "you" of verse 5, addressed specifically to Solomon, is changed to the plural "you" ("ye," KJV), as helpfully indicated by a footnote in the New International Version. Maclaren comments:

The second part of this divine utterance [vv. 3-9] is addressed to the whole nation, as is marked by the "ye" there compared with the "thou" in verse 4, and it lays down for succeeding generations the conditions on which the new Temple, that stood glittering in the bright Easter sunshine, should retain its pristine beauty. While the address to Solomon incited to obedience by painting its blessed consequences, that to the nation reaches the same end by the opposite path of darkly portraying the ruin that would be caused by departure from God. God draws by holding out a handful of good things, and He no less lovingly drives by stretching out a hand armed with lightnings (*Expositions*, II Samuel-II Kings 7, pp. 192-93).

F. Results of Disobedience: v. 7

". . . then I will cut off Israel from the land I have given them and will reject this temple I have consecrated for my Name. Israel will then become a byword and an object of ridicule among all peoples."

Moses had already warned the Israelites of the consequences of disobedience. He told them what would happen if they went into idolatry:

I call heaven and earth as witnesses against you this day that you will quickly perish from the land that you are crossing the Jordan to possess. You will not live there long but will certainly be destroyed. The LORD will scatter you among the peoples, and only a few of you will survive among the nations to which the LORD will drive you (Deut. 4:26-27).

This prediction was fulfilled in the Babylonian captivity and subsequently (cf. II Kings 25:11-12).

God also warned that the Temple would be rejected. Solomon's beautiful Temple was destroyed by Nebuchadnezzar's army in 586 B.C., as recorded in II Chronicles 36:19.

The last sentence of this verse is almost an exact repetition of what Moses had warned the Israelites: "You will become a thing of horror and an object of scorn and ridicule to all the nations where the LORD will drive you" (Deut. 28:37). Later, Micah sounded this warning: "You will bear the scorn of the nations" (Micah 6:16). The results of disobedience are tragic!

G. Disgrace and Dishonor: vv. 8-9

"And though this temple is now imposing, all who pass by will be appalled and will scoff and say, 'Why has the LORD done such a thing to this land and to this temple?' People will answer, 'Because they have forsaken the LORD their God, who brought their fathers out of Egypt, and have embraced other gods, worshiping and serving them—that is why the LORD brought all this disaster on them.'"

In view of the many, many warnings given by Moses and the later prophets, as well as this direct revelation to Solomon, it is difficult indeed to understand why that great king, son of such a godly father, should himself finally fall into the trap of worshiping pagan gods. But he did, as we shall soon see. It is not surprising, then, that later kings, farther removed by time from Moses, Samuel, and David, would lead the nation off into idolatry and precipitate the fulfillment of divine judgment pronounced here.

II. DIVINE JUDGMENT: I Kings 11:9-13

A. God's Anger: v. 9

"The LORD became angry with Solomon because his heart had turned away from the LORD, the God of Israel, who had appeared to him twice."

Solomon had been especially favored. He not only had a godly father, but the Lord had wonderfully favored him by twice appearing to him with an impressive combination of promises and warnings, as we have seen. How could he now turn away from the Lord? It is almost unbelievable!

B. Solomon's Disobedience: v. 10

"Although he had forbidden Solomon to follow other gods, Solomon did not keep the LORD's command."

The sad story of Solomon's lapse into idolatry is related in the first eight verses of this chapter. We are first told:

King Solomon... loved many foreign women besides Pharaoh's daughter— Moabites, Ammonites, Edomites, Sidonians and Hittites. They were from the nations about which the LORD had told the Israelites, "You shall not intermarry with them, because they will surely turn your hearts after their gods." Nevertheless, Solomon held fast to them in love (vv. 1-2).

The quotation here is from Deuteronomy 7:3-4. Solomon had been brought up under the Law and had doubtless heard this passage read many times. Yet he blatantly and extravagantly disobeyed it: "He had seven hundred wives of royal birth and three hundred concubines, and his wives led him astray" (v. 3). This was enough to ruin any man!

What was the consequence of this disobedience? "As Solomon grew old, his wives turned his heart after other gods, and his heart was not fully devoted to the LORD his God, as the heart of David his father had been" (v. 4). It would be hard for any man to resist the pressure of seven hundred beautiful princesses who were now all wives with whom he lived. It is no wonder that Solomon caved in!

DISCUSSION QUESTIONS

1. What are some of the perils of prosperity?
2. How can we avoid bad influence from associates?
3. Was Solomon's wealth an asset or a liability?
4. What were some of the mistakes Solomon made?
5. What are some of the advantages of having only one wife?
6. Why should Christians marry Christians?

We are told specifically: "He followed Ashtoreth the goddess of the Sidonians, and Molech the detestable god of the Ammonites" (v. 5). The Hebrew has "Milcom" (KJV, NASB), but most scholars take this as another name for the more familiar "Molech" (see v. 7 here).

The question has been raised as to whether Solomon himself was actually guilty of idolatry, offering sacrifices to the pagan deities. But we are told in verses 7 and 8:

> On a hill east of Jerusalem [this would normally be the Mount of Olives] Solomon built a high place for Chemosh the detestable god of Moab, and for Molech the detestable god of the Ammonites. He did the same for all his foreign wives, who burned incense and offered sacrifices to their gods.

This was certainly an act of promoting idolatry among God's people. Solomon had fallen a long way!

C. Loss of Kingdom: v. 11

"So the LORD said to Solomon, 'Since this is your attitude and you have not kept my covenant and my decrees, which I commanded you, I will most certainly tear the kingdom away from you and give it to one of your subordinates.'"

When the Lord appeared to Solomon previously He told him that "if" he obeyed, his kingdom would be established (9:4-5). Now he had clearly disobeyed, and so would lose his kingdom.

We are not told how "the LORD [spoke] to Solomon." It seems probable that it was through a prophet, perhaps Ahijah.

D. Delayed Execution: v. 12

"Nevertheless, for the sake of David your father, I will not do it during your lifetime. I will tear it out of the hand of your son."

We find similar incidents of God's mercy in 21:29 and II Kings 22:20. Here the Lord said that He was being especially gracious to Solomon "for the sake of David your father."

E. Retention of One Tribe: v. 13

"Yet I will not tear the whole kingdom from him, but will give him one tribe for the sake of David my servant and for the sake of Jerusalem, which I have chosen."

The story of the fulfillment of this promise is found in our next lesson. We only note here that the "one tribe" was Judah, the tribe from which David came and the tribe from which the Messiah would come. God had made promises to David that must be kept in spite of Solomon's sin. So David's dynasty would continue in the southern kingdom of Judah.

On these last two verses Maclaren comments:

> What a lesson as to God's great patience is here! What a solemn glimpse into man's power to counterwork God's purpose! So soon after its establishment did the house of David prove unworthy, and the experiment fail. Yet that long-suffering purpose is not turned aside, but persistently and patiently goes on its way, altering its methods, but keeping its end unaltered, bending even sin to minister to its design, pitying and warning the sinner ere it strikes the blow that the sinner has made needful (*Expositions*, II Samuel-II Kings 7, p. 207).

CONTEMPORARY APPLICATION

Our lesson today gives us a powerful warning against the dangers of backsliding. Solomon had almost everything in his favor. His father was a godly man who set a good example before him in most ways. God had graciously appeared to him twice, honoring him with His special presence. Furthermore, the Lord had prospered him very greatly. In fact, his life is a vivid example of the perils of prosperity.

Yet Solomon turned away from the Lord to other gods, as people still turn away to false gods of money and pleasure. It was a gradual process of being influenced wrongly by his wives over a period of time. We must stay *close* to the Lord to avoid the dangers of backsliding.

WHY DIVISION CAME

DEVOTIONAL READING	I Kings 12:1-11

ADULTS AND YOUTH

Adult Topic: *Revolt Against Oppression*

Youth Topic: *Let's Split*

Background Scripture: I Kings 11:26—14:31

Scripture Lesson: I Kings 11:29-33; 12:15-16

Memory Verse: *Thus says the Lord, the God of Israel, "Behold, I am about to tear the kingdom from the hand of Solomon, and will give you ten tribes . . . because he has forsaken me."* I Kings 11:31, 33

CHILDREN

Topic: *Not Thinking of Others*

Memory Verse: *But he forsook the counsel which the old men gave him, and took counsel with the young men who had grown up with him and stood before him.* I Kings 12:8

DAILY BIBLE READINGS

July 2 M.: Hadad, Adversary of Solomon. I Kings 11:14-22

July 3 T.: Jeroboam, Adversary of Solomon. I Kings 11:26-40

July 4 W.: Withdrawal of Israel from Judah. I Kings 12:16-20

July 5 T.: Jeroboam's Idolatry. I Kings 12:25-33

July 6 F.: Judgment Against Jeroboam. I Kings 13:1-5

July 7 S.: Conflicting Counsel. I Kings 12:1-11

July 8 S.: Rehoboam's Tragic Decision. I Kings 12:12-15

LESSON AIM

To help us understand the causes of division.

LESSON SETTING

Time: 930 B.C.

Place: Jerusalem

LESSON OUTLINE

Why Division Came

I. **Identification of Jeroboam:** I Kings 11:26-28
   A. One of Solomon's Officials: v. 26
   B. Foreman of Work Force: vv. 27-28

II. **Jeroboam and Ahijah:** I Kings 11:29-30
   A. The Prophet of Shiloh: v. 29
   B. Ahijah's Cloak: v. 30

III. **Prediction of Division:** I Kings 11:31-33
   A. Announcement to Jeroboam: v. 31
   B. One Tribe for David: v. 32
   C. Reason for Division: v. 33

IV. **Further Instructions:** I Kings 11:34-39

V. Rehoboam and the Israelites: I Kings 12:1-11

VI. Division of the Kingdom: I Kings 12:12-17
  A. Final Meeting: v. 12
  B. Rehoboam's Answer: vv. 13-14
  C. Divine Purpose: v. 15
  D. Revolt of the Ten Tribes: v. 16
  E. Judah Under Rehoboam: v. 17

SUGGESTED
INTRODUCTION
FOR ADULTS

Today we begin our study of Unit II: The Two Kingdoms. Under Saul, David, and Solomon all twelve tribes of Israelites formed one kingdom. Each of these first three kings reigned forty years (Acts 13:21; II Sam. 5:4; I Kings 11:42). In his article on "Chronology of the Old Testament" J. B. Payne dates Saul's reign as 1043-1003 B.C., David's as 1010-970 B.C., and Solomon's as 970-930 B.C. (*Zondervan Pictorial Encyclopedia of the Bible*, 1:836).

Between last week's lesson and this one we have an account of two adversaries of Solomon that appeared on the scene before Jeroboam. Because the king countenanced idolatry, "the LORD raised up against Solomon an adversary, Hadad the Edomite, from the royal line of Edom" (11:14). It will be remembered that Edom was another name for Esau, the brother of Jacob (Israel).

The other adversary was Rezon. We are told that he "was Israel's adversary as long as Solomon lived" (v. 25). He ruled in Aram (Syria).

SUGGESTED
INTRODUCTION
FOR YOUTH

"Let's Split" is a bad slogan. We have too many splits today, in both politics and religion.

Instead of creating splits when we sense some difference of opinion, we should try to get together, talk things over, and see if we can come to some kind of agreement on essentials. In writing to the Corinthians the apostle Paul warned strongly against causing divisions within the church. After speaking of the local church at Corinth as God's temple (I Cor. 3:16), he declared, "If anyone destroys God's temple, God will destroy him" (v. 17). In the Greek (contra. KJV) the verb is the same in both clauses. And the subject Paul is discussing in Chapter 3 is divisions in the church. So the context clearly indicates that he is talking about destroying a church by dividing it. May we never be guilty of that sin!

CONCEPTS FOR
CHILDREN

1. Rehoboam was guilty of "Not Thinking of Others."
2. When we fail to think of others, we get ourselves into trouble.
3. We should seek the advice of older, more experienced people.
4. To follow the advice of other young people can be harmful.

THE LESSON COMMENTARY

I. IDENTIFICATION OF JEROBOAM: I Kings 11:26-28

A. One of Solomon's Officials: v. 26

"Also, Jeroboam son of Nebat rebelled against the king. He was one of Solomon's officials, an Ephraimite...." The tribe of Ephraim was the leader of the ten tribes in the north, so that instead of speaking of Judah and Israel we sometimes speak of Judah and Ephraim (e.g. Isa. 7:17; 11:13).

B. Foreman of Work Force: vv. 27-28

"Here is the account of how he rebelled against the king" (v. 27) is really an introduction to a lengthy section (vv. 27-40). The account goes on: "Solomon had built the supporting terraces and had filled in the gap in the wall of the city of David his father." Verse 28 reads, "Now Jeroboam was a man of standing, and when Solomon saw how well the young man did his work, he put him in charge of the whole labor force"—the New American Standard Bible says "forced labor" and has in the margin: "literally, *burden*—of the house of Joseph." This would definitely include the tribes of Ephraim and Manasseh, the two sons of Joseph. But it probably included all the tribes north of Judah and Benjamin (see above).

There may be some sad implications here. Joseph Hammond has this to say:

> The tribe of Ephraim, with its constant envy of Judah, must have been mortified to find themselves employed—though it was but in the modified service of Israelites—on the fortifications of Jerusalem. Their murmurings revealed to Jeroboam the unpopularity of Solomon, and perhaps suggested thoughts of overt rebellion to his mind (*The Pulpit Commentary*, I Kings, p. 236).

In much the same vein Maclaren makes these observations:

> One can easily fancy the grumblings of the Ephraimites dragged up to Jerusalem to the hated labour, which Samuel had predicted (I Samuel viii.16), and how facile it would be for the officer in charge to fan discontent or to win friends by judicious indulgence. How long this went on we do not know, but the fire had smouldered for some time under the unconscious king's very eyes, when it was fanned into flame by Ahijah's breath (*Expositions of Holy Scripture*, II Samuel-II Kings 7, p. 210).

II. JEROBOAM AND AHIJAH: I KINGS 11:29-30

A. The Prophet of Shiloh: v. 29

"About that time Jeroboam was going out of Jerusalem, and Ahijah the prophet of Shiloh met him on the way, wearing a new cloak. The two of them were alone out in the country."

Shiloh was in the tribe of Benjamin, north of Bethel, so Jeroboam would doubtless have known Ahijah.

From the time of Joshua to the time of Levi the sacred Tabernacle was at Shiloh (Josh. 18:1; I Sam. 21:3). So this was a very appropriate place for the prophet of the Lord to be staying.

But there may also be some implications here. Robert Jamieson says this about Ahijah:

> His ministrations were carried on amidst the tribes on the central highlands of Ephraim, among the oldest and most influential families in the country, and in the tribe which was most important, both in respect of its large interest in the prosperity of the state and of its ancestral recollections. Moreover, one of the holy places was possessed by them. Shiloh, with a sacred antiquity now gathering around it, continually reminded them of what was forgotten amid the pomp of the southern city [Jerusalem]. There accordingly an expression of the gathering discontent

of the better spirit of the community was first made public; and it was very naturally first heard there, since "the burden of Joseph," imposed according to the fertility and productiveness of the soil, would, in that garden district of the country, be most irksome and oppressive (Robert Jamieson, A. R. Fausset, and David Brown, *A Commentary, Critical, Experimental, and Practical on the Old and New Testaments,* 2:332).

B. Ahijah's Cloak: v. 30

"And Ahijah took hold of the new cloak he was wearing and tore it into twelve pieces." Some commentators have held that it was Jeroboam who was wearing the new cloak—the uniform for his new position. But most scholars agree that it was clearly Ahijah's cloak.

Regarding the new cloak we read in Lange's *Commentary on the Holy Scriptures:* "A new garment is one that is whole and complete . . . , without a rent or hole; the kingdom was hitherto without split or division, but was now to be torn and divided" (I Kings, p. 136). Maclaren elaborates this point further:

How pathetic is the newness of the garment! Unworn, strong, and fresh, it is yet rent in pieces. So the kingdom is so recent, with such possibilities of duration, and yet it must be shattered! Thus quickly has the experiment broken down! It is little more than a century since Saul's anointing, little more than seventy years since the choice of David, and already the fabric, which had such fair promise of perpetuity, is ready to vanish away. If we may say so, that "new garment" represents the divine disappointment and sorrow over the swift corruption of the kingdom (*Expositions,* II Samuel–II Kings 7, 210–11).

Ahijah tore his own new cloak he was wearing "into twelve pieces." These would represent the twelve tribes of Israel. They had been molded into one nation by Saul and David, and perhaps further solidified by Solomon, but now

there was to be a division. It was indeed a sad day in Israel's history, with unhappy consequences.

III. PREDICTION OF DIVISION: I Kings 11:31-33

A. Announcement to Jeroboam: v. 31

Then Ahijah said to Jeroboam: "Take ten pieces for yourself, for this is what the LORD, the God of Israel, says: 'See, I am going to tear the kingdom out of Solomon's hand and give you ten tribes.'"

Solomon had brought this trouble on himself. Jamieson says this about his reign:

The severity of his despotic rule, rivaling the magnificence of the ancient Oriental autocrats, and oppressing his people by grinding exactions to maintain his numerous harem, as well as outraging the feelings of the better classes by his woeful idolatries, trampling upon the national constitution [the Law of Moses], and altering the character and destiny of Israel by his commercial and unrestricted intercourse with other nations; above all, having failed to consolidate his wide-spread empire by the bond of the true religion, his government neither enjoyed the blessing of God, nor secured the attachment of the people, and so it declined. Solomon's great sagacity, enlarged by the experience of a long reign, enabled him to foresee the outburst of impending calamities . . ." (*Commentary,* 2:332–33).

B. One Tribe for David: v. 32

"But for the sake of my servant David and the city of Jerusalem, which I have chosen out of all the tribes of Israel, he will have one tribe."

This was the tribe of Judah, in the south. But there were twelve tribes. How is it that "ten tribes" (v. 31) were promised to Jeroboam and "one tribe" to David's heir?

The answer is that the small tribe of Benjamin stayed with Judah. In

Lange's *Commentary* we read: "Little Benjamin, over against Judah, came scarcely into consideration; and as, besides, the capital of the kingdom (Jerusalem) lay on the border of both tribes, they might very well be reckoned as one" (I Kings, p. 136).

The result was that after the death of Solomon the Israelites were divided into two kingdoms—Israel in the north and Judah in the south. The descendants of David ruled over Judah until the Babylonian captivity (586 B.C.). In the north there were several different dynasties on the throne until the kingdom of Israel came to an end with the Assyrian capture of its capital, Samaria, in 722 B.C. Both kingdoms failed God and so were destroyed.

C. Reason for Division: v. 33

"I will do this because they have forsaken me and worshiped Ashtoreth the goddess of the Sidonians, Chemosh the god of the Moabites, and Molech the god of the Ammonites, and have not walked in my ways, nor done what is right in my eyes, nor kept my statutes and laws as David, Solomon's father, did."

As we noted in a previous lesson, "Milcom" (Hebrew, KJV, NASB) is probably another name for the more familiar "Molech," which is found in the Hebrew text of verse 7.

In last week's lesson we saw how Solomon had turned away to the worship of these pagan gods (11:4–8). Now it seems that the people are charged with this same idolatry. It is true that the early versions (Septuagint, Vulgate, and Syriac; see footnote in NIV) have the singular "he has" instead of "they have" (Hebrew). But Hammond says that "the plural is to be retained, the import being that Solomon was not alone in his idolatrous leanings; or it may turn our thoughts to the actual idolaters—his wives— whose guilt he shared" (*PC*, I Kings, pp. 236–37).

IV. FURTHER INSTRUCTIONS: I Kings 11:34-39

Through Ahijah the prophet the Lord told Jeroboam that Solomon would remain as king "all the days of his life for the sake of David my servant" (v. 34). But the kingdom would be taken from his son, and ten tribes given to Jeroboam (v. 35). The Lord said: "I will give one tribe to his son so that David my servant may always have a lamp before me in Jerusalem, the city where I chose to put my name" (v. 36). Jeroboam would be "king over Israel" (v. 37).

Then the Lord promise Jeroboam: "If you do whatever I command you and walk in my ways and do what is right in my eyes by keeping my statutes and commands, as David my servant did, I will be with you. I will build you a dynasty as enduring as the one I built for David and will give Israel to you" (v. 38).

Unfortunately, Jeroboam failed to meet these conditions. He made two golden calves, placed them in Bethel and Dan, and told his subjects to worship these idols (12:28-33). This plunged the northern kingdom of Israel into idolatry right away. So Jeroboam's dynasty did not last long.

V. REHOBOAM AND THE ISRAELITES: I Kings 12:1-11

After the death of Solomon (11:41– 43), "Rehoboam went to Shechem, for all the Israelites had gone there to make him king" (v. 1). When Jeroboam heard of this, he returned from Egypt, where he had fled from King Solomon (v. 2; cf. 11:40). The people sent for Jeroboam (v. 3), and he joined the assembly at Shechem, near Samaria (which became the capital of the northern kingdom).

With Jeroboam as their leader, the people asked Rehoboam to "lighten the harsh labor and the heavy yoke" that Solomon had put on them. If he did so, "we will serve you" (v. 4).

Rehoboam asked for three days to consider the matter (v. 5). He then consulted the older men who had served Solomon (v. 6). They advised him to grant the people's request (v. 7).

Foolishly, Rehoboam "rejected the advice the elders gave him and consulted the young men who had grown up with him" (vv. 8-9). They advised him to tell the people: "My little finger is thicker than my father's waist. My father laid on you a heavy yoke; I will make it even heavier..." (vv. 10-11).

VI. DIVISION OF THE KINGDOM: I Kings 12:12-17

A. Final Meeting: v. 12

"Three days later Jeroboam and all the people returned to Rehoboam, as the king had said, 'Come back to me in three days.'"

Three days gave plenty of time for a lot of thinking. We have just seen what Rehoboam did during that period. But we can only conjecture as to what the people were thinking. Were their expectations raised? We don't know. At any rate, they returned at the appointed time.

B. Rehoboam's Answer: vv. 13-14

The king answered the people harshly. Rejecting the advice given him by the elders, he followed the advice of the young men and said, "My father made your yoke heavy; I will make it even heavier. My father scourged you with whips; I will scourge you with scorpions."

One can hardly imagine a more stupid response by a new king to the justifiable request of his subjects. Any ruler who would answer "harshly" was unworthy of the throne. And the rest of Rehoboam's answer sounds like the words of a smart aleck, not a king.

Solomon scourged the people with "whips"; his son was going to scourge them with "scorpions." Lange's *Commentary* says, "The king was to use

instead of whips for servants the thorn-whip used for criminals alone, and which was called *scorpio* by the Romans" (I Kings, p. 146). Jamieson spells it out more fully:

The latter, as contrasted with the former, are supposed to mean thongs thickly set with hard knots and sharp iron points, used in the castigation of slaves; sometimes in after-times inflicted on Christian martyrs [Septuagint, *scorpiois*]. Scourging was performed by prostrating the victim on the ground at full length; while his limbs were kept down by force, a person with a whip lashed him on the bare back (2:334).

A king who would talk that way to his subjects deserved the consequences that Rehoboam reaped. One cannot blame these people for their reaction. Rehoboam was utterly unfit to be king. He showed that he was a spoiled brat, not a wise, mature person. He was not fit to be king over God's chosen people.

C. Divine Purpose: v. 15

"So the king did not listen to the people, for this turn of events was from the LORD, to fulfill the word the LORD had spoken to Jeroboam son of Nebat through Ahijah the Shilonite."

This is a significant statement. Maclaren writes:

The separation of the kingdom of Solomon into two weak and hostile

DISCUSSION QUESTIONS

1. How would you analyze Jeroboam?
2. What was Rehoboam's greatest fault?
3. What should be the true role of a leader (12:7)?
4. Why did Rehoboam take the advice of the young men?
5. What were the consequences of Rehoboam's response?
6. How can we help to improve our government?

states is, in one aspect, a wretched story of folly and selfishness wrecking a nation, and, in another, a solemn instance of divine retribution working its designs by men's sins. The greater part of this account deals with it in the former aspect, and shows the despicable motives of the men in whose hands was the nation's fate; but one sentence (verse 15) draws back the curtain for a moment, and shows us the true cause. There is something striking in that one flash, which reveals the enthroned God, working through the ignoble strife which makes up the rest of the story (II Samuel-II Kings 7, pp. 216-17).

D. Revolt of the Ten Tribes: v. 16

When all Israel saw that the king refused to listen to them, they answered the king:

"What share do we have in David,
    what part in Jesse's son?
To your tents, O Israel!
    Look after your own house,
        O David!"

So the Israelites went home.

The great tragedy finally took place. Rehoboam had a golden opportunity to repudiate his father's unreasonable burden on the people and offer them a fair, kind regime. He failed, threatening greater hardships instead. The people were fully justified in rejecting him, as he had rejected them.

E. Judah Under Rehoboam: v. 17

"But as for the Israelites who were living in the towns of Judah, Rehoboam still ruled over them."

There is a concensus among commentators that "Israelites" here means members of the ten tribes, not all twelve tribes. Those from the north who happened to be living in the territory of Judah submitted to the rule of Rehoboam. But Jeroboam became king of the kingdom of Israel (the ten tribes).

CONTEMPORARY APPLICATION

There are several applications of this lesson that are painfully obvious. The first relates to young people. When they have crucial, life-determining decisions to make, they should not seek and follow the advice of their peers, who know no more than they do. Rather they should listen to what more experienced, mature people have to say, and follow their advice.

For all of us there is the warning that when we treat people harshly we are asking for trouble. Many a politician, employer, or boss has treated his subordinates in an unkind way, and has thereby himself become the loser.

Above all, we should seek God's guidance. Nothing is said of Rehoboam praying about the matter!

AN ERA OF EVIL

DEVOTIONAL READING	I Kings 19:9-18

Adult Topic: *Bad Times for God's People*

Youth Topic: *Bad Times for God's People*

ADULTS AND YOUTH

Background Scripture: I Kings 16:15—22:40

Scripture Lesson: I Kings 16:21-25, 29-33; 22:37-39

Memory Verse: *How long will you go limping with two different opinions? If the Lord is God, follow him; but if Baal, then follow him.* I Kings 18:21

CHILDREN

Topic: *Bad Times for God's People*

Memory Verse: *Omri did what was evil in the sight of the Lord, and did more evil than all who were before him.* I Kings 16:25

DAILY BIBLE READINGS

July 9 M.: Reign of Nadab of Israel. I Kings 15:25-32
July 10 T.: Reign of Baasha of Israel. I Kings 15:33—16:7
July 11 W.: Reign of Elah of Israel. I Kings 16:8-14
July 12 T.: Consequences of Zimri's Coup. I Kings 16:15-22
July 13 F.: Reign of Amri of Israel. I Kings 16:23-28
July 14 S.: Reign of Ahab of Israel. I Kings 16:29-34
July 15 S.: The Death of Ahab. I Kings 22:30-40

LESSON AIM | To show the sad consequences of evil in high places.

LESSON SETTING

Time: ninth century B.C. (about 885-850 B.C.)

Place: Tirzah and Samaria

LESSON OUTLINE

An Era of Evil

   I. Rivals for the Throne: I Kings 16:21-22
     A. Two Factions: v. 21
     B. The Winner: v. 22

  II. Omri's Reign: I Kings 16:23-26
     A. Twelve-year Reign: v. 23
     B. Purchase of Samaria: v. 24
     C. An Evil Reign: v. 25
     D. Prevalent Idolatry: v. 26

 III. Ahab's Evil Reign: I Kings 16:29-33
     A. A Long Reign: v. 29
     B. The Wickedest King: v. 30
     C. Marriage to Jezebel: v. 31
     D. Worship of Baal: v. 32
     E. An Asherah Pole: v. 33

IV. **The End of Ahab's Life:** I Kings 22:37-39
   A. Burial at Samaria: v. 37
   B. Fulfillment of Prophecy: v. 38
   C. Luxurious Palace: v. 39

SUGGESTED
INTRODUCTION
FOR ADULTS

Last week we studied the division of the nation of Israel into two kingdoms following Solomon's death. The southern kingdom of Judah remained loyal to the family of David, so that his descendants reigned over Judah until that kingdom came to an end with the destruction of Jerusalem by the Babylonians in 586 B.C. There was only one dynasty in Judah.

The case was very different in the northern kingdom of Israel. There several dynasties reigned. Jeroboam was the first king and reigned twenty-two years, about 922-901 B.C. (I Kings 14:20). To keep his people from going to Jerusalem to worship, and so perhaps reverting to the Davidic dynasty, he set up golden calves at Bethel and Dan (12:26-33). Because of this, the northern kingdom of Israel went into idolatry from the start.

Jeroboam's son Nadab succeeded him, but his evil reign lasted for only two years (15:25-26). Baasha killed Nadab and all of Jeroboam's family (v. 29). But he also led Israel more deeply into sin during his reign of twenty-four years (vv. 33-34). In turn, Baasha's son Elah, after a two-year reign, was assassinated by Zimri, who proceeded to kill all of Baasha's family (16:8-13). The kingdom of Israel had a very bad beginning!

SUGGESTED
INTRODUCTION
FOR YOUTH

The lesson today deals with "Bad Times for God's People." That is what we certainly find in the reigns of Omri and Ahab in the northern kingdom of Israel. The people were worshiping idols and living sinful lives. It was a bad time for those who were supposed to be God's people.

The situation is not so bad, of course, in the United States today. But the prevalence of immorality and false religion does make it difficult for Christian young people. However, God is on our side!

CONCEPTS FOR
CHILDREN

1. We live in days of confusion and strife.
2. We need to keep close to God.
3. We should not follow bad examples.
4. Poor leadership in politics brings division.

THE LESSON COMMENTARY

I. RIVALS FOR THE THRONE: I Kings 16:21-22

A. Two Factions: v. 21

"Then the people of Israel were split into two factions; half supported Tibni son of Ginath for king, and the other half supported Omri."

We really know nothing further about Tibni, who is mentioned only here (vv. 21-22). Omri, however, founded a new dynasty.

B. The Winner: v. 22

"But Omri's followers proved stronger than those of Tibni son of Ginath. So Tibni died and Omri became king."

There is a complicated chronological problem here, but it is thought that this rivalry for the throne lasted about four years. Finally Omri won.

We know little of Omri's background. In verse 16 we are told that he was "the commander of the army," evidently a popular man. The soldiers proclaimed him king (v. 16), but it took him some time to become the sole ruler.

II. OMRI'S REIGN:
I Kings 16:23-26

A. Twelve-year Reign: v. 23

"In the thirty-first year of Asa king of Judah, Omri became king of Israel, and he reigned twelve years, six of them in Tirzah."

Throughout much of I Kings and II Kings (originally one book in Hebrew) we have accounts of the reigns of the kings of Judah and Israel. As here, the beginning of the reign of a king is dated according to the reign of the ruler in the other kingdom.

We are informed here that Omri "reigned twelve years" and that he became king of Israel "in the thirty-first year of Asa king of Judah." But in verse 29 we read that Ahab, the son and successor of Omri, became king of Israel "in the thirty-eighth year of Asa king of Judah." That makes only seven years for Omri's reign. But if we assume that the "twelve years" began with the army's proclamation of Omri as king "in the twenty-seventh year of Asa king of Judah" (vv. 15-16), the chronological problem is solved. The "twelve years include the four or five years of Omri's rivalry with Tibni.

Verse 23 indicates that for the first six years of his reign Omri's capital was "Tirzah," where the upstart Zimri (vv. 9-10) had reigned for "seven days" (v. 15)! The name "Tirzah" means

"pleasantness" or "a delight." The site of the city has been identified with the ruins at Tell el-Fara, about seven miles northeast of Nablus (ancient Shechem). It was near the Jordan River, and so was not a good central location for the capital of the northern kingdom. Jeroboam had a residence there (14:17), and it became the capital of the kingdom of Israel from the days of Baasha, Elah, and Zimri (16:8, 9, 15), so it was natural that Omri started his reign there. Unfortunately, Zimri had burned the royal palace when Omri laid siege to Tirzah (16:17-18).

B. Purchase of Samaria: v. 24

"He bought the hill of Samaria from Shemer for two talents of silver and built a city on the hill, calling it Samaria, after Shemer, the name of the former owner of the hill."

This was a very smart move on Omri's part. As we have just noted, Tirzah was off to one side. Omri wisely chose a central location and built his capital city there.

Samaria was not only centrally located, but it was on a high hill. As one stands today at the site of ancient Samaria, he is thrilled with the vast panoramic view of the countryside. One can look westward to the Mediterranean Sea, northward to the hill Megiddo, eastward to the Jordan Valley, and southward toward Jerusalem. The traveler today feels that Omri's choice was a stroke of genius. From his palace windows the king could see the beautiful Mediterranean, about twenty-five miles away. The city was on an oval hilltop about three-hundred-feet high. It is mentioned over one hundred times in the Old Testament.

One of the many things that have impressed me as I have stood on this magnificent hilltop is the steep slope on most sides. No enemy army could rush this hill without superhuman effort. Omri chose an almost impregnable site for his capital city. Several times the Syrians tried to capture the city, but without success. It took the Assyrians three years to finally succeed in overthrowing it in 722 B.C. (II Kings 17:5).

Shortly before the birth of Christ, Herod the Great recognized the strategic importance of the site. He rebuilt the city and renamed it Sebaste, in honor of Augustus Caesar. (Sebaste is Greek for Augustus.) The present Arab village at the east end of the site is called Sebastiyeh. The impressive ruins of Herod's magnificent building can still be seen on this memorable hilltop.

Way back then, Omri paid "two talents of silver" for the hill. This would be about one hundred pounds of silver, a sum of considerable value.

C. An Evil Reign: v. 25

"But Omri did evil in the eyes of the LORD and sinned more than all those before him."

While some of the kings of Judah were godly men, almost all the kings of Israel were wicked. Omri was no exception. We are told that he "sinned more than all those before him." In Micah 6:16 the Lord says to Israel, "You have observed the statutes of Omri." This is generally thought to mean that Omri enforced the worship of the golden calves at Bethel and Dan more than his predecessors had done. These calves were claimed to represent the gods who delivered the Israelites from Egyptian slavery (12:28), but they were a form of idolatry.

D. Prevalent Idolatry: v. 26

It is said of Omri: "He walked in all the ways of Jeroboam son of Nebat and in his sin, which he had caused Israel to commit, so that they provoked the LORD, the God of Israel, to anger by their worthless idols."

The northern kingdom of Israel started off on the wrong track under its first king, Jeroboam, and it continued on that trail through most of its history. This kingdom included by far the larger part of the Israelites—ten tribes in all. With Judah in the south was only the little tribe of Benjamin. So the vast majority of God's chosen people, by His covenant with Abraham, were living in open sin and idolatry.

The literal Hebrew of "worthless idols" (NIV) is "vanities" (KJV), but even the highly literalistic New American Standard Bible has "idols." All scholars are pretty well agreed that this is the true meaning.

III. AHAB'S EVIL REIGN: I Kings 16:29-33

A. A Long Reign: v. 29

"In the thirty-eighth year of Asa king of Judah, Ahab son of Omri became king of Israel, and he reigned in Samaria over Israel twenty-two years."

The name *Ahab* means "brother of father." It seems that Ahab almost acted as the brother of his father Omri, joining him in his sin and idolatry, as well as in his great accomplishments. Both were very capable men. Secular documents of that period tell of the exploits of Omri, and Ahab was a well-known figure of his time.

B. The Wickedest King: v. 30

"Ahab son of Omri did more evil in the eyes of the LORD than any of those before him."

Both Omri and Ahab have the same divine condemnation: they were more wicked than their predecessors. Sin has a way of reproducing itself in abundance. "Like father, like son" has a way of becoming "Like father, like son—only much worse!" Omri set the wrong example, and Ahab followed it zealously.

C. Marriage to Jezebel: v. 31

Of Ahab it is said: "He not only considered it trivial to commit the sins of Jeroboam son of Nebat, but he also married Jezebel daughter of Ethbaal king of the Sidonians, and began to serve Baal and worship him."

Through Moses, God had specifically commanded the Israelites not to marry pagans (Deut. 7:3-4). Yet Ahab deliberately disobeyed and reaped consequences that Moses said would follow.

Ahab could hardly have made a worse marriage. His father-in-law, "Ethbaal king of the Sidonians," is said to have gone so far as to act as priest of Baal.

The name *Baal* means "owner, master, lord." It was sometimes used as a personal name (I Chron. 5:5; 8:30; 9:36). But it usually refers to the Canaanite deity, the great nature-god. He was supposed to control rainfall and fertility. He is sometimes described as "the rider of the clouds." In the sculptures Baal is pictured with a helmet decorated with the horns of a bull, the symbol of strength and fertility.

When Ahab married Jezebel, he "began to serve Baal and worship him." His bad marriage proved to be the cause of his ultimate downfall. Jezebel was a domineering wife, as we see in the chapters that follow. She had far more than a passive influence on her husband. So wicked was she that the worst thing we can now say about a woman is that she is a "Jezebel." Her name has become a synonym for the lowest and vilest in life.

D. Worship of Baal: v. 32

Ahab went so far as to "set up an altar for Baal in the temple of Baal that he built in Samaria." Ahab not only worshiped Baal himself but promoted the worship of this god by the masses of the people. Instead of building a temple for Israel's true God, he built a temple for the pagan Baal. He could hardly have stooped lower in leading the Israelites astray. This temple was later destroyed by Jehu (II Kings 10:27).

E. An Asherah Pole: v. 33

"Ahab also made an Asherah pole and did more to provoke the LORD, the God of Israel, to anger than did all the kings of Israel before him."

The King James Version says that Ahab made "a grove." But the Hebrew says "an *Asherah.*" This was an image of Astarte, a female deity, as Baal was the image of a male deity. As might be surmised, the worship of these two images easily led to sexual immorality on the part of the worshipers.

In the Old Testament we frequently find idolatry and immorality going hand in hand. When people depart from the worship of the one true, holy God, they quickly descend into the depths of sin. That was the tragedy of idolatry in Israel and Judah.

IV. THE END OF AHAB'S LIFE: I Kings 22:37-39

A. Burial at Samaria: v. 37

"So the king died and was brought to Samaria, and they buried him there."

In between the two parts of our printed lesson we find the story of Elijah's appearance on the scene. He confronted Ahab with the announcement: "As the LORD, the God of Israel, lives, whom I serve, there will be neither dew nor rain in the next few years except at my word" (17:1). Then the Lord told Elijah to hide in the

---

DISCUSSION QUESTIONS

1. Why did the Israelites go into idolatry?
2. How would you characterize Omri?
3. Why did Ahab marry Jezebel?
4. What kind of training did Ahab probably have as a child?
5. Why did Ahab become so wicked?
6. What idols do modern Americans worship?

Kerith Ravine, east of the Jordan (17:2). This was because Ahab would seek to kill him.

When the brook dried up, the Lord instructed His prophet to go north to Zarephath, near Sidon in Phoenicia. There a widow would supply him with food (17:7-9). Elijah repaid her handsomely by restoring her dead son to life (17:17-23). The grateful mother acknowledged that Elijah was a man of God (17:24).

Chapter eighteen describes one of the dramatic crises in Israel's history, when Elijah challenged the 450 prophets of Baal and the 400 prophets of Asherah (18:16-10).

The historic meeting took place on Mount Carmel. Elijah said to the assembled crowd: "How long will you waver between two opinions? If the LORD is God, follow him; but if Baal is God, follow him" (18:21, our memory verse for today).

The scene is a familiar one to every Bible reader, but it is filled with spiritual significance. We need to recognize the true God and then give our full allegiance to Him. We cannot go on trying to serve two masters. We must make the choice as to who is going to be Lord of our lives.

When the people saw the fire of the Lord fall miraculously on the altar of sacrifice, they cried out: "The LORD, he is God! The LORD—he is God!" (v. 39). People today need to sense God's power and acknowledge Him as the true Lord.

Finally wicked Ahab's life came to a close when he was shot by an arrow in battle (22:34). He was brought back to his capital, Samaria, and buried there.

B. Fulfillment of Prophecy: v. 38

"They washed the chariot at a pool in Samaria (where the prostitutes bathed) and the dogs licked up his blood, as the word of the LORD had declared." (The reference is to 21:19.) The king's blood flowed onto the floor of his chariot after he was shot (v. 35).

C. Luxurious Palace: v. 39

We find a reference in this verse to "the palace he built and inlaid with ivory" (cf. Amos 3:15). This is thought to refer especially to ivory inlay furniture. Archaeologists have found over five hundred ivory plaques or fragments in the ruins of Ahab's palace on top of the hill Samaria. It is an impressive sight.

Ahab was a great builder, but his life finally came to a sad end. So it is with all who disobey God.

CONTEMPORARY APPLICATION

Our memory verse today challenges us with the crucial question: "Which God will you serve?" Today it is not God or Baal, but too often it is God or money.

The fact we need to face is that money can't buy the best things in life. You can pay for lust, but you can't buy love. You can pay for a house, but you can't buy a home. You can pay for false friends, but you can't buy true friendship. You can pay for thrills, but you can't buy happiness.

Oscar Wilde once said: "A cynic is a man who knows the *price* of everything and the *value* of nothing."

Much the same things as above can be said about God *versus* pleasure. Pleasure is for a moment, but God is forever.

REFORM: BY FORCE?

DEVOTIONAL READING	Psalm 37:1-9

ADULTS AND YOUTH

Adult Topic: *Reform: By Force?*

Youth Topic: *Reform: By Force?*

Background Scripture: II Kings 9-10; Hos. 1:4-5

Scripture Lesson: II Kings 10:18-19, 24b-31

Memory Verse: *A wise man is mightier than a strong man, and a man of knowledge than he who has strength.* Prov. 24:5

CHILDREN

Topic: *Living for God*

Background Scripture: II Kings 9-10

Scripture Lesson: II Kings 10:18-19, 23-24, 27-31

Memory Verse: *Jehu was not careful to walk in the law of the Lord the God of Israel with all his heart.* II Kings 10:31

DAILY BIBLE READINGS

July 16 M.: Fomenting a Political Revolution. I Kings 19:14-21

July 17 T.: Condemning the Oppressive Dynasty. I Kings 21:17-24

July 18 W.: Anointing of Jehu in Israel. II Kings 9:1-13

July 19 T.: Assassination of Joram and Ahaziah. II Kings 9:17-29

July 20 F.: Assassination of Jezebel. II Kings 9:30-37

July 21 S.: Extermination of House of Amri. II Kings 10:1-17

July 22 S.: Massacre of Baal Worshipers. II Kings 10:18-31

LESSON AIM | To show the tragic results of wrong motives.

LESSON SETTING

Time: about 842-814 B.C.

Place: northern kingdom of Israel

LESSON OUTLINE

Reform: By Force?

   I. **Jehu Anointed King of Israel:** II Kings 9:1-13

   II. **Jehu Kills Joram and Ahaziah:** II Kings 9:14-29

III. **Jezebel Killed:** II Kings 9:30-37

  IV. **Ahab's Family Killed:** II Kings 10:1-17

   V. **Jehu's Deception:** II Kings 10:18-19
     A. A Deliberate Lie: v. 18
     B. A Sweeping Order: v. 19

VI. The Setting for Slaughter: II Kings 10:20-24

VII. Slaughter of the Prophets of Baal: II Kings 10:25-27
   A. Killed with the Sword: v. 25
   B. Sacred Stone Burned: v. 26
   C. Temple of Baal Destroyed: v. 27

VIII. Half-way Reform: II Kings 10:28-31
   A. Baal Worship Destroyed: v. 28
   B. Idolatry Continued: v. 29
   C. Reward for Obedience: v. 30
   D. Halfhearted Obedience: v. 31

SUGGESTED
INTRODUCTION
FOR ADULTS

The Second Book of Kings begins with Elijah's prediction that Ahaziah, Ahab's son and king of Israel, would die (c. 1). Then we have the stirring account of Elijah being taken up to heaven and Elisha taking his place as God's prophet in Israel (c. 2).

The next few chapters record many miracles performed by Elisha: the supplying of water to the armies fighting against Moab (c. 3), multiplying the widow's oil (4:1-7), bringing the Shunammite's son back to life (4:8-37), restoring bad food (4:38-41), feeding a hundred men (4:42-44), healing Naaman of his leprosy (c. 5), causing a borrowed axhead to float (6:1-7), striking the Arameans with blindness (6:8-23), and lifting the siege of Samaria (6:24-7:20).

Then an unfortunate thing happened: Jehoram, the son of good king Jehoshaphat of Judah, married a daughter of wicked Ahab of Israel (8:16-18). In turn, his son Ahaziah "walked in the ways of the house of Ahab and did evil in the eyes of the LORD" (8:27). Judah was forsaking God, as Israel had. This gives us the background for our lesson today.

SUGGESTED
INTRODUCTION
FOR YOUTH

"Reform: By Force?" No! That is not the best way to undertake reform. It should be done by seeking God's help and employing spiritual means for accomplishing the desired result.

Jehu allowed selfish motives to govern his actions. He wanted to rule with absolute authority. He followed God part way, but not completely (10:31). We must obey God fully.

CONCEPTS FOR
CHILDREN

1. We should be careful not to do the right thing for wrong reasons.
2. We should see the wrong in ourselves, as well as in other people.
3. Children need to take their stand for what is right.
4. The most important thing is to live for God.

THE LESSON COMMENTARY

I. JEHU ANOINTED KING OF ISRAEL: II Kings 9:1-13

Elisha summoned one of the young prophets and gave him careful instructions. "Tuck your cloak into your belt"—so he could run fast—"take this flask of oil with you and go to Ramoth Gilead" (v. 1). There he was to find Jehu and take him into an inner room (v. 2). Then he was to pour the oil on Jehu's head and give him the divine message: "I anoint you king over Israel" (v. 3).

The young man did as he was told. He went to Ramoth Gilead (v. 4), "found the army officers sitting together" (v. 5), and anointed Jehu privately (v. 6). He also gave Jehu the divine commission:

"You are to destroy the house [family] of Ahab your master, and I will avenge the blood of my servants the prophets and the blood of all the LORD's servants shed by Jezebel. The whole house of Ahab will perish. I will cut off from Ahab every last male in Israel—slave or free" (vv. 7-8).

He added the divine prediction: "As for Jezebel, dogs will devour her on the plot of ground at Jezreel, and no one will bury her" (v. 10).

When Jehu reported to his fellow officers, they blew the trumpet and shouted, "Jehu is king!" (v. 13). They were evidently happy to see one of their own number receiving this honor.

II. JEHU KILLS JORAM AND AHAZIAH: II Kings 9:14-29

Israel's reigning king, Joram, had gone to Jezreel to recover from wounds received in battle (vv. 14-15; cf. 8:29). Jehu gave the careful order: ". . . don't let anyone slip out of the city to go and tell the news in Jezreel" (v. 15). "Then he got into his chariot and rode to Jezreel" (v. 16).

There he confronted King Joram, who rode out to meet him, accompanied by Ahaziah king of Judah (v. 21). Jehu shot (with an arrow) and killed Joram (v. 24). He ordered that the king's dead body be thrown on the field of Naboth, whose vineyard Ahab had murderously taken (vv. 25-26; cf. I Kings 21:1-19). Jehu also had Ahaziah king of Judah killed (vv. 27-28).

III. JEZEBEL KILLED: II Kings 9:30-37

Jehu went on into Jezreel. "When Jezebel heard about it, she painted her eyes, arranged her hair and looked out of a window" (v. 30). As Jehu entered the gate, she asked, "Have you come in peace, Zimri, you murderer of your master?" (v. 31).

Jehu looked up at the window and called out, "Who is on my side? Who?" (v. 32). When two or three eunuchs looked down at him, he commanded, "Throw her down!" They complied, "and some of her blood spattered the wall and the horses as they trampled her underfoot" (v. 33).

Jehu ordered that Jezebel be buried because she was a king's daughter (v. 34), but when some men went out to do this, "they found nothing except her skull, her feet and her hands" (v. 35). On hearing this, Jehu recalled the Lord's prophecy through Elijah: "On the plot of ground at Jezreel dogs will devour Jezebel's flesh" (v. 36; cf. I Kings 21:23). Thus ended the life of this wicked woman.

IV. AHAB'S FAMILY KILLED: II Kings 10:1-17

At the capital city, Samaria, there were "seventy sons of the house of Ahab." Jehu wrote letters to the city officials, "to the elders and to the guardians of Ahab's children" (v. 1). He told them to "choose the best and most worthy of your master's sons and set him on his father's throne. Then fight for your master's house" (v. 3).

This "terrified" the recipients, as they recalled how Jehu had killed two kings already (v. 41).

So the palace administrator, the city governor, the elders and the guardians sent this message to Jehu: "We are your servants and we will do anything you say. We will not appoint anyone as king; you do whatever you think best" (v. 5).

In response Jehu wrote: "If you are on my side and will obey me, take the heads of your master's sons and come to me in Jezreel by this time tomorrow" (v. 6). The men complied, and the heads of the seventy royal princes were taken in baskets to Jezreel (v. 7).

Jehu ordered the heads to be put "in two piles at the entrance of the city gate until morning" (v. 8). The next morning he stood before the people and defended his action (vv. 9-10). Then we read the sweeping statement: "So Jehu killed everyone in Jezreel who remained of the house of Ahab, as well as all his chief men, his close friends and his priests, leaving him no survivor" (v. 11).

On Jehu's way to the capital city, Samaria, "he met some relatives of Ahaziah king of Judah" (vv. 12-13). He ordered them all slaughtered—all "forty-two men" (v. 14). There was no justification for this. Jehu went far beyond what he was told to do.

Then we read, "When Jehu came to Samaria, he killed all who were left there of Ahab's family; he destroyed them, according to the word of the LORD spoken to Elijah" (v. 17). This duplicated what he had done in Jezreel. Both actions were in line with what Elijah had predicted (I Kings 21:21) and Elisha had ordered (II Kings 9:7).

V. JEHU'S DECEPTION: II Kings 10:18-19

A. A Deliberate Lie: v. 18

"Then Jehu brought all the people together and said to them, 'Ahab served Baal a little; Jehu will serve him much.'"

There was no excuse for this lie. The methods Jehu used to carry out his reform were immoral. The end does not justify the means.

Evidently the people were unaware of Jehu's deception. In Lange's *Commentary on the Holy Scriptures* we read:

The fact that Jehu was believed, when he said that he would serve Baal far more than Ahab had done, is explained by the consideration that his entire enterprise was regarded as a military revolution, like that of Baasha and Zimri, in which the thing at stake was the supreme power and the throne, not a religious reform and the restoration of the service of Jehovah. No one any longer thought of that as a possibility (II Kings, p. 113).

B. A Sweeping Order: v. 19

"Now summon all the prophets of Baal, all his ministers and all his priests. See that no one is missing, because I am going to hold a great sacrifice for Baal. Anyone who fails to come will no longer live." Then we are told, "But Jehu was acting deceptively in order to destroy the ministers of Baal."

George Rawlinson comments:

"Subtilty" was characteristic of Jehu, who always preferred to gain his ends by cunning rather than in a straightforward way. Idolaters were by the Law liable to death, and Jehu would have had a perfect right to crush the Baal-worship throughout the land, by sending his emissaries everywhere, with orders to slay all whom they found engaged in it. But to draw some thousands of his subjects by false pretences into a trap, and then to kill them in it for doing what he had himself invited them to do, was an act that was wholly unjustifiable.... Jehu's religious reformation did not succeed, and it was conducted in such a way that it did not deserve to succeed (*The Pulpit Commentary,* II Kings, pp. 211-12).

VI. THE SETTING FOR SLAUGHTER: II Kings 10:20-24

Jehu told the people to "call an assembly in honor of Baal," and they complied (v. 20). "Then he sent word throughout Israel, and all the ministers of Baal came; not one stayed away. They crowded into the temple of Baal until it was full from one end to the other" (v. 21). He even had religious robes put on them (v. 22).

Jehu wanted to make sure of two things: first, that all the ministers of Baal would be killed; and second, that no others would lose their lives. So he issued another order: "Look around and see that no servants of the LORD are here with you—only ministers of Baal" (v. 23).

With that done, "they went in to make sacrifices and burnt offerings" (v. 24). Now all the ministers of Baal were inside.

To make doubly sure he got them all, Jehu posted eighty men outside the doors. He warned them: "If one of you lets any of the men I am placing in your hands escape, it will be your life for his life." Everything was now secure.

VII. SLAUGHTER OF THE PROPHETS OF BAAL: II Kings 10:25-27

A. Killed with the Sword: v. 25

As soon as Jehu had finished making the burnt offering, he ordered the guards and officers: "Go in and kill them; let no one escape." So they cut them down with the sword. The guards and officers threw the bodies out and then entered the inner shrine of the temple of Baal.

To quiet any possible fears, Jehu carried his deception right through to the end: He went into the temple and offered burnt offering to Baal. It seemed certain that the Baal worshipers were in the favor of the new king.

But then Jehu issued the order for the wholesale massacre of all the ministers of Baal, who had gathered in the temple in obedience to his orders. In perpetrating this deception, Jehu really acted more immorally than the Baal worshipers themselves. Once more we note that the end does not justify the means.

The guards and officers cut down the worshipers with the sword and threw their bodies outside the temple of Baal. Then they entered the very exclusive "inner shrine," thus desecrating it.

Instead of "inner shrine" the King James Version has "city." The Hebrew word originally meant "fortress." It then came to be used for a "city," because cities were usually fortified with walls. In Lange's *Commentary* we read:

In this place, however, it refers to that part of the entire sacred enclosure, which, in contrast with the outer courts, was firmly surrounded by a wall, the temple strictly speaking, in which was the chief image of Baal (II Kings, p. 114).

Rawlinson comments:

It is to be remembered that the assembled multitude occupied the court or courts of the temple, within which, in a commanding position, was the "house" or "sanctuary"—perhaps reserved for the priests only (*PC*, II Kings, p. 213).

B. Sacred Stone Burned: v. 26

"They brought the sacred stone out of the temple of Baal and burned it."

This act was proper, of course, and in line with the Law. God told the Israelites through Moses: "Break down their idols, smash their sacred stones, cut down their Asherah poles and burn their idols in the fire.... The images of their gods you are to burn in the fire" (Deut.7:5, 25). These strong commands are repeated in Deuteronomy 12:2-3. Idolatry was one of the greatest threats to Israel's religious life, and so it was to be dealt with severely.

In place of "the sacred stone" (NIV), we would prefer here "the *sacred pillars*" (NASB). A stone cannot be "burned." It (or, they) was probably a wooden pillar.

C. Temple of Baal Destroyed: v. 27

"They demolished the sacred stone of Baal and tore down the temple of Baal, and people have used it for a latrine to this day."

On the first clause of this verse Rawlinson comments, "The representation of Baal, the main *stele* of the temple, being of stone or metal, could not be destroyed by fire, and was therefore broken to pieces" (*PC*, II Kings, p. 213).

In a similar view we find this in Lange's *Commentary:*

> It is to be noticed ... that the images were *burned* (ver. 26), so that they must have been of wood, while the chief image was "broken in pieces" . . . , as the *stone* temple-building was. This image was therefore probably of stone, as indeed we might presume that the large image would be of stone and the smaller ones of wood rather than *vice versa* (II Kings, p. 114).

The temple of Baal was torn down and used for a latrine from that time. This showed the people's utter contempt for their former place of worship.

VIII. HALF-WAY REFORM: II Kings 10:28-31

A. Baal Worship Destroyed: v. 28

"So Jehu destroyed Baal worship in Israel." This was a noble accomplishment. But, as we have just seen, it was done in an ignoble way—through deception. We must do God's work in God's way.

Rawlinson comments on this verse:

> The measures taken were effectual; the worship of Baal was put down, and it is not said to have been revived in the kingdom of the ten tribes. Moloch-worship seems to have taken its place (see ch. xvii.17) (*PC*, II Kings, p. 213).

B. Idolatry Continued: v. 29

"However, he did not turn away from the sins of Jeroboam son of Nebat, which he had caused Israel to commit—the worship of the golden calves at Bethel and Dan."

Why Jehu did this is hard to understand. He probably shared the concern of Jeroboam and Omri that the Israelites in the north might gravitate back to the Temple of the Lord in Jerusalem, and finally the nation be reunited under David's descendants. But he should have realized that the worship of the golden calves was a form of the idolatry which the Mosaic Law strongly condemned. Added to this was the well-known story of what happened at Mount Sinai. When Moses stayed a long time on the mountain, receiving the Law, the Israelites became impatient. The result was that they made "an idol cast in the shape of a calf" (Exod. 32:4).

When Moses returned to the camp, he discovered the golden calf and destroyed it (Exod. 32:19-20). He "saw that the people were running wild and that Aaron had let them get out of control and so become a laughingstock to their enemies" (32:25). As a result, three thousand Israelites were put to death for their idolatry (32:28). Jeroboam and Jehu should both have heeded this warning.

DISCUSSION QUESTIONS

1. Why do you think God selected Jehu?
2. What were some good points in Jehu's character?
3. What were some bad points in Jehu's character?
4. Is deliberate deception ever justifiable?
5. How should we try to bring about reform in our nation today?
6. How is the kingdom to be brought in?

C. Reward for Obedience: v. 30

"The LORD said to Jehu, 'Because you have done well in accomplishing what is right in my eyes and have done to the house of Ahab all I had in mind to do, your descendants will sit on the throne of Israel to the fourth generation.'"

Jehu had carried out God's basic command to him. So his dynasty would last for four generations. This was longer than many of the other dynasties in Israel had lasted.

D. Halfhearted Obedience: v. 31

"Yet Jehu was not careful to keep the law of the LORD, the God of Israel, with all his heart. He did not turn away from the sins of Jeroboam, which he had caused Israel to commit."

It is hard to understand this halfway loyalty on the part of Jehu. He had been specifically selected by God to be the king of Israel. The prophet Elisha had negotiated his anointing as king. Why didn't he keep close to Elisha and get his directions from him? We don't know why.

CONTEMPORARY APPLICATION

This lesson presents a real warning to all of us. A person may zealously carry out an assignment given to him by the Lord. He may have great success at first and win considerable recognition for doing great things for God and the kingdom. And yet he may fail to follow the Lord fully and live as God wants him to live.

We should read God's Word carefully and prayerfully. Then we should seek to live every day according to the divine light that God sheds on our pathway. Let's not be halfway Christians!

WAR BETWEEN THE KINGDOMS

DEVOTIONAL READING	Deuteronomy 24:16-22

Adult Topic: *Boasting in Military Might*

Youth Topic: *I Dare You!*

ADULTS AND YOUTH

Background Scripture: II Kings 14

Scripture Lesson: II Kings 14:1-3, 8-14

Memory Verse: *Pride goes before destruction, and a haughty spirit before a fall.* Prov. 16:18

Topic: *Getting Along with One Another*

Background Scripture: II Kings 14

CHILDREN

Scripture Lesson: II Kings 14:8-14

Memory Verse: *Live in harmony with one another . . . if possible, so far as it depends upon you, live peaceably with all.* Rom. 12:16, 18

DAILY BIBLE READINGS

July 23 M.: The Reign of Jehu in Israel. II Kings 10:28-36
July 24 T.: The Reign of Athaliah. II Kings 11:9-30
July 25 W.: The Reign of Jehoash in Judah. II Kings 12:17-21
July 26 T.: The Reign of Jehoahaz in Israel. II Kings 13:1-9
July 27 F.: The Reign of Joash in Israel. II Kings 13:10-25
July 28 S.: Ambition of Amaziah in Judah. II Kings 14:1-7
July 29 S.: Defeat of Amaziah by Israel. II Kings 14:8-14

LESSON AIM	To show the sad consequences of a haughty spirit.

LESSON SETTING

Time: about 800 B.C.

Place: Jerusalem and Beth Shemesh, both in Judah

LESSON OUTLINE

War Between the Kingdoms

   I. **Beginning of Amaziah's Reign:** II Kings 14:1-4
      A. The Date: v. 1
      B. Length of Reign: v. 2
      C. A Good King: v. 3
      D. Partial Obedience: v. 4

  II. **Execution of Murderers:** II Kings 14:5-6

 III. **Arrogance of Amaziah:** II Kings 14:7-8
      A. Defeat of Edomites: v. 7
      B. Challenge to Jehoash: v. 8

344

IV. **Reply of Jehoash:** II Kings 14:9-10
   A. Parable of the Thistle: v. 9
   B. Wise Advice: v. 10

V. **Consequences of Folly:** II Kings 14:11-14
   A. Confrontation: v. 11
   B. Defeat of Judah: v. 12
   C. Destruction in Jerusalem: v. 13
   D. Sacking of Temple and Palace: v. 14

SUGGESTED INTRODUCTION FOR ADULTS

One of the blackest chapters in the history of the kingdom of Judah resulted from a bad marriage of one of its kings. Jehoram "married a daughter of Ahab" (II Kings 8:18), the notoriously wicked king of Israel. The name of this daughter was Athaliah, and she turned out to be much like her mother Jezebel. When her son Ahaziah king of Judah died, "she proceeded to destroy the whole royal family" (II Kings 11:1). But the deceased king's baby son, Joash, was hidden by his aunt Jehosheba with his nurse in a bedroom, and so escaped death (v. 2). "He remained hidden with his nurse at the temple of the LORD for six years, while Athaliah ruled the land" (v. 3).

Then Jehoiada, the high priest and husband of Jehosheba (II Chron. 22:11), staged an inauguration of Joash as king of Judah at the age of seven (II Kings 11:4-21). It is one of the most fascinating stories in Judah's history.

Joash, brought up under such godly influences, proved to be a good king. He repaired the Temple of the Lord (12:1-16). Yet he had a sad ending: "His officials conspired against him and assassinated him" (12:20).

SUGGESTED INTRODUCTION FOR YOUTH

"I Dare You!"—those are dangerous words to say. But that is about what good King Amaziah of Judah said to Jehoash king of Israel, as we find in today's lesson (II Kings 14:8). He had just won a great victory over the Edomites, his sworn enemies (v. 7), and it seems that his heart was filled with pride because of it.

The results were disastrous for Amaziah and for his capital city, Jerusalem, as well as for the Temple of the Lord (vv. 12-14). It never pays to have a haughty spirit. Proverbs 16:18 warns us:

> Pride goes before destruction,
> a haughty spirit before a fall.

CONCEPTS FOR CHILDREN

1. "Getting Along with One Another" is a very important part of life.
2. This applies to relationships between children and between children and parents.
3. We must work at getting along with others all the time.
4. We should ask the Lord to help us.

THE LESSON COMMENTARY

I. BEGINNING OF AMAZIAH'S REIGN: II Kings 14:1-4

A. The Date: v. 1

Throughout the Books of Kings we find the beginning of the reign of a king of Judah or Israel dated in terms of the reign of the king in the other kingdom. At that time, of course, there was no set calendar such as we have today.

So we read here, "In the second year of Jehoash son of Jehoahaz king of Israel, Amaziah son of Joash king of Judah began to reign."

It will be noted that the King James Version and the New American Standard Bible have "Joash" twice. The footnotes in the New International Version for 11:21—14:1 indicate that the original Hebrew oscillates back and forth between "Joash" and "Johoash" for both kings. To help in quickly recognizing the distinction between the two kings, the New International Version has adopted "Joash" regularly for the king of Judah and "Jehoash" for the king of Israel.

In the field of Old Testament chronology there is much difference of opinion among scholars, but the accession of Amaziah to the throne is to be dated at approximately 800 B.C.

B. Length of Reign: v. 2

We are specifically told that Amaziah "reigned in Jerusalem twenty-nine years." This was longer than most of the kings of that period sat on the throne. It is also stated that he was "twenty-five years old when he became king." So he reigned through the prime of his life.

We find the same figures in II Chronicles 25:1. In fact, II Kings 14:2-6 is closely paralleled in II Chronicles 25:1-4.

It is also stated here: "His mother's name was Jehoaddin; she was from

Jerusalem." We know nothing further about her, but from what we are told of Amaziah, we may assume that she was a godly woman and brought up her son to obey God. The King James Version has "Jehoaddan." This is just another one of the many examples of difficulty in the spelling of Old Testament names.

C. A Good King: v. 3

"He did what was right in the eyes of the LORD, but not as his father David had done. In everything he followed the example of his father Joash."

In keeping with the custom of the times, Amaziah's ancestor David is called his "father." We find this frequently in the Old Testament. Actually, Joash was his real father.

Amaziah was a good king. In general he did what pleased the Lord. But he did not follow God quite so closely as David had done. Things had degenerated a great deal by his day, and so his pattern of life was not all that God intended it should be.

George Rawlinson summarizes the situation well in these words:

Only one King of Judah hitherto, namely Asa, had obtained the praise that he "did that which was right in the eyes of the Lord, *as did David his father*" (1 Kings xv.11). All the others had fallen short more or less; and Amaziah fell short in many respects. He was wanting in "a perfect heart" (2 Chron. xxv.2), that is, a fixed intention to do God's will; he was proud and boastful (v. 10); he gave way to idolatry in his later years (2 Chron. xxv. 14), and he despised the reproof of the prophet who was sent to rebuke his sin (2 Chron. xxv. 16). Though placed among the "good kings" by the authors of both Kings and Chronicles, it is, as it were, under protest, with a distinct intimation that, although better than most of his predecessors, he did not reach a high standard (*The Pulpit Commentary*, II Kings, p. 279).

We are further told that Amaziah "followed the example of his father Joash." Rawlinson points out the following parallels between father and son:

> Both kings began better than they ended. Both were zealous for Jehovah at first, but turned to idolatry at last. Both opposed themselves to prophets, and treated their rebukes with scorn. Both roused conspiracy against them by their misconduct, and were murdered by the malcontents (*PC*, II Kings, p. 279).

D. Partial Obedience: v. 4

"The high places, however, were not removed; the people continued to offer sacrifices and burn incense there."

No king until Hezekiah did away with the high places. We are told that he "removed the high places" (18:4). Even good King Asa failed at this point (I Kings 15:14). Rawlinson says of these high places:

> They were remnants of an old ancestral worship which went back to the time of the judges, and which had been connived at by judges and kings and prophets. Local feeling was everywhere in their favour, since they provided for local needs, and enabled men to dispense with the long and tedious journey to the distant Jerusalem (*PC*, II Kings, p. 279).

Points of high ground were chosen as local places of worship because they gave the people a religious feeling of elevation. Also the burning sacrifices and incense could be seen from a distance.

II. EXECUTION OF MURDERERS: II Kings 14:5-6

After the kingdom was firmly in his grasp, he executed the officials who had murdered his father the king. Yet he did not put the sons of the assassins to death, in accordance with what is written in the Book of the Law of Moses where the LORD commanded: "Fathers shall not be put to death for their children, nor children put to death for their fathers; each is to die for his own sins." (The quotation is from Deut. 24:16.)

Joash had been murdered in Jerusalem by conspirators (12:20), two of whom are named (12:21). Probably these men opposed Amaziah at first. But finally he got a firm grasp on the throne.

It was common in those days to execute the sons of traitors along with their fathers. We even find the practice being carried out among the Israelites. The children of Achan were put to death with their father (Josh. 7:24-25). Later, Naboth's sons suffered the same fate as their father (II Kings 9:24-26) when Jezebel engineered their execution. But Amaziah obeyed the divine command given in Deuteronomy.

III. ARROGANCE OF AMAZIAH: II Kings 14:7-8

A. Defeat of Edomites: v. 7

"He was the one who defeated ten thousand Edomites in the Valley of Salt and captured Sela in battle, calling it Joktheel, the name it has to this day."

The "Valley of Salt" was probably at the south end of the Dead Sea. "Sela," which means "rock," was the capital of Edom (descendants of Esau). It is identified with modern "Petra," the Greek word for "rocks." It was a magnificent mountain fortress, almost inaccessible to enemy armies.

This campaign is described much more fully in II Chronicles 25. There we read that he "mustered those twenty years old or more and found that there were three hundred thousand men ready for military service" (v. 5). But then he did a very unwise thing: "He also hired a hundred thousand fighting men from Israel for a hundred talents of silver" (v. 6). On orders from "a man of God" (v. 7), Amaziah dismissed the soldiers from Israel, though not without protest.

Then we read a shocking thing: "When Amaziah returned from slaughtering the Edomites, he brought back the gods of the people of Seir. He set them up as his own gods, bowed down to them and burned sacrifices to them: (v. 14). Naturally, the Lord was highly displeased and sent a prophet to reprove him (v. 15). Amazingly, Amaziah threatened to kill the prophet (v. 16). Instead, the prophet warned the king that he would be destroyed. Amaziah had become arrogant and defiant.

B. Challenge to Jehoash: v. 8

"Then Amaziah sent messengers to Jehoash son of Jehoahaz, the son of Jehu, king of Israel, with the challenge: 'Come, meet me face to face.'"

The account in Chronicles suggests, as Kings does not, a reason for Amaziah's challenge to the king of Israel. When Amaziah dismissed his mercenaries from Israel, they "were furious with Judah and left for home in a great rage" (II Chron. 25:10). While Amaziah was defeating the Edomites, these disgruntled troops from Israel "raided Judean towns from Samaria to Beth Horon. They killed three thousand people and carried off great quantities of plunder" (v. 13).

Nevertheless, the close sequence of events here in II Kings (vv. 7-8) does suggest that the main cause of the ridiculous challenge was Amaziah's pride and self-confidence after defeating the Edomites.

IV. REPLY OF JEHOASH: II Kings 14:9-10

A. Parable of the Thistle: v. 9

But Jehoash king of Israel replied to Amaziah king of Judah: "A thistle in Lebanon sent a message to a cedar in Lebanon, 'Give your daughter to my son in marriage.' Then a wild beast in Lebanon came along and trampled the thistle underfoot."

This was a very clever parable. The thistle was about the lowliest little plant

on the ground. The cedars of Lebanon were famous for their towering height, as we saw in a previous lesson. For the lowly thistle to ask that the magnificent cedar, "Give your daughter to my son in marriage," was the height of insolence. Rawlinson notes the prevailing rule in the world of that day: "To ask a man's daughter in marriage for one's self or for one's son was to claim to be his equal" (*PC*, II Kings, p. 281).

Amaziah should not have forgotten that he was speaking to the king of a nation much larger than his own. His challenge sounded "cocky," to say the least.

B. Wise Advice: v. 10

"You have indeed defeated Edom and now you are arrogant. Glory in your victory, but stay at home! Why ask for trouble and cause your own downfall and that of Judah also?"

This was a well-deserved rebuke. Jehoash had recently three times defeated the powerful king of Aram (13:25). He knew that he could muster several times as many soldiers for battle as Amaziah could. There was every reason for him to know that he could defeat the armies of Judah. Why then should Amaziah be so foolish as to challenge him to battle?

Throughout both the Old and New Testaments, we find that pride is shown to be the most common besetting sin of humanity. As we noted in the Introduction for Youth, the wise man observed long ago in Proverbs (16:18):

Pride goes before destruction
    a haughty spirit before a fall.

V. CONSEQUENCES OF FOLLY: II Kings 14:11-14

A. Confrontation: v. 11

"Amaziah, however, would not listen, so Jehoash king of Israel attacked. He and Amaziah king of Judah faced each other at Beth Shemesh in Judah."

Amaziah had asked for it and he got it! The confrontation he had demanded quickly took place. He is a good example of a person speaking first and thinking afterwards.

"Beth Shemesh" was assigned to Judah by Joshua (Josh. 19:38). The name means "house of the sun." Archaeologists have identified it with the site now called "Ain Shems," which means "the Well of the Sun." It was on the northern boundary of the territory of Judah. The modern site is about due west of Jerusalem, on the road from Hebron to Jaffa.

Jehoash cleverly marched his troops around through the Philistine area, so as to attack Judah in her back, as it were. It was a wise procedure and it paid off.

B. Defeat of Judah: v. 12

"Judah was routed by Israel, and every man fled to his home."

Picking a quarrel with someone else, especially a stronger person, is never a sign of good judgment. It is hard to understand why Amaziah should have done such a stupid thing.

As often happens, it was not only the proud and provocative king who suffered; it was his subjects as well. When we do unwise things, we often hurt many others besides ourselves.

C. Destruction in Jerusalem: v. 13

Jehoash king of Israel captured Amaziah king of Judah, the son of Joash, the son of Ahaziah, at Beth Shemesh. Then Jehoash went to Jerusalem and broke down the wall of Jerusalem from the Ephraim Gate to the Corner Gate—a section about six hundred feet long.

Josephus, the Jewish historian of the first century, says that Amaziah was deserted by his troops, who fled from the field, leaving him unprotected. It was a tragic hour for the king of Judah.

Josephus also says that Jehoash threatened to kill Amaziah if the gates of Jerusalem were not opened to him,

and that Amaziah arranged the surrender of the city. It was a very humiliating moment in Jerusalem's history.

The "Ephraim Gate" was the main gate in the north wall of Jerusalem, through which travelers would head toward the territory of the tribe of Ephraim. Since one had to go through Benjamin's territory to get to that of Ephraim, it was sometimes called "the Benjamin Gate" (Jer. 37:13; Zech. 14:10).

It is generally thought that the "Corner Gate" was at the northwest corner of the city wall. However, this is uncertain. It appears that there were at least thirteeen gates in the wall around Jerusalem at this time (Neh. 3:1-31; 12:31-39; Zech. 14:10). So "six hundred feet" between these two gates fits the picture very well.

The reason Jehoash broke down this section of the wall was evidently so that the city would be left defenseless. This was the price that Amaziah paid for his senseless act of arrogance.

D. Sacking of Temple and Palace: v. 14

"He took all the gold and silver and all the articles found in the temple of the LORD and in the treasuries of the royal palace. He also took hostages and returned to Samaria."

Some fifteen or twenty years before this, King Joash of Judah had taken "all the gold found in the treasuries of the temple of the LORD and of the royal

---

DISCUSSION QUESTIONS

1. How can we avoid "going bad," as Amaziah did?
2. What do you think caused Amaziah to go wrong?
3. Why is it important that we obey God completely?
4. How can we avoid pride?
5. What happens when we refuse to listen to reason? (II Kings 14:11)
6. What other lessons do you learn from Amaziah's life?

palace" and given them to Hazael to buy him off from capturing Jerusalem (12:18). So Jehoash would not have gained so much as he may have hoped for. But we can certainly surmise that Amaziah would not have challenged Jehoash if he had known what would be the consequences to himself and his nation.

The end of this man's life was also a sad one: "They conspired against him in Jerusalem, and he fled to Lachish, but they sent men after him to Lachish and killed him there: (v. 19). This conspiracy and execution may well have been caused by Amaziah's provoking Jehoash to battle.

CONTEMPORARY APPLICATION

Selfish pride always brings sad consequences. Amaziah made a good beginning in his reign as king, but his life ended in tragedy.

The consequences of self-will are always disastrous. The only safe way to live is to walk daily in humble, loving obedience to God and His Word. It is the big "I" that gets in the way and

brings ruin to our lives and to the lives of others involved. Someone has well said that we should be concerned to promote not "the Big I" but "the Great I Am!" That is our best hope.

When God is at the center of our ambitions, desires, and purposes in life, we are bound to be a blessing. When self is at the center, we are a curse.

LAST DAYS OF A KINGDOM

DEVOTIONAL READING	II Kings 17:34-41

Adult Topic: *Refusing to Face the Consequences*

Youth Topic: *Facing the Consequences*

ADULTS AND YOUTH

Background Scripture: II Kings 16-17

Scripture Lesson: II Kings 17:5-9a, 11b-15a, 17-18

Memory Verse: *The Lord was very angry with Israel, and removed them out of his sight; none was left but the tribe of Judah only.* II Kings 17:18

CHILDREN

Topic: *Sin Brings Unhappiness*

Memory Verse: *Depart from evil and do good; so shall you abide forever.* Ps. 37:27

DAILY BIBLE READINGS

July 30 M.: The Reign of Shallum in Israel. II Kings 15:13-22
July 31 T.: The Reign of Pekahiah in Israel. II Kings 15:23-26
Aug. 1 W.: The Reign of Pekah in Israel. II Kings 15:27-31
Aug. 2 T.: The Reign of Jotham in Judah. II Kings 15:32-38
Aug. 3 F.: The Reign of Ahaz in Judah. II Kings 16:5-20
Aug. 4 S.: The Reign of Hoshea in Israel. II Kings 17:1-6
Aug. 5 S.: The End of the Northern Kingdom. II Kings 17:7-18

LESSON AIM — To show that sin brings tragedy.

LESSON SETTING

Time: about 722 B.C.

Place: Samaria

Last Days of a Kingdom

I. **The Last King of Israel:** II Kings 17:1-2

II. **The End of a Kingdom:** II Kings 17:3-6
A. The King of Assyria: v. 3
B. Hoshea Imprisoned: v. 4
C. Siege of Samaria: v. 5
D. Deportation of Israelites: v. 6

LESSON OUTLINE

III. **Reason for the Captivity:** II Kings 17:7-13
A. Sin Against the Lord: v. 7a
B. Idolatry and Pagan Practices: vv. 7b-8
C. High Places: v. 9
D. False Worship: v. 10
E. Wicked Things: v. 11
F. Worship of Idols: v. 12
G. Warnings of Prophets: v. 13

IV. **Rejection of God's Law:** II Kings 17:14-15
  A. Refusal to Listen: v. 14
  B. Rejection of God's Covenant: v. 15

V. **Gross Idolatry:** II Kings 17:17-18
  A. Molech Worship: v. 17
  B. Resultant Captivity: v. 18

SUGGESTED INTRODUCTION FOR ADULTS

Last week we studied the fourteenth chapter of II Kings. The fifteenth chapter describes the reigns of two kings of Judah and five kings of Israel.

The Background Scripture for today's lesson includes chapter 16. It is taken up entirely with the reign of Ahaz king of Judah.

Right away we are told of him, "Unlike David his father, he did not do what was right in the eyes of the LORD his God" (v. 2). The account goes on to say, "He walked in the ways of the kings of Israel and even sacrificed his son in the fire, following the detestable ways of the nations the LORD had driven out before the Israelites" (v. 3). Judah had become almost as bad as Israel!

Once more the Temple was sacked (v. 8). Ahaz used the silver and gold to hire the king of Assyria to defend Judah from attacks by Aram (Syria) and Israel (v. 7).

The depth of depravity displayed by Ahaz is shown in his copying a pagan altar in Damascus, having one like it constructed in Jerusalem, and then worshiping at it (vv. 10-13). It is sad that Uriah the high priest complied with all this, instead of protesting against it.

SUGGESTED INTRODUCTION FOR YOUTH

We have a very important topic today: "Facing the Consequences." It is something that every young person should think seriously about. Too often we thoughtlessly do things, neglecting to consider carefully what the consequences might be. This can lead to tragedy.

There is a very real sense in which everything that we do has consequences. Are those consequences what we want to live with? If not, we had better not do the things that produce those consequences! This goes not only for alcohol, drugs, and immorality, but for the attitudes we take and the words we say, as well as all our actions.

CONCEPTS FOR CHILDREN

1. "Sin Brings Unhappiness."
2. Sin is disobedience to God's Word.
3. Sin always carries some kind of punishment.
4. As children we can build a good foundation for life.

THE LESSON COMMENTARY

I. **THE LAST KING OF ISRAEL:** II Kings 17:1-2

In the twelfth year of Ahaz king of Judah, Hoshea son of Elah became king of Israel in Samaria, and he reigned nine years. He did evil in the eyes of the LORD, but not like the kings of Israel who preceded him.

This is not the first time that we are told about this last king of Israel.

During the reign of Pekah there was a partial deportation of people from the northern kingdom of Israel to Assyria (15:29). The next statement in the Scripture is this: "Then Hoshea son of Elah conspired against Pekah son of Remaliah. He attacked and assassinated him, and then succeeded him as king" (15:30). This was not a very propitious beginning. Hoshea began his reign as a murderer of the previous king. In other words, he committed murder in order to get the throne. It is no wonder that his reign ended with the demise of his kingdom.

II. THE END OF A KINGDOM: II Kings 17:3-6

A. The King of Assyria: v. 3

"Shalmaneser king of Assyria came up to attack Hoshea, who had been Shalmaneser's vassal and had paid him tribute."

The previous king of Assyria, Tiglath-Pileser III, says in one of his annals that he "placed Hosea as king over them" [the Israelites]. Hoshea paid heavy tribute to him. In 727 B.C. Tiglath-Pileser died and Shalmaneser V succeeded him. Apparently Hoshea considered this a good time to withhold tribute. This caused Shalmaneser to come against Israel in 724 B.C.

B. Hoshea Imprisoned: v. 4

But the king of Assyria discovered that Hoshea was a traitor, for he had sent envoys to So king of Egypt, and he no longer paid tribute to the king of Assyria, as he had done year by year. Therefore Shalmaneser seized him and put him in prison.

The two great enemy empires of that day were Assyria (north of Palestine) and Egypt (south of Palestine). When Shalmaneser learned that Hoshea had sent envoys to Egypt to secure its help against Assyrian domination, it doubtless made him very angry, and he put the king of Israel in prison. He was also punishing Hoshea for failing to pay his annual tribute to Assyria, as an acknowledgment of Assyria's sovereignty over Israel. So there was a twofold reason for the imprisonment.

C. Siege of Samaria: v. 5

"The king of Assyria invaded the entire land, marched against Samaria and laid siege to it for three years."

In another lesson we noted that Samaria, the capital of Israel, had been built on a high hill, with steep slopes and strong walls. That is why it took Shalmaneser three years to capture it.

D. Deportation of Israelites: v. 6

"In the ninth year of Hoshea, the king of Assyria captured Samaria and deported the Israelites to Assyria. He settled them in Halah, in Gozan on the Habor River and in the towns of the Medes."

We have already noted that there was a previous, partial deportation of Israelites to Assyria, when Tiglath-Pileser captured the northern part of the kingdom (15:29). But now Shalmaneser captured the capital city, Samaria, and "deported the Israelites to Assyria." He settled them in various places, including "the towns of the Medes." This would be the eastern part of Mesopotamia.

In verse 24 we are told, "The king of Assyria brought people from Babylon, Cuthah, Avva, Hamath and Sepharvaim and settled them in the towns of Samaria to replace the Israelites." This was an exceedingly cruel procedure. It was the policy of the Assyrians to mix up populations in all the areas they conquered so as to forestall any effective rebellion. But it meant broken ties of family and friends, and worked a real hardship. The later empires of Babylon and Persia did not have such a harsh policy. The Assyrians seem to have been among the cruelest conquerors of ancient times.

The Assyrian capture of Samaria,

which marked the end of the kingdom of Israel, is usually dated 722 B.C. Sargon, king of Assyria, claims in his annals that he took Samaria at that time. If so, Shalmaneser must have died during the three-year siege of that city and Sargon took over as Assyrian king. Both the accounts here and in 18:9-12 state that Shalmaneser began the siege of Samaria but do not specifically say that he was the one who took it. Unfortunately, the annals of Shalmaneser have been so mutilated that they shed no light on this problem.

III. REASON
FOR THE CAPTIVITY:
II Kings 17:7-13

A. Sin Against the Lord: v. 7a

"All this took place because the Israelites had sinned against the LORD their God, who had brought them up out of Egypt from under the power of Pharaoh king of Egypt."

One of the worst sins that the human heart can be guilty of is the sin of ingratitude. The Japanese have traditionally emphasized this, and Americans should certainly face up to this truth.

God had graciously rescued the Israelites from Egyptian slavery, redeemed them at the Red Sea, given them His covenant of Law at Mount Sinai, led them safely through the desert, and given them the land of Canaan as their national home. How had they shown their gratitude? They had grumbled against Him ten times in the desert, disobeyed him frequently during the period of the judges, turned away to pagan gods over and over again, and now they had gone to the depths of idolatry.

B. Idolatry and Pagan Practices: vv. 7b-8

"They worshiped other gods and followed the practices of the nations the LORD had driven out before them, as well as the practices which the kings of Israel had introduced."

George Rawlinson gives the following explanation of this sentence:

> The sins and idolatries of Israel had a double origin. The great majority were derived from the heathen nations with whom they were brought into contact, and were adopted voluntarily by the people themselves. Of this kind were the worship at "high places" (ver. 9), the "images" and "groves" (ver. 10), the causing of their children to "pass through the fire" (ver. 17), the employment of divination and enchantments (ver. 17), and perhaps the "worship of the host of heaven" (ver. 16). A certain number, however, came in from a different source, being imposed upon the people by their kings. To this class belong the desertion of the temple-worship, enforced by Jeroboam (ver. 21), the setting up of the calves at Dan and Bethel (ver.16) by the same, and the Baal and Astarte worship (ver. 16), introduced by Ahab. This last and worst idolatry was not established without a good deal of persecution, as we learn from 1 Kings xviii.4 (*The Pulpit Commentary*, II Kings, p. 332).

One wonders how the Israelites could depart so far from the faith and obedience of their fathers and founders: Abraham, Isaac, Jacob, Moses, and Joshua. It is indeed a sad commentary on the sinful nature of humanity.

C. High Places: v. 9

"The Israelites secretly did things against the LORD their God that were not right. From watchtower to fortified city they built themselves high places in all their towns."

In our previous lesson we had a reference to these "high places" (14:4). Now we are told that the worship there was carried on somewhat "secretly," as if the idolaters did not want God to see what they were doing. What they seemed to forget was that there is no place where we can hide from God. He sees everything we do and hears everything we say—and, yes, knows everything we think!

The basic meaning of the Hebrew word for "high place" (*bamah*) is "back" or "ridge." So it was usually an elevated place. In the Old Testament the word has the specialized meaning of a place of worship, usually on a hill or mountain and used for pagan rites. C. E. DeVries notes that

the selection of an elevated spot seems psychological, for this location put the worshiper above his immediate environment with its mundane associations and placed him nearer the skies, where the ultimate object of worship was believed to reside (*The Zondervan Pictorial Encyclopedia of the Bible*, 3:155).

The Canaanites had worshiped at "high places" before the Israelites conquered their land. But God had commanded His people through Moses to "demolish all their high places" (Num. 33:52). This they failed to do.

We are told that the Israelites built these high places "from watchtower to fortified city." As Rawlinson notes, this means "from the smallest and most solitary place of human abode to the largest and most populous" (*PC*, II Kings, p. 333). We find the same expression in 18:8. The watchtowers were small wooden frame towers on which a watchman would guard the ripened crops of grapes or other fruits. These towers would be located out in the fields and vineyards.

D. False Worship: v. 10

"They set up sacred stones and Asherah poles on every high hill and under every spreading tree."

The King James Version translation "groves" (here and in thirty-eight other places in the Old Testament) is incorrect. One does not set up a "grove" under every tree! The Hebrew for "groves" is *Asherim* (NASB), that is "Asherah poles" (NIV). These were made of wood (Judg. 6:26) and were to be burned (Deut. 12:3; II Kings 23:6, 15). They were "wooden symbols of a female deity" (NASB, marginal note), sometimes referred to in extrabiblical

sources as Asherah, from whom Baal was descended.

Concerning the "sacred stones" Rawlinson says:

The *matsevoth* were stone pillars, anciently connected with the worship of Baal, but in Judah perhaps used in a debased and debasing worship of Jehovah with self-invented rites, instead of those which had the express sanction of God, being commanded in the Law (*PC*, II Kings, p. 333).

E. Wicked Things: v. 11

"At every high place they burned incense, as the nations whom the LORD had driven out before them had done. They did wicked things that provoked the LORD to anger."

Burning incense in high places is referred to frequently as one of the most serious sins of the Israelites (see I Kings 3:3; 22:43; II Kings 12:3; 14:4; 15:4, 35; 16:4). Incense was a symbol of prayer. David prayed (Ps. 141:2):

"May my prayer be set before you
    like incense;
may the lifting up of my hands
    be like the evening
    sacrifice."

At that time incense was to be burnt only on the golden altar of incense in the Holy Place in the Temple at Jerusalem. Rawlinson comments:

The offering of incense to their gods by the Canaanitish nations had not been previously mentioned; but the use of incense in religious worship was so widely spread in the ancient world, that their employment of it might have been assumed as almost certain. The Egyptians used incense largely in the worship of Ammon.... The Babylonians burned a thousand talents' weight of it every year at the great festival of Bel-Merodach.... The Greeks and Romans offered it with every sacrifice (*PC*, II Kings, p. 333).

The "wicked things" the Israelites did are enumerated at length in verses 15-17. We shall look at them there.

F. Worship of Idols: v. 12

"They worshiped idols, though the LORD had said, 'You shall not do this.'"

The reference is to the second of the Ten Commandments (Exod. 20:4-6) where all making and worshiping of idols was strictly forbidden. This injunction is repeated carefully in Deuteronomy 4:16-18. It is difficult to understand the Israelitish obsession with idolatry, as well as the almost universal practice of it among the pagan nations. It doubtless reflects the need that most people have for something tangible that they can see and feel. It is very difficult to get people to be spiritual-minded. "God is spirit" (John 4:24).

G. Warnings of Prophets: v. 13

The LORD warned Israel and Judah through all his prophets and seers: "Turn from your evil ways. Observe my commands and decrees, in accordance with the entire Law that I commanded your fathers to obey and that I delivered to you through my servants the prophets."

On "seers" and "prophets" Rawlinson says: "A 'seer' is, properly, one who *sees* visions; a 'prophet,' one inspired to pour forth utterances. But the words are used as synonyms" (*PC*, II Kings, p. 333).

In II Chronicles we find a long line of no less than nine prophets mentioned by name who prophesied in Judah, and eight who prophesied in Israel. Besides this there were Hosea and Amos, whose books we have. God had been very faithful to His people, constantly warning them through His chosen messengers.

The burden of their messages is given in the latter part of this verse. They warned the people to turn from their evil ways and obey all God's commandments.

IV. REJECTION OF GOD'S LAW: II Kings 17:14-15

A. Refusal to listen: v. 14

"But they would not listen and were as stiff-necked as their fathers, who did not trust in the LORD their God."

Rawlinson comments, "The obstinate perversity of the Israelites . . . is noted through the entire history" (*PC*, II Kings, p. 334). He cites no less than a dozen passages in the Old Testament, where this theme is sounded. The Israelites were a "stiff-necked" people and they paid a high price for it.

B. Rejection of God's Covenant: v. 15

They rejected his decrees and the covenant he had made with their fathers and the warnings he had given them. They followed worthless idols and themselves became worthless. They imitated the nations around them although the LORD had ordered them, "Do not do as they do," and they did the things the LORD had forbidden them to do.

It is a sad story indeed. One would think that as the Israelites recalled God's redeeming love and miraculous care in days gone by, they would have obeyed Him and served Him. But they were ungrateful.

DISCUSSION QUESTIONS

1. What was the main cause of the captivity?
2. What lesson does this have for us?
3. What advantages do we have that the ancient Israelites did not have?
4. What forms of idolatry exist in America today?
5. What should be our attitude toward sorcery?

V. GROSS IDOLATRY:
   II Kings 17:17-18

A. Molech Worship: v. 17

"They sacrificed their sons and daughters in the fire. They practiced divination and sorcery and sold themselves to do evil in the eyes of the LORD, provoking him to anger."

The first sentence describes one of the most diabolical forms of pagan worship, practiced by the Phoenicians, Ammonites, and Moabites. A child, especially a firstborn son, was placed into the fiery arms of a metal image of Molech—a human figure with a bull's head and outstretched arms. The child was a human sacrifice to the god. What our loving God wants is living sacrifices (Rom. 12:1), not dead ones!

B. Resultant Captivity: v. 18

"So the LORD was very angry with Israel and removed them from his presence. Only the tribe of Judah was left."

This concludes the discussion (vv. 7-17) of why the Assyrian captivity of Israel took place. God's chosen people had forsaken Him and turned to the worship of pagan gods. They had refused to listen to His warnings through the prophets.

CONTEMPORARY APPLICATION

Just as God had rescued the helpless Israelites from Egyptian slavery, so God has provided for our redemption from the slavery of sin. But if we refuse to listen to Him, we will suffer the same fate as those we studied about in our lesson today. We will find ourselves the captives of Satan because we chose to follow the prince of this world rather than the eternal Prince of the universe.

Are we guilty of idolatry, as the ancient Israelites were? The facts are clear that the majority of Americans today are worshiping the false idols of money, pleasure, and so on. We need to heed God's voice and turn to Him with all our hearts in full obedience.

REFORM IN RELIGION

DEVOTIONAL READING	Isaiah 1:18-20
ADULTS AND YOUTH	**Adult Topic:** *Reform in Religion* **Youth Topic:** *Changing Directions* **Background Scripture:** II Kings 18-20 **Scripture Lesson:** II Kings 18:1-8; 19:29-31; 20:20 **Memory Verse:** *The surviving remnant of the house of Judah shall again take root downward, and bear fruit upward.* II Kings 19:30
CHILDREN	**Topic:** *A Righteous King* **Background Scripture:** II Kings 18:1—20:21 **Scripture Lesson:** II Kings 18:1-8 **Memory Verse:** *For he held fast to the Lord; he did not depart from following him.* II Kings 18:6
DAILY BIBLE READINGS	**Aug. 6 M.:** Hezekiah's Reforms. II Kings 18:1-12 **Aug. 7 T.:** Invasion of Sennacherib's Army. II Kings 18:13-18 **Aug. 8 W.:** Call for Unconditional Surrender. II Kings 18:28-39 **Aug. 9 T.:** Isaiah's Counsel. II Kings 19:1-7 **Aug. 10 F.:** Sennacherib's Message to Hezekiah. II Kings 19:10-19 **Aug. 11 S.:** Deliverance of Jerusalem. II Kings 19:32-37 **Aug. 12 S.:** Isaiah's Protest Against Babylonian Negotiations. II Kings 20:12-19
LESSON AIM	To show the blessings that come through one man's obedience to the Lord.
LESSON SETTING	**Time:** about 716-687 B.C. **Place:** Jerusalem

LESSON OUTLINE	**Reform in Religion**
	
	I. **King Hezekiah's Reign:** II Kings 18:1-2
	  A. Beginning of Reign: v. 1
	  B. Length of Reign: v. 2
	
	II. **A Religious Reformer:** II Kings 18:3-4
	  A. Doing What Was Right: v. 3
	  B. Destroying Idolatry: v. 4
	
	III. **A Righteous King:** II Kings 18:5-8
	  A. The Best of Judah's Kings: v. 5
	  B. Full Obedience: v. 6

C. Divine Blessing: v. 7
D. Defeat of Philistines: v. 8

IV. **Sennacherib's Threat to Jerusalem:** II Kings 18:17-37

V. **Isaiah's Reassurance:** II Kings 19:1-7

VI. **The Sign to Hezekiah:** II Kings 19:29-31
A. Good Crops: v. 29
B. Bearing Fruit: v. 30
C. A Remnant of Survivors: v. 31

VII. **Hezekiah's Achievements:** II Kings 20:20

SUGGESTED INTRODUCTION FOR ADULTS

In Unit II we studied "The Two Kingdoms"—Israel in the north and Judah in the south. We noted "Why Division Came," and saw how the northern kingdom of Israel went into idolatry and wickedness. This resulted in the Assyrian captivity of Israel, which brought an end to that kingdom (with the fall of Samaria in 722 B.C.).

Today we begin our study of Unit III: "Judah Only." This reflects the last statement in last week's lesson: "Only the tribe of Judah was left." The ten tribes had gone into captivity, leaving only Judah and its small associated tribe, Benjamin. So we now study the fortunes—and misfortunes—of the kingdom of Judah. Our first lesson of Unit III covers the reign of good King Hezekiah who brought about a "Reform in Religion." He was a model of what a ruler should be. Under his guidance, Judah prospered and was protected.

SUGGESTED INTRODUCTION FOR YOUTH

Our topic today is "Changing Directions." That is what most young people need to do. Never has there been a time in the history of our country when so many young people were going in the wrong direction. A great majority of high school youth admit to having used marijuana. An alarming number are drinking alcoholic beverages. Many are on heroin or other drugs. The figures are alarming! And promiscuous sex is also admitted by a high percentage.

What are we to do? If we are tending in these directions at all, or even neglecting God in our daily lives, we need to change directions at once. God will help us!

CONCEPTS FOR CHILDREN

1. After studying some wicked kings, we now look at "A Righteous King."
2. God wants all of us to live righteous lives.
3. He will help us to do so if we ask Him to.
4. Righteous living makes our lives happy.

THE LESSON COMMENTARY

I. KING HEZEKIAH'S REIGN: II Kings 18:1-2

A. Beginning of Reign: v. 1

"In the third year of Hoshea son of Elah king of Israel, Hezekiah son of Ahaz king of Judah began to reign."

As we found in last week's lesson, Hoshea was the last king of the northern kingdom of Israel. At the end of his nine-year reign the Assyrians "captured Samaria and deported the Israelites to Assyria" (17:6). This was in 722 B.C. So the third year of Hoshea would be about 728 B.C., when Hezekiah began to reign.

B. Length of Reign: v. 2

"He was twenty-five years old when he became king, and he reigned in Jerusalem twenty-nine years. His mother's name was Abijah daughter of Zechariah."

"Twenty-five years old" was rather young for a man to assume the responsibilities of a ruler of God's people. His father Ahaz, the previous king, had lived a very wicked life (c. 16). But Hezekiah turned things around.

"Twenty-nine years" was a long reign for those days. But Hezekiah followed the Lord, and the Lord blessed him. His reign ended about 687 B.C.

That Hezekiah was such a good king was probably due mainly to the fact that he had a godly mother: "Abijah daughter of Zechariah." It has been said, "Behind every great man is a godly mother." We find many examples of this. The leading church father of the fourth century was Augustine, whose mother was Monica. Someone has well observed, "Had Monica not prayed, Augustine had not preached."

The King James Version says that the name of Hezekiah's mother was "Abi," which means "my father." But II Chronicles 29:1 gives her name as "Abijah" ("The LORD is my father"), which makes much better sense. It

would seem that she was called "Abi" for short, perhaps as a sort of nickname. She was the daughter of Zechariah, who may be the same man mentioned in Isaiah 8:2.

II. A RELIGIOUS REFORMER: II Kings 18:3-4

A. Doing What Was Right: v. 3

"He did what was right in the eyes of the LORD, just as his father David had done."

Hezekiah not only met the approval of godly people around him, but he did what was right "in the eyes of the LORD." People only see part of what we do and hear most of what we say, but God sees all we do, hears all we say, and even knows all we think. He reads our motives like an open book. So to do what is right in His eyes includes not only our actions but our attitudes—the inner motivation of our lives. Hezekiah passed the test with flying colors.

The last clause of this verse—"just as his father David had done"—is very significant. George Rawlinson comments:

> Such unqualified praise is only assigned to two other kings of Judah—Asa (1 Kings xv.11) and Josiah (ch. xxii.2). It is curious that all three were the sons of wicked fathers. Hezekiah was probably, at an early age, brought under the influence of Isaiah, who was on familiar terms with his father Ahaz (Isa. vii.3-16), and would be likely to do all that lay in his power to turn Hezekiah from his father's evil ways, and to foster all the germs of good in his character (*The Pulpit Commentary*, II Kings, p. 357).

In a previous lesson we noted that Amaziah king of Judah "did what was right in the eyes of the LORD, but not as his father David had done" (II Kings 14:3). Amaziah failed to remove the high places, but Hezekiah met the high standard of David.

B. Destroying Idolatry: v. 4

He removed the high places, smashed the sacred stones and cut down the Asherah poles. He broke in pieces the bronze snake Moses had made, for up to that time the Israelites had been burning incense to it. (It was called Nehushtan.)

We have already noted, in earlier lessons, that the "high places" were local sites of worship, situated on high ground. The Lord had commanded the people to worship Him in Jerusalem, not at local shrines as the pagans did.

Hezekiah had begun his religious reform right away. In II Chronicles 29:3 we read, "in the first month of the first year of his reign, he opened the doors of the temple of the LORD and repaired them." He then assembled the priests and Levites and revived the worship of God in His house that had been neglected so long, purifying the Temple so that it could be used again (vv. 4, 18). He renewed the celebration of the sacred Passover (c. 30). Then the people "went out to the towns of Judah, smashed the sacred stones and cut down the Asherah poles. They destroyed the high places and the altars throughout Judah and Benjamin and in Ephraim and Manasseh" (31:1). It was a religious revival, carried out with great zeal.

In previous lessons we have had references to "Asherah poles." They were symbols of a pagan female deity, worshiped by the people of Canaan.

Hezekiah also "broke into pieces the bronze snake Moses had made." This takes us back to the twenty-first chapter of Numbers. The Israelites had once more grumbled against God and Moses (v. 5). The result was that venomous snakes bit the people and many died (v. 6). When the people confessed their sin (v. 7), the Lord said to Moses, "Make a snake and put it up on a pole; anyone who is bitten can look at it and live" (v. 8). In obedience to this command, "Moses made a bronze snake and put it up on a pole. Then when anyone was bitten by a snake and looked at the bronze snake, he lived" (v. 9).

Jesus explained to Nicodemus the spiritual significance of this: "Just as Moses lifted up the snake in the desert, so the Son of Man must be lifted up, that everyone who believes in him may have eternal life" (John 3:14-15).

Typically, the Israelites had prostituted this symbol by idolatrous practice: "They had been burning incense to it." Again we see the gross, incurable materialism of these people. What God had intended as a symbol of Christ became an object of pagan worship.

For the meaning of Nehushtan see the footnote in the New International Version. "*Nehushtan* sounds like the Hebrew for *bronze* and *snake* and *unclean thing.*" Scholars are pretty well agreed that "he called it" (KJV) should be translated "It was called" (NIV).

III. A RIGHTEOUS KING:
II Kings 18:5-8

A. The Best of Judah's Kings: v. 5

"Hezekiah trusted in the LORD, the God of Israel. There was no one like him among all the kings of Judah, either before him or after him."

This is a sweeping statement. Interestingly, we find almost exactly the same words used of Joash in 23:25. Rawlinson comments:

At first sight there may seem to be contradiction between the two passages... but the context shows that the pre-eminence is not the same in the two cases. To Hezekiah is ascribed pre-eminence in *trust;* to Josiah, pre-eminence in an exact observance of the Law: one excels in faith, the other in works; Josiah's whole life is one of activity, Hezekiah's great merit lies in his being content, in the crisis of his fate, to "stand still, and see the salvation of God" (*PC,* II Kings, p. 358).

It is our challenge to excel in both faith and works. They should complement each other.

B. Full Obedience: v. 6

"He held fast to the LORD, and did not cease to follow him; he kept the commands the LORD had given Moses."

The last statement here indicates that Hezekiah excelled in works as well as faith. He was obedient to all the Law of Moses. But his unique virtue was his implicit trust in God.

We find recorded one sad mistake that Hezekiah made near the end of his life. After his miraculous recovery from a seemingly fatal illness (20:1-7), some envoys from the king of Babylon brought a gift to him (v. 12). Unfortunately, Hezekiah showed the messengers "all that was in his storehouses—the silver, the gold, the spices and the fine oil—his armory and everything found among his treasures" (v. 13). Isaiah had to tell him that the result would be that all these treasures would one day be carried off to Babylon (vv. 16-17). This happened in 586 B.C.

Perhaps we should say that Hezekiah was not guilty of conscious disobedience, but he would have done better to accept God's announcement that he would die (20:1).

C. Divine Blessing: v. 7

"And the LORD was with him: he was successful in whatever he undertook. He rebelled against the king of Assyria and did not serve him."

The secret of Hezekiah's success as king of Judah is found in the first clause of this verse. The statement is not made about any other king of Judah or Israel except David. Of him it is said, "And he became more and more powerful, because the LORD God Almighty was with him" (II Sam. 5:10). But God promised Moses, "I will be with you" (Exod. 3:12). And He repeated the promise to Joshua: "As I was with Moses, so I will be with you; I will never leave you or forsake you" (Josh.

1:5). In II Chronicles 15:2 we find the profound truth given this way to good King Asa: "The LORD is with you when you are with him." It is up to us to stay close to the Lord. When we do so, we have His promise that He will always be at our side to meet our every need.

Hezekiah's rebellion against the king of Assyria probably consisted of his refusal to pay tribute to that monarch. Meanwhile the Assyrians had their hands full with Israel and other nations nearer home, and so at first did not bother with Judah.

D. Defeat of Philistines: v. 8

When the Israelites under Joshua defeated the nations living in Canaan and occupied their territories, they failed to oust the Philistines. These people, for whom "Palestine" is named, lived on the south coast of the Promised Land. During the reigns of Saul and David they continued to be the most persistent enemies of Israel. Now, at a much later time, they were still a problem.

But Hezekiah defeated them, "as far as Gaza and its territory." The name Gaza has become prominent in recent years because of the so-called "Gaza Strip" between Israel and Egypt. An ancient battleground has once more come to the forefront.

IV. SENNACHERIB'S THREAT TO JERUSALEM: II Kings 18:17-37

Probably as a result of Hezekiah's rebellion, "The king of Assyria sent his supreme commander, his chief officer, and his field commander with a large army, from Lachish to King Hezekiah at Jerusalem" (v. 17). When these asked for the king, three of his assistants were sent instead (v. 18).

The Assyrians were insolent in their demands for surrender (vv. 19-25). They even asserted that the Lord had told them to march against Judah and destroy it (v. 25).

Hezekiah's representatives begged

the Assyrians not to use Hebrew, the language of the Israelites, but Aramaic (v. 26). The Assyrian commander's reply was even more disgusting (v. 27). Then he called out in Hebrew, challenging the people to reject Hezekiah and go to Assyria (vv. 28-32). The gods of the other nations had not been able to resist the king of Assyria. "How then can the LORD deliver Jerusalem from my hand?" (v. 35). In obedience to Hezekiah's command, the Israelites remained silent (v. 36).

V. ISAIAH'S REASSURANCE:
II Kings 19:1-7

When Hezekiah heard the report of what the Assyrian military commander had said, "he tore his clothes"—a sign of deep grief (cf. 18:37)—"and put on sackcloth and went into the temple of the LORD" (v. 1). He sent word to Isaiah the prophet, urging him to "pray for the remnant that still survives" (vv. 2-4).

Isaiah was ready with an answer from the Lord:

> "This is what the LORD says: Do not be afraid of what you have heard—those words with which the underlings of the king of Assyria have blasphemed me. Listen! I am going to put such a spirit in him that when he hears a certain report, he will return to his own country, and there I will have him cut down with the sword" (vv. 5-7).

Sure enough, Sennacherib king of Assyria heard that the king of Egypt "was marching out to fight against him" (v. 9). Then an angel of the Lord put to death 185,000 Assyrian soldiers one night (v. 35). Sennacherib returned to his capital, Nineveh (v. 36), where he was assassinated (v. 37).

VI. THE SIGN TO HEZEKIAH:
II Kings 19:29-31

A. Good Crops: v. 29

> "This will be the sign for you,
> O Hezekiah:

> This year you will eat what grows
>   by itself,
>   and the second year what
>   springs from that.
> But in the third year sow and
>   reap,
>   plant vineyards and eat their
>   fruit."

The prophet Isaiah had been sounding forth the Lord's message to Sennacherib king of Assyria in verses 21-28. It ended with the declaration:

> "I will put my hook in your nose
>   and my bit in your mouth,
> and I will make you return
>   by the way you came."

As we have already noted, this prophecy was speedily fulfilled (vv. 35-37).

Now the prophet addresses Hezekiah, and gives him a sign of God's blessing. Concerning verse 29 Rawlinson says:

> The Assyrian invasion, coming early in the spring, as was usual, had prevented the Israelites from sowing their lands. But they would soon be gone, and then the Israelites would gather in such self-sown corn as they might find in the corn-lands. The next year, probably a sabbatical year, they were authorized to do the same, notwithstanding the general prohibition (Lev. xxv.5); the third year they would return to their normal condition (PC, II Kings, p. 389).

DISCUSSION QUESTIONS

1.   What example does Hezekiah set for us today?
2.   Why does God allow trouble to come to us?
3.   Why does God not destroy all the wicked nations on earth?
4.   What is always our resort in times of trouble?
5.   How can we know for certain that God answers prayer?
6.   How can we bring about a spiritual reform in our day?

Rawlinson uses the term "corn" for wheat, as is the custom in the British Isles.

The "sign" that God was giving Hezekiah through Isaiah was that Jerusalem would be free from any further attack at this time. Though Sennacherib reigned for another seventeen years, he never invaded Palestine again.

B. Bearing Fruit: v. 30

"Once more a remnant of the
     house of Judah
   will take root below and bear
     fruit above."

Rawlinson comments:

> Sennacherib, who in his first expedition had carried away out of Judaea 200,150 prisoners ("Eponym Canon," p. 134, line 12) had in his second probably done considerable damage to the towns in the south-west of Palestine—Lachish, for instance, which was a city of Judah. . . . The open country had been wasted, great numbers killed, and many probably carried off by famine and pestilence. Thus both Hezekiah (ver. 4) and Isaiah regard the population still in the land as a mere "remnant" (*PC*, II Kings, p. 389).

"Take root below and bear fruit above" is the picture of a tree. Unless it sends its roots down into the ground, it cannot bear fruit on its branches.

This verse was fulfilled beautifully in the reign of good King Josiah, which soon followed. His was a time of religious revival.

C. A Remnant of Survivors: v. 31

"For out of Jerusalem will come a
     remnant,
   and out of Mount Zion a band of
     survivors.

The zeal of the LORD Almighty will accomplish this."

The last line is found verbatim in Isaiah 9:7c. This is the assurance the Lord gave through Isaiah.

The doctrine of the "remnant" is an integral part of the Old Testament. Even if the masses forsook the Lord, He always had a small remnant who remained true to Him. And this has been true also in the history of the Christian age.

VII. HEZEKIAH'S ACHIEVEMENTS: II Kings 20:20

> As for the other events of Hezekiah's reign, all his achievements and how he made the pool and the tunnel by which he brought water into the city, are they not written in the book of the annals of the kings of Judah?

"The pool" is what is known now as the Pool of Siloam. Today it is south of the southern wall of Jerusalem. But in Hezekiah's day it was inside the city walls. "The tunnel" brought water from the so-called Virgin's Fountain, which was outside the city wall, into the city. It was dug—much of it through rock—in order to provide a supply of water inside Jerusalem during a siege.

When one stands on the edge of the Pool of Siloam today, one can peer into the tunnel and even crawl through it when the water is low. Archaeologists found a Hebrew inscription near the Siloam end of the tunnel stating that it was a thousand cubits in length (about 1,500 feet). Measurements have confirmed this approximate figure.

CONTEMPORARY APPLICATION

The life of Hezekiah proves to us that we can rely on the Lord to take care of us, no matter what dangers may threaten us. But there is one essential condition: We must follow the Lord with all our hearts and obey His commands. Those who are fully in His will are graciously in His care.

One might raise the question: Why, then, do faithful Christians have fatal accidents? We cannot hope to have all the correct answers. But we do believe that God knows what is best in all circumstances, in the light of the final results. When five missionaries were killed by the Aucas, it precipitated a fresh burst of missionary dedication, with many Aucas now converted.

MEASURED BY THE WORD

DEVOTIONAL READING	II Kings 21:1-9

Adult Topic: *Measured by the Word*

Youth Topic: *Living by the Book*

ADULTS AND YOUTH

Background Scripture: II Kings 21:1—23:30

Scripture Lesson: II Kings 22:10-13, 15-16; 23:1-3

Memory Verse: *I have found the book of the law in the house of the Lord.* II Kings 22:8

Topic: *Living by the Word*

Background Scripture: II Kings 21:1—23:3

CHILDREN

Scripture Lesson: II Kings 22:8, 11-13, 15-16; 23:1-3

Memory Verse: *Lead me in the path of thy commandments.* Ps. 119:35

DAILY BIBLE READINGS

Aug. 13 M.: The Wicked Reign of Manasseh. II Kings 21:1-15

Aug. 14 T.: The Wicked Reign of Amon. II Kings 21:19-26

Aug. 15 W.: Discovery of the Book of the Law. II Kings 22:1-10

Aug. 16 T.: Consultation with Huldah. II Kings 22:11-20

Aug. 17 F.: Josiah's Religious Reforms. II Kings 23:1-14

Aug. 18 S.: Extension of Reforms to Northern Kingdom. II Kings 23:15-20

Aug. 19 S.: Final Days of Josiah. II Kings 23:21-30

LESSON AIM

To help us see the importance of living by the Book—the Bible.

LESSON SETTING

Time: about 640-609 B.C.

Place: Jerusalem

LESSON OUTLINE

Measured by the Word

    I. **Good King Josiah:** II Kings 22:1-2

    II. **Command to Repair the Temple:** II Kings 22:3-7

    III. **Finding the Book of the Law:** II Kings 22:8-10
        A. Discovery by the High Priest: v. 8
        B. Report of the Secretary: v. 9
        C. Report of Discovery: v. 10

    IV. **Josiah's Reaction:** II Kings 22:11-13
        A. Deep Sorrow and Concern: v. 11
        B. Inquiring of the Lord: vv. 12-13

V. **Huldah's Reply:** II Kings 22:15-20
  A. Message from God: v. 15
  B. Disaster on Jerusalem: v. 16
  C. Reason for Disaster: v. 17
  D. Kindness to the King: vv. 18-20

VI. **Josiah's Renewal of the Covenant:** II Kings 23:1-3
  A. Assembling the Elders: v. 1
  B. Reading the Book: v. 2
  C. Renewing the Covenant: v. 3

SUGGESTED INTRODUCTION FOR ADULTS

Last week we studied three chapters (18-20) on the reign of good King Hezekiah and the sweeping "Reform in Religion" that he brought about. Today we have nearly two chapters (22-23) on the reign of good King Josiah, who carried through a similar religious reformation. But there is one very important new note: the discovery of the Book of the Law and the resultant renewal of the Covenant.

In between the two lessons (c. 21) we have the dismal story of the long and wicked reign of Hezekiah's son, Manasseh (and the brief reign of his son, Amon). It is difficult to understand how such a godly man as Hezekiah could have had such an atrocious son as Manasseh.

The devastation of true religion that Manasseh brought about was compounded by the fact that he reigned for fifty-five years (21:1).

He rebuilt the high places his father Hezekiah had destroyed; he also erected altars to Baal and made an Asherah pole, as Ahab of Israel had done. He bowed down to all the starry hosts and worshiped them. . . . He sacrificed his own son in the fire, practiced sorcery and divination, and consulted mediums and spiritists (vv. 3-6).

The religious situation in Judah had reached an all-time low.

SUGGESTED INTRODUCTION FOR YOUTH

"Living by the Book"—that's the secret of having a worthwhile life here on earth and enjoying eternal life in heaven.

How do we live by the Book? We must read the Bible every day. Before starting to read we should ask the Lord to help us to understand the truths He has for us and to put these into practice. The Holy Spirit can help us to do both.

CONCEPTS FOR CHILDREN

1. We need to live by the Word of God.
2. To do this we must read the Bible every day.
3. Get a Bible that is easy to read.
4. Ask the Lord to help you to obey His Word.

THE LESSON COMMENTARY

I. GOOD KING JOSIAH:
II Kings 22:1-2

> Josiah was eight years old when he became king, and he reigned in Jerusalem thirty-one years. His mother's name was Jedidah daughter of Adaiah; she was from Bozkath. He did what was right in the eyes of the LORD and walked in all the ways of his father David, not turning aside to the right or to the left.

In the Introduction we expressed surprise that good Hezekiah could have had such a wicked son as Manasseh. Now we register our wonder that wicked Amon (21:20-21) could sire such a good king as Josiah.

Josiah's mother was the one who gave him the right start in life. We are told that her name was Jedidah, which means "Darling." She must have been a darling!

Of verse 2 George Rawlinson says: "This is a stronger expression than any which has been used of any previous king of Judah except Hezekiah, and indicates a very high degree of approval" (*The Pulpit Commentary*, II Kings, p. 435). Josiah was indeed a miracle!

II. COMMAND TO
REPAIR THE TEMPLE:
II Kings 22:3-7

In II Kings we have no record of Josiah's activity until "the eighteenth year of his reign" (v. 3). But in II Chronicles 34:3-4 we read:

> In the eighth year of his reign, while he was still young [only sixteen years old], he began to seek the God of his father David. In his twelfth year [when he was twenty years old] he began to purge Judah and Jerusalem of high places, Asherah poles, carved idols and cast images. Under his direction the altars of the Baals were torn down; he cut to pieces the incense altars that were above them, and smashed the Asherah poles, the idols and the images.

It was a sweeping reform.

Second Chronicles 34:8 agrees with II Kings 22:3-7 that it was in "the eighteenth year of his reign," when Josiah was about twenty-six years old, that he ordered the Temple of the Lord in Jerusalem to be repaired. Money was to be paid to "the carpenters, the builders and the masons" to "repair the temple" (v. 6). "The men appointed to supervise the work on the temple" (v. 5) were trusted to pay the workers (vv. 5-7).

III. FINDING THE BOOK
OF THE LAW:
II Kings 22:8-10

A. Discovery by the High Priest:
v. 8

"Hilkiah the high priest said to Shaphan the secretary, 'I have found the Book of the Law in the temple of the LORD.' He gave it to Shaphan, who read it."

What was "the Book of the Law" that Hilkiah the high priest discovered in the Temple of the Lord? Rawlinson has an excellent discussion of this much-debated question:

> There has been a great difference of opinion as to what it was which Hilkiah had found. Ewald believes it to have been the Book of Deuteronomy, which had, he thinks, been composed some thirty or forty years before in Egypt by a Jewish exile, and had found its way, *by a sort of chance*, into Palestine where "*some priest*" had placed a copy of it in the temple.... Thenius suggests "a collection of the laws and ordinances of Moses, which was afterwards worked up into the Pentateuch"; Bertheau, "the three middle books of the Pentateuch, Exodus, Leviticus, and Numbers"; Gramberg, "Exodus by itself" (*PC*, II Kings, p. 437).

All these are the wild views of extremely liberal German higher critics. And all these groundless assumptions are rejected by evangelical scholars today. The Bible attributes the Pentateuch (first five books of the Bible) to Moses.

Then Rawlinson proceeds to give to our question the answer held by most evangelicals. He says this:

> But there seems to be no sufficient grounds for questioning the ancient opinion—that of Josephus, and of the Jews generally—that it was a copy of the entire Pentateuch. . . . The words, . . . "*the* book of the law," are really sufficient to decide the point; since, as Keil says, they "cannot mean anything else, either grammatically or historically, than the Mosaic book of the Law (the Pentateuch), which is so designated, as is generally admitted, in the Chronicles and the Books of Ezra and Nehemiah" (*PC*, II Kings, p. 437).

B. Report of the Secretary: v. 9

"Then Shaphan the secretary went to the king and reported to him: 'Your officials have paid out the money that was in the temple of the LORD and have entrusted it to the workers and supervisors at the temple.'"

This was in keeping with what the king had commanded his secretary to do: "Have them entrust it [the money collected from the people] to the men appointed to supervise the work on the temple" (v. 5). Now Shaphan reported that this had been done.

C. Report of Discovery: v. 10

"Then Shaphan the secretary informed the king, 'Hilkiah the priest has given me a book.' And Shaphan read from it in the presence of the king."

If this "book" was the entire Pentateuch (the five scrolls of the Law) Shaphan must have "read from it" in the presence of the king rather than "read it" (KJV). Even to have read all of Deuteronomy aloud at one time would have been most unlikely. The secretary read enough from the Law to convince the king that God was displeased with what His people were doing.

IV. JOSIAH'S REACTION: II Kings 22:11-13

A. Deep Sorrow and Concern: v. 11

"When the king heard the words of the Book of the Law, he tore his robes."

We can well believe that "the Book of the Law" had been entirely lost sight of early in the long (fifty-five years) and wicked reign of Manasseh (c. 21). Now its appearance was a new discovery.

We may liken this to the Protestant Reformation. The Roman Catholic Church had forbidden its people to read the Bible. For centuries it was a closed book. Then Martin Luther translated the Bible into German (1522-34). When the people could read the Bible in their own language, a tremendous religious revival began, and the moral complexion of society was changed. Instead of kneeling before images and reciting memorized prayers, the people began to believe in Jesus and find personal salvation in Him.

When King Josiah heard the words of the Book of the Law, "he tore his robes." We find this expression many times in the Old Testament and several times in the New. It expressed grief and concern—an appropriate gesture for the king to make.

B. Inquiring of the Lord: vv. 12-13

> He gave these orders to Hilkiah the priest, Ahikam son of Shaphan, Acbor son of Micaiah, Shaphan the secretary and Asaiah the king's attendant: "Go and inquire of the LORD for me and for the people and for all Judah about what is written in this book that has been found. Great is the LORD's anger that burns against us because our fathers have not obeyed the words of this book; they have not acted in accordance with all that is written there concerning us."

Hilkiah the priest was the high priest at that time (v. 8). Ahikam son of Shaphan was later the supporter and protector of Jeremiah (Jer. 26:24). His father was evidently Shaphan the secretary, mentioned several times in this chapter (vv. 3, 8, 9, 10, 12). Later Ahikam's son Gedaliah became the caretaker of Jeremiah (Jer. 39:14) and was finally appointed by the king of Babylon as governor of Judah (Jer. 40:7). Achor was the father of El-nathan, who was later one of the officials at the royal palace (Jer. 36:12). Asaiah (cf. II Chron. 34:20) was the king's attendant.

These men were commanded by King Josiah: "Go and inquire of the LORD for me and for the people and for all Judah about what is written in this book that has been found" (v. 13). It would seem that perhaps Shaphan the secretary had read Deuteronomy 28:15-68 or Leviticus 26:16-39. There we read extensive, solemn warnings as to the tragic consequences of unbelief and disobedience on the part of the people. Josiah realized that the people of Judah, as well as the people of Israel, had been guilty of the very things that God, through Moses, had warned the people against. Rawlinson writes:

> Josiah recognized that Judah had done, and was still doing, exactly those things against which the threatenings of the Law were directed—had forsaken Jehovah, and gone after other gods, and made themselves high places, and set up images, and done after the customs of the nations whom the Lord had cast out before them. He could not, therefore, doubt but that the wrath of the Lord "was kindled"; but would it blaze forth at once? (PC, II Kings, p. 438).

V. HULDAH'S REPLY: II Kings 22:15-20

A. Message from God: v. 15

The messengers from the king went to "the prophetess Huldah" (v. 14). Those who do not believe in women preachers should note that in every age God has had women who spoke for

Him. In the New Testament church "Philip the evangelist" had "four unmarried daughters who prophesied" (Acts 21:8-9). And in his great sermon on the Day of Pentecost, Peter quoted from Joel 2:28-32: "Your sons and your daughters will prophesy"; and:

> "Even on my servants, both men and women,
> I will pour out my Spirit in those days,
> and they will prophesy" (Acts 2:17, 18).

Huldah "lived in Jerusalem, in the Second District"—literally, "the second city" (not "the college," KJV). This was probably the lower part of Jerusalem. Huldah told the messengers: "This is what the LORD, the God of Israel, says: Tell the man who sent you to me" (v. 15). She knew that she had a message from God for the king.

B. Disaster on Jerusalem: v. 16

"This is what the LORD says: I am going to bring disaster on this place and its people, according to everything written in the book the king of Judah has read."

"This place" obviously meant Jerusalem. It was to suffer disaster, and it did so when destroyed by the Babylonians in 586 B.C.

The parallel passage in II Chronicles 34:24 is a bit stronger. It reads, "This is what the LORD says: I am going to bring disaster on this place and its people—all the curses written in the book that has been read in the presence of the king of Judah." As we noted before, what was read to the king may have included Deuteronomy 28:15-68, which begins with the words: "However, if you do not obey the LORD your God and do not follow all his commands and decrees I am giving you today, all these curses will come upon you and overtake you. . . ." This is followed by four lines of poetry (vv. 16-19), in which the word "cursed" occurs six times. Willful disobedience always brings God's curse on people.

C. Reason for Disaster: v. 17

"Because they have forsaken me and burned incense to other gods and provoked me to anger by all the idols their hands have made, my anger will burn against this place and will not be quenched."

The crowning sin of the people of Judah is stated in the first clause: "Because they have forsaken me." There are many warnings against this in the Scriptures. In Deuteronomy 29:24 we are told that when divine judgment struck the Israelites, all the other nations would ask, "Why has the LORD done this to this land?" The answer would be, "It is because this people abandoned the covenant of the LORD, the God of their fathers" (v. 25). In the period of the judges, God said to the people, "But you have forsaken me and served other gods, so I will no longer save you" (Judg. 10:13).

Now the people had gone so far in rejecting God and turning to idols that the doom of Jerusalem—"this place"—was settled. It would have to be destroyed. And that destruction soon took place.

D. Kindness to the King: vv. 18-20

There was a very different message for good King Josiah:

"Tell the king of Judah, who sent you to inquire of the LORD, 'This is what the LORD, the God of Israel, says concerning the words you heard: Because your heart was responsive and you humbled yourself before the LORD when you heard what I have spoken against this place and its people, that they would become accursed and laid waste, and because you tore your robes and wept in my presence, I have heard you, declared the LORD. Therefore I will gather you to your fathers, and you will be buried in peace. Your eyes will not see all the disaster I am going to bring on this place. . . .'"

Though Josiah, doing his best to reform the nation, could not avert the final disaster, it would be postponed until after his death. He had torn his robes as an outward act of humiliation, but he had also shed tears of repentance for his people. Even though the people were rejecting God, Josiah's heart was responsive, repentant, and humble.

VI. JOSIAH'S RENEWAL OF THE COVENANT: II Kings 23:1-3

A. Assembling the Elders: v. 1

"Then the king called together all the elders of Judah and Jerusalem." The term "elders" is used frequently in I Kings (8:1; 20:7, 8; 21:8, 11; 10:1; et al.). At that time older men had special recognition among the people. But here the term "elders" probably refers to a group of men who acted somewhat as officials, or at least representatives, of the people.

B. Reading the Book: v. 2

He went up to the temple of the LORD with the men of Judah, the people of Jerusalem, the priests and the prophets—all the people from the least to the greatest. He read in their hearing all the words of the Book of the Covenant, which had been found in the temple of the LORD.

DISCUSSION QUESTIONS

1. Why is a godly mother so important in the home?
2. What are properly the religious functions of the father and of the mother?
3. How can a Christian mother with a non-Christian husband raise godly children?
4. How is the importance of youth shown in Josiah's life?
5. How may we rediscover the Bible? (See Contemporary Application.)
6. How may we renew the Covenant with God?

The king "went up to the temple of the LORD" from his royal palace, which was at a lower level (cf. I Kings 10:5). Rawlinson comments:

> No place could be so suitable for the renewal of the covenant between God and his people as the house of God, where God was in a peculiar way present, and the ground was, like the ground at Horeb [Sinai], holy (*PC*, II Kings, p. 451).

All classes of people were there—"from the least to the greatest." Then the king read to the people "all the words of the Book of the Covenant." Since reading all the Pentateuch would take at least ten hours, it seems most reasonable to assume that he read only a part of that. What was found in the Temple has hitherto been referred to as "the Book of the Law" (22:8, 11).

C. Renewing the Covenant: v. 3

> The king stood by the pillar and renewed the covenant in the presence of the LORD—to follow the LORD and keep his commands, regulations and decrees with all his heart and all his soul, thus confirming the words of the covenant written in this book. Then all the people pledged themselves to the covenant.

Renewing the covenant, as we see here, involves promising sincerely to obey all of God's Word with all our heart and soul. Nothing less will do. Ultimately, it must be all or nothing.

The people also pledged themselves. This reminds us of another, earlier scene. In Deuteronomy 24:7 we read of Moses: "Then he took the Book of the Covenant and read it to the people. They responded, 'We will do everything the LORD has said; we will obey.'"

A careful reading of Exodus 24:3-7 convinces us that "the Book of the Covenant" which Josiah read consisted of Exodus 20-23. This would be a reasonable length of Scripture to read in public.

CONTEMPORARY APPLICATION

Have you discovered God's "Book," the Bible? Perhaps you went to Sunday school as a child and studied the Bible. It may have even been read in family worship in the home where you were brought up. But have you become so busy in adult years that you have neglected reading the Bible? If so, today is the time for you to rediscover God's Book and make it your daily companion.

The best way to begin every day is to sit down with your Bible, close your eyes, and ask God to speak to you through His Word, and then carefully, prayerfully read a chapter of it. As you do so, ask the Holy Spirit, who inspired the sacred Scriptures, to help you understand and obey the Bible. This will give you the right start for each day.

INTO EXILE

DEVOTIONAL READING	Jeremiah 12:8-16

ADULTS AND YOUTH

Adult Topic: *Into Exile*

Youth Topic: *Without a Home*

Background Scripture: II Kings 24-25

Scripture Lesson: II Kings 25:1-12

Memory Verse: *Because of the anger of the Lord it came to the point in Jerusalem and Judah that he cast them out from his presence.* II Kings 24:20

CHILDREN

Topic: *Judah Is Captured*

Scripture Lesson: II Kings 25:8-12

Memory Verse: *So Judah was taken into exile out of its land.* II Kings 25:21

DAILY BIBLE READINGS

Aug. 20 M.: The Reign of Jehoiakim in Judah. II Kings 23:36—24:7
Aug. 21 T.: First Deportation Under Jehoiachin. II Kings 24:8-17
Aug. 22 W.: Siege of Jerusalem Under Zedekiah. II Kings 24:18—25:7
Aug. 23 T.: The Sack of Jerusalem. II Kings 24:8-21
Aug. 24 F.: Murder of Gedaliah. II Kings 24:22-26
Aug. 25 S.: The Pardon of Jehoiachin. II Kings 24:27-30
Aug. 26 S.: Prayer for God's Blessing on the King. Ps. 72:1-15

LESSON AIM | To show the sad results of disobeying God.

LESSON SETTING

Time: about 597-586 B.C.

Place: Jerusalem

LESSON OUTLINE

Into Exile

I. **Jehoiachin's Reign:** II Kings 24:8-17
  A. Another Evil King: vv. 8-9
  B. Surrender of Jerusalem: vv. 10-12
  C. Stripping of the Temple: v. 13
  D. Beginning of Exile: v. 14
  E. Captivity of King and Leaders: vv. 15-17

II. **Beginning of Zedekiah's Reign:** II Kings 24:18-20
  A. The Last King of Judah: v. 18
  B. An Evil King: v. 19
  C. Rebellion Against Babylon: v. 20

III. **Siege of Jerusalem:** II Kings 25:1-3
   A. Beginning of Siege: v. 1
   B. Length of Siege: v. 2
   C. Severe Famine: v. 3

IV. **Fall of Jerusalem:** II Kings 25:4-7
   A. Flight of Army: v. 4
   B. Capture of Zedekiah: vv. 5-6
   C. Punishment of Zedekiah: v. 7

V. **Destruction of Jerusalem:** II Kings 25:8-12
   A. Nebuchadnezzar's Official: v. 8
   B. Devastating Fire: v. 9
   C. Destruction of Walls: v. 10
   D. Final Deportation: vv. 11-12

SUGGESTED
INTRODUCTION
FOR ADULTS

In our last lesson we studied about Josiah, the last good king of Judah. As Hezekiah had done (in the previous lesson), Josiah brought about a sweeping reform in the religion of Judah (II Kings 23:4-25).

After Josiah there were only four more kings ruling over Judah, and every one of them was wicked. The first was Jehoahaz (23:31-34), who reigned in Jerusalem only three months (v. 31). Of him it is said: "He did evil in the eyes of the LORD, just as his fathers had done" (v. 32). He ended up as a captive in Egypt (v. 34).

The second of the four kings was Jehoiakim (23:34—24:6). Again we find the dismal refrain: "And he did evil in the eyes of the LORD, just as his fathers had done" (23:37). During his reign, "Nebuchadnezzar king of Babylon invaded the land, and Jehoiakim became his vassal for three years. But then he changed his mind and rebelled against Nebuchadnezzar" (24:1). The stage was being set for the destruction of Jerusalem and the end of the kingdom of Judah.

SUGGESTED
INTRODUCTION
FOR YOUTH

The people of Judah became a people "Without a Home." They refused to obey the Lord, and so they lost the land that God had promised to them through Moses and Joshua. Jerusalem, the holy city, was captured by the Babylonians. The people of Judah became exiles in a foreign, pagan country. All this was because they had rejected the Lord as their God, and He rejected them as His people.

Young people must realize that when they deliberately disobey God they suffer severe penalties. They ruin their lives and become the captives of sin. Our decisions determine our destiny, in this life as well as for eternity. Let's choose God and live in His wonderful will.

CONCEPTS FOR
CHILDREN

1. No one likes to be taken somewhere against his or her will.
2. But if we disobey God, this can happen to us.
3. The people of Judah found this out too late.
4. We should obey God's will, and so enjoy His presence and blessing.

THE LESSON COMMENTARY

I. JEHOIACHIN'S REIGN:
II Kings 24:8-17

A. Another Evil King: vv. 8-9

"Jehoiachin was eighteen years old when he became king, and he reigned in Jerusalem three months. . . . He did evil in the eyes of the LORD, just as his father had done."

Here we find the sad refrain that is voiced with every king from Josiah on.

B. Surrender of Jerusalem:
vv. 10-12

At that time the officers of Nebuchadnezzar king of Babylon advanced on Jerusalem and laid siege to it, and Nebuchadnezzar himself came up to the city while his officers were besieging it. Jehoiachin king of Judah, his mother, his attendants, his nobles and his officials all surrendered to him.

Jehoiachin's short reign of three months ended with the surrender of Jerusalem to Nebuchadnezzar. This was the beginning of the end of Judah.

In verse 12 we find a reference to Jehoiachin's mother, who is named in verse 8. It is thought that she may have been the ruling spirit in Jerusalem during her young son's very brief reign and may have influenced him harmfully.

C. Stripping of the Temple: v. 13

"As the LORD had declared, Nebuchadnezzar removed all the treasures from the temple of the LORD and from the royal palace, and took away all the gold articles that Solomon king of Israel had made for the temple of the LORD."

The voluntary surrender of the king, his mother, and his officials did not prevent Nebuchadnezzar's plunder of the Temple and the royal palace. Solomon had furnished the Temple with what we would say were many millions of dollars' worth of gold articles. These Nebuchadnezzar quickly confiscated. A description of these gold furnishings made by Solomon is given in I Kings 7:48-50.

The Lord had "declared" more than once that this plunder of Jerusalem would take place because the people had forsaken Him (e.g., Jer. 15:13; 20:3). Disobedience is costly!

D. Beginning of Exile: v. 14

"He carried into exile all Jerusalem: all the officers and fighting men, and all the craftsmen and artisans—a total of ten thousand. Only the poorest people of the land were left."

"All Jerusalem" probably means from all over the city, or at least all the important classes of people. "Only the poorest people of the land were left," to care for the vineyards and fields outside the city. "All the officers and fighting men, and all the craftsmen and artisans" were taken to Babylon. The total exile of this time is placed at "ten thousand." This would be most of the population of Jerusalem.

E. Captivity of King
and Leaders: vv.15-17

"Nebuchadnezzar took Jehoiachin captive to Babylon. He also took from Jerusalem to Babylon the king's mother, his wives, his officials and the leading men of the land" (v. 15). Nebuchadnezzar hoped thereby to prevent any uprising or rebellion against him.

"The king of Babylon also deported to Babylon the entire force of seven thousand fighting men, strong and fit for war, and a thousand craftsmen and artisans" (v. 16). This made up the bulk of the ten thousand captives.

Then Nebuchadnezzar provided for the rule of Judah. "He made Mattaniah, Jehoiachin's uncle, king in his place, and changed his name to Zedekiah" (v. 17).

II. BEGINNING
OF ZEDEKIAH'S REIGN:
II Kings 24:18-20

A. The Last King of Judah: v. 18

"Zedekiah was twenty-one years old when he became king, and he reigned in Jerusalem eleven years." These were the final, fatal years of the kingdom of Judah.

B. An Evil King: v. 19

"He did evil in the eyes of the LORD, just as Jehoiakim had done."

Interestingly, Zedekiah is compared to his brother Jehoiakim, rather than to his nephew and predecessor, Jehoiachin. This is perhaps because the latter's reign was so very brief (only three months) that a comparison was hardly relevant.

C. Rebellion Against Babylon: v. 20

Once more we are told the reason for the Babylonian captivity: "It was because of the LORD's anger that all this happened to Jerusalem and Judah, and in the end he thrust them from his presence." Divine anger was provoked by the people's stubborn rejection of God and His law. Punishment was inevitable.

Then we are told: "Now Zedekiah rebelled against the king of Babylon." This set the stage for the destruction of Jerusalem by Nebuchadnezzar.

III. SIEGE OF JERUSALEM:
II Kings 25:1-3

A. Beginning of Siege: v. 1

"So in the ninth year of Zedekiah's reign, on the tenth day of the tenth month, Nebuchadnezzar king of Babylon marched against Jerusalem with his whole army. He encamped outside the city and built siege works all around it."

On the dating in the first part of this verse George Rawlinson comments:

Extreme exactness with respect to a date indicates the extreme importance of the event dated. In the whole range of the history contained in the two Books of the Kings, there is no instance of the year, month, and day being all given excepting in the present chapter, where we find this extreme exactness three times (vers. 1, 4, and 8) (*The Pulpit Commentary,* II Kings, p. 487).

The exact date here is confirmed in Jeremiah 52:4 and Ezekiel 24:1. In the latter place Ezekiel is commanded, "Son of man, record this date, this very date, because the king of Babylon has laid siege to Jerusalem this very day" (v. 2). God considered it important.

Nebuchadnezzar "marched against Jerusalem with his whole army." Jeremiah says that he "and all his army and all the kingdoms and peoples in the empire he ruled were fighting against Jerusalem and all its surrounding towns" (Jer. 34:1) It was a massive assault.

Nebuchadnezzar "built siege works" around Jerusalem. Rawlinson writes:

The towers used in sieges by the Assyrians and Babylonians were movable ones, made of planks, which were pushed up to the walls, so that the assailants might attack their adversaries on a level, with greater advantage. Sometimes they contained battering-rams (*PC,* II Kings, p. 487).

B. Length of Siege: v. 2

"The city was kept under siege until the eleventh year of King Zedekiah."

Putting this with the first part of verse three, we learn that the siege lasted one year and seven months. It was a time of great suffering inside Jerusalem.

C. Severe Famine: v. 3

"By the ninth day of the fourth month the famine in the city had become so severe that there was no food for the people to eat."

The word "fourth" is not in the Hebrew text here. This is indicated in the King James Version by italics and in the New International Version by half-brackets. It has to be restored here from Jeremiah 52:6.

Severe famine held the city in its grip. Rawlinson describes it this way:

> The intensity of the suffering endured may be gathered from Lamentations, Ezekiel and Josephus. The complexions of the men grew black with famine (Lam. iv. 8; v. 10); their skin was shrunk and parched (Lam. iv. 8); the rich and noble women searched the dunghills for scraps of offal (Lam. iv.5); the children perished for want, or were devoured by their parents (Lam. ii. 20; iv. 3, 4, 10; Ezek. v. 10); water was scarce, as well as food, and was sold at a price (Lam. v. 4); a third part of the inhabitants died of the famine, and the plague which grew out of it (Ezek. v. 12) (*PC*, II Kings, pp. 487-88).

This was the darkest hour thus far in the history of Judah. The people were paying a horrible price for having their own way rather than letting God have His way.

IV. FALL OF JERUSALEM: II Kings 25:4-7

A. Flight of Army: v. 4

"Then the city wall was broken through, and the whole army fled at night through the gate between two walls near the king's garden, though the Babylonians were surrounding the city. They fled toward the Arabah."

It is probable that the breach in the walls was made on the north side of the city where the ground is fairly level. There are valleys on the other three sides of Jerusalem.

"The whole army fled at night" through a gate in the southern wall of the city. Here there is a very steep slope and deep valley where they could escape undetected.

"They fled toward the Arabah." This was the popular name then for the Jordan Valley. The escapees rushed down near what is now known as the Jericho Road. It stretches some fifteen miles to near the Jordan River.

B. Capture of Zedekiah: vv. 5-6

But the Babylonian army pursued the king and overtook him in the plains of Jericho. All his soldiers were separated from him and scattered, and he was captured. He was taken to the king of Babylon at Riblah, where sentence was pronounced on him.

When the escape of Zedekiah and his soldiers was discovered, the Babylonians took off in hot pursuit. Nebuchadnezzar had retired to Riblah (v. 6), leaving his commanders in charge at Jerusalem. If Zedekiah escaped from them, they would be held severely responsible. They *had* to capture him, and they finally succeeded in taking him in "the plains of Jericho," west of the Jordan River. It would seem that his soldiers panicked and "scattered," leaving him unprotected.

When caught, Zedekiah "was taken to the king of Babylon at Riblah." Rawlinson notes, "The presentation of rebel kings, when captured, to their suzerain, seated on his throne, is one of the most common subjects of Assyrian and Babylonian sculptures" (*PC*, II Kings, p. 488).

"Riblah" was situated in Syria, on the bands of the Orontes River. It made a convenient headquarters for Nebuchadnezzar at this time. Here "sentence was pronounced" on Zedekiah. He had clearly been guilty of rebellion against the Babylonian king (24:20).

C. Punishment of Zedekiah: v. 7

"They killed the sons of Zedekiah before his eyes. Then they put out his eyes, bound him with bronze shackles and took him to Babylon."

The Lord said through Ezekiel, "I will bring him to Babylonia, the land of the Chaldeans, but he will not see it, and there he will die" (Ezek. 12:13).

On the surface this seems contradictory: Go to Babylon and not see it? But our verse here solves the problem. Zedekiah's eyes were put out, perhaps with a hot iron, so that he did not "see" the land of his captivity.

Blinding prisoners was a common practice at that time. It happened to Samson, whose eyes were "gouged out" (Judg. 16:21).

It seems a bit surprising that Nebuchadnezzar did not have Zedekiah put to death. But what he did was perhaps more cruel. It would appear that the last sight Zedekiah saw was his own young sons being killed. He had to live with this memory the rest of his days, which he spent in prison (Jer. 52:11).

V. DESTRUCTION OF JERUSALEM: II Kings 25:8-12

A. Nebuchadnezzar's Official: v. 8

"On the seventh day of the fifth month, in the nineteenth year of Nebuchadnezzar king of Babylon, Nebuzaradan commander of the imperial guard, an official of the king of Babylon, came to Jerusalem."

Instead or returning to Jerusalem himself, Nebuchadnezzar commissioned his "commander of the imperial guard"—to go in his place. His orders were to destroy the city so that it would never again rise in rebellion against Babylonian sovereignty.

B. Devastating Fire: v. 9

"He set fire to the temple of the LORD, the royal palace and all the houses of Jerusalem. Every important building he burned down."

Some four centuries before this Solomon had built the Temple of the Lord at Jerusalem as one of the most magnificent buildings of all time. As we noted in an earlier lesson, it would be impossible to compute the full monetary value of all the gold, silver,

and bronze that he lavished on the house of the Lord. Now it went up in flames. For fifty years God's chosen people were without any Temple, until a rather meagre one was built by the returning captives, under the sponsorship of Cyrus king of Persia (Ezra 1:2-4). It did not compare at all with the dazzling structure that Solomon had erected.

Nebuzaradan burnt down not only the beautiful temple but also "the royal palace and all the houses of Jerusalem." Rawlinson notes:

> The royal palace was, perhaps, almost as magnificent as the temple; and its destruction was almost as great a loss to art. It doubtless contained Solomon's throne of ivory (1 Kings x.18), to which there was an ascent by six steps, with two sculptured lions on each step (*PC*, II Kings, p. 489).

Nubuzaradan also burned down "every important building." The city must have been a shambles.

C. Destruction of Walls: v. 10

"The whole Babylonian army, under the commander of the imperial guard, broke down the walls around Jerusalem."

That this does not mean that the walls of the city were completely demolished seems to be shown by Nehemiah 2:13-15. The governor was

---

DISCUSSION QUESTIONS

1.   Many other times God had protected Jerusalem. Why did He not do it this time?
2.   How can we be sure that God is on our side?
3.   What were some consequences of the Babylonian captivity?
4.   What lessons can one learn from the life of Zedekiah?
5.   What is the secret of having divine protection?
6.   What did the Jews learn in captivity?

able to examine the walls by night, to see what needed to be done. This was after the captivity period.

D. Final Deportation: vv. 11-12

"Nebuzaradan the commander of the guard carried into exile the people who remained in the city, along with the rest of the populace and those who had gone over to the king of Babylon" (v. 11).

The last group mentioned here would be those who, during the siege or before it, had deserted to the Babylonians, and so were outside the city. The commander also took as captives those who had remained in the city.

"But the commander left behind some of the poorest people of the land to work the vineyards and fields."

The Babylonians hoped to reap some profit from the land of Judah in the years ahead, so they left some paupers to care for the crops.

In the verses that immediately follow (13-14) we read how the Babylonians took copious quantities of the bronze in the Temple and carried it to Babylon. They also took whatever they could find of gold and silver articles that were left (v. 15). We read, "The bronze from the two pillars, the Sea and the movable stands, which Solomon had made for the temple of the LORD, was more than could be weighed. Each pillar was twenty-seven feet high" (vv. 16-17).

But the material loot was not all that was taken. "The commander of the guard took as prisoners Seraiah the chief priest, Zephaniah the priest next in rank and the three doorkeepers" (v. 18). He took some other officials he found in the city, and sixty other men (v. 19). "Nebuzaradan the commander took them all and brought them to the king of Babylon at Riblah. There at Riblah...the king had them executed" (vv. 20-21).

The climax is found at the end of verse 21: "So Judah went into captivity, away from her land." She lost the land because she forsook her God.

CONTEMPORARY APPLICATION

The apostasy and consequent captivity of Judah should be a solemn warning to all people in our so-called Christian land. If we forsake God, as too large a segment of our population has done, we have no right to be surprised when we lose some of our prized liberties. We sometimes wonder how long God can bless America, in the light of what is going on all around us. We need to pray that God will have mercy on our country and help people to turn back to Him in true repentance and obedience.

BIBLIOGRAPHY

The numbers in parentheses following each entry indicate the quarter(s) that reference is used for.

Abbott, T. K. *A Critical and Exegetical Commentary on the Epistles to the Ephesians and to the Colossians.* International Critical Commentary. Edinburgh: T. & T. Clark, 1897. (1)

Abbott-Smith, George. *A Manual Greek Lexicon of the New Testament.* 3d ed. New York: Charles Scribner's Sons, n.d. (1, 3)

Alexander, J. A. *Commentary on the Gospel of Mark.* Grand Rapids: Zondervan Publishing House, n.d. (3)

Alford, Henry. *The Greek Testament.* Revised by E. F. Harrison. 4 vols. Chicago: Moody Press, 1958. (2, 3)

Archer, Gleason. *Encyclopedia of Bible Difficulties.* Grand Rapids: Zondervan Publishing House, 1982. (3)

Arndt, W. F., and Gingrich, F. W. *A Greek-English Lexicon of the New Testament.* Chicago: University of Chicago Press, 1957. (1, 3)

Barrett, C. K. *Commentary on the Epistle to the Romans.* Harper's New Testament Commentary. New York: Harper and Brothers, 1957. (1)

Beacon Bible Commentary. 10 vols. Edited by A. F. Harper. Grand Rapids: Baker Book House, 1965-68. (1, 2, 3)

Branscomb, Bennett Harvie. *The Gospel of St. Mark.* Moffatt New Testament Commentary. New York: Harper and Brothers, 1937. (3)

Clarke, Adam. *Commentary on the Holy Bible.* Abridged by Ralph Earle. Grand Rapids: Baker Book House, 1967. (3)

Douglas, James Dixon, ed. *New Bible Dictionary.* Grand Rapids: Wm. B. Eerdmans Publishing Co., 1962. (2)

Eadie, John. *Commentary on the Epistle of Paul to the Colossians.* Grand Rapids: Zondervan Publishing House, 1957. (1)

——. *Commentary on the Epistle to the Ephesians.* Grand Rapids: Zondervan Publishing House, n.d. (1)

Earle, Ralph. *The Gospel According to Mark.* Evangelical Commentary on the Bible. Grand Rapids: Zondervan Publishing House, 1957. (3)

——. *Meet the Minor Prophets.* Kansas City: Beacon Hill Press, 1955. (1)

——. *The Story of the New Testament.* Kansas City: Beacon Hill Press, 1941. (3)

——. *Word Meanings in the New Testament.* 5 vols. Grand Rapids: Baker Book House, 1974-80. (1, 3)

Edersheim, Alfred. *The Life and Times of Jesus the Messiah.* 2 vols. New York: Longmans, Green & Co., 1903. (3)

Expositor's Bible Commentary. Edited by Frank E. Gaebelein. 12 vols. Grand Rapids: Zondervan Publishing House, 1981. (3)

The Expositor's Greek Testament. 5 vols. Edited by William Robertson Nicoll. Grand Rapids: Wm. B. Eerdmans Publishing Co., 1951. (1)

Godet, F. *Commentary on St. Paul's Epistle to the Romans.* Grand Rapids: Zondervan Publishing House, 1969. (1)

Gould, Ezra. *A Critical and Exegetical Commentary on the Gospel According to St. Mark.* International Critical Commentary. Edinburgh: T. & T. Clark, 1955. (3)

Henry, Matthew. *Commentary on the Whole Bible.* 6 vols. New York: Fleming H.
    Revell, n.d. (1, 2)
Hunter, A. M. *The Gospel According to St. Mark.* Torch Bible Commentaries.
    London: SCM Press, 1949. (3)
——. *Interpreting Paul's Gospel.* Philadelphia: Westminster Press, 1955. (1)
Jamieson, Robert; Fausset, A. R.; and Brown, David. *A Commentary, Critical,
    Experimental, and Practical, on the Old and New Testaments.* 6 vols. Grand
    Rapids: Wm. B. Eerdmans Publishing Co., 1945. (1, 2, 4)
Keil, C. F. and Delitzsch, F. *Biblical Commentary on the Old Testament.* 25 vols.
    Grand Rapids: Wm. B. Eerdmans Publishing Co., reprint. (2)
Kittel, Gerhard, ed. *Theological Dictionary of the New Testament.* Translated and
    edited by Geoffrey W. Bromiley. 10 vols. Grand Rapids: Wm. B. Eerdmans
    Publishing Co., 1964-76. (1)
Lange, John Peter, ed. *Commentary on the Holy Scriptures.* Translated and edited
    by Philip Schaff. 24 vols. Grand Rapids: Zondervan Publishing House, 1960.
    (1, 2, 4)
Lenski, R. C. H. *Interpretation of the New Testament.* 14 vols. Minneapolis: Augsburg
    Publishing House, 1946. (3)
Lewis, C. S. *Reflections on the Psalms.* New York: Harcourt Brace, 1964. (1)
Lock, Walter. *A Critical and Exegetical Commentary on the Pastoral Epistles.*
    International Critical Commentary. Edinburgh: T. & T. Clark, 1924. (1)
Maclaren, Alexander. *Expositions of Holy Scripture.* 17 vols. Grand Rapids:
    Wm. B. Eerdmans Publishing Co., 1944. (2, 3, 4)
Mayor, Joseph B. *The Epistle of James.* Grand Rapids: Zondervan Publishing
    House, 1954. (3)
Meyer, F. B. *Tried by Fire.* Expositions on the First Epistle of Peter. Grand
    Rapids: Zondervan Publishing House, 1950. (1)
Mitton, Charles Leslie. *The Epistle of James.* Grand Rapids: Wm. B. Eerdmans
    Publishing Co., 1966. (3)
Morison, James. *A Practical Commentary on the Gospel According to St. Mark.*
    London: Hodder and Stoughton, 1889. (3)
Moule, H. C. G. *Ephesian Studies: Lessons in Faith and Walk.* London: Hodder
    and Stoughton, n.d. (1)
Oxford English Dictionary. 13 vols. Edited by James Murray, et.al. Oxford:
    Clarendon Press, 1933. (1, 3)
Plummer, Alfred. *The Epistles of St. John.* Cambridge Greek Testament. Cam-
    bridge: University Press, 1894. (1)
——. *The Gospel According to St. Mark.* Cambridge Greek Testament. Cambridge:
    University Press, 1914. (3)
——. *Second Epistle of St. Paul to the Corinthians.* Cambridge: University Press,
    1912. (1)
The Pulpit Commentary. 23 vols. Edited by H. D. M. Spence and Joseph S. Exell.
    Grand Rapids: Wm. B. Eerdmans Publishing Co., 1963. (1, 2, 3, 4)
Robertson, A. T. *Studies in the Epistle of James.* New York: George H. Doran Co.,
    1915. (3)
Ropes, James H. *A Critical and Exegetical Commentary on the Epistle of St.
    James.* International Critical Commentary. Edinburgh: T. & T. Clark, 1916.
    (3)
Ryle, J. C. *Expository Thoughts on the Gospels.* 4 vols. Grand Rapids: Zondervan
    Publishing House, 1951. (3)
Sanday, William, and Headlam, Arthur C. *A Critical and Exegetical Commentary
    on the Epistle to the Romans.* 5th ed. International Critical Commentary.
    Edinburgh: T. & T. Clark, 1895. (1)

Schaff, Philip. *History of the Christian Church.* 8 vols. Grand Rapids: Wm. B. Eerdmans Publishing Co., 1960. (3)

Selwyn, E. G. *First Epistle of St. Peter.* London: Macmillan Co., 1961. (1)

Simpson, E. K., and Bruce, F. F. *Commentary on the Epistles to the Ephesians and Colossians.* New International Commentary on the New Testament. Grand Rapids: Wm. B. Eerdmans Publishing Co., 1965. (1)

Smart, James D. *History and Theology in Second Isaiah.* Philadelphia: Westminster, 1965. (2)

Swete, H. B. *The Gospel According to St. Mark.* London: Macmillan Co., 1898. (3)

Taylor, Vincent. *The Gospel According to St. Mark.* London: Macmillan Co., 1963. (3)

Trench, R. C. *Synonyms of the New Testament.* Grand Rapids: Wm. B. Eerdmans Publishing Co., 1953. (1)

The Wesleyan Bible Commentary. Edited by Charles W. Carter, Ralph Earle, and W. Ralph Thompson. Grand Rapids: Wm. B. Eerdmans Publishing Co., 1964-69. (1, 2)

Westcott, B. F. *The Epistle to the Hebrews.* 2nd ed. London: Macmillan Co., 1892. (1, 3)

———. *Saint Paul's Epistle to the Ephesians.* Grand Rapids: Wm. B. Eerdmans Publishing Co., 1958. (1)

The Zondervan Pictorial Encyclopedia of the Bible. Edited by Merrill C. Tenney. 5 vols. Grand Rapids: Zondervan Publishing House, 1975. (4)